John J. Ó Ríordáin, CSsR.

A TRAGIC TROUBADOUR

Life & Collected Works of Folklorist, Poet & Translator
Edward Walsh (1805-1850)

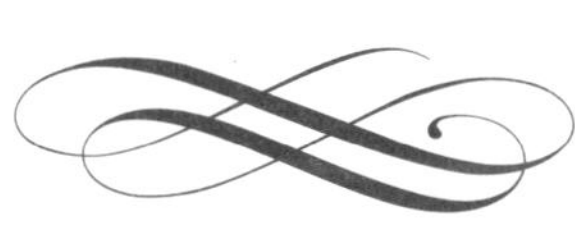

Published in Ireland by John J. Ó Ríordáin, CSSR.
Mt. St. Alphonsus, South Circular Rd., Limerick.
Tel: 061 315099 Mobile: 087 9280849

John J. Ó Ríordáin, CSSR

For my mother
Anne Murphy
(*Nancy the Shamrock*)

and my sisters...
Mary Clare Moriarty
Anne Theresa Leslie
Joan Mary Downes
Margaret Rose Hopkins
Eileen Philomena O'Riordan

SUPPORTED BY
IRD DUHALLOW AND LEADER
FUNDING

ISBN: 0-9551059-0-0

CONTENTS

Part III: Folklore & Other Prose Works

Other Stories by Edward Walsh?

LIST OF ILLUSTRATIONS

LIST OF ABBREVIATIONS

Appreciation =	C.G. Duffy's two-part article on Edward Walsh in the *Nation*, Aug. 24th & Sept. 7th 1850.
CAI =	Cork Archives Institute.
DJTSL =	Dublin Journal of Temperance, Science and Literature.
DPJ =	Dublin Penny Journal.
Ed. =	Editor (Ó Ríordáin).
Gleeson =	"Edward Walsh, the Irish Poet and Translator. A Biographical Sketch with Poetry" in JCHAS, Vol. II (1893), pp. 145-208, & Vol. III (1894), pp. 209-214.
IPJ =	Irish Penny Journal.
JCHAS =	Journal of the Cork Historical and Archaeological Society.
Memoir =	"Edward Walsh" by "J" in the *Celt*, Dec. 1857.
MS =	Manuscript.
MSS =	Manuscripts.
NA =	National Archives.
NHI =	*New History of Ireland* by Moody & Martin.
NLI =	National Library of Ireland.
NUI =	National University of Ireland.
O'Daly (1886) =	2nd edition of *Reliques*
Reliques =	*Reliques of Irish Jacobite Poetry*, by Edward Walsh.
RIA =	Royal Irish Academy.

A Note on Orthography

In his writing and spelling of English as used in Ireland Edward Walsh broke new ground and he did it at a time when English was supplanting the old Gaelic language as the vernacular of the majority of the people. The inevitable linguistic turmoil accompanying such a transition is well reflected both in Walsh's prose and poetic translations. I was loath to tamper with his rendering of Irish words as they found themselves struggling for survival in an Anglo linguistic milieu. Consequently, the purist may find it jarring to see fiana rather than Fianna or mo cailin rather than mo chailín and the almost complete absence of accents, but to rectify these matters would be tantamount to a mutilation of the texts. I have, therefore, made only minimal change in this regard and, to the best of my ability, adhered to standard orthographical practice elsewhere, namely, in all of the Letters section and in editorial footnotes identified by the abbreviation 'Ed.'

FOREWORD AND ACKNOWLEDGMENTS

It is over one hundred and fifty years since a call went out to have the works of Edward Walsh collected and published. Maurice Richard Lyne, a relative of Daniel O'Connell, had the intention of doing so but his untimely death prevented him. Now, in the bicentenary year of Walsh's birth, after nearly forty years of intermittent research, I place an edition of his work before the public.

Edward Walsh was a native of Doire on the eastern bank of the Araglen water in Western Duhallow in the county of Cork. He died at 13 Princes Street, Cork city, at the beginning of August 1850 at the age of forty-five. Many of his relatives still live in Duhallow or its vicinity but since the1860s his immediate family have lived in Australia.

This book contains a *Life*, a substantial body of letters in whole or in part, a rich and vibrant collection of folk stories and over a hundred songs and poems. Many of the songs are Walsh's original compositions while others are translations from the Irish. But the *Life and Collected Works* is more than a record of this distinguished Co. Cork folklorist, poet and translator; it is a window on to the social, political and literary happenings of early and middle 19th century Ireland: the White-boy Disturbances, the Tithe War, the Repeal Movement, the Young Ireland Movement, the Great Famine, the 1848 Revolution and Walsh's own significant contribution in laying the foundations of the Irish Literary Renaissance of late 19th and early 20th century Ireland.

Starting life as a hedge schoolmaster in the 1820s, he got a teaching post in the new National School system towards the end of the following decade. Later, on being befriended by Charles Gavan Duffy, Thomas Davis and Daniel O'Connell, he found employment as a secretary at the headquarters of the Repeal Association in the Dublin Corn Exchange where he was afforded some preferential treatment for the development of his literary potential.

Described as 'second only to Crofton Croker'[1] it was Edward Walsh the folklorist who introduced the Irish public to such charming tales as *The Ford of the White Ship, The Duhallow Cowboy, The City of the Lake, Daniel the Outlaw, The Midwife, The doomed Maiden, Daniel O'Leary, the Duhallow Piper, Paddy Doyle's First trip to Cork, The Headless Horseman of Shanacloch, The Spirit of Lough Deargart, The Chiefs of Clanawley* and more. Some of his original songs were among the most popular in the Dublin of the 1840s, notably *Bríghídín Ban mo Stór* and *Mo Chraoibhín Cnó*, both of which extolled the virtues and loveliness of his wife Brighid.

[1] The *Irishman*, Mar. 14th 1866. The writer is probably C.J. Kickham.

In *An Appreciation*, published in the *Nation* shortly after Walsh's death, Charles Gavan Duffy described him as 'a man of exquisite genius; an unrivalled balladist; a lover of all the old traditions of Erin; an erudite Irish scholar... More, perhaps, than any man who sung in later days of the vanished glory of Éire, of her weird superstitions, of her passionate longings and of her desperate struggles for liberty, Walsh was the representative of the old order of our minstrels. Others had attained by culture, as of a foreign tongue, a competent knowledge and mastery of Irish, and had taught the language of the stranger to catch some tones of the *cláirseach*. But Walsh more than Davis, Mangan, Ferguson, Williams, or McCarthy, sang with voice and passion as intensely native as the bards whom English legislature proscribed.'

***

After the long process of preparing this book the number of people and institutions deserving thanks calls for a booklet in its own right. In the name of all those not mentioned hereunder I appoint John P. Murphy of Kiskeam Post Office, to represent them, and in thanking him I thank one and all. Writing the *Life* of Edward Walsh was not an easy task. Initially it was a matter of assembling isolated snippets of information gleaned from the oral tradition. Indeed it is a source of grief to me that most of those good people have not survived to see the finished work because none would have appreciated it more than they. Among those who come to mind are Dan-Seán O'Keeffe, Sean B. O'Leary, Molly J. Neylon, Molly Hickey and of course my own parents, Jim and Nancy. In those early days neither they nor I had any appreciation of Walsh as a prolific writer or of his varied, colourful and troubled existence.

It was on a visit to the late professor T. P. O'Neill of NUI Galway whose wife was a relative of mine that I began to find a way into Walsh's written sources. In the early 1950s when Tom was a staff-member of the National Library in Dublin he assigned a trainee librarian to note any 'Walsh material' that she might find, and, fortunately for me, he still had the little file of hand-written notes and references. Those few pages of foolscap gave me the entrée that I needed and from that base I kept expanding my literary research into many an Irish library and archive and some beyond the sea.

It is with heartfelt gratitude that I acknowledge the assistance and unfailing courtesy of the library staffs at the National Library of Ireland, the Gilbert Library, the libraries of the Royal Irish Academy, Trinity College and the National Archives; the Cork Archives Institute, the Cork County and City libraries; the Limerick City Library, the Linen Hall St. Library and that of Queen's University in Belfast; the Hardiman Library at NUI Galway, Mary Immaculate College Library, Limerick, the Louth County Library, Dundalk; the Carnegie Libraries in Tralee and Millstreet and the Scottish National Library, Edinburgh.

For work carried out on my behalf I thank Alice Carter and James Callaghan presently of Girvan, Scotland for the translation of some Lowland Scots; Elizabeth Nunn for research in the British Museum and Kew Military Library, Catriona Robinson of Ipswich Genealogical Society Inc., Queensland, Australia, Sr. De Lourdes Gogarty RSM, Cappoquin for some Waterford source material and to Maureen Phibbs of Blessington, Co Wicklow, especially for making her research at *Saor-Ollscoil na hÉireann* available to me.

At *Saor-Ollscoil na hÉireann* I received much encouragement from the Registrar, Mairéad Ní Chíosóig, the Chancellor, Dr. Kevin Byrne, the director Dr. Sean English as well as from Dr. Eoghan McAodh of Saor-Ollscoil and St. Patrick's College, Drumcondra and Dr. Dáithí Ó hÓgáin of the Folklore Department, UCD, before whom I did a viva voce defence of my doctoral thesis on Edward Walsh at *Saor-Ollscoil.*

The photographs of Tourėen School and of 13 Prince's St. Cork, are the gifts respectively of Tim Peterson, late of Lismore, Co. Waterford and George A Healy of 61 Oliver Plunket St. Cork, while family photographs from Australia were provided by Elizabeth Nunn. To all three I say sincere thanks.

I acknowledge with thanks the work of Therese Grisewood of Limerick and Cappawhite, Co. Tipperary, in setting up the music and to Katina Hegarty (Née O'Rourke) of Clonloghan, Newmarket-on-Fergus for her unstinting and indispensable assistance in the final preparation of the text for printing.

Finally, when I approached Councillor Jack Roche of Rockchapel for Leader funding, he first took the wind out of my sails by quoting the late Martin Corry TD who in similar circumstances said 'you're coming to the goat house looking for wool.' But the effervescent Jack went on to offer generous financial assistance from IRD Duhallow and for this I am truly grateful. Having met Jack it was with a lighter heart that I headed for Castleisland to talk business to Patrick Fogarty of *Walsh Colour Print* and to him also and his staff, particularly Kieran O'Donoghue, I say thanks.

John J. Ó Ríordáin, CSSR,
Mt. St. Alphonsus,
South Circular Road,
Limerick.

PREFACE

The massive output of Edward Walsh is one of the storehouses of culture and literature from 19th century Ireland. Readers of literature, both popular and creative, historians, folklorists, anthropologists, and all those who have a special affection for Irish rural and traditional life, have long wished for one compilation of all this work. Now, thanks to Fr. John J. Ó Ríordáin, they have that. This book, which describes the career of Walsh and presents all his known writings, is the result of painstaking and in-depth research and is a major contribution to scholarship. It not only brings together the various and varied works of Walsh, in the realms of poetry and prose, but also places that author in his historical and literary context, clearing up the confusion which has clouded parts of his biography. Not least in value are the unique insights given into the personality and creative urge of an extraordinary man, a man who knew misfortune and misery only too well but whose spirit was indomitable.

All will recognise the book as a valuable source for the study of the history of Irish literature in the English language, particularly in Walsh's own period but also with considerable relevance as background to later writing in Ireland, many of whose worthies were indebted to the work of Walsh and found therein inspiration and a wonderful well of imagery. The book furthermore performs a noted service to the study of the cultural inter-relationship between the Irish and English languages, as Walsh exemplified an epoch in which both languages existed strongly side-by-side (as they did in the north-west Cork of his day). The assembly and editing of these texts has, of course, a special importance for folklore studies, as oral traditional narrative was one of the sources most avidly used by Walsh. Indeed, some of the earliest and best versions of many oral legends and of much general lore were given to us by him.

It is indeed a great honour to a worthy institution of our own time, Saor-Ollscoil na hEireann, to have hosted Ó Ríordáin's researches on Walsh as part of its postgraduate programme, and few doctorates have ever been better earned than that awarded to him by that institution. What Walsh was to Cork and Irish culture in the 19th century, Ó Ríordáin himself has been in the 20th. These are the type of men who add lustre to the culture of their people – their scholarship gently and wisely expressed, their interests generous and inclusive, their selfless commitment to learning obvious to all.

John J. Ó Ríordáin is a priest, a missioner, a lecturer and a counsellor, as well as a writer and scholar. He is native of Walsh's own area and has gained academic recognition at home and abroad. He is especially concerned with spirituality as a constructive and creative force fostered within traditional culture, and has given much time to the study of Irish and Celtic spirituality. His many books on religion and history combine a keen eye for detail with a magnanimous humanism and a fine sense of context and of sympathetic humour. A great storyteller himself, he is the ideal person to introduce the full work of Edward Walsh, having regard to its wealth of detail, local references, and rich imagination always rooted in the community.

A dramatic and legendary figure well known to both Walsh and Ó Ríordáin, to Yeats and Corkery, and indeed to the traditional lore of Munster for many generations, was the 18th-century bohemian poet Eoghan Rua Ó Súilleabháin. Eoghan is reputed to have composed those fine lines:

Friotal na hÉigse ar bhéalaibh maireann go deo,
Is gan ach dorn de Ghaelaibh gréine, taisce na seod!

Which we may translate as: 'The words of the learned live forever in the mouths of the people, although now only a fistful of inspired tradition-bearers are left to store the treasures!'

Thanks to this book, there will be far more than that fistful of people to hand on the memory-trove to future generations…

Dáithí Ó hÓgáin,
Associate Professor,
Department of Irish Folklore,
University College,
Dublin.

PART ONE

· LIFE ·

CHAPTER ONE

AT HOME IN DUHALLOW

Introduction

The life of Edward Walsh didn't quite span half a century (1805-1850), but that half-century was one packed with political, religious, social and cultural change in Ireland. Walsh was directly involved in most of these changes and closely associated with others. In 1800, five years before his birth, the *Act of Union* was carried. When he was an infant the Napoleonic Wars touched his family. During his teens an eruption of the *Whiteboy Movement* saw serious disturbances in his locality and public hangings within walking distance of his home. As his young adult life unfolded, he adopted the role of *Poor Scholar* (hedge-school master), became politically involved, participated in the *Tithe War*, witnessed *Catholic Emancipation*, and got a teaching post in the new National School system. Moving into early middle age he worked for the *Repeal Movement*, was a journalist with the Dublin *Monitor* and wrote for the *Nation* - the *Young Ireland* newspaper. During his short life, he also found time to collect a considerable amount of folklore, and in his literary use of the English language in Ireland, he can be considered a midwife to Hiberno-English and a forerunner of the *Celtic Revival*. Through his songs and translations his contribution towards the preservation of Irish cultural tradition was not inconsiderable. Finally, Edward Walsh not only lived through *The Great Famine* but his letters on the subject have left us harrowing firsthand accounts of it.

When I first 'met' Edward Walsh

To anyone growing up in Kiskeam, in western Duhallow, Co. Cork, in the 1940s, the name of *Walsh the Poet* was as familiar as their own name. I was no exception. My mother sang his songs; my father recited his poems; my maternal great grandmother, Nano Casey, knew him.[1] The site of the house in which he once resided was often pointed out; and it was common knowledge that he was a cousin of the shopkeeper at the west end of the village, Mrs Margaret O'Sullivan, better known by her maiden name, *Maggie Walsh*, or by her husband's church-related office, *Maggie-the-Clerk*. It is little wonder, then, that I had taken for granted that Edward Walsh was born in Kiskeam, and like most of his neighbours, lived more or less within the bounds of Duhallow in North West Co. Cork.

[1] In the summer of 1848 when Nano Casey was about fourteen years of age, she remembered Walsh strolling by the Araglen water and noted that he did not seem to be well in his health. The adult population at that time would have remembered him in happier times by the same beloved river, particularly at the *Glouneen* - the recreation area of old Kiskeam.

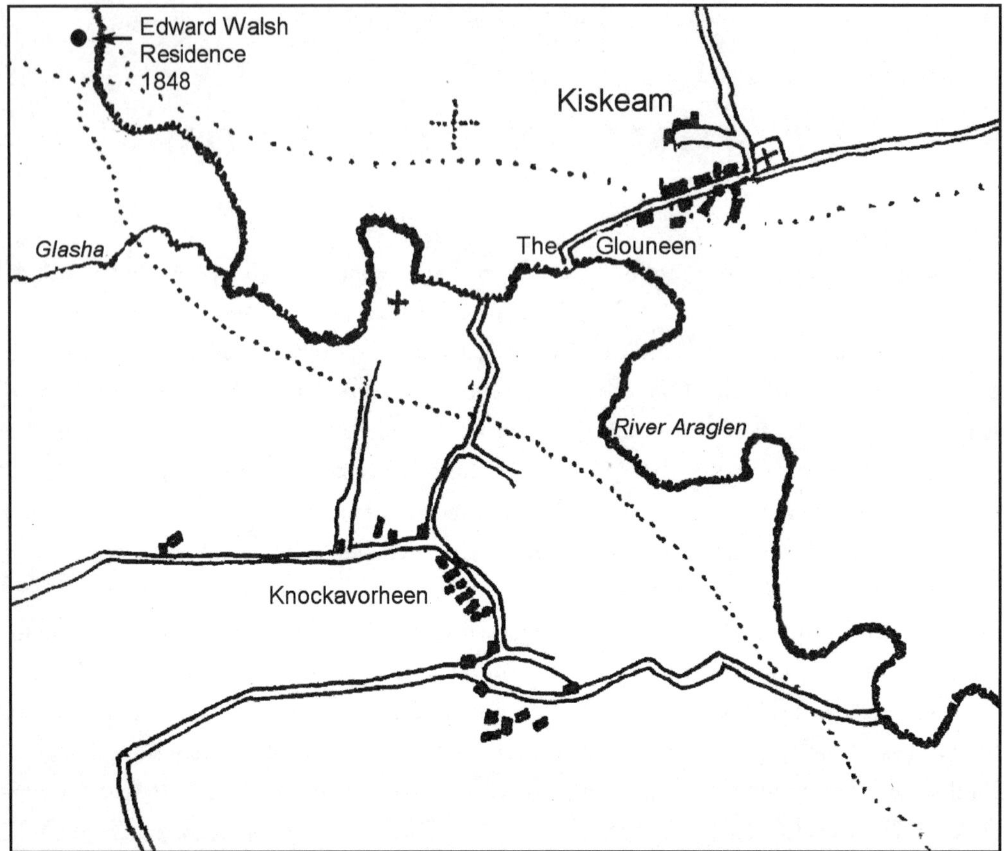

Fig1. Kiskeam and the adjoining settlement of Knockavorheen about 1830. At this time there were no roads in the district, just a few boreens and bridle paths. The structure of the little hamlet of Kiskeam ran in a north-east south-west direction. At the top of the lane was the catholic church and at the lower end was the Glouneen on the river's edge. The dotted lines indicate roadways that were to be constructed in the following decades. The new roadway linking Tralee and Mallow cut right through the little village street and thereafter Kiskeam developed on an east-west axis.

Legend: (a) + The site of a Penal Church dating perhaps from the 17th or 18th Century.

(b) [+] Church built in the 1820's, and in which Edward Walsh Worshipped.

(c) ⁞ Site of present church, built in 1932.

The death of my mother, Nancy Murphy of the *Shamrock House*, in April 1967, brought me face to face with an awareness of the reality that the oral tradition was the poorer for her passing. With her had gone irretrievable data of an historical, genealogical and folkloric nature. I grieved, therefore, not only for her but for all that had gone with her. Yevgeny Yevtushenko's observation became for me a stark reality:

"Not people die but worlds die in them."[1]

Then and there I determined to rescue from oblivion whatever lore I might, particularly in relation to *Walsh the Poet*. The project I set myself on that sad day has by now stretched over three and a half decades.

The Search Begins

My first incursion into this new field of research was a visit to the home of Dan-Seán O'Keeffe in the townland of Urraghilmore East. I knew him to be a man steeped in local history, and if anybody had the words of Walsh's two most popular songs in Duhallow - *Mairéad Ní Cheallaigh* and *O'Donovan's Daughter* - it was he. In this I was not disappointed.

The next phase of inquiry took me to Gortnacreha in the hinterland of *Cuilinn-Uí-Caoimh*, or Cullen, the very next village south of Kiskeam. I had been informed that Molly Hickey would supply me with lots of material that might be helpful. The day I first met Molly marked the beginnings of a strong friendship that only ended with her death. For many years she continued to enrich me by her breadth of knowledge and pleasant disposition. On our first meeting, however, she left me speechless by informing me that Pat Lynch, a well-known and respected local journalist, had recently given a lecture in Cullen in which he claimed that Edward Walsh was born in Derry! This was not simply disturbing news: it didn't make sense; it went against the *entire* oral tradition in Duhallow. But it certainly whetted my appetite for further research.

The Question of Walsh's Birthplace

Almost all, but not all, written sources state that Edward Walsh was born in Derry.[2] At face value this would appear to present a case of considerable strength in favour of the thesis. The position weakens, however, on discovering that all the statements are based on

---

[1] Yevtushenko, Y., *The Collected Poems*, 1952-1990: "People" http:lightning.prohosting.com/~zhenka/035a.html

[2] A limited number of examples include "Edward Walsh" by "J" in the *Celt*, Dec. 1857; "The Poets of Ireland. Edward Walsh" in *The Irishman* Mar. 24th 1866; "Our Irish Poets. No. 1.- Edward Walsh." by C.J. Kickham in the *Emerald*, Dec. 1869, pp. 284-285, 304, 316-317; "Hours with the Irish Poets: XXV - Edward Walsh" by Owen Roe in the *Shamrock*, Feb. 10th, 1877, pp. 298-302; "Edward Walsh, the Irish Poet and Translator" by Timothy Gleeson in the *Journal of the Cork Historical and Archaeological Society*, 1893 (ii); *The Macmillan Dictionary of Irish Literature*; Henry Boylan's *Dictionary of Irish Biography*.

information directly or indirectly traceable to a single source. The argument in favour of Derry is more seriously undermined when, as we shall see below, that source is historically unreliable. The historicity of the source would seem to have gone without question since its publication in 1857.

The source is a memoir by "J", published in four parts in the December 1857 issues of the *Celt*, and within seven years of Walsh's death.[1] In 1890, Charles Gavan Duffy refers to the *Memoir* "afterwards attributed, I do not know on what authority, to Charles Kickham."[2] In the November 1895 issue of the *New Ireland Review*, V. Edwards published an article entitled "Edward Walsh: Poet and Schoolmaster."[3] In it he acknowledges his source as the *Celt* but does not address the identity of "J".

Some sixteen years later, in 1911, a short article entitled "Charles J. Kickham and Edward Walsh," appeared in the *Irish Book Lover*.[4] The author, Daniel Crilly, took up the question of the identity of "J". Arguing in favour of Kickham as the likely author of the *Memoir* Crilly states that "there is circumstantial evidence which practically puts the matter beyond dispute;" and having made several points in favour of his contention he goes on to quote D.J. O'Donoghue's *Poets of Ireland* which states that Kickham: "wrote largely for the *Nation*, *Celt* and *Irishman*, over the signatures of 'Slievenamon' and 'J.' "[5]

On the heels of Crilly's article in *The Irish Book Lover* came one from 'Tasman' offering corroborative evidence in support of Kickham's authorship:

> In the *Shamrock*, and also in the *Irishman*, for the years 1876-7, a series of articles, entitled 'Hours with Irish Poets,' by 'Owen Roe,' was published. One of them was devoted to Edward Walsh. It seems clear from it that the writer was on terms of friendship with C. J. Kickham. He says, in quoting a passage from the Memoir of Walsh which appeared in the *Celt* for 1857: 'The scene of his (Walsh's) death is depicted by no unworthy master hand; and it would be the veriest presumption on our part to write an account, however meagre, of his last moments, while we can give it in the words of Charles J. Kickham.' There is this footnote to the same article: 'The present writer thinks it but right to mention that for the facts of this biography he is indebted to the talented author of *Knocknagow*, Charles J. Kickham, Esq., and to him alone.' "[6]

The discussion of "J" and the authorship of the *Memoir* were finally put to rest by a contribution to the same journal by William Murphy of Abilene Lodge, Blackrock, in which

[1] "J" in the *Celt*, Dec. 1857, Nos. 19 (Dec. 5th), 20 (Dec. 12th), 21 (Dec. 19th), 22 (Dec. 26th).
[2] Duffy, C.G., *The Memoirs of an Irish Patriot 1840-1846*, p. 191.
[3] Edwards, V., *New Ireland Review*, Nov. 1895, p. 158 sq.
[4] Crilly, D., *Irish Book Lover*, Aug. 1911, pp.1-2.
[5] ibid.
[6] 'Tasman,' in *Irish Book Lover*, Sept. 1911, p.192.

he states that: "Kickham's Memoir of Edward Walsh which first appeared in the *Celt* in 1857 was republished, in three instalments, in the New York *Emerald*, in December 1869. It was headed 'Our Irish Poets, by Charles J. Kickham. No. 1. Edward Walsh.' Its appearance in the *Shamrock* was concurrent with the American publication."[1]

Making the authorship of the articles quite clear, the editor of the *Emerald* (27-11-1869) introduces Kickham with the words:

> We are happy to welcome our gifted friend, Charles J. Kickham, who is as accomplished an Irish littérateur as he is a true and tried patriot, as a constant contributor to our pages of the *Emerald*. He proposes to begin his work by a series of articles on the 'Poets and Poetry of Ireland' - a charming subject surely. And, as an earnest of his purpose, he has sent us, as a first contribution, an article of which Edward Walsh is the subject."[2]

The fact that the *Memoir* came from such a prestigious pen as that of the author of *Knocknagow* may perhaps account for the fact that nobody, to my knowledge, has questioned the historical accuracy of its contents. But in fairness to Kickham it must be acknowledged that he described his material as a "hurried and necessarily imperfect memoir"[3] and warns, "this hasty memoir is not the biography of Edward Walsh."[4] He goes on to say that the primary purpose of the *Memoir* was not the writing of history but to enlighten the reader as to the calibre and character of his subject. "It has been our intention from the beginning" he says, "to give the reader an insight into the character of the *man*: of the *poet*...in order that our readers may have as perfect an idea as we can give them of the sterling stuff this poor poet was made up."[5]

How accurate is the biographical data given in the memoir? I suggest that it is not accurate at all. Kickham's use of biographical data was incidental to authoring a *good story*. And a *good story* is his four-part article in the *Celt* of 1857. It is written for the express purpose of stirring responses of the heart calculated to induce readers to make a financial contribution to the welfare of Walsh's widow and children. But Kickham is short on facts, and indeed quit erroneous in most of the biographical information he offers. Reliable sources show him to be mistaken about Walsh's commencement of teaching, his move to Toureen, the beginning of his writing career, the circumstances of his marriage, and matters pertaining to his death.[6]

---

[1] Murphy, W., in *Irish Book Lover*, July 1912, p. 213
[2] ibid.
[3] *Memoir*, Dec. 12th. p. 306.
[4] ibid., Dec. 26th., p. 340.
[5] ibid., p. 337.
[6] e.g. in his surviving letters and administrative records.

Fig. 2. Doire, south of Kiskeam, is on the left bank of the lower Araglen beside the 'dark river' (the Blackwater). Walsh also refers to other local townlands, for example, Kiskeam Dromacarra, Doon and Glentanedowney.

Consider the following examples. Kickham gives 1837 as the "time he commenced to write for the magazines."[1] By 1837 Walsh had been publishing for several years.[2] The *Memoir* also states that, "Poor Walsh was now forced to earn his bread as a schoolmaster. In 1837, and for some years after, we find him teacher of the National School at Toureen, in the County Waterford."[3] The truth is that by 1837 Walsh had already been earning his bread as a schoolmaster for at least eleven or twelve years.[4] Besides, his employment in Toureen did not start in 1837 but two years later in the summer of 1839.[5] And to give yet another example, Kickham's account of Walsh meeting and marrying his wife Brighid,[6] differs from that given by Walsh himself.[7] These factual errors and inaccuracies do not detract from the memoir as a piece of literature. They are, however, more than sufficient to establish that the document is not a reliable historical source.

Concerning the birthplace of Edward Walsh, Kickham's contention in the *Memoir* is as follows:

> Edward Walsh was born in Londonderry, in the year 1805. To account for his first seeing the light in the 'Black North', we must mention an event, which would be invaluable to the novelist - but which we shall hurry over as quickly as may be - a runaway marriage: a not uncommon occurrence, it must be remembered, in those days. The father of the poet, who, it would appear, belonged to the *genus* devil-may-care, induced a young lady of family to elope with him. They were both natives of the county Cork. Shortly after their marriage, Walsh joined the militia, and got the rout to Londonderry, which, in consequence, has the honour, in addition to many other honours, of being the birthplace of the poet... The militia being disbanded the family returned to Millstreet, in their native Cork, again."[8]

In a society where the contracting of marriage was a highly controlled procedure, especially among the propertied classes, elopement was often the only avenue open to couples that were in love and wanted to marry. For that reason, one cannot legitimately conclude that either or both parties to the marriage were feckless or devil-may-care. Timothy Gleeson in his *Biographical Sketch* describes Walsh's father as "a sergeant in the North Cork Militia,

---

[1] *Memoir*, Dec. 5th, p. 292.

[2] It is evident from the *Dublin Penny Journal* that Walsh had been publishing from at least as early as 1833.

[3] *Memoir*, Dec. 5th. p. 293.

[4] 1826 Education Report, ii, p. 954, states that Walsh was then teaching at Knuttery, Knockbrack, south east of Mallow, Co. Cork.

[5] Reports of National Education Commissioners on National School at Toureen, p. 44.

[6] *Memoir*, Dec. 5th. 1857, p. 292.

[7] *The Irishman*, March 14th 1866, "The Poets of Ireland - Edward Walsh;" MS 2261, *Letters*, No. 46.

[8] *Memoir*, Dec. 5th. p. 291.

but was previously a small farmer residing in the vicinity of Millstreet, who had imprudently eloped with a young lady much above his own position in life. Shortly after the marriage he was evicted from his farm, and his difficulties increasing in consequence, he was forced to join the militia as a refuge from starvation."[1] This is the only information at our disposal. While not necessarily denying Kickham's "devil-may-care" speculations it is also a real possibility that in the social milieu of the time Walsh's father may well have been evicted as a punishment for the elopement. But to this we shall return presently.

Concerning the North Cork Militia, it is true that during a goodly portion of the Napoleonic Wars, the bulk of the regular British army was out of Ireland and the guardianship of the country against a possible French invasion fell mostly to militia forces. However, there is no record that the North Cork militia were stationed in Derry in 1805, the year of the poet's birth, nor were they there in the years immediately before or after.[2] Even had they been there it is not at all likely that persons outside of the officer class would enjoy the privilege of having their families with them while on duty. Therefore Kickham's claim that Walsh was born in Derry is not even a plausible hypothesis.

If not in Derry, then, where might Edward Walsh have been born? Certain reliable written sources together with the unanimous voice of oral tradition in and about Kiskeam affirm that Walsh was born in *Doire*, not *Doire Coluim Chille* on the Foyle but *Doire* on the banks of the Araglen water where his father was a tenant farmer. The townland of *Doire* is located in Western Duhallow to the south of Kiskeam and on the eastern bank of the river.[3] During the poet's adult years, the Ordinance Survey anglicised and standardised the name and spelling of the townland as *Derragh* but the pronunciation has ever remained the same, *Doire*.

The Western Duhallow tradition is that Edward Walsh was born in Kiskeam or more specifically in Derragh. When I asked the late Mrs. Molly J. Neylon, N.T., a near contemporary of Walsh and matriarch of Kiskeam in my young days, where the poet was born, she replied simply and directly: "He was born below in Derragh."[4] Besides the oral tradition there are two significant written sources that corroborate it. *Guy's Directory of Munster* for the year 1886 states that "Kiskeam is the birth-place of the poet Edward Walsh,"[5] a statement not inconsistent with that of Molly Neylon since Derragh is in the Kiskeam vicinity. Highly significant also is a statement by Charles Gavan Duffy who was Walsh's long-term and probably closest friend outside of the family. In an article published

---

[1] Gleeson, pp. 145 sq.

[2] I was so informed by the late professor T.P. O'Neill of U.C.G. who instigated the research while employed at the National Library of Ireland.

[3] See map fig. 2, p. 22.

[4] Interview with Mrs. Neylon in 1969.

[5] *Directory of Munster* (Guy & Co) Cork, 1886, p. 609, ii.

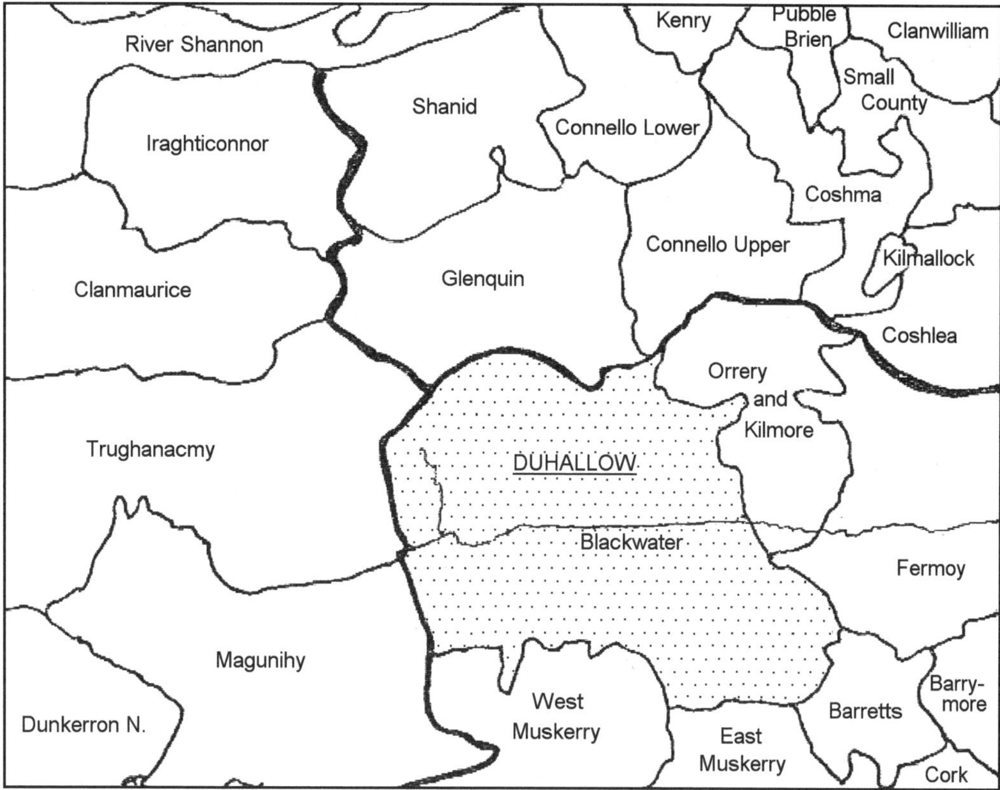

Fig. 3. Duhallow and surrounding baronies - Magunihy and Trughanacamy to the west of the Upper Blackwater are in Co. Kerry; Glenquin and Upper Conello to the north are in Co. Limerick; and the remainder are in Co. Cork. Much of Sliabh Luachra is in Magunihy & Trughanacmy. To the east it tapers off into western Duhallow.

The heavy black line indicates the county boundaries. For the first seven miles of its course, the Blackwater forms the boundary between Cork and Kerry. At Rathmore it turns sharply east. After about three miles it is joined from the north by the river Araglen and thereafter runs through the heart of Duhallow and of Cork county into West Waterford. At Cappoquin it takes a sharp turn south and enters the sea at Youghal where it forms the boundary between Cork and Waterford. Pobal O'Keeffe constitutes the narrow strip of land between the Araglen and Upper Blackwater. Apart from the few years spent in Dublin, Cobh and Cork, Edward Walsh never lived far from the beautiful Blackwater Valley.

in the *Nation* after Walsh's death, Duffy speaks of "that dark river by whose wave he was born"[1] - a reference to the proximity of the Munster Blackwater to his birthplace.[2]

Weighing up the evidence, we are presented on the one hand with Kickham's romantic, inspirational, historically unreliable, and uncorroborated account; on the other hand is the clear unbroken oral tradition corroborated by significant written sources to the effect that Edward Walsh was born 'in Kiskeam' and by 'the dark river,' in the Barony of Duhallow in North Cork. And finally, there is the total absence from the oral tradition of any reference to Kickham's narrative; nor has any location other than Derragh been suggested as the birthplace of Edward Walsh.

So why the Kickham version? Clearly Kickham had heard that Walsh was born in Derragh/*Doire*/Derry, and, knowing nothing of Derragh on the Araglen, simply assumed that it was Derry or Londonderry on the Foyle.

Walsh's 'Weltanschauung'

A government inquiry of 1834 into the condition of the poorer class in Ireland notes that, "the poorer classes in Ireland may be considered as comprehending nearly the whole population."[3] When the Commissioners assigned to the task set to work, interested parties and individuals presented them with a wide variety of remedies for this state of affairs, ranging from the imposition of "rigorous laws against Trades Unions" to the encouragement of coffee drinking.[4] In due time the Commissioners came up with their own assessment of the situation:

> The great proportion of the population about and among whom the Inquiry was to be made is constantly fluctuating between mendicancy and independent labour. In whole districts, scarcely one of that class of substantial capitalist farmers so universal in England, can be found. The small resident gentry are but few, and the substantial tradesman is not to be met with at intervals of two or three miles as in England; for there are but few towns of sufficient trade to create such a class. The clergy of the various persuasions, and the proprietors, when resident, are, in many cases, so much at variance with each other, or with the working population, upon political questions, that great caution was requisite in regard to the manner and degree in which we could avail ourselves of their assistance. Similar difficulties existed with regard to the constabulary, from the frequent collision in which they are placed with the people; and parochial authorities can scarcely be said to exist."[5]

---

[1] *Appreciation*, *Nation*, Aug. 24th 1850.

[2] See map fig. 2, p. 22.

[3] *Commissioners for Inquiring into the condition of the poorer classes in Ireland*, p. 6.

[4] ibid.

[5] ibid., p. 5.

The assessment is a capsule of conditions on the borderlands of East Kerry and Duhallow when Edward Walsh was growing up. The wild bogs and uplands of Sliabh Luachra stretch from Killarney to the Cork county bounds and taper off through Pobal O'Keeffe in Duhallow to the Araglen water. The Walsh farm ran down from the high ground of Derragh to the left bank of the river. It was young Walsh's good fortune, then, to be within the ambit of Sliabh Luachra's high Gaelic culture of which Daniel Corkery said, "Munster was the Attica of Irish Ireland and Sliabh Luachra its Hymettus."[1]

The values held dear by the people of the area hinged on a deep loyalty to the Catholic faith and an equally deep loyalty to the old Gaelic Ireland. In a Parliamentary Report of 1834, James Weale, a government engineer and surveyor working with Richard Griffith stated that the people were "distinguishable for an observance of their religious and moral duties, for the general kindliness of their disposition, and by a deeply implanted affection for their kindred; of all which virtues, I have myself witnessed among them some striking manifestations."[2] Weale's comments are a first hand description of the world in which Walsh was living at that time. Other important cultural characteristics not enumerated by him would have to include poetry, history, folklore, music, song, and dance. Of each of these characteristics Edward Walsh was a distinguished exponent.

The English language had penetrated the eastern portion of Duhallow where Elizabethan and Cromwellian settlers from Britain had taken up residence on the good land. The western part of the barony was more traditional and either wholly Gaelic speaking or bilingual to some degree. In a letter of 1831, James Weale says that in these upper reaches of the Blackwater valley "very few of the native population at present speak English."[3] Fewer still would have spoken it a generation earlier when Walsh was in his infancy.

The transition from Irish to English as the spoken language of the people at large is well illustrated from my own family background. My great-grandfather, Michael Culloty, was a contemporary of Edward Walsh and lived just across the valley from him. Michael spoke no English, although in his latter years he understood a little. (When my father, then a small English-speaking child, would call him to his dinner he would reply *tuigim*, I understand). Michael's daughter Mary, born in 1860, a decade after Walsh's death, was bilingual; and my father, born in 1889 had English only, although his *English* included hundreds of Gaelic words.

The Walsh household in Derragh may have had a greater leaning towards the use of English than most of their neighbours. The following paragraphs will help to substantiate this statement.

---

[1] Corkery, D., *The Hidden Ireland*, p. 185.

[2] *House of Commons Report Crown Land Experimental Improvement (1834)* p. 64.

[3] ibid., p. 13.

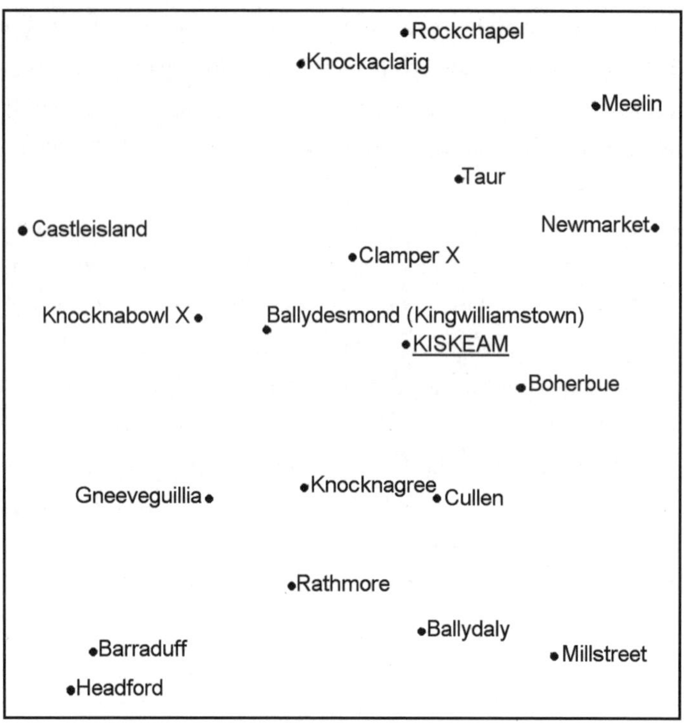

Fig.4.
Kiskeam geographical milieu. The five villages on the left hand side of the map are in Co. Kerry, the remainder are in Co. Cork.

Fig. 5.
The arena of Whiteboy activity in north-west Cork and east Kerry in 1821-1822 when Edward Walsh was in his late teens.

Walsh's Parents

Who were the parents of Edward Walsh? What was their family background? From where did they come to live in Derragh? The pursuit of answers to these questions has so far been an almost fruitless search particularly in terms of factual information. One local tradition attests that he sprung from the Walshs of Glenlara, north-west of Newmarket[1], but there is no certainty about it. The Newmarket tradition is silent on the question. Then again, despite the many families known to be related to Edward, nobody has so far been able to establish every link in the genealogical chain.[2]

Tradition is strangely reticent about the identity of the poet's mother. Perhaps because of the social unacceptability of the marriage it was deliberately neglected. Kickham describes her as "a young lady of family;"[3] in other words, she certainly enjoyed a higher social status than that of the man she married and may have belonged to the ascendancy class.

One of the few rays of light to shine on the subject came from my friend Molly Hickey and her view can be substantiated, partially at least, from independent sources. A Lannett family from Britain settled in the Newmarket area in the 17th or 18th century and about the time of which we write, they leased a 119-acre farm in Derragh from Mr. Leader, the Landlord. This holding was the largest in the townland. Molly maintained that of the three daughters in the Lannett household at this time, one eloped with Walsh, a second married a member of the Verling family of Newmarket, and a third married a Moynihan. The Verlings were a long established Co. Cork family of Nordic or Low Land extraction, and the Moynihans had, for the most part, come into the area as middlemen or landlords' agents and while being tenant farmers themselves were considered to be on a higher rung of the social scale than ordinary lessees.

In the early 19th century the catholic presbytery of Kilmeen parish was in the townland of Acres, north of Boherbue. In those days the parish included the four present-day parishes of Boherbue, Dromtarriffe, Ballydesmond and Knockaclarig.[4] On his appointment as parish priest in 1833, Fr. John McNaughtin explored the possibility of establishing the parochial house in the newly built village of Kingwilliamstown (Ballydesmond) but this came to nothing.[5] Fr. McNaughtin remained parish priest until 1855, and for the years 1841-1846 was assisted by his brother Fr. Richard, curate but also a landlord with a reputation for having diverted famine-relief money for the purchase of land for the aggrandisement of

---

[1] The source of this tradition is from the Shamrock House, Kiskeam, Dan Seán Ó Keeffe of Urraghillmore and Molly Hickey.

[2] Among the known relatives of Edward Walsh are the Walshs of Bogra, near Nadd, the Walshs of Carrig near Nohoval, the Walshs of Derragh, to mention but three of many branches of the family.

[3] *Memoir*, Dec. 5th. 1857, p. 291.

[4] See map, fig. 4, p. 28.

[5] NA: Quit Rental Papers, Letter of Fr. McNaughtin to Richard Griffith, Dec. 1833.

relatives in the parish. The name and reputation of Fr. John McNaughtin on the other hand is held in high regard. Edward Walsh refers to visiting him in the presbytery. The two men may have been relatives but this cannot be satisfactorily established. Be that as it may, probably after the building of Boherbue Presbytery the residence at Acres became the family home of the Moynihan-Lannett couple (Edward Walsh's aunt and uncle-in-law) or their direct descendants, the *Moynihans of Acres.*[1]

Kickham says that Edward was "fond of attributing whatever was good in him"[2] to his mother. This may have had something to do with his education. The implications of being "a lady of family" in the context of the *Memoir* would have meant more than material status. It is likely that she had a certain amount of education, had access to books in English, and was anxious to better her son's prospects in life.[3] In view of her somewhat superior status, it is also likely that she had a bias towards the English tongue, for, as Eamon Kelly, the *seanachaí*, says, "English was thought to be a leg up for the man that wanted to rise and be well thought of in the world."[4] Another "leg up" in acquiring proficiency in English may have come from growing up in the same townland and in close proximity to the principal family in the vicinity, namely, the McCarties of Derragh House who would also have access to books and have a bias towards English. In later years Walsh, while priding himself on his command of English[5] admitted that he was struggling with the use of Irish as a written language.[6]

Walsh received some tuition at one or other hedge school,[7] but his early education seems to derive from private reading in English whereas his knowledge of Irish was acquired through the oral tradition.

The status of the mother may account for another feature in Walsh's character. Although he wrote warmly of the people among whom he lived and moved, he never fully identified with them. They were "the peasantry." He was different. In later years, John Keegan, a fellow poet, would excoriate him for his "overweening ridiculous vanity," for his "upstart demeanour"[8] and for being a "stinking prig."[9] Keegan who came from a poor rural background may have sensed that Walsh's identity was not at one with the 'peasants' about whom he wrote.

---

[1] The above speculations and conjectures must not be taken as factual; further research is required.

[2] Kickham, *Memoir*, Dec. 5th. 1857, p. 291.

[3] O'Donoghue, Dr. Bernard, Cullen & Oxford university: in conversation.

[4] Kelly, E., *English That For Me & Your Humble Servant*, p. 54.

[5] *The Schoolmasters' Magazine*,1840, pp. 340-342.

[6] MS 2261; *Letters*, No. 28: "I hardly know how to form the letter 'r' in Irish."

[7]. Walsh speaks of his early youth "when at the 'noisy mansion' of Phil Sullivan, near the bank of the sliver Araglen, I received my first idea of chivalry and romance." " *Memoir*, Dec. 5th p. 291. See also 'Daniel the Outlaw' in the DPJ, May 18th. 1833

[8] MS. 2261, Keegan to Daly; *Letters*, No. 50.

[9] ibid. No. 57.

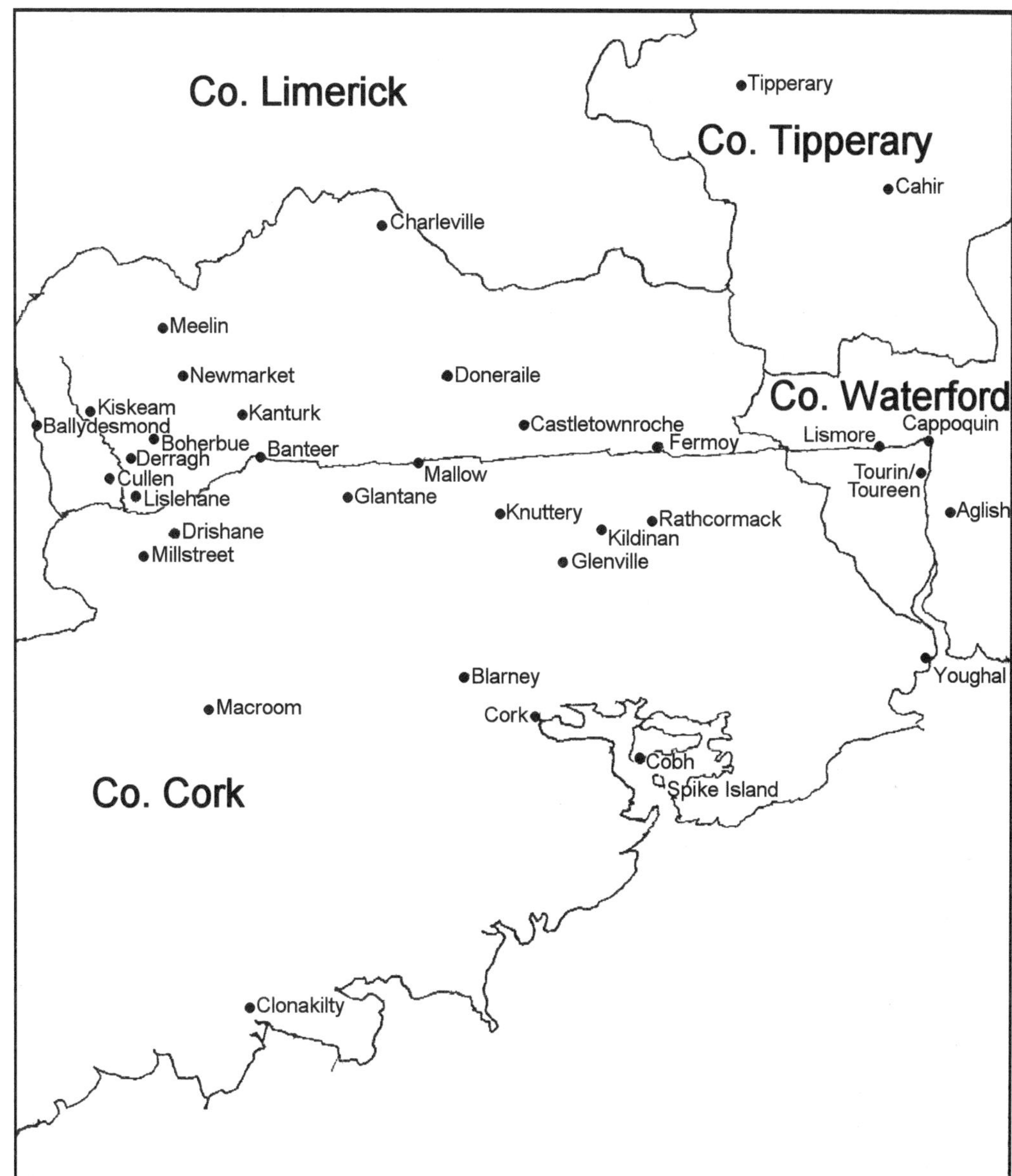

Fig. 6. During his earlier schoolmastering years Walsh rarely departed from the Blackwater valley from its source two miles north of Ballydesmon to its entrance into the Atlantic Ocean at Youghal harbour. After "The Dublin Years" he returned once more to his native county to take up the same profession, first at the Convict Depot in Spike Island and later at the Cork Union Workhouse.

For Edward's father, joining the militia was not necessarily the act of desperation it might appear to us at first sight. The country was in some ferment. The British government and their adherents in Ireland were uneasy. In 1796 when the government passed a bill establishing a new force, 37,000 yeomen, mostly cavalry, enrolled within six weeks.[1] Mr. Walsh's neighbour in the *big house*, Denis McCartie, was 2nd Lieutenant of the Millstreet Cavalry in the Yeomanry Corps of the North Cork Militia. McCartie's brother-in-law, John Leader of Keale, a townland close by, was 1st. Lieutenant, and the captain was John Wallis of Millstreet.[2] So for Mr. Walsh, if joining the militia was not exactly a family affair, it certainly was a local one.

We can only speculate on the sequence of events. The elopement would have been unpopular among the squireen class. Eviction would have been seen as an appropriate punishment for such behaviour. Furthermore, it would not only act as a deterrent for others but would also be an expression of solidarity with the offended people "of family." Finally, putting Mr. Walsh into straitened circumstances might pressurize him into joining the new militia force of which John Leader, the landlord, was 1st Lieutenant.

Mr, now Sergeant, Walsh and his commanding officer survived the campaign and on the disbandment of the militia, (probably after the battle of Waterloo in 1815) they returned to farming in Derragh.[3] At that time Edward Walsh was ten years of age and there is no indication from available sources that he spent any or all of the first decade of his life as a camp follower of the infamous *North Corks*. On the contrary, being of a thoughtful, dreamy disposition the boy drank freely from fountains of fact and fancy in his native Derragh. Writing of those early days he says:

> By the silver Araglen is the oak-crowned cliff of Donall na-Rasca, or the Outlaw, I have been delighted to lie for hours in his retreat in the cliff - to regard, in musing mood, the compartments of the rock which tradition has assigned to his solitary fire, his sword, his gun - to conjure up the days when the decayed oaks cast their umbrageous protection round his rock; when his shrill whistle roused his band to the call of their chief. Here I rehearsed all that has been preserved of his matchless prowess and hairbreadth escapes.[4]

---

[1] Grove White, J. in JCHAS, II, 1993, p. 479.

[2] See Grove White "Account of the Yeomanry of Ireland, 1796-1834" in JCHAS, (II) 1893, pp. 479-512 passim.

[3] Gleeson, p. 149. See also Pat Lynch "The Infamous North Cork Militia," *The Charleville & District Historical Journal*" 4 (1989) pp 94-5: "The folklore of the countryside west of Mallow Bridge, would have it that when being dismissed by a general on their last parade, he bade them farewell with the concluding words: 'You can return now to your respective hovels, jails and poor-houses'. "

[4] *Appreciation, Nation*, Sept. 7th, 1850.

Agrarian Unrest

Walsh's dreaming of days gone by was constantly challenged by the appalling conditions of the people among whom he lived and in the country at large. Agrarian disturbances such as the *Whiteboy Movement* in Munster, the *Terry Alts* west of the Shannon, the *Whitefeet* in Leinster, and the short-lived *Hearts of Steel* or *Steelboys* in Ulster were all symptoms of the underlying grievances of the people.[1] The authorities reacted with repressive legislation by, "making any participation in Whiteboy activities a capital offence."[2] During his middle and late teenage years, the *Whiteboys* of Western Duhallow and Sliabh Luachra were particularly active due to the famine and near famine conditions[3] together with the continuing irritation of paying tithes in a situation "where the great bulk of those who paid regarded the clergy whom they were obliged to support as heretical and alien."[4]

The famine of 1821-22 brought things to a head in Western Duhallow and Sliabh Luachra. "In the year 1822 the district was the focus of disturbance and bloodshed"[5] reported Sir. Richard Griffith, and of the same year, and the same place, his co-worker James Weale wrote, "This very estate of the Crown was the appointed rendezvous of an insurgent force of 6,000 or 7,000 men, which afterwards crossed the Blackwater, and was encamped for several days in the vicinity of that river, committing great destruction of lives and property, and threatening the entire demolition of Millstreet, Killarney and other towns."[6] On August 16th 1824, when Walsh was nineteen, young Thady Cotter, a local boy, was hanged at Shinnagh Cross[7] near Rathmore for alleged involvement in the *Whiteboy Movement.* Indeed it is possible, even likely, that Edward Walsh was among the silent throng gathered to witness the macabre event.

The Hedge-school Master

From as early as the mid 1820s Walsh took up the time-honoured role of *poor scholar* or hedge-school master. In the 1826 Education Report we find him running what were officially called pay schools, first at Kildinan, near Rathcormac, Co. Cork, and later in a similar institution in Knuttery, near Knockbrack, south-east of Mallow while Timothy Gleeson mentions him as conducting a school at Glentane not many miles distant from that

---

[1] See: Ó Tuathaigh, G., *Ireland Before the Famine*, pp. 138-139; Beckett, J.C., *The making of Modern Ireland*, pp. 176-178.

[2] Beckett, J.C., *The Making of Modern Ireland*, p. 177.

[3] Moody, T.W. *A New History of Ireland, VIII*: The year 1816 saw the 'first major famine since 1742' (p. 301). In 1821 the 'Potato crop fails' (p.304). See also: *Crown Land Experimental Improvements*, (1834): Richard Griffith (p.38) "the land was neglected and uncultivated, the people were ill-clothed, ill-fed and wretchedly housed."

[4] Beckett, J.C., op. cit., p. 177.

[5] *Crown Land Experimental Improvements*, (1834), p. 38.

[6] ibid., p.11.

[7] For the story in detail, see: Ó Ríordáin, John J. *Where Araglen So Gently Flows,* pp.149-156.

town.[1] At Kildinan, according to the Protestant Church returns, he taught 56 pupils, all Catholics, 54 boy and two girls. The figures for the Catholic returns are 57 pupils, 55 boys and two girls. The 'school house' is described as "a wretched cabin" estimated to cost £5. He enjoyed the patronage of Mr. Roche, the landlord, at least to the extent that the property was rent free and Walsh's annual income from the school was £22-15-0.[2]

In his school at Knuttery students contributed between one shilling and eight pence to half a crown per quarter - less than 15 cent Euro. The number of students attending is not wholly clear: 40 according to Protestant clergy, 25 boys and 15 girls; 50 according to the Catholic clergy report, 34 boys and 16 girls. In view of Walsh and his students belonging to the Catholic community it is more likely that the figures from his own religious leaders are the more accurate. What is abundantly clear, however, are the conditions under which he and his pupils pursued learning: "A smoky room; wretched accommodation; probably cost £5."[3]

Nearer to home there are traditions of Walsh's schools in Cullen and in the neighbouring townland of Lislehane but no dates are assigned. The oral tradition identifies David Ring's haggart as the site of the Cullen establishment but of the Lislehane site there is no memory.[4] Because of their proximity to Derragh it is possible that these schools marked his first incursions into the role of poor scholar but it cannot be said with certainty.[5]

That he taught school in Kingwilliamstown (now Ballydesmond) is also in the oral tradition.[6] What is unclear is whether it was in a hedge-school or in the new National School or both. A census of the Crown Lands of Pobal O'Keeffe in which Kingwilliamstown was situated, dated September 24th 1834, registers Redmond Walsh, aged 30, as the schoolmaster.[7] Edward (Redmond) Walsh was precisely that age at that time and there can be little doubt that he is the man in question.

Walsh also had a school at Drishane, near Millstreet. The 1835 Education Report states that while there he taught reading, writing and arithmetic, that he depended entirely on

---

[1] Gleeson (p. 145) may be correct in asserting that Walsh taught in Glentane but he was not dismissed from there. However, the song to which Gleeson refers, *What is Repeal Papa*? [*recte*: *What are Repealers*?] (*Nation,* 11-11-43) may have been a factor in his dismissal from Toureen.

[2] 1826 Education Report, ii, pp. 910-911.

[3] ibid., pp. 954-955.

[4] The oral tradition identifies the site of the Cullen school as the paddock at the back of *Lúibín na Rince* near David Ring's house. The identity of the Lislehane site is not preserved. According to the late Molly Hickey of Gortnacreha, Walsh put one of his protégés in charge of the Cullen school before he himself moved elsewhere.

[5] The schools at Cullen and Lislehane were within two miles of his home.

[6] Oral Tradition: in conversation with Michael Cronin, (*Mockie*), Knockeenacurrig, Kiskeam; Seán B. O'Leary, Tureenglanahee, Ballydesmond.

[7] *Census of the Crown Lands of Pobal O'Keeffe in the County of Cork*, 24th September 1834: records 'Redmond Walsh (30) Schoolteacher.' See: A.T. Culloty, *On Broken Wing*, p. 122.

payments from the students and that the numbers attending the school had increased over a five-year period so that by 1835 they numbered 70 boys in summer, 50 in winter.[1]

The Folklore Collector

During his school mastering years Walsh engaged in committing to writing a considerable corpus of folklore. At least as early as February 16th 1833, he started publishing both prose and poetry in George Petrie's newly founded *Dublin Penny Journal.*[2] It is to *the first life* of that Journal, with its all-too-short span of about four years,[3] that we are indebted for the publication of so much of Edward Walsh's fresh and delightful Irish folklore, much of it from his native Duhallow and the county of Cork. Through its pages the public was introduced to "The Ford of the White Ship," "The Duhallow Cowboy," "The City of the Lake," "Daniel the Outlaw," "The Doomed Maiden," "Daniel O'Leary the Duhallow Piper," "Paddy Doyle's first trip to Cork," "The Headless Horseman of Shanacloch," and so much more.[4]

The Tithe War

While Kickham refers to Walsh's involvement in the Tithe War, he gives no indication of exactly when or where this occurred or how long it lasted. The tithes issue was a long running one, a hundred years at least. It was not just a tax; it was a tax for the upkeep of the established church. In other words, the largely Catholic population of Ireland was legally bound to pay for the upkeep of the protestant religious establishment (Church of Ireland) and its clergy. As early as March 1736, the House of Commons in London passed a series of resolutions condemning some extreme aspects of the system, but the concept of tithing in itself was so utterly repugnant to the people that attempts at collecting them frequently led to civil strife. In the 1820s and 1830s the issue came to a head and despite the repressive measures taken by the authorities the people continued to resist paying. The disturbances on the Cork-Kerry border of which James Weale spoke were instances of widespread unrest. In mid-summer of 1831, for example, twelve people were killed in a clash at Bunclody, Co. Wexford, and seventeen at Castlepollard, Co. Westmeath. In December of the same year "a proctor and a dozen police were killed when ambushed by the peasantry at Carrickshock in Co. Kilkenny."[5] According to Kickham, Walsh was an active participant in the Tithe War and "made speeches at the anti-tithe meetings of the county Cork; he used

---

[1] 1835 Education Report, ii p. 142 c.

[2] The Journal was first issued on June 30th 1832.

[3] The *Dublin Penny Journal* ceased publication on June 25th 1836. It was revived at a later date.

[4] See Part III ,"Folklore & Other Prose Works," p. 216ff.

[5] Ó Tuathaigh, *Ireland Before the Famine*, p. 178.

also to write articles for the local journals against tithes...and made himself so active an agitator as to attract the attention of 'the authorities', and get himself imprisoned."[1]

I have so far been unable to find any data on Walsh's involvement other than Kickham's reference and its reproduction in various books and journals. Being a schoolmaster in the mid-nineteenth century would generally qualify a person for a leadership role and it was a schoolmaster who led the notorious Whitefeet ambush on the police at Carrickshock.[2] The *Constitution or Cork Advertiser* of August 7th 1832 reports on an incident near Castletownroche, on the Blackwater:

> On Saturday fourteen men were brought into [Fermoy] from the neighbourhood of Castletownroche, by a party of the 92nd Highlanders, and lodged in the Bridewell, charged with assaulting George B. Low, Esq. some time since, for removing an *anti-tithe* placard. The magistrates of the Petty Sessions offered to take bail, but the fellows refused giving any, until the prosecutors name would be told them which was not complied with. They remained in the Bridewell late on Saturday, but it was supposed that they would gladly tender bail before night, if they accepted. There was a slight attempt made to rescue the prisoners when going through Ballyhooley, and on entering Fermoy the rabble who followed made the air resound with yells of '*No Tithes*,' etc. etc. They appeared to be all comfortable farmers. One of them, named Hennessy, was the person who let the temporary barracks in which the party of the 92nd are quartered in Castletownroche.[3]

A flavour of these tithe-battles can be gleaned from an inquest reported in the same newspaper. Writing of an incident at Wallstown, near Doneraile, Co. Cork, the paper reports that the church of Ireland minister, Rev. John Gavin together with the police and military invaded James Blake's farm and was confronted by the local people. There was a stand off for some hours and eventually the tithe-collectors withdrew to the road. The account continues:

> The people followed them, shouting 'No Tithes - Down with Tithes and Church Rates - no church - no minister.' The people were armed with sticks, stones, [reaping] hooks and pitchforks; there were women too with stones in their aprons... The 92nd charged the assailants with the bayonet, and attempted to disperse them - but the attempt was resisted

---

[1] *Memoir*, Dec. 5th. 1850, p. 291.

[2] NHI, p. 311: Dec. 14th 1831: 'Twelve policemen killed in affray during serving of tithe processes at Carickshock, near Knocktopher, Co. Kilkenny.'

[3] *Constitution or Cork Advertiser*, Aug. 7th. 1832.

> by means of long pitchforks - a general discharge of stones, at the same time, took place.[1]

That particular incident resulted in four deaths, and the sending of sixteen prisoners to Doneraile, thence to Mallow and finally, under strong escort to Cork Jail.

It was probably during such an incident as this that Walsh was captured and imprisoned. We have evidence of Edmund/Edward Walsh serving on a jury panel after the infamous "Rathcormac Massacre" in December 1834. Whether Walsh was back teaching in or about Kildinan, we cannot say, but he would certainly have been known in the district as the resident schoolmaster from some years previously. The *Constitution or Cork Advertiser* relates that on the morning of Thursday the 18th. December,

> The Rev. Archdeacon Ryder [Church of Ireland] proceeded to distrain for tithes due to him from the parish of Gortroe. Two magistrates, Captain Collis and Bagley, assisted him and by a small detachment of the 4th Dragoon Guards under the command of Lieutenant Tait. They were subsequently reinforced by a hundred men of the 29th Depot under Major Walter and also by a small party of police.
>
> For two or three nights preceding to Thursday, horns had been sounded on the hills throughout the country and the night preceding, large bodies of peasantry marched through various towns - distant eight, ten and twenty miles from the threatened parish. On the approach of Mr. Ryder and his party from Bartlemy's Cross, the countrymen on the hills assailed them. The country people then drew down from the hills and in a dense body surrounded the farmyard or haggard of a widow Ryan. When Major Walker and Captain Ailes were wounded the fatal order to fire with ball was given. Twelve [were] killed and eight seriously wounded. The widow Ryan who had been called on so often in vain, now came out and paid the demand (£2-14-0 [3.50 euro]) all the resistance immediately ceased through the parish. The widow Ryan has to deplore the loss of her two sons, fine young men, one 32 and the other 30 years old.[2]

A law case of about two weeks duration ensued and on the jury panel of twenty-two men was Edward/Edmund Walsh. There was a three-way split in the jury verdict: thirteen (including Walsh) for Wilful Murder; seven for Justifiable Homicide and two for Manslaughter.

---

[1] *Constitution or Cork Advertiser*, Sept. 11th. The townland of Wallstown lies between Killavullen and Doneraile but closer to the latter.

[2] NLI, "Joly Pamphlets," No. 2240-2261.

Disappointed Hopes

According to Kickham's *Memoir* Edward Walsh came under the notice of a man with high ambition who employed him as tutor to his family[1] while he himself drew on Walsh's talent and support in order to get elected as a member of parliament for Co. Cork on the basis that if successful he would really represent the ordinary people.[2] Who was that man? None of the sources reveal his identity but circumstantial evidence points to Edward Burke Roche of Kildinan.[3] Walsh, as we have already noted, had the patronage of Mr. Roche and held his school in "a wretched cabin" which Mr. Roche provided rent-free.[4]

It would appear that when Edward Roche stood for parliamentary election as one of Daniel O'Connell's Repeal Candidates he employed the services of Walsh in the election campaign. Kickham's version runs:

> A county Cork politician, who coveted parliamentary honours, took notice of the young poet agitator, and seeing in him a useful ally, became his patron. This gentleman had his ambition gratified. He entered St. Stephen's as a champion of the people, and (we had almost said, as a matter of course) betrayed them. Happy day for Edward Walsh. He had now a patron with government situations innumerable at his disposal. Let him but hold out his hand now and a shower of treasury gold will be his reward.... [But Walsh] would not be an accomplice in the betrayal of the people. He spurned and denounced the recreant patriot.[5]

The reference to entering *St. Stephen's* is an indication that the election in question dates from or after 1834 since in that year the fire in the House of Commons necessitated the use of St. Stephen's Chapel for parliamentary proceedings. Roche became a member of the imperial parliament for the county of Cork in 1837 and held that seat for many years.[6] The seat had previously been held by another anti-Repeal candidate, the colourful *Feargus* [*recte:* Fergus] O'Connor who took up the cause of the people in the "Rathcormac Massacre" and later gained notoriety as the most popular leader of the Chartist movement in England.[7]

O'Connor, like O'Connell was a landlord. Each in his own way was atypical of their class. In times when landlords were liable to be shot O'Connor lived close to his tenants,

---

[1] Gleeson, p. 145, ii.

[2] *Memoir*, Dec. 5th p. 292.

[3] I was alerted to this information by Maureen Phibbs (daughter of my friend Molly Hickey) in her unpublished study for NUI Certificate in Local History: *The Poet Edward Walsh, as a conduit for the study of Education and tradition in the Parish of Cullen, North Cork, 1805-1830.*

[4] See p. 34 above.

[5] *Memoir*, Dec. 5th , p.292.

[6] Copinger, W.A. "Historical Notes" Bk. ii, ch. 9, in JCHAS, 1893, p. 471.

[7] See Read, D., & A. Glasgow, *Feargus O'Connor, Irishman & Chartist*, passim.

cared for his work-force, paid them well and promptly and sometimes worked side by side with them in the fields. He was a supporter of the anti-tithe movement and sincerely stood for universal suffrage, secret ballot and repeal of the Act of Union. A speaker of fine ability, O'Connor could be colourful and lively and not infrequently bombastic; his style is said to have been that of a demagogue. A flavour of it may be gleaned from a short intervention made by him at a Repeal meeting in the Corn Exchange, Dublin, and reported in the *Constitution or Cork Advertiser*:

> Fergus O'Connor Esq. next addressed the meeting. He declared himself - for England, a reformer - for Ireland, a repealer. He was for annual parliament, universal suffrage and vote by ballot. The Union he denounced as the d—d, the odious, the infernal Union! and the aristocracy, as the land-jobbing, the tithe-jobbing, the road-jobbing aristocracy![1]

Daniel O'Connell found Feargus too independent in thought for his liking, and since he was unlikely to have a man of such radical views excluded at the polls he did manage to exclude him from taking his seat in 1835 on the grounds that he failed to meet the property qualifications required at that time.[2]

Most if not all of O'Connell's Repeal candidates elected in 1834 were bought off by being given positions or titles of privilege.[3] The practise can hardly have ended with the 1837 elections. Kickham implies that the new M.P. did not forget the work Walsh had done on his behalf and now from a position of influence extended an invitation to Walsh to share in his good fortune. Walsh, for his part was not happy with the manner in which his erstwhile patron had acquired his new-found privileges, and if we are to believe the *Memoir*, saw the whole process as a betrayal of the Irish people for gold and would have nothing more to do with him or his family.[4]

---

[1] *Constitution or Cork Advertiser*, Dec. 3rd 1831.

[2] See Read, D., & A. Glasgow, *Feargus O'Connor, Irishman & Chartist*, p. 38.

[3] Duffy, C.G., *My Life on two Hemispheres*, vol. I, p. 193. Edward Burke Roche held a seat in the British House of Parliament from 1837 – 1855, and in the following year was created 1st Baron of Fermoy.

[4] See *Memoir*, Dec. 5th, pp. 291- 292.

CHAPTER TWO

THE SCHOOLMASTER IN TOUREEN

In the latter half of the 1830s Edward Walsh moved further down the Blackwater valley into the county Waterford. Where he first settled we do not know but it appears from an article by Timothy Gleeson that it was not a particularly happy experience. He fell madly in love with the daughter of a gardener named Power but was thwarted in whatever romantic or matrimonial designs were taking shape in his heart. "The course of his love was not permitted to run smooth," writes Gleeson, "as some rivals of his plundered his little garden of its contents one night, and heaped insult upon injury by composing a satirical song on the occasion, which is sung to the present day [1893] at pattern and fair. Walsh retaliated in a few cutting verses."[1]

In the fall of 1839 there is hard evidence of his presence in Toureen on the banks of the Blackwater south of Cappoquin.[2] He was employed as a teacher. The school in which he taught was in the townland of Ballynelligan. It had existed for some years but was not part of the new National School system. The owner of the school, Sir Richard Musgrave, was a kindly and well-disposed local protestant gentleman who had supported both Catholic Emancipation and the Repeal Movement. Sir Richard was now anxious to bring his private school under the new arrangement established in 1831.

There were standards to be met both in relation to the quality of buildings and the competence of teachers before approval for such transitions were permitted to take place. Sir Richard was prepared to face the necessary changes and seek National School status for the Toureen institution. On June 22nd 1839, he submitted the following testimony to the Board of Education:

> It [the school] was established about ten years since. It is in the townland of Ballynelligan, part of Toureen, parish of Lismore, Co. Waterford. The nearest post town and Cappoquin are each distances of about two Irish miles. The school was formerly assisted by the Kildare St. Society, but about six years since it ceased to be so connected. It is erected on the estate of Sir Richard Musgrave and not on church or chapel grounds. It is not in connection with any religious establishment. It is built of stone, with lime-mortar, and slated. It is 32 ft. long by 100 wide inside. It was erected at the expense of

[1] Gleeson, pp. 145-146, says that the song *Mo Chraoibhín Cnó* was written for Miss Power. Internal and external evidence indicate that it was written for his wife Brighid after he had moved to Dublin at the end of 1843 while she still remained in Waterford. John Keegan confirms that it was written for Brighid; cf. *Letters*, No. 58. See nt. 4, p. 550.

[2] See fig. 6, p. 31.

John Musgrave. It is not subject to rent. The whole as described above is exclusively employed for the scholars but the schoolmaster's dwelling house is attached. There is one classroom 32ft by 100ft.wide. It is in good repair. There are six desks each accommodating six scholars. Sir Richard Musgrave gives fuel, half an acre of manured potato ground and £10 annually. The children are examined every day in their catechism and on Sunday are instructed by their clergymen. On every day they are thus examined between the hours of nine and ten. Public notification is given for this arrangement. Parents are at liberty to dissent from it but hitherto none have dissented, all the children being Catholics. Six days of each week are thus employed from 10 o'clock to 1.00 and from 2.00 to 5.00 each day. A Register is kept, but the present schoolmaster has not been at school for more than a few weeks. For the past quarter year twenty seven males and ten females have attended. A considerable increase is expected. The name of the present teacher is Patrick Casey. He has not been at Model School. He can produce testimonials from the Rev. E. Condon of Tallow. The schoolmaster states that the scholars pay him at the rate of £12 per annum. The clergy of the established church have not been applied to as being opposed to the national system. The School is under the control of Sir Richard Musgrave whose object is to place it under the superintendence of the board. There are schools in Cappoquin and Lismore but not nearer. The parish population is 16,000.[1]

The fact that Patrick Casey, the incumbent teacher, had "not been at school for more than a few weeks" may mean that his appointment was recent or perhaps that he may not be proving altogether reliable in attendance, a factor all too common to the *poor scholar* fraternity. It is clear that not only the status of the building was of concern to the new Board. Stringent rules governed all aspects of the enterprise; for example, the books to be used in the schools, the choice, of teachers, and a miscellaneous section dealing with such matters as: the encouragement of clergy of different denominations to co-operate; the placing of the words 'National School' in a conspicuous position and having a stone "built into the wall having that inscription cut in it;" and that the school building should not be used for public worship or political meetings.

The section most relevant to Edward Walsh is headed "On the choice of Teachers." It stipulates:

1. Local patrons and committees of schools are expected to select suitable teachers, and to superintend them. But the Commissioners will require to be satisfied of the fitness of the teachers, both in regard to moral character and to literary qualification, by testimonials, and also, if they see fit, by training in a model school, and examination.

---

[1] NA, ED 1/86 no 48.

2. Should the Commissioners judge any teacher employed in a school receiving, occasional aid from them not to possess suitable qualifications for his office, or to be otherwise objectionable, they will feel themselves at liberty to withhold the portion of the salary contributed by them until a fit person shall be appointed. If such a teacher be found employed in a school-house erected partly by the public funds entrusted to them, and vested in Trustees, as above directed, they will require that the teacher be dismissed, and another provided.

3. Salaries granted by the Board are granted to the teachers individually; and therefore, if any teacher be dismissed, or die, or any new teacher be introduced into the school, it is expected that such changes be communicated immediately to the Board, and their sanction obtained for the new teacher.[1]

Here in the idyllic surroundings of Toureen Walsh met Brighid or Bríghídín, the love of his life. She was about eighteen years of age and from Eglish, eight miles from Toureen, the daughter of the schoolmaster Michael Sullivan and his wife Mary Walsh.[2] Of their initial encounter he writes, "I first saw Bríghídín on a quiet Sabbath at her devotions in the quiet country church. Her gentleness and modest air made such an impression on me that I resolved to win her and that day month we stood at the altar man and wife."[3]

Contrary to the expectations of such hasty marriages, this particular one was a model of steadfast love and fidelity through rough ways and smooth, bad times and good, till death did them part. The years at Toureen were probably the best and happiest in the life of Edward Walsh. His residence on the lush banks of the great Blackwater was in a district still enjoying the sobriquet *Irish Rhineland.* He shared this "rural bower"[4] with his young wife Bríghídín and it was here that their two eldest children, Adam and Frances,[5] were born. Here, too, he wrote for his wife what proved to be one of his most popular songs, *Bríghídín Bán Mo Stór*:[6]

---

[1] 1826 Education Report, p. 67.

[2] Letter from Elizabeth Nunn, May 7th 2000.

[3] *The Irishman*, March 24th 1866, "The Poets of Ireland - Edward Walsh"; see: *Letters* No. 46. The entry in the marriage register of the church in Aglish reads: 'In Matr. Conj: Eduardus Walsh et Brigidam Sullivan ex Aglish. Josepho Flyn et Catherina Dower, tests. J. O Meara. Sept. 12th. 1840.'

[4] *Memoir*, Dec. 19th 1857, p. 305-6; *Letters*, No. 33.

[5] Adam's obituary in the *Bundaberg Mail* (Queensland, Australia) of Jan. 22nd 1925 says that he was born in Toureen on June 17th 1841. He was baptised the following day. (See Cappoquin church Register). Frances was baptised in the same church on April 13th 1843, and because of the custom of the time, it is to be presumed that she was born the previous day if not on the day itself.

[6] Published in the *Nation*, Jan. 11th 1845.

I am a wand'ring minstrel man,
And love's my only theme.
I've strayed beside the pleasant Bann,
And eke the Shannon's stream;
I've pip'd and play'd to wife and maid
By Barrow, Suir, and Nore,
But never met a maiden yet
Like Bríghídín bán mo stór.

My girl hath ringlets rich and rare,
By Nature's fingers wove -
Loch-Carra's swan is not so fair
As is her breast of love;
And when she moves, in Sunday sheen,
Beyond our cottage door,
I'd scorn the highborn Saxon queen
For Bríghídín bán mo stór.

It is not that thy smile is sweet,
And soft thy voice of song -
It is not that thou fleest to meet
My coming lone and long!
But that doth rest beneath her breast,
A heart of purest core,
Whose pulse is known to me alone,
My Bríghídín Bán Mo Stór.

The inner worth of Bríghídín, her strength of character and resourcefulness, would manifest itself through their poverty stricken family life and even more so after the poet's death. Bríghídín, or Brighid, was about eighteen years of age when she married. She was not a beauty in the conventional sense, but she was a truly loving and loveable lady. In a letter written some years later, the poet, John Keegan, having visited the Walsh family home in Dublin about 1846 described Bríghídín as,

> a sweet, simple-looking, love-inspiring woman of 26 years of age, though she looks like a *thackeen* [*tachrán*, a waif] of eighteen. She is not a belle or a *blue*, but she is well formed, speaks English prettily and Irish bewitchingly. I am almost in love with the poet's wife myself, and envy him the treasure he enjoys in the once charming and still interesting Bridgid Sullivan of Amhan Mor... Mrs. Walsh is

tall... of pale complexion, with large blue eyes, very prominent and apparently swelled, as if with some radical disease or excessive weeping. She was in her hair, and justly has her husband described that hair when he says: -

My girl has ringlets rich and rare,

for never did lovelier hair decorate Eve herself in Eden than clusters over the fair brow of *Mo Chraoibhín Cnó*. Yet she is not [at] all a beautiful woman. She is not intellectual-looking or graceful, although one must love her at first sight."[1]

Working conditions in Toureen School were relatively good, and the manager, Sir Richard Musgrave, was humane and friendly. The student roll during Walsh's years there was as follows:

Date	No on Roll	Boys	Girls
Sept. 1839	72	40	32
Mar. 1841	69	42	27
Sept. 1841	106	59	47
Mar. 1842	113	60	53
Sept. 1842	113	60	53

His salary was £15 a year. He was paid £8 in 1839, an indication that his contract commenced about half way through that year. In 1842 he received only £13 because of a £2 fine for disrespectful conduct towards the school inspector in the presence of the pupils.[2] In 1843 his salary was also short of the full amount because of the termination of his contract before year's end.[3]

From time to time his income would have been supplemented by writing for magazines. In the summer of 1842 three of his pieces were published in the *Dublin Journal of Temperance, Science and Literature*: "The Buckaugh's Legend; or the wife of the two husbands"[4] - possibly the most entertaining of all his stories - and, under the heading of "Stray chapters of an unfinished story," "The Harper" and "The Bridal."[5]

[1] Keegan, John, quoted in D.J. O'Donoghue's *The Life and Writings of James C. Mangan*, p. 176.

[2] NA, MS. 5531 pp. 309-310

[3] ibid., p. 505.

[4] DJTSL, 4-6-1842.

[5] ibid., July 22nd 1842.

Toureen might have been idyllic from many points of view, but it had one serious drawback. The schoolmaster could not abide a departmental superintendent who literally unnerved him with his 'strut and stare and a' that.'[1] The hostile feelings were mutual and it became evident that it would be a fight to the death. The minutes of the National Board of Education for August 11th 1842 have a plea from the district superintendent for Walsh's dismissal on the basis of his conduct.[2] The nature of the 'conduct' is not specified in the minutes but the Board ordered "that a copy of the Superintendent's statement be sent to the Manager with a letter suggesting the propriety of the teacher's removal."[3] Sir Richard did not act.

In October of the same year the district superintendent again tried to have Walsh dismissed. At a meeting on the 13th of the month, the National Board had three documents read to them on the issue: the report of the superintendent, a memorial from Walsh himself, and a letter from the manager.[4] Walsh survived this attempt as well, but according to the Board minutes it was agreed, "That E. Walsh be fined £2 to be deducted from the current half-year's salary, and that he be reprimanded, and that he be informed that he would have been dismissed had it not been for the favourable representations made with regard to his previous conduct by Sir Richard Musgrave, the manager of the school."[5] And so things rested. The superintendent had failed twice in his objective. Walsh, however, was not to be third time lucky.

After that October debacle peace descended upon the education world in Toureen, at least for the time being. But in that same month of October 1842, another event, of far greater moment, took place. Charles Gavan Duffy, Thomas Osborn Davis and John Blake Dillon founded the *Nation*, a newspaper destined to become an influential Irish journal, and, curiously, to play a part in Walsh's downfall at Toureen.[6]

Walsh was not slow in making an approach to the *Nation* with a sketch, in the hope, no doubt, of earning some much-needed money. (The fine of £2 by the Education Board was severe - about 13% of his annual salary).[7] On February 25th 1843, Gavan Duffy, the editor of the *Nation*, acknowledged the contribution, promised to publish it, and invited more.[8] Thereafter, Walsh was a frequent contributor to the paper.

---

[1] *Memoir*, Dec. 12th p. 305. The inspector *may* have been John Coen, or a Mr. Sheehan. See *Letters* No. 41, and No. 45 and footnote 2 of same.

[2] NA, MS. 5531, pp. 309-310.

[3] ibid.

[4] ibid. p. 339.

[5] ibid.

[6] The first issue of the *Nation* was published on Oct. 15th 1842. The first *Nation* Office was a rented property at 12 Trinity St., Dublin.

[7] His salary was £15 (c 19.05 Euro) per annum.

[8] *Nation*: 25-2-1843, Answers to Correspondents.

At the beginning of that year Daniel O'Connell had promised the people that if they exerted themselves they could make 1843 the Repeal year.[1] The promise set up an air of tangible expectancy among the people. In February, Dublin Corporation passed a motion in favour of Repeal, a fact widely publicised throughout the land; and in April, Edward Walsh, responding to the enthusiasm of the times composed a spirited song entitled *Irish War Song AD 1843* and had it published in the *Nation*.[2] As fortune would have it the publication of the *Irish War Song* furnished the superintendent of district 21 (which included Toureen), with energy for a renewed attack on his quarry.

It happened that an anti-repeal meeting was held in the Rotunda in June, attended by a large crowd. "The body of the house", says a report for the *Nation*, "was principally filled by Orange freemen, composing the Protestant Operative Society, while the more respectable portion of the auditory were accommodated with seats upon the platform."[3] Isaac Butt addressed his enthusiastic hearers and delivered a passionate speech, punctuated by repeated bouts of wild approving cheers. He accused O'Connell of treason and of attempting to carry Repeal "not by any means known to the constitution and the law, but by violence and intimidation."[4] But, he said, Protestants would not be intimidated by the Repeal Movement and by the Repealers employment of massive crowds, rousing songs and ballads hostile to England and the Union, and ignoring the House of Commons and its procedures.[5] He then took up Gavan Duffy's *Spirit of the Nation*[6] and proceeded to denounce two popular songs by Thomas Davis: "The Men of Tipperary" and "The Vow of Tipperary." He reminded his hearers that "They all knew for what the men of Tipperary were noted in the page of Irish crime."[7] The report in the *Nation* continues,

> About his next quotation there could be no mistake; it was, "Irish War Song, A.D. 1843". He implored their solemn attention to this "Irish War Song of 1843." No ante-dating - no attempt at concealment here - no veiling the murderous incentive under the thin disguise of an historical allusion - the date is conspicuously attached: -

Bright sun! before whose glorious ray
Our Pagan fathers bent the knee;

[1] At a meeting of the Repeal Association in the Corn Exchange Rooms on Jan. 2nd. O'Connell declared that year, 1843, to be "The Year of Repeal."

[2] *Nation*: April 15th 1843.

[3] ibid., June 17th 1843, p. 576 i.

[4] ibid.

[5] ibid.

[6] The *Spirit of the Nation* was a collection of songs which had already appeared in the *Nation* and had just been published in book-form by the paper's editor, C.G. Duffy.

[7] Isaac Butt in the *Nation*, June 17th 1843 p. 576 i. London and Tipperary were considered the chief centres of crime in all of Britain and Ireland.

Whose pillar altars yet can say
When time was young our sires were free;
Who seest how fallen their offspring be,
Our matrons' tears, our patriots' gore;
We swear, before high heaven and thee,
The Saxon holds us slaves no more!

Our sunburst on the Roman foe
Flashed vengeance once in foreign field;
On Clontarf's plain lay scathed low
What power the sea kings fierce could wield;
Benburb might say whose cloven shield
'Neath bloody hoofs was trampled o'er,
And, by these memories high, we yield
Our limbs to Saxon chains no more!

The *cláirseach* wild, whose trembling string
Had long the "Song of Sorrow" spoke,
Shall bid the wild *Rosc Catha* sing
The curse and crime of Saxon yoke.
And by each heart his bondage broke -
Each exile's sigh on distant shore -
Each martyr 'neath the headsman's stroke -
The Saxon holds us slaves no more!

Send the loud war cry o'er the main -
Your sunburst to the breezes spread:
That *slogan* rends the heaven in twain -
The earth reels back beneath your tread.
Ye Saxon despots, hear, and dread!
Your march o'er patriot hearts is o'er -
That shout hath told, that tramp hath said
Our country's sons are slaves no more!

"It is impossible, "concludes the *Nation*, "to describe the sensation produced by the reading of those and other extracts."[1]

---

[1] *Nation*: June 17th 1843 p. 576 ii.

The Anti-Repeal Meeting closed but the debate went on. The next question was: Who wrote the offending song? It transpired that it was the work of Edward Walsh.[1] Having the author of such a seditious song teaching in a National School was unlikely to be tolerated, so the superintendent of district 21 made a new bid to unseat his enemy. Again he wrote to the Board accusing Walsh of disrespectful conduct to him (the superintendent) whilst in the discharge of his duty, and in the presence of the pupils.[2] The Board's decision is duly recorded, and dated November 30th 1843: "That the superintend having on two previous occasions brought a similar charge against E. Walsh and for which he was reprimanded and fined, he be dismissed from 1st. Dec. and his salary paid up to that time."[3]

About a quarter of a century later, a writer in the *Irishman*, probably C. J. Kickham, gives the following version of Walsh's departure from Toureen National School:

> Walsh had the pluck and spirit of a man, and though respectful to Mr.— when he [the superintendent] visited his school, he was not subservient. He could not bow and scrape with his hat in his hand, to the great man, and the great man could not forgive this. He found fault with everything that Walsh did and seemed bent on his ruin. The opportunity came. In examining a class he found fault with one of the boys pronunciation, and asked him,
>
> 'Is that the way the master taught you'?
> 'Yes sir,' was the reply.
> 'Mr. Walsh is that the way you pronounce this word?'
> 'Yes sir.'
> 'By what authority?'
> 'It is so pronounced by Webster, by Johnson, by —'
> 'Stop sir, it's wrong and should not be pronounced so. You do not know your pronunciation, sir.'
>
> Walsh ventured to reply upon established authorities. It was no use. Mr — knew better. He at once complained of Walsh to Sir Richard Musgrave, who was the patron of the school. Sir Richard took no notice of it, and Mr. returned to Dublin, bent on Walsh's ruin.
>
> Some time after an altercation took place in the Dublin Corporation between Mr. Butt and O'Connell. Butt in support of his assertions as to the disaffected state of the country, quoted from the *Nation* the "Irish War Song of 43" just published.

---

[1] Walsh's authorship had not been acknowledged in the *Nation* of April 15th 1843.
[2] NA, MS. 5531, p. 505.
[3] ibid.

> In the course of debate it transpired that Walsh was the writer. This was enough for Mr. —. He at once laid the whole case before Sir Richard Musgrave, and demanded Walsh's dismissal. Sir Richard sent for him, and asked was he the author; to which Walsh replied in the affirmative. 'Well, Mr. Walsh,' said Sir Richard, 'I am sorry I cannot do anything for you; they are bent on your dismissal. I think you had better resign and not give them the chance.' Walsh saw that it was his only course and did so.[1]

There was a sequel to the whole sorry affair. Sir Richard obviously hadn't given up. More curious still, the district superintendent of area 21, having finally succeeded in having Walsh removed from office in Toureen, was now prepared to support his reinstatement. An entry in the Board Minutes for December 28th 1843 says, "Read letter from superintendent of the district No. 21 requesting the commissioners to restore the teacher of the Toureen N.S., Mr. E. Walsh, whose dismissal was lately directed by the Board on the superintendent's report - Read also letter 4679K from the Manager Sir Richard Musgrave, joining in the recommendation of the superintendent."[2]

The Board did not yield. The Board minutes of December 28th 1843 record that "disrespectful conduct to [the superintendent] whilst in the discharge of his duty, and in the presence of the pupils" was not to be lightly absolved. It ordered "that Sir R. Musgrave be informed that the teacher referred to having been twice guilty of the same offence the commissioners cannot rescind their order for his removal from the Toureen N.S., Co. Waterford, but they will not object to his appointment to another National School, provided that after a reasonable period he afford satisfactory proof of his good conduct."[3]

So ended Walsh's links with the place in life wherein he seems to have found most contentment.

---

[1] The *Irishman*, March 14th 1866, p 614.

[2] NA, MS.5531, p. 518.

[3] ibid.

Fig. 7. The school-cum-dwelling-house at Toureen, Co. Waterford, where Edward Walsh spent what were probably the happiest years of his life.

Fig. 8. Southern half of Ireland showing many places mentioned in the Life & Letters.

CHAPTER THREE

THE DUBLIN YEARS

Ferment in the Capital

The termination of Walsh's employment at Toureen was a severe blow to him. He had lost his job; he had also lost the family residence that had accompanied it. The world of his dreams "where Amhainn Mhor's waters flow"[1] was in tatters. Added to that, Walsh's sensitive and nervous disposition did not well fit him for the rough and tumble of life and the difficulties between the superintendent and himself in Toureen were but symptomatic of his difficulties in relating.[2] But time for brooding was now in short supply; money was needed in order to provide for the family.

In view of Isaac Butt making political capital out of the "Irish War Song of A.D. 1843," published in the *Nation*, Walsh began to suppose that his connection with that journal had done him a disservice. He communicated this to the editor, Charles Gavan Duffy, and being the man that he was, Duffy took on the responsibility of finding the erstwhile schoolmaster alternative employment.[3] Even though it was a difficult time for himself, he brought Walsh up to Dublin in December of 1843 to begin a new career.

The Dublin of 1843 was one of ferment. The Act of Union of the kingdoms of Great Britain and Ireland had been passed in 1800, thus ending *Grattan's Parliament*, which had sat since 1772. From the late eighteenth century onwards there were moves afoot to repeal the Penal Laws and grant emancipation to the Catholic Church in Ireland after centuries of persecution. In 1813, Henry Grattan introduced a Catholic Relief Bill but it was defeated in the House of Commons in London.[4] Seventeen years later, Daniel O'Connell introduced the Roman Catholic Relief Act, 1829, enabling Catholics to "enter parliament, belong to any corporation, and hold higher civil and military offices - *catholic emancipation*."[5] If Charles Gavan Duffy's assessment is right, Catholic Emancipation, when it was granted was not done so as an act of generosity but "had been yielded to out of fear of insurrection in Ireland."[6]

With the advent of emancipation the expectations of the people rose. They looked towards an improvement in economic conditions to follow, but it didn't. At the beginning

---

[1] *Nation*: 21-12-1843, a line from Walsh's "Mo Chraoibhín Cnó."

[2] Walsh was super-sensitive.

[3] Duffy, C.G. *Thomas Davis*, p. 269; MS 2261, "Duffy you know is my friend through whose wish I came up." See: *Letters*, No.11.

[4] NHI, p. 299.

[5] ibid., p. 309.

[6] Duffy, C.G., *My Life on Two Hemispheres*, I, p. 68.

of 1830 O'Connell founded his Society for the Repeal of the Union, a goal which, for him, did not mean a break with Britain or its monarch, but simply the restoration of an Irish parliament.[1] As a landlord he had no appetite for serious social change; he condemned agrarian secret societies and opposed trade unionism and the reform of factory legislation.[2] His various accommodations with the Whig party in Britain were not working to Ireland's advantage and although he went to the House of Commons in April 1834 with thirty-eight deputies and high hopes of having the Union repealed the House didn't even give his case a serious hearing.[3] Instead, the award of offices and honours from the Government silenced many, if not most of his supporting deputies.[4] As the decade dragged on, the disappointment of the people lapsed into apathy. Then at the beginning of the 1840s the moribund Repeal Association was given new life by an influx of energetic young men[5] so that by the time Walsh arrived at the end of 1843 there were many political factions and viewpoints, notably groups and associations of Repealers and Unionists, Protestants and Catholics, Old Irelanders and Young Irelanders. It was all a far cry from his "rural bower"[6] in Co. Waterford.

The Reluctant Journalist:

The first hard information we have of his presence and whereabouts in the capital is at the beginning of January 1844, where, according to his letters,[7] he was living in rented accommodation in Summerhill, an area at that time outside the city limits.[8] Gavan Duffy had found him journalistic employment with a Mr. James Charles Coffey, a barrister and proprietor of the *Dublin Monitor* with offices at 51 Lower Dominic St. and No. 6, Lower Abbey St. Walsh was appointed sub-editor.[9] He was also engaged with John Daly, a Kilkenny publisher, with whom he had contracted to make metrical translations into English of some Irish poetical works.[10] Furthermore, his friend Gavan Duffy, who with O'Connell and some others were at that time on trial for treason, had assured Walsh that he would procure him "a respectable situation after the trials."[11]

---

[1] Ó Tuathaigh, G., *Ireland before the Famine*, p. 160.

[2] ibid., p. 162

[3] ibid., p. 170.

[4] Duffy, C.G.D., *My Life on Two Hemispheres*, I, p. 193.

[5] Ó Tuathaigh, G., op. cit. p. 186. In April 1840 O'Connell formed the National Association of Ireland which in July was renamed Loyal National Repeal Association. See: NHI, p. 317.

[6] *Memoir*, Dec. 12th p. 305; *Letters*: No. 33.

[7] NLI, MS 2261.

[8] *The Dublin Directory*, 1844, p. 394, nominates the address as 'country.'

[9] *Memoir*, Dec. 12th p. 305; *Letters*, No. 33, 'I procured, through the influence of Mr. Duffy, of the *Nation*, the situation of sub-editor of the *Monitor*.'

[10] ibid., p. 306.

[11] NLI, MS 2261; *Letters*, No. 5.

Walsh's letters to John Daly during the first nine months of 1844 are the chief but not the only source of information about him during this period of his life.[1] Because most of these are undated it is difficult to establish an exact sequence, but it is evident from the overall collection that he was not really settled in Dublin. Initially he saw the move to the capital as a temporary arrangement and lived in the hope of being reinstated at Toureen. On January 2nd he wrote to Daly, "I have no certain knowledge when I leave town, or whether I go at all - I'll know in a week."[2] Three days later he wrote again, "I was in the hope that the board would allow me back to my snug residence at Toureen, but they decided against it yesterday, though Sir Richard and the superintendent applied in my behalf. I am grieved that my poor wife and infants will be disturbed in their calm solitude and sent up here in winter weather God pardon the doers of this injustice."[3] Brigid and the children, Adam and Frances, were not with him initially. They had remained in Co. Waterford.[4]

Once his chances of reinstatement in Toureen school had been frustrated, Walsh's immediate concern was to get the family to join him in Dublin: "I am very lonely and sad away from my beloved wife and children, and cannot well settle down to anything till they come; I have written for them."[5] In another letter he explores the possibility of Daly finding them suitable accommodation in Kilkenny for a stop-over on the journey, but mentions that his wife had been planning on taking the packet steamer from Cork. How they travelled eventually we cannot say.

It was probably in January 1844 when Walsh was alone and pining for his wife and family that he wrote "Mo Chraoibhín Cnó,"[6] (literally 'my cluster of nuts' - a reference to his wife's strikingly beautiful head of curls). The song proved highly popular and 'made his name' in the capital:

My heart is far from Liffey's tide
And Dublin Town;
It strays beyond the southern side
Of Cnoc Maol Donn,
Where Capa Chuinn hath woodlands green,
Where Amhan Mhór's waters flow,
Where dwells unsung, unsought, unseen,
Mo Chraoibhín Cnó,
Lo clustering in her leafy screen,
Mo Chraoibhín Cnó!

---

[1] e.g. His publications in the *Nation* and the *Wexford Independent*; in *An Appreciation* by C.G. Duffy in the *Nation*, in Duffy's *Short Life of Davis*, Kickham's *Memoir*, etc.

[2] NLI, MS 2261; *Letters*, No. 1.

[3] NLI, MS 2261; *Letters*, No. 2.

[4] *Memoir*, Dec. 12th p. 307, mentions that Brighid was 'in her old home on the banks of the Blackwater' i.e. in her parents home in Aglish.

[5] NLI, MS. 2261; *Letters*, No. 2.

[6] *Nation*: Dec. 21st 1844.

The highbred dames of Dublin town
Are rich and fair,
With wavy plume and silken gown,
And stately air;
Can plumes compare thy dark brown hair?
Can silks thy neck of snow?
Or measur'd pace thine artless grace,
Mo Chraoibhín Cnó,
When harebells scarcely show thy trace,
Mo Chraoibhín Cnó?

I've heard the songs by Liffey's wave,
That maidens sung -
They sung their land, the Saxon's slave,
In Saxon tongue -
Oh! bring me here that Gaelic dear
Which cursed the Saxon foe
When thou didst charm my raptured ear,
Mo Chraoibhín Cnó!
And none but God's good angels near
Mo Chraoibhín Cnó!

I've wandered by the rolling Lee!
And Lene's green bowers -
I've seen the Shannon's widespread sea,
And Limerick's towers -
And Liffey's tide, where halls of pride
Frown o'er the flood below;
My wild heart strays to Amhan Mhór's side,
Mo Chraoibhín Cnó!
With love and thee for aye to bide,
Mo Chraoibhín Cnó.

Walsh's career as sub-editor of *The Monitor* was short lived. According to C.G. Duffy, the "employment proved so arduous and uncongenial, that Walsh in a few days resigned it."[1] By January 8th he had quit the job and was feeling the worse for having taken it. "When I left, or rather was driven from my rural bower at Toureen, I procured, through the influence of Mr. Duffy, of the *Nation*, the situation of sub-editor of the *Monitor*. I did not like the employment and quitted it - got then, to vary my life, a severe bilious fever, induced by mental suffering."[2] And again: "I am not well fitted for the bustle of a town life; and

[1] Duffy, C.G., *Life of Davis*, p.269.

[2] *Memoir*, Dec. 12th p. 305; *Letters*, Nos. 7 & 33.

besides, I dread if my health, which is not very robust, should fail. I dread the fate of my family but I must now bear the charge and pray to God to assist me."[1]

Another letter to Daly revealed the final straw that ended his journalistic days: "I have not been employed at the *Monitor* office since Monday last as I refused to report at a meeting at the Mansion House and afterwards at the state trials as I found that I had not skill nor nerve enough to report the public proceedings - Duffy is on his trial. Duffy you know is my friend through whose wish I came up and his heart is broken completely down. He has been complaining for the last two months and with the best intentions of serving me he cannot, even if his health permitted, look out for me."[2] Duffy himself observed of Walsh that "the close work of a newspaper office galled him [Walsh],"[3] and it would appear that the whole episode brought him to the brink of nervous breakdown. Duffy was right. Urban journalism was no life for this man who had spent most of his years in relaxed rural surroundings.

Secretary at the Corn Exchange

Walsh's next post of employment was marginally more relaxed than that of sub-editorship. Gavan Duffy found him a secretarial post in the headquarters of the Repeal Association offices at the Corn Exchange on Burg Quay.[4] Soon afterwards he wrote to a friend:

> "When I could crawl abroad, I procured employment at that great vortex of agitation, the Corn Exchange Rooms, where I am engaged in a purely literary capacity, and am treated with respect. I know it will gratify you to learn that change from the influence of the anti-National Board has tended to my advantage. I have a very pretty cottage of my own. I am almost entirely my own master at the Corn Exchange, and am engaged in translating, during my leisure moments, 'Jacobite poetry', which is being published by Mr. Daly, of Kilkenny. You must have seen the very favourable notice I have had from the newspaper press."[5]

Working in the Repeal Association headquarters meant that Walsh was rubbing shoulders with Daniel O'Connell, Thomas Davis, Gavan Duffy and the cream of Irish literary and political circles. There was a certain prestige in moving among such company but the glitter soon wore off as he found ten hours a day at secretarial work a heavy burden. At this point, another friend in court came to his rescue. Davis, a fellow Corkman, had an appreciation both of Walsh's potential as a poet and of the strain under which he now laboured. Through his influence and with special permission kindly granted by Daniel

---

[1] NLI, MS. 2261; *Letters*, No. 2.

[2] ibid.; *Letters*, No. 11.

[3] Duffy, C.G., *Life of Davis*, p. 269.

[4] The Repeal Association offices were at the Corn Exchange in Burg Quay, Dublin. Early in 1843 the foundations of Conciliation Hall were laid and the building completed before year's end, i.e. just prior to Walsh taking up employment there.

[5] *Memoir*, Dec. 12th p. 305-306; *Letters*: No. 33.

O'Connell himself, shorter hours and better pay were procured for him so that he could pursue things more congenial to his nature.[1]

The secretarial work assigned to him at this early stage seems to have been of a rather casual nature. He complains to Daly, "I am engaged for some time past in copying out Plunkett's speeches which a barrister of the city is going to publish. 'Tis dull work and I know not what I am going to get for my pains."[2] On St. Patrick's Day he complains again, this time of the work-load: "I trust you will pardon me for not replying earlier to your letters, when I assure you that I have, so lengthened are my hours of labour, scarcely have time to say my prayers, which, as a good Catholic, you are aware I am bound to do at least twice a day."[3]

Publishing with John Daly

Though secretarial work was burdensome to Walsh, translating songs energized him, and to that task he devoted himself with enthusiasm. The songs for translation belonged, for the most part, to the rich corpus of literary material emanating from the Jacobite era in Ireland.[4] John Daly supplied the texts, accompanied by a literal translation. Walsh's task was to make metrical translations.

Whether Walsh had come to know John Daly prior to the Dublin years is a moot point. Daly, a native of Farnane in the Sliabh Gua area of West Waterford, was a somewhat controversial character, especially in his younger days.[5] He changed his religion, becoming a member of the "Irish Society for Promoting the Education of the Native Irish through the Medium of their own Language," a Protestant proselytising sect founded in 1818,[6] and worked as a teacher and inspector with that organisation for a time. Some folk suspected that his motives for the religious change were more financial than theological, and when, in 1841, he changed back again to Catholicism, the same motives were suspected. His work with the Bible Society brought him to Youghal where he met his wife, and later to Kilkenny, where in the 1830s he established himself as a bookseller and stationer.[7] Over the next several decades Daly (*alias* O'Daly or Ó Dálaigh) earned for himself a reputation

---

[1] Duffy, C.G., *Life of Davis*, pp. 269-70; C.G. Duffy in *An Appreciation*, *Nation*, Sept. 7th 1850: 'Through the kindness of O'Connell, Edward Walsh was permitted, as a special grace, to devote his evenings to study and self-cultivation.'

[2] NLI, MS 2261: *Letters*, No. 9.

[3] ibid. *Letters*, No. 16.

[4] The *Jacobite Era* in Ireland dates from the late 17th to the mid 18th century and takes its name from King James II. Its political legacy was virtually nil despite the hopes expressed by the bards, but those same bards have left the memory of their high hopes with us to this day in music and song.

[5] Shannan Mangan, E., *James Clarence Mangan*, p. 274.

[6] NHI, p. 302.

[7] Daly, Brendan, in *Sliabh gCua Annual*, 1999, p. 21.

Fig. 9.
Charles Gavan Duffy, born in Monaghan town on Good Friday, 1816, was a barrister at law, a founder of the *Nation*. As editor of that paper he published many of Walsh's songs and was instrumental in having him move to Dublin at the end of 1843 or the turn of the year. Outside of his immediate family circle, Duffy together with Fr. William O'Connor of the South Parish, Cork, were the closest friends Walsh had.

Fig. 10.
Thomas Davis, a native of Mallow, Co. Cork, was also a barrister at law, a founder of the *Nation* and an admirer of Walsh's talent.

as one committed to the Irish language and tradition, and his premises at No. 9 Anglesea St. was an emporium of Irish books and manuscripts scarcely equalled in the country.[1]

The first of Walsh's letters to John Daly is dated January 2nd 1844. At that time Daly was forty-three years old with a considerable degree of expertise in business affairs. It would seem from Walsh's letters that the business arrangement between the two men was verbal only, and from Walsh's point of view, not an altogether satisfactory one, to say the least.[2] It is clear that Walsh is always the weaker party to the agreement and has little choice but to accept whatever Daly stipulates. In his letter of January 5th 1844, Walsh sets out his understanding of the agreement as follows:

> With regard to our projects respecting the songs, I understand you to say that you will bear all the expenses of printing, paper, etc., and after deducting all costs from the sales, you then at the end of six months will equally share the net profits remaining, with me. If this be so I am content. I'll engage to give you spirited translations, - talent is my only stock-in-trade, and I'll be no miser of it. In all other respects, Mr. Daly, reckon me as one who will die rather than lie or deceive.[3]

Daly did not accept this understanding of the agreement, as is evident from Walsh's letter of January 10th, "I have thrown out no hint of your dealing unfairly by me, but I understand from you both 'by word and write', as Burns says, that I was to share half 'the profits'. That you meant so if I paid half the expenses as they occurred, I do not doubt, because you tell me so, but I did not understand it so before. However, I am willing to 'sing' for the thing you mention, that is one-third, as I cannot get more unless I contribute to the outlay. Are you satisfied, Mr. Daly?"[4]

After another exchange of letters, Walsh wrote, "I understand your terms with me now Mr. Daly. You want to engross two thirds simply because you advance cash and some physical and a little mental toil while I that have to invoke the muse without whose inspiration you know, I would bring discredit on myself and your work, get but one third. That was not in 'bond' at first; but I'll take it for the good of - myself perhaps."[5]

Despite the lack of clarity in their business relationship, Walsh treated Daly as a friend from whom he could seek advice. He confided to him that he was "sadly disappointed"[6] with the move to Dublin, and sought his advice on the future. "My wife would wish to leave Dublin for some country town where she could carry on a little business in the millinery

---

[1] Daly, Brendan, in *Sliabh gCua Annual*, 1999, p. 21.
[2] NLI, MS 2261; *Letters*: No. 3.
[3] ibid.; *Letters*: No. 2.
[4] ibid.; *Letters*, No. 3.
[5] ibid.; *Letters*, No. 8
[6] ibid.; *Letters*, No. 7.

line or anything else that may do (she knows millinery) while I could attend to something else or teach school. We could command about £4 at present and I would wish to know from you whether you think the plan a good one; and if so, what town you would recommend us. We don't care in what direction we go and perhaps too you could say what business would be best with our small stocks. Write, dear Mr. Daly, and give us your best advice."[1] On April 7th he expresses his pleasure at his "quiet pretty residence"[2] in Mulgrave Place, but by May 5th the scene has changed again: "I am scribbling this at the Corn Exchange. I have not leisure nor room in my house for my wife has poured in lodgers on me."[3] Indeed, it is hard to blame her; more than likely Walsh's earnings were scarcely ever enough to support even the most frugal living.

John Daly, for his part, felt no obligation to reciprocate the intimacy, nor did he. When he "made a very profitable hit by the sale of some Irish works," Walsh complained that he only heard of it second-hand.[4] At the same time, Daly used the Walsh contact to further his own interests, and a major interest of his at that time was to secure a business premises in the capital. Having done some 'house-hunting' on his behalf, Walsh reported, "I travelled all round the quays and other places in the neighbourhood of the Liffey and could see few shops to be let, only one or two. These were to be let with houses at £100 a year. In Grafton St. near the corner of Galwey St. a shop with 2 or 4 rooms is to be let at £100 a year. I considered these too dear. I should apprise you that I am a bad hand at these concerns of life. If you tell any particular streets you would like to inquire for such in I shall do so again with pleasure."[5] As early as mid February Walsh had found a suitable premises for Daly: "It is a shop in Anglesea St. opposite Duffy's, with a parlour off the shop and either a back or front drawing room. The rent is no instance higher than £30 a year. Anglesea St. is well established and £30 I should suppose low."[6]

Meanwhile, each week, the translations being made by Walsh, together with the original Irish and interlinear literal translations were being printed by Mr. S. J. Machen, 28 Westmoreland St.[7] and released to the public in *penny numbers*. Negotiating the final versions of these by letter was cumbersome. In the exchanges over accuracy of translation, choice of words and phrases, matters of rhyme and metre, Walsh's criticisms were blunt and at times satiric, and although we do not possess Daly's replies, it would appear from Walsh's replies that Daly could give as good as he got. In a letter of April 16th., after a paragraph on the progress of the state trials in which Duffy was involved, Walsh continues:

[1] NLI, MS 2261; *Letters*: No. 11.
[2] ibid.; *Letters*, No. 19.
[3] ibid.; *Letters*, No. 23.
[4] ibid.; *Letters*, No. 16.
[5] ibid., *Letters*, No. 3.
[6] ibid.; *Letters*, No. 13.
[7] Samuel J. Machen, Publisher, 28 Westmoreland St, Dublin.

"Now Sir, why should I not mind your remarks when you have given the occasion? I have expostulated with you on the injustice and disrespect you showed me by checking me as you would a slave."[1] In the same letter he goes on to say, "Your disavowal of my intention of giving offence is sufficient and I accept it and shall resume the songs and I trust that no more bickering shall be between us."[2]

When the songs did come into the public domain, they found favour both in Dublin and in the provincial press.[3] Walsh was encouraged by the fact that the *Nation* carried some of his compositions and translations: "I gave Mr. Davis a few days ago, 'The Expulsion of the Saxon' and he was very polite and said he would publish it."[4]

At the beginning of July, 1844, Walsh expected to receive his first share of the profits from all the hard work he had put into translating over the previous six months. When it did not arrive he sent out a request to Daly on July 8th:

> I have been thinking that you would send me word against the first of July what I might expect to receive for my share of the work I have done for your songs but perhaps you have not yet been furnished with the account from Machen. My time is so occupied that I have not a moment to spare and had I time I should devote it to something that would fetch in a little money. Without a prospect of remuneration I cannot afford to write any more for your work... Send me now *a few pounds* as an earnest of what I may expect hereafter and as an encouragement to sing with something of energy. I shall use the vanity of saying that you will find few more capable of giving so faithful and spirited a version and none more willing but I must have some immediate encouragement."[5]

Daly's reply must have been anything but encouraging because Walsh's next letter reads: "I have had your note of this morning and have to apprise you that I have arrived at no hasty conclusion, but have informed you more than once before that I would not employ my time in writing translations and lives of Irish poets without a prospect of being paid (reasonably at least) for my trouble."[6] He went on to reminded Daly that, "'Tis not your Irish remember that sells the work but the English version,"[7] and at the end of his post script he returns to money matters, expressing the wish that Daly would come up to Dublin to "see whether I am going to get anything for my pains."[8] In his replies Daly tried to give the impression

---

[1] NLI, MS. 2261; *Letters*, No. 21.

[2] ibid.

[3] ibid.; *Letters*, No. 16; *Memoir*, Dec.12th p. 306; *Letters*, No. 33; Belfast *Vindicator*, June 26th. 1844.

[4] ibid.; *Letters*, No. 22.

[5] ibid.; *Letters*, No. 26.

[6] ibid.; *Letters*, No. 27.

[7] ibid.

[8] ibid.

that he had poets in abundance and that Walsh was quite dispensable.[1] As the letters went back and forth, it became evident that the conflict was that of a genuine artist versus a businessman. Walsh's deepest concern was to do justice to the poets he was translating.[2] He was more than anxious to ensure that anything published did honour to the material, to the translator and to the publisher, and one might legitimately conclude that his chief, and perhaps only reason for staying with John Daly was the fear that the latter would otherwise not give justice to the original poets a sufficiently high priority.

In mid-August, John Daly felt the need to put his overall position to the *Nation*, and did so in a letter dated August 14th 1844:

> Dear Sir,
>
> When I began publishing these songs, I was not actuated by pecuniary motives, my object being solely to distribute among my countrymen in a cheap form a large collection of the songs of our bards - songs written when persecution raged - when penal enactments ground the people to the very dust - and written in language which conveyed, in the most glowing manner, the cruel deeds of the hungry adventurer; but if that language were understood by the foe, the poet dare not give utterance to the effusions of his wounded spirit.
>
> Having had a large collection of those songs, which I collected from time to time through the country, and in many instances succeeded in obtaining the original MSS themselves, whose authenticity cannot be doubted - these I issued in penny numbers, to suit the lower classes of the community, who do not very often have many pence to spare, at the same time giving *interlinear* translations, to render those who did not understand the language, and were anxious to learn it, some assistance. A failure in this mode of publication, induced me to make up these numbers into parts, with printed wrappers, at a shilling each, for the respectable classes; and now, after having expended upwards of *twenty pounds* on the undertaking, when getting the account the other day from my publisher, Mr. Machen, Westmoreland-street, the return of the sales only amounted to £2-8s-10d, and 5,935 numbers were returned.
>
> However, this failure will not intimidate me, knowing that the songs will eventually make way for themselves, and that the public ere long will be able to take up the poetic effusions of Seán Claragh, Eoghan Ruadh ua Súilleabháin, Uilliam Dall ua Heifernáin, Seán ua Tuama an ghrinn, the eccentric Mangaire Súgach, and many

[1] NLI, MS. 2261; *Letters*, No. 27.

[2] Walsh was horrified at the prospect of translations being issued which did not do justice to the bards in question. He raised the matter in *Letters*, No. 29 and again in No. 31.

others, with a keener appetite than they do now a Byron or a Scott. With this view I have placed the second part of the songs in my printer's hands, which will be ready for delivery in a few days..."[1]

Walsh saw the letter in the *Nation* and "was much pleased with it."[2] Gavan Duffy was less impressed. He introduced Daly's letter with the comment, "The following letter from Mr. Daly tells a tale which we would have doubted upon less competent authority. But we do not yet believe that the fault was the people's. Was there no mismanagement?"[3]

By withdrawing his labour and talent, Walsh called John Daly's bluff concerning all the wonderful writers who could readily replace Edward Walsh,[4] so that by September, we find Daly trying to coax him back to work on the *Jacobite Reliques*. Walsh invited him to make an offer of a new contract while not rescinding the old. He even suggests a price per unit of work:

> I will engage to give you what you desire 'Sketches and Poetry' in future without any claim to the profits at the rate of £3 (three pounds) for every six numbers... I have spoken with a literary person on this subject and when I spoke of £3 for every six numbers he smiled at the little value I set by my song genius...This does not set aside my claim to be paid according to agreement for the already published numbers. If these terms you should consider not suitable to you, you need not make me a second offer as I will not take less than what I have just now repeated for my future labours."[5]

Daly replied by offering half what Walsh had proposed. At this point, Richard Nethercote, a printer at 75 Marlborough St., entered the picture as a mediator:

> I have seen Mr. Nethercote since the last letter of yours reached me, and when I told him I could not possibly accept the proposal of 5/- a number, he pressed me to come to some terms with you for I believe he has an interest in the repute of the work done at his place. He proposed that I should take the 5/- a number and if the work progressed so as to leave a profit that I should have the *half profit* according to our first agreement deducting of course in what came the 5/- per number from my share of the profit if I found it the more advantageous mode to take the half profit.

---

[1] *Nation*: Aug. 17th 1844.
[2] NLI, MS. 2261: *Letters*, No. 30.
[3] *Nation*: Aug. 17th 1844.
[4] NLI, MS 2261: *Letters*: No. 27.
[5] ibid.; *Letters*: No. 29.

> I would be better pleased that you dropped the songs rather than send them abroad in a manner unsuited to their merits, but as you are determined to persevere in publishing them, few things would give me greater grief than to see the language of your Jacobite poets clothed in such a garb as the rhymes that are now before me. And in short I shall therefore accept the terms which Mr. N——— has mentioned and I suppose you will have no objection to agree to them. I await your reply.[1]

The upshot of this agreement was the final publishing of *Reliques of Irish Jacobite Poetry* with the original Irish version and Walsh's metric translations. The volume was published by S.J. Machen in the autumn of 1844 and appeared in a green cover with floral decorations at the corners.[2] Its publication was the fulfilment of a dream for both parties but particularly for John Daly. It was he who possessed the original vision of such a project and had the practical qualities to see it through to completion. Walsh's growing reputation as a versifier gave Daly's efforts a status they would not otherwise have enjoyed. Much of the material in the book had already been placed before the public, first in the weekly numbers and later in small collections.

In the first *penny number*, Daly's address *To the Public* outlined his vision and motives. It was written from his Kilkenny premises and dated November 1843:

> In undertaking such a work as I am now about laying before my countrymen, I do not feel influenced by any other motive, than that of a sincere desire of preserving our old and soul-stirring songs from decay and destruction;... and leave them on record for posterity.
>
> In bringing out my little work the plan which I intend pursuing will be this: -The work will be printed in numbers, of eight octavo pages, good paper, and beautiful clear type, at the small price of one penny. The first number will be an introduction to the language, comprising a series of short and simple rules, by which any man of common understanding after one or two careful perusals, will be able to read any Irish book with ease. Each succeeding number will contain, at least, two Irish Songs, with short notes and *literal* translations; also, biographical notices of the writers, when practicable. With the last number will be given a title, index, and a general preface to the work, so as to enable purchasers to bind up their volumes at the close of its publication. The price charged will hardly realise the expense incurred by such an undertaking,[3] but Ireland's Sons must feel proud of such an opportunity as the present affords, for possessing themselves of the songs of their country. - On the whole it shall be conducted in such a manner as to render it in every way pleasing and satisfactory to the public, to whom I

---

[1] NLI, MS 2261: *Letters*, No. 31.

[2] NLI, 1st. (1844) edition.

[3] Each 8-page number cost one old English penny, i.e. about half of one cent euro.

> shall at all times feel thankful for any suggestions they may give, or alterations they may deem advisable; because in carrying on such a work, I do not consider myself any more than the servant of the parties for whom it is intended.
>
> Persons having manuscript Songs or Poems in their possession, which they would wish to see in print, will be pleased to have them duly forwarded. Such contributions shall be thankfully received and acknowledged by me, and the names of the contributors shall be mentioned in the number, in which the article appears.[1]

It was a noble task, timely too, as the Irish language and culture were at that time yielding fast to all things English.

The first issue made no reference to Edward Walsh but this was soon remedied. "I would wish, Mr. Daly," wrote Walsh, "when you give the metrical version of the songs, that you gave the name of the troubadour."[2] And adding weight to the request he goes on to invoke the authority of no less a person than Denny Lane the renowned Cork balladeer, "Mr. Lane recommended me not to forget this, as it might procure me notice."[3] Daly was sincere when he invited comment in his address *To the Public*. He was swift to respond, not only to Walsh's request but to some other suggestions too:

> At the suggestion of some friends I have altered my original plan, in order to facilitate the reading of the Songs to those who do not understand the Irish language; and, in the present number, it gives an interlinear translation of the Hamiltonian system, from which I shall not depart in future. A second edition of the second number will shortly appear in this form, and, as the *literal* translation, which accompanied that number is now dispensed with, I have engaged Mr. Edward Walsh, a writer thoroughly conversant with the legends and manners of the peasantry of the South of Ireland, and a principal contributor to the "Nation Newspaper," to furnish the metrical version which now appears, as well as that which will appear hereafter; thus making my penny publication suit the views and wishes of the community.[4]

Sixteen penny numbers in all were published. The press both in the capital and in the provinces warmly welcomed them.[5] The comment in the *Wexford Independent* is illustrative of it:

---

[1] *Reliques*, 1844 ed., pp. i & ii.

[2] *Letters*: No. 2.

[3] ibid.

[4] *Reliques*, 1st. (1844) ed., p. 9.

[5] ibid., Reviews in: *Clare Journal, Cork Examiner, Vindicator* (Belfast), *Chronicle and Munster Advertiser, Drogheda Argus, Kerry Examiner, Wexford Independent, Kilkenny Journal, Nation, Limerick Reporter.*

> Mr. Daly of Kilkenny has published the third number of his collection of Irish Songs, giving translations word for word, accompanied by truly beautiful poetical translations by Edward Walsh. Mr. Walsh has been the author of some of the most admired Songs published in the *Nation* Newspaper, and was previously known to the Irish public, as possessing in a high degree, the talents and acquirements necessary to constitute a successful poet. From the specimens before us, we would anticipate that, in conjunction with Mr. Daly, he will be enabled to make important and truly acceptable additions to the stores of native poetry and music, available to the different classes of the Irish people. The Songs hitherto given are excellent, breathing the genuine spirit of Ireland.[1]

In Daly's vision, the publications had the further purpose of cultivating the Irish language and culture that at that time was being displaced by the English language and the culture and values embodied in it. That language had come of age with the publication of the King James Bible and the plays of Shakespeare in the 17th century. Its value-system was largely rooted in the Anglo-Saxon Puritan culture which was narrow in religious outlook, poor in artistic expression, materialistic in pursuit of wealth, isolationist in relation to Continental Europe; but at the same time it was the culture of an expanding empire destined to stamp the emerging nations of the English speaking world. Daly and Walsh were ambitious enough to attempt the stemming of this brimming tide in the hope of saving Ireland from being swamped by it. The combination of songs with both literal and metrical translation was calculated to operate as a sort of primer for those interested in recovering the use of Irish.

Circulation of the penny numbers ranged from one to two thousand copies. By June there was a change of policy with a view to boosting sales. The Belfast *Vindicator* noted: "We understand Mr. Daly purposes editing his songs for the future in monthly, instead of weekly parts, as he finds they do not pay the outlay upon their publication in the latter form."[2] Because the publisher lacked the skill if not the will to sell the issues, the whole undertaking was proving a financial disaster.[3]

No matter how much one may argue the rights or wrongs of John Daly's dealings with Edward Walsh they can hardly be said to have been generous. Walsh seems to have been willing to accept any conditions in the hope of doing justice to the poets whom he was translating and earning enough on which to survive. There is something almost pathetic in his expression to Daly of a need for a dictionary and other relevant books to assist him in the translations:

---

[1] *Reliques*, 1844 ed., back cover.

[2] *Vindicator*, June 26th 1844.

[3] *Nation*: Aug. 17th 1844: Letter of John Daly with a prefatory comment by C.G. Duffy.

I had a particular reason for writing this letter. My acquaintance with the Jacobite songs makes me desirous of cultivating the language further and I have to request if you have any Irish books by you to send them. I want a dictionary but would not take that imperfect edition of O'Reilly of which I saw some volumes.[1] As a matter of course I would expect books from you to enable me to prosecute any particular subject we were engaged with - or if you demur there I will take a good dictionary at any reasonable price you will charge."[2]

Walsh turns against Davis

Walsh's overly sensitive nature made him his own worst enemy. He always craved approval, and any criticism, even of a friendly nature, threatened him. Gavan Duffy fell foul of him and so did Denis Florence McCarthy - the former because he did not include more of Walsh's compositions in his *Spirit of the Nation*, the latter because of 'a difference in the *Register*.'[3] But Gavan Duffy knew his man and did not cease to befriend him and promote his talent. Davis was next to fall from Edward Walsh's favour, but like Duffy, Davis too, "made allowances for Walsh's temperament but indicated that Walsh was not an easy man to live with because he brooked 'badly the companionship of ill-suited associates, and the rule of officials who had no appreciation for his gifts, no kindly sympathy for his mental torture'."[4]

It was the end of September 1844 when Davis fell from Walsh's favour. Gavan Duffy, together with O'Connell and half a dozen others, having been convicted in January, were sent to jail at the end of May but in early September had their sentence declared invalid by the House of Lords.[5] When released from Richmond Prison in Dublin, Duffy, whose health was in need of special care at the time, took a much needed holiday in Derrynane, Co. Kerry.[6] In his absence Thomas Davis temporarily took over the editorship of the *Nation*. During the weeks of Davis's stewardship Walsh sent in an original poem, *Éire Mo Chroí*, only part of which was published, and that with the following introductory comment: "The writer of *Éire Mo Chroí* is a man of fine ability, but in these verses, as in many of his, he commits two great faults - he uses uncommon dictionary words when he could have more readily used popular words, and he is unequal. Why did he wind up such sweet generalities as these with yesterday's hurra and a mock miracle?"[7] Davis was right on both counts but the blunt reality that he expressed was more than Walsh could take and his fury knew no bounds. He resorted to writing anonymous letters to the provincial press, criticising the

---

[1] Reilly, Edward, *An Irish-English Dictionary* (Minverva Printing Office) Dublin 1821.

[2] NLI, MS 2261; *Letters*, No. 19.

[3] *Appreciation*, *Nation*, Sept. 7th 1850; and *Letters* No. 59.

[4] Ibid.

[5] Duffy, C.G., *My Life on Two Hemispheres*, vol. I, p. 95.

[6] Duffy, C.G., *Nation*, "Answers to Correspondents," Oct. 19th 1844.

[7] *Nation*, Sept. 28th 1844.

Nation. Under "Answers to Correspondents" Gavan Duffy, on his return to the editorial desk, trenchantly rejected the allegations made against Davis and against the *Nation* and its policy and staff:

> The *Waterford Chronicle*, a journal in which we have usually seen extravagant praise of the *Nation*, has recently permitted some writer - certainly of ability, but apparently with a malignant motive - to misrepresent us. A more generous opponent would have preferred some other time than when the editor was notoriously absent in ill health; suffered in the public cause; but he is now at his post, ready to answer for himself and his colleagues. The first charge is, that the *Nation* contained a paragraph injurious to Catholicity, the said paragraph being a declaration for the practical exercise of religious liberty. Does this writer think that all the declarations by O'Connell and the national press, that religion is a question between man and his God, mean nothing, and that when they come to be reduced to practice we must act in direct opposition to them? If he does not, we are at a loss to understand the ground of his complaint. The second charge is, speaking favourably of a popular author who once wrote injuriously of Ireland. We might be content to say that we did not praise his faults; but the fact is, that he has entirely redeemed himself, and done substantial service to the cause of the country, in a work, which will see the light in a few days. In a former number of the *Chronicle* or some other provincial journal, a charge of similar character is made in relation to a phrase used by the editor's representative in rejecting some religio-political verses. Mr. Duffy's absence might have accounted for and excused a single inconsiderate or objectionable paragraph. It is hard if his character is not a shield for his journal against the imputation of damaging a cause that he has served since boyhood. The writers of the *Nation* have judged charitably and written courteously of their contemporaries and of all men; and they are surely not unreasonable in expecting to stand free from misrepresentation in return.[1]

Even though Gavan Duffy was aware of the authorship of Walsh's offending letters he continued to accept his work and have it published in the *Nation*. Through the remainder of 1844 Walsh had a number of items published including three, or possibly four, in December alone.[2] In 1845, his work appeared almost once a month up to July, after which there is a gap of almost a year. Other journals carry little of his work at this time. In the summer of 1846 he published a two-part article in the *Irish National Magazine* entitled "Passages in

---

[1] *Nation*, Oct. 19th 1844. Walsh was not the only writer of anonymous letters and Gavan Duffy's statement defending the *Nation* was directed at more than one.

[2] *Nation*: Dec. 7th, *The Minstrel's Invocation*; Dec. 21st, *Mo Chraoibhín Cnó*; Dec. 28th, *Song of the Mermaid*.

the life of Daniel O'Keeffe, the outlaw; surnamed Domhnall na Casgadh."[1] Finally in 1847 there appeared in the *Nation* a sonnet entitled "I would this dreary pilgrimage were o'er." It is initialled 'W'[2] and the sentiments expressed in it are certainly suited to the plight of Edward Walsh around that time.

During these years, particularly from the autumn of 1844 to the autumn of 1847, biographical details on Walsh are skimpy. According to *The Dublin Almanac, 1845,* he is still resident at No. 9 Mulgrave Place.[3] He became a member of the newly formed *Celtic Society* at its inception in 1847 and remained so for the rest of his life.[4]

The Split in the Repeal Association

During the same period (1844-47), the relationship between the ageing O'Connell and the more radical elements in the Repeal Association were gradually straining to breaking point. O'Connell's "Repeal Year"[5] - 1843 - had come and gone. The young men acknowledged O'Connell's leadership but did not rest easy with what they perceived to be his complicated and compromising involvement with the Whigs.[6] Among the ranks of the young men were many who in later times distinguished themselves on both the national and international scene - men such as Charles Gavan Duffy, Thomas Francis Meagher, Michael Doheny, John Blake Dillon, William Smith-O'Brien, John Mitchel and Richard O'Gorman. The title *Young Irelanders* was used initially as a disparaging one[7] but the level of integrity and dignity with which they conducted their affairs earned an increasing respect for them in their own time and a place of high honour in Ireland's memory of them ever since.

The voice of Young Ireland was the *Nation*, and Thomas Davis, as well as a being co-founder of that journal was also the acknowledged, if unofficial, leader.[8] It was, as we have seen, through the columns of this paper, and particularly with the publication of the "Irish War Song of A.D. 1843," that Edward Walsh was drawn into that lively world.

---

[1] *Irish National Magazine*, June 13th and June 20th 1846.

[2] *Nation*: Feb. 13th 1847.

[3] *The Dublin Almanac & General Register of Ireland, 1845*, p. 758.

[4] O'Donovan, J., *Miscellany of the Celtic Society,* 1849 (published in 1851), gives a list of "members of the Celtic Society since its formation in 1847" in which is named "Walsh (the late) Edward, esq. Dublin. Also, in *Letters,* No. 39, (Nov. 10th 1847) Walsh thanks his wife for sending the receipt for 10/- (the annual subscription) from the Celtic Society.

[5] At a meeting of the Repeal Association in the Corn Exchange Rooms, on Jan. 2nd O'Connell declared that year, 1843, to be "The Year of Repeal."

[6] O Connell's strategy of varying degrees of support for the Whig Party during the middle and late 1830s and into the early 1840s was not seen to bear fruit. In the attitude of the young men, later known as Young Irelanders, there was, in the words of historian Gearóid Ó Tuathaigh, an 'attitude of 'high principle' [and] an implicit condemnation of the wheeling and dealing which was a central feature of O'Connell's political style. Here lay the seeds of future discord.' (see: Ó Tuathaigh, *Ireland before the Famine*, pp.187-188).

[7] Duffy, C.G., *My Life in Two Hemispheres*, vol. I, p.112.

[8] Meagher, T.F. speaks of Davis as 'our prophet and our guide.' see, Arthur Griffith, *Meagher of the Sword*, p. 15.

From the beginning of Walsh's employment in the Corn Exchange in the late winter of 1843 or the early spring of 1844 the conflicts between *Old* and *Young* Ireland were playing themselves out all around him.[1] He did not take sides. His heart was probably with the young men,[2] but it was in the Corn Exchange that he earned his daily bread.

During his imprisonment[3] O'Connell lost faith in the Repeal movement. He was released from prison amid scenes of jubilation, "but from that hour forth," says C.G. Duffy, "he never made one step in advance, or one serious effort to reanimate the National Movement."[4] Between the time of conviction and sentence he had at a private conference proposed the dissolution of the Repeal Association as presently constituted but met with massive opposition and the matter was not raised again. He was old and infirm and may well have believed that Repeal was beyond the bounds of possibility in his lifetime, but, as Duffy says, "it was open to him to proclaim his new conviction, and declare he would get all he could for Ireland before he departed... What he unfortunately determined to do was to maintain in pubic that he was still on the same track, and to conceal from the people, by painful and shameful devices, that he had altogether changed his purpose."[5]

In early 1845, a particularly significant meeting of the Repeal Association was held, one characterised by much rancour and bitterness in the midst of which the chairman, Thomas Davis, was reduced to tears by O'Connell.[6] Despite an apology from the Liberator, the meeting was, in the view of Michael Doheny, a watershed after which "the Association never recovered."[7] A few months later, Davis died. Scarlatina swept him out of this world on September 16th, within a month of his 31st birthday. Referring to him as "our prophet and our guide"[8] Thomas Francis Meagher expressed the Young Irelanders opinion of their lost hero.

Walsh reported further deterioration in the affairs of the Repeal Association in a letter dated July 19th. 1846:

---

[1] In a letter dated July 19th 1846 (*Letters* No. 36) one gets a slight flavour of the atmosphere in which he worked at the Corn Exchange.

[2] Several of Walsh's original songs give a sense of rejoicing in blood and slaughter. I suggest that this mentality was born of romanticism and that he himself was in reality 'a paper tiger.'

[3] O'Connell had planned a *monster* Repeal Meeting for Clontarf on October 8th 1843. Peel, the British prime minister, instructed that the meeting be proclaimed illegal. On the day itself, the British army turned away any would-be attenders and on the following day, October 9th warrants were issued for the arrest of O'Connell, the head of the Repeal Association, Gavan Duffy, the editor of the *Nation*, and others. They were tried in February 1844 by an all-protestant jury, and found guilty. Sentence was passed on May 30th and all were jailed in the Richmond bridewell (near Portobello Bridge, Dublin) until the result of their successful appeal to the House of Lords was announced on September 13th Of that year.

[4] Duffy, C.G., *My Life in Two Hemispheres*, vol. I, p. 95.

[5] ibid., pp. 88-89.

[6] ibid., p. 113.

[7] ibid.

[8] Griffith, A., *Meagher of the Sword*, p. 15.

> I am not sorry that I had not time on Friday to reply to your letter, as I have some political information to send you, which has not yet reached the Dublin papers. At 'a soirée' at Kilrush, in reply to some severe remarks of Mr. Charles O'Connell - a gentleman of Clare and a friend of O'Connell's - upon 'Young Ireland,' Smith O'Brien declared that there were at present three Repeal parties in Ireland, each pursuing its own particular views - O'Connell and his sons, the priests, and lastly, the people. He also loudly condemned the policy of the committee respecting Dungarvan.[1] His language has caused a strange sensation in the Corn Exchange Rooms, and is wholly unaccountable. We may know more after tomorrow's meeting.[2]

At a meeting on July 26th O'Connell demanded a pledge against the use of violence as a means of gaining political objectives. Though violence was not contemplated at the time, the pledge was one the Young Irelanders were not prepared to give.

The result of this quarrelling was a split within the Repeal Association, and the founding, on January 13th 1847, of an *Irish Confederation* to represent the Young Irelanders in the world of politics.[3] At that foundation meeting in the Rotunda, the brilliant young orator, Thomas Frances Meagher, addressed the chair:

> Sir, there was a levee at the Castle this morning. Gentlemen went there to pay their respects to the representative of royalty: we have met here this night, to testify our allegiance to liberty. I will not inquire which is the more honourable act; but I think the latter more useful. Where a court resides a parliament should sit. A court, without a senate, can do little for the public good; it may do much for the public harm. The court of the province may distribute favours, and teach a propriety of demeanour. The senate of the free nation distributes blessings, and inspires the community with virtue...Sir, the Castle has been preserved, whilst the senate has been destroyed, and the blood and poison in which it was destroyed have given birth to a hideous famine.[4]

Whether Edward Walsh was present at that meeting, we cannot say. To the sentiments expressed he would surely have assented. Nor can we say if a conflict of interests created by his position at Corn Exchange and his loyalty to Duffy and the Young Irelanders was a

---

[1] Dungarvan: a reference to a bye-election in which the Repeal Association did not put forward a candidate, thus leaving the seat open to the Whig candidate. In a speech in Conciliation Hall, July 13th 1846, Thomas Francis Meagher said, "I regret exceedingly that the battle for Repeal was not fought upon the hustings of Dungarvan, against all odds, and in the teeth of every risk. The influence of the Duke of Devonshire has been alluded to. If the fear of ducal influence, my lord, is to deter us from the assertion of our rights, farewell, then, say I, to public honour, to public virtue, to public liberty in Ireland. If in the Cavendishes there lies a stronger spell than in the banner of Repeal, our cause, in truth, is hopeless. (See Griffith, A., *Meagher of the Sword*, pp. 21-22)

[2] *Memoir*, Dec. 12th p. 308; *Letters*, No. 36.

[3] NHI, p. 323.

[4] Griffith, A., *Meagher of the Sword*, p. 53. Speech in the Rotunda, Jan. 13th 1847.

factor in his eventual departure from employment at Burg Quay. That move is more likely to have been precipitated by the death of O'Connell in Genoa on May 15th 1847; for Walsh, while having respect for O'Connell, had none for his son and heir, John, on whom the leadership of the Association now devolved. "The only one of O'Connell's sons he had a high opinion of was Maurice" wrote Kickham in his *Memoir*. "He looked upon John with contempt, even when that gentleman 'was his father's favourite', 'the young liberator,' 'the hope,' etc. As another proof of Walsh's correct perception of character, the following anecdote is worth repeating. Mr. J. O'Connell (Walsh, when speaking of him used to call him 'Johnny') rushed up in a flurry to the desk where Walsh was writing, and called, in a hasty, imperious manner, for 'ink, ink'. Walsh, scarcely lifting his head said, quietly: 'Porter, get Mr. O'Connell ink.' The little great man did not like him after."[1]

Another reason why Walsh did not join the Young Irelanders may have been religious. In 1845 the British Prime Minister, Sir Robert Peel, proposed a new educational system for Ireland so that Catholics might enjoy the same privileges as Protestants in relation to colleges and universities. The Catholic bishops were prepared to cooperate with the government provided there were some important amendments. The young men in the Repeal association were delighted but O'Connell opposed the bill and claimed that the bishops were on *his* side.[2] Reflecting on the poisoning of the public mind against Young Ireland that ensued, Duffy says that O'Connell's son John whom he describes as "a feeble, conceited young man who believed that he had inherited with his name the splendid endowments of his father"[3] -

> found time to sow suspicions of Thomas Davis as a dangerous, intriguing infidel, whose friends acquiesced in his dark designs. The young men in towns treated these rumours with contempt, but they made a serious impression on the Catholic clergy. Among a pious people irreligion is the most unpardonable of offences, and from this time rumours were circulating in many parts of the island that the Young Irelanders were the enemies of God and their country.[4]

Bishop William Higgins of Ardagh wrote that in his diocese "there were no physical-force men, nor, he thanked God, any schoolboy philosophers, false and sanguinary Repealers, or Voltairian newspapers; the *Nation* was the most dangerous publication that ever appeared in Ireland."[5] O'Connell went so far as to get George Plunkett Browne, the new bishop of Elphin, to come to the Corn Exchange to denounce the *Nation* and its writers. He came

---

[1] *Memoir*: Dec. 5th 1857, p. 306.

[2] Duffy, C.G., *My Life in Two Hemispheres*, vol. I, pp. 109.

[3] ibid., p.81.

[4] ibid., p. 123.

[5] ibid., p. 176.

there, said the bishop, "to enter his solemn protest against the puny efforts of the Young Irelanders. They are the enemies of religion."[1] Even a decade later John Henry Newman the first Rector of the newly established Catholic University of Ireland in Dublin was reaping the fruits of such malicious or ill-informed pronouncements. In casting about for suitable professorial talent Newman was limited by the knowledge that archbishop Cullen did not want Young Irelanders on the university staff. But Newman found that the best talent in the country was among the ranks of these "enemies of religion." His respect for the archbishop did not deter him from going against the latter's wishes, and even though he suffered for it he did not regret it:

> There was a knot of men who in 1848 had been quasi rebels; they were clever men and had cooled down, most of them. I did not care much for their political opinions. Dr. Moriarty [of Kerry] introduced them to me, and I made them professors. They are the ablest men who have belonged to the university; such are professor O'Curry and professor Sullivan. I can never be sorry for asking their assistance; not to take them would have been preposterous... I cannot pursue these things at this distance of time; but the consequence was that Dr. Cullen became alienated from me, and from an early date either did not write to me, or, if ever he did, wrote by a secretary."[2]

Edward Walsh, a devout and faithful Catholic but no Newman, would scarcely have allowed himself the liberty of conscience to hold out against the views and assertions of powerful church leaders despite what his heart might have dictated.

Irish Popular Songs

Though it cannot be said with certainty, the death of O'Connell in May of 1847 in all probability marked the end or at least 'the beginning of the end' of Edward Walsh's employment at the Repeal Headquarters in Conciliation Hall, if indeed it had not already ended the previous year.[3] It is unthinkable that a man of his temperament, feelings and views, could bring himself to continue in there under the stewardship of John O'Connell, even if faced with starvation. And starvation cannot have been far from his door during that blighted year of *Black '47.*

---

[1] Duffy, C.G., op. cit. 187.

[2] Ward, W., *The Life of John Henry Cardinal Newman*, p. 382.

[3] NLI, MS 2261. An unidentified newspaper cutting attached to the MS refers to Walsh's post of employment in the following terms: "This he held until 1846, when the famous break up of the Irish organization sent the staff of O'Connell adrift."

Fig. 11.
Thomas Francis Meagher, *Meagher of the Sword*, was the flamboyant son of a Waterford merchant. A Young Irelander and compelling orator, Meagher, at the age of twenty four was transported to the convict settlement in Tasmania (Van Diemen's Land) in 1849. After his escape, he rose to high military and civil rank in the U.S.A.

Fig. 12.
William Smith O'Brien, Young Irelander, and prisoner in Tasmania after the 1848 Rebillion. His health broke down but he maintained a stout spirit 'thanks to my Good friend Thomas à Kempis,' a mediaeval writer and author of the ever popular *Imitation of Christ*.

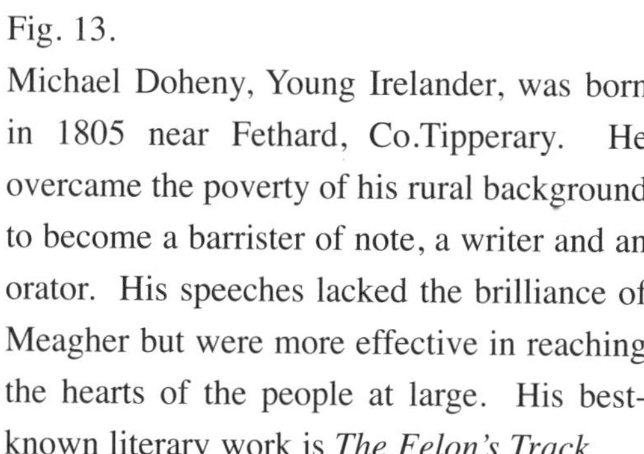

Fig. 13.
Michael Doheny, Young Irelander, was born in 1805 near Fethard, Co.Tipperary. He overcame the poverty of his rural background to become a barrister of note, a writer and an orator. His speeches lacked the brilliance of Meagher but were more effective in reaching the hearts of the people at large. His best-known literary work is *The Felon's Track*.

In that year his second volume of poetry, *Irish Popular Songs*, was published in Dublin by James McGlashan.[1] The volume, as the title indicates, contained some of his original compositions already in print and proving popular particularly in Dublin. It included also a number of translations from his *Jacobite Reliques* and other sources, together with a lengthy introduction in which he expands his view on matters pertaining to Irish poets, poetry and translators. It was dedicated

To
The people of Ireland,
as a tribute to their many virtues,
and
with ardent admiration
of
their high poetic genius,
as evidenced in their songs and legends, this volume
is inscribed
by
their friend and countryman,
EDWARD WALSH.[2]

Reviews in the *Dublin Warder* and the *Dublin Weekly Register* were favourable but superficial. A more substantial review in the *Nation* readily acknowledged Walsh's gifts but went on to point out a range of shortcomings in the content of the book. The unnamed reviewer first expatiates on the general state of Irish poetry and notes that as a literary genre it scarcely merited a mention until the recent past:

> The recognition of a distinct character in Irish literature, not English, and not Scotch, but native and to the manner born of the soil, is altogether modern. However it may have floated in men's minds before, as we were convinced it did, we do not find any distinct enumeration of it till 1843 - the year that sent forth men questioning all English pretensions to supremacy. Up to that time an article on *Irish Poetry*, in the most Irish periodical, would have suggested some pleasant exaggeration or burlesque. Readers would have prepared themselves to enjoy the humour of having the "Groves of Blarney" treated as a National Epic, or a street ballad from the Liberties gravely welcomed as the "latest offspring of the Irish muse."[3]

---

[1] Walsh, E., *Irish Popular Songs*, McGlashan (Dublin); W.S. Orr (London) 1847.
[2] ibid.
[3] *Nation*, June 26th 1847 p. 602.

The reviewer next assesses the merits of *Irish Popular Songs*:

> Mr. Walsh's *Popular Songs* are translations from the Irish, of which, we believe, he is a practised scholar. Nine tenths of the Irish poetry that has come down to us through all the formidable difficulties which stood like barriers and sentinels between the past and present of Irish traditions are untranslated; and three-fourths of what has been translated are so formal, frigid, and pedantic, that the soul of the country acknowledges no affinity with them. Mr. Walsh, therefore, has chosen an honourable and useful task, and one for which his genius fitted him well.[1]

> The reviewer is seriously disappointed to find that he [Walsh] has been less anxious to widen our domain and increase our possessions, than to contend for personal distinction with his predecessors on fields already won... A contest with Ferguson and Mangan brings its own punishment, but the practice and *animus* are so unhealthy that contending with poets inferior to them, and to himself, Mr. Walsh wins no laurels.[2]

A further disappointment is the fact that "nearly the entire collection of Irish originals are taken from Hardiman's *Minstrelsy*,"[3] despite Walsh's own assertion that "our hills and valleys and milking bawns, and every cottager's fireside are vocal with hundreds of songs, which want but the aid of a poet, himself one of the people, speaking their tongue, and familiar with its idioms, to recommend them to public notice in an English dress."[4] The reviewer's advice is that "Mr. Walsh should break new ground, and devote his talents, which are great and original, to make independent accessions to our too scanty store of translations. His *Jacobite Reliques*, many of the pieces in the present collection, but above all his own original poems, justify us in expecting valuable results from labour in this direction."[5] And a final comment: "In purpose and character, Mr. Walsh's labours are entirely Irish, and his zeal is akin to that which sustained the persecuted poets whom he loves to honour. He is their brother in genius and patriotism."[6]

In the Ireland of 1847, however, the Great Famine was reaching its zenith, few were in a mood for singing, many must have wished "this dreary pilgrimage were o'er" and for more than a million people it was.

---

[1] *Nation*, June 26th 1847 p. 602
[2] ibid.
[3] ibid.
[4] ibid.
[5] ibid.
[6] ibid.

I would this dreary pilgrimage were o'er,
Where countless snares my bleeding feet betray.
Sweet dawn arise! my home is far away -
A friendless exile on an alien shore,
I mark the time's advancing breaker's roar;
The tide rolls in to gulf us - yet we stay,
And on a crumbling landmark madly play,
Wasting the priceless hours for evermore.
Rise, sacred dawn! methinks a fresh'ning breeze
From yonder holy mountain skyward springs,
The day is breaking! Courage! now, my heart,
Our lonely skiff shall brave the coldest seas,
For sighs of angels rustle through her wings -
The tear to some, and then in silence we depart.[1]

[1] *Nation*: Feb. 13th 1847; initialled 'W'.

CHAPTER FOUR

UNMERCIFUL DISASTERS[1]

Walsh's fortunes can never be said to have been particularly good, but they turned decidedly worse in the latter part of 1847. Probably at the end of the autumn or the very beginning of winter he left Dublin. Why? We do not know. The move may have been precipitated by the split in the Repeal Association, or more likely, by the death of Daniel O'Connell. To a man of Walsh's sensibilities the thought of serving under John O'Connell, the Liberator's son and successor in the Corn Exchange, could scarcely have been entertained.

Spike Island

In *An Appreciation*, Charles Gavan Duffy said that "subsequent to the cessation of his connection with the Repeal Association, he was driven by the straitened circumstances of his family to accept the situation of schoolmaster of the Convict Depot at Spike Island, procured for him by an attached friend, a Catholic clergyman of the county Dublin, himself a learned Irish antiquarian and genealogist, and passable versifier."[2] The most likely candidate to fit this description is Fr. Charles P. Meehan (1812-1890) who was educated in Rome and served all his life as curate in the parish of Saints Michael and John, with a residence in Lower Exchange St. Meehan, like Walsh, wrote verses for the *Nation*. Among his other literary activities Fr. Meehan edited the *Irish Catholic Magazine*, published translations and historical compilations, edited the poems of Davis and James Clarence Mangan, and was author of *Fate and Fortunes of Hugh O'Neill, Earl of Tyrone, and Rory O'Donnell, Earl of Tyrconnel.*[3]

Before becoming a fortified military post and symbol of oppression, Spike Island, Walsh's new home, was a 180-acre plot of fair and fertile land surrounded by the waters of Cork's lower harbour opposite the picturesque town of Cobh. St. Carthage of Rahan and Lismore founded a monastery there in the 7th century and the island's reputation was that of "a most holy place," having "most holy people reside in it perpetually."[4] Leaping forward to the 18th century, at the outbreak of the French Revolution and the subsequent Napoleonic Wars Spike Island's function as a breakwater for the spacious inner harbour attracted the eye of Britain's defence authorities. In 1791 was begun the erection of Fort Westmoreland (now Fort Mitchel)

---

[1] *Memoir*, Dec. 12th p. 308.

[2] *Appreciation*, *Nation*, Sept. 7th 1850.

[3] Boylan, H., *A Dictionary of Irish Biography*, p. 226.

[4] Coleman, J., in JCHAS, II, No. 13, (Jan. 1893), pp. 1-2.

on the high ground at the centre, and later a barracks and military hospital.[1] The 1831 census shows the island as having forty houses and a population of 205.

As a British naval base the island served many purposes, notably as a defence against invasion, an assembly point for soldiers awaiting transport overseas, and safe harbourage in time of need. During the Great Famine Spike Island was also a convict depot housing prisoners or detaining those destined for transportation to, among other places, Bermuda, Australia, and Van Diemen's Land (Tasmania). It was into this island of sorrow that Edward Walsh arrived as the darkness of winter was closing in over the harbour.

Perhaps the most valuable part of Kickham's *Memoir* is the number of Walsh's letters quoted in whole or in part. It includes four from Spike Island, two from the early winter of 1847, November 10th and 18th respectively, and a further two undated.[2] His eldest son, six-and-a-half-year-old Adam Edward, accompanied him on the island and it was Walsh's hope that Brigid and the rest of his family would be allowed to join him later.

Considering the times, his own living conditions were not so bad at a material level: "Adam and I are just sitting down to our supper of boiled bread and milk. We have both to spare, as the storm did not permit the milkman to land in the morning, and we have now a double portion. Adam says, 'Mamma will be in great glee when she comes here, to find such lots of boiled bread and milk.' "[3] But despite having Adam with him, the absence of the others is a source of pain. To his wife he wrote:

> My Dear Love,
> I sit down to write to you, and the more readily, as the fierce storm that is raging here, at eight o'clock at night, is tremendous; this storm of the elements inclines my heart and its faculties to you, my beloved, and our dear little ones, with a prayer that God may protect you, till you all come to my longing embrace. How awfully it blows! Adam who is now reading some ballad, has started suddenly exclaiming 'Is not that the cry of some one in great pain?' The island is very high, and the winds seize upon it fearfully. I went at three o'clock to look out upon the harbour from the ramparts, and was forced to lie down in the blast. However, we have a warm room, with solid stone walls, and a bomb-proof roof over our heads, and are very snug."[4]

Again he wrote: "I have not had since I left Dublin, those deep and dreamless slumbers which I always had, as a portion of my existence, when you were near me. But they will come again, and you and my children shall yet make my heart leap at the joy of your

---

[1] *The Parliamentary Gazetteer of Ireland*, 1845, vol. III, p. 274; S. Lewis, *Topographical Dictionary*, vol. I, p. 5723.

[2] *Memoir*, Dec. 19th pp. 321-322; *Letters* Nos. 37 & 38.

[3] ibid., *Letters* No. 38.

[4] ibid., *Letters*, No. 37.

presence."[1] And further: "If you were permitted here, you could have nice apartments, coals and candles, and two pounds of bread each day, *gratis*; and then the salary would leave us enough for minor wants. We shall try."[2] As with many of Walsh's dreams, this one never materialised. In another letter to Brigid, he expanded further on the consequences of the family being permitted to share his living quarters: "I think we'd be very happy here till the children would be grown, did they permit you to reside with me. I'd have great leisure; the school business won't be more than four hours a-day."[3] He explored the possibility of finding alternative accommodation for the family on the island but, as two comments testify, it was a fruitless search: "there is no lodging to be got in any of the miserable cabins of the island,"[4] and "I don't think there is a decent room in this whole island."[5]

The routine affairs of domestic and family life irked the schoolmaster: "I am annoyed from little turns I am forced to do about myself and Adam. Fancy me cooking ham and cabbage, and cleaning up the crockery?"[6] And again: "It gives me great hardship to do every little turn of the place, and also to attend Adam, and my public duties, which are now commencing."[7]

Attending to his "public duties" was not only physically demanding but emotionally draining: "I am awake every morning at five o'clock and up at six[8]... I have three hundred persons here, to whom I have given books, etc., before the school regularly opens. Most of the convicts are persons of the south and west, who were driven by hunger to acts of plunder and violence. I wept to-day in one of the wards, when some of the people of Skull and Skibbereen told me the harrowing tale of their sufferings from famine, and the deaths - the fearful deaths - of their wives and little ones. How 'we' should thank the Lord!"[9]

Over and over the letters from Spike Island reveal his feelings of love and expression of tenderness towards Brigid and the children: "Let me know, love, particularly, how you are and how are the children. I hope Fanny will mind Mary and Edward. I hope you won't make yourself vexed or uneasy about that work which always injures your health. Will you promise me now? If you don't, I'll take Fanny and Mary into the Island, and leave you and Edward outside."[10] On hearing that Brigid's own health had improved, he wrote on November 10th: "Need I say how your last letter makes my heart glad? You know how I felt for your illness, and how I must rejoice at your restoration to health. Nothing that could

---

[1] *Memoir*, Dec. 19th p. 321; *Letters*, No. 37.
[2] ibid., p. 323; *Letters*, No. 39.
[3] ibid., p. 321; *Letters*, No. 37.
[4] ibid., p. 324; *Letters*, No. 40.
[5] ibid. p. 323; *Letters*, No. 39.
[6] ibid., p. 322; *Letters*, No. 38.
[7] ibid., p. 320; *Letters*, No. 37.
[8] ibid., *Letters*, No. 37.
[9] ibid., p. 322; *Letters*, No. 38.
[10] ibid., p. 322; *Letters*, No. 38.

befall me on earth would give me such sincere joy as to see you well and happy."[1] He was particularly concerned for the health of Edward Charles, their fourth child and second son:

> How your letter of Monday and Tuesday relieved my wretched heart, thanks to the Almighty Disposer of life and death! You who know my tender love for the children, will understand the boundless gratitude of that heart for such mercy. It is curious that, even after reading your letter announcing his illness, and up to the receipt of your last, I had a strong presentment that the child would not die!
>
> As I feel a wrong, so do I cherish the memory of a good deed done to me or mine. Give my best and most grateful thanks to Dr. McSweeney, who on another occasion acted as my friend. Tell him how I loved my boy, and then he'll conceive my overflowing gratitude; tell Miss Murray's family also how deeply I feel their kindness. God bless and prosper them through life. Write, dear Brigid, at once, and let me know if Edward Walsh, the younger, is well and kicking. Let me know if Fan is minding all the house, and playing with Mary and Edward. Tell Fan, and 'mine mouse', that I'll soon be kissing them. 'Tis now very late at night, for I put Adam to bed and mended his clothes before I set to this. Make haste to me. You have asked me to pray for you; don't you know, love, that twice every day, since you became my wife, a prayer for your welfare has gone to the throne of Heaven, from the unworthy, but fervent heart of your fond husband and truest 'friend' Edward Walsh.[2]

Brigid's tenderness and love communicated itself wonderfully to him by letter: "Your last letter was so gentle and kind, that if your tongue, my fair Brigid (how sweetly that pretty name suits my notion of you!) wagged as tenderly at all times as your pen, your voice would be balm to my bruised and broken spirit, and I would fly to hush, in the white bosom of my gentle dove, all my sorrows for ever!"[3] Brigid's loving care extended beyond words to the point of overworking in order to be able to send him money and supplies of food and clothing: "I have got your parcel in Cork. Why did you not tell me the particular things you sent? I found some coffee and brown sugar in the keg, and some cheese, also a scarf and trousers."[4] But the loneliness dogged him: "I am very lonely here, and don't read nor write, and have scarcely leisure, and no inclination to amuse myself without you and the dear little ones."[5] These sentiments concur with John Mitchel's later assessment that Walsh's life was in tatters,[6] and C.G. Duffy in his *Appreciation* said, "Since that day he has never sung; or if he did he had not the heart to sing aloud."[7]

---

[1] *Memoir*, Dec. 19th, p. 323; *Letters*, No. 399.
[2] ibid., p. 324; *Letters*, No. 40.
[3] ibid., p.324; *Letters*, No. 40.
[4] ibid., p. 321; *Letters*, No. 37.
[5] ibid., p. 322; *Letters*, No. 38.
[6] ibid., p. 30.
[7] *Appreciation*, *Nation*, Sept. 7th 1850.

The Man Most to be Envied - John Mitchel

The political and social ferment in Dublin during Walsh's years there continued long after his departure. In his new employment he was not only separated from his family but from familiar faces and friends. Isolated though he was the high drama continuing to take place in the capital could not have entirely escaped his notice. Then, suddenly, at the end of May 1848 the central character in the drama stepped ashore on Spike Island. That person was John Mitchel. Walsh's excitement knew no bounds when he discovered that Mitchel, "the man in all Ireland most to be envied,"[1] had come ashore from his prison ship.

Mitchel, a native of Camnish, near Dungiven, Co. Derry, was the son of a Presbyterian minister. He was educated in Newry and Trinity College and practised as a lawyer in Newry and Banbridge. He joined the Repeal Association in 1843, started writing for the *Nation* two years later and eventually became its editor. Because he disagreed with Charles Gavan Duffy, the proprietor of the paper, he resigned and in February 1848 established his own newspaper, *The United Irishman.*[2]

Convinced that constitutional politics were achieving nothing, Mitchel first advocated passive resistance and then physical force for the attainment of a free Ireland.[3] In the year 1848 revolution was in the air across Europe and beyond and Mitchel was convinced that it would be in Ireland before year's end because the still hungry population would not take kindly to seeing their grain harvest exported as had been done the previous year.[4] For writing and speaking in this vein he was arrested towards the end of May, detained in Newgate prison and hurriedly tried at Green Street courthouse, Dublin. Before his wife Jenny and several Young Ireland friends he was found guilty by a packed and hostile jury and sentenced to fourteen years transportation. There was a mood for a rescue bid among the large gathering around the court. Mitchel seemed to expect one and he placed the blame for its absence on his former friend Gavan Duffy.[5]

Noting the circumstances of Mitchel's conviction and transportation, the people at large instantly numbered him among the martyrs for Ireland. In a speech in the Music Hall in June, Thomas Francis Meagher expressed himself thus: "Upon the walls of Newgate a fettered hand has inscribed this destiny - we shall be the martyrs or the rulers of a revolution. 'One, two, three - ay, hundreds shall follow me,' exclaimed the glorious citizen who was sentenced to exile and immortality upon the morning of the 27th of May."[6] Before the day of his conviction had passed Mitchel had opened his now famous *Jail Journal*:

---

[1] Mitchel, J., *Jail Journal*, p. 30.

[2] Boylan, H., *A Dictionary of Irish Biography*, p. 227; R. Hogan, *Dictionary of Irish Literature*, pp. 451-452.

[3] ibid., p. 227.

[4] Keneally, T., *The Great Shame*, p. 145.

[5] ibid., p. 148-151.

[6] Griffith, A., *Meagher of the Sword*, p. 162.

"May 27th 1848. - On this day, about four o'clock in the afternoon, I, John Mitchel, was kidnapped, and carried off from Dublin in chains, as a convicted *Felon*."[1] The *Sheerwater*, which bore him away from Dublin's North Wall on that very evening, docked next day beside Spike Island in Cork Harbour. It was against this background that Edward Walsh saw Mitchel as "the man in all Ireland most to be envied."[2]

The prisoner was treated with dignity on Spike. Mr. Grace, the governor of the depot, went to the trouble of getting him a few changes of linen and other necessities. Walsh's desire to meet the patriot drove him to recklessness, and, with the connivance of a jailor he achieved his ambition. Mitchel had known of Walsh as the author of *Mo Chraoibhín Cnó* and other beautiful compositions. But now, looking at him there in his black threadbare clothes, he felt that Walsh was losing the battle for life. In the *Jail Journal* for that day, May 30th, he wrote:

> There is a door in the high wall leading into another enclosure, and, as I was taking a turn through my territory to-day, the turnkey was near the door, and he said to me, in a low voice, 'This way, sir, if you please.' He held the door open, I passed through, and immediately a tall, gentleman-like person in black, but rather over-worn clothes, came up to me and grasped both my hands, with every demonstration of reverence. I knew his face, but could not at first remember who he was. He was Edward Walsh, author of *Mo Chraoibhín Cnó*, and other sweet songs, and of some very musical translations from old Irish ballads. Tears stood in his eyes as he told me he had contrived to get an opportunity of seeing and shaking hands with me before I should leave Ireland. I asked him what he was doing at Spike Island, and he told me he had accepted the office of teacher to a school they kept here for small convicts - a very wretched office, indeed, and to a shy, sensitive creature like Walsh it must be daily torture. He stooped down and kissed my hands. 'Ah!' he said, 'you are now the man in all Ireland most to be envied.' I answered that I thought there might be room for difference of opinion about that; and then, after another kind word or two, being warned by the turnkey, I bade him farewell, and retreated into my own den. Poor Walsh! He has a family of young children; he seems broken in health and spirits. Ruin has been on his traces for years, and, I think, has him in the wind at last. There are more contented galley slaves moiling at Spike Island than the schoolmaster. Perhaps this man does really envy me; and, most assuredly, I do not envy him.[3]

---

[1] Mitchel, J., *Jail Journal*, p. 21.
[2] ibid., p. 30.
[3] ibid., p. 30.

Fig. 14.
John Mitchel, a solicitor of Banbridge, Co. Down, was one of the first Irish protestants of note to join the Repeal Association. After his escape from the convict depot in Tasmania he fought on the Confederate side in the American Civil War. Shortly before his death he returned to Ireland and was elected a member of parliament for Tipperary.

Fig. 15. The gateway to the forbidding fortress on Spike Island where Mitchel and Walsh had their one and only meeting. In the foreground are Elizabeth Nunn of Queensland, Australia, great-great-granddaughter of Edward Walsh chatting with a distant relative, John O'Connell of Stuak, Co. Cork.

Walsh's patriotism, which drove him to seek this illicit interview with the renowned prisoner, cost him his job and plunged him into virtual destitution. Following his dismissal, he went to Kiskeam and spent most of the summer of 1848 there but he does not seem to have had his family with him. His residence was a mud-walled cabin, not dissimilar from many others of the day, located about three hundred metres west of Kiskeam Bridge, on the right hand side of the road, overlooking the river. My great-grandmother, Nano Casey, then in her teens, remembered him at this time as a man broken in health. During the weeks and months of his convalescence, she would observe him stroll by the Araglen water and the Glouneen[1] where in the days of his youth he had danced at the bonfire on St. John's Night.

There is an entry in the Baptismal Register of Saints Michael and John parish that may indicate Walsh's presence in Dublin at the beginning of July and certainly before July 6th.[2] The entry states that Edward and Brigid Walsh were sponsors to a child of John and Mary Walsh. The officiating priest was Fr. C. P. Meehan[3] If indeed it was our Edward Walsh, one can only wonder if he had more than one motive for undertaking the long arduous journey from Kiskeam to Dublin. Perhaps he was in hopes of finding new employment there.

Whether or not Walsh sought work in Dublin, he eventually found it in Cork. On August 24th 1848 he was employed as a teacher in the Cork Union Workhouse (in the grounds of St. Finbarr's Hospital better known perhaps as *The South Infirmary*), a post carrying a salary of £50 per annum.[4] But the conditions! From his four hours a day in Spike Island he was now working fourteen. Then there was the question of numbers. For March 17th 1849, about half way through Walsh's term of employment, the *Minute Book of Cork Union Board of Guardians* records a total Workhouse population of 6,300. Close on half of this number were children, 1,383 boys and 1,264 girls.[5] By January 12th1850, shortly before Walsh's departure on health grounds, the number of children had dropped slightly: 1,261 boys and 1,191 girls. On any other date during his employment there the figures were not dissimilar.

Teaching in the ordinary sense of the word was a secondary consideration as the following report testifies:

> The teachers have...done as much as was possible under the many obstacles in their way: their time is chiefly occupied in distributing rations to the children, and superintending

---

[1] Family tradition through my maternal (*Shamrock House*) line.

[2] NLI, Micro film Baptismal Records, Parish of SS. Michael & John. The dates between July 1st and 6th in the Baptismal Record are partially defaced.

[3] ibid.

[4] Gleeson, p. 148ii

[5] MS: BG69A9, 17-03-1849. The school buildings still stand at St. Finbarr's Hospital. The ground floor of the boy's school is presently the accident and emergency unit; the second floor is a geriatric unit and the top floor is not fully operational. What used to be the girls' school presently caters for some of the hospital's female patients.

them at work and at their meals; school business being but a secondary consideration. The Master can command the children to work whenever he thinks fit; they are employed in breaking stones and grinding corn. It is impossible under such circumstances that any useful effects can spring from the operation of the school."[1]

In a letter dated September 9th 1849, Walsh wrote: "I am worked here from six in the morning till eight at night, and always have to get a pass from the master to go for an instant beyond the gate."[2] And in another, dated October 11th of the same year and from the same dismal spot, he wrote: "I am writing this at half-past five in the evening, with the dull twilight of the school-room closing upon me, and the noise of a hundred pair of iron-bound clogs over my head. Do you not pity your poor, sensitive friend, Dear C...., in this most uncongenial place?"[3] In this latter communication there is a suggestion of seeking a post "in the College" (University?), but nothing came of it.[4]

A year and a half teaching in the Workhouse was as much as the dying man could endure - and now Edward Walsh was really dying. It was probably in late July of 1850 that the family took private lodgings at 13 Princes Street.[5] Bríghídín had also been through years of serious illness, lost her lovely hair in the fever hospital, and had mourned the deaths of the eldest girl and youngest boy - Frances and John Walter, respectively. Yet she worked herself to the bone to provide some little comfort for her 'dear Edward'. Old friends dropped by to see him and discreetly tried to dull the edge of the family poverty while leaving self-respect intact.[6] Gavan Duffy came from Dublin to see him but hesitated at the last moment lest it be too hurtful for Walsh to meet him in such stricken circumstances, and so the great man returned to Dublin without accomplishing the object of his journey.[7] Fr. O'Connor, whom Timothy Gleeson mistakenly took to be the workhouse chaplain and later parish priest of Passage,[8] was a faithful friend[9] and attended the poet at the end.[10]

---

[1] MS: BG69A9, 17-03-1849. January 12th 1850.
[2] *Memoir*, Dec. 26th p. 337; *Letters*, No. 42.
[3] ibid., p. 338; *Letters*, No. 43.
[4] ibid.
[5] Gleeson, p. 148 ii.
[6] ibid., p. 149 i.
[7] *Appreciation*, *Nation*, Aug. 24th 1850; *Memoir*, Dec. 26th p. 338.
[8] Gleeson, p. 149 i. Gleeson is in error in both of the statements as he is in relation to some other matters in his otherwise valuable article. At the time of Walsh's death Fr. George Sheehan was "chaplain to South Parish Convent [Presentation] and poorhouse" (*Catholic Directory* 1846-53). Fr. William O'Connor was curate in the South Parish and later parish priest of Courceys.
[9] ibid., Fr. O'Connor was one of Walsh's two most faithful friends. See *Letters*, No. 43.
[10] Gleeson, p. 149 i.

Describing Walsh's last months and death, Charles J. Kickham wrote - and here we allow free rein to his literary talent for blending fact and fancy because it is all that we have: -

> Come we now to the deathbed of Edward Walsh. It is the autumn of the year. Spring put forth its buds, and the birds sang, and the whitethorn blossomed, and the voice of the cuckoo was heard in the woods. But he pined away mid the dust and buzz and worry of that workhouse school-room; and never once looked upon the gentle, sickly primrose, nor felt the balmy air of the fields upon his cheek. Summer came with its blue skies and dewy evenings, and still,
>
> 'Throbbing for the sea-side billows,
> Or the water-wooing willows;
> Where in laughing and in sobbing
> Glide the streams away,'
>
> he grasped through the live-long day at his wearying, monotonous toil. And now the merry harvest time is at hand; and these poor pauper children are thinking of the stooks in the cornfields, and of the happy homes they were driven from by the cruel landlord. Some of them, who are old and strong enough, will sally forth to seek employment. God help them! and God help Ireland! But the tall schoolmaster, with the mournful eyes, whom they saw wasting away since the springtime, is not there now. They had learned to love him, and they wondered what has happened to him, or whether he will come back any more. They looked upon him with awe, too, for some of the bigger and more intelligent boys had found out that he made a book himself! and was a great poet. They remembered how sometimes he used to forget the lessons altogether and remain with his forehead resting on the desk for a long while; and once or twice they were frightened to see tears dropping upon the book before him. But then he would recover himself, and motion to them so gently with his white hand, to go on, and stroke the little boys' heads and draw them close to him - they could not chose but love him. But his last humiliation is over. The craving for sympathy (which is the very sunlight of genius) is felt no more. Forgotten and neglected as he thought himself, he waits calmly and with resignation the approach of death.
>
> But there is one heart whose truth he never doubted, and whose affection for him shone the brighter for his misfortunes. The tried love of the peasant girl has expanded into heroism. She is with him, and he feels it would be agony to miss her, even for an instant, from his bedside. The priest has entered and beckoned to the weeping children (whom their dying father had over and over blessed), and they leave the room. That pale woman, too, makes a movement to withdraw, but he holds her hand. The priest stoops

down to catch his voice. What does he say? 'He had little to conceal from her during life, and now that he is dying he has nothing!' So the clergyman desires her to remain, and having administered the last rites of the church to the dying man, he retires noiselessly from the room. They are alone now - these two whom God joined long ago in the little chapel by the Blackwater. His lips move - what does he say? 'Pray'! And she does pray, and with her prayers the soul of Edward Walsh is borne upwards to the Throne of light. The bruised and broken heart has ceased to beat. All is over![1]

[1] *Memoir*, Dec. 26th 1857, p. 338-339

CHAPTER FIVE

"SWEET DAWN ARISE! MY HOME IS FAR AWAY"[1]

Business as usual

Edward Walsh died in early August 1850 at the age of forty-five. The news of his death is reported in the Minutes of the Board of Guardians of the Cork Union Workhouse where an entry for Saturday, August 3rd reads: "The Master reports the death of Mr. Walsh, the Schoolmaster."[2] On Tuesday, August 6th he was laid to rest in St. Joseph's cemetery, otherwise known as the Botanic Gardens, in Cork city.[3] The grave contains not only the remains of *Walsh the Poet* but also those of his children Frances and John Walter who predeceased him.[4]

After the Master of the Workhouse had announced the death of the schoolmaster it was 'business as usual.' There was a proposal by J. Henrick and seconded by R. Butcher, "that a schoolmaster at £40 and an assistant at £20 per annum be advertised for and that the present assistant schoolmaster be promoted at a salary of £30 per annum, his conduct being such as to entitle him hereby."[5] One can only hope that the Guardians otherwise paid their respects to the man whose health had broken under the strain of his office in the Workhouse. A letter to the *Nation* gives a revealing eyewitness account of Walsh's tasks there:

> He held as you are aware, the office of Schoolmaster in the workhouse for the last two years [1848-1850], which were years of great misery, and, as a consequence, great labour was imposed on all engaged in the details of administering relief to the poor. No ordinary share of labour devolved on Mr. Walsh. He did not shrink from it, but plied his daily task of toil, with a diligence and patience beyond all praise. I have seen him day after day with untiring energy, endeavouring to enlighten the ignorance, to tame the ferocity, and humanize the savageness, of the masses placed under his care. He has frequently had in the workhouse school as many as 1,200 boys. The great majority of this large number were brought up in ignorance, exposed to all the demoralizing influences which extreme poverty is sure to exercise, and quite unaccustomed to restraint or discipline of any kind. To leaven such a mass as this is no small task, and yet he succeeded, but the success cost him dear. His life was the price at which success

---

[1] *Nation*: Feb. 13th 1847; See poem, p. 76

[2] CAI, MS. BG69A10, Sat. Aug. 3rd.

[3] Gleeson, T., p. 149 i.

[4] ibid.

[5] CAI, MS. BG69A10, Sat. Aug. 3rd.

> was purchased. You know, better even than I do, the gentleness of his nature, and the delicacy of constitution, upon which labour such as he undertook would make terrible inroads.[1]

A Suitable Memorial

In 1857 a group of working men in Cork set about honouring Walsh and keeping his memory green by the erection of a Celtic Cross "over the grave of one who contributed some of our sweetest lyrics to the adornment of our native literature."[2]

> Cork, which has given birth to so many names illustrious in Art and Literature, and whose inhabitants have been distinguished perhaps above those of any of our cities by their sympathy with and appreciation of Native Genius, is just now about to erect a Memorial to one of our sweetest Poets and best Celtic scholars - Edward Walsh. It is proposed to erect a Celtic cross of limestone, with tablets and inscriptions in both Languages, over his grave in the Mathew Cemetery. We sincerely trust that the Subscription set on foot by the Committee will soon enable them to carry their well-merited and patriotic work to completion.[3]

Ralph Varian, a young Cork businessman with an affable disposition and good organizational skills, spearheaded the project. Ralph and his brother Isaac Stephen were of Presbyterian background. They belonged to the Young Ireland movement and were, like Edward Walsh, songwriters and versifiers but, unlike Walsh, were successful business people and combined their gifts for music and song with establishing and operating a brush-manufacturing business at 105 Patrick St., Cork. Prior to the 1848 Young Ireland revolution the Varian brothers together with Denny Lane and a number of others had been arrested and spent four months in prison in their native city. In the course of his life Ralph published at least two volumes of poetry and song, partly of his own composing and partly not. Some of his verses evince an enhanced sense of place; *Ballyvolane*, *Ballinhassig* and *Leemount* being examples in point. An editorial comment on a lengthy and informative letter to the *Nation* in January 1858 reads,

> Mainly through the exertions of one truehearted gentleman in Cork, whose love of country is as strong as his attachment to literature, this monument to Edward Walsh has been raised. That gentleman is Mr. Ralph Varian; his efforts in this undertaking, while they but evidence his warm patriotism and regard for the Bards of Celtic song, will elicit for him the grateful thanks of every Irishman who admires the genius of him over whose ashes this beautiful memorial has been raised.[4]

---

[1] *Nation*: Aug. 31st 1850.

[2] ibid., Jan. 8th 1859: 'The Monument to Edward Walsh.'

[3] NLI, MS 2261: From an unidentified newspaper cutting accompanying the MS.

[4] *Nation*: Jan. 8th 1859; *Letters* No. 66.

Standing nine feet tall (2.75m) this impressive memorial is the work of a draughtsman named O'Leary who designed the template and Mr. Samuel Daly of Cook Street, Cork, who saw to the chisel-work. It seems that O'Leary modelled his work on the ancient high crosses at Kilklispeen, county Kilkenny but deviated from the original by the insertion of "a few shamrocks" and "a small bit of Grecian ornamentation."[1] The above mentioned letter to the *Nation* voices approval for the former and abhorrence of the latter but does not allow these minor details to distort or overshadow the writer's thorough satisfaction with the overall effect. On the day of his visit to St. Joseph's Cemetery the newly erected cross "glittered like white marble in the sun rays; and the beautiful tracery of the shaft, the cross, and the circle, in fine, intricate interlaced work, which is characteristic of ancient Irish art, was admirably thrown out by the light and shade at play upon it."[2] And again:

> But for this one error - the Grecian cross towards the base of the shaft - this Celtic Cross over the grave of Edward Walsh, viewed from the side which is sculptured, and which faces the head of the grave, might be pronounced perfect in its pictorial effect. The ornamentation of the shaft of the cross ends appropriately with the initials E.W. in the Celtic characters, beautifully interlaced. The fine block of limestone from which this cross has been sculptured was cut from the celebrated diamond quarry of Ballintemple. The whole cross - shaft, arms, and circle - is carved from the one block of stone. There is no joining in it. It rests on a rough base, as the Ancient Crosses usually did; and in the base are inserted two tablets of white marble with the inscription to the memory of Edward Walsh, in English on one, in the Gaelic on the other.[3]

On the lower marble slab are the following inscriptions:

Eadbhard Breathnach,
An file agus an Fir-Eirionnach,
D'éag an séisreadh lá do mhí Lúghnasa, MDCCCL.
'San m-bliadhan ceathrachad agus cúig d'a aois.

---

[1] *ibid.*; *Letters*, No. 67. Timothy Gleeson, (p. 149 ii) says "The edges and members of cross are 'roped,' the panels containing interlaced work of Celtic form, and also raised over tracery are five rosettes, with four sprigs of shamrock cut in each. The lower panel of cross has tracery or ornamentation different from upper ones, and in lower half of this panel are two Celtic letters, E.W., beautifully ornamented, and cut in relieved Celtic tracery work. A small palisading enclosing the tomb-flag surrounds all. On the tomb-flag, cut in large capital letters, is the following: - The Burial place of EDWARD WALSH and Family."

[2] ibid.

[3] ibid.

Do tógbhadh an chros-Liag so,
Mar leacht-cuimhne do, le a chárdaibh agus le lucht,
Ag a ribh móir-mheas air.
Go d-tugaidh DIA suaimhneas siorruidhe da anam.

(i.e. Edward Walsh, the poet and true Irishman, died on August 6th 1850, in the 45th year of his age . This cross-slab was erected as a memorial by his friends and those who held him in high regard. May God grant eternal rest to his soul).

And on the upper:

EDWARD WALSH,
The poet and Translator,
Died August, 1850. Aged 45 years.
Erected to his Memory,
By a few admirers of the Patriot and the Bard.
God rest his soul!
Frances and John Walter died the year before.

In 1891 the grave and monument were in need of some refurbishment and at the instigation of C.G. Doran of the city council, a committee undertook to carry out the necessary work. Mr. Fleming, editor of the Gaelic Journal and a Patrick O'Brien of Dublin, added a further inscription: It reads:

Ar n-dul do chaitheamh 'san
Thoirbheirt so
Ó mhuintir na h-Éireann,
I n-díl-chuimhne air an bh-file,
Thar-éis a bháis,
do righneadh athnuaghadh uirre,
le beagán de daoinibh Múinntearadha
'san m-bliadhain, 1891.

(i.e. The monument erected to the memory of the dead poet by the people of Ireland having fallen into decay was renovated by a small band of friends in the year 1891).

After the monument had been erected over the grave, Brighid Walsh, Edward's wife, had a letter published in the *Cork Examiner* expressing her appreciation and thanks:

> I trust and pray that this just tribute to his memory - prompted by a good Providence - may bring a blessing on all who aid the work.
>
> To me it will be a tremendous happiness, during the remainder of my life, to feel he was not forgotten by his countrymen whom he loved so much, and whose good opinion he prized so highly.[1]

On May, 10th 1891, Alderman Horgan, the mayor of Cork, presided over a ceremony at the graveside where Mr. Edward Murphy of Cork delivered an oration as also did Timothy Gleeson.[2] The next assembly of note (as far as I am aware) was on August 6th 2000, (the 150th anniversary of his death) when, in the presence of the Lord Mayor of Cork and a small group of relatives and admirers a wreath was laid at the grave by his great-great-grand-daughter, Elizabeth Nunn, from Queensland, Australia.

Memories

We are unaware of the existence of any photograph or other representation of Edward Walsh but it is possible to build up some mental images from a variety of sources. One of his best loved songs - *Mairéad Ní Cheallaigh* - published in the Belfast *Vindicator* carries the following introductory remarks:

> It seems but the other day, and yet it is a good many years, since we passed the merry day in the sweet town of Fermoy, conning over classical lore, in the company of the author of the following lines, then a fair cheeked, merry, pretty boy, like ourselves , barring the beauty.[3]

Charles Kickham quotes an unnamed woman's pen picture of him in adult life:

> He was tall and not over slight, with a habitual bend. His hair, which was black as night, and straight as a Delaware Indian's fell down over the collar of his coat, and swept with one deep wave over a forehead of surpassing intellectual development. His eyes, black, poor fellow, as his destiny, seldom looked upward, but, under the shadow of remarkably long lashes, retired as it were within - alas! the only bright spot for him - his own soul.

---

[1] *Cork Examiner*, June 16th 1858.

[2] Gleeson, p. 150.

[3] *Vindicator*, Belfast, July 31st 1844

Fig. 16.
Elizabeth Nunn, standing by the grave monument of her great-great-grandfather, Edward Walsh in The Mathew Cemetery, within St. Joseph's Cemetery (alias The Botanic Gardens), Ballyphehane, Cork city.

Fig. 18.
No.13 Princes St.Cork, where Edward Walsh died at the age of 45.

Fig. 17.
Another view of the monument erected to the memory of Walsh by some friends and admirers and the traders of Cork in 1858.

There were moments, however, when, as the fox hunters say, they broke cover, and with such a flash too, as made one start."[1]

Writing to a friend in 1847 John Keegan said: "He is forty-three years of age, tall and elegant in figure, and looks the very essence of feeling and intelligence - he seems, too, like myself, to have suffered much mentally, for his face is worn and his hair is nearly thoroughly silvered.[2] The following year John Mitchel saw him as "a tall, gentleman-like person in black."[3] Writing in the *Nation* after Walsh's death, Charles Gavan Duffy remembers him in "that great room of the Corn Exchange" where:

> [Walsh] might be seen, among some fifty clerks, during the years in which the Repeal Association was at the height of its power and rule in Ireland, the tall, student-like figure of a man of middle age, employed at some task of routine business. Watch for an hour and you saw him labouring on assiduously; with head never raised to notice who it was that had entered, or inquire what had caused the stir and excitement in those about him. Approach and address him, and a pale, saddened face was upturned, and large, deep-thoughtful brown eyes were fixed on yours; then, if you were a friend, a faint smile stole across the comely features; and a gentle recognition met you from a low, but musical voice. The hand you held was fervid; the features, when the brief emotion had passed, wore a heavier gloom than that of abstraction of thought, as of one who had known many griefs, and who was not at home amid the crowd and the drudgery of office toil. The spiritualised countenance; the creative forehead; the depth and meaning of those vision-seeking eyes; the air of habitual reverie; revealed the man of genius. This was Edward Walsh.[4]

Finally, there is Walsh's mildly humorous self-portrait: "My person is tall and thin, my face abstemiously pale, and not a single grog blossom expanding its fiery petals on my nasal organ."[5]

As a personality, Edward Walsh had many conflicts and difficulties both internal and external in the management of his relationships. He was of a nervous disposition, supersensitive,[6] took offence easily, and in general would seem to have been his own worst enemy. From his 1844 letters it seems evident that some of his illnesses at least were

---

[1] *Memoir*, Dec. 5th 1857, p. 291.

[2] Quoted in D.J. O'Donoghue's *Life and Writings of James Clarence Mangan*, p. 176

[3] Mitchel. J. *Jail Journal*, p. 30.

[4] *Appreciation, Nation*, Sept. 7th 1850.

[5] DPJ, Oct. 18th 1834, "Daniel O'Leary the Duhallow Piper." See pp. 225ff.

[6] Kickham refers to his "painfully sensitive nature;" (*Memoir*, Dec. 12th p. 305). He himself refers to 'my delicate overwrought frame,'(*Letters*, No 34). D. J. O'Donoghue: 'Walsh was extraordinarily sensitive.' (*Poems of J.C. Mangan*, p. 177).

related to his disposition.[1] There is no doubt that he was a talented man: in the words of Mangan "a gentleman to whose literary exertions Ireland is indebted almost beyond the power of repayment."[2] He has been charged with overrating his own gifts and taking it badly when others were not as impressed by his work as he might have wished.[3] John Keegan, poet and contemporary, said "I hated him at first sight,"[4] and elsewhere refers to him as "an arrant rascal,"[5] a "stinking prig,"[6] "No son of genius ever yet had his overweening ridiculous vanity or his puppy upstart demeanour."[7] Keegan may have suffered from a degree of professional jealousy - he was equally uncomplimentary to Mangan.[8] But there may be a certain truth in what he says.

Duffy made allowances for Walsh's temperament but indicated that the poet was not an easy man to live with because he brooked "badly the companionship of ill-suited associates, and the rule of officials who had no appreciation for his gifts, no kindly sympathy for his mental torture."[9] Gavan Duffy's patience and patronage never faltered.

The dreamy quality of his personality exhibited in his introduction to the story of *Daniel the Outlaw* emerges from time to time; especially in his letters. Kickham says that while in Toureen, "he used to amuse himself and his friends (like Banim in the streets of Dublin) by guessing at the character and occupation of the people as they passed by his cottage door. His power of reading the human heart through the countenance is said to have been perfectly wonderful."[10] In this assessment Kickham may not have been altogether correct. If he could suggest that Walsh's father belonged "to the *genus* devil-may-care,"[11] perhaps it is permissible to look out for elements of the *dúchas* in his son. In one of his letters Walsh refers to the possibility of making big money - £10 a sheet - half a year's wages! - for a London publishing house.[12] Another letter reveals what can scarcely be described by anything other than gullibility: "a certain friend of mine who is a deep phrenologist says, upon an examination of my skull, that I have 'benevolence' and 'attachment' uncommonly developed."[13]

An unnamed person - who can only be James Clarence Mangan in puckish mood - repeating to him 'passages of the Persian tongue' which Walsh would have sworn to be 'the

---

[1] *Memoir*, Dec. 12th pp. 305-306; *Letters*, No. 33.
[2] Mangan, J.C., in the *Nation*, June 13th 1846.
[3] NLI, MS. 2261; *Letters*, No. 10.
[4] ibid, No. 57.
[5] ibid., No. 56.
[6] ibid., No. 57.
[7] NLI, MS. 2261; *Letters*, No. 50.
[8] O'Donoghue, D.J. *The Life & Writings of J.C. Mangan*, p. 177.
[9] *Appreciation*, Sept. 7th 1850.
[10] *Memoir*, Dec. 5th p. 292.
[11] ibid., p. 291.
[12] NLI, MS. 2261; *Letters*, No. 22.
[13] ibid., *Letters*, No. 16.

language of some province of Ireland so much did it resemble the Irish', likewise overly impressed him.[1] Mangan, if that be he, went on to tell him that he was "the purest and most Saxon writer of English in this country."[2] Walsh could be facetious[3] but lacked a sense of humour. He rebukes John Daly for some flippancy: "never joke with me."[4] Nevertheless, he was capable of indulging in some mild fun, as indicated in his remarks on the amorous antics of Lord Byron[5] or in writing to his brother-in-law, Joe Sullivan, on the subject of his wife's illness: "I knew Brigid would get over the illness. I'm a capital judge of a sick girl's pulse. I've sometimes felt one, Joe!"[6]

Walsh was ever a lonely man. He had many acquaintance but friends were few: "I never made many friends. I have had through life some inborn intuitive perception of the man whom I would and could love; and the number of them I found to be remarkably few."[7] Closest of all, apart from his wife and children, was Charles Gavan Duffy. The little circle extended to Fr. O'Connor in Cork, to Dr. McSweeney in Dublin, and probably included Fr. C. P. Meehan in Sts. Michael and John's presbytery in Meath Street, in the same city.

In a preface to the second edition of Walsh's *Irish Popular Songs*, "J.S.S."[8] gives the following portrait of that lonely man:

> Well we remember (though now forty years since) following Walsh in the twilight of an autumn evening, drinking in the odd chords that came from the little harp that lay on his left arm as he wandered, lonely and unknown, by the then desert, Jones's-road, or reposed himself on one of the seats that at that time were outside the walls of Clonliffe House. It was then we first heard *Casadh an t-Súgáin*, 'The Twisting of the Rope' - that beautiful air to which Moore adapted the no less beautiful words, 'How dear to me the hour when Daylight dies!' We have ever known a difficulty in singing the words of the great poet to the air - there is none in Walsh's version; but then *it* is the pure vintage, and words and music come from the same source.[9]

Perhaps that loneliness was the price of his particular genius.

---

[1] NLI, MS. 2261; *Letters*, No. 19.
[2] ibid.
[3] ibid., *Letters*, Nos. 27, 30, 32.
[4] ibid., No. 13
[5] ibid., No. 28.
[6] *Memoir*, Dec. 26th p. 338; *Letters*, No. 35.
[7] ibid., p. 338; *Letters*, No. 43.
[8] Surgeon O'Sullivan?
[9] Walsh, E., *Irish Popular Songs*, (2nd ed.) p. iv.

CHAPTER SIX

OUT OF THE SHADOWS: BRÍGHÍDÍN & FAMILY

What happened to the Walsh family immediately after Edward's burial is not altogether clear. A letter in the *Nation* of August 26th stated that "she [Mrs. Walsh] and her orphans are now numbered among the inmates of this paupers establishment," i.e. the workhouse.[1] If this be true, it can only have been for a short while because V. Edwards, in his article in the *New Ireland Review* attests that "Charles Gavan Duffy was faithful to Walsh to the last. Walsh's wife, his *Bríghídín bán mo stór*, acknowledges that she should have gone to the Poor-house after his death were it not for Charles Gavan Duffy, God bless him!"[2] Duffy went to Cork and saw to the welfare of Bríghídín and the surviving children, Adam Edward, Mary Frances, Edward Charles and John Joseph (the baby Brighid had been expecting at the time of Edward's death and who was apparently born in Cork).[3] Nor were other friends found wanting. Maurice Leyne, grandnephew to Daniel O'Connell, had yet another small volume of Walsh's poems in preparation for publication when an untimely death snatched him away. However, this book of Irish Songs with English Translations is believed to have been published by Bradford of 44, Patrick Street, Cork.[4]

On the death of her husband, Mrs. Walsh considered emigrating to America and to that end applied to the Board of Guardians for assistance. While the Board acknowledged the justice of her request, they explained that it would have been against the law to accede to it and contented themselves with paying tribute to her late husband's memory![5] An unnamed "Confederate" wrote to the *Nation* appealing for funds on her behalf: "A few pounds will enable Mrs. Walsh to carry out her project of emigrating to America, where she feels confident of supporting her orphans by the fruit of her industry."[6] By this time, however, the *Nation* had already opened a fund for the widow and her children.[7]

The reader of this biography of Walsh may have already concluded that Bríghídín was a formidable character. She was. Through bad times and good, most of them bad, she kept the best side out and was not reduced or defeated by poverty, illness or other misfortune.

---

[1] *Nation*: Aug. 25th 1850.

[2] Edwards, V., in *New Ireland Review*, Nov. 1895, p. 161, n.

[3] Frances and John Walter had died in 1849; see: Daly, J, et al., *Poetry and Legendary Ballads of the South of Ireland*, pp.148-149.

[4] Gleeson, p. 149 i.; C.G. Duffy, *My Life in Two Hemispheres*, II, p. 9.

[5] *Nation*: Aug. 31st 1850; *Letters*, No. 60.

[6] ibid.

[7] *Nation*, Aug 31st 1850.

Much as she loved Edward, his death was not the end of the world for her. She had a life to live and a family to rear and she applied herself to both with spirit.

No further reference is made to emigrating to America but at some point she did move back to Dublin where she had lived and worked and had friends in high places.[1] In the *Memoir,* Kickham quotes a letter from one of her Dublin friends, probably Dr. McSweeney, who more than once had given free medical care to the Walsh family:

> I saw your friend, Mrs. Walsh, several times last week. Her little daughter, a most interesting child of twelve, being ill, I volunteered my services, and as the poor woman was unable to pay a doctor, and too proud to apply for relief at the dispensary, she entrusted her to my care. It is lamentable to see a woman of such a soul and such a heart suffering so much privation. She is dependent on her needle alone for the daily assistance of herself and two children; and though an experienced workwoman,[2] her poverty debars her from profitable employment. Few indeed would wish to be seen walking in the streets where she is compelled to drag on life. Her lodging is the "wretched garret of a wretched locality." Are there no friends of Edward Walsh to undertake the publication (it could be done by subscription) of a volume of his poems and legends, in order to rescue her whose love was the sunshine of his existence, from a fate like this? As if there should be no circumstance wanting to awake sympathy for the widow of Edward Walsh, his eldest son, "poor Adam", is a sailor boy!"[3]

On November 21st 1858, in St. Andrew's Church, Westland Row, Dublin, Brighid Walsh remarried.[4] Her new husband, John William Flynn, was the same age as herself, about thirty eight, and a chemist by profession. There were no children of this second marriage.[5]

The next record we have of Brighídín is on board the *Erin-go-Bragh* on her way to Australia. An interesting but little-known detail of Ireland's checkered history forms a backdrop to the circumstances surrounding her departure. Rev. Dr. James Quin, headmaster of the principal catholic school in Dublin, St. Laurence O'Toole Seminary in Harcourt St., was also a director of the Mater Misericordiae Hospital in the same city. His apostolic spirit manifested itself in recruiting personnel from among the Sisters of Mercy to nurse the sick and wounded during the Crimean War. His pioneering cast of mind and independence of thought was noted by his kinsman, Archbishop Cullen, and in April 1859 he was appointed first bishop of Queensland, Australia. As bishop he played a prominent part in forming the Queensland Immigration Society, which in the course of the 1860s landed

---

[1] C.G. Duffy & Dr. McSwiney, Fr. C.P. Meehan.

[2] Edward Walsh says that his wife "knows millinery"; see: *Letters,* No. 11.

[3] *Memoir*, Dec. 26th 1857, p. 340; *Letters*, No. 63.

[4] Register M/1858-1870.

[5] Elizabeth Nunn's unpublished family history.

nearly 4,000 Irish in his diocese. One of the many ships used in this enterprise was the *Erin-go-Bragh* which set sail from Cobh in Co. Cork, on February 7th 1862. Among those on board were Bríghídín and John William Flynn together with three of the Walsh children, Mary Frances, Edward Charles and John Joseph. After a journey of more than six months (200 days) they arrived at Moreton Bay. The little party also included a young man from Tralee, Matthew O'Sullivan, son of Patrick O'Sullivan and Johanna Savage. Matthew who had studied law at the Irish College in Paris was eventually to marry Mary Frances Walsh.[1] The Walsh family were financed, at least in part, by some Cork traders and other well wishers.[2]

Ever a resourceful woman, once settled in Warwick, Queensland, in 1862, Bríghídín opened a business in millinery, clothing, and jewellery at *Dublin House* in Palmerin Street. To publicise her wares, she placed advertisements in *The Warwick Argus* and *Tenterfield Chronicle* newspapers in the 1870s. Bríghídín outlived her first husband by forty-seven years and her second by twenty. For the last two decades of her life she lived with her daughter Mary Frances and son-in-law Matthew Sullivan. Death came to her on Palm Sunday, April 11th 1897, at the age of seventy-seven. She was buried in Warwick Cemetery.[3] And it is there, in a well-kept grave, far from the 'Irish Rhineland', and her 'dear Edward' that Bríghídín Sullivan of the 'ringlets rich and rare' awaits the Resurrection.

Family Fortunes

Of the six children born to Edward Walsh and his wife Bríghídín Sullivan, we have seen that Frances and John Walter had predeceased their father while John Joseph was born posthumously.[4] In the aftermath of the poet's death, Gavan Duffy was probably instrumental in assisting Adam Edward, then aged eleven, to become a sailor. Adam's first voyage was "made to America, at a time in world history when conditions were not nearly so comfortable for the sailor as is the case today (1925),"[5] but then, hardship was nothing new to the Walshs. At the age of seventeen he joined the United States Revenue Service and at the outbreak of the American Civil War he joined the U.S. Navy, serving sometimes under assumed names, on several different vessels. He was discharged from the Navy near the end of 1863 and soon after took up service with the United States Volunteers until he was finally discharged from military service in 1867. In that year, on hearing that his mother was seriously ill in Australia, he set out from San Francisco and joined the family in Queensland at the end of December.[6] On September 8th 1875, at the age of thirty-three,

---

[1] ibid.

[2] Gleeson, p. 149 i; C.G. Duffy, *My Life in Two Hemispheres*, II, p. 27.

[3] Personal Interview with Elizabeth Nunn.

[4] ibid.

[5] *Bundaberg Mail*, Jan 22nd 1925.

[6] ibid.

Fig. 19. Three generations: Elizabeth Nunn's mother, grandmother and great grandmother. Charlotte JosephineAnderson (Mrs. Adam E. Walsh) Great Grandmother. d. 1932. Hilda Bridget (Mrs Tunstall) Grandmother. d.1961. Mrs C. Hetherington (Mother).

Adam Edward married Charlotte Josephine Anderson of Gothenburg, Sweden in the Lutheran Church, Maryborough, Queensland. Of the eight children born to them, a boy and a girl died in infancy while the remaining six outlived him.[1] Adam was highly respected in Bundaberg. His love for the sea does not seem to have abated on his arrival in Australia, as his subsequent career testifies.[2] His varied and colourful career ended in his eighty-fourth year at his home in Boundary St., Bundaberg, Queensland, on January 21st 1925.[3]

A second family wedding in 1875 was that of Edward Charles, then aged 27. He and Ellen Mary Duggan became husband and wife in the Catholic church at Warwick, Queensland. Of their seven children, three boys and four girls, one, Kathleen, (third daughter and sixth child) did not survive infancy.[4] Edward was a farmer in the Inglewood area and died on December 6th 1898 from a combination of bronchitis, pneumonia and asthenia, aged fifty.[5]

Shortly after his arrival in Queensland, Matthew O'Sullivan, the Traleeman, became a law clerk in Brisbane where he completed his legal training. On February 18th 1867, he and Mary Frances married in St. Stephen's church in that city. Their children, Eugene Edward, and Matthew, died in infancy, the first in 1869 and the second in 1871. They may have had a third child, a boy, who, like his brothers, did not survive infancy. From 1872 until his death on February 24th 1885 at the age of forty-four, Matthew practised as a solicitor in Warwick. Mary Frances herself lived to the age of eighty-eight and might have survived longer were it not for a car accident.[6]

John Joseph, the youngest child of Edward Walsh and Bríghídín, born approximately three months after his father's death,[7] did not marry. He was a miner in the Mount Morgan area in central Queensland, and died on July 2nd 1916, at the age of 65.[8]

* * *

Postscript

For most of my thirty-six years of research I had been hoping some day to trace the fortunes of Bríghídín and the family. For thirty-three years they evaded me. Then in a space of less than a year all came to light. During a casual conversation Alice O'Sullivan, of the Surgery, Ballybunion, made reference to a well-informed and helpful woman in a

[1] His death certificate gives the surviving children as Brian Sarsfield (47), Hilda (45), Minnie (44), Frances (42), Adam Edward (38) and Edward (35).

[2] *Bundaberg Mail*, Jan. 22nd 1925

[3] ibid.

[4] Elizabeth Nunn's unpublished family record.

[5] Death Certificate of Edward Charles Walsh. See p. 105.

[6] Elizabeth Nunn's unpublished family records.

[7] ibid.

[8] ibid.

Fig. 20.
Adam Edward, eldest son of Edward and Brighid. Born in Toureen, Co. Waterford, July 17th., 1841. Died in Bundaberg, Queensland, January 21st.,1925.

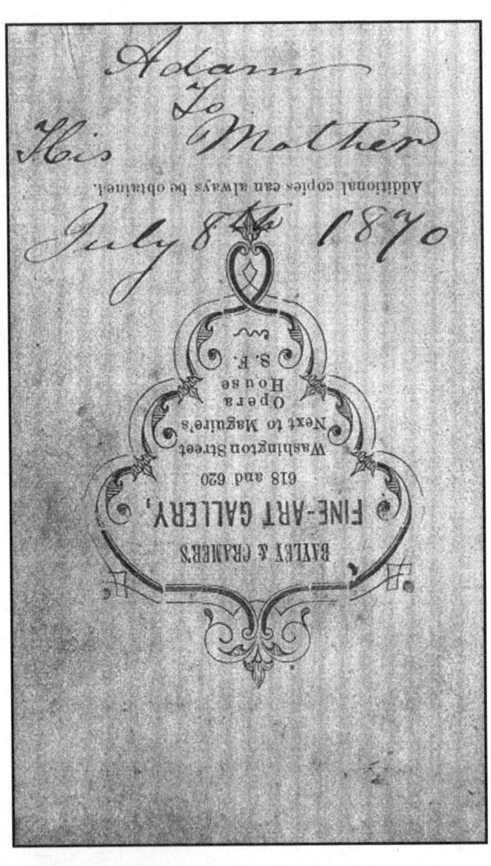

Fig. 21.
Obverse side of the photograph in fig. 20. The inscription "Adam to his Mother July, 8th., 1870" may be the handwriting of Brighid Sullivan, or his own or that of another.

Fig. 22.
Edward Walsh's great-great granddaughter and her brother on their way to school. From an early age Elizabeth Nunn and her brother went to school on horseback. During school hours the horses rested in an adjoining paddock.

genealogical office in Queensland, Mrs Catriona Robinson of Ipswich Genealogical Society. I wrote to this good woman and after some initial disappointment she began to unravel the mystery that had so long evaded me. First came the death certificates of Edward Charles Walsh and Adam Edward Walsh. More data on the Walsh generations followed but no word of a living link and no word of Walsh's wife Bríghídín.

In the early stages of this biography I had occasion to mention Molly Hickey of Gortnacreha, Cullen, Co. Cork. She is long dead but in a way she isn't, because her daughter, Maureen Phibbs, now living in Blessington, Co. Wicklow, is following closely on her mother's footsteps. Maureen wrote to tell me that a Mrs. Elizabeth Nunn from Queensland, Australia, had been advertising in a genealogical magazine for information on her great-great-grandfather, a poet named Edward Walsh.

I immediately wrote to Elizabeth and soon afterwards had a reply that brought joy to my heart: - I had found a living descendant of Edward Walsh, his great-great-granddaughter, Elizabeth Nunn. Among the many things I learned from her was the fact that Bríghídín had married secondly. That solved the question of why Brigid Walsh could not be traced among the records of the dead in Ipswich. She had become Mrs. Flynn prior to her departure from Ireland.

Because the year 2000 was the 150th anniversary of the death of Edward Walsh a number of interested people were determined to honour the poet and folklorist but it was not until a couple of months prior to the anniversary that we were to discover that the principal guest was to be Elizabeth. A week of celebration was held in Western Duhallow during which both Elizabeth and I delivered lectures to the Duhallow Historical Society. John O'Connell, N.T., of Stuak, Co. Cork, himself a distant relative of Elizabeth, had set up appointments with Mayor Hourican of Cork for a grave-side commemoration and with the state authorities in Spike Island for a visit to the convict depot where her illustrious ancestor taught school, and another appointment at St. Finbarr's Hospital in the city which in Walsh's day was the Workhouse. Maureen Phibbs, and I took her on a tour of the ancestral farm in Derragh, the Walsh farm in Glenlara, the monument to Edward Walsh in Kiskeam, the sites of his hedge-schools in Duhallow. I later took Elizabeth on a tour of the Dublin of Edward Walsh, including his rented accommodation in Summer Hill, the *Monitor* office in Abbey St, the Corn Exchange in Burg Quay, and a visit to the Manuscript Department of the National Library of Ireland to see his letters to John Daly. Prior to the tour of Dublin, however, I made sure to take Elizabeth to that *petit coin du paradis* of Edward and Bríghídín - Toureen, Co. Waterford. The old schoolhouse built by John Musgrave still stands. It is now a private residence and beautifully restored. On identifying our mission and ourselves we were graciously invited into the house by a relaxed, graceful and sophisticated young lady who identified herself as Aisling McGrath, a daughter of the house. Over the welcoming cup of tea, the young lady happened to mention that in the course of renovation a sewing kit had been discovered stuck in the rafters but since no one knew the significance of such a find, it was discarded. It was a poignant moment: how often Bríghídín, the seamstress, the young girl of twenty with her baby Adam asleep in the cot and she herself weary from plying her needle, must have stuck that sewing-kit in the rafters and in her hasty departure for Dublin in early 1844 forgotten to retrieve it.

5113856

DEATH

DEATH in the District of Darling Downs East in the Colony of Queensland.
1899 Registered by Patrick Joseph Kennedy, Acting District Registrar

Marginal notes (if any)	Column	
	1 Number	1509 958
	DESCRIPTION - 2 When died and where	6th December 1898 Woodlands, Inglewood
	3 Name and surname; profession, trade, or occupation	Edward Charles WALSH Farmer
	4 Sex and age	Male 50 years 7 months
	5 1. Cause of death	Bronchitis Pneumonia Asthenia
	2. Duration of last illness	7 days
	3. Medical attendant by whom certified	Dr. Orton
	4. When he last saw deceased ..	2nd December 1898
	6 Name and surname of father .. .. Profession, trade, or occupation ..	Edward Walsh Teacher
	Name and maiden surname of mother	Bridget O'Sullivan
	7 Signature, description, and residence of informant	Certified in writing by Ellen Walsh, Wife, Woodlands
	8 1. Signature of Registrar	P.J. Kennedy
	2. Date	3rd January 1891
	3. Place of registration	Warwick
	If Burial or Cremation Registered - 9 When and where buried or cremated	7th December 1898 Inglewood
	By whom certified	Jonas Reibelt
	10 Name and religion of minister, and/or names of two witnesses of burial or cremation	John Hennessey, R.C. Priest S. Thompson, E.W. Dowling
	11 Where born and how long in Australia States, stating which	Dublin, Ireland 36 years in Queensland
	If deceased was married - 12 1. Where	Warwick, Queensland
	2. At what age .. .. .. 3. To whom	27 years Ellen Duggan
	13 Issue living, in order of birth, their names and ages	Living years Edward 21 John Vincent 19 Mary Frances 15 William Charles 17 Ellen Dora 13 Kathleen Winifred 7
	Deceased, number and sex	Deceased 1 Female

CAUTION:- Whosoever shall unlawfully alter any Certified Copy of an entry in any Register of Births, Marriages, or Deaths, whether by erasure, obliteration, removal, addition, or otherwise is guilty of a CRIME, and is liable to the punishment by law provided in that behalf. (Vide Sections 486 and 488 of the "Criminal Code.")

I, Desmond Barry Tanner, Registrar-General, do hereby certify that the above is a true copy of an entry in a Register of Deaths kept in the General Registry Office at Brisbane, and I further certify that I am a person duly authorised by law to issue such certificate.

Extracted on 10 November 1000

Exd. by

Registrar-General

N.B. Not Valid Unless Bearing the Authorised Seal and Signature of the Registrar-General

Fig. 23. Death Certificate of Edward Charles Walsh, son of Edward & Bridget.

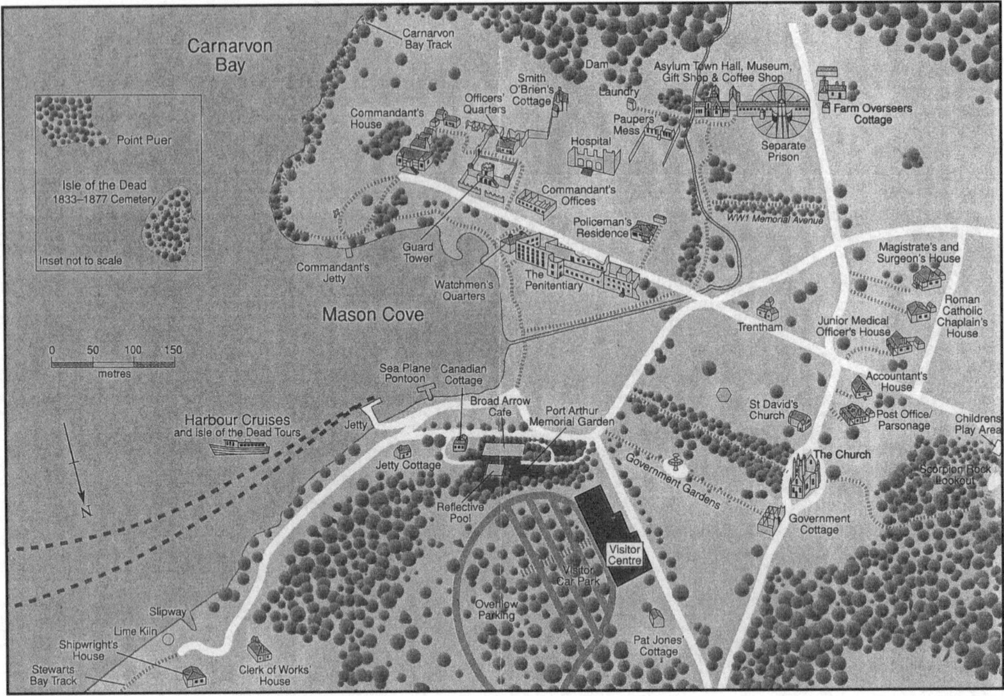

Fig. 24. Port Arthur in Van Diemen's Land, (Tasmania), familiar to Willaim Smith O'Brien, John Mitchel, Kevin O'Doherty and other political prisoners of the Young Ireland era. Familiar to many of the 'young convicts' whom Edward Walsh taught while on Spike Island was Point Peur (insert in upper left corner). Fr. Woolfrey who lived in the Catholic chaplain's house (right hand side of map) managed to smuggle out some of William Smith O'Brien's letters with his own mail, and here O'Brien received a book of Irish Jacobite poetry from Thomas Francis Meagher - Edward Walsh's *Reliques*.

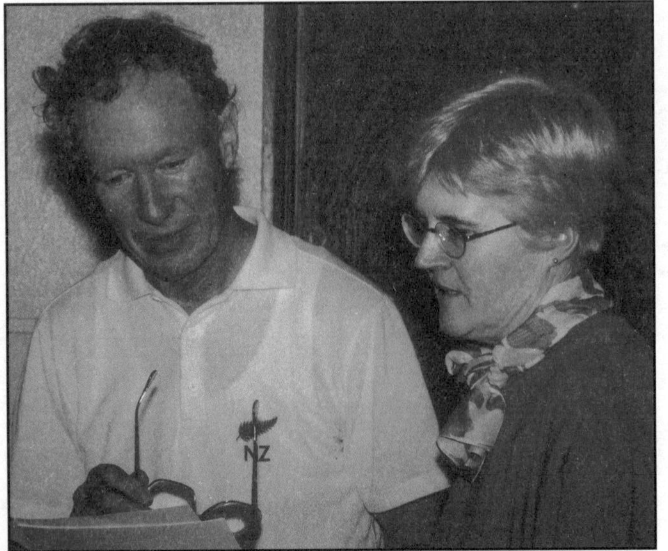

Fig. 25.
The Author John J. Ó Ríordáin with Elizabeth Nunn at the 150th Anniversary Celebration in Cullen, Co. Cork. August 5th 2000.

CHAPTER SEVEN

THE VERDICT OF HISTORY

In *An Appreciation*, published in the *Nation* on August 24th 1850, Gavan Duffy referred to Edward Walsh as 'a man of exquisite genius; an unrivalled balladist; a lover of all the old traditions of Erin; an erudite Irish scholar.'[1] Continuing that *Appreciation* in the September 7th issue of the paper, he wrote, 'More, perhaps, than any man who sung in later days of the vanished glory of Éire, of her weird superstitions, of her passionate longings and of her desperate struggles for liberty, Walsh was the representative of the old order of our minstrels. Others had attained by culture, as of a foreign tongue, a competent knowledge and mastery of Irish, and had taught the language of the stranger to catch some tones of the *cláirseach*. But Walsh more than Davis, Mangan, Ferguson, Williams, or McCarthy, sang with voice and passion as intensely native as the bards whom English legislature proscribed.'[2]

A century and a half has elapsed since the death of Edward Walsh, a century and a half since the above *Appreciation* was published. Now removed by one hundred and fifty years we may well ask if Charles Gavan Duffy's estimation of him has survived the test of time. It is not my intention in this present work to make any definitive pronouncements on the matter but a brief and imperfect exploration of how subsequent writers and scholars have estimated Edward Walsh may be apposite.

Walsh's poetic efforts have earned him no more than the status of a minor Munster poet, despite the most recent attempt to extricate him from this lowly state.[3] Nevertheless, I consider that, in a curious sort of way, Duffy's estimation of *Walsh the Poet* is sustainable.

Biographical data on Walsh, as is evident from the foregoing chapters, is sketchy enough and virtually every source purporting to offer biographical data is flawed. With few exceptions Walsh's extant letters are unpublished and although his folkloric output is very considerable, it rarely receives more than a passing mention from commentators. His *persona* is that of 'poet and translator', but even here, the inclusion of Walsh's work in anthologies of song and verse is minimal.

In the years and decades immediately following his death, Walsh received publicity in a variety of journals. The *Nation*, always favourable towards him in life, did not neglect him in death and throughout the 1850s it printed a number of his poetic compositions hitherto unpublished. Kickham's *memoir* in the *Celt* (1857) became the matrix of several articles

---

[1] *Appreciation*, *Nation*, Aug. 24th 1850.

[2] ibid., Sept. 7th 1850.

[3] See: MacCarthy, Anne, *James Clarence Mangan, Edward Walsh and Nineteenth-century Irish literature in English*. (Edwin Mellen) NY, 2000; reviewed in *Irish Studies Review*, vol. 10, No. 1, (April, 2002) pp. 96-97.

on Walsh, notably in the *Irishman*, the *Emerald*, the *Shamrock* and the *Cork Historical and Archaeological Society Journal* of 1893. Common to all of these is the gratuitous acceptance of the data in the *Celt* as factual - and that despite Kickham's monitum. Besides they carry little by way of critical assessment of Walsh's poetry. Finally, dictionaries of biography more or less ignore Walsh the folklorist, as well as continuing to disseminate the biographical inaccuracies of Kickham's 'hurried memoir'.

In an introduction to *The Book of Irish Poetry*, Alfred Percival Graves refers to 'the fresh flowering of Irish poetry brought about by what has been called the Irish Literary Renaissance, whose first inspirers were Sir Samuel Ferguson, Mangan, Edward Walsh and Aubrey de Vere.'[1] This development he sees rooted in the lesson 'learned by Edward Walsh and Sir Samuel Ferguson, that the use of that poetical Hiberno-English speech, recently made popular by Douglas Hyde, Synge, Lady Gregory and others, was a truer vehicle for the expression in translation or adaptation, of Irish Gaelic poetry.'[2]

During the late nineteenth century, Walsh's songs and translations insinuated themselves into the national psyche. Second editions of both the *Reliques* and *Popular Songs* were published in 1866 and 1883 respectively. Walsh was perceived as belonging, but not wholly belonging,[3] to the culture of the Young Ireland poets and their literary contemporaries. Katherine Tynan, recalling the excitement surrounding the emergence of Yeats, wrote, 'The Ireland of my young days was terribly unexacting in the manner of poetry... Of course there was always Mangan and Ferguson, Callanan and Edward Walsh and the best of de Vere, but these were dead or old and Ireland was placidly accepting for poetry what was merely propagandism or heartless exercises in unsimple simplicity.'[4] And yet, Edward Walsh influenced Tynan herself, as Yeats pointed out, 'The work of the Irish folklorists and the translations of Dr. Hyde and of an earlier poet, the village schoolmaster, Edward Walsh, began to affect her.'[5] Dedicating his *Love Songs of Connaught* to George Sigerson, Hyde wrote, 'Allow me to offer you this slight attempt on my part to do for Connaught what you yourself and the late John O'Daly, following in the footsteps of Edward Walsh, to some extent accomplished for Munster more than thirty years ago.'[6]

In *The Young Douglas Hyde*, Dominic Daly wrote, 'Hyde was fortunate in the timing of his book; the climate was favourable. For almost forty years Anglo-Irish poetry had been weighed down by its burthen of nationalist propaganda. Poets were popular if they bewailed Ireland's wrongs and chanted her virtues. There had been exceptions, of course, Callanan and Walsh had turned to the Gaelic songs of the people, and each had succeeded

---

[1] Graves, A. P. *The Book of Irish Poetry*, p. xxxv.

[2] ibid., pp. xxix-xxx.

[3] Yeats and Hyde, among others point to Walsh as a man apart. See: infra.

[4] See: Daly, D., *The Young Douglas Hyde*, p.132.

[5] The *Bookman*, Sept. 1894, quoted by D. Daly in *The Young Douglas Hyde*, p. 85.

[6] Hyde, D. *Love Songs of Connaught*, Preface.

in a few instances in putting something of the form and flavour of folk song into their English verse.'[1]

In his preface to *A Book of Irish Verse*, Yeats declares that 'Young Ireland poetry is always good teaching and sometimes good poetry,'[2] but he goes on to say that 'Edward Walsh, a village schoolmaster, who hovered, like Mangan, on the edge of the Young Ireland movement, did many beautiful translations from the Gaelic.'[3] Yeats also acknowledges his indebtedness to him, 'I took from Allingham and Walsh their passion for country spiritism, and from Ferguson his pleasure in heroic legend.'[4] In his article on 'Irish National Literature from Callanan to Carleton', Yeats wrote, 'Callanan was followed immediately by other translators, of whom Edward Walsh... was the best.'[5] And Yeats described Douglas Hyde as 'the last of our ballad-writers of the school of Walsh and Callanan - men whose work seems fragrant with turf smoke.'[6]

On the genesis of *Bards of the Gael and Gall*, A. P. Graves notes that 'much of the work had been done in the Sixties, when, following in the footsteps of Edward Walsh, Dr. Sigerson, in co-operation with the late John O'Daly, accomplished for Munster lyrics what Dr. Hyde has since achieved for the Religious and love poetry of Connaught in his two memorable books, *The Love Songs of Connaught* and *The Religious Songs of Connaught.*'[7]

Graves pays tribute to the work of Hardiman's translators and their predecessor Charlotte Brookes, but is critical of their 'over ornate, and often extremely artificial English verse into which they were translated.'[8] He envisages Walsh's *Reliques* (1844) and *Irish Popular Songs* (1847) almost 'as a protest against the artificial character of previous collections of the kind.'[9] By contrast, as Robert Farren expresses it, Walsh 'did not petrify the verses he translated.'[10] In Farren's eyes Walsh enjoyed the advantage of being 'the one fully-orbed Irishman of his day: a Catholic; educated; at one with the peasants except in their limitations; a lover of spoken Irish and of its music, poetry and history; a separatist and all but a martyr; a man so poor and denied that he coveted Mitchel's deportation to Botany Bay.'[11] But it wasn't just the 'fully orbed' nature of Walsh that put him ahead of Davis and the Young Ireland poets. It was in the words of Graves, 'This wise tendency to treat Irish

[1] Daly, D., *The Young Douglas Hyde*, p. 131.
[2] Yeats, W.B., *A Book of Irish Verse*, p. xiv.
[3] ibid., p. xxiii.
[4] Yeats, W.B., *Essays and Introductions*, p. 248.
[5] Yeats, W.B., 'Irish National Literature from Callanan to Carleton,' the *Bookman*, p. 106, col. i.
[6] Yeats, W.B., *Fairy & Folk Tales of the Irish Peasantry*, p. xvi.
[7] Graves, A.P., *The Book of Irish Poetry*, p. xxxix.
[8] ibid, p. xxix.
[9] ibid., p. xxx.
[10] Farren, R., *The Course of Irish Verse in English*, p. 29.
[11] ibid., p. 28.

poetry in an Irish way, through the medium of what I have already called Hiberno-English speech.'[1] More than other poets of the Young Ireland days, including Davis, Moore, Callanan, Gerald Griffin and to some extent, even Mangan, Graves concludes that both Edward Walsh and Ferguson had 'a something;' a something of that special sensitivity to the Gaelic rhythm and flow in its pristine purity which other writers lacked.[2]

Robert Farren tried to put words on that 'something':

> "[Walsh] is remembered as Callanan is, as one who tipped our verse in the way that would lead it to distinction. But Walsh did it consciously, as part of a fervent belief. He appreciated several of the formal virtues of his originals, determined to reproduce them in translating, and did, in fact, do this thing, in a certain degree. That is, he fits the words always to the tune, as Moore did, arriving as did Moore, Callanan and Ferguson at the long, sinuous line; and he 'vowells' well, employing cross-rhyme and assonance. His chief fault was a stiff, often bookish diction; the source of his considerable influence, his relative faithfulness and the completeness, in a given genre - that of Jacobite poetry - of what he attempted.
>
> A stanza from his best poem, *Have you been at Carrick*, will show his quality:

Have you been at Carrick, and saw you my true-love there
And saw you her features, all beautiful, bright and fair?
Saw you the most fragrant, flowering sweet apple-tree?
O! saw you my lov'd one, and pines she in grief like me?[3]

In a substantial chapter on Edward Walsh, professor Robert Welch of the university of Ulster, says that Walsh's 'aim as a translator is to transpose the music of the original into English, keeping the Irish rhythm and phrasing, in some way that will also accommodate the content, meaning and spirit line by line.'[4] He goes on to state that 'The concentration on recreating Irish word-music in English, while it consistently results in beautiful and fascinating aural effects, often distracts Walsh from the details of the original poetry.'[5]

Seamus Deane's monumental *Field Day Anthology of Irish Writings* is typical of other anthologies in that it contains just two translations by Edward Walsh, a Jacobite song from

---

[1] Graves, A.P. *The Book of Irish Poetry*, p. xxx.
[2] ibid p. xxxi-xxxii.
[3] Farren, op. cit. p. 29. For full text of 'Have you been to Carrick?' see p. 632f.
[4] Welch, R., *A History of Verse Translation from the Irish 1789-1897*, p. 124.
[5] ibid., p. 126.

Reliques and, from *Irish Popular Songs*, a translation of Eoghan Rua Ó Súilleabháin's jaunty 'Drinking Song'. He acknowledges Walsh to be 'one of the best and most influential translators of Irish in the nineteenth century'[1] but does not address his importance in terms of pioneering Hiberno-English. Instead, his focus is on his contribution to the attempted revival of the Irish language, subsequently manifested 'particularly in the development of the Gaelic League, founded in 1893, and in the later writings of Daniel Corkery , Frank O'Connor and others.'[2] He also highlights a superficial aspect of Walsh's personality, namely, a certain prudery endemic to Anglo-Saxon Puritan culture since Cromwellian times, but with the retreat of Irish as a spoken language, now infiltrating Irish Catholic culture as well. 'He [Walsh] assures his audience,' says Deane, 'that nothing offensive was ever produced in Irish poetry - that is nothing that would offend a Victorian-catholic sensibility. This was not true, but is of a piece with the development of the notion that Irish represented tradition, purity, fidelity, and a whole combination of sterling values that the modern world has lost.'[3] Interesting as this observation may be, it has little relevance to the survival of Edward Walsh's name in the Irish literary tradition.

As a translator, Walsh 'succeeded with the enthusiasm of genius, in finding for the cumulative methods of Celtic verse adequate means of expression in English. All those delicate shades of colouring, which the old poets expressed by the use of words differing almost imperceptibly in meaning, he has succeeded, with a poet's instinct, in transferring undiminished and unimpaired.'[4]

Virtually unknown among the population of modern Ireland, the name of Edward Walsh will survive for many a day in literary circles, not indeed because of disappointed hopes for a revival of the Irish language, but for his pioneering work in the evolution of a new medium in Ireland. Faced with a cultural and linguistic change after two thousand years of Gaeldom, Walsh was among the first, possibly the very first, to attempt its preservation through translations made with a refined sensibility to the ancient rhythms and in a style of language later to be hailed as Hiberno-English.

---

[1] Deane, S., *Field Anthology of Irish Writings*, vol. ii, p. 112.
[2] ibid., p. 40.
[3] Ibid., p. 41.
[4] Gregg, F.J., "Edward Walsh" in *The Irish Fireside*, 1887, p. 316.

LAMENT FOR EDWARD WALSH[1]

On silver-bosom'd Avon Dhu
Soft shone the rosy morning beam,
And many a leaf impearl'd with dew
Hung weeping o'er the gentle stream;
On shaded rock and misty fell
The sickly hue of autumn hung;
When by the river's pensive swell
I heard this plaintive requiem sung.

"From wild Glengarriffe's fairy strand
To Avon Dhu's romantic side;
From gentle Banna's amber sand
To Liffy's darkly-winding tide;
From Shannon's border to the sea -
From Suir's bright springs to crystal Nore;
Ye sons of song come mourn with me
The bard of legendary lore.

"Ah! gentle star of genius dear,
Where is thy beam of beauty gone?
Tho' clouded in thy kindred sphere,
Thy ray with sweetest splendour shone;
As springs the modest mountain flower
Beneath mild April's dewy ray -
As smiles the wild rose on the brier
Thy genius smiled and passed away.

"Thy country's eyes have tears for thee,
Thy country's soul embalms thy name,
Thy talent grew, a lovely tree,
Fann'd by the genial airs of fame;
Amid a nation's tears and gloom,
The thrilling sweetness of thy lyre
Awoke her gentleness from its tomb,
And stirred her heart's blood into fire.

---

[1] Poem by M.H. Thomond, Banks of Shannon, Jan. 16th 1858, published in the *Celt*, March, 1858, pp. 32-33.

"What human heart can read unmov'd
The record of thy dying hour,
When she, thy partner so belov'd,
Bent o'er thee like a weeping flower;
Alas! that souls so sweetly twined,
Should from each other's love be torn;
Alas! that hearts so pure and kind,
As her's should sigh and weep forlorn.

By silver Avon's misty wave,
He won the treasure of her love,
And noble was the heart he gave,
Unsullied as the skies above;
And gentle as Loch Callan's swan,
Was she his spirits worshipp'd bride,
And love and beauty round her shone,
With youth and virtue at her side.

"The breathings of his lofty soul
Were turned to music in her praise,
His heart was love's own banquet bowl,
And she the bright wine of his days.
For Erin and his Bríghidín fair
His wild harp's notes were poured alone,
For Erin and his Bríghidín dear,
His spirit thrilled with one sweet tone.

"Ye hills and moors and ferny dales,
By fairy Avon's silent tide,
Ye groves and banks and shamrock vales,
No more he'll hail your vernal pride;
His sorrows and his toils are o'er,
And keen privations suffered long,
His gentle heart shall feel no more,
The genial powers of love and song."

PART TWO

· PERSONAL LETTERS · OF EDWARD WALSH

together with
Secondary Source Correspondence Relating to Him.

INTRODUCTION

Over forty of Edward Walsh's letters, in whole or in part, are still extant. Thirty-two of these are in his own handwriting and are contained in MS. 2261 in the National Library of Ireland, Kildare St., Dublin. Among these are to be found a sketch of the life of Eoghan Ruadh Ó Suilleábháin, the Sliabh Luachra poet, and four poetical translations from the Irish. All the handwritten material is addressed to his publisher, John (O') Daly, Bookseller, Kilkenny. The collection was purchased at the sale of Rev. J. Lee's books in Limerick, October 28th 1929.

Of the remaining extant letters and fragments, eleven are contained in an article by C.J. Kickham, published in the *Celt*, December 1857, one is in the *Irishman* of March 14th 1866, one each in C.G. Duffy's papers in the Royal Irish Academy and in the National Library respectively. In the *Wexford Independent*, October 16th 1844, there is an item which *may* be from the hand of Edward Walsh (or possibly based on an earlier letter of his). Among the secondary source letters there is one of particular significance - a letter from Walsh's wife, Brighid, published in the *Cork Examiner*, June 16th 1858.

I have not attempted to impose a sequence either on the MS letters or those from other sources, but the accompanying foot notes indicate both sources and dates in so far as these are possible to ascertain. I give what approximates to a critical edition of the letters to John Daly that are contained in MS 2261, so that from observation of the abbreviations and general hurried style, the reader will be able to pick up a flavour of the pressure of time under which the author so often laboured.

The following brief introduction to some persons featuring in the letters may be of assistance to the reader.

Coffey, James Charles, barrister, proprietor of the *Dublin Monitor*.
Office 6 Lower Abbey St. & 51 Lower Dominick St., Dublin.

Daly, John (O'), Irish Scholar and Bookseller in Kilkenny,
& later in 9 Anglesea St., Dublin.

Davis, Thomas Osborne, barrister, 61, now 67, Lower Baggot St., Dublin.

Duffy, Charles Gavan, 3 Connaught Place, Rathmines.

Geraghty, Bryan, Bookseller and publisher, 11 Anglesea St., Dublin.

Goodwin, C.F., General Printing Office, 33 Eustace St., Dublin.

Machen, Samuel J. Bookseller, publisher, stationer & British & Foreign circulating library, 28 Westmoreland St., Dublin.

McGlashan, James, Bookseller & Publisher, 21 D'Olier St., Dublin.

McSwiney, (McSweeney), Dr. Stephen Myles, M.D. Surgeon, 18 York St., Dublin.

Nethercotte, Richard, printer, 75 Marlborough St., Dublin.

Roe, Peter, Printer & Publisher, proprietor of the *Irish Builder*, 42 Mabbot St.;
residence: 158 North Strand Road, Dublin.

Treanor, Patrick, New & Old Bookseller, 29/30 Essex Quay, Dublin.

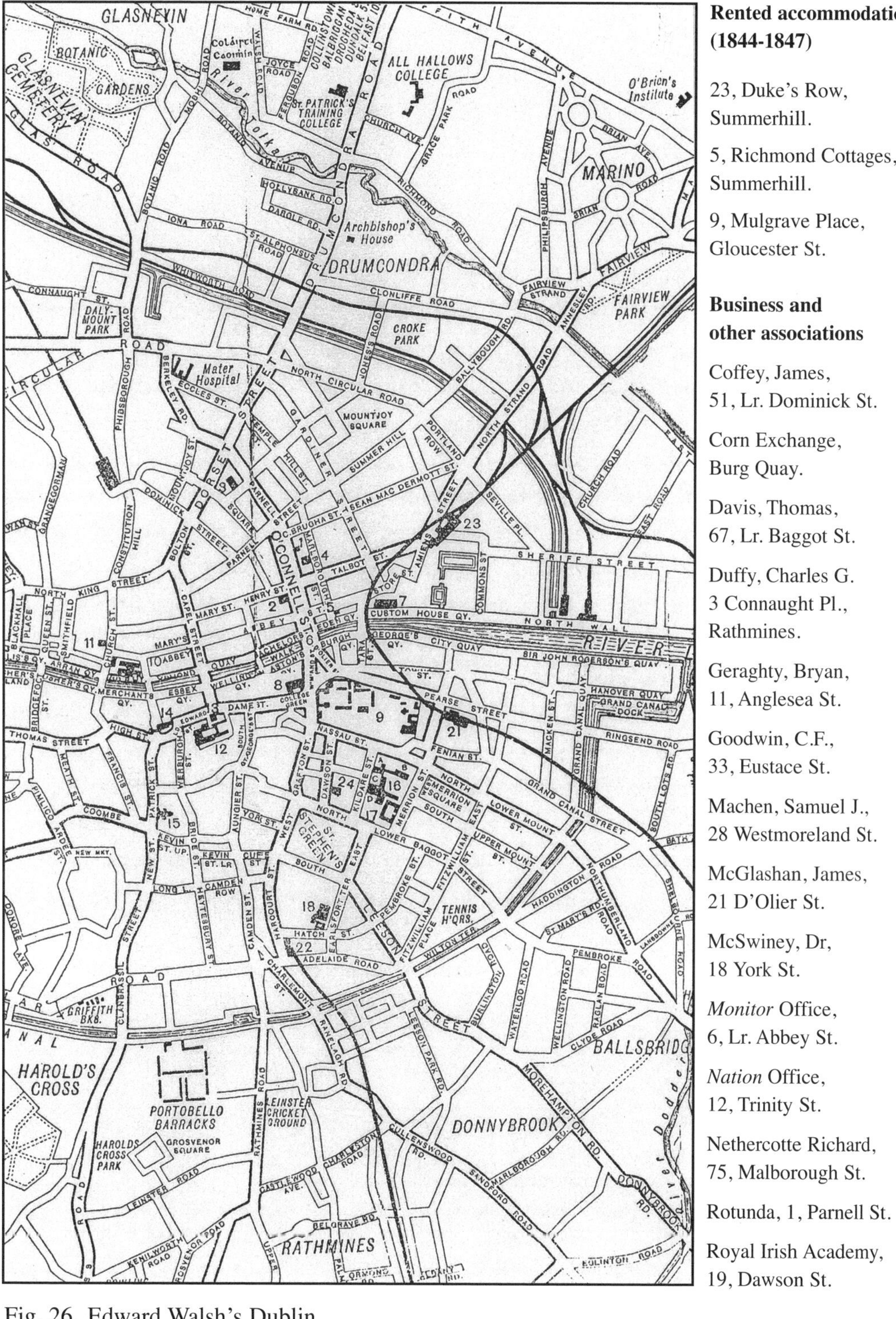

Fig. 26. Edward Walsh's Dublin

Rented accommodation (1844-1847)

23, Duke's Row, Summerhill.

5, Richmond Cottages, Summerhill.

9, Mulgrave Place, Gloucester St.

Business and other associations

Coffey, James, 51, Lr. Dominick St.

Corn Exchange, Burg Quay.

Davis, Thomas, 67, Lr. Baggot St.

Duffy, Charles G. 3 Connaught Pl., Rathmines.

Geraghty, Bryan, 11, Anglesea St.

Goodwin, C.F., 33, Eustace St.

Machen, Samuel J., 28 Westmoreland St.

McGlashan, James, 21 D'Olier St.

McSwiney, Dr, 18 York St.

Monitor Office, 6, Lr. Abbey St.

Nation Office, 12, Trinity St.

Nethercotte Richard, 75, Malborough St.

Rotunda, 1, Parnell St.

Royal Irish Academy, 19, Dawson St.

(1) Walsh to John Daly[1]

Duke's-row
Summer-hill
Dublin,
[Postmarked Jan. 2. 1844]

Dear Sir,

I did not receive your letter till late last night, though left here yesterday morning.

I called at Machen's[2] at 10 to-day. He informed me that the printer did not yet give him your second number, and that many gentlemen called to inquire for it & seemed disappointed — I called at the residence of a barrister of note[3] in the city afterwards — one of those fiery spirits[4] who are carrying out the present movement of freedom & he told me that he likewise called at Machen's for the songs — He begged of me to leave him my metrical version of the songs to show to his friends — He has a high opinion of my abilities & says that my aid in giving an elegant translation would be powerful in recommending them to mere English speaking readers. He says it would be a good plan to interline your literal version with the Irish — that is to give the prose English under the Irish word for word without regard to the arrangement for the use of them who would study the tongue & they would be many. He says Jacobite songs would take well — He has given me some business in the way of writing.

The artist I spoke of informs me that Curry[5] says the last line of the Creevin Evin[6] in your song is not belonging to that song at all — and I am clearly of opinion that it does not suit the measure of the other lines — Curry's remark is that the two first lines are from a long song - the others are from a Jacobite song & the last taken from some other song —

I have to say that it strikes me if the songs were got up in a clever way they would succeed —

You will scarcely be able to read this which I write in a confounded hurry.

Yours faithfully,
E Walsh

---

1 MS 2261, NLI. John Daly (O'Daly) a bookseller in Kilkenny had an agreement with Walsh regarding the publication of translations from the Irish.

2 Samuel J. Machen, Bookseller, publisher, stationer & British & Foreign circulating library, 28 Westmoreland St. Dublin.

3 The "barrister of note" is probably C.G. Duffy.

4 'those fiery spirits,' i.e. the Young Irelanders.

5 Eugene O'Curry, who at that time was employed in the cataloguing and arranging of manuscripts for the Royal Irish Academy, Trinity College, and the British Museum.

6 Song title: the spelling in Walsh's letters varies - Creevin/Craovin/Chroevin Evan/Aoivin/Aoibhinn.

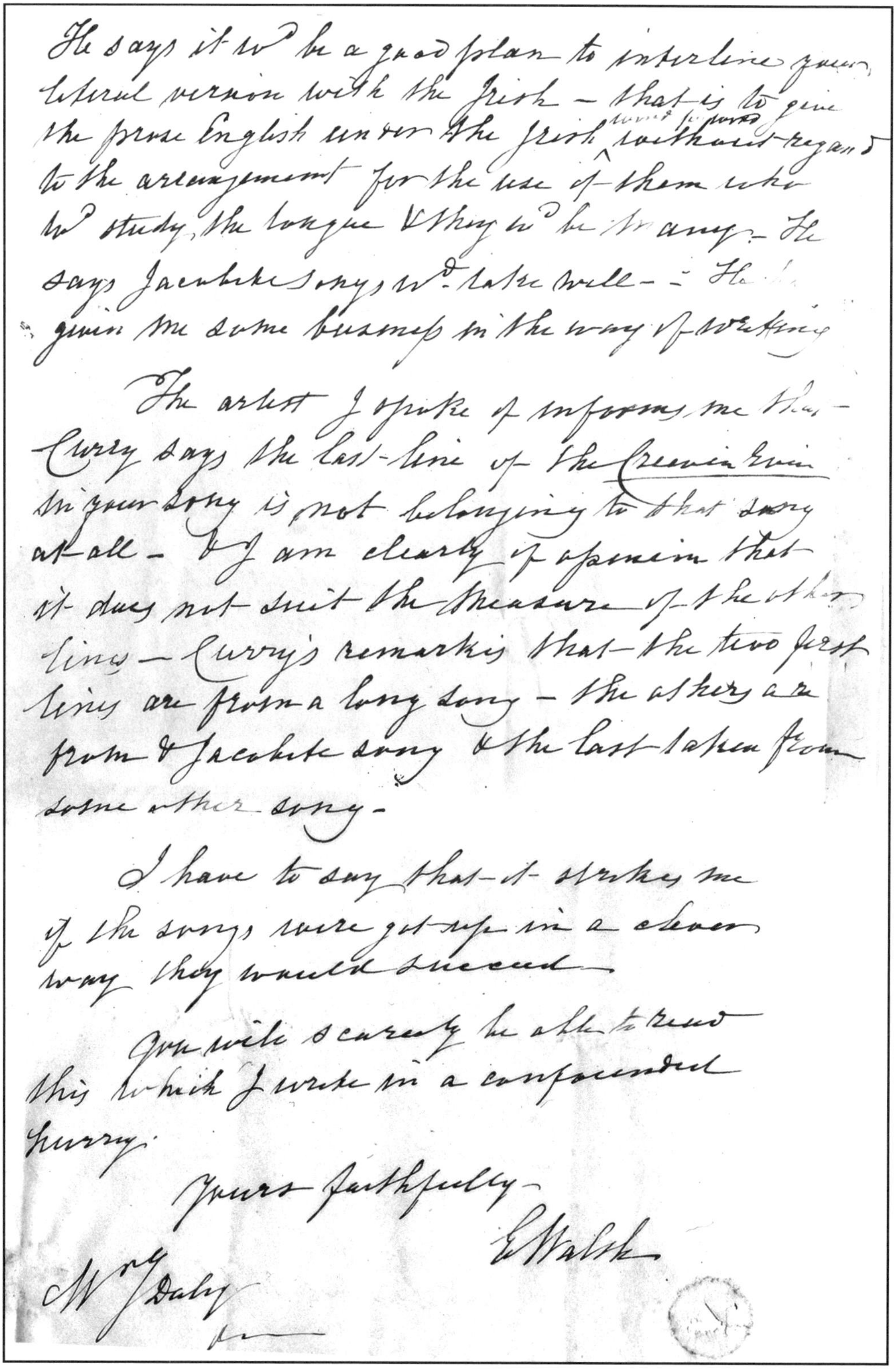

He says it wd be a good plan to interline your literal version with the Irish — that is to give the prose English under the Irish word for word without regard to the arrangement for the use of them who wd study the tongue & they wd be many. — He says Jacobite songs wd take well — He has given me some business in the way of writing

The artist I spoke of informs me that Curry says the last line of the Creevin Evin in your song is not belonging to that song at all — & I am clearly of opinion that it does not suit the measure of the other lines — Curry's remarks that the two first lines are from a long song — the others are from a Jacobite song & the last taken from some other song —

I have to say that it strikes me if the songs were got up in a clever way they would succeed —

You will scarcely be able to read this which I write in a confounded hurry.

Yours faithfully —

E Walsh

Mr J Daly

&c

Fig. 27. Edward Walsh's handwriting. See *Letters*, No. 1.

Mr. Daly esq.

[P.S.] I have no certain knowledge when I leave town, or whether I go at all[1] [.] I'll know in a week [.] The Creevin Evin is in the mouth of all the clever fellows here.

(2) Walsh to John Daly[2]

23 Duke's-row
Summer-hill
Dublin,
[Postmarked Jany 5. 1844]

Dear Sir,

I got your letter this morning & have great pleasure in now replying to that favour.

I called into Machen's at half-past 2 o'clock yesterday & up to that time the printer did not send him your songs. I did not go to hear Mr. W's lecture at the Rotundo — I did not know that you were acquainted with him — I now suppose him to be the person of whom we were speaking & whose brother I know.

I was in the hope that the board would allow me back to my snug residence at Tourin[3] but they decided against it yesterday — though Sir. Rich [ard Musgrave][4] — and the superintendent applied in my behalf. I am grieved that my poor wife & infants will be disturbed in their calm solitude[5] and sent up here in winter weather — God pardon the doers of this injustice — You will say perhaps that it is the best course for my future advancement — It may be so, but I am not well fitted for the bustle of a town life and besides I dread if my health which is not very robust should fail — I dread the fate of my family — but I must now bear the charge and pray to God to assist me.

With regard to our projects respecting the songs I understand you to say that you will bear all the expenses of printing paper etc and after deducting all costs from the sales you then at the end of six months will equally share the net profits remaining, with me — If this be so I am content [.] I'll engage to give you spirited translations — talent is my only stock-in-trade and I'll be no miser of it [.] In all other respects Mr. Daly reckon me as one who will die rather than lie or deceive.

---

[1] When Walsh came to Dublin at the close of 1843, he still had hope of getting back to his school in Tourin, Co. Waterford.

[2] MS 2261.

[3] Tourin, Toureen in Ordinance Survey and present day usage.

[4] Sir Richard Musgrave: The Co. Waterford Landlord who owned Tourin School was a faithful friend to Walsh.

[5] After his resignation from Tourin, Brighid and the children stayed at the parental home in Affane until Edward found them suitable accommodation in Dublin.

I would wish when you give the metrical version of the songs, that you gave the name of the translator — Mr. Lane[1] recommended me not to forget this as it might procure me notice [.]

That Mr. Curry sent the artist I was speaking of to me last night to say that he would wish to know me. I am now about to go to him to the Academy[2] & shall enquire at Machen's about the songs — It still strikes me the last line of the Creevin has not the same measure nor number of feet with the other lines — Try Mr. Daly —

I shall with great pleasure try my hand at your songs Nos 2 & 3 if you send up the Irish & your literal version. I wish you were here & then we would pull harmoniously together.

I am very lonely & sad away from my own beloved wife and children & cannot well settle down to anything till they come [.] I have written for them.

Believe me with all truth, dear Mr. Daly,

Yours faithfully,
E Walsh

Mr. John Daly esq.

[P.S.] I shall keep this open till I see Machens [.]
I have been to Machen, who says that he got the songs at last [.] I called at the Nation office[3] but did not see Mr. Davis[4] — I forgot to ask Machen whether he sent the songs to him.

(3) Walsh to John Daly[5]

23 Duke's-row
Summer-hill
Dublin,
Wednesday, Jan 10. 44

Dear Sir,

I have thrown out no hint of your dealing unfairly by me but I understand from you both "by word and write" as Burns says, that I was to share half the profits. That you meant so if I paid half the expenses as they occurred I do not doubt because you tell me so but I did not understand it so before — However I am willing to sing for the thing you mention that is 1/3 as I cannot get more unless I contribute to the outlay — Are you satisfied, Mr. Daly?

---

[1] Denny Lane (1818-1895), the Co. Cork businessman & balladeer, prominently identified with the Young Ireland cause in Munster..

[2] The Royal Irish Academy, Dawson Street, Dublin.

[3] The *Nation* Office was initially at 12 Trinity St.; later in a premises in Abbey Street (now occupied by the *Independent* Office. The paper was printed by James Duffy.

[4] *Mr. Davis* or *Davis*: Thomas Osborne Davis.

[5] NLI, MS 2261

I am prepared at all times to try my rhyming powers though the vis poetica[1] will not rush forth at my call at all times — however never ask me if I am prepared, but always send without ceremony — send the Irish and the literal version [.] What you translate link in the Creevin I could not for some time understand the meaning of [.] I've learned it means a "ringlet of hair"[.] You should render it ringlet — it is highly poetical [.] Your translation bore me from the meaning.

I have written to Mrs. Walsh, and mentioned you [.] When she calls (if she travels by that way) provide her some decent safe lodging house to sleep in [.] She is anxious to see 'Edward' and I don't think she'll linger on the road. Your civil and kind invitation pleases me Mr. Daly.

I travelled all round the quays and other places in the neighbourhood of the Liffey and could see few shops to be let only one or two. These were to be let with houses at £100 a year — In Grafton St. near the corner of Galwey St. a shop with 3 or 4 rooms is to be let at £100 a year — I considered these too dear — I should apprise you that I am a bad hand at these concerns of life — If you like [?] any particular streets you would like to inquire for such in I shall do so again with pleasure.

I was greatly pleased with your intention of giving the interlinear version according to my first suggestion. If you gave it without regard to the grammatical order of the English but word for word in the Irish — it would be of service to my poetic version by turning the reader from instituting comparisons between your accurate version and my looser one.

I called today at Machens. He tells me the songs are taking right cleverly but he complains of the manner in which the 2nd N° is got up [.] It is not fit for a street ballad, in type or paper — The letter press & paper would damn the best work of the day — I told him you were taking it out of the printer's hands altogether & he seemed pleased. I bought your first N° & am greatly pleased at its cleverness, and also at its respectable appearance —

I earnestly beg of you unless you wish to ruin the Irish character of the work, not to print your Irish in either Roman or Italian character — The old Irish type is the type of their nationality [;] alter that — & you destroy it — These are my own suggestions [.] I have not spoken yet to anyone on the subject but shall perhaps with Mr. Duffy[1] tomorrow.

You will pardon me & attribute to my present situation the manner in which I send your communication.

I beg to remain yours,
E. Walsh.

Mr. J. Daly esq.

[P.S.] I'm confident Mr. Duffy will agree with me in saying that the Irish should be done in Irish type.

---

[1] Unless otherwise stated, references to *Mr. Duffy* or *Duffy* designate Charles (later, Sir Charles) Gavan Duffy.

(4) Walsh to John Daly[1]

23 Dukes Row
Summer Hill
Monday.
[Postmarked January 15th - 44]

Dear Sir

You see I've lost no time — You will oblige me if you send me copies in future that I need not be paging the [...?] book — I have a remark to offer in your future writing avoid all words of contempt or hate to any party [;] it will check the sale of the work whose alone it would harm that is in England & Scotland — When you give strong expressions give them as the words of the bard but not as your own — I had this hint from one who is on the opposite side to us. Also when translating you should take not only the literal meaning but also the genius of the tongue into effect. "Footmanlike" gives to an English reader the idea of a servant or a soldier whereas "bronaire" denotes one who trudges on foot if I mistake not. I have kept the Irish title of the second song in the translation so you see it has a capital effect [.] In fact every allegorical allusion should be preserved in Irish. To print these into English would ruin the effect. The last stanza of the Irish is unworthy of Shane Clarach.[2] There's a [...?] confusion of idea in it — I was forced to alter it to preserve the sense [.] If luib means a lock is it not a lock of hair — three words for the term ringlet.

Yours etc
E. Walsh

[P.S] I would say that when your author is dull or defective in sense I would omit particular passages altogether if I were you.

---

[1] NLI, MS 2261.

[2] Seán Clárach MacDómhnaill (1691-1754), a farmer-cum-poet who lived in the vicinity of Charleville, Co. Cork and who is buried in Ballysally Graveyard in that town. For the most part, Walsh's spelling is *Claragh*.

(5) To John Daly[1]

23 Dukes Row
Summer Hill
Sunday Night.

Sir,

I reply at 9 o'clock at night to your letter of the 25th inst. I have been with Goodwin[2] and & have to say that Christie has not yet brought him the Irish types [.] I shall enquire tomorrow before this leaves and let you know [.] Mr. Machen says the work is repeatedly asked for but that each inquirer concludes as it is not forthcoming that it has gone the way of all Irish works — I said before it should be brought out weekly and so thinks Machen [.] Goodwin says you would not take his types which have done service for Dr. McHale[3] & others — Christie is famous for delays it is said —

I have changed "glaire" & let it stand as I write it "glaive" — I was aware of the spelling "glave" but have preferred the other mode which I have seen in old Romany — You seem to think "wold" a novel word when you give a learned note upon it — It is not so —

I have laid aside the idea of going back — Mr. Duffy set his face in toto against it & said he would consider himself insulted by the expression of any doubt in his wish and favour to procure me a respectable situation after the trials.[4] I will not go — Duffy is a true man.

I sent a sketch of Owen Roe[5] from old snatches fetched from rude memories of the child of song [.] The parallel between him and Burns is perfectly just. I wrote it before my dinner today.

Do not put my name to the heading of any future songs. The first notice is quite sufficient. Any further particulars of Owen you can procure may be added by yourself. I have altered the last line of the last stanza of "Mac an Ceanead"[6] to suit the others.

---

[1] NLI, MS 2261.

[2] C.F. Goodwin, general printing office, 33 Eustace St. & Callenswood Cottages, Cullensville Avenue, Dublin; also, Goodwin, Son & Nethercotte, Printers, 75 Marlborough St., Dublin.

[3] The archbishop of Tuam.

[4] For a full report on the 'trials' see John Flanedy's *A Special Report of the proceedings in the case of The Queen against Daniel O'Connell, ESQ. M.P., John O'Connell, ESQ., M.P., Thomas Steele, Esq., Thomas Matthew Ray, Esq. Charles Gavan Duffy, Esq [et al.] on an Indictment for Conspiracy and Misdemeanour*, (J. Duffy) Dublin, 1844.

[5] A reference to a sketch of the life of the 18-century Sliabh Luachra poet Eoghan Ruadh Ó Súilleabháin, *alias* Owen Roe or Owen the Red and Eoghan an Bheóil Bhinn - Owen of the Sweet Voice.

[6] Mac an Cheannuidhe/ Ceanaidhe/Cheanaighe, an aisling poem by the 18th-century Sliabh Luachra poet, Aogán Ó Rathaille. See final text p. 638f.

You have not said how my version of Shane Claragh's last song pleased you — I love both praise & censure when deserved & am never content with neither.

If you could open a correspondence with Mr. Galwey a farmer living some years ago in the parish of Ardnaguhy near Charleville, he would give you many a relic of Owen Roe.[1]

Gandsey is the Killarney piper & a celebrated one. The Millstreet piper is D [aniel] O'Leary whom I have celebrated in two legends[2] — Get music from Gandsey — Duffy is again calling for it. Get it at once [.] Write and say how you like my slight sketch of Owen — & point out what you approve and what you dislike in my metrical versions.

It strikes me that you should print out the air of each song if possible — the last I did was to the beautiful air of "Shela ny Guiry"[3] —

Your new plan is excellent — Eschew all party expressions [,] give regular weekly songs in future [,] treat your Anglo-Irish rhymer liberally and I have no doubt of your success.

E Walsh.

Mr. J. Daly

---

[1] Owen Roe worked in the Charleville area of Co. Cork as a day labourer. Of three known lady friends in that district, Misses Lynch, Gleeson, and Casey, the poet's eulogy of the latter makes her best remembered:

One evening late it was my fate
To meet a charming creature
Whose airy gait and nice portrait
Excels both art and nature;
Her curling hair in ringlets fair
Down to her waist doth dangle,
The white and rose, united foes,
Her beauteous cheeks bespangle.

Her rolling, glancing, sparkling eyes,
Each gazer's heart at once surprise,
And bind a train of love-sick swains
In Cupid's close enthralling chains.
Whoever views her lovely face
That is bedecked with youth and grace,
Must every hour proclaim the power
Of Molly Casey's charms....

[2] See pp. 225ff.

[3] Shela ny Guira, or Guiry: *Séila Ní Dhuibhir*, the name of a beautiful Irish love song.

6) Walsh to John Daly[1]

The Cruel base-born Tyrant
a Jacobite Relic

What wither'd the pride of my vigour?-
The lowly-sprung tyrant train;
That rule all our border with rigour,
And ravage the fruitful plain!
Yet once when the war-trumpet's rattle
Arous'd the wild clansman's wrath,
They heartless abandon'd the battle,
And fled the fierce foeman's path!

My flocks roam the valley untended. -
There's grief in my native vale -
Hark! heard ye in wild breezes blended,
The brute and the human wail!
Misfortune my temper is trying
This raiment no shelter yields -
And chief o'er my evils undying -
The tyrant that rules my fields.

Alas! on the red hill where perish'd
The offspring of heroes proud
The virtues our forefathers cherish'd
Lie pall'd in their blood-stain'd shroud!
And O! for one hero avenger
With aid o'er the heaving main
To sweep from Clar Fodhla the stranger
And sever his bondage-chain!

[1] NLI, MS 2261. Walsh's missive consists of these two texts only. The poems and accompanying notes may be found on pp. 637.

Mac an Ceanaide
(a Jacobite Relic)

A vision bless'd my eyes erewhile
Revealing scenes sublime and airy! -
The genius of green Erin's isle
Stood by my couch a gorgeous fairy -
Her blue eyes' glow, her ringlets' flow
And pure pale brow exceeding any,
Proclaim'd with pride that at her side
Would sit her true-love Mac an Ceanaide [.]

Her voice is sweetest music's sound
To us who for her love are dying
Proud spouse of Brian conquest-crown'd
I mourn the doom that leaves thee sighing!
When Saxon might assails thy right
I dread, fair queen belov'd of many
That o'er thy brow dark sorrow's plough
Shall come ere cometh Mac an Ceanaide [.]

Myriads languish for her love
And burn to clasp her form of beauty;
For her have kings and heroes strove,
Rivals high in love and duty. -
But joy's bright trace ne'er lights her face
She fears her foemen fierce and many,
No hope-fraught ray to cheer her way,
Will come, till cometh Mac an Ceanaide [.]

"My brethren," said the beauteous maid
"Were kings supreme and chiefs of glory
Conn of the blood-red battle blade
And Art, the theme of ancient story.-
And o'er the deep, where tall barks leap,
shall heroes come renown'd and many"
Alas the day! - thy charms' decay
Shall come ere cometh *Mac an Ceanaide* [.]

"There's glory for thy future day,
The banner green shall yet be flying,"
I cried - but 'neath the vision's sway,
In distant Spain I saw her dying!
As burst my joy she gave reply,
One shriek that spoke her broken-hearted.
My bitter grief found no relief,
Until the vision wild departed [.]

(7) Walsh to John Daly[1]

23 Dukes Row
Summer Hill
[Postmarked January 8th 1844]

Dear Sir

I have had your friendly advice & unless something presents here within a week I shall act upon it — I have been sadly disappointed.

I send this one & hope I have done it well. In the 4th stanza I give in the 1st line your choice of two expressions — It seems from what you say the first is agreeable to history.

When I am confined Mr. Daly to the compass of the stanza to express therein the meaning of the same number of lines in the original you cannot expect that I could deliver line exactly for line — If you glance at Furlong's versions of Hardiman's songs you will see the fidelity of mine — What you have will suit your alteration right well but if you think otherwise here are 4 lines to suit your notion:

The lov'd ones my life would have nourish'd
Are foodless & bare & cold -
My flocks by their fountains that flourish'd,
Decay on the mountain wold. -
Misfortune, etc

I hope I have conveyed the sense of the original in this.

Would you recommend if I go to the south to travel by the canal boat to Athy and on to Clonmel then [.]

I have no news [.] I have not been out today [.] None are permitted to occupy the court I understand. I wanted to see Mr. Duffy one day & was not allowed beyond the barrier & he was obliged to come out to me. & I saw neither judge nor jury — You know I have

[1] NLI, MS 2261.

given up the reporting business [.][1] Would to heaven I never came up here [.] However it will teach me a better understanding of things and that is perhaps worth the purchase.

Yours etc
E. Walsh

Mr. Daly

(8) Walsh to John Daly[2]

23 Dukes Row
Summer Hill
Monday
[Postmarked January 44]

Dear Sir

I have written to my wife to say that you would wish she should call on you in Kilkenny if she comes that way [.] Her letter expresses her wish to travel by the packet - from Cork — I said in reply that I would wish she came by the coach and hope she will.

I understand your terms with me now Mr. Daly — You want to engross 2/3rds (two thirds) simply because you advance cash & some physical & a little mental toil while I that have to invoke the muse without whose inspiration you know, I would bring discredit on myself & your work gets but 1/3 (one third). That was not in the "bond" at first — but I'll take it for the good of — myself perhaps.

I am scribbling in extreme haste as it is up to post hour [.]

Yours etc
E Walsh

Mr Daly

---

[1] Charles Gavan Duffy first secured Walsh a job with Mr. Coffee, proprietor of the *Monitor*. The journalistic work, both inside and outside the office, did not suit Walsh and he resigned it after a very short time.

[2] NLI, MS. 2261.

(9) Walsh to John Daly[1]

Monday Evening
[Postmarked January 29th 1844]

Dear Sir,

I have just been to Goodwins — Christie sent the type on Saturday & I was told that you may expect a proof on Wednesday. I am engaged for some time past in copying out Plunkett's speeches[2] which a barrister[3] of the city is going to publish [.] 'Tis dull work & I know not what I am to get for my pains. Write and let me know how you like the sketch [.] 'Tis of course imperfect [.] I wish you were living here [.] We would pull together cleverly at the songs [.] You must publish weekly and in regular succession if you wish to succeed —
E Walsh

[P.S.] My wife is just singing the song "I was a young charmed Queen John,"[4] which I wrote for the Nation — Have you seen it? — I have seen six imitations of my other song "What are Repealers?" in the papers.

(10) Walsh to John Daly[5]

5 Richmond Cottages,
Summer Hill,
Dublin,
Saturday [Feb.3rd 1844].

Dear Sir,

I have received your letter enclosing the music for which I return thanks [.] I have sent it to Mr Duffy in a letter in which I have mentioned your suggestion regarding the reward offered by the Association for Irish Music [.] When I receive his reply I shall take care to inform you of it [.]

I had none to play off the tune for me. I have scarcely any acquaintance in town but I mentioned to Mr. D [uffy] my wish to hear it played as it would furnish me with some rude judgment of its correctness.

I have now to remark upon your remarks regarding my version of the songs [.] When I begged your opinion of what I was doing for you, I was under the impression that the

---

[1] NLI, MS, 2261.
[2] John Plunkett, Q.C.
[3] The 'barrister' may be Davis or Duffy.
[4] I have so far failed to find this entry in the *Nation*.
[5] MS, 2261, NLI; Postmarked Feb. 3rd. 1844, - a Saturday.

character which my songs in the "Spirit of the Nation"[1] might establish for me as a song writer, would be sufficient to satisfy you of my abilities at transfusing the spirit of the Irish poet into the English version — I wanted your particular criticism as regards the fidelity of the version or the manner in which I had been sometimes obliged to quit the particular words of the original — but I was not prepared for the very general remark that I did not produce you "good poetry" — Perhaps you are perfectly correct — and yet I had no other recommendation to make in the Nation than the merit of my songs there. I feel it painful to be obliged to speak thus of myself but must say that the last stanza of the "Base Born Tyrant" which you have particularly culled out, is one of the best efforts I ever made in verse [.] See Mr. Daly how "doctors differ"[.] Was it any poet of your acquaintance that pointed out that song — Why was the bad rhyme of the "Vision" copied into the provincial papers or why did the Nation give it a place — In poetry Mr. Daly, there can be no such thing as middling — Poetry must be at all times good & carry its distinguishing marks about it — otherwise it is trash fit only to damn the writer and all parties concerned and the sooner it is got rid of the better [.] If the stuff I sent you be bad don't venture to publish it — It would injure your work & ruin the trifling character my verse has already procured me.

I told you that you would not find insincerity one of the sins of your friend Walsh — Does not my present proposal go to sustain me.

Yours truly
E. Walsh

Mr J. Daly

(11) Walsh to John Daly[2]

23 Dukes Row,
Summer Hill.

Dear Sir,

Though I have not the song finished off yet I have a private motive for sending you this[.] The song will be ready tomorrow unless your Anglo-Irish bard be remarkably stupid [.]

I have not been employed at the Monitor office since Monday last as I refused to report at a meeting at the Mansion House and afterwards at the state trials as I found that I had not skill nor nerve enough to report the public proceedings — Duffy is on his trail [.] Duffy you know is my friend through whose wish I came up & his health is broken completely

[1] *The Spirit of the Nation*, edited by C.G. Duffy, contains a selection of songs published in the *Nation*, including some of Walsh's.
[2] NLI, MS 2261.

down [.] He has been complaining for the last two months & with the best intentions of serving me he cannot even if his health permitted look out for me — In addition to this Mrs Walsh and the little ones have come up [.] Now I tell you all this because I think you are one whose advice may assist me — My wife would wish to leave Dublin for some country town where she could carry on a little business in the millinery line or anything else that may do (she knows millinery) while I could attend to something else or teach school. We could command about £4 at present and I would wish to know from you whether you think the plan a good one and if so what town you would recommend us. We don't care in what direction we go and perhaps too you could say what business would be best with our small stocks. Write, dear Mr. Daly, & give us your best advice.

Now I will say something of the song & you will perceive from the style of my letters that I always write in a hurry. I have kept no copy of the poetry I have sent you & the line of the song whose literal version is "My pair are without covering," I have no memory how I turned it into English particularly as I don't know how you first expressed it [.] I think it must be where I said

"Misfortune my temper is trying".

And if it be so you can change the line to what I first by a sort of poetic instinct wrote

"My lov'd ones for shelter are crying,"

which suits the Irish line you sent me quite literally & I hope it is the exact line.

In Mac an Ceanige after seeing the genius of Erin typically dying in Spain I said in the English version "when burst my joy," her death should give no joy [.] Alter it to "when burst my cry [.]" I quote all these from memory as I have no copy.

Now for your last song: I am very sorry that before you sent that you did not consult the accounts in some diffuse history of the battles on the Continent between 1739 & '44, to know who Khevenhuller is, that must be altogether wrong, his being deprived of his possessions and beaten in Sicily could easily furnish a clue to his real name. I have got over the difficulty as the stanza can testify [:]

3rd Stanza[1]

Bavaria is mighty in greatness and glory
The Sultan's in Europe - who'll credit the story?
Vienna's proud ramparts his horsemen beleaguer
Its empress is tearful - its foeman is eager -
From one cruel tyrant his brave lands are tore
Fair Sicily saw his brigands in their gore,
Silesia knows Prussia and Poland's restriction,
And Leopold! thy race feel the Lord's malediction[.]

[1] For full text and notes, see pp. 627ff.

Will that do without printing out the name of the tyrant — I'll finish the other two stanzas tomorrow & send it unless you order otherwise — I did nothing for the last week but mope about in uneasiness. Write to me —

Yours etc.
E. Walsh

[P.S.] I regret that you have altered your mind about not using offensive expressions [.] I'm as ardent an Irishman as ever breathed & I would not even in a private way give offence — But pursue your plans — EW.

(12) Walsh to John Daly[1]

Ye offspring of heroes through centuries olden
Lend an ear to the tale which the muse hath unfolden -
Though landless your nobles - your chiefs lion-hearted,
From fair Inis-Fodla for ever are parted -
There's Philip victorious o'er wide earth and wave
His allies death-dealing, unsheathed the glaive: -
Wild havoc and ruin shall seize the oppressor,
And God's red right Arm shall be Erin's redresser!

Whole armies are banded and heav'n their protector
To scourge the vile soldiers of George the Elector -
By the wrath of the Lord o'er the wild billow driven
His fleets seek their harbours all shattered and riven!
His thousands that march'd to a far foreign shore
Have pil'd the sad fields of defeat in their gore -
Carthagena's dire day gave his brave a red pillow
And his sails sought Sebastian, in vain, o'er the billow!

[1] MS. 2261, NLI. This *letter* contains a text of *The Peril of Britain*. For final text and notes, see pp. 627f.

Bavaria is mighty in greatness and glory,
The Sultan's in Europe - who'll credit the story?
Vienna's proud ramparts his horsemen beleaguer, -
The empress is tearful - its foeman is eager. -
Khevinhuller exil'd has from Sicily fled
Fierce war crush'd his power - his bandits are dead -
Silesia knows Prussia and Poland's infliction,
And Leopold! thy race feel the Lord's malediction!

De Montemar proud (or The Mighty Count Daun) to the field is advancing,
With lion-like leaders - with long lances glancing,
With fire and fierce slaughter - with Mars' mighty thunder
With war's meetest music - with hosts without number -
All Mantua and Milan his mandates obey:
And Tuscany crouches to Philip's high sway
And Naples hath yielded to Charles the glorious,
Prince sage in the council - in battle victorious. - [1]

The torch-tossing Louis - a lion in danger,
Sagacious, unshaken to terror a stranger -
The fierce Gaul has led to the gates of Hanover -
His heel crushes Holland - its glory is over!
And now while unsheathing his far-flashing brand,
Fell carnage, dark demon, starts forth at his hand;
And George is the game the wild war-hound's pursuing
There's an end to my theme - to the Saxon red ruin!

---

[1] Walsh inserts an asterisk here and gives the following note at the end: 'In this stanza the translator has vainly endeavoured to preserve the alliterative grandeur of the Irish. Waiving other considerations, your tamer English cannot compare with Shane Claragh's native tongue, in comp[…?] epithets and alliterative […?]

(13) Walsh to John Daly[1]

5 Richmond Cottages
Summer Hill
Dublin
Tuesday [Feb.13th 1844][2]

Dear Mr. Daly,

I write this short line lest you might attribute my silence to any motive other than the right one, to say that on the day I received yours of the 4th. inst. I was ill of a very serious sickness which still completely prostrates every power of my body, as I am now only supported in bed while I thus show my anxiety to write to you. When I got your letter I went along the streets between Dame St. and the Quay and found a place that I thought would exactly suit you [.] It is a shop in Anglesea St.[3] opposite Duffy's, with a parlour off the shop and either a back or front drawing room. The rent is no instance higher than £30 a year [.] Anglesea St. is well established and £30 I should suppose low — Another shop in Frances St. did not look so well and the owner not within —

I sent since I have been confined to bed, sent for the proof of the 4th N°. and heard in reply that Christie did not supply the types.

I forgot I believe to say that the doctor pronounced my disorder to be severe influenza and that it would take weeks before I regained my strength.

However write to me & if you have work ready send it[.] It would amuse me to exercise my faculties [.] Why have you not written to me [?] Mr. Machen complains of your continued irregularity [.] I am glad you were not serious in your general & sweeping critique but if you love me never joke with me again!

I can do no more
E. Walsh.

Mr. John Daly

---

[1] MS 2261, NLI

[2] The letter is postmarked '13.' As the only Tuesday 13th in the first seven months of 1844 occurs in February and as Walsh is still living in Richmond Cottages, the date of the letter can only be February 13th 1844.

[3] Daly subsequently opened a bookshop in Anglesea St.

(14) Walsh to John Daly[1]

Biographical Sketch of Owen O'Sullivan, surnamed the Red, from the colour of his hair, was a native of Slieve Logher, a wild mountain district situated east of the town of Killarney in the county of Kerry. He flourished in the latter part of the last century. The lot of Owen Roe, as he was commonly called, was cast upon evil days, & in an ungenial clime, for had he belonged to any other country, or creed, or party, than that to which through a life in other respects wild and irregular, he had invariably adhered, his rare natural endowments - his fervid poetic genius, - his acquirements in the highest walks of classic literature, would have procured him notice patronage and fame. The light of a patron's smile never cheered the obscurity of the village bard; but Owen Roe had his fame — his pastoral ballad of rural love yet lives by the streams of the south, at the cottagers hearth, & in the milking bawn of the hamlet, & will live till tenderness and feeling become alien to the artless heart of the village maiden — His powerful satires, rife with scathing denunciation, & severe personal invective, his bold enmity to the Saxon - his yearning for the restoration of the exiled Stuart - his love songs descriptive of his own irregular amours - These varied compositions preserved in the native tongue have cheered the hospitable fireside of the cottier in many a district of Cork, Kerry & Limerick where his memory survives, his poems recited, and the brilliant effusions of his happy wit shine familiar as household words.

There are doubtless many of our readers who now hear of Owen Roe O'Sullivan for the first time. - To them perhaps it will be necessary to say that Owen Roe was to Ireland what Robert Burns, at a somewhat later date was to Scotland, the glory & the shame of his native land [.] I know no two characters in my range of observation, that so closely resemble each other as Burns & Owen Roe — the same poetical temperament - the same love of notoriety - the same ardent sighing for woman's love - the same embracing friendship for the human family - & the same fatal desire for "cheerful tankards foaming" alike distinguished the heaven-taught minstrels — Like Burns, Owen Roe first turned his head [?] to the charms of nature & the joys of woman's love, - like Burns, the irregularity of his life, obliged the clergyman of his persuasion to denounce him, & like him he lashed the priestly order without ruth or remorse[2] — like Burns, he tried the pathetic - the sublime - the humorous

---

[1] NLI, MS. 2261. The letter is a sketch of the life of Eoghan Ruadh Ó Súilleabháin.

[2] Walsh inserts an asterisk and gives the following note: 'On one occasion Owen Roe's conduct had supplied the pastor of a rural congregation with material for a lengthened invective against general Viciousness and the unfortunate rhymers failures in particular. At the close of his pious discourse he inquired in the native tongue if Owen Roe were present – "Yes, replied the irritable son of genius, goaded, [by] the clergyman's <u>exposure</u> to all forgetfulness of the occasion & the time, "Yes, Owen Roe is here - & may you never behold his dyin[g]!"

and like him succeeded in all — Nor does the parallel end here, they were both born in the humble cottage, both toiled through life at the spade & plough, & both fell in the bloom of manhood, in the pride of intellect, the victims of uncontrolled passion.

Owen Roe O'Sullivan, like hundreds of his countrymen followed the occupation of an itinerant potato-digger and made periodical excursions into the County of Limerick and Tipperary in pursuit of this low occupation. On one of these occasions, happening to receive employment at the house of a farmer in the neighbourhood of Charleville, he was brought into notice by settling the meaning of a sentence in some Greek author, which had caused much dispute between his master's son, fresh from a French college & the old priest of the parish — Owen remained here for some time as a teacher of Greek & Latin & received high applause in that capacity, till his evil destiny drove him in the way of Mary Casey, a village beauty - the enamoured poet lost all relish for the teaching of dead languages in contemplation of the living charms of his mistress — the school was given up & Owen's licentiousness denounced from the altar[.] But Mary lives immortal in the well-known English song - (though that tongue was the least of his acquirements) called "Molly Casey's Charms."

It is recorded that Owen Roe committed his first sin of rhyme while a bare-shinned stripling at the school of one of these humble men whom the severity of the period was driven for shelter to the fastnesses of Kerry to teach Greek to cowboys — Owen was <u>mitching</u> all day and as he entered the hedge-seminary long after the prescribed time, the master was about to proceed to the process of "Hoisting" Owen when the truant begged & obtained one hour to render an account of the peccadilloes of the day 'twas then that the embryo poet produced a lyric in a fancied dialogue between two married ladies in which each details with much dramatic effect, the failings of her spouse and the various evils to which matrimony links the wife who would fain move with her yoke-fellow in freer harness.[1]

'Twas at Annagh near Charleville that Owen Roe taught school — While engaged there he wrote some satirical songs in ridicule of the Irish Volunteers & lashed with fearful severity some village rhymers who attempted to break a lance with him — He died of a relapse of fever at Knocknagree in his native district & was buried at Nohaval. I have no means at present of ascertaining the time of his death.

---

[1] This was the final paragraph in the letter as Walsh had written it. However, through the use of a curved line he indicated that he wished it to be transposed into the position in which I have placed it.- Ed.

(15) Walsh to John Daly[1]

5 Richmond Cottages
Summer Hill
[Thurs.] Feb. 22 1844

Dear Sir

I received your letter yesterday in bed from which I have not risen for 17 days. I have got up today for the first time and turned 8 stanzas of the song into English verse [.] I am greatly pleased with the simple beauty of this over any other of Shane's[2] songs that I have yet seen & found it easy and pleasing to render it into English [.] I have tried to turn the dress into English throughout, but found it wanted a sprinkling of Gaelic to render it graceful and so I left a portion of the Irish dress to cover the barren nakedness of the strangers tongue. I send you now a specimen & I beg in your next that you will say whether you approve of the chorus or not & if I have spelled the Irish words wrongly or not according to what would suit an English reader send me what will do.

I'll not reveal my true love's name,
Betimes 'twill swell the voice of fame;
And, O! may heaven, my grief to quell,
Restore my hero safe and well.
My hero brave, ma gile m'ear,
My kindred love, ma gile m'ear,
What wringing woes my bosom knows,
Since cross'd the seas ma gile m'ear.

That will suit an English reader better I presume than any pure English version I could give. I hope you will think so too. Perhaps another stanza or two might please you:

His glancing eyes I may compare
To diamond dews on rose-buds rare -
And love & valour brighten o'er
The features of my bosom's store!
My hero brave, etc.

I would have no business presenting Mars and Cupid to modern readers [.] And here I shall observe that all the love songs of the Jacobite period are disfigured by allusions to gods and

[1] NLI, MS. 2261.
[2] Seán Clárach MacDómhnaill.

goddesses and heroes and heroines of classical mythology — Never meddle or make with one of that stamp. But the renderings & beauty of the present politico-love songs, are very charming — I have rendered "store" literally [.] Tis an expressive epithet — Is not the next and last one I give you a lovely stanza, worthy of Burns himself:

No cuckoo's note by fell or flood,
No hunter's cry through hazel wood,
Nor mist-wrapt valley yields me joy,
Since cross'd the seas my royal boy. -
My hero brave, etc.

Now to something else. Remember to spell the Irish I have retained in the chorus in the English character and as near the sound as possible if you do not let mine stand. With all submission to your Irish learning and all consideration of my own deep ignorance I respectfully say that I cannot submit to your ipse dixit[1] respecting my remarks on the song [.] I studied the first stanza of the song most attentively in order to catch the spirit of the author & the forms of his rhymed metre and I found that these correspond in regular couplets through the eight lines. Hum that stanza to the air "Sheela ny Guira" and you'll perceive how smoothly 'twill flow to the old tune[.] I have not been faithful to the promise of saving the rhyme and measure of the original if you are right — I'll lay the affair before Curry when I am able to crawl out[.] No poet I insist, in Irish measure would make the last line of the stanza correspond with the 4th as you say nor is it done in the first stanza if I have an ear, and I have one which never deceived me [.] I'll submit - but only to conviction. I likewise have to say that in the first line of each stanza of the "Base Born Tyrant" you have given a foot which should belong to the first part of the next succeeding line — look to that & to my version of it where the proper arrangement is followed.

I must go to bed now — I forgot to say while ago that the doctor a few days after pronouncing my case to be influenza, declared I had a bilious fever and treated me accordingly though he said it was not contagious — I could not execute any of your commands and cannot yet venture out for some days[.] I had no word from Mr. Duffy since I sent the "Craovin Evin."[2] Is its music beautiful. Could you send the papers to me where the songs are praised [.] I would return them.

I hope you will give me a call when you come to town [.] Your advice & presence may promote the health of yours truly —

E Walsh

Mr. Daly

---

[1] The boss said it!

[2] *Craovin Evin*, see pp. 547f.

[P.S.] Dear Mr Daly
In the interlinear translation you have used the word 'traces' to express wreaths of hair[.] The word is never used in English to express that sense [.] It should be 'tresses,' locks or curls of hair. I shall take the liberty of changing that before I send it to Goodwin. I submit what I consider an impropriety in the last stanza "Seintear sgairt" you have rendered lit [erally] "sing a roar"— A wind instrument may roar — A stringed one cannot — It should be "sing a loud strain" — I'll not touch this however without leave.

E.W.

(16) Walsh to John Daly[1]

Richmond Cottages
Summer-hill
Dublin
[Sun] March 17. 1844

Dear Sir

I trust you will pardon me for not replying earlier to your letters, when I assure you that I have, so lengthened are my hours of labour, scarcely time to say my prayers, which as a good catholic you are aware, I am bound to do at least twice a day. I thank you for the newspaper which I now return. The notice was good & a very keen logical critic to whom I showed it upon reading the song, said it was in every way equal to the "Craoivin Aoivin"[.] I beg you will send me all the papers you may get containing critical notices of our work & I shall faithfully return them. I took care on Tuesday or Wednesday last (I do not remember which) to write to Mr. Duffy at Rathmines[2] mentioning the honourable testimony which the songs elicited from the Provincial Press and your regret & disappointment the Nation, the powerful leader of public opinion - should not honour you with a single remark. — I accompanied this with a request that he would give us a favourable notice on Saturday's Nation — But Mr. Duffy neither gave the requested notice, as you must already have perceived, nor sent me a private line in answer to my communication — This neglect on Mr. Duffy's part fills me with surprise and I would assuredly have had a personal interview with him to ascertain the cause, had I time sufficient to visit him — This is an unnatural state of society where a man having some pretensions to literary merit, is so chained down to the galley oar of exertion for what heaven allots the wild beast of the hill - his "daily bread" that he has not only no time to think of God and his glorious Kingdom-come - to listen to the communing of heaven's angels with his own immortal spirit - but cannot spare an hour from his task-time to cross a town or a street upon a common errand of business! But so it is.—

[1] NLI, MS. 2261.
[2] Duffy address at that time was at No. 3, Connaught Place, Rathmines, Dublin.

I called at Goodwin's but the proof was not ready. They told me that they would forward you one on Saturday & that I could have another at 6 o'clock on Saturday night but the severe storm of that evening blew the memory of Goodwin and Co. and all his proof sheets clean from my cranium, as I passed along in the sweeping strife of the elements.

I never perceived my cleverness at entering fully into the true spirit of Irish song till I read D'Alton's translation.[1] I have in many stanzas of the translated songs evidently improved upon the old bard & have scarcely ever fell much beneath him in conveying the wrongs and feelings of our race — A portion of this is because I am intimately acquainted with the manners and feelings of the people and feel - indignantly feel myself with all the poet's feeling the curse & crime of the tyrant.

You were scarcely out of town when a friend informed me that you made a very profitable hit by the sale of some Irish works — This rejoiced me exceedingly though I would be better pleased to hear it otherwise than at second-hand — but I am delighted to hear it at any hand — You will believe this when in addition to my own assertion, I assure you that a certain friend of mine who is a deep phrenologist[2] says, upon an examination of my scull that I have "benevolence" and "attachment" uncommonly developed.

I expected Owen Roe my favourite poet before this [.] I am impatient to see how his English suit will fit him [.] Heaven speed the literary tailor.

E Walsh
Mr J Daly

(17) To John Daly[3]

9 Mulgrave Place
Gloucester Street Dublin
[Thu] 28 March 1843 [*recte* 1844]

Dear Sir

I write to let you know that I have removed from the confounded "country quarters"[4] in which you found me at your visit to the city [.] I have taken a small cottage to myself and feel quite buoyant and happy to have once more a house of my own that I stalk about my

---

[1] John D'Alton (1792-1867) did some of the transitions in Hardiman's *Iris Minstrelsy.*

[2] The 'deep phrenologist' is almost certainly James Clarence Mangan having a joke at Walsh's expense.

[3] NLIMS. 2261.

[4] In 1844 the Summer Hill area of Dublin was not within the city limits. Walsh had been living in Summer Hill since his arrival in Dublin, first at 23 Dukes Row, and later at 5 Richmond Cottages. He then moved to 9 Mulgrave Place, Gloucester St., thus bringing him into the heart of the city and within a stone's throw of his work place in the Corn Exchange.

pretty house with somewhat of an important strut and almost exclaiming in the words of the poet

"I'm monarch of all I survey"

but the extent of my dominions is remarkably like that of the "German gentiles"[1] who furnish the regal breed of these happy realms with wives and husbands — I have picked up this disloyal impertinence of observation by coming in contact with your damned Jacobite poets — confound the foolish followers of the faithless Stuart!

Now to Owen the Red - The song you sent me last Mr. Daly is a gorgeous one, but highly unsuitable for reasons which I have already furnished you but which you did not seem to mind — first it breathes a fierce & furious hate of Protestantism so much so that after transposing the meaning and I believe the spirit of the Irish into my version its fiery, intolerance actually frightened me [.] And on shewing it to a friend he said that the publication of it would actually compromise my character — but I have not given up Owen's beautiful song though it pained me to alter his meaning from a religious to a political sense. It likewise contains allusions to Greek and Roman history & heroes — and I would recommend to send musical songs in future — The *Nation* has not forgotten us — I did not see the Argus[2] — Would wish you sent all the papers that contain notices of our work — I have some remarks to make upon your portion of the present song.

Your English notes are in some places highly defective in perspicuity & smoothness of manner & I have changed them in some places & again I don't like your literal translation of some words which I would beg of you to re-consider [.] For instance the word g-carla you rendered "pitched" which in English conveys very different ideas. It should be "expelled" or scattered abroad & in the same stanza in the horrid character drawn of the arch-heretic Luther you render gras inar "bountiful" — Is it not plain that Owen would not blend that epithet with the terms "treacherous - accursed" which follow it? You render aiteas "drollery" which is too vulgar for the style — In fact I object to many of your words from sheer want of elegance & consequent unsuitableness to the beauty of the original — I hope you will take these remarks in the same friendly spirit in which they are given.

Here is my first version of the first stanza:

By Blarney's towers I paus'd to ponder
What deep dark curse our land lies under
Chain'd neath the foreigner foe -
The shameless lord whose guileful knavery

---

[1] German Gentiles': a reference to English royalty taking to themselves German consorts. This letter is written within about three years of Queen Victoria's wedding to Prince Albert in 1840.

[2] The *Drogheda Argus* newspaper. Text uncertain: 'send' or 'see.'

Coil'd ruined hearts the chain of slavery
Whose life-stream from valiant men flow!

Sires whose sons crouch low to those
Sheathed by the church's vengeful thunder
Since Luther first accursed rode
To rend the seamless robe asunder
And steep souls in fathomless woe!

I have altered the concluding part to a political sense. Upon the whole I shall render it a good song & shall I hope finish it off on Sunday. I have no time to spare and the song is remarkably hard in the constitution —

I do not remember anything else [.] I hope you will pardon the freedom I have taken, & believe me yours

E. Walsh

Mr. John Daly

[P.S.] The Nation gave a very incorrect version of the Gille-mar.[1] I would wish you sent me simple songs like that - and our tongue abounds with them — Mr. Gerarty[2] the bookseller repeated to me one of the loveliest songs I ever heard in either English or Irish the other day — He said he would give it to me — I do not think that Sho ho Lul[3] would do well in English — it has too great affectation of historical learning & if I remember rightly scarcely an [y] tenderness of feeling considering the subject — Owen I should suppose would furnish better than such bombast. You have taken capital selections from Shane Claragh and I beg you will bestow judicious attention and taste on Owen - 'tis there the art of the editor lies.

I am scribbling this side at 3 o'clock in the room where I act among twenty-five others.[4] I have got a cover[5] for this - an article you very seldom receive from your very obedient servant

E Walsh

---

[1] *Gille-mar*: Séan Cláragh MacDómhnaill's spirited Jacobite song, *Mo Ghile Mear* (i.e., my heart's delight).

[2] Brian Geraghty, Bookseller and Publisher, 11 Anglesea St.

[3] *Sho ho lul*: a lullaby by Eoghan Rua Ó Súilleabháin.

[4] Conciliation Hall in the Corn Exchange.

[5] Walsh often dispensed with the need for envelopes by folding and sealing his letters, leaving just about enough room for an address.

(18) Walsh to John Daly[1]

9 Mulgrave Place
Gloucester St
[Mon] April 1. 44

Dear Sir

I have just now left your manuscript at Goodwin's who says that he cannot set about printing it until you give him permission to break up the types and he likewise said that you were about to publish 300 copies of the songs in parts of six numbers.

And you say that unless I preserve the "fury and intolerance" of Owen Roe in my version the songs will not be worth a damn [.] I would be glad to hear from you how prose or rhyme or character can be upheld by acrimonious language on the most touchy and tender of all human opinions - religious belief [.] Neither you nor even Owen Roe hate Saxon oppression more than I, but I have ever drawn a line of distinction between hatred of the oppressor and the coarse revilings of the conscientious belief of brave and good men — It is doubtless right to render the original in the English version but when that version would give deep offence to even the most liberal protestant what injury is done the author by just turning his ideas from a religious to a political sense and saying exactly what the bitter feelings of Owen would have prompted had he fallen upon later times [.] Do you think have I "crippled or maimed" the spirit of the author when I altered his virulent invective against the "litter of demons" to the following anti-Saxon strain —

By Blarney's towers I paused to ponder
What deep dark curse the land lies under,
Chain'd neath the foreigner foe -
The shameless hoard whose guileful knavery
Coil'd the festering links of slavery,
Round hearts where pure pulses flow,
From sires whose sons are crouching slaves,
Or wanderers wild or outlaws gory
Mail-clad sires whose green flag waves
O'er blood-red fields of ancient story
Where prone groan their offspring of woe![2]

And listen to the last and the other only stanza in which I have changed the meaning a little to avoid calling "good men and true" cubs of the "demon litter" — and say if I marr[e]d the poetic flow of Owen the Red

[1] NLI, MS. 2261.
[2] Stanza one of the *Expulsion of the Saxon*; for full text see pp. 602ff.

When Spain sends bravest heroes hither
Oppression's arm shall waste & wither
By sea; by shore - the despot's reward,
And slavery's chain shall rive asunder
When Erin's brave 'mid war's with thunder
In gore bathe the green battle sward —
No thought of ruth nor word of peace
By heart be felt by tongue be spoken,
Till quenched in blood his light shall cease,
And Saxon power lie crush'd and broken, -
Shout aloud Amen to the bard![1]

I cannot understand what you mean by "giving the spirit of the poet [.]" You mean probably giving his exact meaning the very thing you are inculcating in your letter [.] I have given the very spirit of Owen in the very stanza where I have departed a little from him. And in some parts where I have been literal I have not succeeded to my satisfaction — what say you now? I have to say that the translation of this song is no joke —

I have spoken to you already of the false and most ridiculous taste on the poets of that period in their allusions to Greek and Roman history and mythology through a wretched affectation of shewing their classical learning. Owen has fallen into it in this song when he enquires if the lady is Deirdre or Helen or Briseis — How the devil could she be either one or the other of them — tis sheer ridiculous nonsense and though I have ventured to translate it if ever you send me a song with such wretched stuff in it I shall <u>sans ceremonie</u> send it back again to you — I shall not degrade the heavenly gifts of nature which is my only inheritance by stooping to translate affectation and false taste into English verse — You think you honour your bard by publishing his trash — A wise editor does no such injury to his poet -

I have used the corrections you allowed and two more but these with great timidity for I have not sufficient knowledge in Irish for the use of such liberty — You have given the word <u>sgail</u> flame and <u>lasa</u> flame [.] Now I have altered the first to <u>tinge</u> and the latter to <u>bloom</u> & shall alter them to anything else you like if these words don't suit —

The incorrect style to which I have alluded appeared in the remarks you appended to the sketch of Owen Roe's life. I have improved the language and rounded the period of your sentences [.]

Send me the "Run of the Husband" at once[.] I am desiring to see it [.] It must be racy of Irish fun — I beg that you will send me the next songs immediately [.] I have no time to spare & must have them by me for a long time to read by snatches and imbibe their spirit —

[1] Stanza seven of the *Expulsion of the Saxon*; see pp. 604f.

& they may receive many a change from after reading instead of immediately sending them to press as I have heretofore done in a hurry [.] I am delighted that Shane Claragh though he dealt very plentifully in visions eschewed the folly of displaying his Roman and Greek acquirements — It shows his noble genius — Owen Roe was a *bulim sciath,*[1] the very type of Ro [bert] Burns who when he got a smattering of drink was eternally jabbering it[.]

Send me work at once the Keen particularly

Yours ever
E Walsh

[P.S.] Tuesday morning. I finished this last nigh — I am now looking over it[.] I wished to remark that I hope you will take no offence at any words I have let drop [.] My heart and pen are plain and I "call a spade a spade."

(19) Walsh to John Daly[2]

9 Mulgrave Place
Gloucester St
[Sun] April 7 . 1843 [*recte* 1844]

Dear Sir,

I sit down at 8 o'clock this morning to write you a letter of which you say I have been so chary of late time & I wish to wipe away from your memory all recollection of any neglect on my part of a correspondent whose provision in very particularly answering each part of my very discursive missives, I much admire and to reveal a secret I have cut letter-writing acquaintance with one or two whose family was the opposite of our virtue [.]

You will have had the proof before this reaches Kilkenny & will see how promptly I put Owen's lines to the priest[3] into English. You will confess how I have improved the poetry by my trifling departure from the exact meaning of the original [.] How Owen the Red's spirit will greet that of his faithful Walsh when summoned to the world of souls to sing the praises of heaven's eternal King in song sublimated and pure from all taint of earthly passion after consecrating his gift of God, to virtue & sacred liberty! Twas an expression of some fierce hater of the Saxon I had in memory which furnished the hint for

"And eke the Saxon tongue up-borne by law
With phrase uncouth distorts the Gaelic jaw."

---

[1] *bulim sciath*: buaileamsciath, braggadocio, empty boaster.

[2] NLI, MS. 2261.

[3] Text on p. 636.

I had time to read only one stanza of 'Shane Buie'[1] & will find no difficulty in rendering it into smooth English verse & shall return 'Shane Buie' at the end of each stanza. It is awfully long and I trust he had given us no gods of the ancients nor put historical questions unpolite to puzzle the visionary lady and his translator [.] I found the "Expulsion of the Saxon"[2] difficult enough and yet I have evidently improved Owen Roe which is saying a great deal [.] He was a man highly gifted but his genius stooped to the false taste of his age in the display of pedantry — I have made the second stanza in my own opinion at least, one of exquisite beauty of imagery though the genius of the tongue would not permit to use Owen's alliterative expressions — Are there any clever men in your city who would pronounce an opinion?

I have see [n] the clever notice of the songs in the Wexford Independent of Wednesday[3] — I take it unkind that you should not send me the papers which have noticed them but you have done it mayhap to punish me for not sending the "Expulsion of the Saxon" as you desired but I have not time to cough.

The lines which are under my vision of Owen's verses to the priest are incorrect in the proof. Leave them to me. I altered your sentences but I entirely defaced it in my pocket and could barely be deciphered —

I had a particular reason for writing this letter — My acquaintance with the Jacobite songs makes me desirous of cultivating the language further and I have to request if you have any Irish books by you to send them — I want a dictionary but would not take that imperfect edition of O'Reilly[4] of which I saw some volumes — As a matter of course I would expect books from you to enable me to prosecute any particular subject we were engaged with - or if you demur there I will take a good dictionary at any reasonable price you will charge.

I am glad you intend to publish the work in parts & I am much deceived if it will not sell better in that state than in single numbers — I always bought weekly periodicals in monthly parts [.] The continuity & quantity of matter pleases —

I have to go to breakfast and shall if any further thought strikes me before I send this dash it in rumbling by —

Yours truly
E Walsh

---

[1] The term *Shane Buie* (or *Buí*) - (*Yellow Jack*) first emerged as a description of the followers of William (III) of Orange, and is a synonym for *John Bull*, meaning *The English Nation*. For full text and notes, see *A Lament for the Gael*, pp. 646f.

[2] see pp. 602ff.

[3] *Wexford Independent*, Wed. April 3rd 1844.

[4] O'Reilly, Edward, *An Irish-English Dictionary*, new ed. (Minerva Printing Office) Dublin 1821.

[P.S.] I feel quite happy and pleased in my quiet pretty residence[.] You will like that — Don't allow that horrid N° 2 to stick in among its betters without alteration. I have now at 6 o'clock been correcting the proof and have seen that the notice which you have added concerning manuscripts places Millstreet in the county of Kerry — Millstreet is in the county of Cork but the village of Gneeveguilla is in the county of Kerry — I have not the manuscript by me so you have to show the proper spelling of Gneeveguilla [.] I have altered the rest [.] I intend to devote an hour this night or perhaps two to the song Shane Buie [.] I have read yet only one stanza - I hope there are no goddesses to stare at[.] I admire Owen's fiery genius much [.] The stanza of Shane Buie is fine.

I was much struck by the beauty of the "Expulsion of the Saxon" as I heard it sung last night the second stanza in particular — A person whom I knew when a boy[1] and who is now residing in Dublin and one skilled in classic literature who knew most modern languages - has repeated to me different passages of the Persian tongue from one of the celebrated parts of that country and only he told me it was Persian I would have sworn twas the language of some province in Ireland so much did it resemble the Irish — He has further told me & has asserted it elsewhere before some literary men that I was the purest and most Saxon writer of English in this country — Do you believe him[?]

E. Walsh

(20) Walsh to John Daly[2]

9 Mulgrave Place
Gloucester Street
[Thu] April 11. 44

Sir

The conclusion of your note of yesterday filled me with surprise and deep regret that you should use me so disrespectfully after such frequent explanation as again to be harping on the string of not translating the songs faithfully and as a proof of my inferior version you say that you "express your doubt as to the title" of the song because & especially that I have not retained the word "White Hall" — !

It is painful to be obliged to say in my own vindication that the stanza to which you allude is the very best I ever wrote for your song, as it conveys the spirit and meaning - and shall further assert that I have and given the original in that same stanza in practical imagery and vehement hate of the Saxon —

---

[1] This reference is tantalising. The person in question can scarcely be any other than James Clarence Mangan, but where was Mangan or where was Walsh 'as a boy' when they knew each other. Perhaps Mangan may have been visiting his Munster relatives as his father was from Shanagolden in West Limerick.

[2] NLI, MS. 2261. The letter is listed as number 30 in the MS.

I shall now drop the subject never again to resume it - and shall say that whatever be your motive for this disrespectful treatment, I have not deserved it.

I do not attribute your conduct to a studied design to break with me so much as to your not entertaining a clear perception of the merit of my version and the extreme difficulty of keeping the spirit and sense of the author within his limited number of lines —

The frequent errors of your own version in the manuscript leads me to this conclusion — I could show you many of them had I time though I scarcely know how to read the Irish tongue.

In conclusion I beg you will find another versifier who will render the literal meaning to your taste — that's not a difficult task [.] Transfusing the spirit is the rub — I sing no longer for you — I do this with regret as I love my country & its neglected bards & their glorious recollections [.]

Yours obediently
E. Walsh

Mr. Daly

(21) Walsh to John Daly[1]

9 Mulgrave Place
Gloucester St.
[Tue] April 16. 1843 [*recte* 1844]

Sir,

I have to say in reply to the enquiry respecting the "convicted conspirators"[2] that they were not probably noticed at all in the court of Queen's Bench yesterday but were privately called upon to receive sentence within four days [.] To this they have replied by giving notice of calling for a new trial & the arguing & "jaw" on his application will occupy many days — The affair will not terminate very soon and the general opinion so far as I could glean information is that there will be no such thing as <u>Kilmainham</u> in the sentence —

Now sir why should I not mind your remarks when you have given the occasion? I have expostulated with you on the injustice and disrespect you showed me by checking me as you would a slave while I was at the same time working my brain to [...?] in rendering the rough strains of your poet fit for the Saxon ear to hear — I did my best [.] I told you so [.]

---

[1] NLI, MS. 2261. Letter number 20 in MS.

[2] By this time the state trials had resulted in finding O'Connell, Duffy and the others guilty, but sentence had not yet been passed.

The public heard the songs and pronounced that I did well — Twas unfair to treat me with injuring your author — I have exceeded him in various places. If I had said that I would refer your manuscript to Curry was it not to know his opinion not of your merits or knowledge of the Irish but to know the particular "air" of the song neither you nor Shane Claragh had any properly in it & I of course could differ from you on the tune of the song without any impeachment of your Irish knowledge —

The remarks I now make are given in no spirit of unkindness but to show that I have not hinted at your not seeing the merits of my translation without a cause and that you may pay more attention to the delicacies of the English tongue [.] In the 3rd stanza[1] you speak of "flame perambulating her cheek [.]" One wishing to throw ridicule over the sentence could not light on a more ludicrous mode of effecting it[.] The flame of passion is good but the blush of beauty is what is meant and the other [...] word is utterly unsound "bias." Rent should be tribute [.] The term you have rendered slumber (a beautiful word) should be sluggard or some reproachful epithet — In the last line of the second stanza is an egregious blunder where you make the son of Jason bear the fleece to Greece [.] 'Twas Jason brought the fleece and not his son. It should be the son of Eson or as it is in Latin, Aeson, who was the father of the hero — I'll not pursue this further - but tis necessary to look well to the sense and the spirit of the tongue —

Your disavowal of my intention of giving offence is sufficient and I accept it and shall resume the songs and I trust that no more bickering shall be between us —

Mr. Duffy said on Sunday that my translations were beautiful and that he considered I acted judiciously in departing where deep offence would be given from the author. I never did so to my knowledge but in the one song where [I] dreaded to translate the author bluntly & even there I succeeded in giving the last lines I ever wrote for you. I'll assure you & so will any judge that my version is close considering the tone of its spirit.

Let me know at what time you would wish to send what I have done to Goodwin [.] I have only five stanzas of Shane Bui translated — Owen is very difficult[.] I think these would eke out the next number.

Yours faithfully
E. Walsh

Mr. Daly

---

[1] The stanza spoken of here is from *The Expected of Ireland* by Eoghan Rua Ó Súilleabháin. For the full text see pp. 640ff.

(22) Walsh to John O'Daly[1]

9 Mulgrave Place
Gloucester St.
[Sat] April 20 [1844].

Dear Sir,

I have just now corrected certain parts of your interlinear version and also changed your English note a little to improve the style and added a line or two on the term Bui which I think will please you [.] I have rendered smearla "churl" which comes pretty close to the sense and now I shall clear the manuscript at Goodwin's as I go to the Corn Exchange.[2] I am annoyed by a violent headache which I have procured by my position at the desk of the Corn Exchange room.

I was with Machen yesterday — He & his clerk apprised me that there was no sale for the songs and that respectable persons bought more of them at his shop than are sold elsewhere [.] Upon the whole Machen's account was quite discouraging. He likewise said that unless you made them up in parts and in a green cover having 3 or 4 N^{os} in each they would never do [.]

I was promised by a literary person to open a communication for me with the London periodicals and that if I wrote a story he would procure me from 8 to 10 pounds for each sheet [.] I have talents and material for prose writing but no time & though I have written part of a tale I did not touch it these 3 days. My head is very bad —

I think I have done justice to Shane Bui which is finished off [.] The next song which you call "The Expected of Ireland" might more strictly be termed "Ireland's Expectation [.]" The chorus of that song hangs a mere "caput mortuum"[3] on the tail of the stanza — It adds nothing to the sense of the song and was I should think the burden of some vulgar trash to that air which Owen found and preserved — I would submit that you leave it entirely out in your Irish giving the stanza without the chorus — You clearly see that the chorus is not in connection with the song and in no way applicable to the subject. An English translation of it would be most absurd to a stranger's ear — I shall omit it and would recommend that you do the same in your portion —

Burns found an old chorus in the same way & has been greatly censured for hanging it upon his beautiful verses —

I thank you for your last letter but you still labour under a misconception regarding my meaning and that of Duffy too — In hate of the Saxon we agree with you but would wish to say nothing of his religious errors — Remember I've sinned in this way in one song only —

I dread from Machen's words that the work will go down — tis ever so with Irish efforts.

---

[1] NLI, MS 2261. Letter number 21 in MS.

[2] The Corn Exchange on Burg Quay, where Walsh was employed, was the headquarters of the Repeal Association.

[3] Useless residue.

I hit Duffy off cleverly at his own house last Sunday upon the frigidity of his praise in his notice of the songs [.]

I gave Mr. Davis a few days ago "The Expulsion of the Saxon" and he was very polite and said he would publish it —

Yours
E. Walsh

[P.S.] I will not give the manuscript till Monday.

(23) Walsh to John Daly[1]

9 Mulgrave Place
Gloucester St
[Sun] May 5. 1843 [*recte*: 1844]

Dear Sir

I sit down on the only day that I have leisure on to write to you and shall not close this until I receive your proof which I expect by tomorrow. I hope my translation of Shane Bui has pleased you. I am heartily tired of Owen Roe notwithstanding all I have said in his praise in the sketch of his life — I find a sameness in his songs that betoken anything but the various aspects under which the beauties of nature present themselves to the man of genius, and you will perceive how he is perpetually presenting us with his "golden fleece" and the "lady of Emania [.]" I have her in "The Expected of Ireland" — Those same dull repetitions shew extreme poverty of imagination and very false taste. I would translate the facile beautiful lines of Shan Claragh as fast and faster sometimes than my pen could commit them to paper and would feel relieved by returning again to him [.] I am much obliged by permitting me to leave out that wretched chorus[2] and I have likewise left the 4th stanza untranslated - the language of it is absolutely ridiculous and it jambs up the connexion between the 3rd & 5th of the song & I beg your permission to omit it in the original also — The last stanza I like much & shall by and by turn into English & send it to you with this — It is quite in the bardic manner of devoting a stanza to the praise of the patron or friend — Lord Byron has done it in his Child Harold on the death of his friend Howard at Waterloo —

Now allow me a passing word upon your translation [.] In the first stanza of the "Expected" I think, "affability" should be joy or pleasure, "smart," lively — In the 3rd

[1] NLI, S 2261. Letter 22 in MS.

[2] 'that wretched chorus' and the lines following are in reference to *The Expected of Ireland*. For full text and notes, see pp. 640ff.

stanza "flame" should be blush & the use of "variety & red" near it, I cannot see — In the same stanza "quarrelling" should be contending or some such expression — And the note you have given on the obscurity of the two last lines in the stanza I have erased, because they beautifully express the ever-varying glow of her cheek struggling with the pale pure white for the mastery in the face of the ideal being of the poet's adoration.

You should have a note on the 6th stanza furnishing some account of the Lady of Emania — In that stanza the words "firm intrigues" are not suitable English[.] "Firm" should be cruel[.] Cruadh hard means cruel also. In the 7th "Chest" should be bosom - "Merriment," joy— Now I correct all these only from my knowledge of the delicacies of the English and if you give me leave I shall alter them for the more appropriate words.

In Shane Bui you have war "sparkling" in the second stanza[.] The word corrugated which means wrinkled I have altered it to coruscant though I would sooner omit it altogether [.] In the 4th you have "perambulatory" which I have changed to varying and the printer's devil[1] to "Carmine" "flame." In the same line I have rendered blush & you have seodhach hurry & quick, two different parts of speech. For the same word I have retained quick, the adjective [.] In the 6th, black neck should be dark neck. In the 7th you have "hames" instead of "yoke [.]" I have already corrected a few of these & want your permission to alter the remainder [.] You will pardon me for saying that you do not attend sufficiently to the delicacies of the English tongue.

I did not know that any part of the "Expulsion" would get into this number [.] I neglected to strike out the chorus [.] Perhaps you would think it well to let it stand in the Irish as the burden, as it has got in but as you please [.] Machen, I forgot to say, has sent the numbers to Waterford and Douglas in Kilkenny. They returned them saying they would not sell.

I like your plan of the Bards — Perhaps you would like to see how I have imitated the Irish in this stanza of the "Expected" —

Her long flowing hair swept her ankle of white,
Golden-ting'd, ringletted braided,
Odorous tresses, before whose rich light
Proud Jason's fam'd treasure had faded —
O! she was the fairest, the brightest, the rarest,
The gentlest, the simplest, the mildest,
The tunefullest, sweetest, the noblest, the meetest,
For poet in vision the wildest![2]

I shall finish this after the receipt of your coming letter.

---

[1] 'Printer's devil': in the circumstances here Walsh seems to refer to himself as the 'printer's devil', i.e., 'a literary hack doing what his or her employer takes the credit and payment for' (cf. *Shorter Oxford Dictionary*).

[2] Second stanza of *The Expected of Ireland*. For full text and notes see pp. 640ff.

Tuesday Morning

I have had your proof and on glancing at it I find you have again written corrugated instead of coruscant though I think neither should be used. Though I resolved not to alter a word without your permission yet rather than detain the proof I shall correct what I deem wrong in your interlinear version — I have omitted coruscant altogether & corrugated is wrinkled and suits not the sense[.] In fact the words are pedantic and inferior to the first — It strikes me that siodhach which you render quick should be peaceful, & if you think so change it in the reverse [?]. It makes no sense near tranquil. I have changed baby again to babe - baby is a nursery word. I have changed alone to lone. The term "high rent" is not appropriate [.] The sense requires tribute & your adjunct crown rent "plays the puck" with the poetry of the thing but I shall not touch them - but you should —

I am scribbling this at the Corn Exchange — I have not leisure nor room in my house for my wife has poured in lodgers[1] on me — I dropped the tale again - partly through want of time & partly that I lost a manuscript story which would suit me, since I came to Dublin. Tis strange that Mr. Duffy or Davis to whom I gave the song did not say twas one of our Irish ones though I wrote to that effect at the front of the song [.] I think Shane Bui would be a good song to send them & they should get the nod — Mr. Duffy learned from me that I was displeased with you & was determined to work no more for you - and perhaps 'twas under that impression he did not notice the source [from] which the song came —

I have just now learned that the motion for a new trial has its further discussion postponed till next term by the judges [.] This shews that a difference of opinion exists among them. I have lost my proof & must set about correcting the parts of my version which you have left untouched in yours [.]

This letter will tire you excessively unless you read it as it has been written by two or three snatches [.]

Your very obedient servant
E. Walsh

Mr. Daly

[P.S.] A very clever person to whom I showed the stanza I sent you has declared that manner of writing unsuited to the English tongue. I have not time to send you the last stanza of the Expected as I promised —

---

[1] Mrs Walsh was a resourceful and hard-working woman. Although she loved her 'dear Edward' she also knew that his earnings were insufficient to support the family.

(24) Walsh to John Daly[1]

Corn Exchange
[Sat] 18th May 1844.

Dear Sir,

I write this hasty line at half past 4 at my desk to say that I have had your note enclosing the notice of the songs. I did not intend that the life of Owen Roe should be understood to have come from my pen [.] I have no objection it should pass as yours and one of the best critics in Dublin has said that it was a very well-written essay — Mr. Green of the Independent it seems is much of your opinion concerning that sorry [...?] which we quarrelled but such is not the opinion of other editors. I wonder at your sympathetic tastes —

I would have written to you this week but that I expected your presence in town and shall now tell you on what subject. I translated the song preceding the "Lullaby"[2] and when I took that in hands I found it full of such inconsistent things that I became satisfied that many of the stanzas were not original but added by succeeding rhymers to Owen's song.

In the first stanza he tells that he will give the child those jewels etc which his royal sires had in the Green Isle of Erin — His object is to keep within the line of Irish story but six of the stanzas describe things found in classical heathen mythology and are doubtless the interpolations of idle rhymers — They bear intrinsic evidence of not being Owen Roe's for the span etc of the genuine lines is used in nearly the same words as those and applied to classical allusions — I have therefore left untranslated these six stanzas and turned into tolerable English rhyme the nine remaining only. I wait for your permission before I send them to Goodwin [.] If you could furnish notes to the Lullaby they would be very curious — The second stanza is not true to history — Falvey fought no battle at Cashel but he went to the rescue of Callaghan Cashel to the mouth of the Boyne where he died gloriously "Cashel of the [order?]" should be from Cashel to Boyne. You can put 'Boyne' into the Irish line which will correct it -

You leave Cu untranslated as if it were the name of a man — It is a hound and its history must be very curious if it were found out [.] I would recommend to give these notes upon the text if possible — I wait your reply hoping that you will agree with me in doing only the nine stanzas which I have retained[.] They are very good & with notes would furnish a curious insight into Irish history — Some research might enable you to give them —

Mr. Gerarty very kindly gave me "Hardiman's Minstrelsy"[3] to read but I had it only one hour in reading when a call for it obliged him to take it [.] I intended from the materials it offered to give a sketch of Shane Claragh for your second number.

Yours etc
E. Walsh

Mr. Daly

---

[1] NLI, S 2261. Letter number 23 in MS.

[2] For full text and notes see pp. 659ff.

[3] James Hardiman (c. 1790-1855) author of *Irish Minstrelsy or Bardic Remains of Ireland,* which he had published in 1831.

(25) Walsh to John Daly[1]

Corn Exchange
[Mon] June 17. 1844

Dear Sir

I have first to inform you that the newspapers of this day announce that the Pit cabinet is dissolved and Lord Melbourne succeeds him — If this be true 'tis a fearful crisis for Ireland & Repeal.

What you call a blunder about the order in which the Jacobite poets are placed is all your own [.] Every one knowing English will see that the words "last but chief" have no reference to time but only to the order in which the names appeared in the sentence. The changes you made in the essay were not needed for I had his epitaph done in the essay & the printer had not room for it so yesterday I struck out 17 lines of the sketch to make room for the epitaph & as you justly complain of the length of the printed page I struck off the song likewise so you'll have brave room & to spare please the printer.

I do not like you should take the trouble of making any changes in my prose or verse [.] Your style is somewhat different from mine and the mixture is easily perceptible.

I did not send you the proof at your bidding for I thought with all respects to your cleverness that you could not arrange my own original composition better than the author. I had a proof of this in the strange attempt you have made now [.] I tried before to bring the second last stanza of the Irish song opposite to the English in N° 3 with which it has no manner of connection in the sense or translation [.] The Irish and English must face one another as I have arranged them by leaving out the stanza which should be omitted even if there were room for it unless you have a mind to make the song and its translator a thorough laughing-stock — Sure the lines on the green paper have no resemblance to the English of the opposite page on N° 3 while what was printed had quite faithfully [.] I fell out with you before for less reason than I now have. Why would you have the reader of this song making a mockery of him who pretended to give translation & did not do it?

Mr. Nethercote[2] complained to me that you altered the word "poetry" to "songs" in the wrapper — Do you know that the change of the term entirely altered the sense of what you meant to convey[.] "reliques of Songs" means remains of songs & poems of which some stanzas where lost, while "reliques of Poetry" means songs or poetry that have come down from earlier times — The printer saw the absurdity & sneered at it — You should not attempt Mr Daly to correct whatever English I write not that I think I am not open to correction but that you have not English enough to do so. "Reliques of Song" would do; but the word "songs" in this sense is absolutely ridiculous [.]

This damnable N° has given me much uneasiness & I shall rejoice if even now I am rid of it.

I beg to remain yours
E. Walsh

---

[1] NLI, MS 2261. Letter number 24 in MS.

[2] Richard Nethercote, printer, 75 Marlborough St., Dublin.

(26) Walsh to John Daly[1]

9 Mulgrave Place
Gloucester St.
[Mon] July 8. 44

Dear Sir

I beg you will pardon me for not replying at once to your communication — I have to say of the sketch of "Owen O Reilly"[2] that it is entirely beneath mediocrity and that the ridiculous way in which the Irish portion is introduced would damn the entire work even though the anecdote were true of the subject of the sketch which it is not. The anecdote is related in Hardiman & the verses are there translated into English and the fact evidently happened in the wars of James when the Irish or rather the Irish rapparees were in the habit of retaliating upon their prisoners the atrocities of the troops of William — The name O Reilly is not known where many a story is told of him but O Rahilly and he is so named in Hardiman. I never before knew him called O'Reilly — Heffernan's[3] sketch is better done but is defective as it tells much more of Damer than of the poet whose life it professes to treat of and depicts him in two mean an attitude [.] The anecdote you sent me in the scrap of paper has not a particle of low humour even to recommend it.

In the proof sheet before me[4] you have either misplaced the note on the line "An tu'n bheith" or else the poet has repeated this same circumstance in the next stanza [.] The first I would suppose has reference to some other amour of Cuchullin while the latter has regard to the subject of your note - but you know better and look to it — In the translation as I have changed it a little the note would suit the second one —

I have just got our proof and I like the anecdote of the blind poet you have sent [.] I have now no time to read them attentively. The first matters are abominable & would absolutely disgrace yourself & the poet together. The secret of writing a good sketch lies here - get a man of imagination to mould the scanty materials in that pleasing shape which talent can bestow & his own story of thought will supply the rest. — I have heard some capital anecdotes of the blind bard but do not remember particularly accurately - for instance the time he went to beg at a church gate to discover a brother bard who had gone to church & when he at once discovered by that persons replying to his holy stanza as he

[1] NLI, MS 2261, Letter number 25 in MS.

[2] i.e. the poet Aogán Ó Rathaille. The general view is that his people are O'Rathailles from Kerry, but there is some question as to whether his ancestry is of the O'Reillys of Cavan.

[3] The 18th century poet Liam Dall Ó hIfearnáin, William Heffernan, the Blind, of Shronehill, some three miles west of Tipperary in the county of that name.

[4] The poem in question is Eoghan Rua Ó Súilleabháin's *Return of Prince Charles*, better known in the living tradition by the opening words, *Im Aonar Seal.*

entered - I think it must be McDonald,[1] have you heard that he ever went to church to avoid the censure of the church. I recollect having reported the stanza for you some time ago — It was not at my bidding that the printer gave the first part of the "Lullaby" but I suppose he had nothing else to eke out the sheet.

I have been thinking that you would send me word against the first of July what I might expect to receive for my share of the work I have done for your songs but perhaps you have not yet been furnished with the account from Machen. My time is so occupied that I have not a moment to spare and had I time I should devote it to something that would fetch in a little money [.] Without a prospect of remuneration I cannot afford to write any more for your work - the sale of the work to this time I am pretty sure is worth little [;] if it were carried on in parts in quick manner it might succeed in future. I have no objection to stick by it for another half year or twelve months if you send me now a few pounds as an earnest of what I may expect hereafter and as an encouragement to sing with something of energy — I shall use the vanity of saying that you will find few more capable of giving so faithful & spirited a version - and none more willing but I must have some immediate encouragement [.][2]

If you should not accede to my proposal and that as a consequence I cease to write for you - I beg that you will not allow the sketches you have sent me to go before the world in their present shape — it would condemn your further efforts when such would be contrasted with the first two sketches.

I beg to remain dear sir

Your very obedient servant
E. Walsh

P.S. I was chagrined to find that in the late numbers you should alter my expressions and alter for the worse so much & that I was very reluctantly obliged to change your alterations back again — I complained of this before. — I mention it now only to show that it was regard for the character of the work that actuated me to differ with you.

O'Connell's affair in the Lord's[3] is postponed for two months - His acquittal is spoken of as a certainty —

---

1 Seán Cláragh Mac Domhnaill.

2 Walsh not only got no encouragement but was bitterly disappointed with the financial disaster which the project proved to be. See John Daly's letter in the *Nation*, Aug. 17th 1844; *Letters*, No. 49, pp. 177f.

3 'O'Connell's affair in the Lords': a reference to an appeal against their sentence by O'Connell and those sentenced with him – a successful appeal as would become evident by early September.

(27) Walsh to John Daly[1]

Loyal National Repeal Association,
Corn Exchange Rooms,[2]
Dublin 2.
Monday 1844

Sir,

I have had your note of this morning and have to apprise you that I have arrived at no hasty conclusion but have informed you more than once before that I would not employ my time in writing translations and Lives of Irish poets without a prospect of being paid (reasonably at least) for my trouble [.] My last letter said no more than what I said before — I have had no communication with Machen and therefore know not whether you have profit or loss — I will write if your profits make it worth while but not till then —

Tis not your Irish remember that sells the work but the English version [.]

I am glad that you have Poets so thick about you - that will enable you to bear the betters with the falling off of so humble an individual as your very obedient servant [.]

It would not become me to comment on the version of Shane Bui you so kindly sent me. I have read the Irish of it at page 50 in "Hardiman's Minstrelsy" and a version by H.G. Curran on the opposite page. Another critic must decide their respective claims.

I have to hope that your future sketches & versions may please as well as those which occupied my time when writing for your work —

If you be serious in what you say of Mrs Daly's opinion of Miss Daly I deeply regret that the daughter of respectable parents should be the subject of such fearful suspicion [.] It is most strange - that one of her manners extensive learning (the best I ever found in any female) and innocence should be mistaken for a "Dublin prostitute"—

I beg to remain yours
E Walsh

Mr. Daly

P.S. You frequently before this have not perceived the errors in your style and language which I have corrected. Let "Nags envious stare" stand if you like - twill make folk stare at the horse at all events. You should be thankful as well as "glad" that I sent Niobe[3] about her business — I wish you came up to settle that I may see whether I am to get anything for my pains [.]

EW

---

[1] NLI, MS 2261. Letter number 26 in MS.
[2] This letter is written on a fragment of headed notepaper - hence the formal address.
[3] A reference to the goddess of that name in Eoghan Rua Ó Súilleabháin's poem, *The Lullaby*.

(28) Walsh to John Daly[1]

9 Mulgrave Place
Gloucester Street
[Sun.] July 21.1844

Dear Sir
I received your Proof on Saturday but as I saw with what reluctance you gave up the translation of all the verses of the Lullaby, I have consented to forego my own opinion in your behalf, kept the proof from Goodwin and have this before morning turned the five remaining stanzas into very decent English — As I am about to take my leave of you I did not chance to have you ungratified in that particular - Goodwin shall receive the proof tomorrow (Monday).

Why did not you endeavour to furnish notes to the more obscure passages in the Lullaby [?] The few notes you gave were so badly written that I was forced to alter them and strike out some words to reduce them to anything like tolerable language — The phases "Gag of a boy" in the sketch of Rahilly and "Main mast of the ship" — 'however dark the night or the occasion." The poet bequeaths his steed & yellow trappings to his offspring, are all deficient and bad. I point out these in order to show you that in your future sketches and notes it will be necessary to keep a strict eye to the style and accuracy of the language to keep up the credit of the work - for any other purpose I would not take them out.

Why have you translated Eadrom, magnanimous - this latter word has reference to mental qualities and does not Eadrom mean "light"[.] I have marked it fleet a quality which I think the poet intended to convey — You have a shocking error in one of the stanzas which I translated today where you have Niobe the cup-bearer of Jove [.] Hebe was goddess of Youth and the cupbearer of Jupiter [.] I must alter that though I hardly know how to form the letter 'r' in Irish — The original stanza is the weakest and worst in the collection but listen to what I've done for it —

For thee shall sparkle in my lays,
Rich nectar from young Hebe's vase,
Who fill'd the cup, in Heaven's abodes
For Jove amid the feast of gods!

I am much pleased that the note on the "Lullaby" has gained your good will. It abounds with some errors of the press which I have now corrected but do not suppose, dear Mr. Daly, that the obnoxious word "enduring" is of the number that you should find fault with [.] This word astonishes me in no small degree, or how a man of your gallantry should spend forty years among the pretty girls of this world, and not understand the meaning of

---

[1] NLI, MS 2261. Letter number 27 in MS.

"one enduring kiss" puzzles my very pericranium — You are hardly two old yet to receive a few short lessons in the divine art & one of the sweetest teachers I could recommend would be your cherry-mouthed namesake from the beautiful south — I, myself shall just furnish you with a dry notion of an "enduring kiss" from Lord Byron - that boy wanted no practice at the game.

"———— A Kiss's strength
Is always to be measured by the length."

Believe me though I intend to write no more translations for fame to be your very sincere obedient etc

E Walsh

Mr J Daly

(29) Walsh to John Daly[1]

9 Mulgrave Place
Gloucester Street
Dublin.
[Sat] Aug. 17th 1844

Dear Sir

I have had your letter of the 15th. instant and have to assure you in reply that it was with great reluctance I withdrew from the "Jacobite Reliques [.]" Yet I felt it imperative that I should not waste my time and talents unprofitably while there were claims upon me superior to any gratification I may feel, & I assure you 'twas no trifling one, of rendering our later writing familiar to the eye of them who should never have forgotten their Celtic costume. I shall now say what I very nearly expressed before, that the writing of which you showed me a specimen would be sufficient to damn the work - & any one careful of the character of our bards would sooner see them for ever forgotten than introduced to modern notice under such circumstances [.] While I contend for carrying on the work if possible my prayer to you would be shun "the gratuitous air of two or three clever writers." There are hundreds who would lick your hand to see themselves in print.

I will candidly say that I consider you now make proposals to me in the hope that the association would patronise the songs [.] I hope it may, yet I made you will remember the like proposal as we stood in the twilight near the "Blessed Church" to whose vicinity I that night called your attention to add the more solemnity to my request — No matter I am

[1] NLI, MS 2261. Letter number 28 in MS.

happy to find you repentant and you will find Walsh like a tender father receiving the prodigal who had left him to herd among swine. You are welcome & chic malheure.[1]

Seriously Mr Daly, my hour is approaching and I have no more jesting time. — I will engage to give you what you desire "Sketches & Poetry" in future without any claim to the profits at the rate of £3 (three pounds) for every six numbers. You know how unreservedly I will apply myself to the work & shall say nothing of my capability to the task.

I have spoken with a literary person on this subject and when I spoke of £3 for every six numbers he smiled at the little value I set by my song genius — However if the Association take up the thing & that it leave a respectable profit let it be understood that you will not see me confined to that trifle —

This does not set aside my claim to be paid according to agreement for the already published numbers. If these terms you should consider not suitable to you you need not make me a second offer as I will not take less than what I have just now repeated for my future labours. —

If you agree with me I would wish you did not allow the sketch or song of the Tipperary Bard[2] to go before the public till I see them [.] I told you I had some anecdotes of your blind poet that would look well in print [.] You see I am not exactly a mere wasting [?] character [.] I would wish to uphold the honour of the Bard.

Yours etc
E. Walsh

Mr Daly

(30) Walsh to John Daly[3]

9 Mulgrave Place
Gloucester Street
August 20. 1844

Sir

That's a horrid pen I took up to say that I have had your letter in reply to my communication. I do not greatly regret the determination to hold by the "Gratuitacy" Gentlemen for my own sake but I do for the fame of men whose characters you intend to

---

[1] In this context, the phrase would seem to mean, *good luck* or *take it and be damned*!

[2] William *Dall* (the blind) O'Heffernan.

[3] NLI, MS 2261. Letter number 29 in MS.

damn through the medium of such verse as you have read to me at the Corn Exchange — I trust that some opportunity may present itself of shewing the public that such is not a faithful transcript of the language of Blind Bill[.] I have read that Shane Bui in the original, and shall say that I have seen nothing yet in Irish verse to compare with that scoffing ballad in silver-sounding lines. "Mar yah" is a very classic phrase to reach the decorous ears of decency when speaking in your version of the dubious chastity of Elizabeth[1] - an idea which the blind old man was too refined to convey to the ears of even untaught peasants[.] May God soothe his blessed spirit if he be aware of the injury done his beautiful song it will chafe him even in Heaven! Why did you not get some one at lest to count the feet in each line for your part that his lines may preserve some rude resemblance to the tune of the Irish song?

God may forgive your worse than Vandalism [.] I cannot. –

I trust you will forgive this outburst but the smooth flow, & silvery sounds of William the Blind's' sweet song betrayed me into it.

My particular reason for sending this is to desire as a matter of course that you will mention in a note that my connexion with you has ceased and that the "Lullaby" was my last effort for you — I have a rhyming character and shall endeavour to preserve it.

But when you publish "Over the Hills and far away,"[2] I trust you will mention that the English version is mine [.] I am proud of Shane Claragh and his sweet song.

I have seen your letter in the Nation[3] and was much pleased with it which is more than I can truthfully say to your notes on Shane Bui — I hope you were equally pleased with "Timothy Scannell's last Words"[4] in the same Journal from the rhyming pen of your very humble servant —

E Walsh

---

[1] Queen Elizabeth I of England.

[2] Full text and notes on pp. 652f.

[3] The letter in the *Nation* is that of Aug. 17th 1844, in which Daly explains the financial losses. See *Letters* No. 49, p. 177 and ft. nt. 1.

[4] Full text and notes on pp. 540f.

(31) Walsh to John Daly[1]

9 Mulgrave Place
Gloucester St.
[Sat] Aug 25.1844

Sir,

I have seen Mr. Nethercote since the last letter of yours reached me, and when I told him I could not possibly accept the proposal of 5/-[2] a number, he pressed me to come to some terms with you for I believe he has an interest in the repute of the work done at his place — He proposed that I should take the 5/- a number and if the work progressed so as to leave a profit that I should have the half profit according to our first agreement deducting of course in that case the 5/- per number from my share of the profit if I found it the more advantageous mode to take the half profit.

I would be better pleased that you dropped the songs rather than send them abroad in a manner unsuited to their merits, but as you are determined to persevere in publishing them few things would give me greater grief than to see the language of your Jacobite poets clothed in such a garb as the rhymes that are now before me — And in short I shall therefore accept the terms which Mr. N——— has mentioned and I suppose you will have no objection to agree to them [.]

I await your reply —

In the mean time I have got the song from Mr. N—— (who says that he has sent the latter part of it to you) as I dare say you will be glad that I dont intend to abandon the songs [.] The heading of the song "Lament for the Gael" is absurd — This is no song of sorrow I should think but a scoffing ballad in ridicule at the rhymers who in that day were making songs & to the tune of Shane Bui [.] Is it not so — In future you are not to take any trouble by the mere English part, leave that to me. Let me know whether the Irish heading you give the songs are your own or are in the manuscripts that reach you — I am confident that you have been looking over Hardiman for titles for your songs. The "Lament for the Gael"[3] is there — Send me the literal translation of your Irish titles & let me christen the English version —

I'll give your blind minstrel from Slievenamon a good Anglo-Irish dress to fit him the brave old boy —

Where the devil did you find Jack Madden in the song — He's to be found there as much as the story of Lusmore is to be discovered in Moore's "Captain Rock [.]"

I wait a reply to this — In the mean time I shall translate Shane Bui [.]

Yours
E. Walsh

Mr J Daly

---

[1] NLI, MS 2261.

[2] 5/- is an abbreviation for 'five shillings' i.e. a quarter of one pound.

[3] Full text and notes on pp. 646ff.

(32) Walsh to John Daly[1]

9 Mulgrave Place
Gloucester St
Dublin
[Sat] 31st Aug 1844

Sir

I am very glad that I have rescued the memory of Blind William from the contact of the "gratuitous gentlemen." You were very near damning both him and your work together [.] I trust that he who came to the rescue will yet find his reward —

I have given the third of the blind poet's songs to Mr. Nethercote — I have read the Tailor[2] etc and have seen no merit in it — Bill had the itch of endeavouring like other men, to show off his learning — I shall however translate it, and would suggest that you furnish notes to the more abstruse parts of Irish History in the song. It strikes me as very singular that you have a trick of giving notes on well-known passages in Irish history while you pass over the other more difficult ones or only refer the reader to the book in which they may be found. You should look better to the way in which you write the notes — the last were very faulty —

You likewise mark the Irish proper names in capitals which confers a most abominable appearance on the lines. It is difficult to have the first letter a capital as in the English - I detest the task of showing you these errors but I must for the credit of the work —

In the interlinear you speak of "treasure of my chest [.]" Chest is the best expression in a spitting of blood but not in amatory poetry —

Furnish notes to the less known points of Irish history in the last song or send me a Keatings History and I shall do it[.] It would save me the trouble of correcting your notes —

I directed Mr. N——— to alter the punctuation in your Irish to suit the sense for your printing made two abstract words one. Tis where Sing and Benny Brit are mentioned.[3]

I saw in the Nation to day that you have given Mr. Duffy the Irish of the "Saxon Shilling." I would thank you much if you had the kindness to send me a copy of it —

I want more of Wms Irish songs for I shall turn the one I have into English tomorrow —

I greatly regret that your sketch of Wm Dall's life should go abroad without my knowledge of his high genius & the scanty materials I possess besides [.] I would weave an interesting chapter for him —

I have called the last song "The Voice of Joy"[4] & have strove to change your Irish to the same meaning [.] "The Vision of the Blind Bard"[5] you have named the lovely amatory

---

[1] NLI, MS 2261.

[2] *The Merry Tailor* by William *Dall* O'Heffernan. Full text and notes on pp. 648ff.

[3] See: *A Lament for the Gael*, stanza 3 & full text and notes on pp. 646ff.

[4] *The Voice of Joy* by William *Dall* O'Heffernan. See pp. 608f.

[5] *The Vision of the Bard* by O'Heffernan was published under the title *Eire's Maid is She*; the Irish version having the title, *Béith Eirionn Í*. See pp. 600f.

strain [.] It has no claim to the title [;] call it "be n Eirin Í" as I have done — I have seen nothing to exceed that song & I have I must [say] done it justice — It came to my heart [.]

Yours in haste
E. Walsh

Mr J Daly

(33) Walsh to -?[1]

When I left, or rather was driven from my rural bower at Tourin, I procured, through the influence of Mr. Duffy, of the 'NATION', the situation of sub-editor of the 'Monitor'. I did not like the employment and quitted it - got then, to vary my life, a severe bilious fever, induced by mental suffering. When I could crawl abroad I procured employment at that great vortex of agitation, the Corn Exchange Rooms, where I am engaged in a purely literary capacity, and am treated with respect. I know it will gratify you to learn that change from the influence of the anti-National Board has tended to my advantage. I have a very pretty cottage of my own. I am almost entirely my own master at the Corn Exchange, and am engaged in translating, during my leisure moments, 'Jacobite poetry', which is being published by Mr. Daly, of Kilkenny. You must have seen the very favourable notice I have had from the newspaper press.

(34) Walsh to -? [2]

If I could make out a school under some gentleman I would accept it, but your parish school in a country district would be the death of my delicate, overwrought frame. I sigh for the fresh, pure air of the fields, and the song of the birds, and the gentle, sickly primrose, and all the glories of the joyous spring!

(35) Walsh to Joe Sullivan[3]

I knew Brighid would get over the illness. I'm a capital judge of a sick girl's pulse. I've sometimes felt one, Joe! Mary is a good girl; all goes on well; but I am fidgety and lonesome when I look about and miss those to whom my affections cling, green and youthful, tho' my head is grey.[4]

---

[1] The *Celt*, Dec. 12th 1857, pp. 305-306.
[2] The *Celt*, Dec. 12th 1857, p. 306.
[3] The *Celt*, Dec. 12th 1857, p. 307. Joe Sullivan was Walsh's brother-in-law.
[4] When Walsh wrote this letter it seems that his wife and children had gone to visit Mrs. Walsh's sister at Cappoquin for the benefit of Brighid's health.

(36) Walsh to - ?[1]

Dublin (?)
[Fri] July 19th. 1846.

I am not sorry that I had not time on Friday to reply to your letter, as I have some political information to send you, which has not yet reached the Dublin papers. At 'a soirée' at Kilrush, in reply to some severe remarks of Mr. Charles O'Connell - a gentleman of Clare and a friend of O'Connell's - upon 'Young Ireland,' Smith O'Brien declared that there were at present three Repeal parties in Ireland, each pursuing its own particular views - O'Connell and his sons, the priests, and lastly, the people. He also loudly condemned the policy of the committee respecting Dungarvan. His language has caused a strange sensation in the Corn Exchange Rooms, and is wholly unaccountable. We may know more after tomorrow's meeting.

(37) Walsh to his wife Brighid[2]

Spike Island,
Convict Depot,
Sunday Night

My Dear Love,

I sit down to write to you, and the more readily, as the fierce storm that is raging here, at eight o'clock at night, is tremendous; this storm of the elements inclines my heart and its faculties to you, my beloved, and our dear little ones, with a prayer that God may protect you, till you all come to my longing embrace. How awfully it blows! Adam who is now reading some ballad, has started suddenly exclaiming 'Is not that the cry of some one in great pain?' The island is very high, and the winds seize upon it fearfully. I went at three o'clock to look out upon the harbour from the ramparts, and was forced to lie down in the blast. However, we have a warm room, with solid stone walls, and a bomb-proof roof over our heads, and are very snug.

We have a Rev. Mr. Walsh here, who comes every Sunday to give Mass - to-day I went to Communion. It gives me great hardship to do every little turn of the place, and also to attend Adam, and my public duties, which are now commencing. I am awake every morning at five o'clock and up at six. I have not had, since I left Dublin, those deep and dreamless slumbers which I always had, as a portion of my existence, when you were near me. But they will come again, and you and my children shall yet make my heart leap at the joy of your presence. I have got your parcel in Cork. Why did you not tell me the

---

[1] The *Celt*. Dec. 12th 1857, p. 307-308.
[2] The *Celt*, Dec. 19th 1857, p. 321.

particular things you sent? I found some coffee and brown sugar in the keg, and some cheese, also a scarf and trousers. I think we'd be very happy here till the children would be grown, did they permit you to reside with me. I'd have great leisure; the school business won't be more than four hours a-day.

Good-bye dear Brighid, I must get Adam his coffee, and put him to bed.

(38) Walsh to his wife Brighid[1]

Spike Island,
Convict Depot,
Monday Night.

My dear Love,

Adam and I are just sitting down to our supper of boiled bread and milk. We have both to spare, as the storm did not permit the milkman to land in the morning, and we have now a double portion. Adam says, 'Mamma will be in great glee when she comes here, to find such lots of boiled bread and milk.' I am annoyed from little turns I am forced to do about myself and Adam. Fancy me cooking ham and cabbage, and cleaning up the crockery? Let me know, my love, when you would be allowed by the doctor to go into the country; that moment you must come down to Cove or Ring for your health's sake. You would wonder how well Adam reads, and his general knowledge is entirely beyond the 'Auld farren wean' in the beautiful Scotch song. I have three hundred persons here, to whom I have given books, etc., before the school regularly opens. Most of the convicts are persons of the south and west, who were driven by hunger to acts of plunder and violence. I wept to-day in one of the wards, when some of the people of Skull and Skibbereen told me the harrowing tale of their sufferings from famine, and the deaths - the fearful deaths - of their wives and little ones. How 'we' should thank the Lord! Let me know, love, particularly, how you are and how are the children. I hope Fanny will mind Mary and Edward. I hope you won't make yourself vexed or uneasy about that work which always injures your health. Will you promise me now? If you don't, I'll take Fanny and Mary into the Island, and leave you and Edward outside. I am very lonely here, and don't read nor write, and have scarcely leisure, and no inclination to amuse myself without you and the dear little ones. Adam sends his love to mamma and Edward first, to Fanny next, to scratch-face Mary last. I send love to Brighid - my own dear Brighid - first, to the little poet and sisters second and alike.

Edward Walsh.

---

[1] The *Celt*, Dec. 19th 1858, pp. 321-322.

(39) Walsh to his wife Brighid[1]

Convict Depot,
Spike Island,
[Wed.] Nov. 10th '47.

My Dear Love,

I received your kind letter yesterday with the enclosed pound, and the receipt for 10s. from the Celtic Society. You will send no more money till I ask for it. I got some beef and groceries in Cork on my word, but have touched none of them yet - I have been living upon your welcome presents. I did not pay for Adam's 'bluchers' yet, but now have money to do so, thanks to my own dear Brighid. I trust they will restrain him like a pair of convict's anklerings. You see I take my figures from native scenery. Need I say how your last letter makes my heart glad? You know how I felt for your illness, and how I must rejoice at your restoration to health. Nothing that could befall me on earth would give me such sincere joy as to see you well and happy...

Now, with regard to your question, whether I would wish you to stay in Dublin till your work ceases - I say that I do not choose that you should stay a moment longer than the doctor holds necessary for the thorough cure of your complaint. When he says that you should get a change of air, you must come down to Cove at least, which is a beautiful place, or to some neighbouring village. I don't think there is a decent room in this whole island. But if you were permitted here, you could have nice apartments, coals and candles, and two pounds of bread each day, 'gratis'; and then the salary would leave us enough for minor wants. We shall try. At all hazards, you will leave Dublin, that, at all events, I may see you and the children; for I would die of grief, if I did not occasionally behold you. What is life to me without you and my children? I am rather concerned that you should have sent away a clean, good servant, to recall an idle, dirty gawky. 'Tis a strange want of good sense in one who is so clever in other ways. I shall now say no more, than to express a hope that the minds of the little girls will not be polluted with such filthy songs and sayings as Poor Adam is every night repeating, and which he said he learned from——. He says, the other night, 'Eliza was very good, she never taught me blackguarding'. I am really astonished at the songs and sayings he has. Now that I have scolded you, I have to say that in coming down, I would not like you'd come by the steamer, the weather is so stormy. It blew a fierce gale to day (Wednesday), and the night is now very wild, though yesterday was mild and beautiful. I have no milk for our coffee - the storm prevented the milkman from coming to day.

Good-bye, love,
E. Walsh.

---

[1] The *Celt*, Dec. 19th 1857, p. 323.

(40) To his wife Brighid[1]

To the Inspector General of Prisons.

Convict Depot,
Spike Island,
[Thu] Nov 18th 1847.

My own Love,

I have no sheet but this, so I trust you will excuse me for sending it - 'tis not, you see, a 'virgin page'. How your letter of Monday and Tuesday relieved my wretched heart, thanks to the Almighty Disposer of life and death! You who know my tender love for the children, will understand the boundless gratitude of that heart for such mercy. It is curious that, even after reading your letter announcing his illness, and up to the receipt of your last, I had a strong presentment that the child would not die! There is no lodging to be got in any of the miserable cabins of the island.

As I feel a wrong, so do I cherish the memory of a good deed done to me or mine. Give my best and most grateful thanks to Dr. McSweeney, who on another occasion acted as my friend. Tell him how I loved my boy, and then he'll conceive my overflowing gratitude; tell Miss Murray's family also how deeply I feel their kindness. God bless and prosper them through life. Write, dear Brighid, at once, and let me know if Edward Walsh, the younger, is well and kicking. Let me know if Fan is minding all the house, and playing with Mary and Edward. Tell Fan, and 'mine mouse', that I'll soon be kissing them. 'Tis now very late at night, for I put Adam to bed and mended his clothes before I set to this. Make haste to me. You have asked me to pray for you; don't you know, love, that twice every day, since you became my wife, a prayer for your welfare has gone to the throne of Heaven, from the unworthy, but fervent heart of your fond husband and truest 'friend' Edward Walsh.

You had no occasion, my dear beloved, to detail the items of your expenses. The few pounds remaining are for you and the little ones. I would pledge my clothes, if needful, to procure my dear wife the food and comforts necessary to her present weak condition. Spare no cost till you are perfectly restored to me in health and spirits.......

Tell little Mary how I love her, and tell Fan to mind her sister and little brother, as she is the eldest and kiss her for me. Your account of Edward's beauty delights me; my young poet must have a better-requited trade than that which sent E.W. to the convict depot (but to this I am perfectly resigned). Your last letter was so gentle and kind, that if your tongue, my fair Brighid (how sweetly that pretty name suits my notion of you!), wagged as tenderly at all times as your pen, your voice would be as balm to my bruised and broken spirit; and I would fly to hush, in the white bosom of my gentle dove, all my sorrows for ever!

---

[1] The *Celt*, Dec. 19th 1857, pp. 323-324.

(41) Walsh to C.G. Duffy[1]

Duke's Row
Summer Hill

Sir

I am getting on at the Monitor office and will be able to walk about now till Tuesday because of the holidays.

My wife has written to say that Sir R Musgrave and his lady express their regret that I should leave them. Mr. Sheehan it seems has expressed regret that I did leave before I made up matters with him. He is not at Cappoquin and is probably in Dublin. Perhaps you could let me know where I could see Mr Caughey who may have some account of him.

I fear it will displease you and give you a low opinion of me to say that I long to go back. God direct me. Mr. Coffey seems pleased with my mode of 'cutting out'. I'd sooner scribble songs for that *Nation* at Tourin.

I have the honour to your
Very obliged and grateful friend
E. Walsh

C G Duffy Esq

(42) Walsh to C. G. Duffy?[2]

Cork Union Workhouse,
Sept. 9th '49.

My Dear Friend,

I have received yours of the 6th. inst. You and Mrs. C—— will be glad to learn that my poor wife is past all danger from her late sickness. I brought her home from the hospital on last Monday, after lying there for weeks. Hers was the worst case of brain fever at the hospital for the last two years. However, she has been out walking to day, and is in excellent spirits, considering her previous sufferings. She has been today regretting her fine, profuse hair, which the nurse-tenders cut off and sold: those

'Ringlets rich and rare,
By nature's finger's wove,'

---

[1] NLI, MS 8005. Although this letter is undated, it was probably written around Christmas 1843.

[2] The *Celt*, Dec. 26th 1857, p. 337. Kickham introduces the recipient of this letter as "an old and unwavering friend of the poet, whose name, at his own request, we withhold." Charles Gavan Duffy is probably the person in question.

which I once celebrated. I need not say how delighted she is at your present prospects, and how she hugs the hope of soon seeing Mrs. C—— in Cork. By the way, I was not prepared for some of the revelations in your letter. Keegan is dead - let me know when and of what he died. He had more 'natural' talent than all 'Young Ireland' to say nothing of the 'ould' section. Tell me, like a good fellow (I did not miscall you there), did the biting rhymer of the 'Mail', or Terry O'Driscoll, of the 'Warder', say nothing of the Queen's smiting with her royal sword the shoulder of Sir Tim, the Lord Mayor and M.P. of Cashel? It was a fertile subject. I am worked here from six in the morning till eight at night, and always have to get a pass from the master to go for an instant beyond the gate.

(43) Walsh to C.G. Duffy?[1]

Cork Union Workhouse,
Oct. 11th '49.

The hint you furnished me of looking for some situation in the College is a good one; a change to such a place would be a great relief and mercy to me. How greatly I could be delighted to be near you, to hear your friendly voice, and look into your benevolent eyes. I hope and pray that God may grant me such a lot. I never made many friends. I have had through life some inborn intuitive perception of the man whom I would and could love; and the number of them I found to be remarkably few. I am writing this at half-past five in the evening, with the dull twilight of the schoolroom closing upon me, and the noise of a hundred pair of iron-bound clogs over my head. Do you not pity your poor, sensitive friend, dear C—— in this most uncongenial place?

My best regards to you and yours, my own dear friend,
Edward Walsh

(44) Walsh to C.G. Duffy?[2]

[The Cork Union Workhouse, Feb. 1850]

How does O'Daly's books sell? You and Father O'Connor are the only men living with whom I have the slightest friendly intercourse.

---

[1] The *Celt*, Dec. 26th 1857, p. 338. The recipient of the letter is most probably C.G.Duffy; the text almost says as much in the expression "dear C—"

[2] The *Celt*, Dec. 26th 1857, p. 338. C.G. Duffy is most likely the recipient.

(45) Walsh to ?[1]

Your hints about "A.B."[2] have wakened in my mind a painful memory of his "strut and stare and a' that."

(46) Walsh to...?[3]

I first saw Bríghídín on a quiet Sabbath at her devotions in the quiet country church. Her gentleness and modest air made such an impression on me that I resolved to win her and that day month we stood at the altar man and wife.

(47) Walsh to C.G. Duffy[4]

July 1844.

I have no objection that my untaught strains should give way to any of the numerous songs of Mr. Davis that adorn the collection, or to that of any other person who may be honoured in a niche in your national temple.

(48) Walsh (?) to the *Wexford Independent*[5]

In a late paper we felt bound to acknowledge the aid afforded us by a contemporary in rescuing from unmerited and ungracious aspersion the character and claims of one of our national lyric poets, whose powers enable him to take no mean place among the enthusiastic successors of our ancient bards. The occasion on which we and our contemporary were

---

[1] Published in the *Celt*, Dec. 5th 1857, p. 305.

[2] "A.B." is the *nom de plume* of John Coen, born on a Roscommon farm in 1809. He graduated with a B.A. from Trinity College in the 1830s and was later principal of the Abbey Hall Classic School, Omagh. Coen, or a Mr. Sheehan with whom Walsh had an unresolved conflict at the time of his departure from Tourin School (see *Letters* No. 41), may have been Walsh's unnamed inspector and *bete noire*.

[3] *The Irishman*, March 14th 1866, "The Poets of Ireland - Edward Walsh."

[4] RIA, MS 12/P/19-20. Letters and Papers of Gavan Duffy, including diaries and the brief for his defence at his trial, 1848. Quoted by E. Shannon-Mangan, p. 273

[5] When Walsh turned against Davis and the *Nation*, he started writing anonymous letters to the provincial press, denouncing the *Nation* and its administration. C.G. Duffy himself refers directly to this in his memoir of Thomas Davis. The title of the above 'letter' is, *National Songs - Organs of National Feeling*, published in the *Wexford Independent* October 16th 1844. It may be the work of Walsh or based on a letter of his to the *Waterford Chronicle*.

called on to interpose in his behalf was this. Two songs from the pen of our gifted friend have been given in our paper. The two stanzas of the first we published were suppressed in the *Nation*, and one of the writers for that paper thought fit to denounce them as containing reference to a "mock miracle". The author of "Ireland and her Rulers since 1829," among the compliments he pays to the "Young Ireland" party, thinks it one of the highest, we presume, to allege, that "there is nothing monkish or crawling in its nature." To this, however, by way of forming a striking contrast, we presume, he adds that "certainly never was any party less liable to the charge of infidelity." He continues further to assert that "it has nothing of the French scoffer in its disposition - it is calmly religious, and sentimentally averse to unbelief." Taking the party generally, we would hope that this description is the true one; and taking the *Nation* as the organ of that party, we would hope that it is by accident, rather than in pursuance of system, that the sentiment we have noticed came to find insertion in its columns, particularly under the imposing guise of editorial comment. Charles Gavan Duffy has been one of the fellow-martyrs of O'Connell in the cause of peace, order-morality, religion. He is now, we regret, in consequence of the low state of his health - sunk still further of course, by his late imprisonment in defiance of justice - obliged to leave the management of his journal in other hands; and we would be sorry to think that injury to his prospects, or to the character of the journal, should be the result. If the *Nation* should become an organ of infidelity, it would cease to be an organ of Irish feeling. The Irish people, however they differ with each other on other subjects, are - with very few exceptions, indeed - unanimous in recoiling with horror from the sentiments of the "French scoffer." The people taken as a whole, are, in reality, "calmly religious and sentimentally averse to unbelief." The sentiments expressed in the stanzas, which the writer in the *Nation* thought fit to reject and denounce, are in accordance with the feelings of the people. National Songs should be the indices of national feelings. Our valued friend, in recognising this principle, and acting on it, has followed the example of his predecessors, and he may take credit to himself for doing so, rather than enter, on any different course. They are not the friends of Ireland, nor the Irish people, who labour to undermine the foundations of their religious belief; and the public journal that may be made the medium of attempts to this effect will not long retain a character as an organ of national feeling. The conductors of the *Nation* should remember the fate of the *Comet*...............

A Correspondent desires to be informed of the meaning of the words. "Ma craoibhin aoibhinn aluin og," prefixed as a title to the second song, and repeated in it so frequently afterwards. In reply, perhaps, we should premise that they are to be *pronounced* as if written "ma chroevin eevin aloooin oag." The words, as we understand them, signify "my tuneful-hearted charming splendid young one." If we be wrong, our valued friend, the author of the song, might have the kindness to set us right. We may imagine that the bard of O'Donnell was supposed, like Scott's Allan Bane, to be addressing his lay of impassioned denunciation to some distinguished daughter of his people - some "Lady of the Lake," the mountain, or the plain - whose noble heart beat in sympathy with his call to honour and to vengeance; or, perhaps we may suppose him, according to the general custom of our country's minstrels, to have personified Ireland, and addressed the language of his inspiration to *her*. In reply to another question, we have to say that the word "Coolin" signifies the long hair falling from the back of the head, and was formed from "cool", signifying "back."...

SECONDARY SOURCE CORRESPONDENCE

(49) John Daly to the *Nation*[1]

Kilkenny, Aug. 14th 1844.

DEAR SIR - Will you permit me, through your columns, to return my sincere thanks to the "Clare Mountaineer," who has evinced such deep interest in behalf of the Irish songs which I have been publishing for some time, and which you have kindly recommended to the favourable notice of the Committee of the Repeal Association, who now appear determined to take active steps for the renovation of the too-long-neglected language and literature of Ireland.

When I began publishing these songs, I was not actuated by pecuniary motives, my object being solely to distribute among my countrymen in a cheap form a large collection of the songs of our bards - songs written when persecution raged - when penal enactments ground the people to the very dust - and written in language which conveyed, in the most glowing manner, the cruel deeds of the hungry adventurer; but if that language were understood by the foe, the poet dare not give utterance to the effusions of his wounded spirit.

Having had a large collection of those songs, which I collected from time to time through the country, and in many instances succeeded in obtaining the original MSS themselves, whose authenticity cannot be doubted - these I issued in penny numbers, to suit the lower classes of the community, who do not very often have many pence to spare, at the same time giving *interlinear* translations, to render those who did not understand the language, and were anxious to learn it, some assistance. A failure in this mode of publication, induced me to make up these numbers into parts, with printed wrappers, at a shilling each, for the respectable classes; and now, after having expended upwards of *twenty pounds* on the undertaking, when getting the account the other day from my publisher, Mr. Machen, Westmoreland-street, the return of the sales only amounted to £2-8s-10d, and 5,935 numbers were returned.

However, this failure will not intimidate me, knowing that the songs will eventually make way for themselves, and that the public ere long will be able to take up the poetic effusions of Seaghan Claragh, Eoghan Ruadh ua Suilliovain, Uilliam Dall ua Heifernain, Seaghan ua Tuama an ghrinn, the eccentric Mangaire Sugach, and many others, with a keener appetite than they do now a Byron or a Scott. With this view I have placed the second part of the songs in my printer's hands, which will be ready for delivery in a few days; and hoping the "Clare Mountaineer" will come forward with that patriotic spirit which induced him to address you, and established a national feeling in behalf of the songs among

[1] Published in the *Nation*, August 17th 1844 and prefaced by Gavan Duffy, the editor, with this comment: "The following letter from Mr. Daly tells a tale which we would have doubted upon less competent authority. But we do not yet believe that the fault was the people's. Was there no mismanagement?"

his tribe on the wild mountains of Clare, and thanking you, sir, for trespassing so far on your kind indulgence,

I remain, your obedient servant,
John Daly.

(50) John Keegan to John Daly[1]

June 10th 1846

I think Mr. Walsh is not the only person of genius in Ireland. The fact is, I never liked the spirit of his poetry - it is acquired by labour not a bit of nature in it - or if inspired at all, it is by the "court fool" of the fairy palace of Knock-shegowna or Carrig-Cleena. No son of genius ever yet had his overweening ridiculous vanity or his puppy, upstart demeanour, and, mark my words! he will have no monument to perpetuate his memory but the remembrance of his own overbearing, repulsive and self-sufficient - I will say "errors" although I thought to employ a harsher term.

I pray God, your intended marriage may conduce to your temporal and eternal weal. I have a still higher opinion of you for your unselfish feelings. Still, for your sake I wish she had the gold, for after all it forms a prime ingredient in the cup of earthly comfort. And yet, I am making myself ridiculous in talking things I could this day or time marry a girl with 70 or 80 shiners in her purse, yet I despise her and them, and am determined to wed another with less beauty, less intelligence and not one-half her fortune. And the former maiden with these advantages combines virtue and good conduct - Yet I prefer the less favoured - why? Faith I cannot say - only that I love her.

I am sure you feel yourself with me, in a predicament not dissimilar to Sindbad the Sailor when the burthen on the 'old man of the sea' - Well blame yourself! had you held your head as stately as Pedagogue Walsh you would never be annoyed by

Your loving friend.
John Keegan.

John Daly Esq
25 Anglesea St.

---

[1] NLI, MS 2261, letter No. 41.
[Keegan's note] 'Of course Mr. W. is not to hear my opinion - at least till he provokes me further.

(51) John Keegan to John Daly[1]

June 11th 1846

My Dear Daly,

Like the "Bottle Imp" of German story, you cannot now get rid of me, unless, indeed, you can contrive like the unfortunate possessor of that celebrated demon, to sell me for less than I cost you. Please send me whatever information you can about Slieve-na-mon, and I shall give it along with the poem. I would prefer putting it in the National Magazine if I thought that periodical would live long enough to bring out a volume. However, I am not fully resolved yet as to which I shall send it - If you like how I succeed in this you will probably favour me with more particularly if you had any old fragment connected with the Co. Kilkenny of which locality I am very fond. Before sending it to print, I will send you a copy for your opinion, but you must not let it into the hands of Mr. Walsh. Do you think I could, at this time of day, be successful in an attempt to study Irish - if you advise me to do so, I will set about it, for I am ashamed of my ignorance of that magnificent language...

You may confide in me. No one shall ever hear a breath of what passed concerning Mr. Walsh. I am certain you have no private pique to that fool but like myself you cannot help deploring the weakness of a man who possesses some talent, some celebrity, and who I expect was possessed of, what is far better, an amiable disposition and a manly soul. But let him go. I am sorry for him, and I feel no worse towards him than you do nor have I reason to feel personal animosity to him but I cannot help regretting the infatuation which involves him and which I fear will ultimately prove ruinous to his prospects and his labours.

I am in no haste to Wed. Indeed I scarcely ever met one whom I would choose 'for better for worse.' Yet, I must soon marry, if my present avocations in life be not changed. But one thing I am certain of - I intend to have a country girl - I never will "take" a "flag-hopper" nor a "blue-stocking." Plain and unassuming in my own habits, the "bone of my bone" must not be a high-flyer.

I have had letters from various friends in England and Ireland on this morning - yet not one more welcome than your's to your

Sincere friend
John Keegan

---

[1] NLI, MS 2261, letter No. 42. A superscription on the letter reads: "Reverend P. Moore, P.P., Johnstown, Co. Kilkenny, who was intimately acquainted with Keegan, told me that he was unfortunate in business and died somewhere in the neighbourhood of Dublin. C.P. Meehan, June 6, 1883.'

(52) John Keegan to John Daly[1]

June 23rd 1846.

I do not recollect having spoken of Mr. Walsh to Mr. Meany. If I did, however, I did not speak my opinion as I did to you. At first sight, Mr. Walsh lost my esteem - perhaps without just cause - but whether or not, however, I may admire his talents, I never can love or respect the man - such are, with me, the effects of first impressions...

Could you form a company yourself for the publication of a weekly magazine. In such hands as yours aided by Mr. Walsh and a few others, it ought to be good. I think if you could once establish it you would succeed. Try the Celtic Atheneum.

(53) John Keegan to John Daly[2]

June 27th 1846.
[referring again to the idea of establishing a new magazine]

I am confident that if the thing was set about spiritedly and carried on before [...] it should succeed. Shew this letter to Mr. Walsh.*

I got on yesterday a letter from Mr. Meany excusing his apparent discourtesy in not communicating with me sooner. He was visiting in Clare. I am to have a long letter from him on tomorrow with a bundle of magazines. But tell Mr. Walsh that I will not write a line for them without the "brass." Let him do so too. I think he is well deserving of payment, and as we say down here "Its a bad day that's not worth a whistle."

*To have his opinion on the matter.

(54) John Keegan to John Daly[3]

[Postmarked July 5th 1846].

And would you believe it? Mr. Walsh honoured me too with an introductory letter in reply to my observations to you about the magazine. I suppose he was telling you.

[1] NLI, MS 2261, excerpt from *Letters* No. 33.
[2] ibid., No. 35.
[3] ibid., No. 34.

(55) John Keegan to John Daly[1]

Aug. 18th 1846.

Remember me to Mr. Walsh.

(56) John Keegan to John Daly[2]

Killeany, Aug. 20th '46.

My dear friend,

"Thou who win may laugh" and I do not envy you your mirth at the news of my marriage with an artless unsophisticated country maiden, when, had I "looked around me", I might perchance have hooked a "fifty-year-old," well skilled in the ways of the world, and competent to induct me with a coup de grace into the mysteries of the bridal chamber. I wish you much joy of your widow, but take care, my good fellow, that as she got the knack of "sowing" husbands that she does not consign you one of those days to the fate of the rotten potatoes - a fate which, bye the bye, hardier fowls than you or I have met with at the hands of "buxom widows."

I hope my Bridget is no "moderagh". I know her since her infancy. We played and danced and went to school together, and on last Saturday night (15th) we went to bed together. She is certainly not the best choice I could have made. I could have got a belle - a "dasher" with veils and chains and eke, some portion of the "yellow dirt." But because I courted Biddy, and won her heart I could not play the rascal or break my honour. I married her despite of my friends, and I hope I won't regret it. She is quiet, mild, unassuming and affectionate. She loved me for my own sake, and I vow she disclaims every wish - every desire to usurp even the liberties becoming to a wife. Indeed I think she will not be what Ireland was to the Peel government - "my chief difficulty," and I hope she will give me no cause to curse the day I met her. Her name is Collins - the fourth daughter of a small farmer (her elder sisters still unmarried) and spent her years in that routine of rustic labour peculiar to girls of her grade in Ireland. Many years ago - in our very childhood - there was an attachment between us, and, then when brighter prospects opened before me, I could not be ungrateful to her who loved me in gloomier hours. Do you approve of my conduct?

I'm surprised at you having to Ledwich so cheap - I thought it would cost three times that. I shall direct a man to call and pay you for it in the course of next week.

I despised Edward Walsh at first - I now abhor him for his ingratitude to poor Duffy. Any crime for me before ingratitude. He is an arrant rascal, that Walsh - pray never mention my name to him.

---

[1] MS 2261, excerpt from *Letters* No. 36.

[2] NLI, MS 2261, letter No. 37.

Reverend Mr Dunn [?] was not in town since. When he goes he will call to look at some books - and before he quits he will contrive to make himself known. He is a perfect gentleman - warm-hearted, and high-spirited.

I long for your forthcoming volume.

Say is my name given in connexion with the Harvest hymn? Or are there many pieces of other writers? Did you include Walsh? I fear you did.

Answer this soon. With respects to Mr Daly, and looking forward to a long-continued and friendly correspondence,

I am my dear Daly yours
John Keegan.

(57) John Keegan to John Daly[1]

Sept. 4th 1846

My dear friend,

Although, on reading your determination to exclude my poem from your forthcoming vol. I felt that sickness of heart which disappointed hopes bringeth, yet you will never find me selfish or ungrateful or unreasonable all of which I would be were I to take umbrage at my friend looking to his own interests in preference to my humour. No doubt, I would be happy, honoured, exalted at the very "idea of being seen in your book, but then when that would clash with your interest, I would blush to press myself upon you...

Although Mr. Walsh may possibly be "a man after God's own heart" he is certainly not one after mine, and though I am no incendiary I am glad that you and he have disagreed. I think that no good "true man" could deal with that stinking prig. I hated him at first sight and on my way home on the coach I wondered often how a man of your apparent stamp could tolerate his effrontery and his ignorance.

If any paper - Pilot or Freeman, should come in your road noticing the September Dolman, will you post it to me, and if necessary I would return it. I know well them two will be on my [...?] as they suspect me of "Young Irelandish" sympathies. I have even been accused by a London writer with Voltaireism, though God knows all I know of Mr. Voltaire is that he was a learned rascal, a philosophic *omedhaun* and a formidable foe to true religion.

Rev. Mr. Moore sent me last week a ballad of his own make and the groundwork of a local tale, with a request I should correspond with him regularly - I will sometimes.

---

[1] NLI, MS 2261, excerpt from *Letters* No. 38.

I never gained [...?] by C.G. Duffy or any of his party, yet I wish him well and am no foe to the others. I know nothing of their private characters - some say they are insignificant, but I look to principles not to men - down here, almost every man of intelligence, except the priests would join them.

One word more - if you retain any modern verses in your book, do not put me out. - I never wrote to Walsh but once in reply to his own letter - never will again unless a necessity should arise.

Yours faithfully
John Keegan.

[P.S.] The spectre famine is stalking over the Land - the appearance of the country is appalling.

[P.P.S.] If I was you I would call on Walsh to return my MSS and if he refuses I would either apply for legal redress or publish in the newspapers a protest against his appropriation of them to his own behoof. Of course I am not dictating to you. However, I hope Mr. D. is well. I am going on pretty fairly - the dove has driven the raven from my heart and I am tranquil. God be with you till you hear again from me.

(58) Keegan to a friend[1]

I met poor Edward Walsh by mere chance in the Northumberland Coffee-room on last Saturday. He dragged me home to see his children (four beautiful little things) and their mother - the far-famed *Bríghídín bán mo sthor*, whose praises he sang so sweetly in the song of that title, and the still more exquisite verses of *Mo Chraoibhín Cnó*. She is a sweet, simple-looking, love-inspiring woman of 26 years of age, though she looks like a *thackeen* of eighteen. She is not a belle or a *blue*, but she is well formed, speaks English prettily and Irish bewitchingly. I am almost in love with the poet's wife myself, and envy him the treasure he enjoys in the once charming and still interesting Bríghídín Sullivan of Amhan Mor. I believe she feels for me in a kindred vein, for she seems enraptured at having me at her fireside, and will not rest if I do not go every day in the week. I never spent a happier hour than at poor Walsh's, though I fear his fortunes are not looking brilliant just now. He is forty-five years of age, tall and elegant in figure, and looks the very essence of feeling and intelligence - he seems, too, like myself, to have suffered much mentally, for his face is worn and his hair is nearly thoroughly silvered. Mrs. Walsh is tall... of pale complexion,

[1] Quoted in D. J. O'Donoghue's *The Life and Writings of James C. Mangan*, p. 176.

with large blue eyes, very prominent and apparently swelled, as if with some radical disease or excessive weeping. She was in her hair, and justly has her husband described that hair when he says: -

My girl has ringlets rich and rare,

For never did lovelier hair decorate Eve herself in Eden than clusters over the fair brow of *Mo Chraoibhín Cnó*. Yet she is not [at] all a beautiful woman. She is not intellectual looking or graceful, although one must love her at first sight.

(59) Keegan to...?[1]

The Rev. C. Meehan is principal editor. Mr. E. Walsh, I am sorry to say, is discarded from its pages, and why? Guess. Because he had a difference in the Register with D.F. McCarthy, who happens to be a special favourite with the Rev. Mr. Meehan. Clarence Mangan is engaged on it, though he is a madman and a drunkard, and without a spark of religion. Worth your while to see Clarence Mangan. I met him in Dublin. He is about forty-two years of age, pale face, little cat-like eyes, sleepy in his appearance, and slovenly, sottish, and clownish in exterior. He is a man of magnificent talent, but of no originality of conception.

(60) To the editor of the *Nation*[2]

Cork,
Aug. 26th 1850.

Sir, In your last number there is a brief memoir of the late Edward Walsh, "one of the most gifted of our National poets." He was head teacher in the Cork workhouse, where he contracted his death illness by too close and zealous a discharge of his humble yet arduous duties. He has left a widow and four young children, friendless and pennyless.

Are you aware that his widow has in vain applied to the guardians of this union for a small grant to enable her and her orphan children to emigrate to America - and that in consequence of their refusal, she and her orphans are now numbered among the inmates of this pauper establishment? The guardians refused the widow's prayer, because to grant it would be a violation of some law, certainly not the law of charity.

---

[1] Quoted in D. J. O'Donoghue's *The Life and Writings of James C. Mangan*, p. 177.

[2] Published in *The Nation*, Saturday, August 31st 1850, with the following comment from the editor: 'If the writer of this letter refer to the last NATION, he will find that his proposal has been anticipated, and a subscription list opened.'

They finally disposed of the question by passing a bald resolution, expressing their sympathy for her sufferings; and their testimony to the zeal and efficiency of her departed husband. And thus the matter rests, and she and her children are consigned to all the horrors and degradation of workhouse existence.

Is it possible that this lady and her children will be suffered thus to perish? I believe with you "that the orphans of such men become the wards of the people" - and therefore I beg of you to give this text a practical meaning - originate a subscription for them.

A few pounds will enable Mrs. Walsh to carry out her project of emigrating to America, where she feels confident of supporting her orphans by the fruits of her industry. Commence this good and generous work - it needs only a beginning. Do you originate it. I have no fears for the result.

A Confederate.

(61) To the Editor of the *Nation*[1]

One who knew poor Edward Walsh well, and who had peculiar facilities of observing his character since he became an official of the Cork workhouse, has written to a friend of his the following summary of the duties which devolved upon him there, and of the way in which he discharged them: - He held as you are aware, the office of Schoolmaster in the workhouse for the last two years, which were years of great misery, and, as a consequence, great labour was imposed on all engaged in the details of administering relief to the poor. No ordinary share of labour devolved on Mr. Walsh. He did not shrink from it, but plied his daily task of toil, with a diligence and patience beyond all praise. I have seen him day after day with untiring energy, endeavouring to enlighten the ignorance, to tame the ferocity, and humanize the savageness, of the masses placed under his care. He has frequently had in the workhouse school as many as 1,200 boys. The great majority of this large number were brought up in ignorance, exposed to all the demoralizing influences which extreme poverty is sure to exercise, and quite unaccustomed to restraint or discipline of any kind. To leaven such a mass as this is no small task, and yet he succeeded, but the success coast him dear. His life was the price at which success was purchased. You know, better even than I do, the gentleness of his nature, and the delicacy of constitution, upon which labour such as he undertook would make terrible inroads. His widow, within a few days it may be, of her confinement, and three very young children, have to bewail the loss of a husband and parent, sacrificed in a holy cause truly, but still sacrificed. An application was made to the guardians by Mrs. Walsh for some aid to enable her to emigrate. The application was

[1] Published in the *Nation*, Saturday, August 31st 1850.

refused, because to grant it would be illegal, but the refusal was conveyed in a resolution admitting the justice of the claim, and paying a just tribute to her husband's memory.

(62) Board of Guardians to Correspondent[1]

Dec. 19th 1850.

Sir,

In reply to your letter of the 17th. inst. No 68893/50 adverting to letter of the 15th. August respecting increase of Assistant Schoolmaster salary, I beg to inform you that there were no advertisements issued but that the increase was reached in this manner -

When Mr. Walsh the late schoolmaster died the Board of G [uardians] appointed his suc [cessor] at £40 a year, that is £10 less than Mr. Walsh got and it was then proposed that as the assistant schoolmaster conducted himself very satisfactorily, and as he would be left in charge of the boys in the workhouse as the head schoolmaster is to be sent in care of the boys to the farm (that his salary of £20 should be increased by the amount of the reduction in the headmaster's salary.

I have the honour
W. Stanley Esq.

(63) To Charles J. Kickham[2]

I saw your friend, Mrs. Walsh, several times last week. Her little daughter, a most interesting child of twelve, being ill, I volunteered my services, and as the poor woman was unable to pay a doctor, and too proud to apply for relief at the dispensary, she entrusted her to my care. It is lamentable to see a woman of such a soul and such a heart suffering so much privation. She is dependent on her needle alone for the daily assistance of herself and two children; and though an experienced workwoman, her poverty debars her from profitable employment. Few indeed would wish to be seen walking in the streets where she is compelled to drag on life. Her lodging is the "wretched garret of a wretched locality." Are there no friends of Edward Walsh to undertake the publication (it could be done by subscription) of a volume of his poems and legends, in order to rescue her whose love was the sunshine of his existence, from a fate like this? As if there should be no circumstance wanting to awake sympathy for the widow of Edward Walsh, his eldest son, "poor Adam", is a sailor boy!

---

[1] CIA, Board of Guardians *Letter Book*, Cork Union, Ref. BG 69 B I.

[2] The *Celt*, Dec. 26th 1857, p. 340. The person in question is probably Dr. McSwiney/McSweeney.

(64) Brighid (Mrs.) Walsh to the *Cork Examiner*[1]

I trust and pray that this just tribute to his memory - prompted by a good Providence - may bring a blessing on all who aid the work.

To me it will be a tremendous happiness, during the remainder of my life, to feel he was not forgotten by his countrymen whom he loved so much, and whose good opinion he prized so highly.

(65) To the Editor of the *Cork Examiner*[2]

Charleville,
June 15th 1858.

Dear Sir,
I beg to enclose my subscription to the monument to Edward Walsh, to which, from the bottom of my heart, I wish God speed.

Poor Walsh, highly gifted as he was, as an original poet, was scarcely less distinguished as the brilliant translator of many of the beautiful Irish poems of the illustrious Shan Clarach. It may be interesting at the present time to mention, that the latter, who flourished more than a century since, is buried in what was once the aisle of the ancient church of Ballysally, near this town. His grave is marked by a plain but massive block of limestone. This, in the lapse of time, had fallen forward and sunk so much, as barely to leave the poet's name visible over the luxuriant turf. Some years ago I had it raised and fixed in what I supposed was its original position; it bears the following inscription: -

Iohanes McDonald cogno
minatus Clarach vir vere
Catholicus et tribus linguis
ornatus nempe Graeca Latina
et Hybernica non Vulgaris
Ingenii poeta tumulatur
ad hunc cippum; obit Aetatis
Anno 63 Salutis 1754 -
Requiescat in Pace

---

[1] *Cork Examiner*, June 16th. 1858. The letter was prefaced with the following: "A letter has been received from Mrs. Walsh in reference to the intended monument to her late husband's memory. In it she says: - [letter follows].

[2] *Cork Examiner*, June 18th 1858.

which may be freely rendered thus, for the convenience of your lady readers: - "John McDonald, surnamed Claurach, a true Catholic, skilled in three languages - to wit, Greek, Latin, and Irish - and a poet of rare genius is buried near this stone. He died in the 63rd. year of his age in the year of Grace, 1754. May he rest in peace."

I am, dear Sir, yours very truly,
C. J. T.

(66) McCarthy Downing to Ralph Varian & W. Carroll[1]

Prospect House,
Skibbereen,
June 15th 1858.

Dear Sir,

I have much pleasure in enclosing you my mite towards the erection of a monument, to mark the spot where so true a heart as that of Edward Walsh's is laid.

Faithfully Yours,
McCarthy Downing.

Messrs R. Varian & W. Carroll.

(67) Correspondent to the *Nation*[2]

Cork,
Jan. 1st 1859.

I have just returned from a visit to the Mathew Cemetery; I went there to see the monument to Edward Walsh; it is erected within the second gateway, and towards the right

---

[1] *Cork Examiner*, June 18th 1858.

[2] The letter was published in the *Nation* on January 8th. 1859 under the headline "The Monument to Edward Walsh" prefaced thus by the editor: "In the following letter there is one omission of some moment; our correspondent does not state what we know to be the fact - that mainly to the exertions of one true-hearted gentleman in Cork, whose love of country is as strong as his attachment to literature, this monument to Edward Walsh has been raised. That gentleman is Mr. Ralph Varian; his efforts in this undertaking, while they but evidence his warm patriotism and regard for the Bards of Celtic song, will elicit for him the grateful thanks of every Irishman who admires the genius of him over whose ashes this beautiful memorial has been raised."

of Father Mathew's grave as you enter the ground. Mid winter though it is, it seemed a mild day in early spring; the sun shone brightly, and the 'dew of high noontide' hung about the grey trees and green laurels. The simple grey limestone cross, which marks the grave of Father Mathew, stood out in grandeur high above the grave of the 'Apostle of Temperance' relieved against the majestic cedar tree which spread over its dark foliage behind it, and sheltered by the solemn cypress trees, the glittering laurels and the cheerful laurestina shrubs, even now in flower. At the foot of the cross several poor people were bent in prayer over the grave of their sainted Father Mathew. I stepped reverently to the side, by a giant tree that spread its arms over the pathway and the inner ivied wall, and pursued my way over the green mound, and through the evergreen shrubs to the grave of Edward Walsh - and here the sculptured white lime stone of the Celtic Cross that stands over the grave, glittered like white marble in the sun rays; and the beautiful tracery of the shaft, the cross, and the circle; in fine, intricate interlaced work, which is characteristic of Ancient Irish Art, was admirably thrown out by the light and shade at play upon it. The Celtic cross is almost a literal transcript of one of the two celebrated ancient crosses at Kilklispeen, county Kilkenny. Mr. O'Leary, the draughtsman who kindly made the working drawing for the stone-cutter, deviated a little from the original; on the boxes of the centre and arms of the Cross, he placed a few shamrocks - these have a pleasing and appropriate effect, and at the base of the shaft he introduced a small bit of Grecian ornamentation - a decided error. Ancient Irish Art owed nothing to Grecian Art. It came to maturity, not by imitation, nor by introduction from without, but by the growth of its own living principles. It was distinct, national and complete in itself; and borrowed nothing and stole nothing. It attained its perfection before the thirteenth century, and declined rapidly after the partial subjugation of the Island by the English Power. It belonged to the island even before the Christian era; and these very Crosses, with the circle connecting the arms and the shaft, were in this land in the Ossian years.

But for this one error - the Grecian cross towards the base of the shaft - this Celtic cross over the grave of Edward Walsh, viewed from the side which is sculptured, and which faces the head of the grave, might be pronounced perfect in its pictorial effect. The ornamentation of the shaft of the cross ends appropriately with the initials E.W. in the Celtic characters, beautifully interlaced. The fine block of limestone from which this cross has been sculptured was cut from the celebrated diamond quarry of Ballintemple. The whole cross - shaft, arms, and circle - is carried from the one block of stone. There is no joining in it. It rests on a rough base, as the ancient crosses usually did; and in the base are inserted two tablets of white marble with the inscription to the memory of Edward Walsh, in English on one, in the Gaelic on the other. These are the inscriptions -

Eadbhard Breathnach,
An file agus an Fir-Eirionnach,

D'éag an séisreadh lá do mhí Lúghnasa, MDCCCL.

'San m-bliadhan ceathrachad agus cúig d'a aois.
Do tógbhadh an chros-Liag so,
Mar leacht-cuimhne do, le a chárdaibh agus le lucht,
Ag a ribh móir-mheas air.
Go d-tugaidh DIA suaimhneas siorruidhe da anam.

EDWARD WALSH,
The poet and Translator,
Died August, 1850. Aged 45 years.

Erected to his Memory, by a few admirers of the
Patriot and the Bard.

God rest his soul!

(The beautiful Gaelic type of THE NATION gave the model of the letters of this inscription.)

It is to be regretted that the other side of the Celtic cross is not sculptured. All the ancient Irish crosses were beautifully wrought at both sides. And the two sides never corresponded exactly in design; but the sculptors of them displayed in their work a fine variety and fertility of invention. However, it is to be presumed that the committee which superintended the erection of this would have had it richly ornamented at the back as it is at the front, if the funds entrusted to them for the purpose had been more abundant. As it stands, it is an ornament to the Mathew Cemetery, and far surpasses in design and workmanship any of the more costly tombs.

It is a fact, which the Editor of THE NATION will be glad to learn, that the idea of erecting this monument, and the subscription for the purpose, originated with some of the workingmen of Cork.

Some time since a gentleman writing to one of our Irish papers, related that on arriving at a hotel in this city, one of the first questions he asked was, 'Where was Gerald Griffin's grave?' and that they could not inform him. He hired a jaunting car; but the driver was as ignorant as the hotelkeeper. At length he recollected having read in Griffin's life that he had died at the North Monastery, and accordingly he had himself driven there, where he saw within the enclosed pasture and village grounds of the monastery, on a green hillside overlooking the city, undistinguished from the few simple head-stones of the now deceased members of the religious order, to which he belonged in his latter years, that stand by its side, the little grey head-stone which marks the grave of 'Brother Gerald Griffin.'

It is gratifying to think that the working men of Cork have, in this instance, taken the lead to remove such like ignorance, by the erection of a suitable monument, in a public cemetery, over the grave of one who contributed some of our sweetest lyrics to the adornment of our native literature, and who dedicated to *them* his volume of *Irish Popular Songs* thus - 'To the People of Ireland, as a tribute to their many virtues, and with ardent admiration of their high poetic genius, as evinced in their songs and legends, this volume is inscribed by their friend and countryman, Edward Walsh.'

Let me express a hope that the people of Cork will, during the year which is opening on us, erect in the Mathew Cemetery a Celtic Cross, dedicated to the memory of J.J. Callanan, a Cork man, who was a poet and a translator from the Gaelic - and of Gerald Griffin, one of our sweetest poets.

I cannot conclude without a word of commendation for the beautiful chisel-work of Mr. Samuel Daly, of Cook Street, Cork, as displayed upon this Celtic Cross to the memory of Edward Walsh.

(68) Patrick Traynor to Peter Roe[1]

29 Essex Quay,
Dublin.
Mar. 24th 1883.

Sir,

From amongst many of Edward Walsh's letters in my possession, I send you four which I have selected for insertion in your new edition of his *Irish Popular Songs*.

These letters are most characteristic of the meekness of the poor fellow in the dark hours of his homeless adversity; in them are to be found traces of the poetic, patriotic, and most tender domestic feelings as well as a spirit of Christian resignation and humility under a load of undeserved punishment.

Poor Walsh! with great talents and goodness of heart, his life experiences in his own dear Isle were anything but pleasurable.

As you aided him in putting his first edition through the press, I don't wonder at your being so anxious to make this edition an interesting and successful one.

With best wishes for the realization of your hopes in connection with the re-issue of Walsh's *Irish Popular Songs*.

Yours,
Patrick Traynor.

---

[1] Published in *Irish Popular Songs*, (2nd ed. 1883) p. 33.

(69) J.S.S to-?[1]

Well we remember (though now forty years since) following Walsh in the twilight of an autumn evening, drinking in the odd chords that came from the little harp that lay on his left arm as he wandered, lonely and unknown, by the then desert, Jones's-road, or reposed himself on one of the seats that at that time were outside the walls of Clonliffe House. It was then we first heard *Casadh an t-Súgáin*, 'The Twisting of the Rope' - that beautiful air to which Moore adapted the no less beautiful words, 'How dear to me the hour when Daylight dies!' We have ever known a difficulty in singing the words of the great poet to the air - there is none in Walsh's version; but then *it* is the pure vintage, and words and music come from the same source.

[1] Walsh, E., *Irish Popular Songs* (2nd. Ed.), p. iv. I have been unable to find the identity of J.S.S. other than speculating that he may be a Surgeon O'Sullivan.

PART THREE

FOLKLORE

& OTHER PROSE WORKS

1
The Midwife[1]

Now cast your eyes around while I dissolve,
The mists and films that mortal eyes involve;
Purge from your sight the dross and make you see,
The shape of each avenging Deity.
Dryden's Virgil.

'Twas on a bright Sunday morning in the latter days of June, that the congregation began to thicken fast, in the neighbourhood of Kiskeam Chapel, the whitewashed walls of the sacred edifice waxed brighter in the rays of the summer sun, over the right bank of the Araglen, whose waters meandering along their green and beautiful banks, appeared in the reflection of the sun, like islets of light gleaming amid an emerald sea, till sweeping round the oak crowned cliff of Daniel the Outlaw, they receded from the sight. The sombre hue of the surrounding mountains was relieved by groups of the peasantry, directing their steps across the purple heather, from every direction towards the chapel, the lively appearance of the females adding greatly to the beauty of the scene.

Among a group that basked in the long grass of the chapel yard, waiting the arrival of the Rev. Father McNaughton, was placed Tim Murphy. Tim was an old man, of infinite humour, and keen remark, the oracle of the hamlet where he resided, and his memory the storehouse of legendary lore, his grey locks hung negligently over his decent frieze coat, the head of his Clegh-alpeen was neatly set with bright brass nails, while the red worsted garters surmounting the blue woollen stockings, just below the knee of the old fashioned breeches, spoke one determined to maintain the fashion of the olden days, in contempt of modern innovations.

---

[1] Published in *The Dublin Penny Journal*, February 16th 1833. Initialled, E.W. It is the first in a series entitled "Popular Legends of the South," and is the first known publication by the author. The legend of *The Midwife* was still told in Kiskeam in my young days, and Danny Guiney of Knocknenaugh, a ganger with the Co. Council, told me that Nell Connor's 'mounting stone' - used to facilitate getting on a horse – was, in his time, still *in situ* in the townland of Islandbrack. Like so many other reliques of the past it has yielded it place to 'progress'. Edward Walsh also wrote a versified version of the tale, but I have been unable to locate it in print. Michael Cronin (*Mockie*) of Knockeenacurrig, recited the opening lines for me:

From Kiskeam to Ballydonnor
Known to all was Nellie Connor;
Midwife to the country round her
Skilful every mother found her;
To Nellie Connor gave no trouble,
Single births or even double. - Ed.

"In truth Nell you were the decent girl when you and I danced a *moneen* together at Cullin, 43 years ago, come next Lateeren's day, many an ould body an' a young one too, wished us married, and said we were the smartest couple on the green, though now we're ould an' stiff, glory be to God."

This apostrophe was directed by Tim to an old woman with a black patch over her right eye, who just had entered the chapel gate, and was directing her tottering steps beyond the circle that surrounded Tim Murphy. She had been time out of mind, the midwife of the neighbouring districts, and though she never studied any of those volumes that treat of the obstetric art, Nell gave universal satisfaction in the way of her profession.

"I wonder" said an arch wag, with a laughter-loving eye, "I wonder Tim, as Nell and you were such a pretty pair of dancers, an' well acquainted av' coorse, that you took no notion to get at the *blind side of her*."

"Arra Andy a vhic," answered Tim, "it does not become the like o' you to crack jokes at elderly people: - your days are not over yet, *ma bochal*, and your own father, God rest his soul in glory; if he lived could say that he saw Nell Connor with two bright blue eyes, till one of the *good people*, at the fair of Millstreet struck out her right eye, with the point of his switch. God between hearers and harm!"

"Never mind the *Dhalteen*," said a voice in the group, "give him up to the clargy; we long to hear how Nell Connor, poor dear woman, lost her eye."

"Why then in less than no time," said Tim, directing his eyes round the circle of anxious auditors, "you shall hear it word for word as it left Nell's mouth, at ould Andrew Hickey's wake, when that young joker there, young Andy with his *gography* and *wild book keeping*, was but a broth of a gomulack, not cute enough to roast a brohogue."

After a hem or two, Tim commenced his narration, the substance of which is as follows: The family of Nell Connor had all retired to bed, on a wet stormy December night, when a loud knocking at the door, and a strange shrill voice demanding the midwife's attendance on a *sick woman*, aroused the inmates from their slumber, the rain pattered against the single pane that formed the only window of the apartment, and the wind whistled mournfully through the chinks of its mud wall. Nell, ever faithful to the duties of her profession, rose unreluctantly, flung her mantle of frieze on her shoulders, and opened the door. "This is a fearful wild night, to venture abroad in," said she, accosting a tall, dark looking man, mounted on a fine grey horse, "but it is strange a cushla I don't know ye; have we far to go?" "Not far," said the dark man, in a super-human tone that thrilled to the midwife's soul. He caught her hand; and Nell felt herself raised as light as a feather into the pinion behind him. They shot along with the lightning's rapidity; and though a pitchy darkness enveloped earth and heaven, the grey horse moved with sure and steady speed. After passing many a hollow dell and rising moor land, during which no sound betrayed the tramp of the horse's hoofs they came to the banks of the swollen and rapid Araglen: - the roaring rush of the muddy river, the blue gleam of the lightning flashing over its troubled wave, and the fitful moaning of the savage blast, struck terror to the midwife's heart. "God and the blessed Virgin preserve me," she exclaimed in a paroxysm of despair; and the hollow cliff that part the dashing waters reverberated the sounds.

"Utter these names again, and abide the consequences," said the mysterious horseman angrily; then plunging into the wild stream, "be silent," he continued, "and fear nothing, though you were sailing in a turf kish on the broad sea." Gaining the opposite bank, they drove at the same rapid rate with which they at first set forward, till they reached the fort of Doon, which Nell well recognized, as the rising moon flung her pale melancholy light athwart the horizon. Alighting from his horse, the tall dark man struck the ground with his foot, which opening, discovered a long flight of steps that led into the bosom of the earth, he instantly descended, and called upon his terrified companion to follow him. They entered a winding passage that led into a lofty hall, illuminated with burning tapers. The tables groaned beneath the splendid feast, the unearthly thrilling of the melting harp, stole softly on the ear, while a circle of lovely ladies and polished gentlemen flew through all the mazes of the dance, to the stirring sound of the "brisk awakening viol," these were the prominent sights that caught Nell's attention, as her conductor led her hastily through the hall, to an inner chamber, where lay the female, whom she was called on to assist in travail. After Nell had announced the birth of a fine boy, the tall dark man, who still remained in the room, gave her a vessel, containing a greenish ointment, with which he ordered her to anoint the new-born babe from head to foot, but he cautioned her to suffer none of it to touch any part of her except the hand that performed the operation. When this unction was concluded, and the child dressed and laid in a superb cradle, Nell Connor feeling a certain twitching sensation in her right eye, instinctively clapped her hand to that organ when she perceived the objects in the chamber suddenly to undergo a strong metamorphosis, and assume an indefinable two-fold appearance, in which the true and unreal were blended together in an indescribable way. She rightly considered that this arose from the virtue of the *ointment*, which gave her right eye the facility of seeing the things of this strange souterrain in their proper shape; upon closing her left eye all this delusion vanished. The beautiful "lady in the straw," appeared a withered hag; the lovely boy a shapeless cross-grained squaller; and the all mysterious horseman was suddenly changed into a little red-haired chap, of three feet high, wearing a comical red cap - his deformed skinny mouth, extended from ear to ear, and his restless piercing eyes seemed to search the midwife's soul, whenever she met their malignant regard. "Nell Connor," said the little red-haired man, "I feel obliged by your civility; and here is a trifle for your trouble," so saying, he put into her hand what seemed to her *left eye* to be two bright pieces of gold; but which the *right one* detected as two ivy leaves, clipped round all the edges. In passing out, the hall and its guests were sadly altered: - the polished gentlemen and lovely ladies were short red-capped fellows and deformed belles-dames. Instead of delicious music, mere villainous discordant sounds; and the bright tapers were twinkling rush-lights; upon entering into moon-light, the "gallant grey" that travelled so fleetly to Doon, proved nothing more than the *beam of an old plough*, which had lain since the preceding spring across the stone gap at the corner of Nell's cabin; quaking with terror she mounted behind her conductor. The beam performed its part to admiration, outstripped the passing wind - recrossed the roaring Araglen, and, after some hard cantering over marsh and moor land, set Nell Connor down pretty much to her satisfaction, at her own door, as the *March cock* upon the roost within proclaimed the decline of the tardy night.

Millstreet fair happened on the next day; and Nell Connor having business there, was surprised on entering the town, to see her little red haired acquaintance busily employed in selecting and carrying off the choicest cows, and substituting in their stead, clods or stones, or other inanimate things, which in the strict resemblance they were made to bear to the animals thus abstracted, deceived every mortal eye but Nell's: she attentively watched his progress during the busy afternoon; at length she entered a crowded tent, where sat a fine looking country girl, and her sweet-heart, refreshing themselves with a cake, and a glass of punch; the busy purloiner of the cows approached the maiden, and thrusting a *thraneen* up her nostril, caused her to sneeze three successive times; he "grinned horrible a ghastly smile," at the first and second sneeze, but at the third, when Nell Connor exclaimed, "Christ and the Blessed Virgin between you an' the evil one, ma colleen bawn," the disappointed fairy gnashed his teeth in anger; his malignant eyes beamed with fury, and darting, like the lightning's flash, through the guests of the crowded tent, to the spot where Nell Connor stood, and striking out her right eye with the point of his switch, immediately disappeared.

At the conclusion of this singular legend, the influx of the crowd to the chapel gate, announced the priest's arrival; the reclining group were soon in motion, and Tim's auditors reluctantly retired to hear Mass.

2
St. Lateerin[1]

"When the *slua-shee*[2] appear in lonely dell,
And revels are rife when mortals dream,
And wizards behold - but dare not tell
The spells that are wrought by haunted stream:

"When the *shee-geehy*[3] rolls its boding cloud,
And arrows unseen in vengeance fly;
When the voice of the *keener* is wild and loud
O'er the maiden that died by the evil eye:

"When the art of the midwife fails to save
The young mother doom'd to *fairy fort*;
When the traveller's lur'd beneath the wave,
Where *Donall na Geela* keeps his court:

"What saves in the hour of faery,
When goblins awake and gnomes have sway?
What scatters the ranks of the dread *slua-shee*,
That circle the midnight traveller's way?

"Supreme o'er the spirits of earth and sea,
When blessed Lateerin's name is spoken, -
The Druid enchantments fade and flee,
And the spell of the midnight hour is broken.

"Thro' regions remote extends her fame,
And many a clime and age can tell,
What pilgrims invoking her holy name,
Drank health at the flow of her *sainted well*!"

---

[1] Published in the *Dublin Penny Journal*, May 4th 1833. Initialled, E.W. It is the third story in the series "Popular Legends of the South." - Ed.

[2] Slua Shee - Fairy Host.

[3] Shee Geehy - Fairy wind or tempest - those whirling eddies which raise dust, straw, etc. and are supposed by the country people to be caused by the fairies.

These lines are a literal translation of the fragment of a song, which rose to a wild and melancholy air amid the tombs and gravestones of Cullin, as I passed through that little village on a fine evening in autumn. The abrupt and irregular spirit of the original Irish, which I have vainly endeavoured to preserve in these stanzas, the stillness of the evening air, the echoes of the holy ruins around, the voice where strength and wild sweetness blended, and which to a fanciful mind, would seem that some supernatural being (for this singer among the tombs remained unseen,) - all conveyed an impulse to my heart which the boasted art of a Catalini[1] would fail of communicating. Alighting from my horse, I clambered over the *stile* into the churchyard, towards the quarter whence the voice proceeded, and discovered my supernatural vocalist in the person of a wild looking country fellow of twenty-two, wearing a broad-brimmed hat made of that particular grass called *thraneen*, and equipped in a tight pair of sheepskin *inexpressibles*. He was stretched at full length along a grass-grown monument, and beat time with a formidable clegh-alpeen, to the music of his wild song on the timeworn slab that surmounted this ancient tomb.

I had travelled across the steep mountains, along the course of the river Araglen, and was anxious to procure the assistance of a *smith*, the horse on which I rode having left a fore-shoe in one of the deep swamps of Pobble O'Keeffe - "Hillo, friend," said I, "have the kindness to direct me to the next smith's forge."

He ceased his song at the sound of my voice, and seeing a well-dressed person before him, mechanically as it were, started on his legs and took off his broad-leafed hat. I always detest that prostration of spirit, which our peasantry too frequently betray by doffing the *caubeen* to broad cloth without reference to the merit of the wearer, so I bid him be covered, with a rather bitter remark upon his meanness of deportment that sent the glow of sensibility to tinge his deeply embrowned cheek.

"Bless your sowl, Sir," said he upon repeating my interrogation respecting the smith's forge, "from whince did you come to enquire for a forge at Cullin? Sure everybody knows that all the coals in Cork, and the *bellowses* o' Munster wouldn't hate iron after the curse of blessed Lateerin."

"Who is blessed Lateerin, and why did she give the curse?"

"O! its myself knows all about it, - often an' many's the time I heard the *Deerhogh*[2] tell it to the strangers that ped rounds at the well forninst you there; but sure a poor *spalapeen* like me, saving your presence, a'nt fit to talk to a dacint jantleman about blessed saints, an' sich things."

I took my seat on the old tomb, and bidding him sit beside me, encouraged him to proceed.

---

[1] Catalini (*recte*: Catalani), 1780-1846, an Italian soprano with a voice of extraordinary quality and range. – Ed.

[2] A Deerhogh is an old woman that takes care of the well and shows others the manner of paying the rounds. She is supported by the donations of Pilgrims.

"Why, Sir, long ago, whin saints an' monasteries were in vogue, three blessed sisters lived in this country, the eldest at Kilmeen, the other at Drumtarif, and Lateerin, the youngest, at Cullin. She kept in a *skalp* here where the ould walls of the church are, an' her business night an' day was praying to God, and curing all the sick that were brought to her far an' near."

Here he called my attention to a clear spring in a small meadow, contiguous to the churchyard. It was shaded by an ancient whitethorn, which presented a strange appearance, every part of it being covered with threads of various colours, which were fastened to the branches by the numerous crowds that had fulfilled their votive pilgrimages to the well.

"That well, they say, sprung up to give her water; and when she wanted to cook the dinner, for she couldn't always be fasting an' praying, she would bring the *seed of the fire* in the fould of her petticoat from the smith's forge, for the houses were very scarce at Cullin thin, by all accounts. The three blessed sisters visited each other reg'lar wance a week; and the holy angels of heaven, honour an' praise be to 'em, made a fine road one night from Kilmeen to Cullin through Drumtarif, because the poor ladies wint barefooted, and the passage was full of wild brakes and deep quagmires.[1] After Lateerin wint to heaven, this blessed well got great vartue from God in the cure of all disorders. The 24th of July is her pathern day, and, ma vrone, thin the blind and the lame get their walk an' seeing here; - sure it was only the last pathern that a poor disabled crather left thim *crutches* there at the well behind him, and galloped home on two good legs like a Mayboy."

"But about the curse - "

"O! is it the curse you mane? Musha, you're right, Sir, didn't I tell you afore; I have no *gumption*, and am a mere *omedhaun* at telling a story.

"Lateerin, Sir, was the youngest of her sisters, as I said a while agone; and, as they say, was a purty, tidy woman, considering a saint, and when she wanted a spark of fire, she always put the coal in her petticoat. The smith could not forbear noticing her legs that for all her fasting were as smooth and as white as ivory, but respect for the blessed saint kept him silent a long time. But one day as she put the living coal into her petticoat as usual to light her fire, the smith said, 'Lateerin, you have a beautiful pair of legs.' The poor saint who never thought of her beauty afore, looked down to see if the smith spoke truth, whin, God bless us! the petticoat caught fire and her garments blazed about her. In her grief and lamentation for the fault, she prayed that Cullin might never again have a smith to tempt the innocent to sin, and though many made the attempt, no iron would *redden* in all the townland from that day to this."

I arose and pursued my way towards Millstreet, and have only to add, that I made close inquiry respecting this strange opinion, and found that though the place is well situated for a *smithy*, being a country village, and a place of much resort, having a chapel, a burying ground and some public houses; it is said that every attempt to carry on the smith's trade at Cullin has proved ineffectual, nor has any forge been seen there within living memory.

---

[1] The remains of an ancient paved way may be traced between the places - it extends to the distance of ten English miles.

3
Daniel the Outlaw.[1]

In the "Legend of the Midwife," which appeared in the 34th. Number of the *Dublin Penny Journal*, I saw an allusion made to the "Oak-crowned cliff of Daniel the Outlaw.' It speedily re-called to my memory, the bye-gone days when that cliff and its surrounding hills and streams were the scenes of my early youth; when at the "noisy mansion" of Phil Sullivan, near the bank of the silver Ariglin, I received my first ideas of chivalry and romance from the perusal of the "Seven Champions of Christendom," - of gallant enterprise and warlike stratagem, from the "Irish Rogues and Rapparees" - and my early fostered and long-matured hatred of tyranny, from the "Genuine History of Ireland." These volumes would be now disregarded; but can the coolness of judgment atone for pleasures enjoyed in the warmth of youthful fancy? I have been delighted to lie for hours together in the Outlaw's retreat of the cliff - to regard in musing mood, the compartments of the rock which tradition had assigned to his solitary fire, his sword and gun, - to conjure up the days when the decayed oaks of the steep cliff cast their umbrageous protection round the rock of his repose; when his shrill silver whistle roused his faithful band to the call of their chief: here I rehearsed all that tradition has preserved of his matchless prowess and "hair-breadth escapes." I shall sketch his story. The recollection of the time when his tale of truth first struck my ear, still affords me a melancholy pleasure. Days of my youth, why have you given place to years which have stamped the premature wrinkle on my brow? But you shall ever lie in the waste of my memory, refreshing as the green neighbourhood of the wells mid the sands of the desert to the weary eye to the African traveller.

The story of Daniel O'Keefe, surnamed the outlaw, is involved in much obscurity. He was, it seems, a follower of that O'Keefe, who, when driven by the Roches from Fermoy, obtained large possessions in these western districts, and that having accidentally slain McDonough, the chieftain of Duhallow, he was forced to betake himself to these mountain fastnesses to shun the vengeance of McDonough's powerful clan. At length having associated with him a band of daring spirits, he gave proof of his Milesian hatred of the Saxon invader, in bold and desperate outrages on the possessions of the intruders on the native right of the Gael. His daring enterprises and extraordinary escapes from the frequent parties of soldiers sent in pursuit of him, and the protection he afforded the weak and defenceless, are yet the theme of many an Irish song. The outlaw himself was a polished scholar and poet; and fragments of his verses yet survive among the more aged dwellers of the glens.

---

[1] Published in *The Dublin Penny Journal*, May, 18th 1833. Initialled 'W'. Charles Gavan Duffy acknowledges Edward Walsh as the author in his *Appreciation*, published in the *Nation*, September 7th 1850. - Ed.

The common mode of depredation practised by this freebooter was to carry off Creaghs, or whole herds of cattle from the enemy until a sufficient sum was sent for their release. The deep glens surrounding his retreat in the cliff, screened the booty, taken in his predatory excursions, from the closest search; but the cave of Gortmore, by the river Blackwater, about fourteen miles from Kiskeam, was his most usual place of resort, because its vicinity to Mallow, then the great thoroughfare between the north and south, and its immediate proximity to the lands of the stranger, rendered it an excellent centre of operation. Likewise, this retreat could afford full security against all attacks. On the side of a huge cliff that fearfully overhangs its base, gaped the opening of the cave; the river which has since receded from the rock, then rolled its wild waters along its base. From the water's edge a few rude steps cut in the limestone rock, led into the cave, but from every other side it was wholly inaccessible. The reader will form an idea of the importance of this retreat, as it could be approached only in a boat or by swimming; and the cave, as tradition relates, extends for many a mile beneath St. Hillary's hills.

Daniel the outlaw had a female companion to soften the horrors of this dark dwelling and share his life of depredation and danger - her name was Margaret Kelly. She is said to have been extremely beautiful, and O'Keefe loved her with a long and faithful affection; but the temptation of a large reward offered for his head, induced her to betray him. It was she who generally procured him provisions from the neighbouring town of Mallow; and she always crossed the river in a boat which was kept concealed in the cave. She agreed one day with the commanding officer at Mallow, to betray O'Keefe into his hands. A few soldiers were to be stationed convenient to the landing-place on the opposite bank, and when the outlaw, on the next occasion, had conveyed his perfidious messenger in the light skiff over the river in her way to town, the soldiers were to shoot him from their place of concealment on his return to the cave. For this service she received an acknowledgement entitling her to the reward on the outlaw's death or apprehension. After concluding this horrid compact, she returned to the cave, when O'Keefe, in a moment of soft dalliance, gently put his hand into her bosom, and was horror stricken to find the parchment that confirmed to the beloved of his heart the price of his blood, and urged to madness at her detestable perfidy, he plunged his skein into her bosom, and she expired with a single groan.

This celebrated freebooter was endued with great swiftness. In one of his southern excursions, being detached from his band and alone, he fell in with a party of horse troops, and was pursued for many miles. He ran towards Gortmore cave, and the troopers pressing close upon him as he reached the fearful cliffs that overhang the broad Blackwater, he bounded at a spring from a rock to the opposite bank; his pursuers durst not follow him. A woman who witnessed this extraordinary feat, exclaimed, in the Irish tongue, - "How great is thy leap, O! man of wonder;" and he quaintly replied - "It is trifling, compared with the length of the run."

Being seized with a violent fever in a wild district to the west of Millstreet, he was betrayed by his nurse-tender. O'Keefe was yet unable to quit his bed, when the hovel to which he was confined was surrounded by armed men; he was wrapped in his blanket and laid upon a cart, to which he was fastened down by strong ropes. The soldiers concluded he was dying, and were the less watchful of their prisoner. Upon reaching Mallow he cut the cords that held him down with the sword which lay close at his side during his illness and which the soldiers had not perceived as they bore him from the bed. His sudden rush from the cart and the bright flashing of his steel, filled them with astonishment; and in the moment of their irresolution and dismay he effected his escape.

At length the hour that was to terminate the career of this extraordinary man approached. A person in whom he reposed great trust, unable to resist the rewards offered for his apprehension, invited O'Keeffe to partake of his hospitality, that he might betray his guest. This man communicated his intention to his wife, who used every means of persuasion to induce him to forego his base design, but in vain - and upon leaving home for the purpose of bringing a strong party to seize O'Keeffe, he bound her on oath to conceal the treachery from the confiding outlaw. In the course of some time, O'Keefe finding himself thirsty, desired to drink and his hostess brought a draught of new-milk. Upon his expressing a wish to have the draught warmed, she pointedly said - *"Má's maith leat a bheith buan caith fuar agus TEITH.* The ambiguity of these words which equally mean "to drink hot and cold," or "to drink and flee," excited his attention: he flung the bowl to the earth - drew his well-tried sword and rushed from the house - but the red coats had that moment arrived, and a well-aimed bullet cut short his speed and his life.

4
The Beggarman's Tale[1]

'Twas varied much with terms of grief,
And eke of blood-congealing fear:
In sooth it was as strange a tale
As ever dwelt on mortal ear.
Old English Ballad.

Almost all our ancient national customs have entirely fled before the new light of what is termed modern improvement. Many of those customs which maintained their footing among the peasantry within my own recollection, and I have been moping about the world for the last sixty years, have totally disappeared, and left not a wreck behind. No longer does the thrifty housewife on the eve of the New Year, strike the boding oat-meal cake three times on the threshold, proclaiming famine to the Turks! I look, in vain, for the fat sheep which the farmers were accustomed to kill on Michaelmas day. The inmates of the peasant's cabin, are no longer clamorous for the cake and sowins, with boiled sheep's milk, which they were wont to indulge in - on "Patrick's day in the morning," before they went abroad to steep the "chosen leaf" in a drop of the *native*. The conquering goals, where the "good men and true" of two baronies, contended for the mastery, - these goals by which the spirit, strength, and swiftness of our peasantry, were improved, have gone the way of the rest. The last of our harpers has wept over the departing genius of music and song; though even yet our ears are regaled by pseudo-bards, who sing of their sounding lyre, and woodland reed, though they never fingered a Jew's-harp, or blew a *dhokawn*.

It were to be wished that the non-existence of these olden customs only were to be deplored: I fear that a few of our national virtues have likewise disappeared. That love of impartial justice, for which this nation was so celebrated, has, at least in many districts within my own knowledge, evaporated into a love of litigation. And our ancient hospitality which welcomes the stranger to the hearth - which displays upon the board the best the cottage affords - which pours the oil and wine of pity into the wounds of the afflicted and houseless; this hospitality has fled to its last refuge, the mountain glens of Connaught and Munster. We, indeed, in modern "tours through Ireland," find frequent mention made of Irish hospitality; but it is such as can be procured at a house of public entertainment, where the degrees of kindness and attention are regulated by the weight of the travellers purse. Another species of this virtue is found among the upper and middle classes, who receive visitors with "*cead mille failthe;*" but *there* may the way-worn traveller, and the houseless

---

[1] Published in *The Dublin Penny Journal,* June 15th 1833. Initialled, E.W. Walsh was but twenty eight years of age at that time but declared himself to be twice that age perhaps because the subject matter in the opening paragraphs is more that of the reminiscences of an older man. - Ed.

child of misfortune, vainly seek admittance: - Modern refinement has completely driven the genuine virtue, as Cromwell did our forefathers, from the cultivated country, and the neighbourhood of towns, to seek shelter in "Hell or Connaught."

Among the many, in the wild mountain district where I reside, that maintain the rites of hospitality in the old Irish spirit, is one friend of mine, whose house is the well-known resort of "all the vagrant train." As I love to observe human nature divested of that veil of insincerity, which a knowledge of the world is apt to fling over the real character, I frequently visit his habitation, and mingle with his guests. In this humble mansion he exercises, rather faintly it is true, all the virtues of an ancient Betagh. Though he cannot boast of the extensive pastures, and numerous herds, which were the indispensable appendages, to a "house of hospitality," yet here may be found lots of pipers, fiddlers, dancing masters, tinkers, pedlars, story-tellers and *boccaughs*, while mealy potatoes, *muskauns* of butter, and gallons of butter-milk, with an occasional piece of beef or pork, are dealt round to the various guests with unsparing profusion. If my reader wants ocular demonstration of the truth of this relation, he has only to pass, on foot, along the road from Newmarket to Castleisland, and any stroller he meets with at the Light-house, will point out the *borheen* to Daniel Mullowney's at Glanalougha.

Seated, one evening, in Daniel Mullowney's great oak chair, my shoes off, and my heels neatly placed on a square deal board, as is the wont of Daniel to treat those whom he "delighteth to honour," - the exclamation of "Let us praise Jesus Christ," and the loud clatter of an iron-shod *wattle*, announced the arrival of Darby Guiry, the Ballyvoorny beggarman. Darby belonged to that class of sturdy beggars called *boccaughs*; his *tribute*, as he termed it, was oatmeal, butter, wool, and flax. Few refused to bestow the wonted donation, but he took care to leave his best benefactors beads, which if not made of the true wood of the cross, were, at least of the same species of timber, crucifixes procured at Lough-derg - and holy pictures of the Blessed Gobnate, patroness of Ballyvoorny.

"God bless the house an' all that's there! I hope the maister an' mistress, an' all's well since I saw yees last," said Darby, entering.

"All well, thank you, Darby. Throw off thim bags, an' tell us the news you brought."

"In troth, 'tis I myself that's never without a story - and at a pinch I 'vint one, having always the fear of what happened to poor Mary Moylan before my eyes."

Darby took his seat in the chimney corner, on a stone bench, neatly covered with a rush mat. On our expressing a wish to hear Mary Moylan's tale, he thus began:

"Some time agone, there lived in Ballyvoorny a tailor, a sinsible, dacent young man he was, they say; and whin he had a thrifle o' money saved to begin house-keeping, he married Mary Roche, as purty an'tidy a girl as you'd get at a fair, an' that's a great word; she was an honest mother's daughter too by all accounts. By good management, an' hard industry, Paddy Moylan, for that was the tailor's name, at the end of seven years, saw himself the owner of a snug bit o' land, where he kept three cows an' four sheep of his own. He had, moreover, three journeymen, and two 'prentice boys, an' the work o' the entire parish. He was famous, besides, for erribs and sich things, for his mother, they say, was an Ulster woman; howsoever, 'tis sartin, he could restore bewitched butther, an' cure animals overlooked by the *evil eye*. Some say he saw the *Good People* reg'lar, at any rate, his name was so high among the neighbours, that Jack Maunsel, the fairy man, wasn't a patch upon him.

"It's an' ould saying, an' a thrue, that a man's life is like an April day, full of changes. Two bad saysins put Paddy Moylan to the pin of his collar. The corn crop was blasted; an' the cattle, God bless us! died mad. Many's the *collough* shook her head 'an said that Paddy's curse didn't serve him. The next summer came wet, an' the praties failed in the ground. Then came the procther hawking afther his tithes; but the landlord's agint, bad luck to his breed! though Paddy gev him a purty *kir-em-brogue-ey* at taking the ground, kim, an' as Paddy couldn't clear up the rint, turned Mary an' the childer out on the belly o' the road, and the sorrow a pratie, nor a shelter did he lave the crathers at all at all. Well, an honest neighbour give thim lave to be in his cabin. But the customers went like every thing else, the journeymen thramped elsewhere, and the 'printice boys took up their indenthurs: no pratie could be had for love or money; the male was mighty dear, and not a *keenogue* had Paddy Moylan, though the *grawls* war crying for food.

As the poor man ris, one morning, from his cowld sop o' straw in the corner, instead of the warm bed he was used to, to look out for a job among the neighbours, says Mary to him, says she, 'Paddy a-cushla, I'll go yonder, bine-by, for a piece of Denis Flyn's cow that died yesterday; 'twill make a drop o' broth a-gragal; an' the childer nor ourselves had'nt this many a day the wetting of our hearts.' 'Mary aroon,' said he, 'I see the mate yesterday; 'tis as black as the hob, and as tough as the gad of a flail. Fough, Mary! sure you wouldn't think of ating a baste that hadn't the blood drawn. I'm going, asthore, to see to do something for yees; but Mary, bring home no part of Denis Flyn's cow, or you may be sorry for it.'

In the coorse o' the day, when Mary Moylan's crathers began to ask their mammy for something to eat, her heart fell down to hear her weeny things crying: 'hould,' says she, 'ye poor hungry garkighs, (unfledged birds) an' the holy mother, an' blessed Gobnate will assist yees.' She crossed over to Denis Flyn's but God bless us! the cow was gone all but the head, and she brought that home to make a dhrink o' broth for the childer; and it was nearly boiled when her husband kim home in the evening. 'You'll blame me aroon manima, (secret of my soul) for bringing the cow's head,' she said, 'but when little Biddy, that you dote upon, was putting her bright black eyes through me, an' Katty and Timmy crying, it wint to my heart. This is no time for us to be proud *a-leah*!' An' she wiped her wet eyes with the corner of her apron.

" 'Woman', said her husband in a bitter tone, 'what would you think if I shewed you that the head in that pot is something more than a cow's head.'

" 'Musha, Paddy, what a dale you pretend to,' was the reply.

" 'Seeing is believing,' says Paddy Moylan, an' stepping out he soon returned with a sprig o' the lusmore, (great herb) which he had between her an' the pot that he desired her to look into. Great was her astonishment, whin inside o' the cow's head, she saw a *christian's* head all bloody, with the skin completely taken off. 'Light o' grace,' she exclaimed, dropping in a *mag* on the flure."

[Here the bustle occasioned by the arrival of Carroll the dancing-master, and his piper, blind Duggan, who was led along by a shin-burnt gorsoon, completely prevented me from catching this part of Darby Guiry's narrative.]

* * * * * * * *

"Mary Moylan thravelled all day with the childer, asking alms by the way. At length, she came to a part o' the country where the houses was thin; and as the evening advanced - the poor girl who was never on the *shachrawn* afore, got quite downhearted; for the sun was going under, and the hour getting as dark as the ace o' spades. She sat down to rest her poor limbs, on a soft, purple bank o' heath. Before her flowed a fine broad river, as smooth as a looking glass; the sides o' the deep glen through which it ran, wor covered with long-armed oak trees, that hadn't a hatchet upon 'em since Adam was a boy. No voice of friend or stranger broke the sleep o' nathur; no twinkling light from the lonely cabin caught her eye; the tall, dark shadows of the trees, seemed to her to be flitting ghosts; she fancied herself in the silent city o' the Dead; and drawing her little ones to her, she hid her face in her lap and wept bitterly.

"When Mary Moylan lifted her head, the moon was rising; and she was glad to perceive a snug-looking house at the other side o' the river, and bright light streaming from the windey. She called up the childer, who had fallen asleep, and easily made her way over the *clachaun*, across the river. The door o' the house was open; and Mary giv the 'God save all here;' but she saw no body, though a voice coming as it war, from the wall near the fire-place, answered 'save you kindly.' She was bid draw down to the blazing fire - an' the same voice, speaking still from the ould place, ordered some one that she couldn't see, to get the thravelling woman her supper. Some invisible hand furnished the table; an' ma-vrone, Mary an' the childer had *lashings-go-lore* of the best, an' to spare. Thin a bed as soft as down, was made on the side o' the house. Mary put the little ones to bed, an' though, 'tis like enough, she shook with terror, prepared to follow them, whin the same voice said 'tell us your new story, Mary Moylan.' 'Musha, sorrow a story have I, plase your reverence,' says Mary, because she was determined to be mighty civil.

" 'Give that honest woman a new story to tell at the next house that entertains her,' said the voice, in anger; and at the moment my poor crathur was spun like a top out o' doors, and brushed through the air like *a sop o' finane*, and left sitting under a tree in the middle of a wild mountain.

" 'O ma-launderig! my crathers, my crathers! O! but I'm the sorrowful mother o' childer. Paddy, Paddy, save your poor Mary! O! but your erribs an' cures is the root of our misfortune; the curse of Cromwell on 'em holus bolus!' Thus she cried; an' her screeching raised the snipe an' the wild plover from their lodging on the heath.

"While Mary Moylan was keening herself, she heard the sound o' strange voices, and shortly afther the splashing of footsteps in the *loughans* of the dark moor. Doubtful whether they wor the living or the dead, she ascended the three under which she sat, and soon perceived in the eye of the night, four min, who carried a spit an' a *bresnagh*. They stooped just under the three, an' afther lighting a fire, three o' the min riz'd upon the fourth, an' sticking the point o' the spit in at his bottom, an' thrusting it out at his mouth, prepared to roast him at the fire they had kindled under the three forninst Mary Moylan, who thrimbled like an aspen lafe at the sight.

"By all accounts the three min had business elsewhere, for one o' thim cried out, 'who'll turn the spit?'

" 'Mary Moylan will,' says the chap on the spit, 'an I can recommend her for as purty a cook as you'd find in a twelve-month. Come down Mary, from your cozy perch on that three, an' roast me.' The poor thing came down, shaking, for all the world, as if she had a fit o' the ague; an' when she caught the spit, the thief she was turning, swore with a horrid grin, that if she singed his beard, or blistered his shins he would be the death of her.

" 'I'll do the best for your honour,' says Mary, says she, for she wanted to throw it over the chap, 'an' thin sure you'll not be afther blaming me.'

"She did the part of turnspit purty well, without giving any raison to the ould boy on the spit to complain; when suddenly turning round at a rustling behind her, the fire saized upon his beard. Up he started, ma-boochil, on his legs, while the poor cook, God help her, ran for her life over the dark mountain. He coorsed her like a greyhound through hill and *carrigawn*, cliff and quagmire, till she heard the spit that stuck in him clattering at her heels, along the stones, as she entered a house which proved to be the very one she was driven from some hours before, to suffer such mortal hardships as no other christian but herself could get through. 'Mary Moylan,' says the man, or the voice rather, because she saw no body in the house at all at all, 'may be you could tell me a new story to-morrow night. You need'nt be on the *shachraun* ma colleen, only for Paddy's cures at Ballyvoorney; but 'tis a pity to see a tidy girl like you in throuble; make the best of your way back to-morrow, an' you will find in your *thrash-bag* a red purse with twenty yallow guineas in it. Let Paddy clear up the rint, and get a *receate* from the agint; let him buy also at Scartaglen fair, which comes next Monday, as many cows an' sheep as ye lost; - Get the guineas off your hands before tin days: - Lie down with the childer now. I'll tell you, you'll be the snug woman yet, Mary Moylan; but harkey, tell Paddy to middle with no more cures, from this day out at his peril.' The voice was hushed; an' Mary retired to bed.

"Whin she woke, in the morning, Mary Moylan found herself on the same bank where she sat down to rest the evening before. The river was flowing calmly fornint her. The song o' the thrush rose beautiful from the wood; the wild bee hummed in the sweet blossoming heath around her; and the childer wor nestled fast asleep at her side. She struv to collect the scattered thoughts o' last night, the strange *accidence* of which she considered as an idle drame, 'til sarching the *thrash-bag,* she found the red purse, an' the twenty yallow guineas shining in it. Upon retching home, Paddy cleared up the rint - got into his snug farm agin - bought the cows an' sheep - an' promised Mary, on his two binded knees, to middle no more with the *Good People*. They got into the world better nor ever they wor; an' if they didn't live happy that we may: - Amen."

5
The Goban Saer[1]

On the left hand, adjacent to the high road that leads from Watergrasshill to Cork, stands a scanty portion of the ruined castle of Rath-Goban, the ancient residence of the Goban Saer, whose sapient remarks have passed into many a proverb. He was a famous architect - but had his fame depended upon the durability of this structure, it must have been a very unstable monument, as no vestige of it remains for the contemplation of the traveller, save the fragment of one tower. But the name of the Goban Saer will live while the Irish race shall retain their vernacular tongue, for his maxims of wisdom are the oracles of unlettered instruction. I have not learned the particular period at which he flourished, but tradition says, that he was superior to all his contemporaries in the art of building: even in that dark age when so little communication existed between countries not so remotely situated, his fame extended to distant lands. A British prince, whose possessions were very extensive, and who felt ambitious of creating a splendid palace to be his regal residence, hearing of the high attainments of the Goban Saer, in his sublime science, invited him to court, and by princely gifts, and magnificent promises, induced him to build a structure, the splendour of which excelled that of all the palaces in the world. But the consummate skill of the artist had nearly cost him his life, for the prince, struck with the matchless beauty of the palace, was determined that it should stand unrivalled on the earth, by putting the architect to death, who alone was capable of constructing such another, after the moment the building received the finishing touches of his skilful hand.

This celebrated individual had a son who was grown up to man's estate, and anxious that this only child should possess in marriage a young woman of sound sense and ready wit, he cared little for the factitious distinctions of birth or fortune, if he found her rich in the gifts of heaven. Having killed a sheep, he sent the young man to sell the skin at the next market town, with this singular injunction, that he should bring home *the skin and its price* at his return. The lad was always accustomed to bow to his father's superior wisdom, and on this occasion did not stop to question the good sense of his commands, but went his way to the town. In these primitive times, it was not unusual to see persons of the highest rank engaging in menial employments, so the town-folk were less surprised to see the young Goban expose a sheep-skin for sale than at the absurdity of the term "*the skin and the price of it.*" He could find no chapman, or rather chapwoman, (to coin a term), for it was women engaged in domestic business that usually purchased such skins for the wool. A young woman at last accosted him, and upon hearing the terms of sale, after pondering a moment agreed to the bargain. She took him to her house, and having stripped off all the wool,

[1] Published in *The Dublin Penny Journal*, July 7th 1833. Initialled, E.W. It is the fourth story in the series entitled, "Popular Legends of the South." - Ed.

returned him the bare skin, and the price for which the young man stipulated. Upon reaching home he returned *the skin and its value* to his father, who learning that a young woman became the purchaser, entertained so high an opinion of her talents, that in a few days she became the wife of his son, and sole mistress of Rath Goban.

Some time after the marriage and towards the period to which we before referred, when the Goban Saer and his son were setting off at the invitation of the British prince to erect his superb palace, this young woman exhibited considerable abilities, and the keenness of her expressions, and the brilliancy of her wit, far outdid, on many occasions, the acumen of the Goban Saer himself; she now cautioned him when his old father, who did not, like modern architects, Bianconi it along Macadamised roads, got tired from the length of the journey, *to shorten the road*; and secondly, not to sleep a third night in any house without securing the interest of *a domestic female friend*. The travellers pursued their way, and after some weary walking over flinty roads, and through intricate passages, the strength of the elder Goban yielded to the fatigue of the journey. The dutiful son would gladly *shorten the road* for the way-worn senior, but felt himself unequal to the task. On acquainting his father with the conjugal precept, the old man unravelled the mystery by bidding him commence some strange legend of romance, whose delightful periods would beguile fatigue and pain into charmed attention. Irishmen, I believe, are the cleverest in Europe at '*throwing it over*' females in foreign places, and it is pretty likely that the younger Goban did not disobey the second precept of his beloved wife. On the second night at their arrival at the king's court, he found in the person of a female of very high rank, (some say she was the king's daughter) a friend who gave her confiding heart to all the dear delights that love and this Irish experimentalist could bestow. As the building proceeded under the skilful superintendence of the elder Goban, the son acquaints him with the progress of his love, and the ardent attachment of the lady. The cautious old man bid him beware of one capable of such violent passion, and take care lest her jealousy or caprice, might not be equally ungovernable, and display more fearful effects. To discover her temper, the father ordered him to sprinkle her face with water as he washed himself in the morning - that if she received the aspersion with a smile, her love was disinterested, and her temper mild; but if she frowned darkly, her love was lust, and her anger formidable. The young man playfully sprinkled the crystal drops on the face of his lover - she smiled gently - and the young Goban rested calmly on that tender bosom, where true love and pitying mildness bore equal sway.

The wisdom of the Goban Saer and his sapient daughter-in-law was soon manifested; for, as the building approached its completion, his lady-love communicated to the young man the fearful intelligence that the king was resolved, by putting them to death when the work was concluded, that they should erect no other such building, and, by that means to enjoy the unrivalled fame of possessing the most splendid palace in the world. These tidings fell heavily on the ear of the Goban Saer, who saw the strong necessity of circumventing this base treachery with all his skill. In an interview with his majesty, he acquaints him that the building was being completed; and that its beauty exceeded every building of the kind he had done before; but that it could not be finished without a certain instrument which he unfortunately left at home, and he requested his royal permission to return for it. The king would, by no means, consent to the Goban Saer's departure; but anxious to have the edifice completed, he was willing to send a trusty messenger into Ireland for that instrument upon which the finishing of the royal edifice depended. The other assured his majesty that it was of so much importance that he would not entrust it into the hands of the greatest of his majesty's subjects. It was finally arranged that the king's closest son should proceed to Rath Goban, and, upon producing his credentials to the lady of the castle, receive the instrument of which she had the keeping, and which the Goban Saer named 'Cur-an-aigh-an-cuim.' Upon his arrival in Ireland, the young prince proceeded to fulfil his errand; but the knowing mistress of Rath Goban, judging from the tenor of the message, and the ambiguous expressions couched under the name of the pretended instrument, that her husband and father-in-law were victims of some deep treachery, she bad him welcome, inquired closely after her absent friends, and told him he should have the object of his mission when he had refreshed himself after the fatigues of his long journey. Beguiled by the suavity of her manners and the wisdom of her words, the prince complied with her invitation to remain all night at Rath Goban. But in the midst of his security, the domestics faithful to the call of their mistress had him bound in chains, and led to the dungeon of the castle. Thus the wisdom of the Goban Saer, and the discrimination of his daughter, completely baffled the wicked designs of the king, who received intimation that his son's life would surely atone for the blood of the architects. He dismissed them to their native country laden with splendid presents; and, on their safe arrival at Rath Goban, the prince was restored to liberty.

6
Carrig-Cleena.[1]

" - Heaven taught poets know
The sprite that sought his clasp and kiss,
Had borne him off from human woe,
To share her own immortal bliss."
Manuscript Poem.

In the parish of Glantane, and three miles northwest of the town of Mallow, in the midst of a wild tract of country, appear certain rocks of a strange and romantic appearance. The dark green drapery of the creeping and ground-ivy, shades the time-bleached sides of these masses; and the lighter tint of the tall fern springing from their deep interstices, marks their different compartments with many a line of green. These rocks lie circularly on the plain, and in the centre rises one towering over the rest, as the graceful height of the pine looks proudly down on its humble fellows of the forest. Its almost inaccessible top is perfectly level, and covered with a carpet of verdant green. At the base of its northern side lie huge stones, which some giant arm seems to have hurled confusedly around; for, from the perpendicular smoothness of the sides, and the table-like flatness of the summit, they could not have fallen down from the rock. Inside these fragments of granite, and level with the plain, yawns a wide opening in the rock. This entrance is softly shaded by the briery branches of the wild rose, and leads, according to the current opinion to the spacious vault within; and some who have climbed to the top, have found it resound deep and hollow, to the stamp of their foot; but the most adventurous never essayed to explore its inner secrets. A large hawthorn, which opens its fragrant white blossoms in this romantic solitude, is tenanted by the wild thrush that pours his song of beauty to the echoes of the rock. Indeed, this seems to be the favourite haunt of the genius of music. Some unseen songster from the green summit of the rock is often heard to blend strains of melting harmony with the wild warbling of the thrush. The cowboy, as he whistles his herd over the neighbouring pastures to the milking bawn, as the gentle summer evening is throwing her russet mantle over the green bosom of the land, frequently hears, in this fairy haunt, the music of some unknown instrument, whose thrilling vibrations, suspending every sense but that of hearing, deprive the limbs of motion, and bind the entranced soul in the magic links of harmony, until the wild strain is hushed, and silence reigns around.

The land immediately surrounding this haunted rock, has been, time out of mind, deemed consecrated ground. Never did the profane hedging-bill of the peasant, invade its

[1] Published in The *Dublin Penny Journal*, July 20th 1833. Initialled, E.W. It is number five in the series entitled "Popular Legends of the South." - Ed.

time-honoured shrubs; the spade of the husbandman never wounded the holy glebe; and though modern improvement is rapidly changing the harsh features of this rough district, cultivation has not yet dared to obtrude where superstition guards her ancient right - for tradition relates that this is the favourite abode of Cleena, a benevolent genius - hence the haunted rock, so famous in fairy lore, has obtained the name of Carrig-Cleena.

The untaught peasants of the surrounding country have ever regarded Cleena as their benefactress. The rustic of the present day, affirms that in her neighbourhood, no cattle die from the malignant influence of the evil eye, or the mischievous power of the unfriendly spirits of air; and that her goodness preserves the harvest crop from the blight which lays prostrate the farmer's hopes, when beings unfriendly to man appropriate to themselves the produce of his fields. The peasantry seem to be the children of her peculiar care: frequently she has been known to veil her celestial beauty, and attired in the homely garb of the country, announce to some night wanderer the expulsion from her confines of the evil spirits of the north, and the consequent abundance of a plentiful harvest.

On the borders of the Shannon, in the County of Limerick, resided a youthful chieftain, one of the Geraldines, the remains of whose castles along the banks of that king of Irish streams, even yet frown defiance on the dashing waves below. He was skilled in all the accomplishments deemed necessary in that age of chivalry in which he lived. Brave as those daring adventurers from whom he claimed descent, and hospitable and generous as the ancient chieftains of the land, his perfections were the theme of many a harp-striking minstrel. The princely chief himself was a bard of the first eminence, and he early taught his harp to breathe, in ardent strains, the charms of Ellen O'Brien. She was the only daughter of one of those unfortunate chiefs whose possessions sunk to insignificance, and whose power crumbled to dust before the prevailing fortune of the Saxon invader. Fitzgerald saw the beauteous Ellen - and loved; nor was his passion unregarded: his splendid accomplishments and noble mien - the soft music of his harp, and tender lay of love, all stole to the heart of the interesting girl, and Ellen beheld in the enemy of her name and race, the only being whose idea twined like a magic spell round her heart and brain, and without whom this earth and its enjoyments seemed but a dreary void.

Tradition records that Cleena beheld this favoured youth; and that gifted being, before whose knowledge the secrets of the earth lay unlocked, bent to a superior power, and obeyed that magic spell which in the olden day, it is said, drew erring angels from their sphere, to bask in the beauty-smiles of the daughters of Adam. She loved Fitzgerald, and resolved that he should share the splendours of her unseen hall, and the greatness of her power. Upon a festival day, when the proud and noble of the land were assembled at "tilt and tourney," a dark cloud descended on the plain, and enveloping young Fitzgerald, bore him from the field. He disappeared - no trace of him could be found; the various messengers who sought intelligence of him returned weary from their fruitless toil. Days and months rolled away in vain expectation, and the most incredulous, at length, believed that a supernatural power had borne the chieftain away, and that he remained the slave of enchantment in some unexplored retreat impervious to mortal feet.

Of all that mourned this strange and melancholy circumstance, none felt more intense sorrow than Ellen O'Brien. When his followers ceased to seek their master - when every mouth forgot the hopeless inquiry, she departed privately from the home of her childhood, resolved, with that tenacity of passion, which belongs to the true and stainless heart of woman, to find her lover or perish in the attempt. In a rocky glen, in Kerry, where resided a wizard, who held strange and unutterable communings with beings of another life, she learned that Cleena had conveyed her lover to her favourite residence in the county of Cork. In the decline of Autumn, Ellen O'Brien reached Carrig-Cleena, her hair floating wildly in the fitful breeze, her garments torn by every shrub and bramble, and her feet bleeding from the roughness of the path. In her native tongue, that language of life and feeling, she poured the extemporaneous effusions of her love-lorn heart in harmonious verse. She feelingly depicted their unquenchable loves, their early vows of plighted faith, and the assurance she received that the object of her pursuit was detained in this enchanted rock. She appealed to Cleena's wonted kindness to the human race, and expressed her firm determination to expire at the foot of that rock, the echoes of which should bear her final groan to the faithful youth whose eternal constancy, she knew no power on earth or air could destroy.

The legend tells that Cleena, moved by Ellen O'Brien's matchless fidelity, and won by the beauty of her person and the mournful melody of her persuasive song, gave the captive lover to the arms of his faithful maid. They departed together. The nuptial tie joined the hands of those whose hearts were long united; and they became the parents of a numerous happy offspring.

7
The Headless Horseman of Shanacloch[1]

It was one of those wild nights which frequently visits us in the month of December, when the floodgates of heaven pour their torrents, the winds rush angrily through the heavens, and the lightning's glance along the air, that a social and happy circle formed round the hospitable hearth of Tom Cahil, of Shanacloch. Though the rafters cracked in the weight of the savage wind, and the lofty ash trees, that rose amid the ruins of the adjacent castle, groaned to the elemental war, and the echoes of the neighbouring cliffs bore to our ear the hollow roaring of the foaming Bride, yet happy in the contemplation of our exemption from the storm, and enlivened by the much loved strains of Jack Piggot, the purblind piper, we turned a deaf ear to nature's present fit of ill-humour. The servants, domestic and outward, were footing it lightly to the music of the pipes in the kitchen. Jack, seated in the broad chimney-corner, had already gulped down five good tumblers of punch, made in the parlour by Mrs. Cahill's own hand. Tom, maugre his alderman-like rotundity of belly, was jigging it among the youngsters. The stacks were well secured, the barns replenished, the snug mansion afforded a bed for a friend, and a keg of whiskey, poteen or parliament as the case may be - the rent was paid, and the house well thatched - in short we may say, with Burns,

"The storm without might rair and rustle,
Tam did na mind the storm a whistle."

Perhaps the gentle reader would grant me a moment's indulgence, while I introduce Shanacloch to his notice. Tom Cahill's snug residence is situated on the bank of the winding river, Bride, between Rathcormac and Glenville. The farm takes its name from the ruins of an old castle which defended the possessions of the Barrys in this quarter. This ruined castle, like almost all others, in Ireland, has many tales of superstition connected with it. It was a strong square building; and its brave garrison made a noble defence, till at length it was taken by treachery, and its defenders murdered in cold blood. The extraordinary breadth of its massive walls has enabled the edifice to partially resist the assaults of time, who has, at length, flung a green mantle of sheltering ivy over the ruin, as if anxious to preserve it from the storm of ages. But the hand of man has effected wide dilapidations - the instruments of war have levelled its front in the dust; and I am sorry to record that the vandalism of my friend, Tom Cahill, has been busy with the rest, a sacrilege which will not be forgiven *by me* either in this world or in the world to come.

---

[1] Published in *The Dublin Penny Journal*, August 3rd 1833. Initialled, E.W. It is the sixth in the series entitled "Popular Legends of the South." Shanacloch is between Rathcormac and Glenville, Co. Cork. - Ed.

At Shanacloch, the duties of that loveliest of virtues, hospitality, is well observed. To its well-known mansion, the homeless wanderer turns his weary feet, certain of receiving food and shelter; the house never lacked a train of strollers; but myself and Pigott, the piper, were the most frequent and welcome visitors. By some strange coincidence, we generally came to Shanacloch at the same time; and it was a remark, that when your humble servant gave the "God save all here," blind Piggot was not far behind. Piggot's features were cast in nature's coarsest mould, but when he turned his pipes to one of his Irish airs, the expression of benevolence and calm delight on his misshapen face was truly interesting. Jack's music, indeed, had a powerful effect upon those who heard his strain. My heart had throbbed, and my eyes swam in tears, as he poured the full tide of the billowy air, Cosh-na-breeda, on my raptured ear; and when he struck up one of the martial tunes by which the minstrel of the olden day roused the clansmen to war and glory, I have seen the rude peasants who hung upon the strain, start forward with a wild shout, and flourish their sticks in the air. My chief motive for these frequent visits was to hear Piggot's matchless music, and glean legendary lore from Biddy Moylan, an ancient retainer of the Shanacloch family.

"God bless us," said Biddy Moylan, from her straw-bottomed chair in the corner, "what a dreadful hour it is at sae! This wild hour will lave many fatherless childer afther it. Jack Piggot, dhrop that music, and let us all pray for the sowls of the poor sailors that are this blessed minute sinking under the waves, to make food for fishes."

"Don't you know Biddy," says Jack, laying his chanter horizontally across his knees, "that music often calmed a storm; and that whin the wicked one had Paddy Barret in the hoult of the devil's cave, when he played up the 'Graces,' instead of the wicked thune the company axed for, their spells were broken, and poor Paddy set at liberty."

"Enough is as good as a faist," rejoined the old woman, "and too much of wan thing is good for nothing. It was coshering and dancing they war, when *Marcach-na-Shanacloch* gave his last visit; the music drowned his voice, and honest people lost their good luck."

As I was a great favourite of old Bridget's, upon expressing a wish to hear the "Legend of the Horseman," she kindly complied. The dancing ceased, and the pipes were bagged. After Biddy Moylan had struck the last ashes from her *dudeen*, and Jack Piggot called out "'Tension," she thus began: -

"Long an' merry ago, when *Shemish-a-cocca,*[1] that lost ould Ireland, bad 'cess to him was fighting it with some Orangeman, or other, that kem from England, with a great army, to destroy the Pope and the Catholics, Shanacloch, that then belonged to the Barrys (the rap McAdamces), was garrishoned with stout boys, that defended the place for James, and well, in their way, they wor to spill their blood, like ditch water for the bad bird that befouled his own nest. The great guns were planted against the castle over-right us there at Bushy-park,

[1] King James II of England is seen as having fled the Battle of the Boyne. Hence the term *Séamus an chaca*, 'James the Coward'; impolitely, 'Jim the Shit'. - Ed.

and they roared night and day; but though the bullets battered the walls, and did a power of damage, the boys at Shanacloch ped thim off in their own coin. So, my dear, one dark night they stole upon the castle, being detarmined by all accounts to take the Barrys at an *amplush*, but they peppered thim with bullets from the port-holes; and whin the inemy drew off, they followed thim down the big field to the Bridge, and ma-vrone, the battle-axes of the Barrys used to strike off heads and arms like tops o' thistles, and they pursued them into the river; and the Bride, that this blessed night is so muddy and dark, was thin red with blood. Soon after the English captain hoist his sails, and off with him, horse an' foot, *with a flay in his ear*. But as the *bodachs* wor passing through Bunkilly in their way to Mallow, a man kim against thim, mounted on a black horse, with a great parcel of brogues in a kish.

" 'Hilloa, friend,' says the captain, 'who are you, and where might you be throtting to at that rate?'

" 'I'm an honest brogue-maker, saving your honour's presence, and carrying this kish of brogues to the garrishon at Shanacloch,' says the horseman.

" 'Will you come back tonight?' says the captain.

" 'Is it to come back your honour manes? By Jaminie, if I put my eyes on Kippins, the boys wouldn't let me quit to night. I'll be bail for lashings of whiskey there, an' hay an' oats galore for this ould baste."

" 'Harkey, friend,' says the Captain, 'you don't seem to be overburthened with money, and if you got a fist-full of yellow guineas, would you have any objection to do me a trifle of service?'

"Yet, to make my long story short, the murdhering thraitor agreed for a sum of money to betray the Barrys, and let the inemy in upon him in the dead o' the night. The poor min that wor harrashed and worn out from long watching and constant fighting, took a dhrop extrornary for joy that the *English bodachs* legged it, and every man wint to sleep, when the brogue-maker promised to keep watch till morning. But by the time the min wor dead asleep, the English returned and the thief of the world opened the gates, and every mother's soul in the castle was murdered in cold blood. Eighteen Redmonds of the Barrys, that were sworn to stand or fall together, were stabbed (the Lord save us!) in their sleep. Whin this *massacree* was finished, the brogue-maker claimed the reward, and requested to be let go, as the daylight was fast approaching. "I'll give you all you bargained for, an' a trifle over," says the captain; an' when he ped the money down on the nail, he struck off the villain's head for betraying the noble fellows, whose blood flowed through every room of the castle that night.

"From that time forward a headless horseman was seen every night riding round Shanacloch, and it is not said that he ever did the laste injury to any body. In the coorse o' years, this very house that I'm telling the story in (God bless all that's in it!) was built upon the *Horseman's Walk*, by the master's gran'father, and every night he entered the kitchen by the door, and wint out through the opposite wall, that closed after him, as if no Christian sowl passed through it, and they always put out the candle, to allow him to go by unnoticed. But the night the masther's aunt (God rest her soul!) was marrying, in the middle of the piping an'dancing, the horseman called out at the door - though I wonder how he could, for he had never a head upon him. The people of the wedding didn't hear, or were afeard to answer him, not knowing, poor, dear people, what trouble they might be brought to. The headless horseman of Shanacloch was never seen or heard of since. They say his time was out, and his horrible threachery atoned for; and that, on this last night, he came to thank them for their past kindness to him.

Thanks be to heaven, spirits and ghosts are going away very fast, bekase wars and murders are at an ind; and the clargy, more power to 'em, has sent a great many sowls to the Red Say!"

8
The City of the Lake[1]

On a fine morning in autumn, Billy Walsh emerged from the sheltering fence of elder and hawthorn that surrounded his father's white-walled house, which overtopped a green field that sloped gently to the bank of the romantic Daloo. He was equipped in a pair of smart pumps; at the knees of his corduroy smallclothes waved a flowing knot of ribbon. His coat was broadcloth, and a new hat, lately purchased at Mitchelstown, rose above his curling yellow locks that shaded his forehead; while the accurate knot of his yellow grinder, proved that the time employed at the looking glass had not been spent in vain. One hand was concealed in the left pocket of the small-clothes, and the right flourished a slender hazel twig, which, tradition taught him to believe, could put to flight all the powers of darkness, as St. Patrick made use of a hazel staff to expel every evil and venomous thing from the favoured island of his adoption.

From the evasive answers which Billy gave to his mother's inquiries concerning his afternoon excursion, the more than usual attention bestowed on his dress, the inmates of the house suspected that he had some very particular affair on hands; and each furnished his own conjecture on the occasion. One supposed he was going to Mara's benefit dance, which was to take place that night; but then why should he set off so early? Another that Kitty Daly of the Commons, had a hand in the affair, else why should he turn out so gaily? A third, that he was certainly going to his uncle's at Broadford, to engage in the conquering goal to-morrow; but this sage remark was given to the winds, for he left his favourite *hurley* behind. The fact was, a few weeks before, he danced at the patron of Coolavoto with Peggy Noonan, a smiling blue-eyed girl, with fine auburn hair. The next Monday he attended and enjoyed the same satisfaction. In short, this blue-eyed dancer had taken such complete possession of his fancy that he could neither work nor eat, nor rest, with thinking of her pretty ankle and graceful air. Peggy was not altogether insensible to his passion, for on this evening she had promised to meet him, about a mile from her father's house, at the church-yard of Killcorkeran.

Billy Walsh moved along with a light foot and elastic tread, whistling his favourite reel, "I wish I never saw you," and decapitating all the unfortunate thistles and wild flowers that grew to the right and left within range of his hazel plant. He left the town of Newmarket to the right, and struck across Barleyhill towards the ruined castle of Carrigcashel. As he crossed a brook that ran gurgling along its pebbly bed, he perceived a stream diverted into a narrow channel, which wound around the sloping sides of the glen. At that time irrigation was unknown in this part of the country; and our *buckeen* considered the stream led to a *poteen still*. He pursued the watercourse, which conducted him to a wretched and nearly

---

[1] Published in *The Dublin Penny Journal*, August 17th 1833. Initialled, E.W. - Ed.

roofless cabin, through every aperture of which the smoke issued, and rising, formed a beautiful blue column in the still air to a considerable height above. As he passed with silent tread over the heaps of grains that rose around, his farther progress was arrested by the appearance of a short, thick-set man; his broad shoulders and expansive chest, indicated considerable strength, his olive-complexioned face, embrowned with smoke, and shaded by enormous whiskers, displayed almost savage ferocity, while with a stern tone he demanded the stranger's business.

"Mybusiness is easily told," answered the other, unhesitatingly, "I'm cutting across the country to Coolavoto, and have followed the strahane, thinking it might lead me to a glass of poteen to help me across the hill."

"May be young man, you're come *spying* about what shouldn't consarn you, and" -

'Tut,tut! Falvey, leave off your *ramish,*" said a man emerging from the smoke of the hovel, and whom Billy recognised as an old boon-companion, 'Billy Walsh's father's son is not the boy to bring honest people to trouble, or give to say that any of his name ever turned spy to a blackguard gauger." The stern expression on Falvey's features now relaxed into a rugged smile, and grasping Walsh's hand, he cordially invited him to a glass of poteen.

Upon removing a stone from the wall of the hovel, they drew forth a small jar and a black wooden cup that supplied the place of a glass. Then Falvey filled the cup, and after drinking to the health of the new comer, drained it dry. The cup was replenished and emptied in quick succession; and Billy Walsh was so taken with his new acquaintance, and the potent beverage which is loved alike throughout every grade in Ireland, from the peasant to the peer, and finds its way into the cellar of some commissioners of excise, flung such spells around him that Peggy Noonan and the trysting-place at the old church of Kilcorkeran, were completely forgotten.

The shadows of tree and tower, were lengthening in the decline of the evening sun, as his engagement flashed across the mind of Billy Walsh. He lightly rose, and bid his companions farewell. He soon crossed the wood and gained the summit of the adjacent hill; the influence of the poteen, and the dread of missing his blue-eyed girl, added wings to his flight, but the sun was gone down, and the evening star twinkled bright in the west, before he reached Kilcorkeran. The burying ground was removed from the road and seated in the midst of extensive fields, and the dim twilight, which was falling fast around, was not calculated to improve the sad and silent scene. He peeped over the style that led into the lonely abode of the dead - he called Peggy Noonan in vain - the echoes of his voice, as they rose from the ivy-clad ruins of the old church, seemed to be unearthly tones mocking his eager call. The wild bird rushing from the sheltering thorn, and the hollow whistle of the autumnal night-blast along the tomb, shook his courage: - all the tales that superstition taught his childhood to believe, rushed upon his imagination. He wished himself far from this fearful church-yard; but the foolish hope of seeing Peggy Noonan, who doubtless, returned home displeased at his breach of promise, chained him to the spot; he sat down at the gateway, and after cursing Falvey, the poteen, and his own intemperate folly, fell fast asleep.

It is not recorded in his authentic story, how long Billy Walsh slept at the gateway of the churchyard, when he was roused by some one that called him by name. He fancied it was Peggy Noonan's voice; but great was his surprise to see an elderly gentleman on horseback, dressed in black, with cloth *leggings*; and his face shaded by a broad-brimmed beaver: "God save you Billy Walsh;" says he, "what brings you to be fast asleep in so lonesome a spot, and so far from your own place at this hour of the night." Billy Walsh rose, and taking off his hat, saluted the priest, for he knew him to be on from his dress, and because he carried the check wallet behind him, containing the vestment and holy utensils used in the celebration of mass; and which, until lately, the priests themselves conveyed from place to place as occasion required.

"I was waiting for a frind, plase your reverence, an' as the place was lonely an' quiet, I fell asleep; but I can't say how your reverence knows me, for I never placed my two-looking eyes on you afore." 'I know more than you may imagine," said the stranger, "and Billy if you left Falvey and the *poteen* in proper time, you need not disappoint Peggy Noonan, but I have a mass to read at 12 o'clock to-night at a distance from this, and I hope you will not refuse to act as clerk."

"Thunderand turf thin! beggin your reverence's pardon, you aren't half so cute as you pretind, (or may be 'tis throwing it over me you are) not to know that Billy Walsh never received no larning, nor answered mass in his life. Besides, if I'm to be *coologue*, to straddle barebacked behind your reverence, would destroy my new breeches."

"I warrant," said the priest, "that you can answer mass in style; and as to the breeches, we shall pass so smoothly along, that not a thread of it will suffer."

Reluctant to refuse his reverence, Billy Walsh mounted behind him; and the priest directed his course northward across the country, without let or hindrance from hedge or river, over which they glided like the morning mist, pursued by the early beams of the sun. Though our hopeful clerk sat quiet at his ease, and altogether unshaken in his seat, he did not much relish this nocturnal ramble, and was never a professed admirer of early masses. So as they passed along by his uncle's place at Broadford, he endeavoured to fling himself off, but found that he was as it were, rivetted to the horse's back. He next attempted to cry out for assistance, but his tongue refused its wonted office, and like Virgil's hero, under nearly similar circumstances, *vox faucibus haesit*. In the course of the night they reached Lough Gur, a romantic lake that expands its broad bosom a few miles below Bruff, and then shone a field of liquid silver beneath the mild influence of the lovely harvest moon. On reaching the bank, his companion bid Billy Walsh hold fast, and fear nothing. The first part of this advice was needless, for he held with might and main, his breath drawn in, and his teeth firmly set. The other he flung to the four winds of heaven, for on taking the fatal plunge, he mentally besought pardon for all his sins, and the help of every saint in the calendar, for he firmly believed that on reaching the bottom, all the eels of the lake would make a supper of his unfortunate carcase.

As the waters closed over their heads, Billy Walsh instead of instant suffocation, and the monstrous ells which his fears taught him to expect, was delighted to find they were travelling along a broad road shaded on each side with spreading trees, and approaching a fine town whose lamps glittered in the distance, like a multitude of bright stars. This town, which consisted of one principal street, exceeded in beauty every idea that he had previously formed of splendid cities. All the windows were lighted, and the richly dressed inhabitants thronged the street, as if it were some great festival. Upon reaching the centre of the street they stopped at a splendid church, at whose ample gate an immense crowd were pouring in. Our travellers also entered by the *sacristy*. Billy assisted the priest in *vesting*, laid the altar with great cleverness, and then taking his place at its lowest step, answered the mass from the *Introibo*, to the last verse of the *De Profundis*, with so much propriety and decorum as would have added credit to the best schoolmaster in Duhallow. When all was concluded, and the check wallet had received its usual contents, the venerable priest turned round and addressed the congregation that crowded the long aisle, and the spacious gallery to the following effect: -

"My brethren, you have seen with what propriety and decorum Billy Walsh has acted the part of *clerk* at the holy service. We have been long endeavouring to procure a suitable person to fill that situation, and you all know how difficult it is to find one capable of discharging its duties properly. I hardly think the young man can have any objection to remaining in this splendid city, and as his merits cannot be enhanced by any recommendation of mine, I am sure there is not an individual in the crowded assembly, but will be delighted to secure his services."

When the priest had ended, the walls of the lofty aisle resounded with the clapping of hands, - the gentlemen nodded assent - and the beautiful ladies waved their white handkerchiefs that streamed like meteors of light in the glare of the brilliant chandeliers, in token of approbation.

'You must be proud," said the clergyman, speaking to Billy Walsh, "you must be proud to find yourself such a favourite with all classes here, and especially the ladies. You shall have in this city every delight - the best eating and drinking - lovely ladies to dance with - and hurling matches to your heart's content. Stay with us Billy Walsh; - I know you are too sensible to throw away your good luck."

"I have given my hand an' word to mind *cool* at the hurling match on the common to-morrow evening; and more than that I wouldn't part Peggy Noonan for all the gold of Damer."

The gentlemen entreated, - the beautiful ladies wept, - and the priest promised that he should have Peggy Noonan with him to-morrow night. He continued as unyielding as the savage rock, round whose brow the winds of heaven rage, and upon whose changeless base the ocean pours its thousand waves in vain. He would be no *clerk* at all at all.

In short, the obstinate Billy Walsh was driven amid groans of disapprobation from the church into the street, and pursued with shouts and yells of anger along the avenue which led to the border of the lake. On arriving thither, a fearful whirlwind caught him up like a straw, and hurled him ashore. The dark waters of the troubled lake rose in angry waves, and the reeds of its sedgy borders waved mournfully to the breeze of the grey morning; as Billy Walsh arose, and pursued his way homewards, giving at every step, his hearty curse to all young men, who, ever again, would form assignations at lonely church yards.

9

Daniel O'Leary, the Duhallow Piper[1]

Mr. Editor - Some years since, while taking a little excursion through certain wild districts of the south, I had the satisfaction of hearing some of the best Irish airs, played on the best set of "organ pipes" by the best piper in Munster - a rich treat, which I certainly could not have enjoyed had I, like Sir Richard Colt Hoare, Bart., travelled in *my own coach* - or, after the fashion of the famous "Terence O'Toole," of the Dublin Penny Journal, perched "*a top o' the mail,*" surveyed the land with eagle's eye, as I glided with eagle's speed by many a tower and abbey grey. No, no, gentle reader –

"If thou on men, their works and ways,
Wouldst throw uncommon light,"

thou must travel as I have done, an humble pedestrian, and learn the unsophisticated feelings of an Irish peasant at his own hospitable hearth. Upon setting forward on my excursion I made some alterations in my usual mode of dress. I doffed my broad brimmer for a hat of narrower leaf. I exchanged white cravat, which I was accustomed to tie with extreme precision behind, for a gay silk neck-cloth, whose well adjusted knot flowed copiously to the wind; and I laid by my black frock for a "blue body-coat," with a "gilt button," a circumstance which I deem necessary to state for the benefit of the uninitiated in Irish affairs, who may have in contemplation a trip similar to the one to which I allude. Among the peasantry a black coat creates rather unpleasant suspicions, unless they know the wearer to be "one of the clargy," - without this descriptive mark, men of all avocations may travel with perfect impunity, and a certainty of the most hospitable reception in our wildest glens, proctors and gaugers always excepted. I was under no apprehension of being mistaken for the last mentioned personage, because my person is tall and thin, my face abstemiously pale, and not a single grog blossom expanding its fiery petals on my nasal organ. Furnished with a choice hazel sapling for my hand and a portfolio for remarks, I sallied forth to see the world,

"And know if books or swains report it right."

During my peregrination I gleaned many a tuneful lay and curious legend, which have lived for hundreds of years in the traditions of the land. The result of my wanderings are yet

[1] Published in *The Dublin Penny Journal*, October 18th 1834. Initialled, E.W. - Ed.

lying by me, and I have not determined whether to print them in a thin quarto, or send them to the Dublin Penny Journal - I think the Journal shall have them.

The glowing sun was going down in the west on a fine evening in the decline of autumn, as I gained the brow of a hill that overlooks the silver Araglen, which flows through the western wilds of Duhallow, in the county of Cork, to join the broad Blackwater. It was a glorious scene, where the light and shade of hill and valley were beautifully linked with the evening mist that curled along the winding stream. I sat down to enjoy the free and boundless prospect, beside one of those ancient mounds called Danish forts, and was soon accosted by a man, wrapt in one of those great coats of olden fame, which an English writer formerly designated as "a fit house for an outlaw - a meet bed for a rebel - and an apt cloak for a thief." He had a long pole in his hand, and seemed to be engaged in the business of herding a number of cattle that grazed peacefully in the extensive common below.

"This silent spot," said I, "was once a busy, bustling scene, when the heathen Dane kept garrison here, and subjected to his rule the surrounding country."

"Ah!" said the intelligent herdsman "it is an error to suppose that all these ancient works are of Danish construction: the Irish must have raised forts also to protect their own possessions, for the Danes were never entire masters of the land at any time. But tradition assigns the erection of this mound to a period when the Danes were without a name in the annals of Europe. - This very fort is said to have been raised by Goul Mac Morna, in the third century upon separating from Fionn Mac Cool who resided at Doon, about a mile farther down the Araglen. The spot where we sit is called in the Irish tongue, 'The Fort of the Hill of Parting,' and that part of the river which glitters in the last rays of the sun, is named 'The Ford of the Glutton,' from the death of one of the Fiana which happened there."

"By what means did this occurrence happen," I enquired.

"When Goul and his adherents retired from Doon to this hill, Fionn, to maintain a friendly correspondence, sent him daily a joint of roast meat; but one evening, as a certain soldier carried the present to Goul, he was greatly tempted by the delicious flavour of the meat, the richness of which appeared mellowed in the hot sun-beam; regardless of the consequences, he gratified his appetite, and after depositing the meat at the fort, he returned back towards Doon. When Goul beheld the mutilated joint he set an arrow to his bow, in revenge of the insult. The fatal missile overtook the poor glutton, as he crossed the stream, and he fell, pierced to his heart."

"Your legend of the roast meat," I observed, "has awakened within me a certain sensation, not strictly connected with the romance of the olden day; and you must now add to the obligations I already owe you, by pointing out the shortest way to the Rev. Father McNaughtin's.

"You could not reach the priest's before night," he rejoined, "you shall have *cead mille failthe,* and the accommodation my cabin can afford, if you kindly accept them. This path will conduct you to yonder humble mansion in the glen, where the smoke rises above the surrounding alders. I can, likewise, promise you a rich treat of national music, from the chanter of Daniel O'Leary, the first piper in Munster, who luckily has paid us a visit. I shall rejoin you when I turn home the cows."

I thankfully accepted the invitation; and as I approached the house of this hospitable and well-informed peasant, the large dogs came wagging their tails, and seemed to bid me welcome. It is worthy of remark how readily these sagacious animals adopt the manners of their masters. By my own experience, I can rightly ascertain the manner of the inmates of each particular residence from the temper of the dogs. Thus, at the house of the inhospitable churl, the surly cur annoys the coming traveller: the dog at the "great house" is disdainful and silent, while that of the hospitable cottager is ever friendly. Within, at the blazing hearth, was seated the piper; a diminutive man, deformed in person like Willie Wattle's wife, who -

'Had a hump upon her breast,
The twin o' that upon her shouther.'

He had a knowing cast of countenance, and a keen, observant eye. When I gave the usual salute, he bid me sit down and take off my shoes, a form of welcome that has prevailed since the earliest times, by which each guest could entitle the last comer to the hospitality of the mansion, on bidding him take off his brogues. O'Leary yoked the pipes to do the stranger courtesy, and, before the arrival of our host, I was gratified to hear "Carolan's Farewell to Music," and the beautiful "Aileen a Roon," exquisitely performed. I have listened to much music, but Jack Pigott's "Cosh-na-Breeda," by the winding Bride, and O'Leary's "Humours of Glin," are, in my estimation, the *ne plus ultra* of bagpipe melody.

In the course of the night our kind host, seeing how much pleased I was with O'Leary's "execution," requested him to favour me with an account of his adventure with the *good people* in the fort of Doon.

"Ah!" said the piper, "this gentleman has read too much to credit such stories, though, in the ancient times, people saw strange sights; and seeing was believing."

As I love legendary lore nearly as well as music, I requested the piper to relate his story; and to show that I was no sceptic in fairy legend, I told the tale of a *Cluhericane*[1] catched by my mother's gossip's grand-aunt, and of a *collough-na luha*[2] at my uncle's house, that had picked the pockets of those who sat near the *ash-pit*. The piper won into an opinion of my

---

[1] The cluherican is a tiny being that mostly practices the shoemaker's craft. When caught he usually shows the fortunate captor a crock of gold, or gives him a purse that is never found empty, as his ransom.

[2] *Collough-na-luha*, an old fairy, of light-fingered notoriety. Her station is near the ashes-corner in ancient dwelling-houses; and it is said that nothing is too hot or too heavy for her in the way of thieving.

orthodoxy, laid the chanter across his knees, and related a tale of which this is the substance.

On a November afternoon Daniel O'Leary was roused from his bed at his sister's house in the little town of Millstreet. He had retired to take a nap, for he was engaged during the preceding night at the "Wallis Arms" playing for a party of gentlemen that dined there, and had scarcely fetched half a dozen snores when his repose met the above-mentioned interruption. It was a message from the Squire of Kilmeen, commanding his attendance at the Castle: he had a grand party, and though a fiddler or two were in requisition, Miss Julia Twoomy, one of the young ladies invited, could abide no other music that O'Leary's. In fact, the estimation in which a "dinner" or wedding is held in Duhallow, is regulated by the circumstances of that piper's absence or attendance there. Though our friend Daniel disrelished this interruption, he had too much respect for the squire to "refuse going," although the evening was hazy, and he had not quite recovered from the effect of the strong whiskey-punch of the "Wallis Arms." He prepared to depart, and, after "treating" the messenger, was just taking the saddle, (for the squire had sent one of the best horses in his stable,) when a blue-eyed *thackeen* from Knocknagree "an ould acquaintance" of O'Leary's passed by, and he directed the squire's servant to walk the horse slowly on before, whilst he whispered a word or two to Nancy Walsh. They entered the public-house at the cross-road, and were so agreeably entertained with each other's conversation, over a glass of punch, that it was dark night before they parted. At length, having taken a parting kiss, the piper pursued his way in the hope of soon overtaking the man with the horse, but he reached Finown, and no servant lingered for him on the bank of its rapid water. Having made his way with difficulty over the high stepping stones, he set forward with accelerated speed in the hope of overtaking him before he reached Blackwater-bridge; for where the broad river rushes through the glen, and sweeps the tall rock at "Justices Castle," the scene is wild and lonely, and the neighbourhood of that ancient building had, time out of mind, been deemed a favourite haunt of the "*good people*." As he approached the bridge the moon was rising, and our pedestrian halted to hear if possible the friendly tramp of the horse's hoofs, and he stretched his view along the road which ascended the rising hill, but in vain; he heard no sound save the distant voice of the watch-dog, and no object met his eye but the ivied towers of the castle, surmounting the fir-trees that crowned the rock, and flung their giant shadows athwart the stream, beneath the pale moon-beams that danced like things of life upon the water.

Though Daniel O'Leary was "purty well, I thank ye," yet the punch he quaffed in Nancy Walsh's company could not make him scorn the dangers that superstition taught him to expect in this fairy haunt. Knowing the power of music on these occasions, he yoked the pipes, intending to raise a sacred melody to scare any evil thing that might hover round his path; but, owing to some unaccountable irregularity of idea, after many vain attempts he could bring out no other tune than Carolan's "Receipt for drinking Whiskey." This beautiful air rose sweetly on the night wind as he journeyed along, and when the tune was nearly concluded, he thought he could distinguish the tramp of horses. He ceased his strain, thinking it was the servant that came trotting in the distance behind; but soon perceived the sound multiplied by a hundred hoofs along the road. He now descried the dim figure of horsemen as they approached nearer, and supposing that he had fallen in with a party of *Rockites,* he withdrew a short distance from the road to the shelter of a furze-bush.

As the long procession moved onward, he thought he could distinguish among the horsemen the shapes of persons whom he had known to be long dead, and who he thought were resting in their quiet graves. But his surprise was considerably increased to behold his friend, Tom Tightly, who conversed with him alive and well that very evening in Millstreet, in the last rank that closed the cavalcade;[1] and, to complete his astonishment, the horse on which Tom rode was drowned in a bog hole to O'Leary's certain knowledge, about a fortnight before. From these circumstances the piper was now convinced that these horsemen were the *slua shee*, (fairy host). Tom wore his usual broad-brimmed beaver that saved his complexion from the summer sun, for he always shone a rustic dandy of the first water. The moon, which that moment emerged from a cloud, gleamed on the large gold ring that circled his fore-finger, and which Tom on all occasions took no small pains to display, for it descended to him through a long line of ancestry, from the sister of *Donall Caum*, whose descendant he was.

"Avirrah deelish! is it dreaming I am, or are my eyes decaving me all out," says the astonished piper, "Tom Tightly, if it's yourself that's there wouldn't you spake to the son of your own blood relation, and not lave him to die with the cowld without the benefit of the clargy, by the high road?"

" 'Tis a bad day I wouldn't do more than that," says Tom, spurring his horse into the ditch to enable the piper to mount with facility; and at that moment a peal of laughter ran through the whole troop. Had the explorer of an ancient catacomb heard the dead of a thousand years bid him welcome to their silent mansions he could not have experienced greater fear than did O'Leary, when this wild burst of unnatural mirth rose from the ranks of the strange cavalcade upon his mortal ear. When he mounted, his fear was further increased to find that neither the horse nor his rider had the solidity of frame common to mere matter; in short, they seemed to form an undefinable something between the shadow and substance of bodies. When they came to the cross road that led to the squire's the horsemen pursued the opposite direction; and when the piper attempted either to alight or expostulate with his

---

[1] The peasantry believe that a person may be pursuing his usual occupations whilst a figure exactly resembling him is seen elsewhere engaged in other business, or moving in the ranks of the *slua shee*. This apparition is called the *fetch*, and is said to forebode the death either of the seer or the seen.
[I have spoken to people both in Ireland and Gaelic Scotland who have had experiences of the *fetch* even in the present day. - Ed.]

friend, Tom, he found both his limbs and tongue equally incapable of motion. They halted at the fort of Doon, near the river Araglen, where rose a stately building, the brilliant light of which put to entire shame the lustre of the stars, and the clear full moon. In the great hall appeared a splendid company of both sexes, listening to the music of the full orchestra, where sat musicians bearing instruments, with which the piper was wholly unacquainted; and bards in white robes whose long beards flowed across their tall harps. An elderly man, bearing a long white wand, announced Daniel O'Leary, the Duhallow piper, and immediately three distinct rounds of cheering rose from the crowded assembly, till the fairy castle shook to the sound, and,

"roof an' rafters a' did dirl."

When the applause had subsided, a beautiful lady rose from her seat, and snatching a certain stringed instrument sung to the music of its chords the following strain, addressed to the astonished piper:

Thy welcome, O'Leary,
Be joyous and high;
As this dwelling of fairy
Can echo reply,
The clarseach and crotal,
And loud Bara-boo,
Shall sound not a note till
We've music from you.

The bara-boo's[1] wildness
Is meet for the fray,
The crotal's soft mildness
For festival gay:
The clairseach is meeter
For bower and hall.
But thy chanter sounds sweeter -
Far sweeter than all.

When thy fingers are flying
The chanter along,
And the keys are replying
In wildness of song;

---

[1] The *cláirseach* is the Irish harp. The crotal was a kind of bell, and the barra-boo an instrument resembling a trumpet.

Thy bagpipes are speaking
Such magical strain,
As minstrels are seeking
To rival in vain.

Shall bards of this dwelling
Admire each sweet tone,
As thy war-notes are swelling,
That erst were their own;
Shall beauties of brightness
And chieftain's of might,
To thy brisk lay of lightness
Dance featly to night.

The wine of Kincorra,[1]
The bior of the Dane[2]
Shall lighten thy sorrow
Or brighten thy strain;
In the hall of our feasting,
Though many shall dine,
We'll deem thee not least in
The banquet divine.

O'er harper and poet
We'll place thy high seat;
O'Leary, we owe it,
To piper so sweet:
And fairies are braiding,
(Such favourite art thou,)
Fresh laurel, unfading,
To circle thy brow.

Thy welcome, O'Leary,

---

[1] Kincorra, the residence of Brian Boro, on the bank of the Shannon, was famous for its wine cellars.
[2] Tradition affirms that the Danes made delicious intoxicating liquor of the mountain heath, called "Bior". The peasant of the present day, when he would assure you of a hearty welcome, says, "were ours the Bior of the Dane, or the wine of Kincorra, it would be poured out for you."

Be joyous and high;
As this dwelling of fairy
Can echo reply;
The clairseach and crotal,
And loud bara-boo,
Shall sound not a note till
We've music from you.

Then a seat that glittered like a throne was prepared for the delighted O'Leary; and a band of beautiful damsels, with laughing blue eyes, placed a garland of shining laurel round his head. The other performers were completely mute during the rest of the night. Fair ladies poured out the red wine, and pressed their favourite musician to quaff the inspiring beverage. Every new tune elicited fresh applause; and, when the dancing ended, the lords and ladies all declared that their hearts bounded lighter, and their feet beat truer time to O'Leary's music than ever before. At length, oppressed with wine, and intoxicated with the incense of applause, the piper sunk into profound repose. When he awoke in the morning, he found himself reclining at the same bush to which he had retired to let the horsemen pass; the pipes were yoked, and his left hand still grasped the chanter. He at first conceived that the scenes of the preceding night, which began to assume a definite shape in his memory, were but the dream of an imagination heated by music, whiskey punch, and his conversation with Nancy Walsh, until he found the unfading wreath yet circling his brow. This wreath of laurel he has preserved, and still exhibits as his fairy meed of musical excellence.

Such was the adventure of Daniel O'Leary. Many opinions are afloat concerning the truth of his narration; but let sceptics examine, as I have done, this curious wreath of laurel, and consider its complicated braiding, and the piper's unimpeachable veracity in all other respects before they presume to try this singular narrative by the test of their philosophy.

10
The Pooka.[1]

"Goblins haunt from fire or fen,
Or mine, or flood, to the walks of men."
Collins.

Now that "the schoolmaster is abroad," there can be no question that the warm sun of education will, in the course of a very few years, dissipate those vapours of superstition, whose wild and shadowy forms have from time immemorial thrown a mysterious mantle around our mountain summits, shed a darker horror through our deepest glens, traced some legendary tale on each unchiselled column of stone that rises on our bleakest hills, and peopled the green border of the wizard stream and sainted well with beings of a spiritual world. While, however, the friends of Ireland cannot but be pleased in thinking that our peasantry should, from being better informed, renounce their belief in these idle tales of superstition, to which they, unfortunately, have for centuries been taught to listen with delight, to the exclusion of matters more rational and more important; it is to be hoped that the two prominent features of our antiquity as a nation, will not be altogether lost sight of - namely, our vernacular language, and those extraordinary legends, which are esteemed by many as going a great length to prove - from their remarkable analogy with the tales of the eastern world - our oriental descent. Although "the good people" still retain a most respectable footing, a peasant may now travel from Cape Clear to Connemara without encountering that once dreaded personage, a ghost. Even the *Pooka*, or Irish goblin, has not for the last forty years, as far as our recollection serves, been known to shake the dripping ooze from his hairy hide, to approach the haunts of men, or to practise by the conscious light of the moon, like the fairies and satyrs of heathen mythology, any of those unlucky tricks upon his mortal neighbours, for which he was at one period so much dreaded in many portions of our island.

The Pooka is described as a frisky mischievous being, having such a turn for roguish fun, as to induce him to be all night in wait for the *carough* returning over the moor from the pleasures of the card-table, or for the frequenter of wakes. His usual appearance was that of a sturdy pony, with a shaggy hide. He generally lay couched like a cat in the pathway of the unfortunate pedestrian, then starting between his legs, he hoisted the unlucky wretch aloft on his crupper, from which no shin-breaking rushings by stone walls, no furious driving through white-thorn hedges, or life-shaking plunges down cliff and quagmire, could

---

[1] Published in *The Dublin Penny Journal*, July 4th 1835. Initialled, E.W. The tale not only throws light on the behaviour of the pooka, but also on some of the hazards facing those on the Butter Road to the renowned Cork butter and beef markets which operated from the mid 17th to early 20th century. - Ed.

unseat him. The first crowing of the March cock respited the sorrowful rider, who generally ended this dear-bought tour by a tremendous fling from the Pooka's back into some deep bog-hole, or thorny-brake, where ten thousand prickles reared their points to drink the blood of his bruised and broken flesh. On the other hand, he is reported to commiserate the lot of the benighted traveller; and there are some instances on record of his having gently trotted beneath the way-faring cottager for many a mile to the neighbourhood of the well-remembered cabin on the heath.

Feah-a-Pooka, in the county of Kerry, was, as its name imports, the haunt of one of those imaginary monsters. This feah, or marsh, belonged to Tim Dorney, a snug farmer, whose ancestors for many years occupied the adjacent farm, and who, honest men, in that golden age, never found it necessary to disturb the goblin in the favourite haunt, by reclaiming his dreary abode. But when the farm which his grandfather tilled came into Tim Dorney's occupation, a taste for improvement, and the necessary expenditure of a large and increasing family, induced him to cross-cut Feah-a-Pooka by drains and ditches; and two summers had hardly passed, when this haunt of the wild goose and the dark mischievous goblin, afforded a heavy sward of hay, and firm footing for man and beast. The pooka, thus beaten up and driven from the marsh, naturally turned his thoughts to the meditation of revenge on him who, with profane hand, rent asunder that sacred veil which the superstition of ages had woven round the dreaded spot.

Tim was a painstaking, industrious, peasant, and accustomed to traverse his farm every night, to ascertain that no neighbouring cattle trespassed on his ground. One night, as he returned along the border of the marsh, he saw something shaped like a dark-coloured, long-tailed pony lie in the narrow way, directly across his path; and before he could slip aside, to shun the lurking apparition, the pooka (for it was he) suddenly started between the legs of the terrified farmer, and bore him off the ground. The goblin rushed along with the speed of the whirlwind, and Tim's first moment of reflection was employed in a fruitless attempt to fling himself to the ground but he found that some invisible hand had bound him to the back of his supernatural enemy. It would be tedious to recount the hard rubbings against stonewalls, and the wild rushing through quickset hedges, that Tim Dorney endured, while the rapidity of his flight completely deprived him of breath and utterance. At last they rushed towards a tall cliff, which frowned in horrid gloom above the deep river, and intercepted, by its giant bulk, the yellow light of the moon that gilt the mountaintops, quivered in the rustling foliage of the trees, and, brightening in its advance, burnished the trembling waters with liquid fire. The pooka pushed with unabated speed to the edge of the rock - then suddenly stopped, as if to add to the death-pang of his agonised victim, by a previous view of the fearful height and the dark waves that curled among the pointed rocks below. Tim Dorney now concluding that all of this life would be ended for him in the next plunge, yelled a shriek of unutterable dismay. The tall cliff returned the piercing sound, which with the scream of the startled wildfowl, and the demon voice of the pooka, that combined the mockery of human laughter with a wild, indescribable howl, blended in horrid unison along the lonely glen. Whether the pooka was satisfied with thus inflicting the pangs of a frightful death by anticipation, or that he possessed no power over human life, does not appear; but in the next moment he started from the fearful cliff, and returning through the deep ravines and tangled underwood, to a furze brake that skirted the border of a standing pool, plunged his unfortunate rider among the sharp bushes. Happy in his deliverance, he heard the troubled waters of the dark pool resound to the plunge of the returning pooka - beheld his uncouth figure glance darkly along the moor, till the lessening form grew dimly faint in the moonshine - and the hurried splashing of his rapid hoof broke the silence of the night no more. Tim, as may naturally be supposed, made the best of his way to the cottage; and being of true Milesian origin, determined on having his revenge upon his fiendish enemy.

It was a fine night in the month of August, when Tim Dorney, having sufficiently recruited himself after his adventure of wild horsemanship, walked forth, like him "that hath his quarrel just," doubly armed. His heels were furnished with a pair of long-necked spurs that bore rowels contrived at the next forge, which could goad a rhinoceros to death. His hand wielded a leaden whip, so called from the handle being set with lead, and in the grasp of a strong man was capable of felling an ox. "He whistled as he went," not, "for want of thought," for his mind was brooding over a plan of revenge against the pooka, who according to his usual habit, started between the farmer's legs, and bore him off. Tim, nothing loth at the abduction, just when the pooka was commencing his antics, twisted the lash of the whip round his hand, and levelled such blows about the goblin's ears, as would have crushed any skull made of mortal, penetrable stuff, while the sharp-rowelled spurs gave ample revenge for the pointed insults of the preceding night. "Dire were the tossings, deep the groans," of the pooka during this unmerciful ride; but Tim Dorney clung to him like a monkey, until the pooka lay down, outmastered by his mortal antagonist. Next night, Tim walked abroad in quest of his acquaintance. He whistled his favourite air of "Tham-a-hulla," to lull the suspicions of the latter, who held aloof, quite on his guard eying the other from his lurking-place, and breaking his usual taciturnity by asking, in an uncouth voice, the well-remembered question, "*A will na gerane urth?*"[1]

Some years had now rolled their seasons round, and the pooka seemed to have entirely forgotten his antagonist, and his ancient dwelling of the marsh, when Tim Dorney had occasion to visit a gossip's sister's cousin's brother-in-law, who had lately come home after an absence of twenty-five years on board a man of war. The credit side of the account-sheet of this seaman's life was fraught with a copious list of wonders - "all his travels; history" - and a pension of nine-pence a day. On the debtor side stood the loss of the right arm, the closing of his starboard eye, and sundry minor details, received in the duty of his boarding

---

[1] 'Have you the sharp thing on?' [i. e., the spurs.- Ed.]

and cutting out, with occasional tavern scuffles. Tim was highly delighted at the "tough yarn" of his old acquaintance - heard with "gaping wonderment" the recital of a battle with a French seventy-four off the island of Elbow (Elba), where the relater lost his precious *arm*; an encounter with a Salee rover, which they sent down to *Old Davy*; and the dreadful storm near the island of *Moll Tow* (Malta); of voyages along the coast of *Tunis*, where the people are all musicianers; by *Tripoli*, famous for its *wrestlers*; and a journey through the desert of *Barka*, where the inhabitants, men and women, have *dog's heads!* The ale of a neighbouring *shebeen* greatly improved the sailor's turn for narration; and though the rain poured in torrents through the grass-grown roof of the cabin, yet

'The night flew on with songs an' clatter,
And aye the ale was growing better.'

But Tim being retained that night to form one of a party that had engaged to play at cards for two hundred of herrings; and as he was a famous carough, he could not disappoint his friends, who mainly depended on Tim's address to carry off the wager. The rain had now ceased, and after grasping the sailor's hand, and requesting his company on a given night at Feah-a-Pooka, he departed. The moon, yet obscured by heavy clouds, cast a sad and sickly gleam along his path, which winding round a precipitous descent, led into the bosom of a deep glen, where the turbid mountain torrents had swelled into muddy waves the clear and beautiful brook, that erewhile had bubbled with soothing murmurs along the yellow pebbles. There was no sound on the hill, save the plaintive howl of the watchdog, baying the broad round moon. The night wind slightly shook the thin foliage of the decaying wood that surmounted the steep sides of the glen, and the hoarse, hollow sound of the roaring river, that would seem to a fanciful ear the boding voice of the water fairy, echoed along the distant banks. Though Tim Dorney's education had taught him to people the loneliest scenes with beings of another life, yet he passed unappalled to the brink of the torrent, and sighed to behold that the force of the stream left him little chance of crossing over with safety. While he loitered along the bank, he was agreeably surprised to behold in a little cove, which led into a ford, a small horse, resembling a Kerry pony. He was tied by a halter, had a *pilleen susa,* or straw saddle, on his back, and into one of the foldings of the straw saddle was stuck a *white-thorn* plant.[1] Tim, grateful for this favourable opportunity of moving homeward, had already his leg raised to mount, when the titter of suppressed laughter behind a crag, shook his heart with terror, and excited his suspicion of the pony.

[1] The white-thorn is said to be an unlucky tree, are the peasantry and particularly careful that none of it forms any part of the roof or doorway of their houses, as such habitations would be liable to fairy visits.

He had not meddled with the white-thorn stick, for he rarely went abroad by day or night unprovided with a choice hazel sapling.[1] This miraculous plant, against which nothing evil can contend, well served this time of need; for retiring a little, Tim Dorney bestowed so hearty a salute on the guileful pooka, (for it was he,) that the laughter sounds were changed into a wild howl, and as the pooka disappeared along the troubled stream, the dashing waters deluged the sounding banks.

But a time arrived when the persevering goblin wreaked cruel revenge on his hitherto fortunate adversary. It was approaching the 25th of March, when the farmers usually pay the rent; and Tim, who was extremely punctual in the payment of the half-year's gale, prepared to send a quantity of the last season's butter to Cork for that purpose. Wheel carriages were then totally unknown in that part of the country - "the sliding car, indebted to no wheels," glided in the vicinity of the farms, while burdens were conveyed to more remote places on the backs of horses. Five or six neighbours at this time were setting off to transmit the produce of the dairy to Cork, and Tim, with four stunted nags that usually ran wild and free on the mountains, fell into their company. Each little horse was generally laden with two *fullbounds* of butter; but one or two, whose owners were unable to furnish the even number of firkins, carried a large stone placed on the opposite side to balance the single one. After journeying all night, on the next morning an accident happened to Tim Dorney in his way through Millstreet, that seemed the type and forerunner of the evening's misfortune. As the *Kerry dragoons* marched in long procession through the single street that composes this little town, the drummer of a company of soldiers stationed in the barrack, "beat the doubling drum," with such "furious heat" as set all the ponies prancing beneath their riders and butter firkins. It happened that the nag on which Tim rode, by an unfortunate curvette on the slippery pavement, had his heels tripped up, and he fell under the load that lumbered on his back. The rider, whose Milesian irascibility was not much allayed at having the accident perpetrated by a *red coat*, drew his trusty *hazel* from its resting-place between the firkins, and by its instantaneous application to the drummer's head forced him to bite the dust. Though the drummer, for certain *striking* reasons, was no favourite with his comrades, yet a sentinel, who witnessed this insult to the *cloth*, levelled Tim with the butt-end of his piece. The alarm being given, the soldiers rushed thick and fast to assault the *Kerry dragoons*, and as quick rushed the town-folk to their support. The reader's imagination must supply what I would fail in delineating: it will suffice to tell, that after some broken heads and bayonet thrusts on both sides, the red-coats retreated to their strong-hold, and the triumphant Kerryonians were escorted by their faithful allies to the summit of Mushera mountain.

---

[1] Tradition says, that the staff with which St. Patrick banished serpents and evil spirits from Ireland, was hazel - that the touch of hazel is instant death to venomous reptiles - and that unholy spirits fly at its approach.

In the evening, the caravan came within view of Blarney Castle, while the last rays of the declining sun tinged its ivied turrets with golden hue. As the night breeze blew keen and fierce, our travellers halted at a small public house on the road, to repel its chilling influence by a glass of spirits. Their delay was hardly for a minute, and they hastened to overtake the horses that moved at a slow pace before them; but suddenly some strange disorder began to prevail among the animals; some fled terrified along the road - others ran across the open common that extended to the right - and Tim Dorney's train, particularly, were observed to reach a fearful and perpendicular descent, from whose edge the road lay about twenty yards. Their terrified owner uttered a shriek of dread and despair, when he beheld the misshapen, hairy pooka urge his cattle to the steep cliff. It was only the work of a moment - they rushed as if by an irresistible impulse to the fatal brink, and, tumbling headlong, one instant beheld their shattered, lifeless carcasses strew the bottom of the stream-worn ravine; the pointed rocks below staved the butter-casks to pieces, and their contents were wholly lost. This was but the commencement of a train of misfortune to Tim Dorney. He was finally ejected from his snug, well-improved farm. Feah-a-Pooka, that had been in the occupation of his family for a hundred and fifty years before, passed into the hands of strangers; and the descendants of Tim Dorney are homeless wanderers on the earth; and such is the account which at this day is given by the remaining members of the family, of the commencement of their misfortune.

11
The Whiteboy[1]
A tale of truth

In the decline of autumn in the year 18 -, two travellers pursued their starlit way by a beaten horse track, that extended eastward from the parish of K - along a dark and undivided heath. The more conspicuous of the two was a horseman, whose garb presented that semi-genteel cut and cloth which usually designate the class of persons in Irish society called half-sirs. A large whip loaden with led graced his right hand, which, with a pair of rusty spurs, that seemed to have been once plated, and whose well-worn rowels were no longer capable of effective duty, was in constant application to the sides of the lean, bony gelding which he bestrode, to enable him to keep up with the active pedestrian that accompanied him, whose agile and firm step outstripped the stumbling pace of his four-footed companion. This man on foot was slender and elegantly formed; his dress indicated him of the better class of peasants, and his olive complexion and thick, though not bushy, whiskers, were well relieved by eyes of uncommon animation; but a nameless expression that lurked round the dark eye and protruding under lip, gave his otherwise pleasing features a somewhat sinister appearance. He bore a short gun on his shoulder, and as the keen night breeze blew aside his loose upper coat, a pair of pistols might be seen stuck in the broad leather belt that circled his waist; his years were less than those of his companion, and they seemed not more than five and twenty.

They passed almost silently along, till they came where the footway descended the side of a glen, which bore the shattered remains of an ancient wood. Right below, a turbid mountain-stream dashed among the shapeless rocks that impeded its narrow bed. Far down, on the opposite side, rose dimly against the dark clouds a thick cluster of trees, and the voice of the watch-dog beyond, gave indication of their approach towards the habitations of men - when he of the gelding suddenly breaking silence, said in an undertone,

"Captain, was it not in a glen deep and rocky like this that the boys waylaid the ammunition-cart, on its way from Fermoy to the barrack at Glanisheen?"

"Yes," answered the other in a whisper scarcely audible; "but the scene there was more wild and lonely, and no fitter spot could be found in which to execute a deed of plunder and revenge. We had information that the police would escort a quantity of powder and ball to the barrack on a certain day, and were determined to intercept them, and thus accomplish a double purpose of revenge on the Peelers, and the supplying of ourselves with ammunition. It was a stormy, lowering day, the rock-strewn river that rushed through the glen was swelled with the rain of the preceding night, and the descent to the ford winded between high ditches that continued to the edge of the stream. Thirty fellows lay inside the ditch by

---

[1] Published in The *Dublin Penny Journal*, July 11th 1835. Initialled, E.W. - Ed.

the ford; twelve of the number bore pikes, and the remainder, who were armed with guns, could bring down a snipe or a swallow in its most irregular flight. In some time we heard the noise of the cartwheels, and the measured military tramp of feet. Down the glen they winded in our view: six men and a sergeant were in front of the cart, and three others moved behind. As they approached the ford, the sergeant, startled by the wild scene, looked round with a keen, commanding eye. Every heart now beat high - every man's hand was on the trigger, waiting my signal to fire, when a gust of wind blew aside the watch-coat of the tall, muscular sergeant, and betrayed his red jacket and white belts.

" 'They are soldiers,' I whispered, 'rush before them with a loud hurrah, but fire not at your peril.'

" 'Sure, Captain, you were not afraid to fire at the soldiers?" rejoined the first speaker.

"Afraid! Why I had as good boys as ever drew a trigger or flourished a pike - if we were so inclined, they would not have borne our attack for three minutes; but we had no enmity against the soldiers, and were determined to secure the contents of the cart without hurting its guard. When our shrill yell resounded through the glen, and the sergeant saw the wild troop burst upon his front, he with admirable coolness retired with his men to the rear, where, screened behind the cart, he waited the expected attack. I motioned the boys to halt, and advancing a step or two bid the soldiers retire, and leave us possession of the cart. I further observed, that resistance on their part would be but to rashly sacrifice their lives, and that we did not intend them the slightest injury.

" 'We will not yield our convoy but with our lives, and we are resolved to fight to the last drop of our blood,' said the intrepid sergeant.

" 'Captain darling,' cried the boys, 'as we can't have a slap at the Peelers, welcome be the grace of God; but we don't like to touch the sogers, or bring the brave fellows to trouble at all at all.'

" 'I was right glad to find the temper of the boys coincide with my own feelings; and I ordered them to move slowly up the glen by the river's side, while I followed behind; and as we retired the soldiers gave us three cheers, which the boys returned, till the piercing cry seemed multiplied fifty-fold, as it swept from cliff to cliff along the intricacies of that wild glen."

Our travellers had now reached the stream, and pursuing the path that traversed the side of the glen in nearly the direction of the river, they gained the clump of trees already mentioned; and after crossing a field, and passing a haggard that contained some ricks of corn and hay, they entered a house, the glazed windows of which, and well thatched roof, bespoke a comfortable residence, according to the estimate generally formed of Irish comforts. This was the habitation of the horseman to whom we have introduced the reader. They entered silently, and when beyond the porch, glided suddenly into an inner apartment, where the mistress of the house, a good-looking woman, waited their arrival. The table was laid, and a piece of beef and a barn-door fowl shrunk to narrow dimensions beneath the sharp knife and keen appetites of the two. When the cloth was removed, and a decanter of sparkling whiskey and a pair of those drinking glasses called tumblers (probably from the levelling quality of their contents) were placed on the board, the host said,

"Captain, I fear you have done nothing; however, the dinner, though poor, was not a churlish one, and you have a welcome and twenty."

"Thankyou, Mr. Sellman," the guest replied, "the dinner carries its own excuse; and I have not felt more at ease, nor eaten a heartier meal, since I was forced four years ago from my father's house, and driven upon the *schachraune*."

The hostess, who was retiring with the fragments of the dinner, stood still, evidently affected by the stifled tone of the stranger. Then casting a look of keen reproach at her husband, and then a glance of commiseration at the guest, she retired, wiping off the tear that stood in her large blue eye. The glasses were filled and emptied in quick succession; and the host, by his example and urgent solicitation, seemed desirous of making his guest drink deeply.

"You mentioned," said the farmer, "that you were driven from your father's house four years ago; but you have never told me by what events you were obliged to adopt your present mode of life."

"My story is a short but melancholy one. My father was the most respectable farmer in the parish of —. He gave me a liberal education, and it was the dearest wish of his heart that I should enter into holy orders: but fate had otherwise ordained. Happening to dine on a summer's evening with the parish priest, I was returning homeward, when the shrieks of a female excited my attention. They proceeded from a clump of trees that grew near a pathway which formed a short cut across the fields to meet the high road. As I approached, the cries rose faint and short, and I soon discovered a female struggling violently with a well-dressed ruffian. I rushed to the spot, and wielding a knotty blackthorn, bid the ruffian turn and defend himself. Great was my astonishment to discover Squire Craven, my father's landlord, in the person before me. He turned with the rage of a tiger, and snatching a pistol from his bosom discharged it at me. Fortunately, the ball only grazed my temple; and before he could present the second pistol, I rushed upon him and levelled him to the earth. I beat him severely, and leaving him nearly motionless, I assisted the fainting object of his violence home. She was my near relation. I was delighted at being the instrument of preserving the poor girl from his brutal treatment. But the squire soon had his revenge. He was a justice of the peace, and had informations sworn against me before the board of magistrates at the next town, for an unprovoked and felonious assault on him. He likewise procured a perjured ruffian to swear that I was a captain of whiteboys. The police were engaged in close and constant search of me, and I was obliged to abscond and seek concealment in the most retired parts of the country. My family, by unceasing oppression, were ejected from their snug farm. My father died heart-broken, and my aged mother and sisters beg their bread, homeless and unprotected. The villainy of those who should set a good example to my class in society, had driven me to deeds at which my soul revolts; and for my own preservation I am become, what I was at first falsely sworn to be, a whiteboy, and a man of blood. I would fain erase from my memory many a deed of violence, but recollection haunts me even as the shadow pursues its substance. Would to heaven I could escape to a land, where my grievous wrongs and my many crimes are unknown; but the vigilance of the police will hardly permit this last resource, and I dread that the large reward offered for my apprehension will induce some miscreant to betray me. But to anticipate evil is folly: here let us fill a bumper, and toast high hanging to all informers."

The whiteboy captain raised his glass - his host hesitated - the blood of his cheek retreated to his heart, as he lifted the brimmer in his trembling hand, the sparkling punch sprinkled the table; but the next moment saw him regain his self-possession - the blood returned from its citadel to light his blanched cheek and pallid lip, while with unfaltering tone he drank the toast, and drained the tumbler dry.

The night was now far advanced, and the owner of the house retired, leaving his guest to occupy a bed, which stood in the apartment. The whiteboy, though strongly under the influence of the deep potations of the night, forgot not to examine the state of his trusty gun and pistols, which he placed on a table beside his bed. Heavy with drink, he was soon asleep; but his slumber was restless, and his dreams oppressive. Many an undefined and painful appearance was presenting to his mind's view, inflicting terror on his troubled soul. The vague and formless images at length rolled along as clouds before the compelling wind, and the following scene arose before the unfortunate sleeper.

He dreamed that he stood upon the seashore of his own beloved land. On one side rose rocky eminences whose summits seemed to pierce the clouds. On the other, the smooth beautiful sea extended far into the land, forming a harbour, studded with many a lovely islet, within which a forest of masts and a beautiful city seemed to emerge from the deep. Beyond appeared an extensive country, containing villas, groves, and winding rivers on the banks of which grazed many a fat and peaceful herd; before him lay the sea - the calm, crystal sea - over whose bright bosom many a white sail flitted towards some distant land. As he gazed on this scene of beauty, a tall bark touched the shore, and its crew seemed to beckon him on board, that he might flee to

"Some safer world, in depth of woods embraced -
Some happier island in the watery waste."

He wept at his sad destiny, and he wept at the tantalizing offers of those strange mariners who would tempt him to his destruction into the deep sea. Suddenly the fair view vanished before him - the vessel disappears - the sky lowers and the wind lashes into foam the gigantic waves, which culminate nearly to the mountaintops. Anon the trampling of horses, and the shouts of the pursuers resound fearfully in his ear - he flies - the enemy gain fast upon his fainting, faltering footsteps. He reaches a tall cliff - before him yawns a horrid chasm, behind approaches certain destruction, with the pursuing shout and sabre of the Saxon soldier - he plunges into the dark and undefined gulf, and awakes with the horrid exertion. Panting and breathless with mental agony, he felt relieved to find the frightful scene which his fancy had created, vanished with his sleep; but the trampling of the horsemen yet resounded in his ears; he strove to shake off the trammels of this mental delusion. It was dreadful reality; for the horses' hoofs beat thick and heavy on the pavement outside. Prepared for the worst, he started from the bed, and vainly groped for the firearms which he had laid beside him as he went to repose. Then he heard whispers, and saw the light streaming through the doorway of his apartment, which had been left open to facilitate the entrance of his captors. He now knew that his treacherous host had betrayed him, and he resolved not to be taken alive. Standing behind the door, as a tall sergeant of dragoons entered, with a lantern in one hand, and his drawn sabre in the other, the whiteboy struck him so powerful a blow of his clenched fist under the ear, that he extended him on the floor; then snatching the sword from the grasp of the prostrate soldier, he rushed upon the file that pressed forward thick and fierce in alarm at the clash produced by the heavy accoutrements of the fallen dragoon. He rushed upon them with the wildness of despair - cut the right shoulder of the foremost man nearly in two, and laid open the cheek of the second. The soldiers, astonished at this unexpected attack, reeled backward from their single enemy - they beheld with superstitious awe the naked apparition, and shrunk from his flashing steel. Aided by their irresolution he gained the door unhurt, and sprung over the large ditch in front. A dozen carbines were discharged at him, and some drove forward in pursuit; but he soon gained the glen, where the tall rocks and stunted trees of the decayed wood soon hid him from his pursuers.

The dragoons now proceeded to explore the glen. There was no light of the moon, and the whiteboy could easily baffle their pursuit, did not the treacherous Sellman lead them along all the windings of the way. The object of their search had now stolen to the edge of the river, where the stream winded within a high projecting bank. The shouts of the soldiers intermixed with occasional execrations on the bloody rebel and their own eyes and limbs, sounded nearer and nearer. He now saw no chance of escape but by plunging into the stream - down he went, and couching beneath the willows that shaded the bank, with his head only above the water, he awaited the approach of his pursuers. Led by their guide, they explored every nook around; the strong glare of the bog-deal torches with which the farmers are furnished in the decline of autumn for the spearing of salmon in the streams, and which the dragoons bore from Sellman's to light them in their search, fell full before his lurking place, and illuminated the stream around. Secure from observation, he held his post, till the receding torch-light left him in pitchy darkness, the heavy tramp of the dismounted dragoons ceased to strike his ear, and the loud halloo and the uncouth oath came fainter and fainter in the distance, as the soldiers returned to their horses, weary and disappointed. When the whiteboy found his enemies gone, he crawled, after an immersion of two hours, from his lurking place, stiff and trembling: the cold had nearly frozen the life in his heart, and his limbs for some time refused their wonted motion; but as he moved along, the vital glow returned. He crossed the river, and moving at a quick rate along the heath which he traversed the preceding evening with his traitor friend, at length arrived at a hospitable cabin by break of day, after having travelled six miles in his shirt. Here he was furnished with some articles of dress, which enabled him to pass on to a haunt of greater safety.

In three months after this singular escape, and about break of day, a strong party of foot police were observed to direct their course to a hamlet situated at the foot of a hill, which forms a link in that mountain chain extending from Fermoy towards the Atlantic on the west. Two persons accompanied them, whose dress indicated no connection with the police establishment. The less considerable of these personages was a long-legged, shoeless fellow: his upper garment was like Joseph's raiment, "a coat of many colours" - the shapeless caubeen surmounted his lank, thin locks, between which gleamed two grey eyes of sinister cast and various obliquity. This was a spy, induced by the promise of some reward, to betray the whiteboy captain. The other, who was mounted on a spirited horse, and carried a gun, and whose garb was that of the country gentleman, was no other than Squire Craven, the captain's redoubtable foe, and the sole cause of his misfortunes and crime.

As the party advanced towards the cluster of cabins, that sent forth from many a roof and door the deep blue smoke of the morning fire into the brightening atmosphere, they perceived a man armed with a long gun rush beyond them. It was the unfortunate whiteboy. He crossed the fields with great rapidity, and left the police far behind; but Squire Craven, who led the pursuit, drove forward, unimpeded by ditch or fence. The whiteboy was now at one extremity of a large field, while his determined persecutor entered at the other, and the police came on slowly and far behind. The captain was long celebrated for the accuracy of his aim, and it was said that he could hit the smallest mark within range of his gun. Panting and fatigued, he turned, and saw Squire Craven alone continue the pursuit, and he resolved to await his enemy's approach. Squire Craven now checked his career, and they stood for one moment regarding each other with fierce malignity. The whiteboy then presented his gun; but anxious to avoid the slaughter of his enemy, he fired only at his horse. The unerring ball pierced his breast; and the animal sprung forward in the struggle of death, and fell. His rider disengaged himself from the dying horse, and falling upon one knee, discharged his gun at his adversary, who by this time had gained the gripe of the ditch. The ball entered at his back, and arrested his further flight. He fell: then tottering forward, he fired the remaining shot of his double-barrelled gun at the advancing foe; but his aim was no longer true, for the film of death passed thick and heavy over his eye-balls. Loud shouts soon announced the approach of the police. With one dying effort he broke his faithful gun, and scattered his cartridges to the wind, resolving that no stranger hand should bear away one trophy of his defeat. Then, when the foe drew near, he raised his arm, and flourished in fierce defiance the fragment of the broken gun which remained in his grasp; and as the last stream of life ebbed from his heart, he expired, as he had lived, desperate and unsubdued.

12
Paddy Doyle's First Trip to Cork[1]

Mr. Editor. As I saw in an ould number of the Dublin Penny Journal, a letter from Darby Doyle, giving an account of his thrip to Quebec; - an' as Darby was my own blood relation, being my first cousin jarmin, by the father's side, I said to myself, if this Dublin jantleman printed Darby's letther, about his voyage to America, why shouldn't I make bould to throuble him with an account of my trip to Cork; for I'm sure an' sartin, if it was written out fairly by the schoolmaster above, an' if you, yourself, would take to thrubble of correcting it, it would be just as amusing as my cousin Darby's.

Afther Jillian Murphy, the mother o' my little grawls, went from us, I was forced to give up the sod of ground for want o' help. Jillian an' I wor tied for nine years, an' we had, in that time, as many little girls; for she was very fond, afther a way she had of having twins, poor dear woman, an' in all that time, "ill you did it," wasn't between us. I left the ground, as I was saying, an' took a cabin on the road side, an' kept a bit of a baste at work on the new line that was thin carrying on by Mr. Griffith, (I suppose Sir, you hard tell of him,) an' a little dhrop o' whiskey to sell to the masons an' boys that worked on the road. In the course o' time, I picked up my crums so well entirely, that I put a stone facing to the mud wall of my cabin, struck a bit of a pavement from the dure to the road, to make my place cumfortable for thravellers; got a settle-bed in the kitchen, an' if the little girls didn't garnish the new dhresser with all kinds an' sizes of crockery-ware, 'tisn't day yet! an' instead ov buying me little gallon of christened whiskey, at John Sullivan's, in Millstreet, I used to sind for it to Mr. Punch, the spirit seller, at Malla-lane, an' thin to another in Cork: an' at last, as I got stronger, nothing would plaze me, but to hoist off my sails to the beautiful city itself, for a full cask, from the fountain head, at Murphy's still. So getting Shaune into the ould car, an' putting a few good yellow boys into the heel of an ould stocking, I commenced my journey.

On arriving in Cork, I put up my horse at a frind's house, an' turned down Goulasporra, towards the ould jail, that is, where the ould jail was, for they took it out to the counthry some time ago, to give the pris'ners a taste of fresh air, I suppose. As I turned Goulasporra, as I was saying, who should I meet, but my gossip, Jim Connor.

"Well met, Jim," sis I, "I'm going a bit beyant here, to dhrop a letther from Father Foley, (which was thrue for me, at a sartin house,) an' thin we'll take the wetting of our lips together." Jim pushed on with me, an' on our return, afther laving the letther, we passed through a fine sthreet, where all the shops were crowded with rumps o' beef, an' legs o' mutton, an' beautiful fish; but the sight o' the roast beef, an' delightful parfume, knocked me up entirely.

---

[1] Published in *The Dublin Penny Journal*, July, 25th 1835. Initialled, E.W. - Ed.

"Jim, avic," sis I, "that's a grand sight, I wondher what soart o' people ates all that mate."

"Thrue for ye Pad," sis he, "I suppose they must be people that have teeth an' stummucks like ourselves."

"O, more sorra to ye," sis I, Jim Connor, "for Egan O'Rahilly wouldn't bate you at a joke, - but I wondher would they let two *cabogues* (vulgar persons) like us, taste it at-all, at-all."

"Jist as the words left my mouth, an I standin' in the street, a fine flahool lady came to the dure.

"Walk in Pad," sis she, "and take a bit o' dinner, - you must have an appetite afther your journey."

"Long life, an' a thousand thanks to yer ladyship," sis I, taking off my hat, an' making a ginteel scrape with my leg, that sent the gutther five yards beyant me, an' a bow a little below my knees.

"Your ladyship must be from Duhallow, to know my name, - do ye belong, madam, to the O'Driscolls, or the grate Kelihers of that counthry?"

"O! I hard tell o'thim," sis she, "an' many's the Duhallow man, besides you, throubles me here."

"Walk in an' make much o' yourself, Jim" sis I, "for what do ye stand grinnin' there like a Kerry goat, sure you know a man can take a stocach (an attendant) with him any where he's invited, - be bowld man.

In we wint.

"What'll ye choose, sir," says the lady, "would ye have some beef an' cabbage, a nice bit o' mutton an' colicflower, (cauliflower,) or a porcupine o' vale, or — "

"Go no further, madam a-chree," sis I, "as to the porcupine, the sorra a wan I ever saw cooked, let alone ate - we'll pass that - the colicflour must be good for the stummuck - and by the same token, I had a spice o' the gripe all day: - so we'll thry that an' the mutton, with your lave, afther we taste a thrifle o' the beef an' cabbage."

"Molly," sis she, "shew the gintlemen up stairs, into the small room."

Molly was a good-looking girl, with a mighty roguish bit of an eye, an' a smile that id coax a wild plover.

"Molly," sis I, ma colleen bawn, (she had fair hair, beautifully curled,) "I wish I had you in the sporting barenny of Duhallow, where I have a snug stone-wall house o' my own, d' ye see; - I'd keep ye like the first lady o' the land."

"Keep yer freedom, my good man," sis she, "till ye meet your own equals." An' she looked mighty grand, and tossed her curls, and whisked out o' the room.

"Jim, a vrahir," (cousin,) sis I, "we're dished; I'm sure an' sartin that is nobody else but her ladyship's daughter that I affrinted with my rolliciking."

The dinner kem up in grate style, but the colicflour was neyther flour nor male, but bunches of some stuff, like the tops of eldher; the musthard would make you hould your nose for an hour, and the beer was mighty tart, 'twould fissick a snipe, and the mutton, 'id make you keep your head a good bit from the wall; so Jim and I stuck to the beef an'cabbage, till we left short commons of it.

As soon as we had done, "Jim, avourneen," sis I, "let us gather up our scrapers an' be going, I don't feel quite at aise here." We walked down stairs as softly as our brogues would let us - but who should be standing at the bottom, but the landlady herself. Sis the lady, sis she,

"I hope your dinner was to yir liking."

"Long life to yer ladyship," sis I, "that was what you may call a flahool dinner - the sorra betther from this to the Causeway; an' whin we go home to Duhallow, I'll let O'Collins's seven plough-lands, at any rate, know yer hospitality."

"Yehave only wan shilling and six-pence a piece to pay," sis she, "an' I'll expect yer custom in future."

"What, madam," sis I, "sure you wouldn't be afther axing us in to our own expinse."

"Pay down the money, honest man," sis she, "there's nothin' for nothin' on Cork stones."

"O, musha, bad manners to ye," sis I, "ye brandy-faced — if that's yer hospitality, to take in at such a rate, a pair of simple counthry gomuls, that havn't a cross o' money, goold, silver, or brass, to bless themselves with, we wor the two unlooky crathurs to be so deceived by such an imposther."

"Where is yer husband?" sis I, flourishing my blackthorn, an' slapping up the lafe o' my hat, at the same time, to see the betther before me. "Where is yer husband?" sis I, "an' as sure as you're livin', if it was any wan waring a britches, that took such an unfair hoult of a poor soft boy like me, but I'd dust his jacket for him."

But what do you think, my hunny, she sint for a constable, underhand.

"Mr. Slyman," sis she, "here's two counthry spalpeens came a sconcing my house, an' running off with the reckoning, and 'saulting a respectable housekeeper."

"Pay the woman, my good fellow," sis he, "or come before the Mare."

"Yis,"sis I, "I'll go before any mare or horse in Ireland, agin the garrin that took an advantage, an' soothered me into her house, an' not a keenogue in my pocket."

So he boned me by the collar, for fear I'd give leg bail, d' ye see; - Mr. Jim, like a sleeveen, med off.

When we kem before the mare - "meela milloon mulla! sis I to myself, "what a wondherful city this is; "this mare is a rele jintleman, what a dhroll name they call him." So I up and toult him my story, and she up an' toult hers, and afther a power of fending and proving, the mare - long life to his honour, afther larning that I hadn't a pinny in my pocket, - an' that was raal truth, for I slipt every marvidy of my money, notes an' silver, into my brogues, - the mare said she had no right to thripan (that was his word,) poor simple counthry people into her house, and dismissed the case altogether, and my kishough[1] waddled home like a grampus, with her finger in her mouth.

---

[1] Shapeless mass. [*ciseog*, a round shallow basket. – Ed.]

So far, so well! for I left the mare-ill-three-house with flying colours - picked my thrifle o' money out of my brogues, at a convenient place, and wint to the still for my whiskey, an' took out my permit, an' was dhriving up Blarney-lane, thinkin;' of nothing at all, whin a talla-faced man kim up frinting the horse an' load - my baste stopt up.

"Wheeps Shawn," (Jack,) sis I, "do ye think I stole you."

"Is your name Paddy Doyle," sis the talla-faced man?

"Yis," sis I, "what's yer will o' me? My name is Paddy Doyle of Shandangin, above board: - Paddy Doyle that's neyther afeard nor ashamed of no man." I spoke big, for I didn't like the cast of the fellow's eye, and thought he was wanting to throw the gawmogue over me.

"I don't at all doubt it," sis he, "for if you had fear or shame in your forred, you wouldn't be afther robbing that jantleman yonder on the flags," - an' he pointed with his finger across the street.

"None of yer tricks upon thravellers, my gay fellow," sis I, "I never put the two eyes of my head on him afore."

"That's Mr. Punch the publican, from Malla-lane," sis he, "an' he has taken out a decree agin ye for a debt of four pounds, due for goods sowld and delivered, an' I must seize upon the whiskey."

I kept a stiff hoult o' the horse's head, an' Mr. Punch drew near-

"Are you Mr. Punch, Sir," sis I; for I didn't know him an' taking off my hat, "may-be your honour would have marcy on an unfortunate angishore, that wouldn't intend to desave you at-all, and I'll pray for marcy on your sowl, an' the sowls o' the seven ginerations that left you."

Mr. Punch shook his head.

"For the sowls of all your nearest an' dearest relations, your gran' father, an'gran' mother, your uncle an' aunt, your brothers and sisters, the father that reared you, the mother that bore you, an' if there be blot or blame, pain or punishment, consequence o' confession, missing o' mass, pinnance unperformed, or freaks o' folly on their sowls, the prayers o' the poor widdy, (widower,) an' the blessing of the orphans, go to their cumfort for ever an' ever, an' don't be the ruinashun of an industrus man, with a cabin full of femul grawls."

Another shake o' the head.

"The blisssing o' the motherless children 'ithin an' 'ithout ye, above an' below ye, over an' undher ye, lying an' rising, sitting an' standing, sleeping and waking, eating an' dhrinking, late an' airly, dhrunk an' sober, an' let go the dhrop o'whiskey to Jillian Murphy's crathers."

Here Mr. Punch smiled, which made me think I softened him a thrifle, an' thin I detarmined to stick a little longer to the blessed litany I was saying for him.

"The blessin o' the twelve thribes, the twelve patriarchs, the twelve prophits, the twelve apostles, the twelve martyrs, an' the twelve heavenly signs o' the zodiac on your seed an' breed, an' don't dhrive me on the belly o' the high road - Mr. Punch avourneen,[1] by taking the support o' the heavy femul burthin from me."

Not aword from the Buddha. "I'll take all the bravery's (breviaries) in Rome, all the books in Father Foley's house, the holy Batha Phadrig, an' the wondherful Ranigh O'Reefe that id twist the mouth o' the false swearer *west*, where his pole should be, that I'll pay you yer money, an' don't take me short, an' that death mightn't take you short."

It was all to no use to butther Mr. Punch up; if I prached a sarmunt, and said a high mass for him, I couldn't soften his nayther, an' he beckened to the thief o' a bailiff, who wheeled about the horse an' car; an' my taste o' whiskey was taken before me face, and lodged in his consarns; but my poor baste was let go. I left Shaune at the ould place, and strolled into the city, jest to look at the Yall(a?) House. I was quite down-hearted, an' looked for all the world like a motherless calf. I stood on Parliament Bridge, an' as I laned over the battlements, it ran into my head, some how or other, to dhrown myself, out an' out, but the height o' the bridge made me afraid of braking my nick in the wather. At last, I turned about to dhrive away wicked thoughts, whin I saw a fine-looking jantleman coming up the bridge; I rec'lected that I seen him in the morning, whin I took out the *permit.*

"Now's the time!" sis I, "that's a gauger, if I live, and I'll make Mr. Punch sup sorrow."

I up, an' off with my hat, an' sis I,

"Would it be the wil of yer honour to let a poor man know where he'd be likely to meet a gantleman o' the oxcise, (excise.)"

"I'm shuperwiser, (supervisor,) myself," sis he, "put on yer hat, poor man."

"Sur," sis I, "don't suspect me for an informer, at all, at all; my seed, breed, an' gineration always scorned the like, but a scoundhrel in Malla-lane, has played the puck with me, an' I want a little revinge on him."

"It's all nathral," sis he, "if he ill-used ye."

"He's the ruinashon of myself, an' nine motherless grawls; an' he has, at this blessid minit that I spake to ye, forty gallons o' whiskey, in his back-house, unnonst to the gauger."

The gentleman's eye glistened with delight. "Come along," sis he, "an' if we make a sayshure, I'll give you a guinea to boot."

"Long life to your noble honour," sis I, "I knew yer honour looked like some grand jantleman, an', p'rhaps, yer honour would want a baste to remove the whiskey, an' I have a snug horse an' car at yer honour's sarvice."

"My hand for ye, we let no grass grow undher us, till we come to the right place, an' I had Shaune an' the car ready in a jiffy.

The whiskey was saised an' conveyed into my car; an' as we came down towards the guard-house, the shuperwiser slipt the guinea into my fist.

"You desarve it," sis he, "an' here's a crown to dhrink the king's health, besides."

---

[1] Beloved.

"O, you're the jewel of a jantleman," sis I, "long life an' good luck to your noble honour - wheep Shaune - an' I turned up Blarney-lane. The jantleman turned on his heel."

"This is our way, over the bridge," sis he.

"But this is my way up the hill, Sur," sis I, - "wheep, Shaune."

The jintleman got into a high passion, an' collared me.

"Fair an' easy, ma boohil," sis I, "that's my whiskey, an' here's my permit; an' if I hear another word coming out o' your ugly mouth, I'll get a *posse* o' them thripe-women below, to cool your courage in the river."

But for all that, he throttled me still, an' flung a hawk's eye round for a constable. A crowd o' brogue-makers an' thripe women now gathered round us.

"Jack Begly," sis a fat thripe woman, to a big brogue-maker, "Jack Begly, have ye the spirit o' a man to stand on yer two pins there an' see a blagard gauger, throttle any fellow Christian?"

"Let us have at him Poll Dooly, the squinting thief," sis another fierce virago, brandishing a large thripe knife, an' before ye could say Jack Robinson, he received a shower of thripes right in his face.

The sogers at the guard-house, hearing the row, rushed out to see the sport, an' while the thripe-women, an' brogue-makers were busy amusing themselves wid the gauger, I slipt away the car as quietly as possible, an' whipt Shaune to the top of his speed, up Blarney-lane. Stopping for a minit to brathe the horse, I heard below, at the distance of half a mile, the roar o' the thripe-women - the clash o' the sodgers' bagnits, an' the rattling o' the stones along the sthreet. While hundreds came rushing agin me to the bottom of Blarney-lane, I was clearing out at the top of it, an' laving all the fun behind me. From that day to this, I never inthered Cork - nor, if I can help it, will I ever again, till the day o' my death. An' wishing you long life an' prosperity,

I remain yer humble sarvant,
For Paddy Doyle.

E.W.
Shandangin, May, 1835.

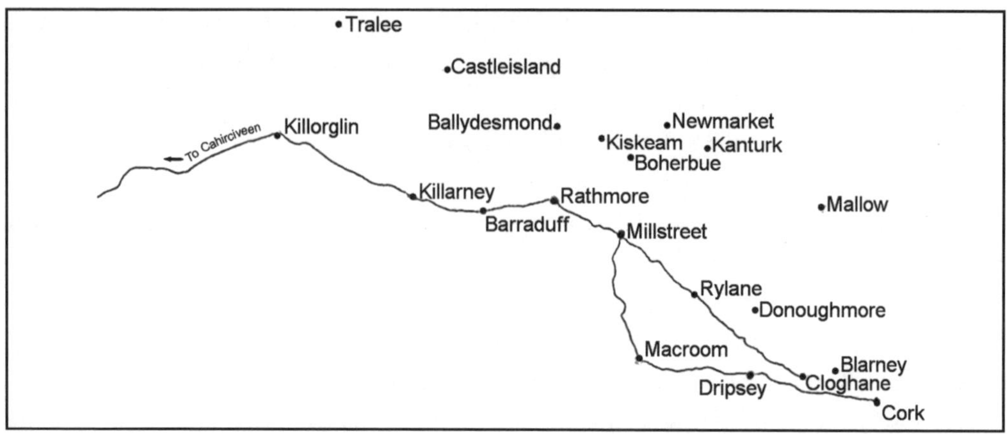

Fig. 28. From the 18th to the 20th century the phenomenon popularly known as the *Cork Butter Market* attracted large numbers of suppliers from all over Cork, Kerry, Limerick and Tipperary. Pack-horses and car-men , together with drovers with their cattle for the beef market were such a regular and frequent sight that their roads and bridle paths are still vividly remembered, none better, perhaps, than the mountain road between Millstreet and Rylane. At a conspicuous slab of bare rock the long distance travellers *(Kerry Dragoons)* paused for rest and refreshment for man and beast. Ever since that slab is affectionately known as The Kerryman's Table.

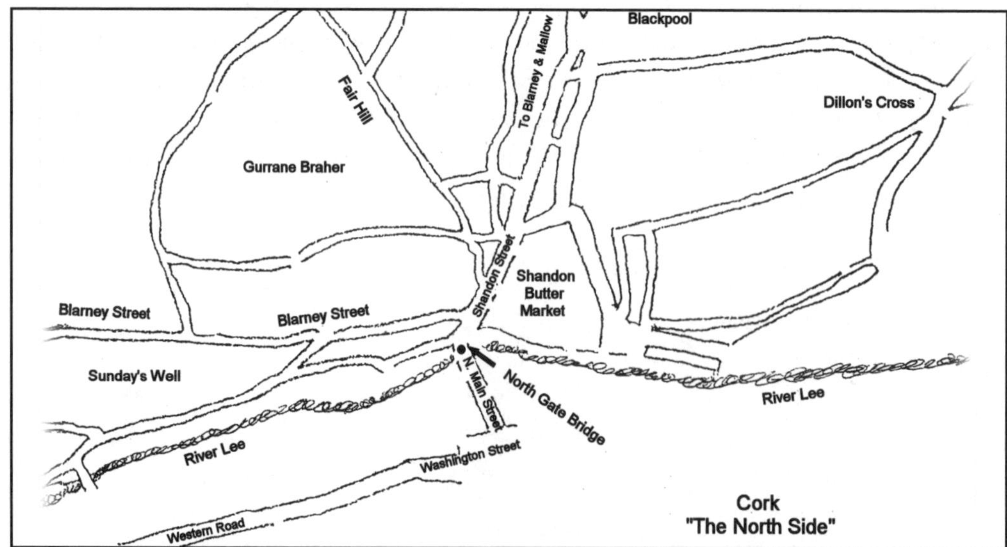

Fig. 29. The Cork Butter Exchange is the official name for the Butter Market. Located in *The North Side*, its business was transacted in the shadow of Shandon's bell tower. The market had a lifespan of about two centuries and in its heyday was the largest butter market in the world. It reached its zenith in the late 19th century when it handled close on half a million firkins of butter a year. Its export market ranged from the arctic to the equator and points south. The streets, lanes, and general commercial activities of cork form a backdrop to some of Edward Walsh's delightful folklore, notable, *The Pooka, Paddy Doyle's first trip to Cork,* and *The Demon Nailer.*

13
The Duhallow Cowboy.[1]

"For thine was the legend of valley and fountain -
The fairy song thine of the streamlet and rill."
Manuscript Poems.

The words were Irish - and the voice of the singer recalled to my memory the strange legends which delighted my childhood, of supernatural visitants awaking tones of entrancing power in haunted glens, and its effect was greatly heightened to my excited imagination by the surrounding scenery. The wild strain seemed to issue from the base of a steep precipice, which gave back the song with additional sweetness; and from the topmost branch of a hawthorn that crowned the cliff, a thrush blended his own wild notes with the wilder harmony that rose in sweet companionship from below. Before, the purple heath, smooth as if the tasteful hand of art had completed nature's workmanship, gradually receded to the Araglen, and gently melted its dark hues into the beautiful banks that held the silver waters; and then I thought that this wild spot was but a compartment of God's own temple - its cupola the blue heavens - its lamp the bright sun - its pavement the solid earth, where nature had spread a rich purple carpet, beautifully bordered with wavy silver and green - and the wild song of the thrush, and the wilder human voice, mixed in harmonious discord, the choral song of praise to the great Maker of all. But I could soon distinguish in the human strain, the querulous outpourings of some heart of sorrow; and on approaching the cliff along the winding stream, I looked around for the singer, but in vain, though this stanza, which caught my attention, seemed to proceed from some one immediately near:

"The moss couch I brought thee
To day from the mountain,
Has drank the last drop
Of thy young heart's red fountain,
For this good *skien* beside me
Struck deep and rung hollow
In thy bosom of treason
Young Mauriade ny Kallagh!"

The song suddenly ceased, and up started almost at my feet, and as it then seemed to me, from beneath the earth, a human figure. It was that of a person advanced to that undefinable season of life between the ungraceful softness of youth and the hirsute strength

---

[1] Published in *The Dublin Penny Journal*, August 29th 1835. Initialled, E.W. - Ed.

of manhood. He was tall and well proportioned - his caubeen had refused to perform the wonted office in its pristine shape, and the wearer had contrived to turn it upside down by forcing his head upward through the crown, while the tattered leaf circled like a border above with a pleasing and picturesque effect, and the long matted hair, guiltless of the comb, fell back on his shoulders, after the manner of the ancient *coolin*,

"Whare *horn* nor *bane*, ne'er dare unsettle
The thick plantations."

A great coat, girt at the waist with a hair cincture, fell succinct and loose to the knee, and being open at the breast, gave full view of the flannel shirt, collared with coarse unbleached linen. Of the other appendages of dress he had none, save a pair of traheens, or hose, used by the natives of these glens to preserve the feet from excoriation - they cover the leg and foot, and drawn through the toes, leave the sole bare. He had been lying within a narrow embankment, the sides of which were overgrown with tall fern, that formed a sort of bower which effectually shut out the sun's rays; and the next step would have sent me upon him through the green retreat in which he sung.

"Do not be alarmed, my boy," I said, looking distrustfully at a long clegh alpeen which he grasped with both hands, "I was only following the course of the river when your singing attracted my notice." "Mulla gudoa! how could my ramaish of a song turn a dhinusal (noble person) out of his way; and by the same token, since I caught a cowld afther heatin' myself dancin' a moneen to Daniel Leary's music, I have no more voice than a frog." 'The Irish words you sung to that mournful air are very simple - could you tell me what gave occasion to them?" "Och, 'tis only a bit of deanthuis (composition) that Donall na Rasca,[1] a great robber, an' a fine poet of the ould times, made whin he plunged his *skien* to the hilt in the heart of Mauriade ny Kallagh, a colleen dubh dhas who soult (betrayed) him for goold, and who had the sweetness of the muruigh (mermaid) in her voice, and the poison of the Aithir Nimhe[2] in her heart! There's a cliff above where he scooped his hard bed in the cowld rock, and here's his song, agus meela failthe."

The boy now sunk his voice to a low and querulous kind of recitative in repeating the following stanzas in Irish, the simplicity of which I have endeavoured to preserve in the translation.

"Thy neck was, lost maid!
Than the kanavane[3] whiter;
And the glow of thy cheek

---

[1] For the story of *Daniel the Outlaw*, see, pp. 201ff. - Ed.

[2] Serpent - literally, the father of poison. [i.e. 'the devil' – Ed.]

[3] A Plant found in bogs, the top of which bears a substance resembling cotton, and as white as snow.

Than the monadan[1] brighter:
But Death's chain hath bound thee
Thine eye glazed and hollow
That shone like a sunburst,
Young Mauriade ny Kallagh,

"At the dance in the village
Thy white foot was fleetest;
Thy voice mid the concert
Of maidens was sweetest;
The swell of thy white breast
Made rich lovers follow;
And thy raven hair bound them,
Young Mauriade ny Kallagh.

"No more shall mine ear drink
Thy melody swelling;
Nor thy beamy eye brighten
The outlaw's dark dwelling;
Or thy soft heaving bosom
My destiny hallow,
When thine arms twine around me,
Young Mauriade ny Kallagh.

"The Moss couch I brought thee
To day from the mountain,
Has drank the last drop
Of thy young heart's red fountain,
For this good *skien* beside me
Struck deep and rung hollow
In thy bosom of treason,
Young Mauriade ny Kallagh.

"With strings of rich pearls
Thy white neck was laden,
And thy fingers with spoils

[1] The Monadan is a red berry that is found on wild marshy mountains. It grows on an humble creeping plant.

Of the Sasanach maiden:
Such rich silks enrob'd not
The proud dames of Mallow -
Such pure gold they wore not
As Mauriade ny Kallagh.

"Alas! that my loved one
Her outlaw would injure -
Alas! that he e'er proved
Her treason's avenger!
That this right hand should make thee
A bed cold and hollow,
When in Death's sleep it laid thee,
Young Mauriade ny Kallagh!

"And while to this lone cave
My deep grief I'm venting,
The Saxon's keen bandog
My footsteps is scenting:
But true men await me
Afar in Duhallow.
Farewell, cave of slaughter
And Mauriade ny Kallagh."

As this young man ended the outlaw's song of sorrow, a gust of eddying wind that whirled aloft every light and loose substance within its reach, swept past, and blowing back the skirts of his belted coat, disclosed his fair and finely formed thigh. He shrunk with evident dread, and plucking a sprig of the fern which grew beside him, threw it after the blast that hurried by, muttering at the same time, some inarticulate words.

"I am sorry" said I "to see a clever boy like you, destitute of a most indespensable part of dress - but why did you fling the fern after the blast that bared your thigh?" "Oh! that was the shee-geehy -(a fairy wind), an the Dhineushla - (noble people), took the gosh-rahinee, (fern stalk), instead of myself. But, in regard of the breeches - it was a load of poneens - (patches), and the weather was rale hot - so yesterday morning I flung it down the river, and now your poor gorsoon-bo, (cow boy,) is as cool and as fresh as a trout."

"Blessed stoicism," said I, "of my unfortunate countrymen, which enables them to meet privation and distress without a murmur." But, addressing the boy, "could you find no better employment than herding cows?" "Ulligone! what employment is betther than ateing grugh (curds), and new milk in the morning - roasting a brohogue[1] at dinner time, and thin sucking the teat of drimin-dubh[2] to wash down the roasters - and thin stretching in this cool shade from the hate of the sun, an' singing ould cronans - and thin driving home my cows at night to the milking bawn - thin afther supper telling a skail feenight, (a tale of romance) - and thin sleeping in a bed of soft finan[3] till the first song of the lark - Fuan-ma-Cool hadn't such a pleasant hour of it whin he was herding in this very glin."

"How could that be? Fuan was the leader of warriors, not a keeper of cows."

"Och, bless your sowl, a vorneen, 'twas all a scheme of the ould boy's. - If you arn't in haste, Sir, dear, I'll tell you in less than no time what made him turn cow-boy - but I couldn't till to-morrow morning, tell you half the thricks he pled whin it would go hard on him, to overcome his enemies."

I assented.

"Fuan, as all the world knows, was a famous hero an' a great gineral, though at first, he was but a lump of a gorsoon like myself, till he ate the *salmon of knowledge*, that the great king Cormac spint half his life sthriving to get to himself - and ever afther that, he could foretell, like any shoun-dreed, (ancient Druid) - so that no hero of the 'varsal world could hould a candle for him, by raison of his gift of prophecy; an' whin he wasn't slicing the throats of his inemies to keep thim quiet, he an' his min would spind their summer saison fishing an' hunting in these wild glins - beyond are the mountains, where the swift footed Bran[4] levelled the red deer in the pride of his strength; and there the deep marshes, where the fiery boar whetted his tusks of slaughter. But wan day, about this time o' year, Fuan-ma-Cool felt himself quiet downhearted, and very heavy entirely - so he knew there was some cloud over him, and he put the thumb of his right hand, in which all the vartue of fortelling lay, in his mouth and began to chew the flesh; but he got quite bewildered and could make out nothing. Then he chewed from the flesh to the bone - from the bone to the marrow - from the marrow to the *smusagh* - and after making an example of his poor thumb, marcy on us! - he found out that the great king of the eastern world had sworn, by the sun an' moon, never to stop two nights in wan place till he took a trial out o' the heroes of the western island, and that he thin was actually anchoring his fair one-masted bark, in the famous port called Vintry Harbour - and that before he sint to demand fight an' fierce war, the king of the east had sint wan of his dreadful warriors to inspect the country, and report if the Fenian soldiers were such min as fame reported them, and that this spy would reach the camp before another sun went down. Fuan likewise knew from his thumb of truth, that these invaders were a race of giants, and the spy in question, would think nothin' at his return, of stringing Fuan himself, and half a dozen of his best min on a spear, like

[1] A meal of potatoes roasted under hot embers.
[2] A black spotted cow.
[3] A kind of soft grass that withers to a pale yellow colour in the early harvest.
[4] Fuan Macool's celebrated dog, said to live to this day enchanted in the Lake of Killarney.

rabbits on a pole. You may be sure he was at a great amplush; but he put on a bould face, and ordered the min to spind the nixt six days about Mangerton and the sweet Lough Lane. Whin the boys were gone, an' the chief heroes, by name, Osshine and Oscar, the son of Osshine and Dermid O'Duin, an' Goul-mac-morin, an' Kyleta-mac-Ronan, an' Conan Maol, the evil-hearted - had departed; Fuan, assisted by his housekeeper, removed a large wicker bed, in which a dozen of the soldiers slept at night, from its resting place to the fire side, and thin he lay in the cradle at full length, and a fine slibberigh (a very tall person) he was. Thin the woman prepared a mighty cake, in which she put a large iron griddle. In the course of the day enthered a man of vast bulk, as tall as a pine tree, and as firm in his bearing as Irish oak. But the woman took no notice at all, only began cronaning for the chap in the cradle.

"God save all here," says the big man. "Save ye kindly, maboohil," says she; "sit down an' count your money."

"Thank ye, ma'aam, kindly," says he; "but the sorrow a marvedy, goold, silver, or brass, came in my road with me."

"I don't at all doubt it," says she; "chaps o' your inches an' figure, ma cobberigh, (crabbed fellow), don't be over-burdened that way."

"Are the min of this camp,' sis he - affrinted at being called a cobberigh - 'are the min of this camp bigger than your humble sarvunt?"

"They could ate their dinner an' bless thimselves afther it over your head," sis she: "you must be some foreign *sisciple* of a thing to ax sich a question, an' I'm very sorry they are all from home to day, or you'd know that by eye-sight."

"Whin will they be back?' sis he. "They might be back to-night," sis she, "or they might be away a full year an' a day - 'tis the habit of our heroes never to tell whin they intend to return."

"What sports and trials of strinth do they indulge in whin at home?" sis he.

"I never watch their motions," sis she, "that garlagh in the cradle there, gives me full and plinty to do - but whin the wind blows in at the dure, wan o' them puts his finger into the kayhole and turns the raythilagh[1] round to the conthrary side - an' I often see thim for a bit o' pastime, take that lump of a *finger-stone* abroad, and afther flinging it into the air, run round the raythilagh, and receive it before it falls to the ground!" The big man thin got up an' put his finger in the key hole, but could not stir the house from its foundation - small blame to him. The finger-stone was a Carrig that tin min could not remove; but the stranger raised it without much difficulty, and heaved it over the house, but failed in attimpting to ketch it in its fall.

"I find, honest woman," sis he, "that your min are active and strong, an' upon my sowkins, I'm sorry I haven't the pleasure of seeing thim exercise before I go."

---

[1] A low oblong building.

"Och, a vorneen," sis she, "there's some o' thim would squeeze crude an' whey out o' the very stones, they're so main strong; an' talkin' o' cruds an' whey, in throth I'm sorry I haven't a bit o' food within, worth your notice; but as no one ever left Fuan, the king of the brave min's house, without ating an' drinking, you will plaze to sit down, an' take this kustha-basha[1] I had for the grawl, an' his mether o' milk." The big man was rale hungry - an' down he sat with the cake on his knee, an' the mether under his arm. The cake was hard galore, by raison o' the griddle in it - but the big man was ashamed to give up, and he cranched an' chawed it to the last bit.

"That was a very tough cake," sis he.

"A hard crust is good for children breeding teeth," sis she.

"I doubt that any crathur could ate sich a crust," sis he, "barring he had all his teeth."

"If you wish to take his dimensions in rigard of the teeth," sis she, "you can put a finger in his mouth an' welcome." The big gomul did so to satisfy his curiosity, an' Fuan bit off his finger clane from the hand. He scorned to complain, and only said in a cool way, "if the grawl in the cradle has no teeth, he has the jiwel of a dhroundel (jaw.)" He got afeard that Fuan an' his min would return before he could get off - an' he took to his scrapers without saying, by your lave or good by, only axing where the stock (cattle) were; an' the housekeeper tould him that the gorsoon turned thim down the glin in the morning.

"Whin the spy of the king of the eastern world had directed his coorse to the glin, Fuan jumped from the cradle, threw a cota-more on him, took a stout clegh alpeen in his hand, and made every short cut to the cows. Whin the big man arrived, afther viewing the beauty of the herd, he chose one of the finest bulls to take home to his master, as a proof of his visit to the Fenian camp. Thin Fuin springing across the river at wan thrislogue, (step), cried, "hillo gaffer, where are you carrying the bull?" "To my master, the great king of the eastern world whose corohan (vessel) is anchored at Fuin-traugh, who sint me to bring him a sample of Irish cattle," says tother. - "If he sint you to us," says Fuan, "as a sample of his min, I'm thinking ye're no great shakes at home, an' depind upon it, if the owner of the bull was here, you'd have a new story to take back with you - but, any-how, leave the bull there." But the big man scorning to reply to the gorsoon, as he thought him, druv on the bull, an' Fuan faced him like a man, an' as the animal passed he grasped him firmly by one horn; the big man instantly seized the other - the struggle was but for a moment, for, as each put forth the highest pitch of his strength - the bull was split in two from head to tail in one long and vengeful pull. "You may take *your* half," sis Fuan, "for you pulled hard for it, but take a friend's advice to boot, an' cut your stick for the east now, an' tell him that sint you 'twas Fuan-ma-Cool's gorsoon that halved the bull with you."

"Whin the big man arrived at Vintry Harbour he tould all that befel him, an' produced his half of the torn bull to witness the truth of his story. Thin the king of the eastern world,

[1] A small cake kneaded and formed on the hand.

alarmed for his safety, hoisted his sails from ould Ireland; - but whether he was lost at sea or landed safe at home in the hot country of the sun, no one living can tell."

As the cow-boy concluded this ancient legend, the lowing of cattle - the clashing of horns, and the deep and hollow bellowing that resounded from glen to craig, announced a fierce struggle for mastery between the bulls of two different herds. My companion started to his legs - stood still for a moment - and yelling a fierce shout of incitement to battle, set off to the scene of combat with the speed of a greyhound - while I, not enamoured of such savage conflict, pursued my musing way, along the green banks of the silver Araglen.

14
Darby Dooly and his White Horse[1]

I was on my way to my own cabin on the mountain as I gained the summit of a hill which rises about three miles west of Kanturk in the county of Cork, on the most luxurious harvest evening I ever enjoyed. The last rays of the setting sun shed their mellow richness on the surrounding landscape. The clouds in the west were varied with every form and colour that fancy could create - not a breath of air was abroad - the very zephyr seemed sunk into repose - and the holy calm diffused around, stole insensibly to my soul. The lonely stars twinkled in the sky, and the harvest-moon rose, a globe of liquid fire. I sat down to rest my wearied limbs, and contemplate the surrounding picture of the Almighty's goodness to man, and repeated these beautiful lines of the poet –

"The sun had gone down to his valley of night,
And evening arose in her sombre hued vest -
Her zone with the rubies of ether was bright -
Her hair shone with gold, and on zephyrs so light
Stream'd lovely and fair in the west."

My meditations were interrupted by the approach of a peasant, returning from the labours of the harvest-field. With that natural politeness which marks the Irish native superior in social feeling to the inhabitants of most countries of Europe, he gave me the usual salutation,

"God save ye, Sir."

"God save kindly, honest man," I returned, "what is the name of this handsome hill which affords so fresh and free a prospect?"

"I can't tell you it's name in the ould times, 'cause I'm not very clever at *shanacha*, but it is now called Knock-an-geran-bawn, (the hill of the white gelding,) from Darby Dooly's white horse - of coorse, Sir, you've often hard of Darby Dooly an' his white horse."

"Never," I replied.

"O! meela murther! any Christian not to hear tell of Darby Dooly's white horse; an' how Darby let on that the horse could produce silver; an' about the ram's horn that was the manes of cutting Mrs. Purcell's throath; an' how the honest pedlar was dhrowned; an' how Darby Dooly an' all his ancestors became rale gintlemin! Musha if you didn't, but that bangs banagher."

I smiled involuntarily.

---

[1] Published in *The Dublin Penny Journal*, September 19th 1835. Initialled, E.W. - Ed.

"O! Sir, you may laugh, but there's the name o' the place, an' here's the raison of it. I'll tell it in a jiffy. Here Norry, (to a yellow-haired little girl that emerged from the smoke of a neighbouring cabin, to peep at the stranger), milk the goat, there's a gintleman here dhry;" and eyeing my lank figure an' sallow cheek, "goat's milk has great vartue, an' cures inward complaints like Mallow spa. But here's the story.

"Darby Dooly lived forninst you there where you see the *fuheroch* (unroofed walls) near the ould road; he was a rale poor man, an' like myself, had a house full of little girls, (I have seven thackeens,) an' not a *marvedi* had he to support 'em, but a small field he was too lazy to till, an a one-horned ram, an' a sheep that thried to pick a blade o' grass between the stones that covered it. He had a white garran, too; an' his business, when he wasn't roasting his shins, was cutting turf in that bog below; an' taking a thruckle load of it whin dhry to Kanturk to buy male for the little females, an snuff for Kate Murphy his wife. Darby had a raison for keeping Kate up to snuff for whin without it, they say she had a tongue that would bother a rookery. But, sure enough, one day whin Darby sould his turf, an' put the horse's head into the flannel bag that held the feed of oats, he strolled into the square to buy the male an' snuff.

" 'Sorra taste of my silver have I,' says Darby, feeling every corner of his mouth for his *three thirteens* - for why? He hadn't a smite of a pocket, nor a tack o' the tail to his ould shirt, that he could tie them in like a dacent man. 'A virra-na-glora! is it draming I am,' says he to himself that way, 'or did I let the silver slip between my teeth down my throath?'

"At last, after a bit of a study, he recollected that he put the money to hould in the mouth o' the bag before he hung it round the horse's neck; an' on his return, he found the oats finished, and not a keenogue in the bag.

" 'The curse o' Cromwell on ye, ye greedy vagabone, how much ye wanted silver for the change o' diet; but I must leather it out o' ye, or Kate Murphy 'ill be the death o' me.'

"He slipped into the twig-yard that then grew where the range of houses is in Paycock-lane, as ye came up from the square, Sir, for half a dozen twigs; and afther lading the white horse to the square, comminced bating him at a terrible rate. And though the people knew not his rason for leathering the poor garran, yet whin they saw him draw his hand through every dung he made the poor baste dhrop, he soon had sich a crowd about him as wasn't seen in Kanturk since the month o' the seven Sundays. A sarvent of Mr. Purcell's came jist as Darby picked up one o' the *thirteens*, who hastens to acquaint his masther with it. Purcell, a grand gintleman, came up jist as Darby found the second, and shortly afther he saw him poke out the third.

" 'Darby avick,' says Mr. Purcell, for he knew him very well, 'is it witchcraft you have to desave people, or is your horse actually making goold?'

" 'Oh, not at all, Sir,' says Darby, very sharply, 'only bits o' silver.'

" 'Is your horse in the habit of doing that?' says he.

" 'Whiniver I bates him well,' says Darby.

" 'And does your horse ever dhrop goold?' says t'other, mighty pullite.

" 'Yes at a sartin time of the moon,' says Darby.

" 'Where did you get the horse, Darby?'

" 'Oh, there's telling of that, a vourneen.'

" 'Would you sell him for a good penny, Darby?'

" 'Oh, bedad, masther avick, my horn is harder than that comes to. If you'd insure me aginst Kate Murphy's putting her tin commandments in my face for the bargain, I'd talk to yer honour about it.'

" 'Does Kate wear the *breeches*?' says he.

" 'I don't say as much,' says Darby; 'but you see, with fighting for it, this ould poneen (patched garment) on me is torn to rags.'

" 'Well, sure enough, with one palaver and another, Darby threw his come-hedher over him, till Mr. Purcell gev him twenty yallow guineas for his ould garran, and Darby walked home with the money in his fist, as proud as a paycock.

"I won't delay you, Sir, to tell how Mr. Purcell sent out a procklymation, I think they call it, inviting all the grandees to see the performance of the wonderful horse - how all the gintlemin laughed at Mr. Purcell's madness - how the poor horse died ov the bating he got, and how Mr. Purcell brought a guard ov sogers to take and hang Darby at the square of Kanturk.

"A frind tould Darby that Purcell was bringing the guard to hang him.

" 'Bedhershin,' says he, 'sure they aren't *Shemus a cocca's*[1] times with us, to hang a man without the benefit of a judge and jury. I gev him the worth of his bargain any how. Kate Murphy, that thief of a ram picks up every blade of grass from the poor sheep, so I think we'll put him out o' the cowld. Juggy, turn in the ram; and Kauth, take this yallow boy and bring us a dhrop o' whiskey to wet the ram, and a grain of coffee to make a dhrop of tay for your mother, poor woman; and, Sheela, lay legs to ground, an' tell my gossy, (gossip,) Teig More, (Great Timothy,) to be here aginst evening, dead or alive; and, Maura, step over to Duarigil for Sheemeen O'Shine, and bid him remimber not to forget the bag-pipes; and in your way home call to Aileen a Keenta, (Eleanor the Mourner,) and bid her be over here bine-by at her peril - Darby Dooly's fathers would blush in their graves if their son left the world without a blast of the pipes, the cry o' the keener, and a dacent wake at his going!'

"Whin the ram was kilt, Darby put the blood in the drisheen,[2] an' ties it up very tidy round Kate Murphy's throath, and pinned her futhill[3] tight, so that her neck looked quite

[1] The Peasantry of Ireland still retain, what I may be guilty of a pun by calling, the most *sovereign* contempt for the memory of James the Second, and loudly execrate his cowardly fight, when they discourse concerning "the break of the Boyne."

[2] The stomach of a sheep.

[3] A garment worn on the neck.

nathral. Thin he takes the horn, an' scrapes it so smooth and purty that you'd swear it was in use since the days of Fion ma Cuil.

"But to come to my story - just as the mutton was cooked, and Sheemeen O'Shine giving the last bar of *Saggart na Bootishy,* who should call to the door but Mr. Purcell.

" 'Darby Dooly, you abominable villain,' says he, mighty grand. 'I'll hang you as high as Hymen, (Hangman, probably,) for chating a gintleman. Come out here, you spalpeen.'

" 'Murther meela,' says Darby, who was *making buttons*, though he put a bould face upon the mather, 'what a pirsecuted man I am! Kate Murphy is pulling out my daylights for selling the horse - and your honour frickens me with them nicknames, that Darby Dooly's father's son never desarved. Howsomever, Sir, your honour won't be above letting these gintlemin (maning the sogers) come in to a bit of mutton, an' a dhrop of rale parl'amint.'

"The sogers, well became 'em, up and tould Mr. Purcell to indulge the poor man; and whin they inthered, my dear, they got hould-belly-hould of mutton and whiskey - the gintleman himself was prevailed on to taste a cup o' Kate's coffee, with a rale good *stick* in it.

" 'Kate Murphy, honey,' says he, (that's Darby,) for he always gev her her own name, 'I must be going, heaven speed all thravellers. Bring us t'other bottle, and thin I'll kiss yourself an' the poor childhre, that I won't see no more;' and he let on to wipe his eyes.

" 'Darby, a goun,' says she, 'yer belly lost upon ye.'

" 'Kate Murphy,' says he, 'maybe you want a dhrop of eye-wather to help your sight to behould your poor man hanging like a scal'crow on a windy day.'

" 'Dear knows Darby, you often wronged me, and gev me a sore heart, afore now,' says she.

" 'Badhershin, avourneen,' says he; and one word borryed another, and Darby Dooley, who let on to be in a rale passion, riz, and saized a knife and stuck Kate a prod in the right place, and she fell spouting blood and kicking her legs like any thing. The sogers saized upon Darby.

" 'Less of yer freedom, my boys,' says he, 'till we're better acquainted. Let her cool a bit.'

"Whin Kate stopped kicking, he pulled out his ram's horn, and blew two or three puffs in her ear, whin up started ma colleen before you could say Jack Robinson.

" 'Darby Dooly,' says Mr. Purcell, says he, 'do ye dale with the divil, to kill yer wife an' bring her to life agin?'

" 'I'd scorn the likes, plase yer honour,' says he, rather cute, 'though I might meet with a worse dailer.'

" 'Sell me the horn, Darby, and I'll forgive and forget all.'

" 'Oh, that's a thing ompossible; for if I gev Kate Murphy a prod as usual, I'd be hanged for murdher.'

" 'Oh, never fear that, Darby - I can bring a man every year from the gallis, (and *so* he could, they say,) and I'll be your frind for ever, Darby.'

"Kate joined the gintleman, and promised never more to fret Darby; and Purcell carried off the ram's horn, after paying a considerable sum on the nail for it."

The peasant had proceeded thus far in his story, when the little girl before-mentioned appeared with a piggin[1] of delicious goat's milk, which she presented me, dropping at the same time a low courtesy, when the peasant, altering his voice from the narrative tone to a sharp, quick mode of expression, said,

"O, ye crathur, one would think it was making that milk ye war. Where is your manners, ye thackeen, not to put that dhrop of milk in the blue basin?' Then turning to me, "Ohone, the dew is falling, and ye'll get cowld, Sir, and my story not tould.

"When Mr. Purcell got home, he invited all the gintlemen, and they had a grand coshering; and in the middle of the inthertainmint he picked a quarrel with his lady, whin he caught up a knife, and stabbed her in rale airnest, and if he was blowing the *ram's horn* in her ear till doomsday, he couldn't revive her at all at all. But the poor gintleman was determined upon revenge, (and no wondher;) so he came upon Darby as sly as a Peeler, and before you could say thrap-stick he was bagged like a fox, and carried down to Kanturk to be dhrowned, while Kate and the childhre riz the seven parishes with their ullagoning. The sogers left poor Darby bound up to his good behaviour, I warrant ye, at the door of a public house in the town, while they stepped in to take a dhram. An honest pedlar, passing down in the dusk of the evening, stumbled across the bag that lay in the footpath.

" 'Hangor dhrown me,' says the man within, 'but the sorra take me, if I marry yer daughter now or evermore, amin.'

" 'Mother of mercy,' says t'other, 'what daughter are ye spaking of?'

" 'Musha, is that all you know ov it,' says he of the bag; 'you must be a *furriner* in these parts at that rate.'

"So he up and toult him how Mr. Purcell's daughter fell in love with him, and was mighty sick - how her father, to preserve her life, pinned him, (meaning Darby), an' that he had his choice to dhrown, or marry the dying, love-sick lady.

" 'Let me in,' says the pedlar, 'and I'll give you my *pack of soft goods* into the bargain.'

" 'Agreed,' says Darby.

"So whin my jockey got out, he fastened the gad upon the pedlar.

" 'There,' says Darby, says he, 'much good may it do ye. Bud it's how I think, it's cowld comfort you'll have with the *garran*, after all, I'm afeared.'

"Thin Darby set off with the pack, and the poor pedlar was taken and pitched into the river, though he offered fifty times to marry Miss Purcell; and by the same token, the hole he was dhrowned in is called the 'pedlar's hole' to this day.

"In a year, or thereabouts, afther, whin Darby Dooly had the pack of goods sould, he returns home. It was a fine harvest night like this, and he never stops nor stays till he comes to Mr. Purcell's and taps at his room windy. Mr. Purcell, hearing the rap, gets up with a blunderbush; but when he sees Darby Dooley, with a little box at his back, standing quite

[1] A small drinking vessel composed of staves and wooden hoops.

nath'rl on his own two legs, the blunderbush dhrops from his hand, his jaws begin to play a tune, and the cowld prospiration runs down his face.

" 'Heaven an' ayrth! Darby Dooly,' says he, 'spake, if it's yerself that's there that I dhrownded in the Allo, or is it yer ghost? Ye war the unloocky man to me - I kilt my wife through yer manes, and I dhrowneded yerself - and I suppose that's your ghost that's come to haunt me.'

" 'It's all thrue ye say,' says Darby, says he; 'but it all turned out for the betther - I'm now a blessed saint in heaven' says he, the thief of the world.

" 'Have ye any news of the misthress, Darby avourneen?' says he.

" 'That's the business that brought me,' says t'other: 'she's purty well, only that she's not clear out o' Purgatory yet. She got lave for me to come for the thrifle of money you have in the desk, to get masses said for her sowl; and to warn your honour to prepare for death, for you havn't long on this ayrth. The money, if you plase, and here's the box to put it in.'

"And, sure enough, Darby gothered away the cash; and the warning saized so much on Mr. Purcell's mind that he died in a month. And there's the story of Darby Dooly and his white horse."

An humble and solitary shilling yet lingered in my pocket. It survived the casual expenses of a little tour from which I was now returning, and in which "all its lovely companions were faded and gone," I instinctively slipped the little piece between my fore-finger and thumb to give the cottager in return for his hospitality, when recollecting from experience how the offer of pecuniary recompense upon these occasions insults the Irish peasant, the shilling fell noiseless to its former resting-place.

I arose, grasped the hand of my new acquaintance, and pursued homeward my solitary way.[1]

---

[1] The foregoing is a fair specimen of the description of stories narrated, and implicitly believed, by the peasantry in many districts of our country. Indeed, in many places they have little else to do, than to tell and listen to such tales. We trust that the efforts at present making to impart real knowledge, and to instruct as well as to amuse, will have the effect of turning their attention to matters of real utility.

[Note: At the time Edward Walsh penned the above foot-note, a virtual revolution was taking place in his native area on the Cork-Kerry border and to some extent in the nation at large. Catholic Emancipation in 1829, the setting up of a National School System in 1831, the development of the *Crown Estate* in Pobal O'Keefe during these years, the building of the new village of Kingwilliamstown (Ballydesmond) in 1832, and the opening up of an elaborate new road network through Sliabh Luachra, all contributed to an air of hope and new dawn. Walsh's final word in that note - 'utility' was also a harbinger of a new philosophy which dominated and still dominates the English speaking world - utilitarianism and the new kind of *poverty* of the mind and heart that accompanies it. - Ed.]

15
The Faithful Lovers.[1]

"Had we never lov'd sae kindly,
Had we never lov'd sae blindly,
We had ne'er been broken-hearted."
Burns.

In the barony of Fermoy, and on the bank of the river Funcheon, lie the ruins of the ancient church of Molaga, celebrated for the crowds of devotees that resort there to testify their respect for the saint, and to invoke his intercession. An ancient tradition of the country also relates that this cemetery contains the remains of two lovers whose matchless constancy and melancholy fate will only be forgotten when the currents of the rapid Funcheon cease to flow.

Mary Fleming was the daughter of a rich farmer that held extensive lands in the fair and fertile tract of Glanworth, or the golden vale, so called from its yellow harvests. He claimed descent from the Flemings, the magnificent remains of whose stately castle crown the bank of the Funcheon at the village of Glanworth, which anciently was a considerable town. Mary Fleming was an only child, and her father, a sordid man, was anxious to procure for her the hand of a wealthy suitor - one whose herds and pastures would equal his own. Many of the neighbouring farmers, no less smitten with Mary's fortune than captivated by her pleasing exterior, and graceful unaffected manners, at the occasional patron or rural dance of the Sunday afternoon, offered her those tender attentions, the meaning of which the most untaught of Eve's daughters are not slow in understanding; but she received their advances with cold civility. Some young men ventured to make formal proposals to Fleming, and though the character and means of these suitors were unexceptionable, yet she unaccountably rejected them. At length a wealthy person from a remote district came and sued for her hand. The advantages of this proposal were too obvious to be contemned: Fleming accepted him as his future son-in-law, and when he placed in review before his daughter, the good qualities and extensive pastures of her suitor, she declared with that bluntness of simplicity which is characteristic of the female mind, when untainted by the simulating affectation of refinement, that she would not wed the greatest man in the five provinces; for it would be the death of Shemus Oge O'Keeffe, who she knew loved her better than his own life.

Some ten months after this, in the twilight of a gloomy November evening, a tall figure, wrapped in a large dark cloak, was seen slowly to wind his course along the Funcheon, towards the well of St. Molaga. It was Shemus Oge O'Keeffe, in whose favour Mary

[1] Published in *The Dublin Penny Journal*, October 24th 1835. Initialled, E.W. - Ed.

Fleming declared herself, as above related. At that time he was a tall commanding figure, where strength and agility finely blended. His family were in decaying circumstances at his birth; but he received a liberal education, for he had been brought up by his uncle, a Roman Catholic ecclesiastic, who, dying when he was young, left Shemus no other inheritance than poverty; and he returned to his widowed mother's cottage, to share her scanty means, and assist in the cultivation of a few fields which remained from the wreck of their ruined fortunes. When her father heard Mary's abrupt declaration in favour of Shemus Oge O'Keeffe, he stood aghast with surprise; for though that young man, immediately after his return to his mother's cottage, was fortunate enough to preserve Mary Fleming from drowning, a stranger to the warmth of gratitude himself, he hardly reflected on the extent of the obligation due to Shemus Oge, or thought that his daughter's intimacy with her deliverer exceeded the bounds of mere acquaintance. He procured one whose influence ought to have been directed to better ends, to tamper with the simplicity of the untaught girl; who, by authority and persuasion, so wrought upon her religious feelings, that she was induced to believe, that entertaining a secret passion for any person contrary to the wishes of her father, was in direct opposition to the laws of God; and that to atone in some measure for her crime, and avoid eternal misery hereafter, she should promise to marry the husband of her father's choice. The weak girl, terrified by the artful representations of one whom she was taught to look up to as the interpreter of every doubt, yielded reluctant consent - promised to abandon Shemus Oge O'Keeffe for ever - and the day was already fixed for her marriage with the wealthy stranger to whom we before alluded. During the progress of this baleful proceeding, her unfortunate lover made frequent attempts to see her, but his endeavours were baffled by her father's vigilance. The ruin of his hopes, the rumoured inconstancy of the maid he idolized - the consuming, restless flame that burned within his breast - all preyed with fatal activity upon his constitution. At length he heard that the day had been fixed for Mary Fleming's wedding: he resolved to see her once more - to bid her an eternal adieu - to catch a parting view of one he loved so tenderly - and then return to his bed of death, or to eternal exile from his native land. Let fate do its worst, he was prepared to suffer. For this he sought an interview, and Mary promised to meet him by the twilight hour on this day, at the well of St. Molaga.

When Mary Fleming arrived in the haze of the twilight gloom at the appointed place, she could scarce believe that the emaciated figure which bent before her, was the gay and accomplished youth who delighted her eye a few short months before. The calm despair that sat on his marble brow - the death-like paleness of his cheek - and the faint glare of his glazed and sunken eye, appalled her, and, flinging herself upon the chilly sward, wild and broken bursts of feeling seemed to convulse her very soul.

"O, Shemus Oge! is this the reward of your faithful love? Are that sunken cheek and hollow eye Mary Fleming's gifts for rescuing her from certain death, on that day when the waters of the rapid Funcheon were closing over her head? O! had I then died, I should not now be the ruin of your health, and the destruction of my own soul."

"Surely you do not apprehend that to trample on my sacred feelings, and, with more than woman's inconstancy, despise that honourable passion which you yourself have approved and encouraged, can merit the exemplary punishment you mention."

"O, poor bewildered heart! - did not Father Florence, the priest of God, who knows more than a thousand like me - did not he say, that there was an eternity of pain for disobedient children? - that I could not innocently have a liking for any young man, unless with my father's approbation; - that what young people call love, is but a snare of the tempter's to lead souls to perdition. O! he bewildered my brain - every night in my dreams I saw hell open to receive us; and last Sunday I swore to renounce you for ever, and marry Myles Mahony."

"Mary," said he, with a calm and collected tone, "I forgive you; and God forgive them that practise on your simplicity of heart. My feelings are not like those of other men: my love has been as fierce as the lava-fire which burns in the bowels of Etna - it has consumed the marrow of my bones. This is the last time I shall obtrude my accents on your ear - never, never more shall this unfortunate wretch cross the pathway of your future life. Mary, farewell for ever."

The wretched Mary Fleming gave her reluctant hand to Myles Mahony on the next Sunday, and it is said that the unfortunate girl heard the mournful howling of *O'Keeffe's little dogs*[1] during the marriage ceremony. This denoted that a descendant of the race of O'Keeffe was dead; and the report soon prevailed, that Shemus Oge had breathed his last. The bride, in all the settled calmness of despair, with a firm, subdued tone, and tearless eye, requested her husband's permission to weep one half hour over the corpse of Shemus Oge O'Keeffe. It was the request of her bridal night; nor did he deny the melancholy boon. She came - and the following is a literal translation of the dirge or cione she uttered over her

---

[1] It is said that the approaching death of an O'Keeffe is announced by a supernatural melancholy cry, resembling the howling of dogs. A man in Duhallow lately assured me, that he both saw the three little dogs and heard their howling at the time the last representative of the O'Keeffe family died.

[Note: The phenomenon to which Walsh refers here is still experienced. Despite the change of language, it is still referred to as the *Gadhairín Uí Chaoimh* - the little dogs of the O'Keeffes. My late sister Peggy Hopkins, when nursing Arthur O'Keeffe in Kiskeam village, experienced it. On the night that he died she heard, as she thought, a great deal of barking of dogs; and, since she then knew nothing of the *Gadhairín Uí Chaoimh* tradition, wondered why it should be so. In the morning, Peggy mentioned the fact to the man's niece, and the woman replied, "Oh, that was the *Gadhairín Uí Chaoimh*, and proceeded to explain the tradition to her. Had my sister known that at the time of the barking phenomenon, she would have been less attentive to the dying man; in fact, I fear that he might have died alone! - Ed.]

beloved youth. The original words are sung to a melancholy air by the peasantry of Roche's country.

"O! deep despair! O, dreadful doom, to view thee laid low in death, bedewed by the tears of thy wretched Mary. I little thought when I gave thee the vow, that I should send thee to an untimely grave; but heaven beholds I would yield my life to preserve thine.

"We exchanged in mutual love a token, and never shall I break the holy promise. I will prize forever the sacred pledge that bound me when thy chaste modest arm circled my waist.

"Ye fair maidens whose pearly tears are falling, whose bosoms are melting with generous compassion, ye are sensible that Shemus Oge had many a charm to win me, and warm into love the heart that breaks in my bosom.

"His was the speed of the wild roe of the mountain, the unrivalled blush of the rose, the mildness of the dove, the retiring modesty of the cowslip. Many a virgin sighed for his love.

"Our favourite thorn has heard the vows we plighted, and though artifice has doomed me the bride of another, I shall be thine, pure and undefiled. Though my father basely sold me for gold, I shall fly to thy embrace - no power of earth can restrain me.

"A hated husband - let other arms embrace him - the virgin's bridal bed shall be the grave of her lover. His blest spirit shall hover on the wing, till his bethrothed fly to his eternal society.

"Wait, wait awhile! my soul warm sighs to rejoin thee. Our greetings shall be unalloyed in the realms of peace, and our bridal sleep shall know no waking. This song of sorrow shall cease, For Shemus Oge calls his beloved - I go! I go!"

Her song of lamentation was hushed; she laid her bosom on that of her lifeless lover, and heaved one deep sigh - it was her last; for when the mourners that attended the corpse sought to remove her, they found her heart and its sorrows hushed in eternal repose.

Fleming would not permit that the remains of his unfortunate daughter should repose in the same grave with Shemus Oge O'Keeffe; they rest in the respective burying-places of their families, which were contiguous; and the next spring beheld two trees planted by unknown hands, unite in midway, and form by their intertwining branches the figure called *a true lover's knot*, emblematic of their changeless fidelity in life and death.

16
The Ford of the White Ship.[1]

"Large was his bounty, and his soul sincere,
Heaven did a recompense as largely send." - *Gray*.

The chords of Dermid Dhu's wild harp had ceased to pour their tide of harmony into the captive ears of the listeners, in the hospitable mansion of Donough More O'Daly, who, about a century ago, occupied a considerable portion of that mountain tract, which extends from the Araglen to the village of Knocknagree, in the western part of the barony of Duhallow. O'Daly inherited in an eminent degree the generous spirit of his ancestors; and though the patrimonial estate had dwindled to insignificance, compared with the extensive domains of his fathers, yet he still upheld their unbounded hospitality. His ample hearth was the resting-place of the houseless and many an itinerant of the decaying minstrel race, and many a carough, and boccagh, and story-teller - talented vagrants, who now exist only linked with the memory of bye-gone times - spread far and wide the fame of his ample hall - for genuine usquebaugh, home-brewed ale, fresh beef, and beds of soft finane, were attractions sufficient [to] induce crowds of stollers to throng the well known residence of Donough More O'Daly.

"Dermid Dhu, man," said the generous host, "lay aside the harp, and fill thy goblet - this red wine is generous and free. Our harpers are departing fast to join the heroes they celebrated so well; but may Dermid Dhu live forever to cheer our days with the light of song. Take thy wine, while Andriesh Bawn gives us one of his inimitable stories."

"Shall it be a Fenian or a fairy legend?" said the storyteller, an old, grey-haird man, who sat at the lower end of the long table.

"Neither, Andriesh Bawn - thy last tale, which combined the romance and superstition of both, was so fearful, that no servant of mine, man or maid, since that hour would venture abroad after dusk, even though he expected a clurikawn to bestow a hidden treasure, or the *sporan nu schilling* as the reward of his daring."

The story-teller inclined forward from his seat, and supporting his bent figure over the board with a slender white staff, thus began:

"Inthe days of old, when the rivers flowed with milk and honey - the untilled earth produced spontaneous fruits - when the sons of men were unrestricted by human laws, because the villains of society had not yet raised their head - when birds and beasts held mutual converse with man, and unvitiated man enjoyed the society of superior beings - in that golden time, their lived a field mouse in a snug retreat under a hedge, among the thick branches of which dwelt a female wren. It is said that at this period all mortal things possessed one common language; and the mouse and wren would love to converse together

[1] Published in *The Dublin Penny Journal*, November 23rd 1835. Initialled, E.W. - Ed.

for whole hours, when the evening sun had sunk behind the huge hill, and the grey twilight advanced with dewy feet to sanctify the mystic hour that intervenes between light and dark. Though philosophers deem it one of the absurdities of civilized society to prevent females from "popping the question" in affairs of the heart, yet tradition, faithful to the native modesty of the sex, declares that females, whether feathered, furred, or fig-leaved, have ever maintained, doubtless in accordance to the dictates of nature, a strict reserve on these occasions. So it remained with the mouse to open his proposal of an immediate conjugation, which he accomplished in his very best way, much to the relief of Miss Wren, who really began to wonder at his extreme dullness in taking a hint.

" 'What shall we prepare for the nuptial feast, my dear,' said the wren, raising her eye and voice for the first time after giving reluctant assent for fixing the happy day.

" 'I have a good winter store of corn,' said the delighted lover, 'and if ground and winnowed, it would furnish a sumptuous feast.'

" 'While you have got teeth, and I a pair of wings,' said the bride, with a vivacity natural to her, 'I trust our corn shall be ground and winnowed.'

"The mouse chewed the corn in his very best manner, and his gay betrothed lightened his labour by taking the sifting business to herself.

" 'Now, my dear,' said the mouse, 'call your friends to the feast, while I invite mine.'

"Then the lover popped into the next hole, where lived a matronly mouse and six young ones. These came without much ado; while the foolish wren beat up every bush in the land, for her relatives were extremely numerous; and she returned on the third day followed by an almost innumerable host of cousins. On the first evening the mouse waited with all the impatience natural to a young bridegroom until night, when he and his party dined. Another and another day lingered past them on tardy feet; and at last, when the bride and her friends arrived the lessening heap of corn had entirely disappeared. The bride was extremely wroth at the affront put upon her, and averred if justice could be found on earth she would procure it. Then the dispute was left to an arbitration; for in that time there were no lawyers to bless society - a circumstance the more to be deplored as their decision in this instance would have afforded an excellent precedent to future times."

When the story-teller had rounded this last period, a loud laugh arose a little below him at the same side of the board; but the ill-timed burst was instantly suppressed, and Andreish Bawn, in order to continue his narration, resumed the posture from which he had been startled. "Weel a weel, Andreish Bawn," said a voice from the spot whence the laughter burst proceeded, "the de'il be in ye, hinny, to ding us wi' your auld warld clavers of mice making love to wrens in guid braid words, like a tappitless swankie to a kimmer under a birken shaw. I dinna ken wha can bide your crack, mon."[1]

---

[1] Lowland Scots, perhaps from the Borders-Newcastle area, meaning: "Well, well, the devil's in you, dear, to drive us mad with your silly tales of mice making love to wrens in good broad Scots, like an immature stripling to a dwarf under a birch-grove. I don't know who can put up with your boast man. - Ed.

This interruption was occasioned by Sandy Roe, a Scotch pedlar, whose national caution was completely swamped in deep potations of usquebaugh. He had been an inmate of the house for six months before, when O'Daly purchased some of his goods, for which, through some unaccountable neglect he had forgotten to pay; and though the pedlar resolved not to depart without payment, he hoped the circumstance would leave O'Daly's memory for ever, so much did usquebaugh and fresh beef delight him. But Andreish Bawn sat in speechless anger, till a senachie at the upper end of the board replied:

"I hopeAndreish Bawn will pardon thy behaviour, especially as it proceeds from a stranger, and a native of Scotland - a nation which was originally a colony of Ireland, and tributary to her; but you should know, Sandy Roe, that allegory was a favourite mode of conveying instruction, adopted from the earliest times by the wisest men. The Saviour discoursed in parables; in the Old Testament it is said that the trees of the forest chose the myrtle for their king; and old Menenius Agrippa, as it is recorded by Livy, appeased a sedition of the Roman people, by the celebrated fable of the belly and the other members of the body."

"Butwha ever heard," said Sandy, hiccupping, "of streams and rivers flowing wi' milk and honey. Andrew is a right gibgabbit chiel, doubtless; but such witless whigmileeries are downright thrashrie."

"Hadstthou read thy Bible attentively," rejoined the shanachie, with some severity, "or known the Gaelic, or read Homer or Ovid, thou wouldst have been better acquainted with the figurative language of antiquity, for -"

"Dermid Dhu," said Donough More, fearful of violating the hospitality of his mansion in the person of the stranger, "we must prevent what our new friend Sandy would term *clashmaclaver*;[1] give us one of thy beautiful airs."

The harper obeyed, and after hurrying the curiously scooped nails of his fingers across the strings, began thus:

"Long years have passed o'er thy winding water,
And Crom's[2] dark worship did fade and flee,
Since Feale the modest, green Erin's daughter,
Consigned her name, lovely stream, to thee."

"Dermid Dhu, thy harp has not a single note of gladness to-night. If thou give us that tune of sorrow, with thy own mournful accompaniment, of the beautiful Feale, who died of shame at being perceived by her husband bathing in that river which bears her name, I need not wish with Jeremiah that mine eyes were a fountain of tears. Where is the spirit-thrilling war-song of thy younger days, which aroused the clans of Duhallow to shed their best blood for a coward king?"

---

[1] Clashmaclaver, (Lowland Scots) gossip. -Ed.
[2] Crom, the god of thunder, was the chief deity of the heathen Irish.

A slight crimson flush dyed the cheek of the harper, as he bent forward in acquiescence to the will of his patron. It was but the hectic of a moment - but whether that of shame, or approval, or resentment, shall not be told by me. But he rushed into his sea of song in the following stanzas, adapted to a warlike air:

"Harp of Erin! quit thy slumbers
At the call of Dermid Dhu;
Bid the voice of flowing numbers
Rouse to war the martial crew,
From loud Allo's echoing water,
From sacred Ceadsrue's gentle floods,
From Carrigcashel's ford of slaughter,
From winding Daloo's waving woods;

"From Earl of Desmond's mist-wrapt mountain,
Where gushes broad Blackwater's spring;
From blest Lateerin's sainted fountain;
From the silvery Araglen:
O'er craggy hill and purple heather
Rush like torrents from the rock,
Led by many a valiant leader,
Bulwark in the battle's shock.

"McDonough, prince of wide Duhallow,
Rouse thy chieftains to the fight;
McAuliff's clansman soon shall follow -
From their marshy mountains' height
The war-cry shrill full wildly waxes,
Where O'Keeffe's towering castles soar;
McSweeny's beamy battle-axes
Thirst to drink the foeman's gore!

"Vassals! leave your valleys wasted -
March at freedom's sacred call;
Leave the genial feast untasted,
Diners in the banquet hall -
The eagle craves his banquet gory,
Dash the wine-bowl to the floor,
And feast him in a feast of glory,
Stalwart, kern, and crahadore.

"I see the rushing squadrons dealing
Dreadful death and ghastly scar -
I see the firm-set phalanx reeling
'Neath the iron shock of war;
Spears pursuing - Saxons flying -
The sabre's clash - the axe's stroke -
Erin victor - foemen dying
Shrouded in the cannon's smoke!

"Terror of the mighty Roman[1] -
Conqueror of the warlike Dane[2] -
Art[3] the scourge of Saxon foeman -
O'Moore,[4] the shield of battle-plain -
Heroes high in Erin's story -
Source of song to Dermid Dhu -
O! may the memory of your glory
Rouse to war the martial crew!"

Some days after, as Donough More was loitering about his fields in the early afternoon, he beheld, to his surprise, groups of persons, some mounted on stately horses, and others on foot, advancing leisurely from every point in the direction of his house.

"Who are these?" said he, addressing a tall, barefoot stocach that followed at his heels.

"I can discern," said the sharp-eyed attendant, "among the nearest groups, O'Keeffe and his followers coming from the south - McAuliff from the east - McSweeny from the west - and

---

[1] Daithi, who succeeded to the monarchy of Ireland in 406, was a prince of the most warlike disposition, and unbounded generosity. In his reign considerable tracts of territory were assigned the ancient Britons that sought shelter in Ireland, as the only country where peace and hospitality were preserved. These grants of land yet retain the names of *Sliabh na mBreathneach*, or the Welsh Mountains, *Graig na mBreathneach*, etc. etc. It was the great object of the Irish to give the Romans so much employment abroad, that they would never think of bringing the war into Ireland. It was in the enforcement of this national maxim, that Daithi carried terror and ruin to the foot of the Alps, where he was struck dead by lightning in a thunder-storm.

[2] Brian Boro, the Alfred of Ireland, who fell in the memorable Battle of Clontarf in 1014, in which 1400 Danes died.

[3] Art MacMurchad O'Cavanagh, prince of Leinster, who assumed the crown of that province in the reign of Richard the Second, king of England. He cut out sufficient employment for the Saxons during the three succeeding reigns, and died during the minority of Henry the Sixth. It was strongly suspected that he was poisoned by English influence.

[4] Roger O'Moore, a Leinster chieftain contemporary with Edward the Sixth. The unconquered Irish of that period were accustomed to say, "Our trust is in God, our Lady, and Roger O'Moore.

O'Broshnihan from the north. The others appear too dim in the distance to be particularly distinguished."

"O, that I were within reach of that scoundrel, Andreish Bawn," said O'Daly, stamping in a paroxysm of rage, "he has taken this method of revenge for the fancied insult I gave him in not checking the impertinence of the Scotch pedlar. I have no preparation made for so many guests - the wine and brandy gone - not a second sheep or cow killed. Run and tell Dermid Dhu to receive these high visitors, and bid him form some excuse for my absence. O, that the earth would open to receive me, before my credit were lost, and my character irrecoverably ruined!"

Donough More O'Daly, overwhelmed with shame and sorrow at his inability to receive, as became the hospitality of his house, this unusual overflow of high-born guests, wandered, unknowing whither he went, till he reached an eminence that overlooked a small stream which formed the boundary of his land on the west. One of his own numerous herds grazed peacefully along the surrounding heath, among the purple blossoms of which the wild bee hummed at her work of sweetness; and right below him the waters of the dark rill shone at intervals between the narrow banks like virgin silver in the lovely splendour of the declining sun. The herd grazed unnoticed, and the song of the bee passed his ear unregarded; but his eyes were fixed where the glistening stream expanded into a broad and shallow pool, and he wished that it were deep enough to hide himself and his shame and sorrow forever. Suddenly his attention was arrested by a sight which rose to his astonished view, as though it were called up by the magic wand of some powerful enchanter in Fenian romance. Had O'Daly beheld it in another place, it would not claim his slightest regard; but to see this strange apparition on the bosom of the shallow pool, which the fervour of a hot summer, would drain to emptiness and so far remote from any sea-port or navigable river, filled him with exceedingly great astonishment, for it was no other than a large well-rigged sloop, as white as snow - the brightness of her sails and stern seemed heightened in the sun's ray, and the prow bore the figure of Hope leaning on a golden anchor. The deck was crowded with men dressed in white; and one who from his proud demeanour, and superb raiment, seemed to be the chief, beckoned to the astonished man to approach.

Donough More O'Daly did approach, and the captain of the white ship thus addressed him:

"I am sorry, O'Daly, that any circumstances should occur to check thy hosptable spirit. Thy fathers were long famous for the generous shelter they afforded the stranger and the houseless; and there are powers unseen and mighty that behold the son emulate the virtues of his ancestors, and that delight to contemplate such hospitality yet lingering among the degenerate race of man. A being before whose nod I bend, has ordered me to relieve thy present distress, if the spices of the East, rich wines, and well-flavoured brandy, can achieve it. Take the good provided thee - but ask no questions."

"Mysterious being," said Donough More "thy benevolent aspect precludes the slightest dread, and proclaims thee the friend of man; but the ancestors of Donough More O'Daly, never received aught to support their house save by purchase or tribute. Their son shall not depart from the customs of his race - choose out the best and bravest of yonder herd in return for thy wine and brandy, and relieve me from a weight of grief."

"Mortal," said the captain of the white ship, "thy herds are valueless in our estimation. Accept these gifts as an earnest of the approval of superior beings, and continue the unrestrained exercise of genuine hospitality."

Thus saying, he beckoned to his attendants, who landed from the vessel many pipes of wine and brandy. When the cargo was discharged, the crew from the tall deck waved their snowy caps in a parting salute, and the white ship immediately vanished. Hardly daring to trust the evidence of his senses, O'Daly returned homeward, and procured three or four of those sliding-cars which at that time plied swiftly over the smooth and marshy moors of the country, to convey the liquor privately home. Snatched from despair by supernatural aid, he tasted the liquor of each pipe, and found its contents genuine and true as his own manly heart. Then commenced the slaying of sheep, and the felling of cattle, and all the bustle of preparation. The hour of dinner was hardly protracted beyond the usual time; and the delighted host heard every tongue rejoice, and every eye glisten in the racy influence of the gladdening wine. Long did the memory of this splendid feast of ten days' continuance live in the recollection of the gratified guests. But O'Daly's strange adventure soon transpired; and that part of the stream which crosses the Killarney road eastward of Knocknagree, where the phantom vessel blessed his sight, yet retains, in commemoration of that event, the name of *Atha-na-linga-bauna*, or the Ford of the White Ship. With such stories is the idea of hospitality to strangers kept alive throughout the country.

17
Legend of Osheen the Son of Fionn.[1]

"Of all the numerous ills that wait on age,
What stamps the wrinkle deepest on the brow?
To find each lov'd one blotted from life's page,
And be alone on earth, as I am now." - *Byron*.

When St. Patrick was labouring to extend the Christian faith in Ireland, the legend says, that in his peregrination he met a very aged man, whose gigantic dimensions far exceeded the ordinary stature of the men who lived in that age. He described himself to be Ossheen the son of Fionn mac Cumhal, the famous king or commander of the Fiana Eirion, the celebrated domestic troops of the kingdom[2] that flourished in the commencement of the third century of the Christian era. These brave "heroes of the western isle" had disappeared from the earth, and the fame of their extraordinary prowess lived then, as now, in the traditionary records of the land. Ossheen alone survived the lapse of ages, borne down by the weight of years, and the melancholy memory of bye-gone days, among a strange and degenerate race. He had been conveyed to *Tire-nan-Oge*, the Elysium of the heathen Irish, and on this permitted return to earth, the gallant band which he left in all the pride of chivalry were gone,

"And of their name and race,
Scarce left a token or a trace."

The passage of Ossheen to the "Country of the Immortals," and his return to earth, happened in the following manner.

The Fiana Eirion, which formed the national guard to defend the land against foreign invasion or domestic treachery, were, it is said, quartered on the people during the winter season; but from May to November they lived on their romantic hills, supported by the produce of the chase. Lough Lene was a favourite summer haunt, and often did the hunter's

---

[1] Published in *The Dublin Penny Journal*, January 9th 1836. Initialled, E.W. - Ed.

[2] Fionn Mac Cumhal, the Fingal of Macpherson, flourished in the beginning of the third century, during the reign of Cormac, monarch of Ireland. The Irish knew no titles of nobility, and the commander of the troops was called Righ mor Fiana, or the great king of the soldiery. From this title of Fionn, Macpherson borrowed the sounding epithet of King of Morven by which he distinguished Fingal. The heaps of burnt stones which are frequently found near the border of a well are called Fulah Fian, and they are said to be the remains of the heated stones with which these hardy warriors baked the produce of the chase in deep pits, exactly in the manner in which the natives of the south Sea Islands prepare their hogs.

cry, and the matchless speed of the tall Bran[1] force the mountain deer to lave his panting breast in the waters of the lake. The wild district by the banks of the western Araglen, in the county of Cork, where the writer of this legend resides, bears testimony to the trace of their footsteps. Dromscarra, or the parting hill of heroes, near that stream, is yet pointed out as the fort to which Goul Mac Morna, the leader of the northern troops, retired, when he withdrew in anger from Fionn. The troops were hunting in the last-mentioned district in the harvest-season, when they received intelligence that a corn-field in the neighbourhood of the camp was on different nights much trodden down by some unaccountable means; for though the field was well minded, the perpetrator of the mischief remained undiscovered. Many of the soldiers watched in vain, and at last Ossheen, the son of Fionn, volunteered his service. In the stillness of the night he heard a rustling in the corn, and by the light of the moon he discovered a beautiful white colt, without a spot. The hero advanced, and the colt slowly retreated; but as they approached the ditch, he bounded forward and seized the animal by the mane, which floated in the midnight breeze. The alarmed colt fled with an eagle's speed, and the pursuer perseveringly followed. The chase had not continued long when the earth suddenly opened - he held by the floating mane, and shortly after their descent, he found himself in a fair, extensive country, and the white colt, the object of his pursuit, metamorphosed into a beautiful lady, whose yellow ringlets were yet strained in his determined grasp, with an ineffable smile, whose magic completely took away the intention of returning, she welcomed him to Tire-nan-Oge; and the pleasures of the chase, and the society of his brothers in war, were things forgotten as if they had never been.

When Ossheen had spent some time in this region of immortal youth, and unfading spring, he felt strongly inclined to visit the green land of his birth, and regain the society of his former friends. Upon intimating this wish to the lady, she assured him that to seek the Fiana Eirion would be fruitless toil, for the race of heroes had long since disappeared from the earth.

"Ah!" said he, "why attempt to deceive me? Fionn, the king of men - Oscar, my dauntless son - Dearmid, of the eagle's speed - Conan, the subtle - heroes whom I left only twelve months since, are not surely dead."

"You have already spent three hundred years here," said she; "for the longest measure of duration on earth is but as a moment in our estimation: yet if you are determined to revisit your favourite haunts, you may proceed - this horse will safely convey you to earth; but if you alight from his back during the journey, it will preclude your return to this place, and you will find your youth and strength vanished, and yourself laden with three centuries of years and infirmities."

---

[1] Bran was a dog of great swiftness and courage. Tradition affirms that he remains yet alive, enchanted in the Lake of Killarney.

He departed - revisited the cloudy Mangerton - winded his course beneath savage Torc - stretched his view into the far prospect from romantic Clara - and roused the red deer of the Galtys - but in vain. No long-remembered friend met his eye - the land was occupied by a feeble and diminutive race - the very face of nature was changed - rivers had abandoned their ancient channels - deep valleys were level plains and the wavy forests became barren moors - he had not known it as the land of his love, had not the multiform hills, and the firm-set, everlasting mountains, been the unchangeable landmarks of his memory to guide him through the altered scene.

Filled with the deepest melancholy, he retraced his footsteps to Tire-nan-Oge; but as he came to the bank of a deep river, he saw one of the degenerate men of that time, vainly endeavouring to raise a sack of corn which had slipped from his horse's back into the middle of the stream. Ossheen had not forgotten his military oath, one clause of which bound the ancient Irish soldier to assist the distressed. He spurred into the current, and endeavoured without alighting to raise the sack with his foot; but it remained unmoved. Surprised that a weight so apparently light should mock his effort, he sprung into the water, when both his horse and the treacherous apparition disappeared, and left him a wretched and forlorn being bent beneath a load of years.

"The Dialogue of Ossheen and Patrick" can tell the difficulty that apostle had in converting the haughty worshipper of Crom to the mild and humble doctrines of the Christian religion. He became a member of the saint's household; and when he lost his sight through extreme old age, he had a servant to conduct his steps. It appears that Ossheen's appetite corresponded with his stature, and that the saint's housekeeper dealt his portion with a niggard hand, for when the old man expostulated with her one day on the scantiness of his repast, she bitterly replied, that his large oat cake, his quarter of beef, and *miscawn* of butter, would suffice a better man.

"Ah," said he, his memory adverting to the days of his strength, "I could yet show you an *ivy-leaf* broader than your cake, *a berry of the quickbeam* larger than your *miscawn*, and the leg of a *blackbird* that would outweigh your quarter of beef."

With that want of respect to the aged and destitute which indicates the ill-tempered and rude of that sex, she gave him the *lie direct* -but Ossheen remained silent.

Some time after, Ossheen directed his attendant to nail a raw hide against the wall, and to dash the puppies of a bitch of the wolf-dog species, that had lately littered, against it. They in succession fell howling and helpless to the ground, except one, that clung with tooth and nail in the hide. He was carefully reared, and when he was full-grown and vigorous, Ossheen one day told his attendant to conduct him to the plain of Kildare, and to lead the dog in a leash. As they went along, Ossheen at a certain place asked his guide if he beheld any thing deserving of particular notice; and he replied, that he saw a monstrous plant resembling ivy, that projected from a huge rock, and almost hid the light of the sun, and also a large tree by a neighbouring stream, which bore a red fruit of enormous bulk.

Ossheen carried away the leaf and the fruit. They shortly reached the plain of Kildare, and he again demanded whether any strange object met his servant's attention.

"Yes," said the other, "I perceive a *dallan* of extraordinary size."

He then desired to be led to the stone; and after removing it from its place with one giant effort, he took from the cavity beneath a *Cran-tubal*, or sling,[1] a ball, and an ancient trumpet. Sitting on the upturned *dallan*, he blew the musical instrument. The loud blast seemed to pierce the concave sky, and though the sound appeared to sweep the extended earth, it was sweet and harmonious. After the lapse of some hours, the blind musician inquired if his attendant beheld any thing uncommon.

"I perceive," said he, "the flight of birds advancing from every quarter of the heavens, and alighting on the plain before us."

He continued the magic strain, when his attendant exclaimed, that a monstrous bird, the shadow of whose bulk darkened the field, was approaching.

"That is the object of our expectation," said Ossheen, "let slip the dog as that bird alights."

The wolf dog bounded with open jaws to the fight, and the bird received his attack with matchless force. The thrilling blasts of the trumpet seemed to inspire the combatants with renewed rage; they fought all day, and at the going down of the sun the victorious wolf dog drank the life-blood of his prostrate foe.

"The bird is dead," said the affrighted servant, "and the dog, bathed in blood, is approaching to devour us."

"Direct my aim," said the hero, "towards the dog." Then launching the ball from the cran-tubal, it arrested the rapid progress of the savage animal, and felled him lifeless to the earth.

The leaf, the berry, and the leg of this amazing blackbird, were the *spolia optima* he produced to the housekeeper in proof of his veracity. This was the expiring effort of the warrior bard; for the legend records, that indignation at this woman's insulting language shortly afterwards broke his heart.

Such is the legend of Ossheen the son of Fionn, and which, in some of the more distant districts of our country, is handed down from father to son, as being the true history of this last of the noble race to whom it alludes.

[1] The Irish, from the accuracy of their aim, and their uncommon strength of arm, were famous slingers. The missiles discharged from the *Cran-tubal* were a composition of blood, lime and sand.

18
Jack o' the Lantern.[1]

"There are more things in heaven and earth, Horatio,
Than are dreamt of in your philosophy." - *Shakespeare.*

My uncle, kind, generous soul! was deeply imbued with superstition - was a firm believer in supernatural influences, a circulating library of legendary lore, and a living chronicle of all the compacts made with the "ould boy" from the days of "Doctor Fosther" (Faustus) up to those of the Witch of Endor. He very rarely diverged into the light and amusing fictions of fairyism, for his genius, and, by consequence, his course of studies, were entirely of the German school, wild, dark, and horrific. The reader will be pleased to take notice, that I do not use the word *studies* in the vanity of showing that this dear and near relation was possessed of book-learning; on the contrary, I roundly assert, that his lore was not derived from books, for though, as I have heard himself assert, he mastered the horn-book at "ould Tim Casey's" hedge seminary, and spelled his weary way as far as the "Oliphant" (Elephant) through a three-penny primer at the age of fifteen, the dread of flagellation for an unfortunate boxing bout with a red-shinned fellow of seventeen, whom he forced to bite the dust, made him bid adieu to book-learning and Tim Casey before he could take the "Rhinoceros," and all his natural history, by the horn. I may observe, by way of parenthesis, that my revered uncle was celebrated in after life for his skill in the noble science of defence; and shall take this opportunity of testifying, that whatever share of dexterity I possess at handling the fist or cudgel, has been entirely owing to his fostering care. He had a sovereign contempt for the Newtonian philosophy; laughed to scorn the manner in which the learned account for a great deal of what is called natural phenomena; could show you with half an eye the man who was translated to the exalted sphere of the moon for stealing a bush from his gossip's fence, but totally denied the existence of any other living being in that planet; and could descry there none of the seas and mountains which all astronomers so easily perceive. In short, he declared it to be as dangerous to follow these lights of learning in their aerial voyages of discovery, as to pursue that misguiding traveller, Jack-o'-the-Lantern, in his devious excursion through the faithless mazes of an Irish shaking bog.

Whether it was that my uncle perceived me the inheritor of his own eccentric temper, or that he always found me the greedy devourer of all his tales of wonder, certain it is, that I was his special favourite; and he rarely took a nightly excursion to any neighbouring wake, shebeen-house, or card-party, without securing my company. Indeed, I improved so much under his auspices, that at fifteen, very few of double my years could boast half my

---

[1] Published in *The Dublin Penny Journal*, January, 16th 1836. Initialled, E.W. - Ed.

dexterity at spinning a tough yarn, handling a pack of cards, or throwing off a draught of poteen. But Truth, "my fair mistress," obliges me to confess, that I have forgotten a third of these accomplishments. Through long disuse, I can now hardly distinguish a *king* from a *knave;* but the tales and legends of my beloved country still possess a charm for me, which neither time nor misfortune can diminish.

One night in October, when returning home from Darby McAuliffe's wake, where my uncle amused a numerous circle of gaping auditors by reciting the wonderful adventures of *Aodh beg an Bridán*, we found ourselves on the border of a mountain-stream, which afforded an outlet to the waters of a deep morass, that extended from a considerable distance to its very edge, when that meteoric light, which the learned denominate *ignis fatuus*, but which in vulgar parlance is called *Jack-o'-the-Lantern*, suddenly started before us. My uncle stopped, and eyeing the irregular motions of the strange light that glided around us, said,

"Well, my ould boy, I didn't think ye'd ever again tempt me to pursue ye; but, howsomever, as I'm growing stiff in the limbs, we'll take the aisy way for getting rid o' yer thricks. Eamon, a vick O! (meaning myself,) mind your eye - off with your coat, an' turn it inside out, or, as sure as your living, the chap yonder will give us a cowld bath in the nixt bog-hole;" then, suiting the action to the word, he deliberately took off his coat and breeches, turned them inside out, and slipped into them *instanter*; while I could scarcely keep my feet, I was so convulsed with laughter at the grotesque appearance presented by my uncle in this strange mode of equipment. "Eamon, a vick," resumed my uncle, upon seeing my extravagant contortions - "Eamon, is it yer books that tayches ye to laugh at yer uncle, ma boochal? I seen, in my own time, some conceated chaps o' yer kitney (kidney) turn their *coats* for a worse reason than this."

The sharpness of the last remark showed that I had greatly offended; and I endeavoured to sooth his irritation, by expressing deep contrition for my ill-timed laughter fit, and by literally turning my coat, leaving, however, the nether garment undisturbed; but my toilet was hardly completed, when the wandering light, after a few curves along the stream, dashed into a small glen that opened into the brook, and finally disappeared.

As we strode homeward along the well-known pathway, my uncle, now relieved from those fears which the presence of the meteor had occasioned, said,

"Now wouldn't ye give yer uncle a *speciment* of yer larning, and tell us what the books you read say about Jack-o'-the-Lantern."

"Why, uncle, the *ignis fatuus* is only a harmless light - a gaseous vapour arising from putrid vegetable bodies, which, ignited by the damps of the night, wanders on in brightness till the inflammable air is consumed."

"Eamon, a hagur, your hard words have bothered me entirely. Thim nateral phil - what do ye call 'em, have *filled* your head, a leagh, with nonsense. Jack-o'-the-Lantern a gaslight - isn't it, asthore? Eamon, a chora, (and his tone grew tremulous with feeling,) - Eamon, if you knew the sufferings of that forsaken crather, since the time the poor sowl was doomed to wandher, with a lanthern in his hand, on this cowld earth, without rest for his foot, or shelter for his head, until the day of judgment - ullayone! oh, it 'ud soften the heart of stone, to see him as I once did, the poor ould *dunawn* - his feet blistered and bleeding, his poneens[1] all flying about him, and the rains of heaven beating on his ould white head."

This burst of emotion would have given me real delight, could a reasonable motive be assigned for it; but in his enthusiastic feeling for the fabled being of his commiseration, I really concluded my uncle was beside himself.

"I was coming home one night," he continued, "from a christening at Tim Fowler's - it was about twelve at night - and I had not taken any thing extraordinary, but was just, as you may say, right enough, whin up started the light before me, on the very spot where we met it to-night; and it was this night twenty years, of all nights in the year. I knew, if I tried to get homeward, that treacherous lanthern would lead me through all the bogs and corraghs of the place, for the night was pitchy dark, and the roar of the mountain streams, as they dashed through their rocky beds, sounded deep and lonely. - "Bedad," sis I, "ma boochal, I'll run no risks in striving to avoid ye, but I'll hunt you down fairly; for, you see, avick, if you shun him, he'll follow ye, but if you purshue him, he'll cut away. I jist slipt off my brogues, (by the same token, I never got tidings of them since,) and dashed towards him in my thraheens. Well became him, he up and runs for the bare life over hill and valley, cummer and carigaun. I stuck to him like his shadow. Sometimes I came rattling down a steep cliff; thin, after picking up my legs, ran headlong into a bog-hole. Now, I got stuck into a furze brake; and the moment after soused head an' ears in a running sthrame. At length, as I retched the bank of a rapid river, I saw him, by the light of his own lanthern, hiding on the very edge of the water, under shelter of a *sally* bush. As I dashed like a greyhound towards him through the loughans of the inch, his eye seemed rivetted on me in wild terror - his face was frightful to look at, and his white beard and whiter hair streamed in the rough blast that swept down the glin along the river. The next step would have brought me straight upon him; but, at that instant, the March cock upon a neighbouring roost gave a notice of day - the lanthern wint out, and the poor crather that carried it disappeared, and I was left in pitchy darkness."

As we journeyed homeward, I introduced various topics to put my companion's sanity to the test; but he displayed his usual acuteness upon every subject, save that of the *sprite* whose lot the reader has heard him so feelingly deplore. Upon this point he was impregnable to all argument, and I gave up the struggle, astonished at this instance of mental delusion. Next day he favoured me with the history of Jack-o'-the-Lantern, which I wrote down at leisure while the facts were fresh in my memory. I greatly regret that I did not write the strange legend in my uncle's rich and imaginative dialect; but the manuscript

---

[1] Wretched garments.

is now before me - and even had I leisure and inclination to revise it, so many years have since elapsed, that I could not recollect my uncle's varied phraseology - so, reader, you have it as it is.

The Legend

Once upon a time there lived a man, whose natural disposition was churlish and morose, and the asperities of whose soul had not been softened down by the influence of a knowledge of God; and his acquirements in the things of this world did not much exceed the narrow skill which enabled him to cultivate the farm on which he lived. He was known throughout the country for his unsocial manners - his blazing hearth never cheered the way-worn stranger - and the repulsed beggar never again sought his inhospitable door. In short, he lived the reproach of humanity, and his name was a bye-word in the land.

Jack, for so this churl was named, was returning home one night from a neighbouring fair, when, as he approached a dark and rapid stream at a particular ford, which the imagination of the people of that time had associated with some tales of murder and superstition, he heard a groan that, to his fancy, proceeded from some tortured spirit. He suddenly drew in the mare on which he rode - all the horrid tales recorded of that dark glen rushed to his memory - and as a second and a third sound of agony smote his ear, his bristling hair stood erect, the cold beads of dismay oozed at every pore - nor did the whiskey which he quaffed that evening in his own sordid way, prevent the current of his blood from freezing at his very heart; but when the horrid sounds were again repeated, he summoned nerve sufficient to inquire what he could do for the tortured soul that crossed his path in that glen of gloom and horror. "For the love of heaven," said the voice, "take me to some human habitation; for I am no tortured spirit, but a poor homeless wanderer who have lost my way on the wild moor, and have lain down here to die, for I durst not cross this rapid water. So may mercy be shown you in your hour of need, and in the day of your distress."

Delivered from supernatural terrors, the peasant's soul softened into humanity. With an indescribable feeling of pity, which never till that hour reached his heart, he dismounted, and saw extended on the damp earth a very aged man, with a white beard, who was evidently borne down with the load of years and misery. He wrapped the aged sufferer in his warm great coat, placed him on the saddle, and then mounting on the crupper, he supported the object of his pity till he reached home. His wife smiled to behold her gruff husband engaged in the unusual office of hospitality, and wondered much what charm could have soothed his unsocial soul to kindness. The miserable stranger received every necessary that her cupboard afforded - was laid to rest in a warm bed, and in a short time his grief and infirmities were forgotten in sound repose.

About the dawn of day, Jack was awakened from his sleep by a bright blaze of light that shone through all the cabin. Unable to account for this sudden illumination, he started to his feet from the bed, when his progress was instantly checked, and his astonishment greatly augmented to behold a young man of celestial beauty, wrapt in white garments. His shoulders were furnished with wings, the plumage of which exceeded in whiteness the down of swans; and as he spoke, his words stole like the notes of a heavenly harp, to the soul of the wondering cottager. "Mortal," said the celestial visitant, "I am one of the angels commissioned to watch over the sons of Adam. I heard thy brethren exclaim against thy unsocial temper, and utter disregard of the sacred virtue of hospitality; but I find that some generous seeds of virtue have lain uncultivated with thee. In me thou beholdest the miserable senior whom thy generous humanity relieved - I have shared thy frugal fare and lowly bed: my blessing shall remain with thy house, but to thyself in particular I bestow three wishes - then freely ask, as I shall freely give. May wisdom bound the desire of thy soul."

Jack paused for a moment, and then said, "There's a sycamore tree before the door, fair and wide-spreading, but every passer-by must pluck a bough from it - grant that every one touching it with such intent, may cling to the tree till I release him. Secondly, I do wish that any person who sits in my elbow chair, may never be able to leave it, nor the chair to leave the ground, without my consent. There's a wooden box on the wall - I keep it to hold the thread, and awls, and hammer, with which I mend my brogues, but the moment I turn my back, every clown comes here cobbling for himself: my third request is, that the person who puts his hand into the box, might not withdraw it, and that the box may stick to the wall, during my pleasure. My wishes are ended."

The angel sighed as he granted the boon; and the legend further adds, that Jack was from that hour excluded from all hope of heaven, because he had eternal happiness within his wish, and neglected to secure the vast gift; but the angel's blessing remained with his house - his children were many, and his crops and cattle throve with large increase.

Twenty years after, as Jack sat one evening in his elbow-chair, musing on his earthly affairs, a strange and unearthly smell of brimstone assailed his nose; and when he turned round to ascertain the cause, the appearance of a tall, dark-looking being, graced with a pair of horns, a cloven foot, and a long tail, which he carried rather genteelly tucked under his arm, further increased his astonishment. The stranger immediately opened his message - mentioned Jack's exclusion from heaven, and spoke of his infernal master's anxiety to see him speedily at his own hot home.

When Jack heard these awful tidings, he repressed every symptom of alarm, and, starting to his feet, bid the stranger welcome. "I hope," he continued, "your honour won't be above sitting in the elbow-chair, and tasting a drop of poteen this cold evening, while I put on my Sunday clothes." The demon complied. "There," said his host, "is a real drop of the native. The sorra a gauger ever set his ugly face on it. Why then would your honour tell me if ye have any gaugers in - your native place?" "We have lots of them," replied he of the cloven hoof; but we give them other employment than still-hunting; but come, the road is long, and we must away."

So saying, he motioned to leave his seat, but found himself immovably fixed therein, while the guileful mortal set his flail to work on his captive enemy. Vain every entreaty for mercy - in vain he kicked, and flung his arms around; the swift descending instrument of vengeance smashed every bone in his skin; and it was only when exhausted, and unable to prosecute his task, that he consented to liberate the miserable being, on his solemn oath, that he would never more visit this upper world on a similar errand.

Satan has more than one courier to do his errands. A second messenger, provided with the necessary instruction for shunning the fatal chair and flail, was despatched to fetch the doomed mortal, who was ruminating, next day, on the adventure of the preceding evening, when the latch was raised, and a stranger cautiously entered. When he had explained his business, Jack requested that he would be seated, and expressed his willingness to depart when he had put a stitch or two in his old brogue. The courier was too cautious, and declined to sit; but Jack took the chair, pulled off his broken shoe, and requested the demon to hand him an awl from the small box. The infernal visitant obeyed; but found that he could neither withdraw his hand, nor remove the box from the wall. He cast a glance of dismay at his mortal antagonist, who sprung to the flail, and bestowed such discipline as forced the present visitor to submit to the same conditions for his release, that his brother devil had done.

It is said that his sable majesty was greatly surprised at the discomfiture of his two trusty messengers; and, like a skilful general, he resolved to go in person and explore the enemy's camp. He ascended from the nether world through Mangerton mountain, near Killarney, where that barren and bottomless pool, called the Hole of Hell,[1] now fills up the funnel which formed his upward passage. He looked round from the lofty height into the far country, and with the sagacity of the vulture in quest of his prey, directed his course to Jack's habitation. It was a sunny morning, and a heavy frost of some days' continuance had congealed all the waters, and rendered the surface of the land hard and slippery. Aware of Jack's wiles, he rapped at the door and, in a voice of thunder, bid the miserable mortal come forth.

"I will go whithersoever your Lordship commands me," he answered, awed by the threatening voice and formidable manner of his summoner; "but the road is slippery, and you will permit me in to fetch my cane; besides, I would wish to kiss my wife and little ones before I go."

The fiend was inexorable, and urged the wretched being on before him.

---

[1] The Devil's Punch-Bowl, called by the peasantry, "The Hole of Hell."

"If I walk without the support of a stick," he resumed, hobbling on before his captor; "I shall speedily break my bones; and if there are no carmen on the road to hell, how would your Lordship wish to fetch my carcase on your princely shoulders? Oh, that I had even a bough from yonder sycamore to support my poor old limbs!"

To stay his murmuring, and furnish the desired support, Satan laid hold on a fair branch of the tree, but immediately found that he was unable either to break the bough, or quit his hold; and Jack, with a yell of joy, returned to fetch his favourite flail. In the words of the legend, whoever would come from the remote ends of the earth to hear the most fearful howling, occasioned by the most dreadful castigation, would here have ample gratification. Jack broke his three best flails on the occasion; and though the miserable fiend cried loudly for mercy, he continued his toil till the going down of the sun, when on his promising neither to seek Jack on earth, or permit his entrance into hell, the arch-fiend was released, and the fortunate man retired to rest, more fatigued from that day's thrashing than ever he had been before.

Our story draws near its close - Jack, with all his skill, could not baffle the assault of Death. He paid the debt of nature; but when his soul was dismissed to its final residence, the porter at the gate of the infernal regions stoutly denied him admittance - the fiends turned pale with affright - and even Satan himself fled within the lowest depths to hide his head from the dreaded enemy. Then, because he was unfit for heaven, and that hell refused to take him, he was decreed to walk the earth with a lantern to light him on his nightly way till the day of judgment. - Such reader, is the legend relative to Jack-o'-the-Lantern, commonly believed by the peasantry in many districts of Ireland.

19
Phelim McCarthy[1]

"Foreign cows wear long horns." - *Irish Proverb.*

The last faint rays of a November sun shed their sickly influence on two travellers that journeyed over a wild and trackless moor in a western district of the County of Middlesex. They were two, who from difference of dress, feature, and habits, could not be supposed to have existed in a long bond of companionship, but to have been brought together by one of those accidents which frequently jumble into contact, for an hour, travellers, who hold very little in common, save the mere outline of humanity. One, who led the way, was a man of colossal stature; his dress was that of a sailor, and his flat nose, thick lip and ebon countenance proclaimed him of African descent, but that toil had not rendered rigid his supple nerves, or marred the light freedom of his vigorous frame.

The haze and gloom of the short twilight now succeeded the transient gleam which lately shot athwart their pathway. They had wandered far from the common thoroughfare; and no human habitation, nor trace of living thing, broke the unvaried sameness of the low, monotonous heath, over which the African pressed with lusty stride, but the other traveller seemed to be borne down by fatigue and despondency.

"We had better sit down for an hour," said the latter, "that respite will enable us to pursue our course with fresh vigour, and the moon, which will rise by that time, will afford us light sufficient to find our way to the high road or explore some cottage that will afford us shelter."

"A vast heaving there," replied the black man, "to turn in to this here cold birth on the moor would set aside the necessity of ever turning out again. We may be thankful, master, that we have not gone down with the Fanny and our messmates to Davy's locker. This lee-gale may yet chop about, and bear us snug into port; but a good seaman would not lie waterlogged, while he could grasp an oar, or snatch at a towrope.

The first speaker now silently followed the gigantic strides of the black man, till the deep roar of a waterfall struck their ear, and they found they had crossed the extent of the bleak moor, and reached the border of a rapid stream. The gloom of night brooded deep and dark over the surrounding scene; but beyond the river, an ascent, that seemed to be covered with wood, rose against the lowering clouds; on this eminence the figures of rock and tree were dark and undefined - but the murmur of the waving boughs, as the dying gust rustled along the decaying foliage, and anon the wild whistle of the hurrying blast, rushing past the columnar tree or projecting crag, gave indication that the dusky rising space was wooded land. While they stood, irresolute whether to gain the rising ground in front, or shape their course along the border of the stream, their attention was suddenly caught by a

[1] Published in *The Dublin Penny Journal*, February, 20th 1836. Initialled, E.W. - Ed.

weak but steady light that shone at some distance, amid the vague and formless gloom. Considering that this light must proceed from some human habitation, the travellers determined upon reaching it if possible. They crossed the stream, and forcing their way with extreme difficulty through the trees and tangled underwood, at length reached the object of their search. During their toilsome progress, the light frequently disappeared, and as often again caught their eye - now seeming to change its position, and then to become stationary; these various appearances were owing probably to an optical delusion, occasioned by their own frequent change of situation from the irregularity of the ground, for it proved to be the light of a fire which burned on the hearth of a cabin, partly formed of sods and trees, and partly hollowed into the high cliff against which it rested. This was the beacon that guided the weary feet of the wanderers to a place of shelter from the inclement air, but such were the intricacies of the path, and the manner in which huge masses of granite shielded the house from observation, that even at mid-day none but one previously acquainted with the spot, would suppose that human being had ever lingered there, or sought shelter in its loneliness.

Never did knight of romance, after a midnight excursion through the windings of some enchanted forest, greet the warder's cry from the tower of a sumptuous castle with greater joy, than did our wanderers the humble fire that gleamed in this wretched habitation. As they reached the low door, they stopped to hear if haply the sound of human voice, or the noise of human toil would reach their ear - but stillness, deep as that of death, presided there. They entered, and beheld nothing within to indicate its being the late dwelling of men, except the decaying fire, that seemed to have been supplied from a heap of wood which occupied one corner of this outer apartment, and a fat hog that had been lately killed, and hung by the hind legs on the opposite side. Within this was another room, doorless, damp, and vacant, save that a bed of fresh-gathered moss lay on the floor - no other trace of human thing was here, and all was silent and solitary.

After having explored every part of the cabin, the Negro replenished the fire, and selecting a larger billet than ordinary from the heap of wood, placed it as a seat for his companion, while he stretched his own giant length along the hearth, and, like Milton's goblin,

"Basked at the fire his hairy strength."

They waited for some time in the hope of finding the tenant of this lonely cabin return - a quarter of an hour had elapsed, then another, and another, but no tread of feet relieved their anxiety; at last the Negro, whom we have hitherto seen act the leader and spokesman, and whose appetite had been excited by a toilsome day's journey, cast the whites of his eyes in sidelong regard at the dead hog, and said, "Master, you see we have run into this snug little cove, after the dangers of a dark night, and a lee shore, without any prog under hatches, and as this keen north-easter must have given us a shark's appetite, what would you say to a slice or two of yon grinning fellow?"

"I would be much gratified to try a cut of the hog," answered his pensive companion, "if I could reconcile it to the principles of honesty, to take what does not belong to me."

"Lookye, master," rejoined the other "you are, mayhap, a deep clerk, and Thomas the black knows nothing of book-learning. But if you chopped logic till doomsday, it would fail to convince me that the Providence which preserved us, almost by miracle, when the Fanny went down, and our messmates were sent to feed the fishes, would be at all gratified at seeing us refuse its good gifts, and die of hunger and fatigue, with a soft bed of moss, and a prepared fat hog within our reach."

The Negro rose without waiting for a reply, and pulling out a large clasp knife, cut enormous collops from the hog - then he drew forth the burning embers, and with all the adroitness of a practitioner in the culinary art, he laid the slices thereon, and after a due share of turning and broiling, he made two equal dividends of the meat, and presented one portion to his companion, whose scruples soon evaporated into thin air before the savoury steam of the broiled pork. They ate heartily, and without a murmur at the sameness of the fare, except one ejaculation on the part of the black man, for a crust of bread and a draught of grog, while his white messmate only poured a short petition for a mealy potato.

After various conjectures on both sides, which our scanty page permits us not to detail, respecting the absence of the supposed inhabitants of the cabin, they both agreed, now that their hunger was appeased, to indulge their limbs on the soft moss; but upon the land's-man's expressing reluctance to seek repose under such circumstances, the black man of the sea bid him turn in fearlessly, for they would keep watch and watch, and that should any danger appear during his hour of sleeping, he should be roused at its first approach. His companion was soon asleep, and after an hour's watching, the Negro heard the sound of approaching voices, and nearer, the quick tramp of feet, and in the next moment half a dozen voices were heard in the outer room. They talked loud and quick, and seemed to express with uncouth phrase and wild oath, their joy at the success of some business in which they were engaged. The black now shook his sleeping bed-fellow, and enjoined silence by laying his ebon palm across his mouth; then, to the surprise of the other, he slipt off his dress, and lay at full length, naked in the bed. When the bustle and hurried discourse of their first entrance had subsided, one of the men bid another prepare super - a strong glare of torchlight now shone around, which enabled our travellers to observe the figures of five ferocious, wild-looking men, all with pistols in their belts, a portmanteau, that lay on the floor, and some guns which stood against the wall. They supposed that these fierce men were thieves, and this lonesome spot their place of resort. Their suspicion was confirmed on seeing a man of advanced years extended on the floor. He was well dressed - his hands were pinioned down - his eyes bound with a handkerchief, and the blood flowed pretty freely from a deep gash in his head.

"Captain," said a fellow who was deputed to furnish the supper, "I'm blest if this here pig ar'n't cut up to the very bones."

"Cut up! Is it the hog we left whole and untouched this morning? - Jack Watson, who last left this can account for it. Watson, have you disposed of the hog? Now mind you, my lad, if you have broken the laws of our society, by alienating the least portion of our goods or booty, you shall abide the consequences. Ho! two men to the door, lest any pass out."

"May I never eat pork or mutton!" returned the accused, "if I meddled or made with it - and come what will, Captain, I am as innocent of this charge as the child unborn. The old boy himself was certainly here, for no mortal man could discover our haunt."

"Yes,and I am not gone yet!" roared a powerful and hollow voice behind them - the wondering thieves turned, and beheld a naked being of gigantic dimensions, black as the prince of darkness himself - his massive arms were raised in a threatening attitude, while he drew up his vast bulk to its topmost stretch. A shout of dismay succeeded the first paroxysm of terror - then a rush to the door, where some tumbled headlong over the threshold, while at their heels rose a loud laugh, deriding as the arch fiends' scoff. They fled - happy to escape from a scene filled up, as they supposed, with the presence of man's ancient enemy. The exulting negro, the author of their dismay, then retired to dress, while he requested his friend in the moss, to restore the old gentleman the use of his hands and eyes. Grateful for his release from impending death, he informed his deliverers that he was a merchant of London, travelling on business to the next town, and attended by his servant; that they were attacked by robbers, and after a fierce struggle, in which the faithless servant had fled, he was overpowered, dragged from his horse, and reduced to the situation from which they had rescued him. The Negro gave immediate directions to have the gentleman's wound bound up, while he himself kept watch at the door for the returning robbers - but the first faint streaks in the east appeared, and no footsteps disturbed the wary sentinel. They now prepared to depart, after breakfast on a few additional slices of the hog. - The Negro led the way, having first strapped on the gentleman's portmanteau, which remained unopened, and shouldered a pair of loaded guns, the merchant and our other acquaintance similarly armed, bringing up the rear.

They passed without molestation through a wild and wooded country, until they reached the high road, and at the next town the merchant procured horses to London, where they arrived safely. Having learned that his deliverers had been shipwrecked on the western coast of England, and had been travelling up to London - the one to enter on board some sailing vessel, and the other to procure in that great mart of literature and commerce, some employment for his literary abilities, when Providence made them the instrument of his deliverance from the hands of the robbers, he forced the Negro to forego his nautical intentions and accept the station of porter in his warehouse, where the other filled the situation of clerk with a respectable salary.

Perhaps the reader has been curious to know who this salaried clerk is; but though extremely anxious at all times to oblige, we have been so hurried in our narration, as not to have a moment to spare for that occasion till now. Phelim McCarthy was an Irishman, the son of the tenant of a wretched hovel in Glenflesk, a wild and picturesque glen in the county of Kerry. Owing to certain political causes, which it is not within our provenance to mention, the wildest valleys in Ireland were, from immemorial time, the places where Roman Catholic schoolmasters instructed the youth of their persuasion, and where all who could afford to pay, and all who could not, were instructed in Greek and Latin, Mathematics and Accounts. Phelim was of the last-mentioned class of pupils - they were denominated poor scholars; and after learning the usual course in these rustic seminaries, were furnished, by a subscription raised in their native parish, with the means of completing their studies, and taking priest's orders on the Continent, to qualify them for the Irish Mission. Phelim was a young man of considerable parts. After pursuing the usual routine of the poor scholar, he was supplied, through the influence of the parish priest, with a decent suit of black, and a tolerable sum of money; but having no vocation for the church, he resolved to try his fortune in London. For this purpose, he embarked at Cork; in a severe gale, the vessel was driven upon the English coast, and all on board perished excepting Phelim and his black friend. They had travelled under adverse circumstances, till they lost their way on the heath, where they at first attracted notice, having strayed from the highway to solicit shelter in one or two farm-houses, whence they were rudely repulsed. In three years from the date of his arrival in London, McCarthy had risen through some subordinate gradations, to the place of head clerk in Mr. Wilson's employment. He had conciliated the regard of all that knew him. His brother clerks beheld his quick promotion without envy - the grey-headed domestics placed him only beneath their master in estimation - the great house-dog barked hearty welcome at his approach - and even the demure old cat purred her complacency, as he took his seat at the parlour-fire after the fatigues of the day. But there was one being beyond all, whose smile and welcome Phelim McCarthy cherished with deep and silent devotion. This was Eliza Wilson, the only daughter of his employer; she was a lovely creature, of retired habits, and lived as deeply secluded in the great city of London as if she were the inhabitant of a desert. She had long beheld with partiality the graceful person and naturally polite manner of the Irishman. Upon those holidays when the family would retire from the bustle of the city to Mr. Wilson's country-house, they had frequent opportunities of being together, and an explanation of mutual affection was the result. Their favourite walk was in a romantic glen, in a certain spot of which a large cypress-tree shaded the grave of an unfortunate female, who, after coquetting her lover away, died of a broken heart. Once, as Phelim accompanied Mr. Wilson and his daughter to this retreat, Eliza repeated the story of the mouldering resident below; and next day, when the youthful pair sought their favourite haunt, McCarthy led the lady to a rustic seat opposite to the melancholy cypress, and seating himself beside her, sung the following song, which he had composed, to one of the sad and beautiful airs of his own native land of melody.

Beneath yon sad cypress, where cowslips are dying,
And green grass is glistening with dew,
Low couched in the cold earth, a maiden is lying,
Who once bloom'd as lovely as you;
Till her scorn quench'd the flame of her own constant true love.
He bade the sly traitress a final adieu,
Tho' his flame was but equalled by my flame for you, love,
So tender, so ardent, and true!

When a fond heart more kind caught his faithful devotion,
What wild woes distracted her brain!
Were hers the rich gems in the bosom of ocean,
She'd yield them to bind him again.
He smil'd at her folly - she linger'd forsaken,
And wept, as before wept her lover his woe!
Unpitied - when hopeless her bosom was breaking,
No tear did in sympathy flow.

Beneath yon sad cypress, where cowslips are dying,
And green grass is glistening with dew,
Low couch'd in the cold earth, that maiden is lying,
Who once bloom'd as lovely as you.
Be warn'd by that maid, in her dark bed of sleeping -
Deny not forever the promise I crave,
Lest the warm bridal touch, be the cold reptile's creeping,
Thy gay nuptial pillow - the grave!

The mellowed softness of the singer's voice, the wild and melancholy air, and her own peculiar situation, overpowered the listener, and she gave vent to her feelings in tears.

Mr. Wilson had observed his daughter's growing partiality for the young man. He had a high esteem for McCarthy, and did not discourage this intercourse, for he sought no wealthy son-in-law, and resolved not to sacrifice his daughter's happiness at the shrine of riches. The Irish peasantry pride themselves on their high descent, and Phelim, upon frequent occasions, gave such magnificent descriptions of the heritage of his fathers, that the honest Londoner conceived that half a barony at least would fall to Phelim on the demise of his father. He at length resolved privately to dispatch a trusty messenger to Ireland, intending to satisfy himself respecting the situation of Phelim's friends, before he determined finally regarding the contemplated alliance. The messenger set forward on his voyage of discovery, towards the El Dorado of Phelim McCarthy; and after crossing the channel, and many a road and river in South Munster, through which we shall spare our reader the fatigue of following him, he found himself, on a fine sunny noon in the month of August, at the foot of one of those wild and multiform hills between Millstreet and Killarney, which form a portion of that continuous chain, extending from sea to sea, through the counties of Cork and Kerry. Over this hill a passage led into Glenflesk, so close and precipitous, that hardly any living thing, save a Kerry goat, or a Kerry goatherd, would venture thereon. This messenger was himself born of Irish parents, natives of Kerry. I cannot determine whether it was a hereditary love of climbing at the risk of his neck, or the imperative commands of his master, that urged him on, but up he toiled the perpendicular steep with unabated vigour. He stopped to rest at intervals under the shade of a friendly holly or mountain-ash, that sprung luxuriantly from the compact, flinty rock, and quenched his thirst at the sparkling cascade, that plunged, as if poured from the clouds, over many a steep cliff. As he turned to pause upon the fearful depth below, the scream of the eagle, sailing in mid air, ascended to his ear, and groups of wild goats, and their wilder keepers, gazed upon the intruder on their haunts with mutual astonishment. At length he mastered the way, and perched among the clouds on the wild and rocky summit, near the border of a lake, he descried the habitation, if habitation it could be called, of Fineen McCarthy. The front wall of the hovel, which was composed of alternate layers of huge stones and turf, rose about three feet in height. On this rude wall were the rafters, that inclined backward to a huge perpendicular cliff. The roof was thatched with heath; and over that extended a curious network of straw-rope, having the meshes about a foot square; the lateral ropes were secured by wooden pegs, and those that traversed downward, had attached to them stones of moderate size, which depended over the eves. Beyond the cabin were seen a few patches of potato-ground enclosed by walls of large loose stones, that rose very high, doubtless to preserve them from incursions of goats and such four-legged marauders.

The evening sun had gone down behind the huge Mangerton, to bathe his yellow rays in the broad waters of Kenmare, as the Anglo-Irishman approached the cabin by a long and uneven causeway. At each side of this passage were collected two flocks of goats; at intervals along the rough pathway, a patriarchal he-goat sallied forth, as if to dare the leaders of the opposite herd to single combat. Nor was the challenge unanswered: the combatants met in midway, shaggy and fierce, reared on their hinder legs, and clashed their long horns in mock encounter, while a boy of fifteen years, in no other covering than a dirty woollen tunic, seemed to regulate their movements by the rude music of a horn. Within, the family were discussing their evening repast. Fineen was seated near a huge smokeless fire, on a bench strewn with new rushes - the oval, shallow basket, called skeehogue, nearly filled with potatoes, rested on his knees - between his forearm and side was lodged a long wooden mug, the ancient Irish mether, filled with goat's milk. At the opposite side, Mrs. McCarthy and her four daughters formed a goodly group round the potato-pot, while another mether of milk went briskly from hand to hand along the circle. Further down the floor, a long-legged pig grunted - a gander, with his wife, and a numerous progeny, cackled in chorus - and a cock, occupying a front position, strutted and cock-a-doodled with all due importance before the ladies of his harem. When the stranger entered, Fineen invited him to the contents of the skeehogue. The mealy potatoes and fragrant goat's-milk were gratefully accepted; and when the meal was concluded, Fineen plucked a handful of rushes from the couch on which he reclined, to cleanse his hands from the gluey matter they had accumulated in the toil of skinning the potatoes during dinner; and then, with the yawn of one crammed to repletion, flung the rushes into the fire. After some hours spent in social converse, of which the traditional tales of the country formed a part, the traveller forgot, in a soft bed of that particular grass called Finane, all the fatigues of his journey. In the morning, another repast of potatoes, goat's milk, and eggs, greeted the stranger. Without furnishing a single hint of the object of his visit, he departed, accompanied by his host, who engaged to show him an easy course through the glens to meet the road to Cork. Fineen beguiled the way by pointing out the castle of O'Donoghue of the Glens, and the rocky throne of Owen the Outlaw, of whose life and death he furnished a brief outline; then, with many a friendly "God speed," he left the stranger to pursue his route southwards.

In that day, before the vapour of hot water was taught to whirl the traveller over land and sea, a journey from Glenflesk to London, was no trifle, but Mr. Wilson's man performed the task with zeal and perseverance, for in three months after his departure, he related to his master's private ear the result of his mission.

"I shall not," said he, "detain your honour by relating all my hardships on board the packet, nor the way in which Irish innkeepers practice Christian charity, by 'taking in' the wayfaring man, but shall solely confine my narrative to all I saw at the mansion of Mr. McCarthy's father. It stands on a vast and lofty eminence, surrounded by immense precipices, and no human habitation exists within a circumference of six miles around it. This loneliness, I understand is a remnant of feudal grandeur, for the McCarthys were the hereditary king's of South Munster, the fairest province in Ireland, where all the men are brave - the women beautiful - the valleys waving with yellow corn - and the lofty hills always green. The abode of McCarthy was the strangest I ever beheld! It would have puzzled our best modern builders to determine to what order of architecture it might belong - and a net-work of some shining yellow material covered the roof. On one side lay a large lake, stored, as I was informed, with rare fish[1] - on the other, were gardens filled with curious trans-Atlantic productions, and enclosed by lofty walls of very strange

[1] In Kerry are large lakes on the tops of mountains, stored with a rare species of trout, that never rise to a fly.

workmanship - between stretched a long avenue, paved with immense stones, on each side of which two large parties, vassals and dependants of the chieftain's doubtless, were drawn up in warlike array and fierce attitude. The chiefs of these singled out in midway to oppose each other like the ancient knights of chivalry at tilt and tourney. They were the wildest combatants the imagination can conceive. The weapons which they clashed in playful combat were falcated and sharp-pointed. Beards as white as snow, and of considerable length, depended from their chins, and the shaggy hides of some wild mountain animals, enveloped their bodies. McCarthy was at dinner; and he reclined, after the oriental fashion, at his repast, on a green couch - green, I understand is the national colour. He sat alone - for the princes of the land, from time immemorial, deigned not to sit at table with their inferiors. His lady and daughters occupied a place below him on the floor.[1] This fashion, I have been told, prevails in all the East, and these proud islanders trace down their descent from some Scythian or Tartan invaders that landed on the coast more than three thousand years ago. Beyond these, towards the door of the apartment, a train of dependants waited, till their liege lord should dine, for the fragments of the feast. Such a table as McCarthy's was never seen in the palace of the kings of Great Britain; this might seem exaggerated, only that I can testify on oath that the united wealth of London would not purchase the legs on which it rested; and what greatly excited my surprise, and showed the extravagant pride of these semi-barbarous Irish was, that, when at dinner, he flung the napkin in which he wiped his fingers into the fire. You might tax your poor servant with vanity were I to recount my hospitable reception - the high honours paid me - how I dined with McCarthy himself, and had a new and rare bed fitted up for my reception, though I tarried at his mansion but one night. In conclusion, I shall say, that Mr. McCarthy's hints respecting the greatness of his ancestors are totally different from the real truth of his father's circumstances, and that I have given but a faint outline of what fell under my observation."

Mr. Wilson, convinced of the young man's high descent, gave him his fair daughter in marriage; and the faithful messenger, for obvious reasons, was ever after honoured with the special confidence and unbounded friendship of Phelim McCarthy.

---

[1] In the wild districts of Kerry and Cork through which I have passed, I have generally observed all the females eat apart from the males of the same family. It is a strong presumption that our ancestors brought this custom from the East.

20
The Demon Nailer[1]

It was on a fine day of June in some old year, of which chronology has taken no note, that a stranger was seen to proceed with a light and lengthy stride along the rough pavement of that toilsome street which leads from Blackpool to the North-gate bridge of the city of Cork. In this most populous outlet of the city, a passenger attracts very little attention, unless his outward bearing entitle him to especial notice, but this traveller was not one whom a Blackpool lounger would pass with unregarding eye. His limbs would appear of massive size, were it not for his elastic tread, his uncommon tallness, and noble and commanding figure. The idle gossips that sat in groups on the rough footway, nursing their half-naked urchins, or sending the cutting jibe after some "nymph of quality," whom the industry of her father had elevated to the enviable splendour of a jaunting-car, shrunk with instinctive dread, as the passing glance of the traveller cast its piercing regards among them, and the boys abandoned the footway with their taws and slashing tops at his approach. His very dark complexion furnished strong proof that he must have long sojourned in some burning climate. Tradition is silent respecting his beard and moustaches, if any he wore; but he was clothed in a suit of rusty black, and a discoloured leather apron, such as smiths and nailers use, and which folded up, seemed to contain his movables, dangled at his back, suspended from the end of a well-seasoned walking-stick. I am grieved that I cannot gratify my readers with a particular description of the stick which this formidable personage bore, for I know that my countrymen are a cudgel-loving race, as many a broken head of friend and foe can testify; but veracity forces me to stick close by the letter of tradition. All agreed, from the cut of his *kilt*, that he must be a journeyman nailer. Though every one shunned his approach, yet all followed at a respectable distance behind, urged forward, perhaps, by the same strange principle of attraction by which the feathered tenants of the grove follow in the wake of the merciless bird of prey.

Up the long street proceeded the mysterious-looking man until he reached that ascent called "The height o' Mallow-lane," from whence he that has been in Cork for the first time

---

[1] Published in *The Dublin Penny Journal*, March, 12th 1836. Initialled, E.W. At the end of the text Walsh gives the following note – Ed.

"Although sometimes ridiculous in the extreme, we have no doubt that many of the legends, yet current among the peasantry of our country, had their origin in a good intention. We should imagine that this must have been observed in several of those we have recently inserted - *The Ford of the White Ship*; *Jack-o'-the-Lantern*; *The Man in the Moon*; and, though last not least, *The Demon Nailer*. In this last, the evil effects of frequenting whiskey shops is apparent. It was at one of those sinks of iniquity that the 'old boy' halted, in the hope of meeting 'a man to his mind;' and little did Peter think, when invocating the devil, and speaking of hell, that the evil one was at that very moment at his elbow; and that he was just fitting himself for the place about which he was so thoughtlessly speaking. We trust the moral of the legend may have the effect originally intended."

may pause, if he chooses to contemplate the picturesque irregularity of the city below, with its lofty spires, and shelving roofs, and antique gables, and innumerable chimneys, from which the deep blue smoke-wreaths of as many fires ascend to crown the whole with a dun canopy. Its beautiful quays starting, as if by necromantic power, from the deep waters, and the tall masts of many an anchoring bark extending north and south, like the lofty pines of an ancient forest, which the desolation of winter had left scathed, dry and barren. The beautiful estuary formed by the rolling Lee, its peaceful bosom studded with green summer islands, lovely as the fabled Elysium, where poets have fixed the abodes of the disembodied spirits of the just - its opposite shore decked with fair villas - lawns stretching their green extent to kiss the cool wave, and woodlands crowning the far ascent, till earth and sky seemed to blend in close companionship. Then, after his bird's-eye view of this enchanting region, he may pause to list the deep sound of the noise and bustle and myriad voices of the city hive, rising on the mid-air like the far roar of a troubled ocean. The dark journeying man did pause - but neither the hum of the city caught his ear, nor did his eye rest for a moment on the desert of multiform roofs, the clustering masts, the sky-reflecting bay, its verdant shores, or beautiful islets; but it rested with attentive gaze on Tom Tracey's sign, "The Glory of the World," on which a flaming copper-coloured sun, touched off with a broad, good-humoured face and eyes, showed his round orb. He stood a minute or two, as if studying the motto that circled below the rude painting, when Peter Finigan, a nailer by trade, and a confirmed drunkard by habit, reeled forward, singing, or rather shouting at the top of his voice, that Irish song of most unseemly name, which the native modesty of my pen will hardly permit me to mention, namely, "The Devil stick the Minister."

I have said that Peter Finigan was a nailer by trade, and a drunkard by habit - he likewise had his intervals of sobriety, during which he worked with all the proverbial diligence of the aproned class to which he belonged; but in his conversation upon all occasions, trivial or important, he was remarkable for his frequent invocation of the great enemy of mankind. Well-disposed persons of my acquaintance, on whose veracity I always place implicit reliance, have informed me, that the "ould boy" must approach within three paces of him who foolishly pronounces his evil name - if so, Peter Finigan at this time must have kept him in a state of constant activity; for he had, during some time past, a new and powerful source of irritation, for Peter, in consequence of some irregularity, had incurred the displeasure of the "Trades' Union" of that day, and had been expelled the society, and placed under the ban of the Cork nailers.

At this time (it was many years before the "Union") the nailers of Cork were in active employment. The demand for nails was so extraordinary, that though all the journeymen nailers of Munster, allured by the promise of very high wages, and the desire of striking the iron while 'twas hot, had visited "the beautiful city," yet, instead of being glutted with this *dark* inundation, the prevailing cry of the master nailers was, "more, more." I have taken uncommon pains to discover the cause of this unprecedented demand for nails, but without any satisfactory result. "The Cork Remembrancer" has failed to remember it; and I have busied myself for six entire weeks in perusing certain records belonging to the most ancient and right worshipful the Corporation of Cork, but to no purpose. Yet certain it is, that the nailers of that ancient city seemed to have realized all the splendid imaginings of adepts respecting the philosopher's stone - for the merchants who fitted out adventures in nails, stood ready to pour the yellow gold into the aprons of the master-nailers in lieu of the baser metal. But amid this golden harvest, the proscribed Peter, after laying in a good stock of rod iron, found none to work for him - every "tramper" shunned his door, or if he chanced to allure a Connaught or an Ulster man by superior wages, he quickly left him, scared, probably, by the fearful denunciations of that league which outlawed Peter from its society. The unfortunate nailer yielded to the unequal contest, abandoned his shop for the tap-room, and when *heated* with liquor would be frequently heard to exclaim, "I'm a lost man - I'm a lost man - all sorts of sizes is shunning me - and if the ould boy himself turned nailer, he'd scorn to work with me."

Out reeled Peter Finigan, singing that song with the ugly name, when his attention was suddenly arrested by the figure of the tall, dark man who stood musing on the sign. He ceased his discordant strain, and approached the stranger, muttering with a sort of repressed exultation, "it's quare if I don't secure this chap."

"Well, honest man," said Finigan, "I daar say you're on the thramp, and if you want a good run o' work, I'm your man. My name is Pether Finigan, and the sorra sweeter pay you'll find in Cork, though I say it myself. From whince did ye come to these parts?"

"I came up the country," said the other ambiguously, and with a distant sort of civility; "I'd have no objection to move farther into the city, but 'tis no harm to ask what wages you give?"

"What wages do I give my men is it? Why, there's not a man in town would give you so much. You might as well turn them up in the city, and stop with ourselves, my ould boy, in sweet Malla-lane, where you shall make twelve-penny nails at ten pence a hundred, and so on for other sizes, and get lashings and lavings of good diet. Give us yer hand, now, ma *bouhil*, and we'll settle the difference over a half-pint at 'The Glory o' the World.' Ta an Dhiel urth, if my wages and Tom Tracey's whiskey won't satisfy you."

"I never drink whiskey," said the journeyman nailer; "but we'll settle about the wages, provided you are able to give me employment enough - for when you have not work to give me, at this moment you shall be bound to pay me up, and dismiss me."

"The devil's in your arm if you can work up my present stock of rod iron for the next six months," said Finigan; "but where the hell did you come from, that you never larned to drink whiskey?"

"My temperance in that respect cannot prejudice others," said the stranger, gravely; "but why do you talk so freely of hell, and of him whose name human creatures should be slow to pronounce?"

"Why," said Finigan in reply, "I hard ould Misther Shine say - by the same token, I'll introduce ye to him to-morrow, an' ould Shine knows as much Latin as any priest at the big chapel - I hard him say, that the devil, more sport to him, is forced three times through the fire whenever ye dhraw him through yer mouth. Is not that a proper raison for talking of the ould sarpint?"

"Your motive for such use of that name," said the strange nailer, with a grim smile, "seems very proper, and will, probably, meet its reward. I accept your terms, Mr. Finigan; but if you fail to pay me up immediately when you cannot furnish employment, what are you willing to forfeit?"

"To forfeit? Why you have as many conditions, Mr. What-ye-call-um, as an ould lawyer. The devil may take me, man, if I don't clear up to the farthing when I can't give you work - and that'ill take some time, I think. So come along."

"Agreed!" said the tall stranger exultingly, and he extended his hand to Finigan, who shook it heartily, and then staggered on before his new journeyman towards the workshop.

The journeyman, in the mean time, unbound his travelling paraphernalia, slipped on his leather apron, placed some coals on the hearth, and strange to relate, blew them into fiery heat with his burning breath. Then began the hoarse voice of the bellows, and the quick stroke of the hammer, whose incessant falls on the glowing iron no ear could separately distinguish; while the well-formed nails rose in little pyramids beneath his practised hand. Anon the bellows blew faster, the strokes fell thicker, and the hammer of the strange workman seemed but a magic wand, beneath the influence of which the iron was instantaneously converted into heaps of nails, and the following song, which he sung to a strange air, the dark incantation that gave potency to the spell: -

"Oft since that fatal time
When Eden's tenants rued me,
Through many an age and clime
I've weary ways pursued me;
On many a heart,
With fraudful art,
I've left a witness token,
That marks it, aye,
My destin'd prey,
If truth on high be spoken.
For this I've to and fro
The earth in many a shape run
But never took, I trow,
Till now, a nailer's apron.

"I bid the bellows blow -
I set the hammer ringing -
If one be doomed to woe,
To me is profit springing;
For human souls,
Like these bright coals,
My fiery breath sets glowing -
But oh! the breath
Of woe and death
Through tortur'd spirits blowing!
For this I've to and fro
The earth in many a shape run;
But never took, I trow
Till now, a nailer's apron!

"I smooth the murderer's path
That to his errand bears him;
I rouse the ruffian's wrath
When baleful passion tears him;
O'er many a sleep
I vigil keep,
Suggesting thoughts unholy;
And oft I wear
An aspect fair,
To catch a sinner solely.
For this I've to and fro
The earth in many a shape run;
But never took, I trow,
Till now, a nailer's apron!

By the time these verses were thrice repeated, all the iron that lay in the shop had been wrought into twelve-penny nails, and when the song and the last rod were ended, the workman lustily called out for more iron. Mrs. Finigan, answering to the call, came quickly out; but great was her astonishment to behold the heaps of nails that rose before her. She uttered a shrill exclamation, and casting a timid glance at her new journeyman, said,

"In the name" -

"Mind no names at present," interrupted the tall, dark man angrily; and then in a softer tone he said, "Mrs. Finigan, get me more iron quickly."

Mrs. Finigan retired, and after rousing Peter, told him that the journeyman had wrought all the iron, and was demanding more.

"Sorrow's in you," said Peter, "you spoilt my beautiful dhrame. The fellow must be some sleight-o'-hand man, that's playing thrick's on your eyes; but here's the key o' the back-house, and let him hammer away at what's there."

The lofty spire that surmounts the tower of the church of Upper Shandon, had greatly lengthened its giant shadow, when Mrs. Finigan heard the fearful voice of the workman loudly demanding more iron. Unwilling to encounter the keen glance of his unearthly eye, she replied from within that there was no more to be had.

"Then,ma'am," says he, "it was hardly worth your husband's while to turn a quick tradesman from his path. Tell him that I must be paid in five minutes."

Mrs. Finigan retired; and such value did the mysterious man attach to his time, that all the tools of the workshop, and every bit of iron around, were beaten into nails in a few minutes, and as Finigan himself entered, the very pipe of the bellows was undergoing the metamorphosis of all its kindred.

"Who the mischief are you, friend?" exclaimed the half-drunken employer, as he viewed the extraordinary scene before him - "Tell us who or what are you, that want to desave people's sight like a Freemason?"

"You may know me better before we part, unless you pay me immediately for the little job I've done for you," said the workman.

"I have not a shilling - you must wait till I sell these nails," said Finigan.

"Then you must comply with the second clause of our agreement, by which you gave yourself to me," said the fiend; and at that instant his frame dilated - his stature stretched beyond human dimensions - and all the demon stood confessed before the horrified Finegan.

"Enemy of God and man, I defy you," returned Finigan, rousing up his retreating energies - "I defy you in the name of the blessed Saviour - you and all the spirits of darkness!"

Saying this, Finigan displayed a small Bible, with which, notwithstanding his irregularity of life, he had never parted. The advancing demon quailed as he opened it - and instantly disappeared.

What became of the nails which the infernal workman so expeditiously wrought, will probably be the subject of a future legend.

21
The Doomed Maiden[1]

Father Prout's congregation were all assembled at Glenville, a little village lying eight miles north of the city of Cork. Men and matrons were ranged along the street; the latter were wrapped in blue cloaks, and had silk handkerchiefs tied loosely under the chin, and floating behind in a very picturesque manner. I must observe, parenthetically, that this method of wearing the shawl must be of eastern origin, for travellers inform us that it prevails at the present day among the females of the islands of Greece. Along the white wall, and round the gate that fronted the chapel, were ranged the choicest lasses, who stood in due array, rosy-cheeked and laughing-eyed, displaying many a bleached cap and well-greased shoe, for Leghorn bonnets and Warren's jet blacking had not yet found their way among the dwellers of the mountainous districts that skirts Glan-a-Phrecauan[2] to the west. Some nymphs of quality, indeed, in imitation of the queen of Sheba, did come from the south to hear the wisdom, not of Solomon, but of Father Prout; but those tripped it with dignified ease through the admiring files to occupy a seat within the narrow railing that separated the priest from the people. The choice spirits of the parish - the village politicians, antiquaries, seanachies, story-tellers, wits, and lovers of fun, (for such there are in every congregation,) were reclining in groups, according to their respective classes, along the greensward of the chapel-yard. The presiding spirit that enlivened the largest and most dense circle on the green, was Conohore Mac Lien Dorgan. He was a grandfather, and his white locks fell over his blue frieze cotamore; but the snows of time had failed to wither the rose of his cheek, or chill the lustre of the grey eyes, where fire and fun seemed to peep forth as if from two transparent windows. Beside him reclined Denis Buckley; or, as he always styled himself, Dionysius O'Buckley, the hedge-teacher of the glens. This personage was ridiculously slow in his gait, solemn in his deportment, and his language an extravagant medley of lengthy and learned words, gleaned solely from Johnson and Bailey's Dictionaries, and dealt forth without much regard to their proper application. His unintelligible language won him great sway over the understandings of the peasantry, and procured him credit for a greater share of learning than his advertisement announced, though it proclaimed that -

"Dionysius O'Buckley, Cosmopolite, and Scientifical Professor, will open an academical institution for the revelation of the sequential branches of scholastic lore to such ratiocinating bipeds as might be consigned to his administration, superintendence, correction, and jurisdiction-

To Wit:

---

[1] Published by *The Dublin Penny Journal*, April, 23rd 1836. Initialled, E.W. – Ed.

[2] Glenville, literally the Valley of the Raven.

Penmanship, plain, chain, and ornamental; English Grammar according to the most improved idiomatic construction; Arithmetic in all its ramifications; Globes, celestial, terrestrial, and tartarian (!!!); Astronomy, Newtonian, Copernican, and Ptolemean; Geometry, Trigonometry, Hydrometry, Stereometry, Cosmography, Stenography, etc. etc.; with a variegation of matter reposited in his pericranium, too tedious for enrolment or recapitulation."

"Why, thin, Mr. Buckley, you never laugh at all at all," said Conohore Mac Lien, in a pause occasioned by perfect weariness of laughter; "now wouldn't you tell us of the sacking you gave that *bulim sciath*,[1] Daniel Long, the other day?"

The pedagogue was not communicative, and he shortly answered, with a peculiar solemnity of manner,

"O! it had been nothing more than a short interlocution, in which we had a reciprocation of science, in which he seemed to soar beyond the galaxy of Newtonian sublimation; but when I perambulated his path, he had a stercoraceous retrogradation, and received a Phaetonic fall, and a woeful elongation of physiognomy."

At this instant a female advanced from the gateway towards the chapel-door. She wore a plain bonnet and shawl, and, though somewhat gone into "the sear and yellow leaf," was still a handsome and interesting woman. She seemed to be a stranger; for, when she approached the group that surrounded Conohore Mac Lien, the inquiry, "Who is she? who is she?" went round in audible whispers.

"Manners, ye caubogues," said Conohore, authoritatively, "lower yer voice. That's Mary Roche, from the foot of Carn Thierna. See how light she moves along, like an angel or a fairy - her tread wouldn't crush the head of a daisy. Yet, ullagone ma collen doun! (alas, my brown girl!) what a grief to your own soft heart, and to the heart of the mother that bore ye, that you are doomed to linger a cowld old maid, though many a man of spur and saddle proposed for you. But God is good, and welcome be his grace -'tis surely all for the better. Mary's moist lips shall never meet a husband's kiss - her first childbirth would be her certain death, for so promised the angry fairy of Lisroe."

"Conohore Mac Lien - Conohore Mac Lien," said a dozen voices in a breath, "let us hear that strange story."

"I'llgive it readily, boys," said the senior; "and so I can, in troth, for Mary Roche's mother, poor thing, was a double gossip of Maura Ny Tieg, my first wife, and often and often I hard it from her own lips.

"Mary Roche was a purty curly-headed thing, with fine blue eyes, and her skin as white as the swan; and every one, young and ould, that saw her, would spit in her face for fear of the evil eye, and say, 'brien banaha urth a liniv frein,[2] ye'll be the pride o' the barony.'

[1] A boaster, literally a shield-bearer.

[2] A blessed drop upon you, fair child.

Sweet bad luck to the spiteful sheaf - but 'tis bad to curse the *gintlemin*, and I'll leave all to Heaven. Very well, she was a fine napachan, as I said, and was at this time going with her two eldest brothers to Eamon O'Haneen's school, with her primmer and sod o' turf under her arm. After they crossed the river one morning in their way to school, she stopped behind her brothers, looking at this thing and that, and picking noneens (daisies), and hunting pilechans (butterflies), and by and by she had no account of the boys. The path led by the big fort of Lisroe, (Lisroe had always an airy name,) and whin she was passing by, she saw a fine lady, beautifully dressed, and smiling like an angel, on the ditch before her. Mary at once dropt her curtshie, and said, 'God save you, ma'am,' for scholars in that time (glancing at Mr. Dionysius O'Buckley) were more polite than now, and Eamon would be the death of any scholar that wouldn't salute a stranger.

" 'Gra bawn, (fair love,) you are Mary Roche,' said the lady, 'how is yer mother, and all the family; and are ye very sorry for Jemmeen (little James)?'

" 'I used to cry every day for the little crathur,' answered Mary, 'till my mammy tould me every tear I dropped would wear a hole through the poor baby, and I cried no more since.'

" 'If you wish to see your little brother,' said the lady, 'come in, and you can kiss him, and play with him all day.'

"So the lady took Mary's hand, and led her into the fort, where there was a grand house; and, after passing through many rooms, they entered a chamber, where Mary saw her little brother, that had died about a week before, laid in a rich cradle, and a young woman singing as she rocked him to sleep. And this was the song of the fairy nurse:[1]

"Sweet babe! a golden cradle holds thee,
Shuheen sho, lulo lo!
And soft the snow-white fleece enfolds thee!
Shuheen sho, lulo lo!
In airy bower I'll watch thy sleeping,
Shuheen sho, lulo lo!
Where branchy trees to the breeze are sweeping,
Shuheen sho, lulo lo!

When mothers languish broken-hearted,
Shuheen sho, lulo lo!
When young wives are from husbands parted,
Shuheen sho, lulo lo!
Ah! little think the keeners lonely,

[1] I have taken the liberty of giving an English version of the nurse's song, which Conohore Mac Lien repeated in Irish.

Shuheen sho, lulo lo!
They weep some time-worn fairy only,
Shuheen sho, lulo lo!

Within our magic halls of brightness,
Shuheen sho, lulo lo!
Trips many a foot of snowy whiteness,
Shuheen sho, lulo lo!
Stolen maidens, queens of Faery,
Shuheen sho, lulo lo!
And kings and chiefs, a Slua-shee[1] airy,
Shuheen sho, lulo lo!

Rest thee, babe! I love thee dearly,
Shuheen sho, lulo lo!
And as thy mortal mother nearly,
Shuheen sho, lulo lo!
Ours is the swiftest steed and proudest,
Shuheen sho, lulo lo!
That moves where the tramp of the host is loudest,
Shuheen sho, lulo lo!

Rest thee, babe! for soon thy slumbers,
Shuheen sho, lulo lo!
Shall flee at the magic koelshee's[2] numbers
Shuheen sho, lulo lo!
In airy bower I'll watch thy sleeping,
Shuheen sho, lulo lo!
Where branchy trees to the breeze are sweeping,
Shuheen sho, lulo lo!

"Mary remained all day in the fairy castle, fondling and playing with the baby; and when evening came, the lady promised she should see him to-morrow; and then she brought her outside the fort, just as her brothers were returning home from school. They were much surprised where Mary could have spent the day; and whin they wint home, she tould how

[1] Fairy host.
[2] Fairy music.

she mit the lady, and how she saw the little baby, and how the lady made her promise to call again to-morrow.

"For some time before this, James Roche's cattle were dying very fast of the Karugh dubh; and whin the little girl was going with the boys in the morning, her mother bid her not go into the fort till the lady would first promise to give her a cure for the cows. So she wint to school, and passing by Lisroe, she saw the lady at the ould place.

" 'Mary,' says she, 'how's all at home? Won't you step in to see your little brother, the crather?'

" 'I can't go in to-day, Ma'am,' sis Mary, 'for the boys tould o' me yesterday, and then my mammy scowlded me; and she's has raison enough, ma'am, to be cross these times.'

" 'What raison, avourneen bawn?' said the lady.

" 'Why, Ma'am, there's hardly a day that one of the cows doesn't dhrop dead; and though my father wint all the way to Kerry to Jack Maunsel that sees all the good people, he could do nothing for them.'

" 'Well, come in, a cuid,' said the lady, 'and play with the baby, and I'll give you a beautiful cure for the cows in the evening.'

"Whin Mary Roche came home, and tould her mother the *resate* for the cows, the honest woman, well became her, put down a fine boiler, and filled it with water; and whin it was very hot, she added to it soot from the cool-lughta, dung from the hen-roost, three handfuls of thatch from over the door, and nine cloheena-greena[1] throwing away the tenth. Thin she stript her little girl mother-naked, and plunged her over head and ears, and washed and cleaned her well in it; and whin she put her to bed, she washed the cows all over in the same manner, according to the direction Mary got. The little thing was sent to school next day all unwashed, and smelling shockingly from last night's bathing. The lady of Lisroe stood smiling at the gap of the fort; but, as Mary drew nigh, she started back in horror, and, houlding her nose with signs of great disgust, beckoned the little girl to depart; and thin raising her voice in anger, 'Dunis duish er da Diavunah,[2] she cried; and as the child ran away, 'Mary Roche,' sis she, 'thank yer own nastiness for your safety, but you shall not entirely escape, for your first childbirth makes you mine for ever.' "

The arrival of the priest had now put the various crowd into motion; but while his auditors hastened to secure their places in the chapel, the story-teller advanced to salute the priest; for Conohore Mac Lien at no time neglected to pay due veneration to Father Prout.[3]

---

[1] *Clogh-grena*, or sun-stone, is the small semi-transparent stone found scattered over the surface of our fields. It is supposed to be of powerful effect in obviating the force of fairyism.

[2] The primal curse attend your teacher.

[3] Notwithstanding all that has been done in the way of education, every syllable of the foregoing is implicitly credited by the peasantry of the neighbourhood in which the occurrence is said to have taken place.

22
Paddy Corbett's First Smuggling Trip[1]

"Then on the 'tither hand present her,
A blackguard smuggler right behind her,
And cheek-for-chow a chuffie vintner,
Colleaguin' join. - *Burns.*

No order of men has experienced severer treatment from the various classes into which society is divided, than that of excise men, or, as they are vulgarly denominated, gaugers. If, unlike the son of the Hebrew patriarch, their hand is not raised against every man, yet they may be truly said to inherit a portion of Ishmael's destiny, for every man's hand is against them. The cordial and unmitigated hostility of the lower classes follows the gauger at every point of his dangerous career, whether his pursuit be smuggled goods, poteen, or unpermitted parliament. Literary men have catered to the gratification of the public at his expense, by exhibiting him in their stories of Irish life under such circumstances that the good-natured reader scarcely knows whether to laugh or weep most at his ludicrous distress. The varied powers of rhyme have been pressed into the service by the man of genius and the lover of fun. The "Diel's awa' wi' the Excise men" of Burns, and the Irishman's "Paddy was up to the Gauger," will ever remain to prove the truth of the foregoing assertion.

But the humble historian of this unpretending narrative is happy to record one instance of retributory justice on the part of an individual of this devoted class, which would have procured him a statue in the temple of Nemesis, had his lot been cast among the ancients. Many instances of the generosity, justice, and self-abandonment of the gauger, have come to the writer's knowledge, and these acts of virtue shall not be utterly forgotten. The readers of the Irish Penny Journal shall blush to find men, whose qualities might reconcile the estranged misanthrope to the human family, rendered the butt of ridicule, and their many virtues lost and unknown.

On a foggy evening in the November of a year of which Irish tradition, not being critically learned in chronology, has not furnished the date, two men pursued their way along a bridle road that led through a wild mountain tract in a remote and far westward district of Kerry. The scene was savage, and lonely. Far before them extended the broad Atlantic, upon whose wild and heaving bosom the lowering clouds seemed to settle in fitful repose. Round and beyond, on the dark and barren heath, rose picturesque masses of rock - the finger-stones which nature, it would seem, in some wayward frolic, had tossed into pinnacled heaps of strange and multiform construction. About their base, and in the deep

[1] Published in *The Irish Penny Journal*, March, 6th 1841. Initialled, E.W. - Ed.

interstices of their sides, grew the holly and the hardy mountain ash, and on their topmost peaks frisked the agile goat in all the pride of unfettered liberty.

These men, each of whom led a Kerry pony that bore an empty sack along the difficult pathway, were as dissimilar in form and appearance as any two of Adam's descendants possibly could be. One was a low-sized, thickset man; his broad shoulders and muscular limbs gave indication of considerable strength; but the mild expression of his large blue eyes and broad, good-humoured countenance, told, as plain as the human face divine could, that the fierce and stormy passions of our kind never exerted the strength of that muscular arm in deeds of violence. A jacket and trousers of brown frieze, and a broad-brimmed hat made of that particular grass named *thraneen*, completed his dress. It would be difficult to conceive a more strange or unseemly figure than the other: he exceeded in height the usual size of men; but his limbs, which hung loosely together, and seemed to accompany his emaciated body with evident reluctance, were literally nothing but skin and bone; his long conical head was thinly strewed with rusty-coloured hair that waved in the evening breeze about a haggard face of greasy, sallow hue, where the rheumy sunken eye, the highly prominent nose, the thin and livid lip, half disclosing a few rotten straggling teeth, significantly seemed to tell how disease and misery can attenuate the human frame. He moved, a living skeleton: yet, strange to say, the smart nag which he led was hardy and kept pace with the swinging unequal stride of the gaunt pedestrian, though his limbs were so fleshless that his clothes flapped and fluttered around him as he stalked along the chilly moor.

As the travellers proceeded, the road, which had lately been pent within the huge masses of granite, now expanded sufficiently to allow them a little side-by-side discourse; and the first-mentioned person pushed forward to renew a conversation which seemed to have been interrupted by the inequalities of the narrow pathway.

"An' so ye war saying, Shane Glas," he said, advancing in a straight line with his spectre-looking companion, "ye war saying that face of yours would be the means of keeping the gauger from our taste of tibaccy."

"The devil resave-the gauger will ever squint at a lafe of it," says Shane Glas, "if I'm in yer road. There was never a cloud over Tim Casey for the twelve months I thravelled with him; and if the foolish man had had me the day his taste o' brandy was taken, he'd have the fat boiling over his pot today, 'tis'n't that I say it myself."

"The sorrow from me, Shane Glas," returned his friend with a hearty laugh, and a roguish glance of his funny eye at the angular and sallow countenance of the other, "the sorrow be from me if it's much of Tim's *fat* came in your way, at any rate, though I don't say as much for the *graise*."

"It's laughin at the crucked side o' yer mouth ye'd be, I'm thinking, Paddy Corbett," said Shane Glas, "if the thief of a gauger smelt your taste o' tibaccy - Crush Chriest duin! and I not there to fricken him off, as I often done afore."

"But couldn't we take our lafe o' tibaccy on our ponies' backs in panniers, and throw a few hake or some oysters over 'em, and let on that we're fish-joulting?"

"Now, mark my words, Paddy Corbett: there's a chap in Killarney as knowledgeable as a jailor; Ould Nick wouldn't bate him in roguery. So put your goods in the thruckle, shake a wisp over 'em, lay me down over that in the fould o' the quilt, and say that I kem from Decie's counthry to pay a round at Tubber-na-Treenoda, and that I caught a faver, and that ye're taking me home to die, for the love o' God and yer mother's sowl. Say, that Father Darby, who prepared me, said I had the worst spotted faver that kem to the counthry these seven years. If that doesn't fricken him off, ye're sowld" (betrayed.)

By this time they had reached a deep ravine, through which a narrow stream pursued its murmuring course. Here they left the horses, and, furnished with the empty sacks, pursued their onward route till they reached a steep cliff. Far below in the dark and undefined space sounded the hollow roar of the heaving ocean, as its billowy volume broke upon its granite barrier, and formed along the dark outline a zone of foam, beneath whose snowy crest the ever-impelled and angry wave yielded its last strength in myriad flashes of phosphoric light, that sparkled and danced in arrowy splendour to the wild and sullen music of the dashing sea.

"Paddy Corbett, avick," said Shane Glas, "pull yer legs fair an' aisy afther ye; one inch iv a mistake, achorra, might send ye a long step of two hundred feet to furnish a could supper for the sharks. The sorrow a many would vinture down here, avourneen, barring the red fox of the hill and the honest smuggler; they are both poor persecuted crathurs, but God has given thim *gumpshun* to find a place of shelter for the fruits of their honest industhry, glory be to his holy name!

Shane Glas was quite correct in his estimation of the height of this fearful cliff. It overhung the deep Atlantic, and the narrow pathway wound its sinuous way round and beneath so many frightful precipices, that had the unpractised feet of Paddy Corbett treaded the mazy declivity in the clear light of day, he would in all probability have performed the saltation, and furnished the banquet of which Shane Glas gave him a passing hint. But ignorance of his fearful situation saved his life. His companion, in addition to his knowledge of this secret route, had a limberness of muscle, and a pliancy of uncouth motion, that enabled him to pursue every winding of the awful slope with all the activity of a weasel. In their descent, the wild sea-fowl, roused by the unusual approach of living things from their couch of repose, swept past on sounding wing into the void and dreary space abroad, uttering discordant cries, which roused the more distant slumberers of the rocks. As they farther descended round the foot of the cliff, where the projecting crags formed the sides of a little cove, a voice, harsh and threatening, demanded "who goes there?" The echo of the questioner's interrogation, reverberating along the receding wall of rocks, would seem to a fanciful ear the challenge of the guardian spirit of the coast pursuing his nightly round. The wild words blended in horrid unison through the mid air with the sigh of waving wings and discordant screams, which the echoes of the cliffs multiplied a thousand fold, as though all the demons of the viewless world had chosen that hour and place of loneliness to give their baneful pinions and shrieks of terror to the wind.

"Who goes there?" again demanded this strange warder of the savage scene; and again the scream of the sea bird and the echo of human tones sounded wildly along the sea.

"A friend, avick machree," replied Shane Glas. "Paudh, achorra, what beautiful lungs you have! But keep your voice a thrifle lower, ma bouchal, or the wather-guards might be after staling a march on ye, sharp as ye are."

"Shane Glas, ye slinging thief," rejoined the other, "is that yerself? Honest man," addressing the new comer, "take care of that talla-faced schamer. My hand for ye, Shane will see his own funeral yet, for the devil another crathur, barring a fox, could creep down the cliff till the moon rises, anyhow. But I know what saved yer bacon; he that's born to be hanged - you can repate the rest o' the thrue ould saying yerself, ye poor atomy!"

"Corp an Doul," said Shane Glas, rather chafed by the severe raillery of the other, "is it because ye shoulder an ould gun that an honest man can't tell you what a Judy ye make o' yerself, swaggering like a raw Peeler, and frightening every shag on the cliff with yer foolish bull-scuttering! Make way there, or I'll stick that ould barrel in yez - make way there, ye spalpeen."

"Away to yer masther with ye, ye miserable disciple," returned the unsparing jiber. "Arrah, by the hole o' my coat, afther you have danced yer last jig upon nothing, with yer purty himp cravat on. I'll coax yer miserable carcass from the hangman to frighten the crows with."

When the emaciated man and his companion had proceeded a few paces along the narrow ledge that lay between the steep cliff and the sea, they entered a huge excavation in the rock, which seemed to have been formed by volcanic agency, when the infant world heaved in some dire convulsion of its distempered bowels. The footway of the subterranean vault was strewn with the finest sand, which, hardened by frequent pressure, sent the tramp of the intruder's feet reverberating along the gloomy vacancy. On before gleamed a strong light, which, piercing the surrounding darkness, partially revealed the sides of the cavern, while the far space beneath the loft roof, impervious to the powerful ray, extended dark and undefined. Then came the sound of human voices mixed in uproarious confusion; and anon, within a receding angle, a strange scene burst upon their view.

Before a huge fire which lighted all the deep recess of the high over-arching rock that rose sublime as the lofty roof of a Gothic cathedral, sat five wild-looking men of strange semi-nautical raiment. Between them extended a large sea-chest, on which stood an earthen flagon, from which one, who seemed the president of the revel, poured sparkling brandy into a single glass that circled in quick succession, while the jest and laugh and song swelled in mingled confusion, till the dinsome cavern rang again to the roar of the subterranean bacchanals.

"God save all her!" said Shane Glas, approaching the festive group. "O wisha! Misther Cronin, but you and the boys is up to fun. The devil a naither glass o' brandy; no wonder ye should laugh and sing over it. How goes the Colleen Ayrigh, and her Bochal Fadda, that knows how to bark so purty at thim plundering thieves, the wather-guards?"

"Ah! welcome, Shane," replied the person addressed; "the customer you've brought may be depinded on, I hope. Sit down, boys."

" 'Tis ourselves that will, and welkim," rejoined Shane.

"Depinded on! why, 'scure to the dacenther father's son from this to himself than Paddy Corbett, 'tisn't that he's to the fore."

"Come, taste our brandy, lads, while I help you to some ham," said the smuggler. "Shane, you have the stomach of a shark, the digestion of an ostrich, and the *gout* of an epicure."

"By gar ye may say that wid yer own purty mouth, Misther Cronin," responded the garrulous Shane. "Here, gintlemin, here is free thrade to honest min, an' high hangin' to all informers! O! murdher maura (smacking his lips), how it tastes! O! avirra yealish (laying his bony hand across his shrunken paunch), how it hates the stummuck!"

"You are welcome to our mansion, Paddy Corbett," interrupted the hospitable master of the cavern; "the house is covered in, the rent paid, and the cruiskeen of brandy unadulterated; so eat, drink, and be merry. When the moon rises, we can proceed to business."

Paddy Corbett was about to return thanks when the interminable Shane Glas again broke in.

"I never saw a man, beggin' yer pardon, Misther Cronin, lade a finer or rollickinger life than your own four bones - drinking an' coorting on land, and spreading the canvass of the Cooleen Ayrigh over the salt say, for the good o' thrade. *Manim syr Shyre*, if I had Trig Dowl the piper forninst me there, near the cruiskeen, but I'd drink an dance till morning. But here's God bless us, an' success to our thrip, Paddy, avrahir;" and he drained his glass. Then when many a successive round went past, and the famished-looking wretch grew intoxicated, he called out at the top of his voice, "Silence for a song," and in a tone somewhat between the squeak of a pig and the drone of a bagpipe, poured forth a lyric, of which we shall present one or two stanzas to the read.

I thravelled France an' Spain, an' likewise in Asia,
Fal de ral, etc. etc.
And spint many a long day at my aise in Arabia,
Fal de ral, etc. etc.
Pur-shoeing of their ways, teir sates an' their farims,
But sich another place as the lakes o' Killarney
I never saw elsewhere, the air being most charming,
Fal de ral, etc. etc.
There the Muses came to make it their quarthers,
Fal de ral, etc. etc.

An' for their ray-creation they came from Castalia,
Fal de ral, etc. etc.
With congratulations playing for his lordship,
A viewing of that place, I mean sweet Killarney,
That the music been so sweet, the lake became enchanted,
Fal de ral, etc. etc.

Early on a clear sunny morning after this, a man with a horse and truckle car was observed to enter the town of Killarney from the west. He trolled forth before the animal, which, checked by some instinctive dread, with much reluctance allowed himself to be dragged along at the full length of his hair halter. On the rude vehicle was laid what seemed a quantity of straw, upon which was extended a human being, whose greatly attenuated frame appeared fully developed beneath an old flannel quilt. His face, that appeared above its tattered hem, looked the embodiment of disease and famine, which seemed to have gnawed, in horrid union, into his inmost vitals. His distorted features portrayed rending agony; and as the rude vehicle jolted along the rugged pavement, he groaned hideously. This miserable man was our acquaintance Shane Glas, and he that led the strange procession no other than Paddy Corbett, who thus experimented to smuggle his "taste o' tibaccy," which lay concealed in well-packed bales beneath the sick couch of the wretched simulator.

As they proceeded along, Shane Glas uttered a groan, conveying such a feeling of real agony that his startled companion, supposing that he had in verity received the sudden judgment of his deception, rushed back to ascertain whether he had not been suddenly stricken to death.

"Paddy, a chora-na-nea," he muttered in an undergrowl, "here's the vagabone thief of a gauger down sthreet! Exert yerself, a-lea, to baffle the schamer, an' don't forget 'tis the spotted faver I have.

Sure enough, the gauger did come; and noticing, as he passed along, the confusion and averted features of Paddy Corbett, he immediately drew up.

"Where do you live, honest man, an' how far might you be goin'?" said the keen excise man.

"O, wisha! may the heavens be yer honour's bed! - ye must be one o' the good ould stock, to ax afther the consarns of a poor angishore like me: but, a yinusal-a-chree, 'tis'nt where I lives is worse to me, but where that donan in the thruckle will die with me."

"But how far are you taking him"

"O, 'tis myself would offer a pather an' ave on my two binded knees for yer honour's soul, if yer honour would tell me that. I forgot to ax the crathur where he *should* be berrid when we kim away, an' now he's speechless out an' out.

"Come, say where is your residence," said the other, whose suspicion was increased by the countryman's prevarication.

"By jamine, yer honour's larnin' bothers me intirely; but if yer honour manes where the woman that owns me and the childre is, 'tis that way, west at Tubber-na-Treenoda; yer honour has heard tell o' Tubber-na-Treenoda, by coorse?"

"Never, indeed."

"O wisha! don't let yer honour be a day longer that way. If the sickness, God betune us an' harum, kim an ye, ''twould be betther for yer honour give a testher to the durhogh there, to offer up a rosary for ye, than to *shell out* three pounds to Doctor Crump.

"Perhaps you have some *soft goods* concealed under the sick man," said the gauger, approaching the car. "I frequently catch smuggled wares in such situations."

"The devil a taste *good* or *saft* under him, sir dear, but the could sop from the top o' the stack. *Ketch*! why, the devil a haporth ye'll *ketch* here but the spotted faver."

"Fever!" repeated the startled excise man, retiring a step or two.

"Yes, faver, yer honour; what else? Didn't Father Darby that prepared him say that he had spotted faver enough for a thousand min! Do, yer honour, come look in his face, an' thin throw the poor dying crathur, that kem all the way from Decie's counthry, by raisin of a dhream, to pay a round for his wife's sowl at Tubber-na-Treenoda: yes, throw him out an the belly o' the road, an' let his blood, the blood o' the stranger, be on yer soul an' his faver in yer body."

Paddy Corbett's eloquence operating on the excise man's dread of contagion, saved the tobacco.

Our adventurers considering it rather dangerous to seek a buyer in Killarney, directed their course eastward to Kanturk. The hour of evening was rather advanced as they entered the town; and Shane, who could spell his way without much difficulty through the letters of a sign-board, seeing "entertainment for man and horse" over the door, said they would put up there for the night, and then directed Paddy to the shop of the only tobacconist in town, whither for some private motive he declined to attend him. Mr. Pigtail was after dispatching a batch of customers when Paddy entered, who, seeing the coast clear, gave him the "God save all here," which is the usual phrase of greeting in the kingdom of Kerry. Mr. Pigtail was startled at the rude salutation, which, though a beautiful benediction, and characteristic of a highly religious people, is yet too uncouth for modern "ears polite," and has, excepting among the lowest class of peasants, entirely given way to that very sincere and expressive phrase of address, "your servant."

Now, Mr. Pigtail, who meted out the length of his replies in exact proportion to the several ranks and degrees of his querists, upon hearing the vulgar voice that uttered the more vulgar salute, hesitated to deign the slightest notice, but, measuring with a glance the outward man of the saluter, he gave a slight nod of acknowledgement, and the disyllabic response "servant;" but seeing Paddy Corbett with gaping mouth about to open his embassy, and that, like Burns's Death,

"He seemed to make a kind o' stan',
But naething spak,"

he immediately added, "Honest man, you came from the west, I believe?"

"Thrue enough for yer honour," said Pat; "my next door neighbours at that side are the wild Ingins of Immeriky. A wet and could foot an' a dhry heart I had coming to ye; but welkim be the grace o' God, sure poor people should make out an honest bit an' sup for the weeny crathurs at home; an' I have thirteen o' thim, all thackeens, praise be to the Maker."

"And I dare say you have brought a trifle in my line of business in your road?"

"Faith, ''tis yerself may book it: I have the natest lafe o' tibaccy that ever left Connor Cro-ab-a-bo. I was going to *skin* an the honest man - Lord betune us an' harum, I'd be the first informer of my name, any how. But, talking o' the tibaccy, the man that give it said a sweether taste never left the hould of his ship, an' that's a great word. I'll give it dog chape, by raison o' the long road it thravelled to yer honour"

"You don't seem to be long in this business," said Mr. Pigtail.

"Thrue for ye there agin, a-yinusal; 'tis yourself may say so. Since the priest christened Paddy an me, an' that's longer than I can remimber, I never wint an the sachrawn afore. God comfort poor Jillian Dawly, the crathur, an' the grawls I left her. Amin, a-hierna!"

Now, Mr. Pigtail supposed from the man's seeming simplicity, and his inexperience in running smuggled goods, that he should drive a very profitable adventure with him. He ordered him to bring the goods privately to the back way that led to his premises; and Paddy, who had the fear of the gauger vividly before him, lost no time in obeying the mandate. But when Mr. Pigtail examined the several packages, he turns round upon poor Paddy with a look of disapprobation, and exclaims, "This article will not suit, good man - entirely damaged by sea water - never do."

"*See* wather, anagh!" returns Paddy Corbett; "bad luck to the dhrop o' water, salt or fresh, did my taste o' tibaccy ever *see*. The Colleen Ayrigh that brought it could dip an' skim along the waves like a sea-gull. There are two things she never yet let in, Mr. Pigtail, avourneen - wather nor wather-guards: the one ships of her, all as one as a duck; and the Boochal Fadda on her deck keeps 'tother a good mile off, more spunk to him." This piece of nautical information Paddy had ventured from gleanings collected from the rich stores which the conversation of Shane Glas presented along the road, and in the smugglers' cave.

"But, my good man, you cannot instruct me in the way of my business. Take it away - no man in the trade would venture an article like it. But I shall make a sacrifice, rather than let a poor ignorant man fall into the hands of the gauger. I shall give you five pounds for the lot."

Paddy Corbett, who had been buoyed up by the hope of making two hundred per cent of his lading, now seeing all his gainful views vanish into thin air, was loud and impassioned in the expression of his disappointment. "O Jillian Dawly!" he cried, swinging his body to and fro, "Jillian, a roon manima, what'll ye say to yer man, afther throwing out of his hand the half year's rint that he had to give the agint? O! what'll ye say, aveen, but that I med a purty padder-na-peka of myself, listening to Shane Glas, the yellow schamer; or what'll Sheelabeg, the crathur, say, whin Tim Murphy wont take her without the cows that I wont have to give her? O, Misther Pigtail, avourneen, be marciful to an honest father's son; don't take me short, avourneen, an' that God might take you short. Give me the tin pounds it cost me, and I'll pray for yer sowl, both now an' in the world to come. O! Jillian, Jillian, I'll never face ye, nor Sheelabeg, nor any o' the crathurs agin, without the tin pound, any how. I'll take the vestmint, an' all the books in Father Darby's house of it.

"Well, if you don't give the tobacco to me for less than that, you can call on one Mr. Prywell, at the other side of the bridge; he deals in such articles too. You see I cannot do more for you, but you may go farther and fare worse," said the perfidious tobacconist, as he directed the unfortunate man to the residence of Mr. Paul Prywell, the officer of excise.

With heavy heart, and anxious eye peering in every direction beneath his broad-leafed hat, Paddy Corbett proceeded till he reached a private residence having a green door and a brass knocker. He hesitated, seeing no shop nor appearance of a business there; but on being assured that this was indeed the house of Mr. Prywell, he approached, and gave the door three thundering-knocks with the butt end of his holly-handled whip. The owner of the domicile, roused by this very unceremonious mode of announcement, came forth to demand the intruder's business, and to wonder that he would not prefer giving a single rap with the brass knocker, as was the wont of persons in his grade of society, instead of sledging away at the door like a "peep-o'-day-boy."

"Yer honour will excuse my bouldness," said Paddy, taking off his hat, and scraping the mud before and behind him a full yard; "excuse my bouldness, for I never seed such curifixes on a dure afore, an' I wouldn't throuble yer honour's house at all at all, only in regard of a taste of goods that I was tould would *shoot* yer honour. Ye can have it, a yinusal, for less than nothing, 'case I don't find myself in heart to push on farther; for the baste is slow, the crathur, an' myself that's saying it making buttons for fear o' the gauger."

"Who might I ask," said the astonished officer of excise, "directed you here to sell smuggled tobacco?"

"A very honest gintleman, but a bad buyer, over the bridge, sir. He'd give but five pound for what cost myself tin - foreer dhota, that I had ever had a hand in it! I put the half year's rint in it, yer honour; and my thirteen femul grawls an' their mother, God help 'em, will be soon on the sachrawn. I'll never go home without the tin pound, any how. High hanging to ye, Shane Glas, ye tallow-faced thief, that sint me smuggling. O! Jillian, 'tis sogering I'll soon be, with a gun an my shoulder."

"Shane Glas!" said the excise man; "do you know Shane Glas; I'd give ten pounds to see the villain."

" 'Tis myself does, yer honour, an' could put yer finger an him, if I had ye at Tubber-na-Treenoda, saving yer presence; but as I was setting away, he was lying undher an ould quilt, an' I heard him telling that the priest said he had spotted faver enough for a thousand min."

"That villain will never die of spotted fever, in my humble opinion," said the excise man.

"A good judgment in yer mouth, sir, achree. I heard the rogue himself say, 'Bad cess to the thief! that a cup-tosser tould him he'd die of stoppage of breath.' But wont yer honour allow me to turn in the lafe o' tibaccy?"

The officer of excise was struck with deep indignation at the villainy of him who would ruin a comparatively innocent man when he failed in circumventing him, and was resolved to punish his treachery. "My good fellow," said he, "you are now before the gauger, you dreaded so much, and I must do my duty, and seize upon the tobacco. However, it is but common justice to punish the false-hearted traitor that sent you hither. Go back quickly, and say that he can have the lot at his own terms; I shall follow close, and yield him the reward of his treachery. Act discreetly in this good work of biting the biter, and on the word of a gentleman I shall give you ten pounds more."

Paddy was on his knees in a twinkling, his hands uplifted in the attitude of prayer, and his mouth opened, but totally unable between terror and delight to utter a syllable of thanks.

"Up, I say," exclaimed the excise man, "up and be doing; go earn your ten pounds, and have your sweet revenge on the thief that betrayed you."

Paddy rapidly retraced his steps, ejaculating as he went along, "O, the noble gintleman, may the Lord make a bed in Heaven for his sowl in glory! O, that chating imposthor, 'twas sinding the fox to mind the hins sure enough. O, high hanging to him of a windy day! - the informer o' the world, I'll make him sup sorrow."

"Have you seen the gentleman I directed to you?" said Mr. Pigtail.

"Arrah, sir dear, whin I came to the bridge an looked about me, I thought that every roguish-looking fellow I met was the thief of a gauger, an' thin afther standing a while, quite amplushed, with the botheration and the dread upon me, I forgot yer friend's name, an' so kim back agin to ax it, if ye plase."

"You had better take the five pounds than venture again; there's a gauger in town, and your situation is somewhat dangerous."

"A gauger in town!" cried Paddy Corbett, with well-affected surprise, "Isas Mauri! what'll I do at all at all? now I'm a gone man all out. Take it for any thing ye like, sir dear, an' if any throuble like this should ever come down an ye, it will be a comfort an' a raycreation to yer heart to know that ye had a poor man's blessing, *avick deelish machree*, an' I give it to ye on the knees of my heart, as ye desarved it, an' that it may go in yer road, an' yer childre's road, late an' early, eating an' dhrinking, lying an' rising, buying an' selling."

Our story has approached its close: the tobacco was safely stowed inside, in order to be consigned to Mr. Pigtail's private receptacle for such contraband articles. Paddy had just pocketed his five pounds, and at that moment in burst Mr. Prywell. The execration which ever after pursued the tobacconist for his treacherous conduct, and the heavy fine in which he was amerced, so wrought upon his health and circumstances, that in a short time he died in extreme poverty. His descendants became homeless wanderers, and it is upon record, among the brave and high-minded men of Duhallow, that Jeffrey Pigtail of Kanturk was the only betrayer that ever disgraced the barony.

23
The Bald Barrys, or The Blessed Thorn of Kildinan[1]

"———— Make curl'd-pate ruffians
Quite bald."*Shakespeare.*

The breeze of the declining March day blew keenly, as I strode across the extensive fields towards the old burial ground of Kildinan, in the county of Cork. On reaching the ancient church, I rested on the broken bank that enclosed the cemetery, to contemplate the scene before me, and pause upon the generations of men that have been impelled along the stream of time towards the voiceless ocean of eternity, since the day on which an altar was first erected on this desolate spot, in worship of the Deity. The most accurate observer would scarcely suppose that this enclosure had ever been a place of interment, save that certain little hillocks of two or three spans long, and defined by a rude stone, were scattered along its surface. To a fanciful imagination these would seem to have been the graves of some pigmy nation, concerning which tradition had lost all remembrance. But the little sepulchres were the resting-places of unfortunate babies that die in the birth, or but wake to a consciousness of life - utter the brief cry of pain, and sleep in death forever. These anabaptised ones are never permitted to mingle with Christian clay, and are always consigned to these disused cemeteries. With this exception, the old churchyard had long ceased to receive a human tenant, and its foundation could scarcely be traced beneath the rank grass. The father of the present proprietor of the land had planted the whole space with fir-trees, and these flourishing in the rich soil formed by decomposed human bodies for many a foot beneath, have shot up an unusual size, and furnish a proof that even in death man is not wholly useless, and that, when his labour is ended, his carcase may fertilize the sod impoverished by his greedy toil. In these tall firs a colony of rocks had established their airy city, and while the young settlers were building new habitations, the old citizens of the grove were engaged in repairing the damage their homes had received from the storms of winter; and the shrill discordant voices of the sable multitude seemed to mock the repose of them that occupied the low and silent mansions beneath.

While indulging these *grave* reflections, I saw a man approach by the path I lately trod. He was far advanced in the decline of life; his tall figure, which he supported with a long staff, was wrapped in a blue-grey coat that folded close under a hair cincture, and the woollen hat, susceptible of every impression, was drawn over his face, as if to screen it from the sharp blast that rushed athwart his way. He suddenly stopped, then fixed his glance upon a certain spot of the burial ground where stood a blasted and branchless whitethorn, that seemed to have

[1] Published in *The Irish Penny Journal*, April, 17th 1841. Initialled, E.W. - Ed.

partaken of the ruin of the ancient fabric, over whose grass-grown foundation it yet lingered. Then raising his eyes to heaven, he sank upon his knees, while his lips moved as if in the utterance of some fervid ejaculation. Surely, thought I, this old man's elevated devotion, at such a place and time, proceeds not solely from the ordinary motives that induce the penitent to pray - some circumstances, some tradition connected with this ancient place, has wrought his piety to this pitch of enthusiasm. Thus did my fancy conjecture at the moment, nor was I mistaken.

As the old man rose from his attitude of supplication, I approached and said, "My friend, I hope you will pardon this intrusion, for your sudden and impassioned devotion has greatly awakened my curiosity."

He immediately answered in the Irish tongue, "I was only begging mercy and pardon for the souls who in the close darkness of the prison-house cannot relieve themselves, and beseeching the heaven would cease to visit upon the children the guilt of their fathers. This spot brought to my memory an act of sacrilege which my forefathers perpetrated, and for which their descendants yet suffer; and I did not conceive at the moment that a living being beheld me but God.

"perhaps," he continued, "as you seem to be a stranger in these parts, you have never heard of the Bald Barrys, and the blessed Whitethorn of Kildinan. It is an old tradition, and you may be inclined to name it a legend of superstition; but yonder is the whitethorn, blasted and decayed from the contact of my ancestors' unholy hands; and here stands the last of their name, a homeless wanderer, with no other inheritance than this mark of the curse and crime of his race." So saying, he pulled off the old woollen hat, and exhibited his head perfectly smooth and guiltless of a single hair.

"Thatold heads should become bald, is no uncommon occurrence," I observed, "and I have seen younger heads as hairless as yours."

"My head," he returned, "from my birth to this moment, never knew a single hair; my father and grandfather endured the same privation, while my great-grandfather was deprived of his long and copious locks in one fearful moment. I shall tell you the story as we go along, if your course lies in the direction of this pathway."

As we proceeded, he delivered the following legend. The old man's phraseology was copious and energetic, qualities which I have vainly striven to infuse into the translation; for an abler pen would fail in our colder English of doing justice to the very poetical language of the narrator.

"Many a biting March has passed over the heads of men since Colonel Barry lived at Lisnegar. He was of the true blood of the old Strongbow chiefs, who became sovereign princes in the land; and forming alliances with the ancient owners of the soil, renounced the

Saxon connection and name. This noble family gloried in the title of McAdam;[1] and the colonel did not shame his descent. He kept open house for all comers, and every day an ox was killed and consumed at Lisnegar. All the gentlemen of the province thronged thither, hunting and hawking, and feasting and coshering; while the hall was crowded with harpers and pipers, *caroughs* and *buckaughs*, and *shanachies* and story-tellers, who came and went as they pleased in constant succession. I myself," said the old man, sighing, "have seen a remnant of these good old times, but now they are vanished for ever; the genius of hospitality has retired from the chieftain's hall to the hovel on the moor; and the wanderer turns with a sigh from lofty groves and stately towers, to the shelter of the peasant's shed!

"David Barry and his seven brothers lived with McAdam, and were of his own name and race; and whether he enjoyed the sport of the chase, or took the diversion of shooting, or moved among the high and titled of the land, they always accompanied him, and formed a sort of body-guard, to share his sports or assert his quarrels. At that time, on the banks of the Bride, near the ruined tower of Shanacloch, lived a man named Edmund Barry. A thick and briary covert on his farm had been for many years the haunt of a fox celebrated all over the south of Ireland for the extraordinary speed and prowess he evinced in the many attempts made to hunt him down. Many gallant and noble huntsmen sought the honour of bearing home his brush, but in vain; and it was a remarkable fact, that after tiring out both hounds and horses in the arduous pursuit, and though his flight might extend over a considerable part of the province, he invariably returned at night to his favourite covert. A treaty of peace, it would seem, had been tacitly instituted between Edmund Barry and the fox. Barry's poultry for a series of years, whether they sought the banks of the Bride or the neighbourhood of the barn door, never suffered by the dangerous vicinity: Reynard would mix with Barry's dogs and spend an hour of social intercourse with them, as familiarly as if he belonged to the same species; and Barry gave his wild crafty friend the same protection and licence that he permitted his own domestic curs. The fame of this strange union of interests was well known; and to this day the memory of Barry's *madra roe* survives in the traditions of the country.

One evening as McAdam and his train returned from a long and unsuccessful chase of Edmund Barry's fox, their route lay by the ruins of the ancient church of Kildinan; near this sacred spot a whitethorn tree had stood, and its beauty and bloom were the theme of every

[1] Dr. Smith, in his History of the County of Cork, thus mentions Colonel Barry: - "The town of Rathcormack also belongs to this gentleman, who is descended from an ancient branch of the Barry family, commonly called McAdam, who have been seated here 500 years, and formerly sat in parliament; particularly David de Barry of Rathcormack, who sat in the upper house, in a parliament held 30th Edward I, 1302. South of Rathcormack is a fair stone bridge over the *Bride*, upon which is this inscription, - 'The foundation of this bridge was laid June 22, 1734, Colonel Redmund Barry, Jonas Devonshire, and James Barry, gentlemen, being overseers thereof."

tongue. The simple devotee who poured his orisons to God beneath its holy shade believed that the hands of the guardian spirits pruned its luxuriance and developed its form of beauty - that dews from heaven were sprinkled by angel hands to produce its rich and beautiful blossoms, which, like those of the thorn of Glastonbury, loaded the black winds of December with many a token of holy fragrance, in welcome of the heavenly advent of HIM who left his Father's throne to restore to the sons of Adam the lost inheritance of heaven. McAdam was charmed with the beauty of the tree, and little regarding the sanctity or the superstitious awe attached to its character, was resolved to transfer it to Lisnegar, that his lawn might possess that rare species of thorn which blooms in beauty when all its sisters of the field are bare and barren.

"Next day, when McAdam signified his intention of removing the whitethorn of Kildinan, his people stood aghast at his impiety, and one and all declared they would suffer a thousand deaths rather than perpetrate so audacious a sacrilege. Now, McAdam was a man of high blood and haughty bearing, and accustomed at all times to the most rigid enforcement of his commands. When he found his men unhesitatingly refuse to obey him, his anger sent the glow of resentment to flush his cheek; he spurned the earth in a paroxysm of rage, exclaiming, 'Varlets! of all that have eaten the bread of McAdam, and reposed under the shadow of his protection, are there none free from the trammels of superstitious folly, to execute his commands?'

'Here are seven of your own name and race,' cried David Barry, 'men sworn to stand and fall together, who obey no commands but yours, and acknowledge no law but your will. The whitethorn of Kildinan shall leave its sacred tenement, if strong hands and brave hearts can effect its removal. If it be profanation to disturb the tree which generations have reverenced, the curse for sacrilege rests not with us: and did McAdam command us to tear the blessed gold from the shrine of a saint, we would not hesitate to obey - we were but executing the will of our legal chief.'

Such was the flattering unction which the retainers of McAdam applied to their souls, as they proceeded to desecrate the spot hallowed by the reverence of ages, and around whose holy thorn superstition had drawn a mystic circle, within whose limit human foot may not intrude. Men have not yet forgotten this lesson of the feudal school; the sack of cities, the shrieks of women, the slaughter of thousands, are yet perpetrated without ruth or remorse in obedience to superior command, and the sublime *Te Deum* swells to consecrate the savage atrocity.

On that evening McAdam saw the beautiful whitethorn planted in his lawn, and many were the thanks and high the reward of the faithful few who rose superior to the terrors of superstition in the execution of his commands. But his surprise was great when David Barry broke in upon his morning's repose, to announce that the tree had disappeared during the night, and was again planted where it had stood for ages before, in the ancient cemetery of Kildinan. McAdam conjecturing that this object of the people's veneration had been secretly conveyed by them during the night to its former abode, dispatched his retainers again to fetch it, with strict injunctions to lie in watch around it till morning. The brothers, obedient to the call of their chief, brought the whitethorn back, and having supported its stem, and carefully covered its roots with rich mould, after the most approved method of planting, prepared to watch round it all night, under the bare canopy of heaven. The night was long and dark, and there eyes sleepless; the night-breeze had sunk to repose, and all nature seemed hushed in mysterious awe. A deep and undefinable feeling of dread stole over the hearts of the midnight watchers; and they who could have rejoiced in the din of battle, were appalled by this fearful calm. Obedience to the commands of McAdam could not steel their bosoms against the goadings of remorse, and the ill-suppressed murmur rose against their sacrilegious chief. As the night advanced, impelled by some strange fear, they extended their circle round the mysterious tree. At length David, the eldest and bravest of the brothers, fell asleep. His short and fitful snatches of repose were disturbed by wild and indistinct dreams; but as his slumbers settled, these vague images passed away, and the following vision was presented to the sleeper's imagination: - He dreamt that as he was keeping watch where he lay, by the blessed thorn of Kildinan, there stood before him a venerable man; his radiant features and shining vesture lighted all the space around, and pierced awful and far into the surrounding darkness. His hand held a crosier; his head was crowned with a towering mitre; his white beard descended to the girdle that encircled his rich pontificals; and he looked, in his embroidered 'sandal shoon' and gorgeous array, the mitred abbot of some ancient monastery, which the holy rage of the Saxon reformation had levelled in the dust. But the visage of the sainted man was fearfully severe in its expression, and the sleeping mortal fell prostrate before the unearthly eye that sent its piercing regards to search his inmost soul.

"'Wretch,' said the shining apparition, in a voice of thunder, 'raise thy head and hear thy doom, and that of thy sacrilegious brothers.'

"Barry did raise his head in obedience to the terrific mandate, though his soul sank within him, before his dreadful voice and eye of terror.

" 'Because you,' continued the holy man,' 'have violated the sanctity of the place consecrated to God, you and your race shall wander homeless vagabonds, and your devoted heads, as a sign and a warning to future times, shall abide the pelting of every storm, and the severity of every changing season, unprotected by the defence which nature has bestowed upon all men, till your name and race be faded from the land.'

"At this wrathful denunciation the terrified man falls prostrate to deprecate the fearful malediction, and awakes with a cry of terror which alarms the listeners. As he proceeds to reveal the terrible vision which his sleeping eyes beheld, the crash of thunder, the flash of lightning, and the sweep of the whirlwind, enveloped them. As the day dawns, they are found senseless, at a considerable distance from the spot where they had lain the preceding night to guard the fatal tree. The thorn had likewise disappeared; and, strange to relate, the raven hair which clustered in long ringlets, that any wearer of the ancient *coolin* might well have envied, no longer adorns their manly heads. The fierce whirlwind, that in mockery of human daring had tossed them, like the stubble of the field, had realized the dream of the sleeper, and borne off their long profuse hair in its vengeful sweep."

Such was the narrative of the last representative of the "Bald Barrys." I bequeath it to the reader without note or comment. He of course will regard it according to his particular bias - will wonder how an imaginative people will attribute the downfall of families, or the entailment of hereditary disease, to the effect of supernatural intervention; or exclaim, as some very pious and moral men have done, that

"There are more things in heaven and earth, Horatio,
Than are dreamt of in your philosophy."

24
The Buckaugh's Legend or, The Wife of Two Husbands[1]

First neist the fire, in auld red rags,
Ane sat weel brac'd wi'mealy bags,
And knapsack a' in order. — BURNS.

That the events of real life are sometimes as wild and romantic as the fancy of an imaginative writer ever portrayed, has been frequently observed; but that strange and singular occurrences will sometimes vary the existence of the humblest peasant that dwells upon the bleakest hill of our dark mountains, the following narration of facts, that happened within living memory, will sufficiently show. The strange story came to my ear in the following manner: —

About four years ago, I had been engaged in preparing material for the lives of some of these unfortunate gentlemen who, after the war of the revolution, refused to submit to the government of the prevailing party, and were consequently outlawed. After sketching off the story of Galloping Hogan, Iron McCabe, and Ned of the Hills, I resolved to visit Glenflesk, a wild and picturesque district in the county of Kerry, to glean from the living voice of tradition whatever particulars of the life and death of the celebrated Owen O'Donoghue, or Owen the outlaw, (as he was more generally called), might have existed from the wreck of years among the rude dwellers of the glen. I viewed Labig-Owen, the inaccessible rock where the outlaw had made him a home and a place of refuge - where his bed of repose was scooped into the living stone, and which was approached only by a ladder. From this rocky throne, he laughed to scorn every attempt made to effect his capture, till the O'Donoghue of the Glens, to purchase the favour of the government, destroyed the ladder of oak saplings by which the outlaw gained his place of retreat. Thus, treachery completed what force had failed to effect. Poor Owen was taken and executed, and his head spiked, among those of other brave fellows, upon the south gate of the city of Cork. But to return to my story.

In the noon of a fine day in July, I left Labig-Owen, to approach the high road which leads through Glenflesk to Killarney. The sun shone fiercely from his meridian height; the hum of the bee rose among the blossoming heather; the blacknosed mountain sheep lay panting in the shadow of the tall cliff, and the Flesk glided smoothly along its rocky bed, save where the plunge of the silver trout broke its glassy surface. But the wave-work channel of the sunken stream could well proclaim how the winter floods of countless centuries had played the part of the sculptor's chisel, in hollowing the intercepting rock into

[1] Published in *The Dublin Journal of Temperance, Science, and Literature*, June 4th 1842. It was signed, 'Edward Walsh.' - Ed.

strange forms of bowl, and vase, and goblet, as if the genius of the stream in some moonlight revel, had ordered his fantastic wand to furnish wine-cups from the solid rock to the sylphs and fairies of the haunted dell.

Upon emerging from the glen, I saw approaching, along the high road, a buckaugh - the last lingering representative of that amusing batch of vagabond idlers of other days, who reared their hydra heads in every district under the various names of minstrels, rhymers, carroughs, and Irish gentlemen. The influence of penal enactments and modern innovation has swept these itinerants from the surface of society - all save the buckaugh. He, in the teeth of foreign refinement, yet maintains his ground, and ever shall, till the matron forgets to give alms for the repose of the soul of her deceased friend; or the young have ceased to indulge in that tender passion which holds equal sway over the untutored heart of the artless country maid, and that of the romance-reading Miss, who fancies herself some chivalry dame, and her stiff-necked woer, her knight of the lance. The Irish buckaugh is a most varied and amusing character. His range extends through some baronies; he is the bearer of dispatches between contending factions; proclaims peace, or denounces war, and appoints the time and place of battle; he is the constant go-between in all contemplated alliances; and almost all the runaway matches of the country are of his manufacturing. Meal, and wool, and butter, with occasional silver shillings, are the reward of his exertions for the public weal, or the fruit of his pious aspirations. Keenly conversant in character, artful and intelligent, he obtains great sway over the understanding of the simple peasantry. For my own part, I can truly affirm, that whatever I know of legendary lore, Irish character, or rustic amours, has been gleaned from this rich mine of knowledge; and that the schoolmaster has been truly abroad for me in the person of the buckaugh.

The individual of this singular tribe, seeing a well dressed person approach, mechanically threw himself into an attitude of supplication, and commenced chanting forth in musical cadence the following petition: -

"Give yer charity, honourable sir, to the poor cripple, and may the MAN ABOVE that left me to crawl a cowld, ould *dunnawn* an this ayrth, give yer blessed sowl wings o' brightness to fly among the cherry-bam, and the serry-fam, an the throwns, and the dummy-nations in the ragings of eternal glory for ever more. Amen.

"O! may every hay-pinny yer gracious honour bestows on a poor vartuous, dissolute crather; be turned and transmugger-afied into a silver *crown*, as a stock an' a store, an' a loan on the long road that's agin yer noble sowl in its way to the world to come.

"O! if there be any smoke o' sin, or cloud o' youthful folly on yer sowl, (here he looked archly into my face as I approached) may God an' the Angels, an' the Virgin Mother, an' the prayers o' the cripple left without power o' limb, or strinth o' body, disparse them as the light o' the sun disparses the mist o' the morning."

I dropped a sixpence into the *caubeen* which he held before me, and took a passing glance at his form and raiment, while he poured a deluge of blessings on my head.

His outer garment, which extended over the woolbag and meal-pouch that lumbered at his back, and were confined at the throat by an iron brooch or *dealg-falline*, was indeed a "coat of many colours" - a patchwork so diversified in hue and texture of material, that it was impossible to say what its pristine "cloth and colour" had been, if any of either yet held possession, amid the strange medley of shreds and patches. His waist was cinctured by a broad belt, from which depended two wooden cans, containing his butter. One muscular, finely-formed leg, fixed at the knee into a socket of a timber prop, of rude workmanship, stuck out behind - while his herculean form leaned forward on two iron-shod crutches, armed with huge spikes that clattered on the stony footway as he strode along.

I had travelled that sultry morning over the steep hill which encloses Glenflesk on the north; and being rather fatigued, and not at that time a disciple of father Mathew, I requested the buckaugh to direct me to the next *shebeen*.

" 'Tis here at your elbow, yer honour - Nance o' the Rock, yonder there, keeps as unlawful an' heathenish a dhrop as ever was taken - fur why? 's curse to the christening it ever resaved, nor the devil a gauger ever squinted at it! You're a parliament-man, I suppose, yer honour; but sartinly in a case o' disthress like this, you wouldn't sneeze at a glass of poteen."

Nancy o' the Rock's habitation was a sort of cave, formed by spars, placed against a huge excavated cliff, from a natural fissure of which the smoke of a large turf fire issued, and formed in the still upper sky a beautiful blue column.

"Nance," said the buckaugh, to the troglodyte who kept this strange *auberge*, "there's a jantleman here of the rale, ould stock, that wants a dhrop to help him over the hill - and I hadn't the wetting of my heart this last week myself, so fetch us out half-a-pint of the right soart."

"I can't," says Nance, stroking back the dark and tangled elf-locks that fell over her bare and smoke-embrowned bosom, "Jack Donoghue an' Darby Cayreen, broke glasses an' all in a *scrimmage* last night, high hanging to 'em av a windy day! and besides -"

"An' besides what?" - interrupted the buckaugh; tatteration to ye, ye born *ounshugh*! do ye sispect his honour, there, that has the face of a clargy, for a blackguard gauger, or sich like varmint? I'll be bail that my mouth houlds an even glass, Irish mishure, to a tint - and the shell of circ-a-soppa's egg there, (pointing to a crested hen) contains as thrue an impayril, as if it was laid by Act o' Parliament, so bring us the crather, in less than no time."

"The shell will make an even glass enough," said Nance, "but with regard to *your* mishure, Darby Guirey, I'd rather not thrust the big hole that's at the bottom of it."

"Now, Nancy, tell God's thruth before the jantleman - though many's the jar of yer poteen wint down that same hole on *charda* - I lave it on the nick o' yer sowl, do I owe ye a testher? or did I ever take an unfair hoult of yer bottle, to let down a dhrop, barrin' the bare stint, whin short-taken for a mishure?"

" 'Tis all thrue for ye, Darby, avourneen," rejoined Nance, soothingly; "yer the shurest an' wettest customer I have; I'd thrust ye as soon as I would father Maurice; but now, Darby, it wouldn't be right to put the bottle an yer throath an' the strange jantleman tasting it along wid ye."

"Nancy a cushla, yer right. By jaminy ye have the breeding any how! though ye never read the Read-a-maw-Daisy, or Rhunart the Fox, or the Irish Rogues an' Robberies at Mr. Casey's school, as I did; let's have a purty big egg now, an' I'll suck it clane - raw eggs sarves the lungs they say."

We sat in the open air, screened from the sun's fierce heat, by the shadow of the tall cliff in which Nance o' the Rock had constructed her habitation. Immediately over our head, and midway in the cliff, projected the ruins of an ancient oak, whose scathed trunk and blasted branches seemed as old and enduring as their parent rock. Upon its craggy pinnacle stood a patriarchal he-goat, whose descending beard and redundant hair were swept by the light breeze that sported past him in "his pride of place;" and further down the receding ledges, the females of his harem clashed their horns in playful combat beneath his lordly eye. Before us rose the tall form of the wild-looking woman, so thin and loosely clad, that every motion of her limbs brought into view some portion of her naked person: while her long raven tresses fell profusely down her shoulders, forming a sort of natural covering to her dark-coloured bosom, on which the smoky reek of bog-deal fires had successfully contended for mastery with the natural tint of white. Farther rearward sounded a descending rill, that sparkled, foamed, and fritted adown its rocky path, till winding round the green sward on which we reclined, it formed a broad basin where some snow-white geese dressed their oily plumage, or stemmed with breast of pride the glassy waves.

The eggshell of poteen, diluted with a cup of the pure stream that meandered past our feet, furnished a cool and exhilarating draught. But my new friend, Darby Guirey, whose garrulity now began to flow quite unreserved at this feast of shells, observed "that it was a sin agin naythur, so it was, to mix sich a nate dhrop with cowld water. It was enough to bring on a spice o' the gripes, or a fit of the collar of morbus."

The itinerant now drew from beneath the band of his *caubeen*, a curiosity I had not observed before. It was a musical tin pipe, about eighteen inches long, having the usual ventages of a flagelet, to which it bore a rude resemblance. This he applied to his mouth; and, whether it was that the artless music harmonized with the rude scene around, or that the uncouth pipe possessed some hidden spirit of melody, certain it is, that the *mundivigant* master of the tune modulated the pitch of his instrument to a great degree of sweetness, and soon the echo repeated the lively strain of the "*Colleen dhas Down*," along the curvature of the rock. I was however, not much surprised at my partiality for the buckaugh's strain, as the rude blast of a *dhoukaun*, the hum of the bee, or the lowing of the peaceful herd, is sweeter music to the sensitive heart; but I was really surprised at the effect of Darby Guirey's pipe on our wild landlady. When the first bar of the "*Colleen dhas Down*" was repeated, she started to her legs, and beat time with one naked foot - then footed the second bar with its fellow - "till first ane caper, syne anither," when with all the enthusiasm so peculiar to the Irish character, she flung her whole soul and body into the living dance, displaying, in her partnerless motions, a foot and ankle and natural grace that I have sought for, in vain, in far more crowded, though not loftier saloons. Here our canopy was the wide cope of heaven; our dancing floor the velvet sward from the workshop of spring; and our chandelier, that wondrous orb to which the nations have bent the knee of adoration. As the tune progressed, there evidently appeared on the part of each performer a desire to earn the renown of tiring down the other, for -

"The piper loud and louder blew,
The dancer quick and quicker flew,"

with each succeeding repetition of the tune, till the master of the pipe, at length, yielded the contest, in exhaustion of breath.

"Mu ceol tu Nance!" exclaimed Darby Guirey, when he had fetched breath sufficient for a talking effort; "You're the girl, any how, for welting the flure. Ma Clorp an slieve! but my heart is bouncing with blowing for ye. Bring us out another *cnogeen*, a cushla! an' thin we'll give his honour the 'Humours o' Glin.'

"Shude urth a Nance," continued the buckaugh, as he filled out a fresh shell full; "we must drink to the ladies, first, sir, an' yer health an' long life, sir, likewise, an' may we have many happy returns of your company in the glin. Here, Nance, (handing a sixpence), I needn't run tick this turn; may the MAN ABOVE give a chamber of goold in the palace of glory to him that gev it! Take the cash, Nance - 'pay all ye owe,' says Moses to Nebby Codnezar. There's a wee sup o' the poteen too, a *colleen*, ye desarve it, for the divarshun ye med his honour; the sup will polish up the diamons of yer dark eyes, an' give a lighter step in the moneen. 'Tis a murdher, Nance to have ye jigging it alone, and may be his honour here would stand to ye - Whoo! yer sowl to glory! did ye ever dhrame of sich a partner?"

I declined the proffered honour, but at the same time knew the etiquette of rustic dancing-parties too well to neglect paying the piper.

"Well, look at that," exclaimed the gratified buckaugh, "Whoo! the piper that played before Moses, wasn't so well sarved. To the devil I'd pitch poverty, if I always mit the likes o' yer noble self. Nance, I'll batther the 'Humours o' Glin' with ye myself, all for his honour's divarshun." And while I mused how the maimed and helpless man could move his own music he unbuckled a belt attached to his wooden prop, which he flung beyond him with a jerk, and springing to his feet, the knave, in the unguarded moment of gratitude and ebriety, confronted Nance, and "battered and trebled" and cut figures with an agility and power of limb which I never saw equalled, while the beat of his feet, seemed but an accompaniment of the music of his pipe. This new transformation of the buckaugh, had such irresistible effect on my risibility, that I actually rolled along the grass, convulsed with laughter, and literally "holding both my sides."

Darby Guirey could not hold out for ever: and when the dance was concluded, he sat down to buckle on the wooden leg, he so little needed; observing deprecatingly that now he feared my honour would set him down as a schaming vagabone all out; but in bad times the sons of honest min must practice a little legerly-main (legerdemain), for a decent livelihood. But "tell God's thruth, sir," he continued, "how did ye like the Humours o' Glin?"

"The music and dancing," I said, "were executed in capital style. That sweet Irish air is touchingly pathetic, when sung or played to slow time, as I frequently heard it."

"Ohone! I sispected yer honour for a thrue Iris ayr (ear). Be coorse he have hard how some sweet harper o' the aunshint times, med that same thune for one o' the knights o' Glin. I have the owld words he med to it - an' p'rhaps yer honour wouldn't mislike a specimint of my singing after the music an' dancing."

I assented- and Darby Guirey, after a few preliminary hems, chanted forth in a rich, untutored tone, mellow as the soft flute, and deep as the billowy organ, the effusion of the Irish bard, of which I here present the reader with a close translation: -

HUMOURS OF GLIN

O'er dark-wooded valley and sky-kissing mountain,
I've borne the sweet clarseach my father once bore;
From Nephin's wild heather, and Moy's chrystal fountain
To Sene's summer islands, and Bera's rough shore,
Where chieftain's proud towers rise famous in story;
Where full silver wine-cups sweet minstrels may win;
But high o'er each chief swell's the Geraldine's glory,
When the harp of his hall, tells the Humours of Glin.

By Liffey's green border, my wild harp was sounding,
High lord's heard its voice by the beautiful Nore; -
I've stray'd where high towers and towns are abounding,
By the dark-rolling Lee, and the broad Avonmore:
Be mine over mansion, green vales, or dark highlands,
Or all the gay revels I oft had been in,
The Geraldine's feast, by the Shannon of Islands
When the harp of his hall, tells the Humours of Glin.

The clarseach I bear, from my fathers descended,
It oft woke the praises of heroes before; -
And long shall thy fame with its verse-wreath be blended,

High knight of the valley by wide Shannon's shore.
These "Humours" shall flourish in poetic story: -
When red win is flowing, and banquets begin,
Shall wine-striking bards sing the Geraldine's story,
When the harp of his hall, told the Humours of Glin.

The Buckaugh now became quite communicative; and in the unreserved flow of his conversation, furnished an outline of his manner of living. He mentioned that when he fell in with me, he was travelling to Killarney, to dispose of his trubute, as he termed the butter, wool, and meal which he had gleaned in his accustomed route. "I have here," said he, pointing to a private pouch, "a few things that will fetch me a thrifle of cash, if they take" - and he shook out half a dozen letters. The superscription of one of them particularly struck my attention; it ran thus: "To Mr. Denis Fihilly, Philomath and rambling student at the Academy of Mr. Casey, Professor of Languages and Science, Clohoreen."

"That's not a penny in my way," said Darby Guirey: " 'tis for Tim Fihilly's grandson. Tim was once in a snug way; and people little thought that any of his seed, breed, or gineration, would be an' the *shachrawn*. A quare story Tim had to tell in his day."

On my expressing a wish to hear Tim Fihilly's story, the buckaugh quaffed another shell of poteen, till he should not, as he said, "interrupt himself byne-by" and then delivered a narration of which this is the substance: -

About forty years ago, Tim Fihilly tenanted a farm in Glenflesk, which consisted of a few fields that produced, by much spade labour, some potatoes, and a few patches of oats, while the rest included a wide tract of swamp and rock, where some sixty or seventy goats frisked in all their native independence, and one or two Kerry ponies, and a few stunted cows, ranged free and unconfined.

Tim Fihilly was a pains-taking and industrious man; and having saved a few pounds, and borrowed a few more, he commenced a very profitable trade, which many persons of his class in life, follow with great advantage to this day, - namely, buying the small cows of his own country, and selling them to graziers in the different districts of Leinster. These stunted cattle thrive admirably in the fertile fields of the east country, and furnish, considering the size of the animal, extraordinary quantities of milk. Each trading adventure usually occupies two months; and Fihilly had pursued the employment, and gone these stated rounds until he realized a large sum of money.

It was in the month of August, that Tim set out from his residence in Glenflesk, to go to Killorglin, a village on the river Laune, nine computed miles from Killarney, famous for its great fair of Kerry cows and stunted ponies. Kate Kearney, his wife, and the mother of his nine children, had that morning given him sixty yellow George's in a weasel-skin purse. - A weasel-skin purse, they say, is very lucky. I have been told, but I do not assert it as a positive fact, that Mrs Fehilly was a cousin-germane to the celebrated Kate Kearney, the fair swan of Killarney, and the theme of amatory song. Leaving this point undecided, we hasten to narrate, that Tim Fihilly, after bestriding his long-tailed pony, whose hairy hide unconscious of brush or currycomb, retained all its primitive shagginess, directed his course towards the high road to Killarney, after promising to return next day. Happy would it have been for Tim, had his evil destiny not urged him to assume the pretence of going to Killorglin; and happy, thrice happy, had it been for Kate, his wife, had he never returned to witness her shame and sorrow; but where he had been during the interval of his absence, Tim Fihilly never breathed to mortal ear.

To-morrow evening came, and the Glenflesk drover returned not; another day, and another, passed heavily on; and neither wife nor child, heard the tramp of his pony's hoofs approaching the comfortable rooftree. Messengers were despatched all over the country. No trace of him could be discovered at the village of Killorglin. Every sainted well and holy road in the seven parishes, was explored, in the hope that he might have performed a pilgrimage to these places of devotion. A travelling pedlar, it was asserted, met him at Thomond Gate, in Limerick, inquiring about the shortest route to Lough Dearg; but the author of this very important intelligence was not to be found. Shane Wounsheal, the fairyman, stoutly denied that Donall na Geela,[1] or the gintlemn, had cognisance of the affair. The only intelligence had of him, was from the bottle-woman in Slieveluachra, who shewed Mrs Fihilly, in her magic phial, a man very like Tim, mounted on a long-tailed pony, and a high hill behind, and a long road before him. A month thus passed on in cruel suspense - had his affectionate wife received certain intelligence of his death, she could summon every aid which reason and religion offered to the unhappy; but this tantalizing uncertainty respecting the man of her house, was more than flesh and blood could bear; and her sorrow, dear woman, was inconsolable. At first the neighbours and friends of the lost Tim Fihilly were close and anxious in their enquiries, but by degrees they waxed less attention, and finally forgot to drop in for an hour to console the wailing woman and her nine fatherless children - all but Shane O'Shine, the parish tailor. He was hardly out of the house since the hour in which Tim was missing; and that was no wonder, for Shane had no better stage in his walk: he had some heavy work there in his periodical round; and besides he always made Mrs Fihilly's Sunday gowns and those of her seven thackuns in the newest style of fashion. It is not wonderful, then, that he should pay the debt of gratitude to a family to which he owed so many obligations. Whether any warmer motive were blended with this grateful feeling, will perhaps appear in the sequel.

An event not uncommon in hilly countries, happened at the time in Glenflesk; a waterspout burst upon the mountain, and the descending deluge swept along the rocky valley, bearing in its destructive course, the cattle of the pasture and the labours of the husbandman. Shane O'Shine was abroad to ascertain that none of the absent Tim Fihilly's cattle were lost in the late disastrous flood, when he saw, in a deep ravine near the bank of the yet swollen Flesk, a lifeless corpse. Shane immediately recognised, in the dead body

[1] O'Donoghue, the enchanted prince of the Lake of Killarney.

before him, the remains of the much lamented drover, the uncertainty of whose fate had wrung the heart of Kate Kearney almost to breaking; for though the features were so disfigured as to be no longer distinguishable, yet Shane could "kiss the Manual" on the identity of the coat and breeches of his own cut and make. In short the corpse was conveyed home, had "a decent wake, an' a beautiful berrin;" and was deposited among the seven generations that preceded Tim Fihilly, in the churchyard of Muckross Abbey - and this is the keen or death-song which the inconsolable widow raised over what she fondly supposed to be the corpse of her dear husband, in the presence of her wailing children, and weeping friends: -

THE KEEN

One Monday morning, the flowers were gaily springing,
The skylark's hymn in middle air was singing,
When, grief of griefs! my wedded husband left me,
And since that hour of hope and health bereft me.
Ulla gulla, gulla g'one! etc. etc.[1]

Light of my eyes! my bleeding bosom's pulses;
Calf of the soul which wild despair convulses!
'Twas little thought thy lov'd return would bring me
The heart-ache and the thousand pangs that wring me.
Ulla gulla, gulla g'one! etc. etc.

Above the board, when thou art low reclining,
Have parish priests and horsemen high been dining,
And wine and usquebaugh, while they were able,
They quaffed with thee - the soul of all the table. -
Ulla gulla, gulla g'one! etc. etc.

Why did ye die? Could wedded dame adore thee
With purer love than that my bosom bore thee?
Thy children's cheeks were peaches ripe and mellow,
And threads of gold, their tresses long and yellow,
Ulla gulla, gulla g'one! etc. etc.

Why did ye die? where Sabbath crowds were brightest,
Thy brogues were blackest, and they shirt was whitest: -
At town and fair, what looks of envy won thee
The fair great coat, these hands I wring had spun thee!
Ulla gulla, gulla g'one! etc. etc.

[1] Mrs Fihilly alone sung the extempore death-song; and the burden of the ullagone, or chorus, was taken up by all the females present.

In vain for me are pregnant heifer's lowing;
In vain for me are yellow harvests growing;
Or thy nine gifts of love in beauty blooming, -
Tears blind my eyes, and grief my heart's consuming!
Ulla gulla, gulla g'one! etc. etc.

Pity has plaints whose wailing voice is broken,
Whose finger holds our early wedding token,
The torrents of whose tears have drain'd their fountain,
Whose pil'd-up grief on grief is past recounting,
Ulla gulla, gulla g'one! etc. etc.

I still might hope, did I not thus behold thee,
That high Knockferin's airy peak might hold thee,
Or Crohan's fairy halls, or Corrin's towers
Or Lene's bright caves, or Cleana's magic bowers.[1]
Ulla gulla, gulla g'one! etc. etc.

But O! my black despair! when thou wert dying
O'er thee no tear was wept, no heart was sighing, -
No breath of prayer did waft thy soul to glory;
But lonely thou didst lie, and maim'd and gory!
Ulla gulla, gulla g'one! etc. etc.

O! may thy dove-like soul, on whitest pinions,
Pursue her upward flight to God's dominions
Where saints' and martyrs' hands shall gifts provide thee -
And, O! my grief, that I am not beside thee!
Ulla gulla, gulla g'one! etc. etc.

Tim Fihilly's was the largest funeral that visited Muckross Abbey since the death of O'Donoghue of the glens. As the long procession winded past the foot of the hills, the *ullalue* of the keeners swelled beautifully wild; but over all the voices that rose in mournful unison on this sad occasion, the cry of Kate Kearney, who rode on her own pillion behind the faithful Shane, was eminently distinguished. When the coffin was lowered into the deep grave, her wild and broken bursts of feeling and shrieks of despair, were so long, and loud, and heart-rending, that the patient endurance of friend and gossip, could hold out no longer;

[1] Places celebrated in fairy topography.

and when at length the fountain of her tears was dried up, and her bosom could have no other sob; the vast crowd had departed - all, save Shane, who, attached and faithful to his departed friend, mixed his sorrows with those of the disconsolate widow, in many a responsive tear and groan.

The tailor tore her away with much reluctance from the spot in which all her hopes of happiness lay interred. She mounted behind him; and as they slowly directed their course homeward, the widow, whose judgment was, in all probability, impaired by excessive grief, was prevailed upon to alight at a public house in the village of Clohoreen. Shane O'Shine called for "a wake jug o' punch;" and when the distressed woman tasted the consoling beverage, her tears, as if receiving further supply from the *drop*, burst out afresh. Tradition saith, forming her testimony probably on this single circumstance, that Shane had the reputation of a very sly fellow. He wept again in companionship with Mrs. Fihilly, and

"Pity melts the soul to love.!"

The humble historian of this simple page would willingly draw a veil over this scene for ever; but the love of strict veracity, and the honour of a chronicler, obliges him to declare, which he does with the conscious blush of shame for the frailty of lovely woman, that Mrs. Fihilly, on this evening of her tears and grief, promised to become the wedded wife of Shane O'Shine.

Three months had now gone their tedious round, when Shane O'Shine, one hazy evening paid a visit at the residence of Father Darby O'Leary, the parish priest of Glenflesk. His reverence was luckily at home; and Shane being a great favourite of Father Darby's, who often publicly asserted, that he never met a man in Rome or Paris could handle shears like Shane O'Shine, in the formation of a pair of leggings. Shane was asked into the parlour, where, after taking a glass of French brandy, and dispatching a few preliminary hems, he introduced the business of his present visit, having previously cast a few inquisitive glances towards the door and window, to ascertain that no curious eves dropper lingered within earshot.

Shane passed in no mean degree all the natural eloquence of his nation; he was, moreover, a perfect master of his own native tongue of feeling; and it is not to be questioned that he performed the purpose of an embassy in which his own personal interest was involved with all diplomatic accuracy. He promised, by adverting to the late unhappy vacancy in Mrs. Fihilly's household - glanced at the many obligations he owed the family of his deceased benefactor, and his disinterested attachment to their interests - shewed his "reverence's honour" how matters would go to sixes and sevens with the hapless widow, unless she had some honest man to look after herself and the little children - indignantly hinted at the uncharitable reports of the Glensters who were already feasting on "the raw flesh" of Mrs. Fihilly's reputation, because of his friendly efforts in her behalf - that to rescue her neighbours' souls from the horrid crime of slander, the widow had consented to make him the partner of her future joys and sorrows; and, finally, concluded by observing that as his reverence was vicar, the marriage ceremony could be performed without delay, and with all due secrecy, till the usual time of mourning should expire.

The good clergyman knew more of human passion and human frailty, and the windings of every avenue of the heart, than a whole host of your modern professors of mental philosophy; and having perceived that the character of a respectable parishioner was at stake; for, indeed, rumours of Shane's over attention to the concerns of Mrs. Fihilly had reached his own ear, he consented to unite them that very evening. Shane returned highly gratified at the issue of his interview with Father Darby; but still, an obstacle lay between the fond pair, and the gratification of their mutual wishes, and this was the lack of the marriage fee; for, in many parts of Kerry, even to this day, coined money has little currency; and the natives, in their various dealings, like the rude nations of antiquity, frequently resorted to payment in kind or give their superfluous commodities in lieu of personal service, instead of the circulating medium.

Now, there resided, adjacent to the bridle-road that led from Mrs. Fihilly's to the house of Father Darby, and about midway between both habitations, a person named Paddher Curran, or Peter Curwin, as he delighted to be called. He had amassed a round sum of money, which common fame multiplied exceedingly by driving, as the late Tim Fihilly was wont to do, a trade in Kerry cows. Yet, in his retirement, he loved "to change the penny," by furnishing small sums to the Glensters in lieu of chattel property, whenever the particular occasion, such as church-rates, county-cess, etc. obliged them to provide the ready cash, usually making cent. per cent. by the transaction. To this Glenflesk money broker, Mrs. Fihilly betook herself, having previously wrapped her form in the folds of her new dickey cloak, like a discreet and decent matron, in order to escape the prying gaze of curious passers-by.

When the widow reached Paddher's domicile, and received the friendly welcome of her gossip, for Curran was the godfather of Mrs. Fihilly's eldest child, she informed him that she had occasion to see him on some private business; he led her to a rude seat beneath an ancient white thorn, that grew in the angle of his kitchen garden; thither he always led those who wanted to discuss money matters, or any other private affair - this high priest of Plutus having never chosen to introduce to the *penetralia* of his temple, the votaries who came to consult him.

"How goes scores with ye, Mrs. Fihilly, in these bad times? I hope there's nothin' amiss with you, nor the childre, nor the substance?" enquired Curran.

"*Wisha cardo chreist deelish*! what 'id go well wid me, an' the man o' my house taken from me, an' the nine grawls o' childre crying round me? But the blow that's making at me now, will kill me out an' out, if ye don't have marcy on me, an' thry to make out a little money for me."

"Upon my sowkins, and that's as good as my oath on me, Kate Kearney, *a vourneen sa chardas Chreist*! that's ompossible. The pinny's too scarce now, a colleen, and ye know three o' the strippers died o' the *carhu duff*."

"O! what is the loss of cattle to the death o' Christians," sobbed Mrs. Fihilly. "There's a demand coming on me for the church-rates." (Here Mrs. Fihilly conceived that she remained within the line of strict veracity, for she very logically inferred that a fee given to any minister of religion must be a church rate). O! *Paddher a chree*, if yer not a little soft in yer hoult o' me, ye'll have me at a great amplush entirely. Three guineas would just do me, but I haven't a cross, gold, silver, or brass, to bless myself with. Oh! the berrin, the berrin, stript me of every teasther!" And here her sobs and sighs burst out afresh.

"Howld, now," interrupted the usurer, appearing to be somewhat softened by his gossip's distress, "all's not lost that's in danger. On what terms will ye take the three guineas, if I can make 'em out?"

"There's two fat pigs in the out-house, just fit for the knife," replied the matron; "they'd make four guineas, if this push that's on me id give me leave to wait till the fair of Clohoreen - but welcome be the grace o' God!"

Paddher finally paid his gossip the three guineas she "was in a hoult for," and agreed to drive the pigs homeward in a private way after nightfall, as Kate did not choose that a third party should take cognisance of her present distress. On that evening, Father Darby bound the happy pair in holy wedlock; and being a person of extreme hospitality, and wishing to compliment the new married couple, he invited them to dinner, and at a rather late hour, they departed full of love and Father Darby's hospitality.

Shortly after Kate Kearney had retired to rest, and forgotten all her sorrow in the sweet oblivion of repose, Tim Fihilly in his own proper person, alive and well, returned, and loudly demanded admittance at his own door.

"Who is that abroad?" exclaimed Kate Kearney, rather angrily, from the pillow - "Who is that abroad?"

"I'm Tim Fihilly - let me in Kate, avourneen."

'Tim, Tim, ulligone!
You're under the stone,
Cowld an' alone!'

responded Kate Kearney, in mournful recitative.

"Let us in, let us in!" thundered Tim at the door, after a lengthy pause.

"Who's that abroad?" enquired Kate Kearney; for it seems, Shane O'Shine, poor man, was all this time fast asleep.

"Thunder and turf! Kate Kearney, 'tis I," was the angry reply; "don't ye know the voice of yer own man, ye *sauvaun* of an ounsha! Death-an-ages! isn't it a cruel case, that a man must be roarin' like a parish bull, for admittance at his own dure? O, *corp-an-phlaig*! Kate Kearney, won't ye let Denis Fihilly into his own house - sha-nu-nah? (yes, or no).

'Tim, Tim, ulligone!
You're under the stone,
Cowld, an' alone!'

rejoined Kate Kearney, in a voice of mournful melody.

In short, after an hour or two had been exhausted in Tim's loud demand for admittance, and Kate's responsive rhymes, the unfortunate drover, unable to fathom the cause of his wife's strange procedure, retired to the shelter of the hayloft in the out-house. He was just sinking into repose, among the soft *finane*, when the loud grunting of the pigs below aroused him. Looking down from his couch, he saw by the clear light of the moon, a long-shanked *strathaire*, engaged in driving off his two fat pigs along the *borheen*, that led to his gossip, Paddher's. Tim Fihilly never went abroad, either on foot or horseback, unprovided with a tough hazel sapling. When he left his own rocky valley, some months before, his favourite hand-stick quickened the tardigrade motion of his reluctant pony; and now the same faithful weapon fills the grasp of the passion-driven man, as he sallies forth, lustily bawling after the thief. The boy turns round, and beholding what he deems the ghost of Tim Fihilly, sinks upon the footway, deprived of sense or feeling. Tim turned back the pigs, and again sought his couch of repose.

When the boy, whom Paddher had dispatched for the pigs, returned to his master, and told with many exaggerated circumstances his rencounter with the ghost of Tim Fihilly, he ridiculed the boy's superstitious fears - and anxious to secure the pigs within his own homestead, walked abroad into the moonshine, provided with the long whip that he had brandished for many a day in his occupation of drover.

Paddher reached the out-house just as the drover was composed a second time in rest. The smacking of a whip, and loud discontented whine of the pigs, shortly roused his attention. But great and wonderful was his astonishment to behold his gossip, Paddher Curran, who could count out five hundred guineas as easily as he would two pence, engaged in the shameful crime of pig-stealing. Mad with indignation, at the villainy of mankind, his anger knew no respect of affinity or gossipred; and poor Paddher's bones rung beneath the hazel, till the rocks of Glenflesk echoed to the voice of his lamentation.

Tim Fihilly slept till morning, and when he arose, and said his prayers, for he was always remarkable for devotion, he saw the people advancing in all directions to hear Father Darby's first mass; and as Tim, either abroad or at home, never neglected to hear first mass, he immediately directed his course towards the chapel. But beyond all the strange events that lately excited his surprise, that which most astonished him was to find, that as he approached the various groups they fled terrifies at his presence, as if he were the incarnation of every thing foul and horrible in nature.

Now, since Paddher Curran had surceased his perambulating duties, and begun to enjoy the ease of dignified retirement, he had been much annoyed by visitations of that racking disease which is yclept either sciatica or rheumatism,, according to the particular grade of its victim. Latterly this cruel tormentor had twitched his nerves so severely, that Father Darby, in consideration of his growing maladies, favoured him with a seat within the railing, where his diseased member could loll apart from the pressure of the crowd. He was now ensconced in his snug position, and the service was being commenced at the precise time that the bewildered Tim Fihilly entered the chapel: and as Paddher stooped forward to strike his breast (as well he may) at the *mea culpa*, he perceived a sudden rush at the right-hand door. Turning round a little to ascertain the cause, he saw the ghost of the deceased drover enter at the other. This was too much for human endurance. Uttering a horrid roar, he leaped over the railing which enclosed the altar, as if the gout had never visited his thigh; but before he could gain the door, Tim had seized him by the skirt of his garment, exclaiming, 'for the love of the blessed and Holy Virgin, Paddher a Chardas! what's the maining of all this?"

"Heaven and earth!" ejaculated the astonished priest, roused from the deep abstraction of prayer, by the mugient voice of the terrified Paddher Curran, "Heaven and earth, what can that cry mean?" And turning round, he beheld his flock dispersed, and the chapel vacant, save where Tim Fihilly hung upon the cota-more of his gossip, Paddher. "Powers eternal!" reiterated father Darby, "is that Tim Fihilly's voice I hear? and do the dead, indeed, forsake their peaceful graves to mingle with the living?"

After some mutual explanation, the priest called back the dispersed and terrified congregation to hear mass. That afternoon, it is said, Tim Fihilly, Kate Kearney, and Shane O'Shine, dined together at father Darby's hospitable board - and further, that Shane O'Shine went off to Cork next morning, and took shipping for Newfoundland - this marriage with Mrs. Fihilly never having transpired (Tim and father Darby only being in the secret) till her death, which happened not till many long years after the happy return of Tim Fihilly from his secret excursion.

25
The Harper[1]

'Love came with all his frantic fire,
And wild romance of vain desire -
The baron's daughter heard my lyre,
And prais'd its tone:
What could presumptuous hope inspire? -
My harp alone.'

On a fine evening in the month of May, in the year 1691, two travellers were seen to ascend the western side of Mullough-Nesha, a craggy mountain that stretches its cheerless form of swamp and rock into the far country, between Bantry and Dunmanway, in the south of Ireland. He who led the way some paces in advance of his companion, was one whom an observer would hesitate to pronounce either a stranger or a dweller of the southern highlands; for this pedestrian combined the massive proportions of a giant with the elastic tread of the wild and half-civilised men of these rocky tracts, who climb the cloud-touching cliffs, with all the agility of their own mountain goats. Unlike these middle-sized, grey-eyed, and light-complexioned sons of the soil, his lustrous and deep-set eye flashed, large and dark, beneath his ebon-brow - his coal-black, elflocks, that strayed from beneath the leather cap, shaded his swart and manly features, before they reached his shoulder to sport in every breeze that fanned this careless climber of the devious and rocky ascent. The close-fitting truise and doublet met beneath a leather belt that bound his waist, and held within its cincture two large iron pistols, and a skein or dirk, the handle of which, curiously carved from the horn of a red deer, appeared above the left hip; the brogues of half-tanned cow-hide, worn more to preserve the feet from excoriation than to cater to the comforts which we of later times attach to shoe-wearing, completed his dress. He assisted his progress up the lengthening pathway by springing from swamp to rock, on a javelin or half-pike, with all the dexterity of a well-practised posture-master. We may observe that from the use of this weapon, the desperate men called rapparees have been named. These, like the descendants of the "wild man" of old, had their hand raised against every man, and every man's hand against them. These hunted men were at this period the terror of William's regular troops; when taken in battle they were immediately hung up without even the mockery of a trial - receiving no mercy, they returned none - destruction went before their attack, and in the retreat, they vanished among their bogs, in the face of their pursuers,

[1] Published in *The Dublin Journal of Temperance, Science, and Literature*, as 'Chapter I' of "Stray Chapters of an Unfinished Story," July 23rd 1842. It appeared under the authorship of Edward Walsh. - Ed.

like shapes of air. We do not assert that our new acquaintance belonged to this devoted class, the half-pike alone betraying such fraternity.

Having reached the topmost peak of Mullagh-Nesha, the traveller of the half-pike suddenly halted, and flinging his giant frame athwart a projecting ledge of rock, waited the approach of his companion; in the mean time, while he treads the rapid footsteps of his precursor, we shall take a passing glance at his form and raiment.

His stature, though above the middle size, was low, compared with that of the fierce-looking man who reclined on the rock, waiting his approach. His slight and elegant form was well developed by his green vest; a light mantle of the same national colour floated over his shoulders in the evening breeze, and was confined at the throat by a highly chased silver broach or dealg fallainne. Upon his pale, pure countenance sat an expression of the mildest benevolence, blended with a deep melancholy, the effect perhaps of habitual thought or health-consuming grief. None need question why the pilgrims of this earth, should bear the impress of sorrow. The sinless Being who for our salvation left his Father's throne and assumed the form of man, was never known to smile; but it has been recorded, that the tear of sorrow had often bedewed his divine cheek, and shall we, the children of sin and shame, seek exemption from the Saviour's lot!

As the pensive-looking young man reached the rocky couch of his fellow-traveller, he unclasped a belt which held something suspended at his back beneath the green mantle. It proved to be a harp of very antique workmanship; and as the breeze which blew aside the drapery that covered it, hurried through the strings, they produced one long note of melancholy; when the tall, dark man half-serious, half-playful, said —

"Hemish Bane O'Daly, this is the haunt of fairies; match me the mortal hand to wake the coel-shee of that lovely note which floats past us. The fairy host are, doubtless, pursuing their airy way from the hill of Corrin to the enchanted halls of Slieve Goul! But, Hemish, man! what has so fixed your attention? Do your gifted eyes behold visions concealed from vulgar sight, and are the shades of your minstrel fathers beckoning their last lingering child of song to wake the harp of your inheritance to the spirits of long-departed warriors?"

The harper heard him not, for all his faculties were absorbed in contemplating the splendid panoramic scene that lay outstretched beneath his raptured view. Far towards the wild ocean lay the wide-extended bay of Bantry, the waters of which, by a visual description, seemed to lave the rocky base of Mullaugh-Nesha - its broad bosom studded with lovely islets. Bear, interposing its rude cliffs against the tremendous billowy volume which the Atlantic pours in from the south-west; and the fertile and populous Whiddy, reposing like an emerald gem in its calm summer sea, and the battlement wall of its ancient castle, yet bearing the green pennon of its once powerful hereditary chieftain, the O'Sullivan Bear. Almost beneath the feet of the gazer lay the town of Bantry, as if newly emerged from the peaceful bosom of the deep. Westward bloomed Glengariff, with all its enchantment of cliff, and valley, and sea-lake, yet unrevealed to the tourist's eye. Farther on the south-west, rose Slieve Goul's tall fragmented peak - the smooth roundness of the Sugarloaf mountain, bright and beautiful in its flinty barrenness - the dark and distant outline of Hungry Hill, on whose topmost peak the evening sun seemed to rest his broad disk, and down whose perpendicular descent foamed the rushing cataract of Adrigole, in one wild fall of eight hundred feet - relieving, with gleams of light, the dark mural back ground that seemed to rear its giant head within the heavens - while, on the opposite shore, the distant outline of water, cliff, and undulating greensward, shone under the mellow light of the declining sun, a silver mirror, set in a superb chasing of burnished gold.

"God and the Virgin preserve us!" said the tall dark man, after a few minutes' pause. "Hemish Bane, two of your five senses have already departed; I must try whether that of feeling have not followed them;" and he shook the harper with vigorous grasp, who, roused from his deep abstraction, turned on his companion, his grey eye moistened with the dews of emotion, and mournfully replied:

"Pardonme, Dermid More, I was lost in the contemplation of the beautiful scene that extends beneath us; and I indulged the sad anticipation that another summer's sun may never again light up that glorious view of land and wave to us."

"But 'twas not by craven anticipations like these," said Dermid More, "that the hereditary bards of the O'Sullivan Bear were wont to rouse the clansmen to battle for their country and their lawful chief."

"True Dermid More; nor shall Heamish Bane disgrace his fathers or their hereditary harp; but the days of chivalry are gone - the glory of Erin exists only in the song of the bard - conquering or conquered, we remain an appendage of Great Britain - the Saxon James loves us not, and the blood that flows in his cause shall flow in vain. Would it avail my country, I could gladly die, as more than one of my ancestors have done, beneath that broad banner which floats afar from the battlemented wall of the last stronghold of the O'Sullivans."

"Mutinyby the mass!" exclaimed Dermid More, "did not our senachi prove last night, before chief and vassal, that the pulse of Righ Shemus beats high with Irish blood; but how eagerly will O'Sullivan's new regiment, its Sullivans, and Driscolls, and Donovans, march to the music of your modern tune, instead of the thrilling war-song of your father's clairseach, the O'Sullivan's March."

"It were better, Dermid More O'Donovan," said the harper pensively, "that our clansmen stayed at home to till their rocky fields, and rear up a new race of bondsmen for the Dutch or Saxon master that may chance to rule us, than have their carcasses to feed the crows in the battle fields of him whom his own children have abandoned."

"And therefore, the better entitled to the hospitality of Irishmen. But, Hemish, what lost a hero his honour, and the sceptre of the world, now causes your recreancy from the cause of God and the Virgin. It is whispered that the young swan of Castle Donovan has not been insensible to the merit of O'Sullivan's bard, and that the sweet harper would more delight to sing the light of the peerless Mary's eyes, than wake the Ross Catha in the van of battle."

The blood of the young man retreated to his heart, as the lady's name sounded on his ear, and again rushed forth to suffuse his face and betray the talismanic effect which that simple word has wrought upon his heart and feelings.

"No more of that," said the harper angrily, as he turned round, as if to adjust the cloth that covered his instrument, but in reality to hide his glowing cheek and awakened feelings from the keen eye of his companion; then in a suppressed tone he said — "the snow of Slieve Esk is not purer than the heart that beats within the bosom of O'Donovan's daughter; and never shall the homeless descendant of bards, whose possessions were extensive, and whose gold wine cups, the gifts of heroes, were many - never shall he raise his eye in aught but deep and distant respect to the heiresss of yonder stately tower."

"I craveyour pardon, Hemish Bane, for the rude jest," said Dermid More. "My own heart's blood is not dearer to me than the pure honour of O'Donovan's house; but were my fair foster-sister the daughter of the Saxon king, she needs not blush to avow that Hemish Bane's merits would create an interest in the proudest heart. But as you have left Whiddy at the wish of your chief, to assist at my brother Hugh's nuptials, shall not the fame of O'Donovan, and the peerless Mary's praise, once more wake the echoes of the Castle-hall, blent with the marriage song, whose holy sound chases away every evil thing that may hover round the couch of happy wedded love!"

"Be it so, Dermid More," answered the minstrel. "As death has hushed the song of Shane Dhoul for ever, the voice of my harp shall bless the youthful pair; and then we turn from banquet scenes and marriage hymns to the tented field and bloody strife of battle."

So saying, he resumed his harp, and the travellers pursued their rugged way down the eastern side of Mullaugh-Nesha, that descends to the vale of Castle Donovan.

It would be difficult for the imagination to conceive a scene of more savage sterility, than is the valley in which rises the tall tower of Castle Donovan. This ancient edifice is found on a rough crag, the surface of which forms the floor of the vaulted hall, rugged with all its natural inequalities. A spiral stair ascends to the top, and leads to a large room on the first story, which is open to the heavens. Around the tower are traces of extensive buildings - and beyond, towards the foot of the hill extends a swampy meadow. No tree or shrub cheers with its soft and eye-consoling green, the dreary barrenness of this wild valley - no music of bird or voice of man, breaks the sad loneliness, save at intervals the melancholy note of the lapwing, or the shrill whistle of the wild goat-herd, as he drives his scarcely wilder flock from the craggy heights towards the distant hamlet.

But the vale of Castle Donovan was not always the dreary, desolate spot we have just described. Within the vaulted hall of that lonely tower, nightly arose the voice of revelry, and the song of joy. The deep indentations and rude inequalities of its pavement of living rock, were hidden by the tessellated oaken floor of curious workmanship. That spacious apartment on the first story, the canopy of whose wall is the wide cope of heaven, was once adorned with the richest arras of the Flemish loom. The discordant notes of the jackdaw did not then awake its slumbering echoes; but here sat the O'Donovan in the pride of his strength, pouring the red wine of Spain, and the soft courtesy of welcome to his honoured guests. And Mary, the proud heiress of his extensive patrimonial lands blended the charm of her beautiful voice with the wild strain of the family harp in the thrilling melodies of her own native land of song. That deep and splashy field which, even in summer, affords no firm footing to man or beast, was once a beautiful lawn studded with clumps of evergreens and flowering shrubs; and the rills that trickle from the rocky sides of the mountain, and soak their silent course through its wide extent, was diversed into one main channel which fritted and wound its murmuring way to the deep glen beneath, where rock and waterfall - the embowering oak - the rich green of the laurel - the lighter tinge of the yew - the red-stemmed arbutus - and the dark and mournful cypress - all combined in one luxuriant scene, where art, affecting the wild irregularity of nature, had dressed a dark valley from which the busy hum and bustle of men seemed for ever excluded, and where a painter or a poet would love to repose. To this beautiful glen did the pensive harper direct his footsteps to take on this mild May eve one last view of a spot associated with the dearest memories of his heart, and while he wound his devious way along the gurgling stream, Dermid More sought the hospitable hall of his chief.

As Hemish Bane O'Daly had gained the deep shades of the romantic valley, the last rays of the declining sun had retired over the craggy head of Mullaugh-Nesha, and ceased to burnish with yellow gleam the high and pointed windows of the castle. He marked the young moon as it shewed its scarcely defined crescent, and dwelt on the fain liquid lustre of one twinkling star that shone lonely and far on the blue sky. A bright star has a powerful charm over the heart and feelings of the lone watcher who contemplates its pure and lustrous beauty; and of all the created things that have been the objects of the false worship of the nations, surely the adoration of the whole host of heaven, was the most excusable. The harper regarded that beautiful star with the sad reflection, that the hours of delight when his and another pure and sparkling eye traced its bright course through the heavens, from the battlement of the tower or the depth of the valley, would never again return. He remembered that one revolving year had gone by since in that very bower, beneath the mild lustre of that distant star, he had sung to an unreluctant ear his unpremeditated lay of love. Unconsciously his fingers sported along the trembling wires of his father's harp; then mingled his voice with the quivering sounds, till forming one harmonious flow these "wood-notes wild" aroused the echoes that slumbered beside the dark stream of the valley:

Thou seest where the planets have motion,
In heaven's high vault of night;
The star of my fervent devotion,
One islet of love and light:
O! had I the wing of an angel,

I'd seek yon blue boundless sea,
To dwell in that beautiful islet,
If Mary would fly with me!

Though sorrow too early hath known us,
And gloom wraps our future lot;
Though the children of prudence my blame us,
And proud ones regard us not;
When the magic of hearts that hath bound us
Can scatter these griefs afar -
O! think what a heaven would surround us
In yonder bright lonely star!

Whatever in summer is fairest
Of flower, or shade or green;
Whatever in beauty is rarest,
Should brighten the blissful scene;
We'd slumber in bowers of roses,
Where fountains fall murmuring,
And harps of wild melody waken
When swept by the zephyr's wing.

There's a voice in that star for us only,
An eye in its liquid ray;
This weeps o'er our destiny lonely -
That whispers us both away!
O! had I the wing of an angel,
I'd seek yon blue boundless sea,
To dwell in that beautiful islet,
If Mary would fly with me!

The echo of the song had died away along the tall cliffs that rise above the streamlet, when a wild thrush, emulous in song, poured his evening anthem to the twilight hour; and Hemish Bane, as if in sportive rivalry, again accompanied the music of his harp in the following extempore strain: -

There's a bird in the deep valley singing,
That charms by his soft vesper song,
And a floweret thrice beautiful springing,

The fairest - the deep vales among:
But the primrose may flourish forsaken,
The thrush vainly sing from his tree;
If Mary were there to awaken
Her wild notes of sweetness for me.

O'er the rock are the bright waters sweeping -
Below waves the green alder grove;
Yon cliff holds the wild echoes sleeping,
That oft wake to accents I love:
The starlight of magical power
Still streams through the old trysting tree;
But Mary, fair star of the bower,
Hath fled the deep valley and me.

We met - and have parted for ever -
We lov'd - and howe'er be her heart,
From mine shall the memory never
Of beautiful Mary depart!
Nor canst thou O'Donovan's daughter,
Permit from remembrance to flee!
The twilight - the rush of wild water -
The bright star - the bower - and me!

"Ye echoes!——————————!

Hemish Bane O'Daly, in accordance with a rule of the bardic school which abhorred odd numbers, was proceeding to a fourth stanza, when a rustling among the surrounding foliage excited his attention, and as he suspended his song at the unwelcome intrusion, a female figure, rich in all the beauty of sylph-like form, coal-black eye, and raven tresses, stood confessed before him - 'twas Mary O'Donovan!

26
The Bridal[1]

What! though no sacred earth allow thee room,
Nor hallow'd dirge be mutter'd o'er thy tomb;
Yet, shall thy grave with rising flowers he drest,
And the green turf lie lightly o'er thy breast. - POPE.

About eight years prior to the time at which our narration begins, the chieftain of Castle Donovan was visited with severe illness. Tradition hath not told the nature of his particular complaint - and we, ever faithful to its living voice, shall neither add unto, nor take away from the words delivered unto us, while collecting materials for our true story through the glens of the south, by many a garrulous matron, and itinerant *baccach*. We of modern times have fallen upon evil days, and must be content to receive our clipped and curtailed stories from chance informers, since the degenerate manners of latter times have consigned to the tomb of all the Capulets, these bright and burning lights of tradition - our hereditary sennachaies. But certain it is, that O'Donovan lay at the point of death; the leech declared that the chieftain's disease had baffled his art; and the priest was now called in to administer the rites which religion has instituted to smooth the pillow of dying penitence, and to breathe peace to the sufferer, in the final struggle, when the angel of death tears the soul from its mortal tenement, to abide the judgment of an all-discerning God.

In that hour of grief and gloom to the inmates of the castle, a strange woman, accompanied by two girls, entered the hall, and moving towards the ample chimney-vent, seated herself on the upper end of the bench, which had been newly strewn with green rushes and sweet-flowering plants from the marsh, according to an ancient custom, which, at that period, had not been laid aside, and took off her brogues, as though she would claim the hospitality of the mansion. When the woman and her children had eaten, (for food was always set before every one that entered), she raised her voice in fervid prayer, that God would long preserve the health of him who provided that comfortable repast.

"Your prayer," groaned an ancient female on the opposite bench, "has come too late; the stranger never left this kitchen dry or hungry; the long table groaned under the brown roast meat; the strong ale flowed in tankards, to comfort her heart - but this hand, the hand of his wretched nurse, will soon close his eyes, and stretch his limbs in death, while this aged breast, that fed him with its own heart's juice, must break to behold my noble horseman, the son of kings and the brother of heroes, laid low under the table;" and she sung herself to and fro, as is the wont of Irish matrons, to express the agony of their grief, or the depth of their despair.

---

[1] Published *in The Dublin Journal of Temperance, Science, and Literature*, as 'Chapter II' of "Stray Chapters of an Unfinished Story," July 23rd 1842. It appeared under the authorship of Edward Walsh. - Ed.

"Peace," said the stranger; "God's mercy is always at hand; I know O'Donovan's disease, though the leech cannot; and he who knows the disease may procure the remedy."

"Mayheaven send a good judgment in your mouth, honest woman," said the afflicted nurse of O'Donovan.

The stranger rose from the green bench on which she sat, and erecting her tall, thin form, flung back the garment that partly concealed her face, displaying features that once were beautiful and eyes of wild unearthly lustre, as she gracefully raised her attenuated arm, to address herself to the wondering listeners.

"Godmay yield that knowledge to a nameless wanderer, which He witholds from the proud and the learned. There never was poison without its antidote; God never sent a disease, without its accompanying cure;" and her eye flashed wildly, and her bosom heaved like the possessed Pythian of old, as she stooped to the bench, on which she had been sitting, and culled from among its green garniture, a simple grey flower.

"Behold," she exclaimed with increased energy; "behold, where lay the herb that restores O'Donovan to his daughter's embrace, and the love of his people! Thus lies virtue unnoticed and unknown, while the worthless or the vicious rear their haughty heads! What will the nurse of O'Donovan promise in the name of her chief to the homeless woman who restores him to health and happiness?"

"Every thing in his power to bestow, but his fair daughter and his own immortal soul," replied the aged domestic.

"I claim but a resting-place, and protection for myself and those two orphans; and as ye fulfil the terms, so may God deal by you, in your hour of need;" so saying, the strange woman directed that some new milk should be set to boil; into this she put the little herb already mentioned, and muttering some inarticulate sounds over the potion, directed that it should be drunk by the patient. He had scarcely swallowed the draught when a convulsive fit ensued; then came on a gentle perspiration, and finally, a refreshing sleep, from which he awoke completely restored.

These wise women who pretend to cure diseases by means of herbs and charms, even yet bear great sway among the lower orders of the Irish; but formerly they were held in still higher repute by all classes. Many of their extraordinary cures, circumstantially described and well attested, are upon record; and Camden speaks of those "skilful women, who, by means of charms, give more certain judgment of disease than many of our physicians can." It is certain that many learned men have borne testimony to the sovereign virtues of plants; but the inhabitants of savage or half-civilized countries have applied their knowledge of healing plants to the cure of diseases, blent with charms and spells, to overawe the vulgar, and wrap in a mantle of mystery that simple power which nature has given to particular plants, over the many diseases that afflict the children of Adam. It is needless to say, that O'Donovan granted Mable M'Donnel the protection she sought. His extraordinary recovery won her great sway among the rude people of the district. Whispers were heard that she held converse with beings of another life, and though she restored some little ones that were said to be fairy-stricken, and some herds of cattle seized with the plague, yet she was greatly dreaded. The hardy mountaineer, when he met the tall form of Mable M'Donnel, as she culled her herbs in the dewy twilight, would gladly turn his footsteps away, to avoid the possibility of incurring the resentment of one possessed of superior means of injury. Her daughters were at this time young and beautiful women, dark-eyed and raven-haired, like their mother. Hugh Donovan, the foster-brother of O'Donovan's daughter, and the youngest of seven brothers of his own blood, had fallen in love with the eldest of these fair damsels. The chief's consent was obtained, and the marriage night fixed.

A writer of romance would embellish his page with a lengthened description of the Gothic chapel of the castle, adorned with arched recesses, sculptured saints, and all the splendid tracery of the finely painted windows, festooned with garlands of living ivy; but the humble historian of this veracious narrative, having no knowledge of ecclesiastical architecture, whether Saxon or Gothic, or of that strange mongrel style which some modern churches and ancient ruins display, is happy to observe, that Castle Donovan had no place of worship within its precincts, and that its inmates paid their Sunday devotions in the chantry or small chapel of Loughduff, whenever it pleased the gout to permit father Phelim abroad to chant his Sabbath Mass, for the repose of the soul of Donald Fuin O'Donovan.

This chantry or shrine likewise served the purpose of a parochial chapel for the people of the surrounding district. It lay about a quarter of a mile from the castle, and was of rather confined dimensions, having a large east window, besides two small narrow ones on the south. The sides of the stone altar were rudely sculptured with figures of mitred saints, and on the right hand was a recess formed in the thickness of the wall, furnished with a drawer, in which the priests' vestments, the missal, and the holy utensils of the altar were deposited. The waters of the brook which murmured past the meadow of the castle, and fretted and foamed its winding course along the roaring romantic dell we have attempted to describe, expanded into a large and deep pool, a few yards below the chapel. Its border was fringed with aquatic plants, and the drooping willow and dark alder were mirrored in its wave. The chapel of the dark lake, the lake itself, its alders and border of waving plants, have disappeared before the inexorable destroyer - time; there memory has nearly faded with the past generation. One time-and-travel-worn *bacach* only could point me out their site. The foundation of the chapel could scarcely be traced along the heathy sward; and the alder-circled pool had disappeared, because the beautiful stream that supplied its dark bosom, has forgotten its ancient channel, and bewrays, with ooze and sedge, the once verdant lawn, that like a carpet of green far overspread the valley.

It was night when the youthful pair kneeled to plight their troth in holy wedlock, before the sculptured altar of the old chantry. Hugh Donovan was tall and slightly formed, his features prepossessing, and his manners far beyond those of the rude retainers of the castle; he and his brothers were educated, and their fosterage, which, according to Sir John Davies, was considered a stronger alliance than blood, gave these young men, and Hugh in particular, opportunities to which, under less favourable circumstances, they could have no access. Though scarcely twenty-three, his manly beauty won many a sigh from the hearts of his female acquaintances, yet he passed his early years an unfixed rover, till the interesting features, jetty eye, and dark luxuriant hair of Ellen McDonnel captivated his heart, though fame had said that her charms were inferior to those of her younger sister, who was educated with Mary O'Donovan, and was now her favourite attendant.

They kneel before the altar, which was adorned with festoons of spring flowers, and lighted brilliantly, whilst the attendants on the nuptial train held torches that, shedding a red glare around the circle of tall forms and eager faces wrapped in a dun smoke-wreath the immediate vicinity, while the eye would vainly endeavour to pierce the dark and seemingly undefined space which extended above and beyond the solemn and silent group that circled the kneeling pair.

As Father Phelim delivered the opening exhortation, impressing on the bride and bridegroom an idea of the solemn obligations which they were about to contract, every sound was so hushed in mute attention, that only the long-drawn respiration of the bride broke upon the stillness of the time - but when the priest in conclusion uttered these impressive words; "If any man can show just cause why they may not be lawfully joined together, let him now speak or else hereafter for ever hold his peace," he paused as if for a reply; and at that moment a groan of anguish burst from the dark gloom beyond, and reverberated along the hollow roof. That groan shot, like a sting of bodily pain through the nerves of the wondering circle; but the momentary pang and pause passed away with the fearful sound that occasioned them; and Fr. Phelim resumed the ceremony from which he had been startled.

Then the bridegroom proceeded to plight his faith in the following words: -

"I , Hugh, take thee, Ellen, to [be] my wedded wife, to have and to hold, from this day forward, for better for worse, for richer for poorer, in sickness and in health, to love and to cherish, till death do us part."

But the conclusion was either lost to the listeners ears, or never spoken; for at the moment that Hugh had plighted his faith till death to Ellen McDonnel, a female figure was seen to rush from the chapel, and one shrill and lengthened shriek, that to the horror-struck group seemed the yell of a tortured spirit, smote the ear. The ill-omened rites were suspended - the bride fell fainting to the floor - the book of his office dropped from the nerveless hand of the priest - the unearthly cry reverberated from crag to cliff - then was heard the sound of a plunge, and the dashing of the troubled waters of the dark pool - and all was silent.

"Merciful heaven!" shouted Dermid More, "that's the cry of Martha McDonnel;" and he rushed from the chapel.

"Save her! - save her! for the love of God and the Virgin," said the chieftain who attended the nuptials - but whom, in the hurry of description, we have forgotten to introduce to our reader - "a well-stocked farm to him who saves her life."

The light of twenty torches gleamed amid the alders of the lake, and flung the red reflection on the broken wave; when Dermid More, having cast off his upper garment, jumped into the pool, and instantly disappeared.

"There goes the brave diver," said a female exultingly; "Dermid will bring up the daughter of the strange woman, though the monster at the bottom of Paula-pheasta held her in his grasp."

"But they say that Lough-duff is a fathomless pool," replied another, "and 'twould be the hard *creach*, and the dark day to his family, if Dermid More rested below with the destroyer of her own life - the daughter of the woman of spells and *piseogs*."

"He has her! he has her!" shouted many a voice, as the fearless man arose, buffeting the waves with one manly hand, while the other was twined in the long streaming tresses of the unfortunate maiden; and shouts of joy and cries of grief rose strange and high from the living forms that circled the pool. Their wild gestures and blazing torches would remind the reader of classic song, of the Bacchantes, who, in a drunken fit of religious enthusiasm, scattered the palpitating limbs of the Tracian bard along the banks of the rapid Hebrus.

When the body of this youthful victim of some deep mysterious despair was brought to shore, and conveyed to the castle, all means employed to restore animation proved ineffectual. Her right hand was observed to hold something within its grasp attached to a black ribbon that circled her neck, and the bystanders essayed to release it from her grasp - but in vain. The hall, which the generous hospitality of O'Donovan had prepared for the bridal feast, now echoed the sharp cry of grief, and the lengthened ullalu of the keener; the bride lay gasping in strong convulsions; the fearful shriek struck like a deathpang to her heart - for in that cry she recognised the despair of her lost sister; the bridegroom had unaccountably disappeared; Mabel McDonnel also stood not beside her daughter's bier. None did question, nor could any reply, why so young and beautiful a being committed suicide. Suddenly the strange woman, accompanied by Hugh Donovan, enters; silent, as if her grief were too great for expression, she approaches the cold remains of what lately was so lovely and full of life, and takes from the fast-closed hand, that at once relaxes its hold, a small silk purse from which she draws forth a ringlet of jetty hair and one part of a broken silver ring; then raising her tall form to its topmost stretch, and fixing her awful eye on the shrinking bridegroom, she exclaimed in the low restrained tone of subdued feeling -

"Is that ringlet thine? - black as thy own foul heart, and severed as my lost one's hopes of heaven! and this thy pledge of early devotion to a heart of purity - ruin - broken - lost to God and me by thy faithless perjury!"

Hugh Donovan heard no more; he reeled like one intoxicated, and fell senseless to the floor.

27
The Rockite Leader[1]

Within that land dwelt many a malcontent
Who curs'd the tyranny to which he bent;
That land full many a writing despot saw,
Who worked his wantonness in form of law.
- *Byron.*

Many of our readers will recollect the winter of 18—, when the Rockite insurrection, which had its rise in the barbarities practised on the peasantry by the agent of Lord C—'s estates, had spread its fearful influence along the far districts of the south. In this season of deep gloom and distrustful fear and cruel suspicion, a terror pervaded the minds of the upper and middle classes of men, the squire and the *shoneen*, which had no parallel even in the disastrous scenes of '98. When the unfortunate peasantry, goaded to madness by wholesale extermination, and unredressed by the laws of the land, rose without leaders, without a definite aim, the terror of all the anti-national class, the descendants of Cromwell's soldiers and the Dutchman's followers, was extreme. Every man's house literally became his castle - supernumerary windows were closed, portholes prepared, and all the munitions of war provided. In every drawing-room window and gilded saloon, the harp, the piano, the elegant ornament, had given place to the paraphernalia of horrid Mars. "Pistols, blunderbuss, and thunder," and rough granite, for the devoted head of Captain Rock, were the order of the night, while the gay quadrille and voluptuous waltz fled frightened to France and Germany. Tender things, whose utmost stretch of enterprise was to flirt an opera fan, now actually leaned to pull a trigger and give fire, without fainting at the sounds themselves had made. Many and ludicrous are the instances recorded of the panic fears of these bold defenders. The patter of the hail on the casement, the shriek of Minerva's moping bird, the howl of the mastiff baying the melancholy moon, filled entire households with terror. Every succeeding morning brought ominous accounts of the tramp of thousands marching, none knew whither - of deeds of revenge and fearful retaliation. In short, the desultory movements of the goaded population were regarded by their rural tyrants as the first manifestation of a deep-set and well-planned conspiracy, formed by men of talent and station, who only abided their time to rise and sweep into the sea the insatiate locusts that eat up every green thing of the land.

In the December of that winter to which we have made allusion, a single horseman was observed to pursue his solitary course along a monotonous heath that extended its dark,

[1] Published in the *Nation*, June 24th 1843. No authorship is recorded, but Charles Gavan Duffy, in his personal bound volume of the *Nation*, has pencilled in Edward Walsh as the writer. - Ed.

undefinable outline towards a distant mountain chain that formed the southern boundary of one of those beautiful vales which divide into green zones the spaces that separate our romantic hills, and which, are at intervals veined by boggy streaks, the remains of ancient forests. The hour was past nightfall; and though the moon was on the sky, the clouds completely hid her light, excepting when in her quick transit through the dark rainfraught vapours, her rushing orb would shed its streaky gleam to burnish the recent waters of the moor, or fling a passing light on the lonely traveller and his horse. Then might an observer catch a transitory glimpse of the form and raiment of the man, and note the small head, arched neck, and well-bent back of the noble brute he bestrode. The horseman was young - the tall, spare form, dark eye, and olive complexion, indicating the pure unmixed blood of the Celtic race - the arched brow, the Roman nose, the firm-set lip of pride, betokened a man of spirit - and the strange semi-military equipment, the costume of the Rockite leader. The deadly blunderbuss filled the hollow of his left arm as he pricked along; and whenever the fitful gusts played along the folds of his Irish mantle, the quick transit of the clear moon would reveal the polished ends of a pair of pistols rising in relief within the cincture of the broad belt that bound his finely formed waist. In fact, that rider, in form, costume, and bearing, would recall to memory one of those Guerilla chiefs of Spain, whose battle cry and pealing death-shot had often borne terror to the ear of the French invader.

At length, having gained the edge of the moor, and entered upon the green upland that skirted the base of the mountain, the horseman, by a sudden turn, entered a deep gorge, where a calm lake reposed in the shelter of the hills, and the ruins of an ancient tower, interposing behind, relieved the dark outline of the background. He had evidently trod this haunt before; habit seemed to have blunted every feeling which an unfamiliar eye must have communicated to the casual visitant of the savage scene. The smooth expanse of the reed-fringed lake - the rush of the cataract that fed its ample sheet - the scream of the disturbed eagle, wrathful at man's unwonted intrusion - the time-shattered tower, robed in mantling ivy - all failed to interest the wanderer. Suddenly he stops, and leaps lightly to the earth. A few paces bring him to an angle of the cliff, where man and horse instantly disappear. In two minutes he again emerges, having left his horse concealed in the subterraneous recess, and wended his way by the reedy margin of the lake towards the dark ruin, that at intervals flung its giant shadow athwart whenever the moon shed its fitful glimpses of brightness upon that lonely sheet of water.

"Who goes there?" cried a mellow voice, issuing from the dim obscurity in which the tower had shadowed its immediate vicinity - a voice which an imaginative ear might recognise as that of the guardian spirit of the ruined fortalice, had not its Munster *patois* sounded so naturally familiar as to instantly dissipate the idea of a supernatural night-watcher.

"Who goes there?" reiterated the guardian of the savage scene; but no reply did the strange intruder vouchsafe, so much had he been rapt in mental abstraction that the night breeze bandied the idle interrogatory in many a wild echo along the opposing cliffs, unmarked by his listless ear.

"Advance another pace and you die!" exclaimed the challenger firmly, and the returning sound of the final syllable 'die' blended fearfully with the cry of the unsocial eagle, that still refused to snuff the gale tainted by the presence of humankind. Yet the young traveller pursued his onward way, as if no sound had gone abroad to warn him of danger.

"Then be your blood on your own head," said the defender of the pass - and at the instant the sharp report of a rifle, and the heavy clash of the fallen stranger's weapons upon the rugged pathway, resounded through the rocks. Then succeeded a wild yell, and a rush, of wilder men, as though that gunshot had evoked from the long slumber of ages the forms of the devoted warriors who, as tradition tells, had battled and bled - aye, bled - by the treachery of the invader within that castle's walls!

At that moment a sudden gleam pierced the surrounding darkness, and displayed the tall forms of ferocious men, who stood suddenly fixed in their headlong rush, as the person of the prostrate intruder was revealed in the light of the moon, while this quick exclamation burst from the wild group - "Oh! the curse o' Cromwell on ye, Martin Dawly, ye kilt the captain!"

"O Mother o' Mercy!" cried the individual accused of the homicide of his chief, "I to kill the captain - I, that 'id go to death's dures at his command. Oh! captain, *achree na drolin*, why did'nt ye spake when I challenged ye? Will ye spake now to yer own fostherer? Wasn't it the nat'ral breast I should suck myself that reared ye? O, marciful Heaven!" he continued, as he burst into the circle that surrounded the fallen man - "marciful Heaven! there's blood flowing from his head - flowing by this wicked hand; the pure ould blood, without a taint of the Sassenach in its course. Spake to me, *a vhic deelish machree* - spake, I say, or by the blessed night I'll murther myself!"

"You had better wait, Martin, till the next occasion," said the object of all this eager oratory, as he raised himself slowly from the earth. "My own absence of mind and the ball from your rifle had nearly given me a *quietus* from this world and its cares for ever. Don't be alarmed, Martin, 'tis nothing - a mere pin's point along the skin."

"O, the Virgin, glory to her! wouldn't let me do it," exclaimed the delighted follower. "To the devil I pitch powdher an' ball. O! my heavy curse on thim, this blessid minit. I'll take the vestment this night, plase God, agin all soarts of firearms, barrin' the poker. Nothing worse than a long, purty ash, with a pike or baynit on the top of it, shall inther this hand for evermore, amin! There's my rejisthered oath for it. But come in, captain, the boys are all waiting in the ould waut (vault). We have a sup to hale ye after the night; and I'll put a beautiful *Patrick's lafe* or a bit of *slainlus* to yer head, that'll hale ye in a jiffy. Glory to him that gev'em the vartue, and druv the sarpints of ould Ireland into the say! Wouldn't we want him agin, captain, to banish the foreign snakes that lave their dhirty thrall upon the green fields of our fathers?

The captain did not reply to the interrogatory of Martin Dawley. Whether it was that he did not entirely relish the blunt, unmilitary familiarity of his talkative subordinate in the presence of his fellows, or that he was again rapt in a fit of abstraction like that from which Martin Dawley's bullet had so lately roused him, tradition saith not, nor shall the present narrator attempt to decide. But certain it is, that the entire party sought, in silence that part of the ancient fortalice of which Martin Dawley made casual mention.

Within that vaulted chamber stood fifty fierce men, whose forms and features were clearly developed in the glare of a fire composed of turf and bogwood, which glare in the huge chimney vent. All were armed with gun, or pike, or bayonet; some reclined against the rude wall, wrapped in the eternal great-coat, the peasant's protection from the cold of winter and the heat of summer, and which now, as in the olden times, furnished "a meet bed for a rebel." Others were dressed in short jackets of grey frieze; the variously-moulded woollen *caubeen* rose grotesque and wild amid the group, and all were shod with the ancient thong-stitched brogue, indebted to no heel, and well fitted to traverse the marshy swamps, in which it has not yet been wholly cast aside.

The majority of these lawless men were the victims of that wholesale system of extermination by which landlords, even yet, seek to consolidate the holdings of ten or twenty families into one extensive occupancy, leaving the aged and helpless to die of destitution - the reckless and bold to swear eternal enmity against the destroyer, to concoct schemes of midnight revenge, when the fiery furnace of passion glows ragingly with the unhallowed fuel of strong drink. A son was in that group, who saw his aged mother expire shelterless when the home of her youth was levelled to the earth - a husband, who beheld the wife of his bosom yield her life on the roadside in that fatal throe which gave another Irish starveling to the Saxon master. Some were there to revenge a son or brother whose neck had been broken by the shameful cord, or who toiled in chains under the burning sun of New South Wales; and more were found in the banded troop, led by that spirit of wild adventure - that misdirected love of romantic emprise which holds, even in his hour of degredation, unbounded sway over the heart and feelings of the Irish peasant.

But who is he, the youthful leader, whose head rises above the giant forms around him? Are the intelligence and education written upon that broad brow and these expressive features properly mated in the rude companions of this dark divan? Patience, reader; perhaps the belted chief of the Rockite band may himself furnish a clue to guide your inquiry.

Martin Dawley, upon whom, it would seem, the commissariat department of the band had devolved, now removed a few stones from the wall, within which lay a recess containing a keg of that contraband distillation, named *poteen*, and a few wooden drinking vessels. The exciting draught went round, and the captain signified his intention of addressing them on the business which induced him to demand their present attendance.

Silence boys! the captain is going to give us a beautiful speech. Hurroo! more power to his silver tongue, and strength to his manly arm, the darling!" shouted twenty of that imaginative peasantry, whose natural rhetorical powers and impassioned love of oratory exceed those of all the nations of the earth.

"Boys," cried the leader to his eager auditory, "since oppression has driven us to seek at our own hands, according to the natural law of justice, that redress which the laws of our tyrants deny us, we have had trials of our truth and bravery in many a daring attack and 'hair-breadth 'scape,' For my own part I have to say that the men whom I now address have proved on all occasions firm and true (what true Irishman does not?), and I trust, boys, your leader has shown himself not unworthy to lead bold hearts to the front of danger. If a man be here who knows me to have ever wavered, like the pliant willow, between the motive of paltry dread or the fear of personal responsibility, let him speak his thoughts without fear or favour."

"Sorra one, indeed. There never was a better head to form a plan, nor a braver hand to put that plan into action," was the simultaneous response. "This tottering ruin," continued the captain, "which shields our hunted heads from the pursuing eye of the spy and the peeler, was once the hospitable hall of my proud fathers. Here the last chief of a glorious line of heroes hurled defiance at the Dutchman's followers. These rent towers, had they a tongue, could say how fierce was the assault - how spirited the resistance, till, yielding to overpowering numbers, the defenders capitulated, and then my noble ancestor and his brave followers were butchered by the Saxon invader in cold blood! Their broad lands were shared among base assassins. When the relaxation of the penal code permitted the Catholic to hold land, my grandfather was allowed to rent a farm on his patrimonial grounds from the descendant of his ancestor's murderer. To this spot, held by such degrading tenure, my family had clung with desperate tenacity, till, by a system of refined and tireless persecution, I, the last representative of a princely race, was finally ejected to gratify the private revenge of Squire Crushem, the detested agent of the Earl of Faraway."

At the mention of this hated name, the yell of execration which burst from the wild men before him obliged the speaker to suspend his discourse.

"Squire Crushem has swore away the life of my innocent boy," cried a grey-haired man, who held a long fowling-piece in one hand while he wildly waved the other above his head; "whin my guiltless boy swung in the rope, I shed no tear; but, as I stood outside the fence of baynits that surrounded him, I swore by the blessed sun that saw that deed of murder, to have blood for blood; and, by the staff of St. Patrick, I shall religiously observe the oath."

"He has hanged the brave, and seduced the virgin," said a bland-featured, blue-eyed youth, whose face glowed red as scarlet as he spoke; "his gould and his villainy overcame poor Mary Connor, and thin he left her, a bird alone, to shame and sorrow! O, Mary ye war wance mild an' beautiful - the joy o' my soul and the light of my eyes - till the seducer crossed your path; may the hearth-stone of pain be his bed for ever!"

"We'll make a riddle of the villain's body - we'll send him tonight to that hell which is gaping to get him," roared the infuriated Rockites.

"Hould boys," interposed Martin Dawley, "don't interrupt the captain, I'll be bail he has another *augisheen* (addition) concerning Squire Crushem's villany."

"Boys," resumed the captain, the thread of whose narration had been suddenly snapped asunder by this outbreak of indignant feeling, "I have somewhat more to say - will you hear me in patience?"

"Say nothing, captain, dear, for yer always checking us - say nothing agin the revenge I have sworn for the blood of my tall, strong boy," exclaimed Tim Murphy. "Pulse of yer mother's heart ye wor ma boochil bawn, when the strong hand o' the traitor tore ye from her arms to the gallis;" and the hollow sobbings of the weeping old man reverberated along the ruined walls.

"Isa is Maura!" exclaimed twenty voices in a breath, "we can stand this no longer. Captain, won't ye lade us agin the murderer of ould Tim Murphy's son?"

"These interruptions will ruin the object of this night's meeting," said the captain. "The hour of revenge has come in vain - will you not hear me?"

A deep silence pervaded the group so lately clamorous, as though some baleful power had suddenly changed each living form that composed it to breathless stone, and the captain resumed: -

"There is one beautiful being dearer to my eyes than the light of heaven. I have loved her long and ardently - and she, fallen as were my fortunes, did not distain me. Squire Crushem sought her hand in vain. The villain, learning that I was the chief impediment to his hopes, suborned men to swear that I was a Rockite leader. I was denounced and hunted like the felon wolf. I turned on my pursuers, and sought safety in aggression. But the wiles of Crushem have succeeded - her father's authority has obliged the deceived girl to renounce forever the outlaw she once preferred. This is the wedding night of her who once pledged her faith to me - the partner of her bridal bed is the brutal, bloodstained Crushem. Shall it be so? or will you fly to save the beloved of my heart from the foul embrace of a ruffian?"

"Lead us on - lead us on," was the general cry; "but we must share the spoil with you, captain. The lady is yours, if strong hands can drag her from the traitor's grasp; but we must also help ould Tim Murphy to fulfil the oath that entered heaven with the soul of his boy from the height o' Gallis-green!"

"Tim Murphy," returned the leader of the vengeful men, "your foot is upon the verge of the grave. God is the avenger of blood - forbear to grasp his prerogative. Unless you religiously promise to shed no blood tonight, except in self-defence, I move not from this. Let Squire Crushem enjoy his triumph."

A low murmur of disapprobation manifested the ill reception of this proposal, till the old man whose wrongs they were resolved to avenge, cried, "Boys let us be said by the captain; he knows more of the laws of God and man than scores of us - he's wan o' the ould stock - his fathers and ours have struggled and bled together before. We're bound to obey him, boys, and we will."

"You're right Tim Murphy - you're right," was the general cry, and three cheers for the captain arose so high and sudden, that the wild starlings of the ruins, aroused by the unusual sounds, rose upon the night wind and mixed their notes of alarm with the shrill huzza of the wilder men beneath.

Within an ample hall glittering with sparkling lustre - adorned with all the elegancies of modern refinement - where blushed the costly wines of France and the Peninsula - where sounds of sweet music stole from the fingers of unseen minstrels - where female forms of beauty delighted the gazer's eye, was assembled, according to the ancient Irish usage, a wedding circle. A venerable priest was there, robed in the vestments of his sacred office - a book was in his hand. Before the holy man stood a large, coarsely featured individual, and by that individual's side was a lady of surpassing beauty, whose bridal dress and glittering ornaments but ill accorded with her pale cheek, and tearful eye, and shrinking timidity. That ill-assorted pair are the bridegroom and bride. God help thee, hapless maiden, the link that binds thee to thy ill-matched mate was never woven in heaven. Thy dove-like bosom never sought the shelter of that vulture's wing. His impudent eye gloats over the proximate sacrifice - there's a scowl of hate and triumph on his brow. God comfort thee, abandoned, weeping child of sorrow! Thou hast no mother to mix her tears with thine - no father to sustain, to snatch thee from the hated clasp of that brutal man. Poor girl! thou never knewest a mother's pitying care; and thy other parent, the dupe of a villain's wiles, the inheritor of ruined fortunes and a despised creed, is there, not to sustain and cherish, but to urge thee to thy doom.

As the reverend man had concluded an exhortation suitable to the importance of the occasion, the clattering tramp of a horse's hoof came quick and clear along the stony avenue to the ear of the guests that filled the wedding chamber. The priest paused, the bridegroom started, and then hastily motioned the clergyman to finish the ceremony. The holy rite proceeded, but at each successive pause came the measured tramp louder, and quicker, and nearer, till, as the bridegroom was about to pledge his troth to the fainting being beside him in the usual form, the advancing sounds suddenly ceased - the doors flew open - a youth of tall stature and noble bearing confronted the inmates of that crowded room. The curiously carved haft of an antique dagger jutted out at his side, and bright steel pistols shone at his belted waist.

"Hold, there!" cried the bold intruder; "cease that unholy rite which consigns youth and innocence to the arms of a monster! I forbid this marriage."

"And who are you?" demanded the bridegroom, when his stifling rage permitted utterance. "Who are you, who dare to obtrude your presence and advice when neither are desired?"

"Behold me, villain, and tremble," rejoined the other - "behold him whom your villainy would consign to an ignominious death. Have you forgotten James O'Brien, whom you sent abroad a homeless wanderer from his father's roof-tree?"

"Ha! most redoubtable captain, I know you now," he returned. "This fortunate occasion, which gives you into my power, adds new zest to the cup of my happiness. Gentlemen," turning to the assembled guests, "as a magistrate , I command you in the king's name to seize upon this Rockite leader" - and he moved to secure the door.

At that instant the stranger blew a small silver whistle that hung at his breast. Its shrill sound was answered by one wild yell, and then came a rush of feet, till the hall and anteroom were filled with fierce men.

"Move but an arm," said the young man, "and my authority over these excited men will fail to save your body from being the target of forty guns!"

A cry of execration burst from the armed throng at the sight of the detested Crushem. Now they had the foe - the exterminator - within their grasp; the hour of vengeance was come - the foremost of the party rushed to drag him forth, and glut their vengeance in his blood; and the coward retreated for shelter behind the priest.

"If the villain that ruined Mary Connor hung on the robes o' the Pope o' Rome, I'd haul him to the death he desarves," said the blue-eyed youth whom we have already heard deploring the fate of the rustic beauty that became the victim of Squire Crushem's seduction.

"He transported the Widow Cronin's son, and murdered a born nat'ral (a simpleton), and hanged the ould man's boy," exclaimed another. "We've a gad for his neck at the first tree; he must die the dog's death he brought upon the innocent! Give the villain up, Father; or, by the souls of the innocent men he hung, I'll shoot him where he stands!"

"Save me, save me," cried the abject wretch, addressing the leader of the furious Rockites; "Mr. O'Brien, save me from these terrible men and by all that's sacred I will be your friend for ever."

A sign from their leader quickly restrained the fierce intruders, "I acknowledge no friendship with base scoundrels," casting a glance of contempt on the terrified suppliant. "I have come not to wreak revenge on your abject head, but to save this unfortunate lady from your polluted touch. Anna McCarthy, fraud and force must have driven you to this. Have you consented to be the bride of Squire Crushem?"

The person he apostrophised had remained since his first entrance like one suddenly deprived of all her faculties; her bosom heaved, her eye dilated, and her arms extended, as she stood in motionless astonishment. She sought to speak, but her feelings forbade all utterance.

"Anna, the companion of my childhood - the cherished jewel of my riper years, have you forgotten James O'Brien?" cried the impassioned youth.

"When I cease to remember you, my heart shall forget to beat," replied the weeping girl, as her tears burst forth, and her words found expression. "They told me a tale of fear and guilt concerning you, and how you were shot down in some midnight attack, and died of your wounds in prison. My father, influenced by that wicked man, has forced me to this. They bewildered my brain and crushed my heart, God forgive them."

"Anna, then, would not willingly link her fate with my mortal foe, nor abandon one, because he is poor and persecuted, who loves her with deep and fond affection?"

"O!" she cried, with energy, and with all the truthful candour of an Irish girl, "I would sooner be the vilest reptile that fattens in the dampest charnel-house, than the wife of that man. Now that we've met, no earthly power shall divide us."

"Dearest and best of girls," cried the enraptured lover, "welcome to my heart. I had concerted measures for sailing immediately to America, where a large property was bequeathed me, but was determined if possible to see you before my departure. This night has Providence favoured me, and your fidelity crowns my success. Tomorrow we sail for a land of freedom. I am now your protector - your natural one has basely sold you for gold to the worst of villains."

But the young lady exclaimed, "it cannot be, James; I will not quit my father. I can never abandon him in his old age to shame and sorrow. Stay with us; my father will be reconciled to our union, and all will yet be well."

"Aye, and gratify my deadly foe, when he beholds my lifeless body swing from a gibbet," said O'Brien.

"Anna, tenderest of daughters," said the softened father of the maid, "I am unworthy of such kindness - I give you both my blessing - I have scarce much more to bestow. O'Brien has no safety here, and you shall not be divided. Father John shall join your hands. May God's blessing be with you!"

The overawed circle gazed in silent wonder - the ceremony which united the lovers was soon performed - Squire Crushem, thankful for his personal safety, hung his guilty head - the bride was soon lifted to the saddle-bow of her exulting lover - the Rockite troop formed in thick phalanx round their precious charge, and with one wild shout of triumph departed.

28
Passages in the life of Daniel O'Keefe, the Outlaw;[1] surnamed Domhnall na Casgadh[2]

The bright sun of a day in the month of August poured a gorgeous flood of light over the woody valley of the Araglen, a stream which, rising in the marshy heights of Pobble O'Keeffe, winds, as though it were a huge silver serpent, its devious course through the wild glens of Kiskeam, till it gives its tributary waters to the beautiful Blackwater, below Cullen, a village famous in traditionary lore, as the residence of the blessed Laterin, a female saint, who, in some long-forgotten age, presided over a convent of nuns in this place, where her memory survives in the recollection of the glensters, green as the tender sward that wraps the long-forgotten site of her holy house from the eye of the curious antiquary.

The sun that shed its golden glories over the silver Araglen, and burnished the dun leaves of its bordering oaks with molten gold, glanced on the compact ray of a party of military men, whose equipment betokened them the soldiers of him who now held undisputed sway through the land. Limerick had capitulated, and James's followers joined their master's fortunes in a foreign country. The presence of this military party, in the far recesses of the west, created terror in the breasts of the unprotected dwellers of the glens; and, as the instruments of death flashed bright in the sunlight, when emerging from the sheltering copses of the valley, the soldiers rounded a declivity, or wheeled into lengthening file to avoid a marsh, the cowboy's light carol, as he drove his flock towards the pasturing vale from the milking-bawn of the distant hamlet, would suddenly cease, and the songster vanish, as though the pitying earth had opened its kindly breast, to receive the son of the stricken Celt, from the terrible view of the Saxon *Saigheadoir Dearg.* [3]

The leader of the party was a tall, athletic young man, whose broad-fronted head, fair hair, and florid complexion, bespoke his Saxon origin. His short velvet cloak, beneath which fitted the tight leather jerkin; his embroidered sword-belt thrown over the right shoulder, from which depended a Spanish rapier; his flapping beaver-hat, overtopped by the

---

[1] Published in two parts in *The Irish National Magazine*, June 13th & part II on June 20th respectively, 1846. Initialled, E.W. - Ed.

[2] The story of 'Daniel the Outlaw,' and the precise time at which he lived, is involved in much obscurity; however, I trust I am correct in placing him in the time of William and James. He was of the noble line of O'Keefe, whose broad lands extended along the western part of Duhallow, in the county of Cork. His usual retreat was a cave on the edge of the Blackwater, near the wood of Gurtmore, near Mallow. Here he slew *Maighrad ne Challéadh*, or Margaret Kelly, his mistress, who had agreed to betray him to the English... His other retreat was at a place near Pobble O'Keefe, on the Araglen, where the people yet point out his lurking-place, which they call *Foil Domhnall na Casgadh*, or the Den of Donall the Queller. He was a polished scholar, and an excellent poet. Tradition says that he composed a poem on the death of the fair, traitress, Margaret Kelly; but I could not discover it, though many fragments of his poetry yet linger in the memory of the peasantry.

[3] Red Soldier; from *saighead*, a dart, and *darg*, red.

waving plume, which a costly jewel held confined, betokened him a gallant cavalier. The state of his lower habiliments, however, seemed not quite in keeping with the gay seeming of the upper garments: for his boots, even to their ruffled tops, that met the fringed breeches, were dark and heavy with the grime of bog-stuff.

At the side of the young officer, stalked another person, wholly dissimilar in dress, feature, and complexion, to his companion. In his bold, fearless bearing alone, he seemed to resemble his military companion: the olive complexion, the tall wiry form, the partially large mouth, the quick-glancing grey eye, told his Celtic origin. A blue bonnet formed his head-dress; the finely-formed waist was well developed by his close fitting woollen tunic, the many skirts of which fell in double folds over the light *triubhas*,[1] that decked his chiselled limb, and, falling into the heelless thong-stitched *brog*,[2] supplied the use to which, in later times, the hose and galligaskin have been applied. The Irish mantle fell in ample folds around his person, or waved in the swelling breeze, revealing the hilt of the formidable *scian*[3] that glistened in his broad leathern belt, as he bounded with a sort of native elasticity over the protuberance that studded the patches of bog, which, at intervals, darkened the green banks of the stream; and a gleam of humour would twinkle in his bright eye, as he offered an admonitory remark to the soldier, whose late acquaintance with Irish quagmires was darkly impressed on the habiliments of his lower man.

"I really think friend," said the English officer to the young native, who appeared to guide the course of their band of soldiers through the glen; "I really think that thou art another feathered Mercury, thou movest with such elastic tread, and unerring precision. By what peculiar sleight of legs, art thou enabled to glide, like a passing shadow, along the rushy mounds, that stud these cursed swamps, from which myself and my unlucky fellows are submerged into the black mire below, at every other step?"

"The facility of motion which you are pleased to compliment so highly, is owing, I conceive, to early training, captain," said the Irishman; "and somewhat might, perhaps, be also added," he continued, "to the credit of our peculiar climate, whose humid atmosphere, while it promotes the growth of bogs, gives our people that suppleness of joint, and strength of limb, for which our warriors in the olden time received the distinguishing title of the 'heroes of the Western Isle.' "

"Your heroes of the Western Isle had most probably their existence in the songs of the bards alone," returned the Englishman.

"But," said the young Irishman, "has the present day produced no testimony of our bravery, which may give currency to our ancient claim? Was Aughrim well contested? Did the Boyne furnish an easy victory? and, captain, have you forgotten the walls of Limerick?"

"It would ill become me to gainsay thy boast, friend," replied the generous soldier; "in the late wars, thy nation behaved with honour and humanity - the Rapparee hordes always

---

[1] Pantaloons; pronounced *truis*.

[2] Shoe.

[3] The Irish dagger.

excepted - night and darkness hovered round *their* guilty path; they struck like assassins, and glided from the attack, like shapes of air."

"The unfortunate Rapparees," returned the guide, "were men driven by famine to deeds of desperation. Proscribed by both parties, they hung upon the rear of your armies, like wolves on the trail of their prey; fated, like that felon beast, instant death awaited their capture; and, like him, too, heaven lent them faculties to elude the foe."

Thus discoursing, the leader of the party and his guide treaded along the rude pathway; when suddenly opened before their way an extensive sward, so level, so smooth, so deliciously green, that it required no stretch of fancy to suppose that the hand of taste had cultivated that beauteous spot, to shame the brown barrenness of the desert wold, within which it lay, in eye-consoling verdure. The young stranger, uttering an exclamation of delight at the beauty of the smooth green surface before him, prepared to step forward, anxious to comfort his weary foot on that fair spot, when the guide, laying a hand on his shoulder, suddenly checked his progress.

"Captain," he said, "another pace forward is as much as your life is worth! You know not what deep chasm lies beneath that which is so invitingly fair."

So saying, the young man, standing on one extremity of the quaking-bog, pressed one foot on the green covering, when suddenly the whole extent, which had so lately reposed in placid beauty, now arose at the pressure of the intruder's foot, as though it were endued with animal life; while the dark waters of the gulf below rambled and growled like a pent monster, wrathful at human intrusion!

"I have never seen anything so deceptive as that green sward," said the officer: "it is a true type of perfidy. Have not the bogs become proverbial of treachery in your land?" and he continued, as though in self-communion - "I detest treachery in all its forms."

"Our antiquaries and philosophers," said the guide, "have left us but one proverb expressive of that un-Irish vice; it is comparatively of modern origin. When our people would typify base treachery, they say, '*'tis like the smile of the Englishman*!' "

"I detest perfidy," repeated the soldier; "I opine, young man, that the proverb-mongers of thy nation never need roam abroad for types of treachery: art not thou thyself, sir, a trafficker in blood?"

The eye of the guide flashed as if it were a bolt of fire; the blood of his heart rushed to his cheek and brow; and as suddenly retired, to leave that brow and cheek pale as cold marble!

"Your present position," he returned, "alone gives you the power, but not the right thus to upbraid me. True, I have agreed to show you the haunt of the dreaded outlaw, who defies your laws, and braves your boldest attempts to effect his capture; but do you suppose I do this, moved by the motive of a scoundrel informer?"

"I only know," the other replied, "that thou hast agreed to point out the retreat of him for whose apprehension a rich reward has been offered."

"Captain," resumed the young man, "I see about you that which inclines me, though conscious of not deserving your esteem, to lengthen at least the obloquy which must ever attach, in the estimation of the generous and true, to him who betrays his fellow-man."

"Speak on," said the Englishman.

"That outlaw has marred my hopes of happiness here, and endangered those of a hereafter. He stole from my affection her for whom I would have resigned the wealth of worlds, quenched in her pure soul the light of faithful love, and kindled there instead the fire of unholy passion. I have sworn on the blessed relic of our sept to quench my just revenge in his heart's blood. I have hunted him down with the same unalterable impulse that precipitates the bloodhound on the track of the murderer. Our swords have crossed in the conflict of death. I sought him at the Boyne, at Aughrim, and Limerick, still some controlling power warps me from my purpose. I have had an additional incentive in this pursuit in the recent death of the unfortunate female by his hand. To glut my just revenge, I am become what you see me, and yet I would not resort to this vile means, save that it furnishes the surest prospect of redress, when all others have failed. Such is my tale. I leave you now to judge if I be a *trafficker in blood*."

"I can now perceive," returned the officer, "the motives of thy conduct. But to me, it seems that the woman whose loss thou dost so greatly regret, is an object not worth a single sigh. She abandoned thee for another, and afterwards sold the blood of that favoured lover for gold!"

"You little know," said the young man, with a deep sigh - "you little know the blandishments of the seducer who wiled her from the ways of virtue - tall, elegant, accomplished, his very tones are melody, and the music of his harp rivals what popular superstition conceives of the *coel sia*."

"The what!" interrupted the Englishman.

"Ah!" said the other laughing, "I beg pardon for the use of the native phrase; *coel sia*, means *fairy music*, and the term is used in allusion to these strange sounds, which the imaginative peasant fancies he hears, on summer evenings, by haunted rath or stream."

The party had now left the bank of the river to enter upon a bridle-road that wound along the border of a thick wood, which clothed the sides of a precipitous descent, that extended, for miles, along the course of the stream. On the opposite side, the land rose gently from the water, and, swelling into rude undulations, mingled its verdant tints with the dark brown of the heaths that stretched far west and north beyond the vision. On the right, towards the east, extended elevated mountain ridges, on whose swampy backs lurked the brown bogberry, and the cotton-plant waved its glistening spikelets in the evening breeze, whilst along the deep intervals grazed herds of cattle on the rich mountain grass that grew even to the border of each dark rivulet, that served as a channel to the waters of the marshy heights. This was the aspect of the country for miles around.

At length, the party, preceded by their officer and his guide, reached a projecting point of that headland along which they had for some time been travelling. This abrupt eminence was formed of huge masses of rock, through the deep interstices of whose rugged sides, tall oaks rose, clothing in one garb of green the savage face of stone. Above the topmost point of the precipice, stood one tree of surpassing beauty, forming, by its overreaching branches, a sort of natural bower which completely excluded the rays of the sun. Below the masses of stone to the edge of the river, thick foliage clothed the steep; and beyond the steep, and far away, swept the undulations of the smooth, grassy moors.

The guide stood beside the spreading tree to which we have alluded, and then, pointing downward, said in suppressed tone, "There is the retreat of Daniel the Outlaw."

"Where?" interrogated the leader of the party, "There are no traces of human foot here, and I see that the sides of the erect rock are perfectly inaccessible."

"He is caverned just beneath our feet," said the guide, "and the only passage thither winds round the bend of the cliff, and is formed by steps cut into the solid rock, which can be treaded by no more than one person in front."

"And the passage terminates—?"

"On a narrow platform before the cavity chosen as his retreat. This entrance can be disputed by a single man against fearful odds."

"I perceive," said the captain, "that the capture of this redoubtable outlaw is a work of some difficulty; thou hast been here before?"

"I have already waited two whole days in the outlaw's retreat in the hope of meeting him, but I waited in vain; I know by certain marks here, that O'Keefe is not now abroad. It will be necessary that your party follow my descent, step by step. Numbers are here nearly useless in effecting his capture, save only as they furnish fresh assailants in the encounter. I have now one favour to beg."

"Name it."

"That none interfere in that mortal conflict which must necessarily ensue between O'Keeffe and me, till one of us be dead; and should I fall, I request that you will tell the world that I died, like a brave man, avenging the ruin of female purity."

"Thou shalt be obeyed," said the officer, "but I must arm thee for the fight."

"More than this would only encumber me," returned the young man as he drew his dagger - an antique weapon, consisting of a blade twelve inches in length, and a hilt curiously carved from the horn of a red deer; "a longer weapon would scarce suffice on that narrow platform, where O'Keeffe shall hug, in deadly embrace, his unbidden visitant."

This dialogue, which was carried on in low whispers, being terminated, the guide removed some branches which had been artfully contrived to hide the entrance to the outlaw's place of concealment. He crept cautiously on, his drawn dagger in his hand, his mantle rolled in many folds about his arm, presenting a target of no contemptible power of defence against the blows of an enemy. The soldiers, with uncertain step, followed close behind.

II

As they winded slowly, round the side of the cliff, and approached beneath the table rock that stretched in front of the outlaw's cell, the sounds of a human voice break suddenly forth. The tongue was the Irish, and the words sounded wild and incoherent among the startled echoes. The guide paused to listen. Above him rose the projecting mass of rock within which lay the retreat of his enemy, concealed by its screen of oak, and into which a single step would have introduced him; and these were the words that caught his startled ear: -

"Who art thou that sittest before me, and ever and anon regardest me with eyes of pity? Thou are not Margaret Kelly! - no no! Thy brow is wrinkled - hers is smoother than the polished ivory; thy hair is matted and grey - hers full, branchy as the oak-bough of our dwelling, and dark as the wing of the raven! Thou art not my beloved Margaret, my lamb of mildness, *mo cuish ma chroide*! Hast thou seen a swan on a broad blue lake, dipping her fair bosom in the limpid wave, and arching her neck of beauty in the bright sunlight? That was the grace of my beautiful love, as she sought her outlaw in his ferny retreat. Thy *falluinn* (short cloak) is flannel; thy *cartall* (close gown) is grey woollen; but I brought her a *céibhin* (frontlet) for her forehead that glittered with gems, and a *seal* (kercher) of Indian silk for her white bosom. But see - oh, see! - she stands before me, pale and speechless, her fair bosom red with her heart's blood! Stay, and I will staunch thy wound with moss! - stay, Margaret, stay, and cast one pitying glance on thy murderer!"

Then came these stanzas, blended with the music of a harp: -

"With strings of rich pearls
Thy white neck was laden,
And thy fingers with spoils
Of the *Sasanach* maiden;
Such fair silks enrob'd not
The dames of Moyalla,
Such proud gold they wore not
As *Mairgread ne Challeadh.*

"The moss couch I brought thee
To day from the mountain,
Has drunk the last drop
Of thy young heart's red fountain;
For this good *scian* beside me
Struck deep and rung hollow
In thy bosom of treason,
Young *Mairgread ne Challeadh*!

The feelings of the listener were now wound up to a fearful pitch of excitement, and, rushing to wreak his revenge on the slayer of her he loved, he ascended to the level rock. The soldiers prepared to move after, when a sign from their leader restrained them. The intruder advanced cautiously forward, expecting the instant rush of his enemy; then came a rustling among the thick foliage within, and pausing, with teeth set and dagger firmly clutched, he stood on his defence. But instead of his expected foe, an old woman, wearing a close-fitting short gown, and a petticoat of woollen stuff, with long grey hair streaming beneath the napkin that formed her head-dress, approached, and the young man at once recognized her as the *beanleigh* or doctress of the surrounding district.

She was one of those mysterious women of Ulster, whose name, even yet, among the districts of the south, is but another word for knowledge in the healing art. Their skill in sanatory plants was extraordinary, and the application of this knowledge, through the medium of superstitious forms, had won them great sway over the people. This woman came forth with arms extended, as if to warn the intruder away, and her dark eye lighted, and her tall form seemed to expand, as she addressed him in the native tongue.

"James O'Danaher,"[1] she said, "what motive urgeth thee to intrude where the FEVER hath come to dry up the blood of the strong man, and burn the marrow of his bones? Surely thine is some evil errand; but thou dost need no shield nor arm-protecting cloak against that enemy who lies bound in the burning chain of the FEVER! Go, James O'Danaher," she continued. "Son of noble fathers, leave vengeance to heaven, lest the trophy of thy victory here be disease and death."

"I have heard Domhnall na Casgadh speaking, but this very moment," returned the youth.

" 'Twas the fever demon that worked within him," she answered with energy. "His were the ravings of madness; and now, till the workings of the next fit commence, he lies as powerless as a corpse."

"I must see if all this be true," said O'Danaher.

"Not," said the old woman, "while thou leavest me life to resist thy murderous intent! Monster, dost thou come hither to anticipate the fever stroke - to plunge thy *scian* in him whom the hand of the Lord hath already stricken? If my words be true - when, friend, was the daughter of Myles McSwiney found to utter a falsehood?"

"Then, God and his angels forbid," said the young man, that I should do so dark a deed. Though I would give worlds to shed his blood in fair battle, I shall never be his slayer when disease yields him to my grasp."

"Then, swear by the sacred cross of your *scian dubh*" cried the old leech, "that while he lies under this fever, thou wilt attempt nought against the life or liberty of Domhnall na Casgadh."

"Alas," returned O'Danaher, "I cannot answer."

---

[1] The O'Danahers were chiefs in the neighbouring locality.

"And why not?" she returned. "If thy words be not lying snares, thou wilt swear by the blessed sign to spare the outlaw while the chain of sickness holds him. Swear quickly, James O'Danaher; why would thy father's son hesitate?"

"Look through the screen, over the edge of the platform," said O'Danaher, "and you will find the solution of the difficulty."

The old woman stepped forward towards the verge of the table rock, and her cry of horror rung loudly among the recesses of the cliff, as she saw, below the platform, the bright weapons and red coats of the hated Saxon soldiers.

"Traitor," she exclaimed, fixing her keen eye upon him who stood stricken in conscious shame before her - "traitor, who hast brought the red soldiers to the border of thy tribe, mayest thou be marked by the curse and crime of him who, in pursuit of revenge, first brought to our shore the foreign foeman; and may that curse and crime walk in thy daily path, and haunt the dream of thy sleep." So saying, she fled, striking through the thick wood, while rock and valley echoed to hear wild cry.

"Captain," said O'Danaher, returning to the soldiers, "the outlaw is dying of fever, and it would be dangerous to the health of your men to remove him."

"I agree with thee," returned the other, "that to bear him away in his present condition is dangerous, and very inconvenient; so we can obviate this by striking off his head, the production of which to the Governor of Mallow will entitle us to a round sum."

"Surely, sir, you would not cut the throat of a dying man," exclaimed O'Danaher.

"My order is to bring the Outlaw to Mallow, alive or dead; thou has shown me the impolicy of now acting upon one stipulation of these, and of necessity I must choose the other."

"For the love of the saints do not stain your soul with so foul a deed!" entreated the Irishman.

"I have known much of the versatile character of thy nation," said the officer, "but yet I can hardly conceive why thou dost now plead for the life of him thou didst so lately doom to destruction."

"To slay' him, under these circumstances, would be downright murder," replied O'Danagher.

"He has been placed beyond the pale of all law," returned the officer - "is he not a hunted rapparee, a proclaimed outlaw? He therefore can be slain with as much freedom as a wolf; besides we have no means of conveying him from these wild glens."

"In ten minutes," said O'Danagher, catching eagerly at the thought - "in ten minutes I can make a litter of the boughs of trees, on which he may be easily removed."

"I will comply with thy wishes in this regard," said the officer, "meantime lead me to the den of this formidable outlaw."

Within the branches of the thick oak that nearly concealed the entrance to the outlaw's retreat, was a natural excavation in the rock, which served as an outer porch. Here were the embers of a small fire in a sort of chimney vent, which had a funnel artfully worked through the natural interstices of the cliff; over the fire was a brazen cauldron nearly filled with whey; within was a recess upon which lay a bed of moss. Upon this was extended the motionless form of a man in the prime of life; his cheek was pale as marble, but no trace of emaciation was yet produced there by the rapid sickness; his stature was tall and finely developed beneath the light woollen covering that wrapped his limbs, a dark *moustache* surmounted his upper lip, the recent growth of beard on the rest of his face showed that he had, till very lately, been wont to prune that appendage of the rough sex - long, dark brown hair, through whose tangled curls a few grey hairs intertwined, fell over his broad shoulders, contrasting with the marble whiteness of the broad bosom it shaded, - that bosom whose slight heaving a close observer alone would notice. Above them, on a natural ledge of the rock, was laid a long gun, and beside him stood a harp of antique workmanship.

"He is a fine fellow," whispered the officer, stretching his own tall figure to its full height, as he regarded the unconscious form beneath him, "and this the harp with which he cultivates the gentle art of the poet."

"Alas, alas!" said O'Danaher, " 'twas that manly form, that poet's craft, and melting harp, which seduced my heart's dear treasure, and left my soul a prey to the demons of hell!" and he rushed into the open air.

In a short time, the soldiers, under the direction of James O'Danaher, prepared a portable bed on which to place their unresisting prisoner. The unconscious man was removed in his blankets from his retreat, and bound upon the litter with bands, formed of twisted oak saplings: the soldiers raise their burden - the leader of the party gives the word to move - and looks around for his guide to marshal the way - but James O'Danaher was nowhere to be found!

29
Mielane's Rock[1]
An Irish Legend

A short distance to the west of the little town of Newmarket, and on the left side of the road to Blackwater-bridge, are the ruins of Castle M'Auliffe, formerly the stronghold of the old, and, in these parts, once powerful family of that name. It is situated nearly on the verge of a steep precipice, at the bottom of which glides the "*Oun Dalua*," or double stream, which winds beautifully along the glen, until it falls into the Blackwater, a little below Kanturk. It was once a large and handsome pile, around which were placed, at equal distances, watch-towers, that communicated by a rampart over the whole length of the main building, and which served to give instant warning of any unfriendly approach. The walls were of immense thickness, and seemed to have been built almost entirely for security, and from its commanding situation could, at that time, have sustained an attack for several days. Indeed from the great steep on which it was erected, and the river (which in winter was almost continually swollen) rolling beneath, it may be said to have been inaccessible at that side; while the approach at the other being also rather high, rendered it even there capable of defence for some time by a few men against a numerous enemy. Its last inhabitant of that family was said to be a man of rather a morose and oppressive disposition, and on that account much dreaded, if not hated, by his immediate neighbours and dependants. The heiress of his possessions, his daughter Mielane, was the only person in the world for whom he felt interested. She was regarded by him with such a love almost approaching to idolatry, and being the counterpart of her deceased mother, whose memory he still cherished with the fondest affection, she in a great measure filled up the void in his heart occasioned by her death. Mielane, at the time to which the story alludes, was about nineteen years of age. Her person was under the middle size, but formed with the most exact symmetry. The *contour* of her face was rather oval, with the nose inclined to the Grecian. Her lips, which were small and of a deep vermilion colour, were generally compressed, and seemed to be an index to her mind, which was high and enthusiastic. Her broad and radiant forehead, which vied with the purest alabaster in whiteness, seemed further to indicate the soul that resided in that fairy mould, while the whole was lit up with such eyes,

"As might have looked from heaven,
But ne'er were turn'd to it before."

---

[1] Published in *The Irish National Magazine*, June 20th 1846. The authorship is not acknowledged. However, since we are aware that Walsh wrote both a prose and verse account of *The Midwife*; and we have his verse account of the present story, this unacknowledged prose account would also seem to be his.- Ed.

They were of a deep blue, and overshadowed with uncommonly long eyelashes, that gave a sort of plaintive melancholy to her beautiful expressive countenance. But what she was particularly remarkable for, was the length and beauty of her hair, which was of a bright flaxen colour, and which descended in vast profusion almost to the ground. Indeed her appearance altogether had something in it so airy and sylph-like, that she might well have seemed an inhabitant of another world. As may be readily supposed, Mielane was not without suitors, but, as her father left her in this respect entirely to her own choice, she had formed an attachment to the young chieftain of the clan "*O'Hierly,*" by whom she was in turn beloved with the greatest ardour. His father, with the chieftainry, had inherited the demesne of his ancestors, in the west part of the County of Cork; but was, some time after the arrival of Cromwell, dispossessed in common with others, and all that now remained to him was a small farm, which, on account of his age, was left by the person that succeeded him. The young lover of Mielane was an only son, and as he saw nothing left for him in his own country, he determined on entering the French service, at that time the refugium of all expatriated Irishmen, and wherein their merit was sure to be fully appreciated. Though he felt the bitterest agony at the idea of the long years which should necessarily intervene ere he should see her again, and though he could have made her his wife at once, the thought was insupportable, that she who from infancy had been accustomed to have every little wish gratified, and even anticipated, should now be obliged to follow the fortunes of a wanderer, whose only wealth was the unsullied honour of his name, and the sword which hung by his side. On the evening of his departure, he bent his steps towards Castle McAuliffe, to bid farewell to its inmates, and to take a last look of her, whom, perhaps, he might now behold for the last time. The day, which had been uncommonly warm, gave place to a cool and beautiful evening, while the crimson rays of the setting sun were reflected in the Blackwater: -

'To gold converting one by one
The ripples of that mighty river;'

and nought remained to disturb the almost breathless silence of the air, save the sudden and solitary plunge of the salmon, as it emerged from its watery pillow, or the shrill whistle of the cow-boy, as he slowly drove along his herd to their place of shelter for the night. O'Hierly beheld the scene with a sort of melancholy pride, that he could call such a country his; and of sorrow, that he, the descendant of a long and almost regal line of ancestors, should be obliged to go forth a wanderer and an outcast from the home of his fathers, and leave the fruits and the flowers which he had planted, to regale the taste and charm the senses of a stranger and an usurper. "Sweet river," said he, in his fullness of heart, "with what different feelings do I now behold thee, from those of my boyhood years? - when life was a day dream of happiness, from which I never thought to be awakened - when all existence to me wore a face of enchantment, as lovely and as bright as the sparkling waters, which now glide at my feet. Thou wilt roll on calmly and undisturbed to thy resting place in the ocean; - while I must depart from thy banks, perhaps never more to behold thee - to find a name among strangers, worthy of those who gave me birth, and which it is in vain to look for at home."

Indulging in all the bitter luxury of such feelings, he arrived at the Castle, and a few minutes found him in the presence of Mielane. She was employed in plaiting a ringlet of her hair, from which her miniature was to be suspended, and given to him as a parting pledge of her affection. So deeply were her thoughts engaged in the task before her, and such was the intensity of her feeling, that she was not aware of his presence until she felt the touch of his lips as he kissed off the tears that were starting in her eyes. - "My beloved Mielane, why will you take so much to heart that which is inevitable? - our separation, I trust, will be but for a short time, - and then, with what delight will I come to claim my affianced bride, and lay the spoils of my victories at her feet; and how will she receive her returning wanderer! With what ecstasy will she clasp him to her bosom, when she hers that he has earned a name not unworthy of her, nor of his country!"

"Oh, Redmond! I feel as if that rich and glorious orb, now about to set, will go down on my last day of earthly happiness - perhaps you will say, 'tis from the agitation of my spirits, and the extreme dejection from which your so sanguine hopes have endeavoured to relieve me - and perhaps it is so; but still the feeling intrudes itself so strongly upon me, that, do or think of what I will, in vain I try to shun it - it comes and secures possession of my imagination, as if it proceeded from some more important cause."

"Rouse yourself, my dear girl, and do not sadden the few moments that now remain to us, by such gloomy anticipations; believe me, 'tis nothing more than the generally usual attendant on partings like ours, and the fallacy of which, in a short time, I hope to prove to you. And now my beloved Mielane, that I press thee to my heart the last time for a long period, say that when far away from you, and journeying in a distant land, your thoughts will sometimes revert to him who, amidst storm or calm, the raging of the battle, or the stillness of the midnight hush, will turn to you, as the star to which his hopes and fears will always be directed."

"It seems you do not know me, Redmond - no, you cannot know my love. Mine is not an every-day one, that changes with time, or is cooled by absence. No! where I love, I shall love for ever! And now shall I tell it? In parting with you, I part with happiness and joy, and everything that made life of value to me; yet still would I not detain you; go, and make me proud of Ireland and still prouder of my own Redmond, my betrothed husband. I will not say be true, because to doubt your love would indeed be agony; but let me not be absent from your thoughts until we meet again, if fate permits it, when you will return to claim a heart that beats but for you alone. Take this," said she, putting the woven tresses around his neck - "forget not the donor - and may He who guides the lightening and stills the tempest, may He protect you from every danger - to His care I commit thee. Farewell, my dearest

Redmond, farewell! while I can say the word," and waving her hand, "our parting is over." She paused, looked at him for a moment and then darted from his sight through a side door that led to her chamber. O'Hierly tottered out, and approaching his steed, which stood neighing and pawing the ground impatiently in the castle yard, vaulted into the saddle, and, as if he could escape from his feelings, was instantly out of sight and on his way to Cork, where he was to embark for the Continent.

We shall hastily pass over the various scenes and dangers through which he had, during an absence of more than three years, attained a high rank in the French army. He continued to correspond with the object of his affections, and all his letters breathed the most ardent attachment. At length the long wished for day arrived, when he had the delight of pressing to his bosom a being whose thoughts dwelt only on him; and as no obstacle now intervened to prevent their union, a month from the day of his arrival was fixed on for its celebration, and preparations on the largest scale, and in the most profuse style of genuine Irish hospitality, were made to do due honour to the occasion. Direful was the havoc made among cattle of all kinds, from the lordly bullock to the quiet and peaceful lamb; and the unfortunate inmates of the poultry yard, might be seen huddled together, and cackling in the most doleful manner, as if conscious of the dreadful doom which awaited them; while several dozen barrels of home brewed ale stood ready waiting in the most inviting manner to be tapped, to allay the thirst which those gastric preparations were so well calculated to excite. We do not descend to the minutiae of the affair, as it certainly would require a much abler pen than ours to do adequate justice to every particular dish that bore a part in the entertainment; and especially as we may be glanced over by some exquisite and critical gourmand, who may perhaps be excited to frenzy by the description. We shall therefore forbear, and content ourselves with saying that the most profuse prodigality reigned throughout; while besides having all the surrounding gentry as guests, notices were put on the road, inviting all passing travellers to repair to the Castle, and to remain there as long as they found it agreeable.

On the eve of the day preceding that of her union, Mielane, accompanied by her foster sister, who was the only female companion she had in the Castle - as the state of society at this period did not admit of much intercourse with the country about - proposed a short walk. She had been confined for some days before, in consequence of the almost continual rain which made it impossible to stir any distance from home. It was towards the beginning of harvest, when the fields were glowing with the rich and mellow tints of autumn, in the warm and vivifying rays of an evening sun. Mielane, as she contemplated the beauty of the surrounding landscape, could with difficulty forbear giving vent to the transports which swelled her heart; but the presence of her friend restrained her, as she could not enter into her feelings, and therefore might be induced to smile at what she would call her folly. They had now reached the end of their walk, and sat down in a sort of natural grotto, which Mielane had handsomely decorated with shells and moss, and where she generally brought her *clairsach*, or harp, to while away the hours of summer. The approach to it was by a small lane of evergreens, planted on either side with different kinds of flowers, and so thickly shaded as scarcely to admit the rays of the sun; while a little from the entrance, ran a small rivulet of crystal water, which dashed sparkling along, now over its bed of red pebbles, and now over some few large stones, which caused it to resemble a distant waterfall: then rushing with impetuous force down a small declivity until it was lost in the river below.

The sun was just sinking below the horizon, and tinged with a fiery red the clouds which were slowly rolling in the western heavens, while his declining beams shed a bright purple on the surrounding hills. Mielane sat in the deepest part of the grotto, and was conversing on the approaching fulfilment of all her wishes - when she stopped suddenly, and turning to her companion asked - who that lady could be, so richly attired, that was approaching so slowly? The other, astonished at what she had heard, looked about in every direction, but in vain, for the supposed object. She could discern nothing save the slight movement of a few cypresses which were agitated by the evening breeze. Supposing it to arise from the enthusiastic imagination of her young friend, she smiling told her that she ought to restrain the exuberant joy with which she was so elated, as to call such fanciful forms before her. - "It is not fancy, nor is it imagination," answered Mielane. "I see her clearly and distinctly before me, and you cannot but behold her too. See, there she is just before us - observe her majestic step and pale but beautiful countenance, and oh! what misfortunes can have crossed the path of so young and lovely a creature, as to leave such traces of sorrow as are there so deeply imprinted; and yet withal, that wildness in her glance seems almost unearthly - and her gaze is so intensely fixed on me, that I find it equally impossible to withstand it, or to withdraw my eyes from her, even for a moment." Indeed the hour which was now verging fast into the gloaming - the almost breathless silence of the air, and the broad glowing and brilliant full moon which had just arisen, and which shone out in all its splendour on the entrance of the grotto, gave a sort of fairy light to the scene, while the spot was precisely that calculated to realize the fanciful description of the place that a poetical imagination would, in idea, assign to the objects of this fine and romantic superstition. It is well known what a degree of belief is attached by the lower order of the Irish peasantry, particularly those of the South, to those various orders of elves which come altogether under the denomination of the *dhine m'athe*, or good people, and the numerous legends which are related of them, which for the luxuriant wildness that pervades them all, are by no means inferior to the most gorgeous descriptions of oriental romance. Eliza (the name of her companion) seeing her persevere so obstinately, as she thought in such a wild delusion, not being exactly insensible to the many stories that she had heard so frequently of these unearthly powers, from the belief in which even the high classes at this period were not exempt, began to get a little alarmed, and said she thought they had best return home, as the night was getting late, and their long absence might alarm her father; but Mielane heeded not what she spoke, and did not even seem to hear her - she continued to stare with dilated and fixed eyes in the direction of the little path. “My dearest girl,” said Eliza, her alarm increasing, though she wished to conceal it, “I fear you are unwell, and that our long walk, from being unaccustomed to it lately, has disagreed with you, else why is your cheek so blanched?”

“Hush!” said Mielane, laying her finger on the lips of her friend, “hush, she is just close to us.” In a low and tremulous tone, as if fearful of being overheard, she continued - “she is just close to us - see she beckons me to her, and oh! she says I must go with her.” Now seriously terrified, her companion pulled her to go home, but she, unmindful of her presence, or, of aught besides, stood trembling, pale, and immovable, her face became livid, her lips quivering and bloodless, while her bosom heaved violently, her breath became short and stifling, and the words *I'm going, yes, I'm going!* came from her with rapidity; but Eliza, who saw her every moment becoming worse, and was apprehensive of her fainting, flew to the little rivulet we before have mentioned, and returned in a few seconds with water to revive her; but what was her horror and astonishment, when no trace of Mielane could be seen in the spot where she had that moment left her, nor in any other part of the grotto. Almost dead with terror, she searched about, calling, or rather shrieking her name, while her cries having attracted the attention of some persons accidentally passing, they came to her assistance, and she told them, in words hardly articulate, what had happened; they immediately commenced a search with the utmost diligence, but in vain.

Eliza was conveyed to the castle half inanimate and exhausted, where we will leave it to our readers to imagine the scene that ensued. All the joyous preparations which were making for the wedding, were now turned into grief and sorrow for her untimely loss. There was no one who did not bitterly bewail the lost Mielane, as she was almost adored for her goodness of heart and disposition. But her father was not to be comforted, being bereft of her,

“The only being who kept his heart unclosed,”

to whom he looked forward for every comfort which could make his old days joyous and happy, was too overwhelming a misery for him to contend with, and after the first paroxysm of grief had subsided, he relaxed into a sullen gloom, which nothing could divert. For whole days would he shut himself up in his chamber, where no one dared to disturb him. We shall not attempt to describe O'Hierly's despair on this occasion, for it would be vain. He seemed as if all the ties that had bound him to earth had been severed, and was no longer desirous of staying in a world, where for a long time he had felt nothing but coldness and chilliness of heart. All his hopes seemed now gone for ever, without the slightest remnant of one which might bring back but for a moment those fairy scenes of joy, in which a short time before he had so largely indulged. And who is there that does not at one period or other remember with ecstatic, but sorrowful feelings, some form that glided before him in his noon of existence, when life appeared all glowing with the schemes of happiness he had planned, when it presented but its fair side of hope and pleasure, and when that form was the sun which shone so brightly upon, and gave so rich a colouring to the sweet but delusive visions which his youthful and ardent fancy conjured up before him? Who is there, that, let him be elevated to the highest pitch of joy, or sunk to the lowest depths of sadness, will not turn, and with feelings which no other occurrence of his life can ever again call forth, bring before his "mind's eye" the being which he enshrined deep in his heart's core? - Too true

' 'Tis a light that ne'er can shine again'
On life's dull stream.'

But we are digressing. O'Hierly's mind was not one of those which, no matter what events may chance to disturb it, can easily recover its usual tone; and things made a far deeper impression on him than, from his appearance, a common observer would be inclined to conclude; and as he imagined the world could not contain another being like the one whom he had lost, he became silent and reserved, and began to conceive an utter distaste to all society. His favourite amusement was in repairing to the spot where she had disappeared, and in gazing upon every thing connected with her, even the most trivial, that could in any degree tend to keep her remembrance fresh in her memory. He would daily pay a visit to the little grotto, and there sit for hours, lost in a reverie on the strange and supernatural manner of her disappearance, utterly regardless of time, until the thickening shades of evening would warn him to depart, that he might not give them cause to animadvert on his absence at the castle. He now determined to bid an eternal farewell to his country, and on entering again into the French service, there to lose, if possible, among the duties and activity of a military life, all thoughts of the happiness that once awaited him at home. His violent grief was now beginning to subside into a deep melancholy, when he by chance heard that she had been seen to appear near the rock which now bears her name. Thinking it was nothing but a mere delusion, particularly from their strong belief in the supernatural, he treated it as a mere bagatelle, and was convinced that it must have been some inanimate object which their heated imaginations, and the extraordinary manner of her disappearance helped to conjure into a belief that it was really she whom they had beheld; so he entirely disregarded the report, and began preparing for his departure. It had now gradually died away, and seemed to be quite forgotten, when again rumours were abroad that she had been distinctly seen leaning against the rock, and singing, in the manner usually attributed to the banshee. Not knowing well what to think of it, after it had been thus confirmed by many who professed themselves to have been eyewitnesses of what they related, and prompted by curiosity, he determined on going himself, and discovering if possible, what had given rise to their terror. He accordingly went, and after remaining a considerable time in anxious expectation of seeing the object of his wishes start up before him, he was obliged to return without success. He repeated it often, but to as little purpose; when giving it up as a mere chimera, and wondering how he could be induced to give the least credence to it, he endeavoured to forget that such a story had ever existed. He had now every thing prepared, and was on the eve of his departure, when, not wishing (as he was about to take a last farewell of his country) to go without again visiting the scene of so many dear recollections, he repaired once more to the spot. It was in the beginning of winter, and at an hour when the family had all retired, he set out. The evening had been extremely cold, and towards night, the clouds threatened an approaching story. The moon, which was nearly full, was quite obscured, except at intervals, when it partially burst forth for a moment, and but served to show more clearly the dreariness of the scene before him, while a few distant and prolonged claps of thunder seemed to give warning of what was to follow; but it was unheeded by O'Hierly, whose mind was quite in unison with the tempest, as almost in despair at the thoughts of his long cherished, but now ruined hopes, he leaned against a tree, in indescribable emotion. An immense rock stood just near the spot, which was fronted by the now foaming river, and near it a large and thick wood. He thought at this moment he could hear the sound of a human voice, which seemed to rise at no great distance from him; and approaching somewhat nearer, he perceived a female form leaning on a fragment of the rock. With breathless agitation he now advanced, and hid himself behind a small cluster of trees, but a few yards from the object, where he could, unperceived, clearly discover every thing. But what were his feelings on finding in the seemingly unearthly being that stood before him, his own love. Her elbow rested against the rock, with which she supported her drooping head. Her features were of an ashy paleness, exhibiting the same deep and plaintive cast as was their wont; but the glance that once was joy to whoever it beamed upon was now vague and wild - her lips were closed - and her whole appearance denoted the extreme of agony. After remaining some moments in the posture just described, she clasped her hands together, and in a wild, but beautiful tone of voice, broke into a sort of *caoin*, or dirge. O'Hierly, whose feelings were now wound up to the highest degree of excitation, could withhold no longer, but calling on her name, threw himself before her. She stopped suddenly, as if to recollect his features - gave a kind of hysteric cry - and putting her hand to the rock, it opened, and on her gliding into it, instantly closed over her! The thunder had now fearfully increased; while the flashes of lightning became every moment more vivid and frequent. He saw no more - his head became dizzy - perspiration poured in large drops down his forehead - his knees trembled under him - and he sunk senseless to the earth.

30
A Legend of Blarney[1]

"Why thin, ye tell me you never heard tell o' the famous Castle o' Blarney, the town itself, or any o' the fine sights about it," says Paddy O'Callaghan, with a look of surprise, at the extreme ignorance of his companions, seated snug and saurtha, after dinner, before a fine fire in the servants' hall of a wealthy squire, in the North of England, "never heard o' the Castle of Blarney? Meilla murther, wisha may be so; why, thin, I thought, sarten sure all the world hard o' the place: the groves so charming - the sweet silent streams - the grottos - the rock close, an the witches' stairs o'Blarney, not forgetting the lake,

'With boat on,
So calm to float on,'

A lookin down on the fishes as they sport along. Zure I'd be tired before I'd be half done, if I was to give a description av it; ye should go there yourselves, and take a day or two to it, so you should, indeed - for, as I said, there's a world o' fine things to be seen in Blarney. Well, I'm going to tell you a story about the castle or the manshin, that's where the ould Macs used to live, long ago, an sure you don't know who they were, small blame to you, but that's no matter 'tis about the manchin, as I say, all the same as the castle, stuck up to it, as may be the wings o' their house (as you call 'im) make part o' the court itself. Well, you know the bearings of the case well as myself, now. Easy awhile, till I tell ye: - There was a great man there last summer, from a near these parts, as I could hear from a sisthers sun o'mine, who came up here from Lunun, where he was at work, to see me, why, thin, he tould me 'this gentleman come all the ways from Scotland to see Blarney;' curiz to see it. Well, a great man he was, bee the powers as Jim tould me, (that's my sister's sun), an a heel an a foot to boot. He wint to see the castle, an the town, an the lake, an all the fine sights; an sure enough, he was greatly divarted and wonderfully pleased wid all he seen, no doubt. An he wint to the top o' the castle, and he seen where

'Oliver Cromwell,
He did it pom well,
And made a great brached in the battlement.'

There he seen where Oliver hot the castle a fair clout ov a cannon ball, from a hill opposite, and the iron strap put there to keep the stones together, for they got a great shake be razon o' the ball not haven far to travel, you see. Why, thin, the identical stone the ball hit, that's the Blarney stone, as they call it, that if any one kisses, he'll be sure to have a sweet tongue all the dear days ov his life; that is, he'll have plinty o' the plain maurh' on the top ov it, as

[1] Published in *The Dublin Penny Journal*, March 23rd 1833, as the second in the series of six stories entitled "Popular Legends of the South." The other five are initialled 'E.W.' but the authorship of this story is not acknowledged. However, having compared it with other work by Walsh, I deem it to be his. - Ed.

they say in Ireland. Well, he walked about on the top ov the castle for some time, with his stick in his hand; takin a fine view for himself av the country round, from it, for it's murtherin high, you see; so as that the highest tree does not reach half way up the walls, no indeed. Why, thin, he wint down be the dark stairs, and faix it give him enough to do, that same, cause of their be'n very narrow, and slippery for stones, and his havin a lame foot, and be'en an ungainly sort o' man that way in himself. Nevertheless, he was mighty courageous an very eager to see every thing curiz, that was to be seen. He wint into the Earl Clancarthy's room, and it's no easy matter to get there, as you'd know if you knew the castle as well as myself. Well, he got into it some way or other, and he see it, an he axed a great many questshins about it, and he see the nails that held the velvet covering the walls, the ould people must be very grand, long ago, you'd think and to have velvet a papaerin their walls. Why, thin, so they had, for you can see to this day the little bits o' velvet a hanging to the nails, is indeed; sure his honour axed Jim to draw out one av um 'till he'd look at it, so he did, an he admired greatly to see the bit o' velvet a hanging to it. He was very curis in other respects, about the castle, an axed Jim a power o'questshions; an faix answered the half ov um himself, he was so knowledgeable a man about all concarning ould buildings, an the good times long ago. Well, he wint out o' the castle, an down to see the caves in the prison, and have a view o' the castle from the west side, for tis from that side it looks best; an, my dear life, all his company follin him: one here, and another there, admiring at every thing. But the ould gentleman himself kept close to Jim, puttin questshions to him about what he knew and hard o' the place. Why, thin, they came into the rock-close, to see it, an 'tis a very contrary sort o' spot, that you'd go asthray in, in a minute, between the ongainly trees, an the rocks, and the sirpintine walks av it, so you would; an, sure enough, the company, one here, an another there, as their curiosity drove um, not mindin the guide, but follying their own inclinashions, soon got scattered about the place, an lost Jim an the poet, who havin seen every thing worth while, left the close, an walked on t'wards the castle agin. Why, thin, whin his honor got opposite the manshin, he stops, and he ses to Jim: - 'James,' says he, as he was pleased to call him, for he was a mighty civil sort av a gentleman that was in himself, 'James,' says he to my sisther's sun, 'I'spose that's a ruin many a day now?' 'Wish, faix, thin it isn't, nor long at all, at all, so it aint; for 'was the prisint man that threw it down, sir, for a dirty trifle o' lucre, not worth the spakin about; bad manners to him.' 'Oh! dear,' says the ould gentleman, clapping his hands, 'what could ha' bewitched him to do the like? O, my!' 'I d'know; af it were not for the lucre, it must be the spirit he seen in it, that made him do it.' 'A spirit,' says his honor. 'Is, indeed, sir,' says Jim; 'a ghost he met in the king o' Sweden's room; there is the windey av it, right fornentin you, (pointing it out to him), there it is, and the room idin it was a fine spashis one too. I was often in it; they called it the king o' Sweden's room, afthur the king that dined in it an a time, sir.' 'The king o' Sweden,' says his honor, 'and did he dine in it, ayea?' 'Faix thin he did,' ses Jim, 'an he come all the way from Sweden to dine at Blarney Castle, never a one av him but did,' says Jim, 'An do you give belief to that, James?' ses he.

'Surely,' says Jim, 'or how would it come to be called the king o' Sweden's room? 'Be gosh, that's true,' ses his honor. 'True as you'r stannin there,' ses Jim. 'The king o' Sweden, my dear,' ses he. 'The king and nobody else, make sure av it,' ses my sisther's sun. 'Wisha, faix, 'may be so,' ses he. 'Devil a doubt on it,' ses Jim. 'Ecod, then, he come a good way to see the groves o' Blarney,' ses he. 'I'spose he did,' ses Jim, 'but people come from furren parts to see the same, I can tell y'r honor.' 'Why, thin, will you point out where it was to me?' ses he. Jim did, and show'd him the diminshions. 'By gosh, thin it must be a fine room; ar, I see,' ses he, 'an worty to dine a king in,' ses he. 'You may say that ,' ses Jim. 'Many's the fine ould anshint prince feasted in it, in the good times; is faix, good as ever the king o' Sweden was for the life av him, died there, I'd make bould to tell you - an many's the fine lady an gentleman 'stirred the foot' to the music of the harp, (for twas that instrimint we used long ago, y'r honor. But, no matter them times are gone - our glory is gone, an that av the manshin av Blarney Castle to boot!' 'Well, well,' ses his honor, ses he, 'ther's no help for misforthin - no help for those things, James; they threw down a site ov ould castles an fine places in my country - dismantled and disordered um - bad luck to um; so, you see, 'tisnt you have a story to tell. 'But,' ses he, sitten down, an becknin to Jim to do the same be him, 'come,' ses he, 'an tell me something about the ghost that struck such fear into that 'GOTH' av a man, as I can't help callin of him, that threw down that fine ould relic of a place.' 'Tis well you call him or the likes of him,' ses Jim. 'I'spose that word 'gath,' have a very ondacent significash in the Scottish tongue.' 'You may bible it,' says his honor, 'that any man in my country would be ashamed av his life to be called be it.' 'Why, then,' ses Jim, 'more luck to y'r honor, to bring it over to Ireland with you for we wanted it badly-or-worse for a friend o' mine, to call him by - that deserves the title well; but no mathur, the shame ov his work will follow him, an maybe that's enough.' 'Quite enough,' ses the gentleman, ses he; 'and now for the story, James, fore the company come upon us.' 'Very well, y'r honor shall have it as I heard it from my aunt, Nance Callaghan, that was their-servant in the house, and knew a deal o' the goings on, no doubt to be able to gi' me a corrict account; sure she hard the masther, himself, tell ev'ry word av it.

"Why, thin, 'twas on a Sathurday night, av all nights in the year, and the masthur come from Cork, afthur selling some o' the timber there; for he was beginning the work o' disthrucshin 'bout this time. Why, thin, he dismounted from his horse, an he very wet all over, be raison ov a great deal ov rain that fell durin the day; an in, my dear life, he walks to the king o' Sweden's room, and sits down to the fire, blazin fine, to dry himself. Why, thin, he reqisted ov the sarvents to bring him his dinner - they did - and he dined there, and took a couple o' tumblers, or may be more, very hearty; an been fatigued, he lay down upon the chairs, (a custom of his), to take a sauvauneen after his meal. Well, he slept very sound and very long, and by gosh, they were loath to wake him; but they left his man, Tady Hegarty, up be the fire in the servants' hall, if he should call or want any thing - 'cause, your honor, all the bells in the house rung in that part - an, faix, the other sarvants went to bed. Very well, the masther slept mighty sound 'till he woke, just 12 be the castle clock, and shakin himself, he laid hould o' the bell to give it a pull for Tady. Why, thin, he had his hand 'pon the bell-rope, when he heard a step on the stair, an look'n over agin him to the door, who should he see enter'n the room, for him, but a tall, fine, grand-lookin ould gentleman av a man, dressed in a shuit of black clothes of the ould cut, with a pouthered wig on his head, and a goold headed cane in his fist. Whin he come into the room, which he did very robustic, as if 'twas his own, (an sure 'twas), he shut the door athur him as he found it, and giv'n a nod to the masthur, (look'n mighty bewildered over be the fire-place, with the bell-handle in his hand still), he walked very consequented, straight a head, over to the windees fornentin him, and look'd out for a while on the plain below him. Well, my dear life, when he sees, for he could not help seein, all the fine threes cut down, an sthrewed on the ground, he shook his head, and turnin round to the masther, (cock-a-northa, in the corner), the Earl, (for 'twas the Earl Clancarty himself), give him a bithur look that made his very heart's blood run could and his body to tremble like one in the aigey, for the bare fright. He thin pointed with his goold headed stick to the plain; drawing his attenshin sure, to the threes he destroyed there, all the while starin at him, an shaken his head. Why, thin, the ould man stood this way a spell; and at long last, he beg'n to move over to the fire place, with his stick over head, and his eyes roulin, an fierce enough to take the complexshin aff any man. Well, while you'd be saying 'be your leave,' he stood wden arms lenth o' the masther, ready to slain him, Lord save us! Och, the masthur give himself up for lost, an the passparashin a flow'n from him, like a well, whin he seen has condition; but, twas nothing 'till the Earl giv'n a mighty stamp on the floor, that made it shake agin, so as to floor the masthur, with the strength ov it - be the powers, down he came, dead as a door nail: bell-rope, wires, an all roulin topsy turvy under the chairs he was sleep'n on; table, decanters, mugs and jugs down a tap ov him - there he lay in a dead faint, snug and snurtha, under um all. Well, beyant that he could'n tell what became o' the Earl Clancarty, whether he remained athur the racket, or walked aff whin he had his revinge ov him, or what, he could not tell; but, no matter, he got enough to remember all the dear days ov his life, tho' there wasn't a word between um, only by signs. Well, there he lay on his hard bed, an all the racket over him, as I said; an he was warm enough, I'll be bound, be raisin av his be'n in a high fever from the thraitment he got. Very well, there he lay 'till mornin break, 'till one o' the sarvants, Judy Casey, be name, came into the room to clane it: and whin she found himself unther all the furniture, an in the state he was in, she got a great fright, no doubt, been a narvous frightful young woman, that way in herself; she gave a bithur scream, (whin she see him for dead as she thought), that brought all the other sarvants a runin up to the king's room, to see what 'twas all about. Why, thin, they rubbed him all over wid whiskey, an got a drop, be a great deal to do, down his throat; an at long last he give signs av the life in him, an come to himself agin. But he was very weak for a long time afthur, on account av the fright, and the cruel usage he got from the Earl Clancarty's ghost; an that day night he was removed to a neighbour's house, for he swore he never u'd give another night in the castle - an sure he didn't, for 'twas thrown down be his orders soon afthur, so it was; an there's my story for you, an the raisin, they say, the manshin was disthroyed, sir. But, indeed, I hear some people, knowledgeable people too, an those that come from the city to see the place, say, 'twas all in my eye 'bout the ghost, but that the masther give it out as excuse for what he done. Well, bless me, af I know wich story to give belief to; but I think 'twas a dirty onnathural thing to spile the pride o' Blarney, even af it was thro' the fear atself.' 'I concur in y'r apinion,' James, ses the gentleman, 'an I say it here an above boord,' ses he, hittin his stick agin the ground, 'an I'm ashamed ov him, for the like,' ses he. "Be this time the company were comin up to him. 'I thank you for your story, an you'll accept o' this trifle for y'r civility, (handin him a crown piece) an I'm indebted to you in the bargain, so I am.' 'Don't minshin a word about it, y'r honor,' ses Jim, 'I'd do more than that to sarve y'r honor, so I would; but ther's one favour I'd be afthur axin y'r honor'. 'Why then, what's that?' ses he. 'Fex, just thin, just y'r name, y'r honor, av you please; for I intinds, this very identical evening, af I'm a livin man to do it, to dhrink your honor's health, over yonder in the village, that I mighn't do an ill turn but I do.' 'Why, thin, 'tis a queer name they calls me by, Jim,' ses his honor, 'an I'll tell it to you.' 'Af y'r honor pleazes.' 'Why, thin, they call me the 'Great Unknown,' now.' 'Great Unknown; by gor, than it is an odd name, no doubt,' ses Jim; '' 'Isn't it now,' ses his honor, 'Devil a doubt av it,' ses Jim; 'Great Unknown, mauriagh. I'd make bould to ask what country y'r honor come from.' I'll tell you that, too, Jim,' ses he; from Scotland, thin, all the ways.' 'Is, so I thought,' ses Jim, 'I'spose your family ar a sthrongfacshin over there; but I never hard o' one o' your name before now; no mathur, y'ere dacent people, I make no doubt in your own country; an more luck to you an yours, every day ye rises, I say; an God speed you on y'r road, y'r honor an I'm obliged to you.' By this time, his honor was in the carriage, an all the company wid him; an never a one of him but kissed hands to my sisther's son, at his goin; an aff they wint, himself an his company, very well pleased with all they see, and the attenshin Jim ped um. So theyre's what I had to tell you, genteels, about Blarney, (that you never hard of before); an how do you like my story, now?" says Paddy, addressing his company, when he had finished. They all, indeed, I am happy to inform the reader, expressed themselves much pleased with it; and one from among them, the butler, a chiel from the land o' Cakes, proposed the health of Mr. Patrick O'Callaghan, which was received with great applause; and Paddy returned thanks in neat words, on the occasien. I was near forgetting, though, to inform the reader, that the butler, in proposing the health of Mr. O'Callaghan intimated to the company, that he knew who Mr. Great Unknown was, very well, (the person alluded to in the tale) and begged leave to thank our friend, for the kind manner in which he had spoken of his countryman.

31
The Steel Boy[1]
Founded on fact

On some fond breast the parting soul relies,
Some pious drops the closing eye requires;
E'en from the tomb the voice of nature cries,
E'en in our ashes live their wonted fires.
Gray.

Walking, one fine day in autumn, through a retired part of the county of — , I saw , at some distance, a verdant hill, crowned by a couple of trees and something like ruins, which tempted me to turn off the road, and take a nearer view.

A genuine old Irish boreen (road), composed, as they usually are, of large stones in a kind of irregular pavement, led from the highway to the foot of the hill, and traversing the green sward to the summit, I found, on a closer approach, that what appeared to be ruins was, in fact, a receptacle for the ruins of human nature, i.e. a burial ground; the trees, two noble ash, planted by some sorrowing children of man, to mark the spot of earth that contained the remains of a beloved object.

Somewhat fatigued by a long walk, I sat on an elevated tomb, and, from the lofty situation of the place, commanded an extensive prospect of the surrounding country, which was not remarkable for the picturesque; its features were rather wild and bare, save that on the south-west there was some planting, and the varied hues of the foliage appeared to peculiar advantage in the light of a brilliant sun and cloudless sky.

With such sad mementos as those by which I was surrounded, I naturally fell into a train of serious reflection on the vanity and uncertainty of all sublunary things; and I felt inclined to exclaim, with the poet,

"Dust to dust concludes the noblest song."

While ruminating on "days of langsyne," I was aroused to the recollection of existing circumstances by hearing the funeral cry, harmonized by distance, like the wild notes of the Aeolian harp. I can well recollect when I would run any length to avoid hearing the funeral cry, from a foolish dread of it imbibed during childhood, and many years elapsed ere I became reconciled to its wild tones, which, at a distance, are not unharmonious. I cannot say so much when in its immediate vicinity. I turned round, and beheld a long procession ascending the hill. There were, in front, a number of females, in white and very light coloured gowns - the two first carrying what is called a garland, viz., a pole, with hoops

---

[1] Published in *The Dublin Penny Journal*, March 16th 1833. Initialled, W. - Ed.

horizontally fastened to the upper part, covered with curled paper - with the figures of long and short gloves, cut in paper, suspended to it - surmounted by a cross. Following these, were a good many girls, two and two, each bearing a white rod tipped with curled paper. This part of the procession appeared to be regulated by a man on each side, who kept the crowd from mingling with the garland bearers. There was no regularity among those who followed, save that, as is usual in this part of the country, the females take the lead at funerals.

I should have liked to witness the ceremonies of this interment unperceived; but here there was no chance; so I went forth to meet them, and returned among the crowd.

It was melancholy to witness the apathy and levity with which most persons, both high and low, attend the remains of their fellow mortals to the tomb; but among the lower orders, whose habits are free from the restraints of etiquette, this indecency of behaviour (I can give it no milder epithet) is most visible.

I joined a group of men, on one side, who seemed rather surprised at meeting a person of my appearance in such a retired spot; however, it was but momentary; for the conversation was soon resumed by the younger part of them.

"Bad luck t'ye Barney," said a fine-looking young fellow, with a set of teeth that rivalled the whitest ivory, "but that was a nice trick ye pled on the girls last night; myself was kilt out wid the laughin'."

"I'm the boy to plase them," replied Barney, a bold, dissipated-looking young man, with his hat set upon the back of his head. "Fwhisper, boys," and he added something I could not hear, which set them a-laughing.

"Isn't a wondher but ye're ashamed iv sich behaviour," said an old man, "an' doesn't know how soon ye'r own turn 'll come."

"Soon enough to bid the devil the time iv day, fwhen ye meet 'im," retorted Barney, and then, with his companions fell behind.

I suppose it was in reply to the old man's remark that another said, "Och! the Lord fit an' prepare us for that day! amen, achierrnah. Arrah, Billy, had ye's a good fair? fwhat way was the pigs?"

The person addressed made a suitable answer, and these sober men entered into a discussion on the probable rise and fall of swine, which disgusted me just as much as the hilarity of the youths, and I passed on to the rear of the females.

Two young girls, who just left the criers, next engaged my attention.

"That's a purty pathern in Peggy Burke's gown," said one. "D'ye know fwhere did she buy it, Biddy?"

"Musha, then, it'd be hard for me, an' it not her own," replied the other.

"O virra! an' as grand as she is," continued the first.

"Aye, faix, shure its fwhat she borret (borrowed) from the cook at the big house," said the other. "An' afther all she got from the gentleman, ye know, sorra dacent faggot she has now, barrin' that red shawl, an' that same's no great thing vid the constant washin."

Two old women came between me and the young ones, talking vehemently. Now, I shall hear some sympathy for the friends of the deceased, thought I.

"Molly, avourneen, the heart widin me is sore," said one, as they pushed before me.

"Och! an' shure its no wondher," returned the other.

"Strugglin' an' slavin' from daylight tal night, in could an' wet," continued the first, "an afther all to think iv one's arnin' going' sich a way."

"The girls is a great throuble to us any way, " said the other.

"Ne'er a word iv a lie ye say, Molly; and wid my will, sorra ring ever Barney Doyle'll put on my little girl's finger," replied the first.

"There worse nor him in the world," said the other; "he's not a bad doin' boy."

"Sugh! bad luck to his breed," cried the first, spitting on the ground. "He'll never join any one belonging to me. I'd sooner cry over my little girl on the table, nor a beggarly Doyle id have her."

Young and old, thought I, are the same, each solely occupied in their own concerns. I moved hastily forward, and entered the cemetery among the foremost.

The usual ceremony of going thrice round the site of the ruined edifice was performed, and then the coffin was set down on a tomb-stone, until the grave was dug. During this process, a number of women rushed to different parts of the yard, some to scream, and some to pray at the graves of their relatives. The uproar was really astounding; and, to be as much away from it as possible, I went to the most remote corner, and seated myself, by an old man, on a stone.

"A poor sight, Sir," said he. "God help us, an'look down on the sore hearts this day."

"Death,"I replied, "is an awful event; we cannot tell when his stroke may fall on ourselves; we should, therefore, strive to be always ready to meet him."

"Och, och! thrue for ye, Sir - thrue for ye, dear. Lord, prepare us for that hour!"

"This is an unmarried person they are interring?" said I.

"Aye, Sir, as purty a young girl as you could see in the three parishes, God rest her soul! she didn't lave her fellow afther her. Och! more's the pity she to be taken, an' sich as me left on the world."

"We should not question the will of God." I remarked.

"No, no, Sir; I ax His pardon. Sure, fwhy wouldn't he know fwhat's best. Only, Sir, it's a sore sight to look at the poor young girl's mother; an' she has none but her, God comfort her this day."

"What caused her death?" I asked.

"Faix, Sir, mysel' doesn't rightly know; some says one thing, and some says another: any way, I think it was throuble kilt her entirely."

"That is strange in a young person," said I.

"Young enough, Sir - not two score out; for all that, she had throuble plenty."

"Was she deceived by any person?"

"Och! no, Sir. God forbid! It's a long story, Sir. Didn't ye hear iv the night-walkers that was goin' through the counthry, callin' themselves Steel Boys?"

I replied in the affirmative, adding, that I was surprised - having imagined the country quiet.

"An' so it ought, Sir an' every counthry. Fwhat's the use in night walkin'? Ne'er a ha'porth, only bringin' throuble on all belongin' to them, as ye may see, Sir, afore ye now. My heavy hathred on them that couldn't let us alone."

My curiosity was aroused; and finding the old man went home by the way I intended to go, we set out together, and, during a long walk, I learned from him the following particulars, which I shall communicate in my own way, divesting them of the endless "says he" and "says she" that accompanied the narration.

Thomas Molloy was the youngest son of a widow, and resided with his mother, in the mud-wall cabin where he first saw the light. Tom, as he was generally called, was good tempered, sober, and industrious. I do not mean to say that he was a *rara avis*; he loved sport as well as most young men, and frequented the ball-alley, fairs, markets, wakes, and dances; but still he contrived to have his work regularly done, and was ready to pay the rent when called on. Moreover, Tom was a well made, handsome, young fellow, who had a good coat, black silk cravat, and other appropriate necessaries for dress, which so captivated the matrons, on their way to the chapel on Sundays, that they usually remarked, "Tom Molly's a clane, dacent boy; an' it'll be happy for the girl that gets 'im."

In consequence of such remarks, the girls, one and all, were throwing sheep's eyes at Tom, but in vain - so at least thought the fair ones. However, one Sunday, at a cake, he proved himself not insensible.

For the information of those who may not be erudite in country amusements, I may observe that, in rustic dialect, cake and dance are synonymous terms. When a cottage vender of the native, viz. poteen, has a good stock on hand, she (for in this case the female is the active partner) gets a large cake made, containing plenty of sugar and caraway seeds. This, on the appointed day, generally Sunday afternoon, is covered with as white a cloth as can be had, and placed on a churn-dash stuck in the ground. A fiddler is engaged, young people collect, and dancing commences.

Now, among all ranks dancing is a thirsty amusement; therefore, there are frequent demands on the native. The evening is concluded by a general drinking bout; and the young man who conceives he has most money to spend, takes down the cake, puts it into the lap of the girl he most prefers, who makes a division of it among their friends.

It was on an occasion of this nature that Tom provoked the envy of half the girls in the parish, by gallantly taking down the cake, and putting it into the lap of Mary Collins, a blooming, black-eyed damsel of eighteen. From this time they were all in all to each other. But when did the course of true love run smooth? Mary's father was averse to the match.

Collins was what is called well to do in the world, and looking higher for his daughter. He acknowledged Tom Molloy was "a likely (handsome) cleverly boy, that no one could fault; but he'd like a young couple to have something to begin wid."

"It's little was between yersel' an' me the first day," his wife would reply, who was won over by her daughter's importunity, "an' fwhat are we the worse iv it now?"

"Sorra hair I care," was the reply. "Iv I was a fool, its no reason I'd let my child be one, nor I wont."

But after much importunity and caviling, and on the widow's giving up the bit of land, Collins at length was brought round. The bride's clothes were bought, and every thing was settled for the marriage.

Two days before, there was a market in a neighbouring town, to which Tom went on some business. He set out alone, and light of heart, whistled as he went, not for want of thought; for the delightful idea that Mary was to be his own in two days, was never absent a moment.

I have said Tom was sober; but he met many acquaintances, and could not avoid sharing in many treats of spirits; for among a certain class of our countrymen, friendship and good neighbourhood are nothing, if not occasionally cemented by a glass.

When evening drew on, and he was about to return, he encountered a neighbouring young man.

"Shure, Paddy," said Tom, "I didn't know ye wor for the market, an' we might be together."

"I didn't know it mysel' at the time," replied the other.

"An' fwhere's this ye're for now, boy."

"Home."

"Whooh! time enough this two hours; wait for me, an' I'll be wid ye. Come in, and take a dhrop iv somethin'."

"Thank ye, kindly, Paddy, but I tuk plenty - sora dhrop I could take."

"Well, come in any way - shure we wont eat ye."

"No, nor drink me, I'll warrant, fwhere ye can get better stuff," said Tom, as they entered the public house.

In one of the rooms they met a company of seven or eight men, among whom, it appeared, Paddy had previously been.

Just about this time, the hitherto peaceable country had been disturbed by parties of the deluded peasantry, assuming the name of Steel Boys, and going about at night, taking up arms.

Tom had been repeatedly solicited to join them, but always declined, which exasperated some of the leading spirits, who swore that he should be one of them by the way of no thanks.

It was into a party of these midnight legislators that Tom was now introduced; but they did not at once betray the cloven foot. His approaching marriage was no secret, and, for some time, furnished a theme of conversation and country wit.

Tom had already drank more than usual, and a few extra glasses put him so much off his guard, that they administered the oath which bound him to their cause.

Sometime after night had fallen they all left the town, and being neighbours, took the road that led to their own townland, but, at a certain crossroad, turned out of the direct way.

"Fwhere are ye's goin', boys?" asked Tom who was not so much elevated as to mistake the road. "Shure this isn't the way home"

"He's in a hurry to his darlin," said one. "Take id asy, Tom; many' the day in seven years."

"Aye, faix, an' night too," responded another.

"Sure it can't be ye're goin' to do any thin' the night, boys," continued Tom.

"An' what iv we have a bit iv a spree? We're the boys that's steel to the back bone!" cried two or three together.

"Ye may go then," said Tom; "sorra av I'll go wid ye."

"Arra,wont ye?" replied his friend Paddy. "But all the books that ever was shut an' opened, ye'll never sleep tal we see fwhat stuff ye're med iv. Now turn back, iv ye dare."

"Iv ye didn't like to be on iv us, fwhat med ye swear, Tom?" asked one of the men.

"Swear! - an' did I swear?" said Tom. "Shure it's jokin ye are?"

"There's no joke like a true one; an'ye swore without doubt," replied the same man.

"That's enough, boys; no goin' beyant an oath," returned Tom, and accompanied them in silence.

"Have a care iv him," whispered Paddy to the next man.

"Never fear; he'll not part from us alive, replied the other.

Surprise, at finding himself thus trepanned, completely sobered Tom; and after a train of most uneasy reflection, he resolved that this night once over, he never would be in the same situation again. "I'll do fwhat a man ought," though he, "an' not lave it in any one's power to say I'm a coward."

The first essay, on that night, was at the porter's lodge of a gentleman's demesne, where, their scouts informed them, there ware only women in the house; and so little were they expected, that the iron gate was only latched, it not being quite nine o'clock. They had no difficulty in possessing themselves of a gun, the only arms the lodge contained. The poor woman was much frightened, and offered them whatever money she had, begging of them to spare her life.

"We're no robbers," one of them replied; "ye may put up the money; we're dacent boys; sorra hair o' yer head we'll touch; only give us all the arms."

At length they departed, in high glee at their success, and proceeded across the country, to another house they had set. But here they entered not so easily. The family were in bed, and the party on the outside had some work ere they forced in the door, and secured two men who were in the house; but, ere they found the arms, one of the men left to watch on the outside ran in, saying, there were some persons approaching - the night was so dark he could not say how many. Friends they could not be, as they knew not of any other party out that night; therefore, there was a general rush to the door. The last man had just gained the outside, and the light of two candles, gleaming through the open door, revealed them to the approaching party, who were so near that they plainly heard a voice exclaim, "There they are! Fire, boys!" And in an instant the report of more than one musket was heard, followed by a heavy fall and deep groan. The gallant steel boys waited not to assist the fallen, but, without delay, escaped, favoured by darkness.

The police, for such the other party were, headed by the gentleman whose lodge had been attacked, leaving two men to secure the wounded gave instant chase, but in vain.

In the mean while, the wounded man, for there was but one, was carried into the house in a state of insensibility, and various were the comments passed on him. An old woman, holding a candle over his face, exclaimed, "Och, och! but he's the purty boy! - more was the pity! - the Lord between us an' harm."

"Is he kilt out?" asked another.

"Only wounded, I think," said a policeman; "he's beginning to come to. If he stayed quiet at home, this wouldn't happen him."

"Thruefor ye, sir, dear," replied the old woman; "sorra good ever cum out iv night-walking. Forreer gair! the youngsters doesn't think so."

"Och! God help every poor sinner that must go through fwhats allotted for im," said another woman.

This doctrine of fatalism is too prevalent among the lower orders of our country; and one of the policemen was about to show the error of it, when the wounded man, slowly unclosing his eyes, murmured, "Mother, avourneen! Mary, darlint! fwhere am I? - fwhat happened me at all? Mary, asthore machree! don't cry - I wont go from ye; we'll be marret the morra, agrah, girl. Och! the pain about my heart!" and feebly putting his hand on his side, he remained silent.

The women were greatly affected, and with streaming eyes, frequently exclaimed, "Wirra strua!" The men, albeit unused to the melting mood, were seen to draw the backs of their hands across their eyes.

The policemen endeavoured to moralize on the occurrence, and point out the evils that this system of lawlessness brought on families and the country generally. But they talked to the winds; for the women, though they seemed to assent, saying, "Thrue for ye, sir," and "Ne'era word iv a lie in it," knew not well what they said, but constantly interrupted them thus: "Oh! wirra! wirra! God look down on yer poor mother this night, but it's she has the sore heart afore her! and the little girl fwhat'll she do afther ye? Och, hone! The Lord purtect all belongin' to us."

It was a considerable time before the party returned from the pursuit, and unsuccessful. On the first appearance of day-light, the wounded man was conveyed, on a car, to the next town, for the benefit of medical assistance.

The magistrate vainly endeavoured to make him confess who were his accomplices. But, during the intervals of consciousness, the poor young man uttered only lamentations, calling on his mother and Mary, pleading with them, in the most heart-felt tones, not to forsake him.

The opinion of the medical man was decidedly unfavourable; the wound he pronounced mortal, and that the patient could not survive many hours.

It is to be supposed the men who were poor Tom's companions gave information to his family of what had occurred; for early in the day his mother and brother made application to see him. That the interview was a most affecting one, may be imagined; but my informant knew no more of it than that Tom bitterly lamented his folly in being tempted to drink so much; for if he had been sober he never would have joined the steel boys. And the old man added, "Och! my curse on the fwhiskey! it's it kilt him out an' out."

I afterwards learned, from another person, that his poor mother was like one distracted, and unable to speak or weep, sat with his hand in hers the image of despair. After the first ebullition of the feeling was past, the brother appeared to think more of the safety of Tom's accomplices than any thing else.

"Tom, dear," he said, "it was a sore lot was laid out for ye, an' ye must go through it. Oh, virra! it's soon for ye to die; but there's no help for it; any way, ye'll die like a man."

"Och, och! Ned, dear," replied the sufferer, "must I leave the world an' my darlint Mary."

"Tom, avourneen! mind fwhat I tell ye: the doctor says, there's no help for ye in this world; then die like a man - don't let any one be cursin' yer bones in the ground."

"Fwhy should they be cursin' me?" demanded Tom.

"Fwhy , wouldn't they iv ye turn informer - fwhat good wll it do ye, or any one belongin' t'ye? Och, Tom, darlint don't disgrace yer family an' yer own bones in the clay."

His mother made no request, but she pressed his hand, and the young man groaned deeply, but did not reply. Before he spoke again, a minister of his church came to give him its last rites.

It is astonishing how anxious people, in general, are to communicate bad news. Poor Mary Collins was, early that day, abruptly informed her betrothed was killed; and, for hours, she was attacked by fainting fits. Next morning when it seemed necessary to preserve her life, her parents reluctantly consented that she should see Tom; but they had not gone more than halfway to the town, when they met his remains conveying to his father's house. He had died the evening before, and, much to his friends' satisfaction carried the secret of his accomplices to the grave. The heartrending scene that followed may be supposed. Poor Mary's hopes of happiness were buried with him, on the day that was to have been her bridal one. She never held up her head, and, in a very short time, followed him. Her's was the interment I witnessed in the lonely churchyard.

32

The Charm[1]

A true story

"He would
Cure warts and corns with application
Of medicine to th' imagination;
Fright agues into dogs, and scare
With rhymes the toothache and catarrh."
Hudibras.

In the vicinity of the chief town of a northwestern county in Ireland resided a widow, with a large family, two of whom were sons. The father of this family had been a labourer with a gentleman, on whose property he resided. At his death, the widow was not disturbed, though unable to pay the usual rent for her house and garden.

The landlord's wife who was a benevolent woman, endeavoured to benefit the lower orders by every means in her power, and took much interest in the family of the widow Morriss; but they were so ignorant and averse to be instructed in any way that she despaired of being able to do any thing for them. She frequently employed the boys about the house and endeavoured to impress them with habits of industry; but her good counsel was undone by the folly of their mother. In her walks the lady of the manor frequently called at the different cottages, and one day entered the cabin of the widow Morriss.

"Good day, Betty, how are your family?" was her salutation.

"Musha, then, misthress dear, ye're hundred welcomes. Nelly, brin a chair; fwhy but ye rub yer apron to it, ye ignorant ape," replied Betty, as she dressed up the fire. "Wont ye cum by, madam, an' take an air iv the fire - the day's cowld."

"Thank you, Betty, my walk has completely warmed me. What are your boys employed about to-day?"

"Faix,mysel doesn't know ma'am; its little they can do, an' less they're inclined for, barrin runnin to town afther sport. God help them, and all the poor iv the world.!"

"Don't you know, Betty, it is wrong thus to permit your children to roam about in idleness, which will certainly lead them into wickedness?"

"A cushla machree, how can I help them, an' has nothin for them to do tal the pretes is diggin?"

"During those seasons when work is slack, could you not send them to school? - it would keep them out of mischief, and, in the end, be beneficial."

"Send them to school! Arra, madam, avourneen, fwhat way cud I sind them an' hasn't one penny to pay the masther? To school, anagh![2]

---

[1] Published in *The Dublin Penny Journal*, April, 20th 1833. Initialled, 'W' - Ed.

[2] An expression of doubt, used here to imply impossibility.

"You cannot be ignorant, Betty, that there are free schools, where the children are provided with every necessary, and attended by good masters. In the town is one of these, where your children may be educated without expense."

"Lord reward them that's so good to the poor! But, misthress a cushla, fwhat wud the leks iv my little boys want wid larnin?"

"It is not burdensome, Betty, and is frequently the means of forwarding young men in the world."

"Faix, an' that's thrue for ye, ma'am," said Betty, with a short pipe in her mouth, and speaking between the puffs. "There's the widdy Kinnedy's son, they say, has the life iv a gentleman in farren parts; an' fwhat is he bether nor my own little boys."

"You have been rightly informed; the young man has a good sitution, and is much esteemed. What do you suppose has raised him thus? Education and good conduct."

"Well, well; but some people is lucky, an' he only a poor scholard afther all."

"And surely, Betty, this does not lessen his merit."

"Troth, an' misthress dear, its not every one id lik to sind the childer to a poor school, an' maybe have it cast up in their teeth."

"This is nonsense, Betty; you should be rejoiced such places are open for the benefit of your children, and send them there."

"Ah, then, madam, I was thinkin to do that same, only the neighbours crassed me, an' that's the truth entirely."

"In my opinion, Betty, you should not let what any person says, prevent your benefiting your children; and depend upon it, if they are not usefully employed in some way, they will be doing wrong."

"Thrue for ye, ma'am dear - och! och! thrue for ye any way," was Betty's reply. And after some further conversation, the lady finding she could effect no good, left the house.

"Wirra! wirra!" muttered Betty, after her departure, "but the misthress is bad about the schoolin. There father an' all afore them had no larnin, and fwhy but they cud do 'idout it? Sorra poor-school thrashel (threshold) ever they'll crass wid my will." And she kept her word. Her sons were consequently continually in bad company; and the younger, who was infinitely the most wicked, while a mere boy, received sentence of transportation for life, for being concerned in sheep-stealing. This was a great affliction to Betty, nor could she be persuaded by her mistress to believe that she was, in a great measure, the cause of this fatal event by denying the boy the opportunity of improving his mind.

It might be supposed that, after this melancholy example, Betty's repugnance to education would give way, and that she would wish to see her remaining son usefully employed; but no such thing. The fate of her younger son was not imputed to his own bad conduct, but to the extreme severity of the laws; and the elder son was allowed still to go on in the same way, frequenting the dance-house, cock-pit, bull-alley, and toss-pit, until he attained the age of nineteen, when, in a drunken brawl at one of those places, his leg was so much injured by a fall that he was laid up for months. The wound was not properly treated - Betty preferring the quack remedies of all the old women in the parish, to sending the young man at once to the infirmary. "Bad scran to them fur aspitls" (hospitals), she would say, "fwhat good was in them at all? Nera one ever wint in cum out alive; an' maybe ids fwhat they'd cut off my little boy's leg, an' sure he might as well be dead entirely - sorra good id be in him afther."

And, in consequence, though the wound appears to heal, on the least exertion it broke out again, and, for a time remained very sore. However, in process of time, the young man married, and still continued to live in his mother's house.

About three years after her son's accident, Betty and her daughter-in-law were one day seated at their wheels, when a man in rusty black clothes, an old hat, and a bundle in one of his hands, entered the cabin with the usual salutation, "God save all here!" "God save ye kindly!" was responded by the old woman, and a seat offered by the young one.

After a short silence, during which the stranger cast keen glances around the house from a pair of sleepy looking eyes, almost concealed beneath a heavy brow. Betty said, "A fine day, sir, God be thanked."

"Very fine," replied the man, and paused, still looking about, as if in expectation of seeing some other person.

"Great weather for dryin the turf," continued Betty, "an plentiness there'll be iv id the year; an' the pretes an' the oats look finely, Lord be praised!"

The man murmured something, and Betty proceeded: "Happy for them that has the turf, an' pretes, an' oats growin for them in lashins! God look down on the poor widdy that has none, and every poor crathur in the world."

"No cattle, no care," was the dry response of the stranger.

"Thrue for ye, dear; but its hard for the poor to knock the bit and the sup, let alone the rags iv clothes, out if the dozens[1] and they so chape, and flax dear." "There's nothing but grumbling in the world," said the man; "rich or poor, its all the same with them."

"Och! och! sir, dear, shure its the poor that's smashed entirely, an' has nothin at all but the day-light an' the wather, God comport (comfort) them."

"There's plenty of water in this country, any way," replied the man.

"A reasonable share," said Betty. "Ids like, sir, ye're not of this counthry."

"No," was the answer.

"Humph! no doubt ye're a thraveller," continued Betty, and without waiting his reply, took the pipe from her mouth, rubbed it with the disengaged hand, and held it to him adding, "Will ye take a blast, sir? To be sure ye cum a good piece the day."

He took the pipe, put it in his mouth, and said, "I am indeed a great traveller - seldom off the fut."

---

[1] Hanks of yarn are called dozens, in allusion, we suppose, to their containing twelve cuts.

"I'll warrant ye're a dealer; they're ever an' always walkin. God prosper them an' every poor sinner that's sthriven to arn in honesty," replied Betty.

"I'm not a dealer in the way you mean," said the man.

"Well, dear, in fwhatever ye are, its no harum to say good luck t'ye. Maybe ids for the good of yer sowl ye're a thraveller."

"For that and for the good of others," he said.

"The mother iv God reward ye the last day," responded Betty.

"Isn't there some person sick in the house?" asked the man, after a pause.

The woman exchanged a rapid glance of astonishment," and Betty answered, "Och, foreer (alas)! there is, sir, dear; my little boy is very bad entirely, an' sorra one iv uz knows fwhats the mather wid 'im at all."

"What does he complain of?"

"All in the leg, avourneen - all in the leg. He got a hurt in id three years agone, but that was cured an' he was finely tal this turn."

"Can I see him?"

"Sir dear, his gone to the spensary (dispensary) the day."

"Nerra go from them for doctors; there's no satisfaction out iv them. Fwhat one goes to the spensary, sorra haporth they get, barrin a powder or a pill, an' bid ye go home, iv ye ax what ails ye."

"What would you give to one who could cure your son?"

"Och, sir, acushla, any thin at all, an' my blessin to boot."

"Give me a shilling, and I'll do it."

"O wirra, wirra, sir, dear, there's not a pinny, gould, silver, nor brass inunder one roof wid me this day; och hone! I'd give ye tin iv I had it."

"I'm sorry for it; I can do nothing without touching silver," replied the man, standing up, and taking his bundle, as if to depart.

"Och, avourneen machree," said Betty, also leaving her seat "iv ye can do any thin, for the love iv God, don't go."

"I told you, I could not, except I touched silver; you say you have not any, so there's no use in my staying longer."

"An' sorra word iv lie I tould (told) ye, dear. O wirra! its hard for the poor to have money; an' iv a poor widdy doesn't get somethin for the love iv God, fwhat'll she do."

The man remained standing, but made no reply, and Betty, who seldom continued long silent, resumed.

"An' ye cud cure my little boy, iv ye got a shillin?"

"I have no doubt of it." replied the man.

"Arra, Judy, dear," said Betty, turning to the young woman, "d'ye hear that, an' fwhat'll we do at all, an' hasn't a pinny?"

"Maybe I'd borry (borrow) id from Winny Berne, an' pay her fwhen we sell the dozens a Thursday," returned Judy.

"I doubt she wont have id," said Betty.

"She's not a good warrant to sarve a neighbour on an amplush (nonplus). Thady Carty is far reddier only its a piece off."

"Iv the gantleman's not in a hurry," replied Judy, "I'll not be a fwhip away, an' be shure to have it back wid me."

"I'll wait a little longer," said the man; "though in a hurry, I'd like to serve you if I can; its more for that than the value of the money, but I'm sworn not to perform any cure without touching silver,"

"The heavens may be yer bed, avourneen," answered Betty, "Run, Judy, a hegar, and iv ye can't get a shillin'; maybe a tester id do - its silver, ye know."

"I cannot take less than a shilling," said the man.

"I'll do my best, sir," replied Judy, as she left the house, and set over the fields in a half trot, the usual pace of our countrywomen.

Betty, who delighted in hearing herself talk, was no sooner left alone with the man, than laying aside the wheel and putting a coal in the pipe, she began: "A then, sir, dear, fwhat way did ye know my little boy was sick - maybe the neighbours toul ye?"

"I did not speak to any of your neighbours," he replied.

"Wirra, wirra! but that's quare; an' no one tould ye."

"Not one."

She then plied him with question, as to where he came from - whether he was a doctor, and such like, in every form her ingenuity could devise; but received very laconic answers; he evidently was not disposed to be communicative.

After waiting some time he asked, whether the woman had far to go.

"Hooh! don't be unasy, dear," replied Betty; "its only a little piece wid a mile; she'll not be a minit away."

But the "little piece wid a mile" extended to somewhat beyond two, so that Judy returned not so quickly as her mother-in-law said. The man began to grow impatient, and was just on the point of departing, though Betty used all her efforts to detain him when the messenger returned out of breath with speed.

"Fwhat luck acushla?" exclaimed Betty, as Judy came to the outside of the door.

"Good luck! good luck! answered the other.

"Didn't I tell ye Thady Carty is a good man on a pinch," continued Betty.

"Sorra, sight I seen iv 'im good or bad; he went to the corp-house," said Judy.

"Chrish chriestha erin! who's dead?" interrupted Betty.

"A first cousin to his aunt's husband's uncle, in the manor," was the reply.

"Sau well dhea er in, I freckoned," said Betty; "an Judy, avourneen, fwhere did ye get id."

"Comin back iv me, I slipped over to Winny Berne; fwhen I tould the amplush we wor in, she borrit id from a neighbour tal Thursday. I kep id in my mouth all the way - there was a hole in my pocket;" and she gave the shilling to her mother-in-law.

"The Lord reward Winny Berne any way," said Betty, and handing the money to the man, who seemed impatiently waiting to touch it, added, "Here, sir, may God give you good luck iv id, an' prosper fwhat ye're to do. Amin, achiernah!"

The operator deliberately rubbed the shilling over the palm of both his hands, then deposited it in his pocket, and said, "I want two clean plates and some spring water."

These were given; he placed them on a stool by him, and pausing a few moments continued: "I must have three clean articles of clothes belonging to the sick man, or his nearest relation, before I can do any thing."

The women looked at each other in some surprise, and Betty said, "Is there any thin clean belonging to 'im in the box, Judy?"

On inspection, Judy reported that "the nera fagget was in id, barrin one handkercher."

"Fwhat'll we do now?" cried Betty.

"If there is any thing clean belonging to his nearest relation, I said it would do," remarked the man.

"Here's my new coat an' my red shawl," said Judy.

"Are you a relation?" asked the man.

"Shure, isn't she the little boy's wife," exclaimed Betty.

"Oh, then, they'll do just as well - give them to me."

The three articles were handed to him; he folded and placed them on the stool by the plates. He then said, "Now turn round to the fire, and be sure don't look at me until I speak."

They turned their backs on him; but the younger female possessing a good portion of mother Eve's frailty, could not resist an occasional side peep, and perceived that he first took off his hat; then searched his vest pocket, and produced something rolled in paper; his lips were moving, as if he spoke to himself. She was afraid to look steadily, for he frequently turned to try if they were observing him. She saw that he tied up the clothes they had given him in his bundle, and that he kept rubbing one of the plates for some time with his finger. Betty never once looked round, but continued repeating her prayers with great vehemence.

At length he called them. "See, there is your friend's blood dropping from the plates; you may depend upon it he'll soon be as well as ever, the cure is granted to me."

They were not long in obeying the summons, and beheld some liquid, like blood, falling drop by drop from the plates, which were placed one over the other.

"Chrish chriestha erin! an' is that my little boy's blood - Lord save 'im!" said Betty.

"Certainly," returned the operator.

"And he's cured now?" exclaimed the wife.

"All as one," replied the man. "I'll see him in the morning, and finish it. Let no one look into these plates till I come to-morrow."

He placed them on the top shelf of a dresser that stood near, put on his hat, and taking up his bundle, was quitting the house, when Betty said, "The Lord reward ye, sir, avourneen, ye'll shurely come the morrow mornin; the little boy'll be home then any way."

"You may be sure I wont leave the thing half done," replied the man, as he went from the door.

He was not many minutes gone, when Betty, being reminded by Judy, ran after him exclaiming, "Sir, dear, ye forgot to leave the rags the little girl giv ye - the coat, an' the shawl, and the handkecher."

"I didnot forget, (he said), I'll bring them in the morning, the cure cannot be finished without them - don't fear."

"No, dear; only be shure to bring them; she has nera dacent stitch but the one."

The man did not wait to hear what she said, but hurried on; and she returned to the house assuring Judy the things would be brought back in the morning; however, Judy was not so sure of this matter, but made no comment.

Betty was so firmly persuaded the charm would effect her son's cure, that when he returned from the dispensary, she scarcely permitted him to enter the door, ere she called out to know whether he did not feel himself much better.

"I'm not so long away that I could know whether or no," he replied.

"Any way," she said, "ye're not worse, an'll soon be betther entirely, thanks be go God."

"How do ye know?" returned the son. "Ye're not a witch nor a fortin-teller."

"No, agrah, foreer, I haven't that luck; only I am shure ye'll soon be well, thanks an' praise be to the Lord."

The man began to imagine his mother was either drunk or doting; he looked to his wife; she felt the appeal, and told what had occurred, only omitting what related to the clothes, fearing they had been too credulous. The man set up a loud laugh, when he heard the tale; and Betty, rather indignantly, asked why he laughed.

"A then is id any wondher," he replied. "Shure no one ever heard iv two sich own shaughs, to give a shillin to a common streeler (stroller), that's afther makin a hare (fool) iv ye."

"Ye needn't speak that away," said Betty; "sure didn't he show us yer blood droppin' from betune two plates; and them that cud do that id do more."

"Show ye the divil!" returned her son. "Did ever ye see fwhite blood comin from the cat? An' he'll cum back the morra! O yes, to be shure, fwhat a fool he is! See now the way ye'll pay the shillin ye were so ready to borry."

The women looked rather blank at this speech, but were wise enough to be silent. They were in a feverish state of anxiety all that day, and never did day and night appear of such interminable length. But the longest term must have an end; the next morning dawned, and they were up with the sun; hour after hour flew by; the breakfast was eaten and still no man appeared.

Betty's confidence began to waver. "Fwhat'll we do?" she said to her daughter-in-law; "Jemmy id be mad entirely iv he heard iv the clothes."

"Nera one iv me knows," replied Judy. "I dread we'll never see a stitch iv them." Then, after a pause, she added, "I'll slip over to Billy; maybe he'll tell me fwhat to do."

"Run acushla; tell 'm the amplush we are in. O wirra, iv the clothes is gone, Jemmy will kill uz out."

Judy lost no time in consulting her friend; his advice was to follow the charmer without delay, and he offered to accompany her.

They set out, and at a little town, a few miles off, traced him; and following the route they heard he had taken, were fortunate enough to come up with him two miles farther on. Billy at once seized on and carried him before the nearest magistrate, who committed him to the county jail. The clothes were secured, but the shilling had been spent, except two-pence, and the only other article he had on his person was a paper, containing a small quantity of rose-pink, with which he caused the appearance of blood that had deceived the women, as the sediment was found on the plates.

The principal events of the foregoing were, as nearly as I can recollect them, given in evidence before the assistant barrister of the county of —. When the swindler, or charmer, whichever term may seem most appropriate, was brought to trial he made no defence, and appeared to care very little for the sentence of imprisonment passed on him.

Judy recovered her clothes, much to the satisfaction of Betty, who declared she never would put faith in streelers no more. They were obliged to spin hard for some time to repay the shilling. And, in the end, poor Judy was left a widow, her husband soon after dying of mortification in the sore leg.

33
Fitzstephen's Tower[1]

The County Wexford is bounded by the sea along the whole of its eastern, and south eastern, and southern frontier: on the west by the Waterford rivers Suire, Nore, and Barrow, from the Hook-point till it joins the County Carlow.

Thus connected by its northern frontier only, it appears isolated from the rest of its province, and would seem the very spot, of all others, where all traces of old Irish customs, manners, and traditions, would most tenaciously remain, and be now most distinctly visible: such, however, is not the case, and I think I may safely say that scarcely any part of Ireland exhibits fewer remains of Milesian antiquities or traditions than the County Wexford. The Irish language is never spoken in it, except by a Munster stranger, and the Irish customs of clanship, fosterage, etc., are unknown. This seeming paradox of a district, separated by nature from the rest of the country, abandoning rights, habits, and language, whilst the part of the country more exposed to change still tenaciously clings to them, may, however, be easily explained. Wexford has been the country where each successive swarm of invaders landed, from the days of Strongbow to those of Cromwell. It was in Wexford soil Maurice Fitzstephen first imprinted a Saxon footstep in hostility; 'twas on Wexford's cliffs a Saxon camp first was fortified; 'twas at Wexford a Saxon tower first reared its battlemented walls.

Thus rendered insecure for the natives, by new hosts of invaders, they left the country to them, and Wexford was the first part of Ireland colonized by the English, being ceded to them by the treacherous Mac Murrough, as the dowry of his daughter.

If, however, there are few traces of the genuine Irish antiquities in Wexford, it abounds in remains of Saxon architecture, every leader in Strongbow's army having erected a fortalice or square tower, at once a residence for himself, and protection to his dependants.

The whole line of coast, south of Wexford town, is studded with these forts always built in such situations, that each fort is visible from at least the two nearest ones, so that an uninterrupted chain of signal posts was thus established to watch and curb the native Irish. Something on the same principle in later days have the Martello towers been erected round the coast, the use of which having been once asked of Curran, his answer was 'to puzzle posterity!'

Two miles from the town of Wexford the river Slaney is suddenly narrowed by hills on either side, forming a gorge or narrow pass about 150 yards across; above and below this the river expands into wide bays. Often have I on a calm summer's evening wandered by the river bank, and been delighted by the surrounding scenery – a wooden bridge spanning the narrow stream, connects the two sides, over the northern extremity of which nods the almost perfect ruins of Carrig Castle, or Fitzstephen's Tower, one of those square forts I have described as erected by the English strangers to protect their newly-acquired territory,

[1] Published in the *Irish Penny Magazine*, May 25th 1833. Initialled, W. – Ed.

and a place of great strength it must have been in those days, before the invention of artillery enabled man to destroy his fellows by wholesale.

Maurice Fitzstephen, as the story goes, soon after taking possession of Wexford, finding the town unfit for defence, and inhabited by a race of people adverse to his sway, erected this tower to curb them, and at the same time afford protection to his navy, both from hostile attacks, and from the stormy weather then approaching.

One fine evening in the month of August, 183-, I was leaning over the rails of the wooden bridge I have mentioned, looking at some fishermen below me, and anxiously watching the fate of a very fine salmon I had seen leaping a few minutes before within the scope of their nets, when I heard a voice close by my side, saying – "Why, then, the devil a fish they'll have after all!'

"And why so, friend?" said I, turning round.

"Oh, no matter," said he, "Devil a salmon they'll catch there this blessed night. I'll be bail to roast on my finger all the fish they catch, barring a fluke or two."

"Why then true for you, Jim Lacy," said another, "and sure if they warn't rale omedauns they wouldn't expect to kill a salmon in the castle-hole, and the dhurrus on it iver so long."

What do you mean by the dhurrus, neighbour?" said I.

"Och sure, your honour must have hard of the dhurrus, that's the curse, I mean, put upon the castle-hole, by the blessed Saint Patrick, when he was banishing the snakes and varmint. Musha maybe, Tim, he ant wanted agin here; but did your honour niver hear of the dhurrus?"

"Never," said I, "will you tell me all about it?"

"Wud pleasure, your honour," said he, "but let us stay, and see what Terry has in the nit first, and maybe you'll believe me the better whin you see I'm right. ''Twon't keep us long, for you see he has the twang of it in his fist – aye, that's right, Terry," said he, shouting out, "hould the cork rope high up, and keep the leads down to the bottom, and divil a fish you'll catch after all your trouble; - sure I tould you so," he continued, as the disappointed men drew in the bag of the net full of weeds and mud, with an eel here and there working its way out.

"Sure I tould you so, and it's great luck you have intirely that she didn't tear the bag out of the ould nit, as often she did before, and will agin 'till her time comes – God protect us from all hurt and harum. Well, now, your honour, I'll tell you all about it. Once upon a time whin Saint Patrick was on the quest for the snakes and toads, driving them all out of the country afore him, God bless him for that same, anyhow. Well, as I was saying, he was driving them all afore him from Enniscorthy, and the Duffry, and upper country; well, he managed thim asy enough till he came here to the river, just under the castle, and thın, your honour, divil a foot farther they'd go, pretending, the spalpeens, they couldn't swim. 'Sure your rivirence,' says the snake, 'you wouldn't ax me to wet myself, and swim across this wide river; your rivirence knows I doesn't know how to swim, and I havn't fins, your rivirence.'

'Musha, your honour, says the toads, ''twould be the death of me to vinture into the salt water; if it's fresh your honour, I havn't the smallest objection in life, maybe your honour's rivirence would just taste it for me.' For your see he knew the Saint was under a vow not to take any thing till after sunset, and a mighty great vow it was of him, if ''twas as hot as to-day. I'll engage M'Daniell here, of the ferry, wouldn't like many passengers like him, for it's he has the proper beer, and the whiskey too, though it's seldom I tastes it, barrin a gentleman was to trate me."

"Here," said I, "go and see if it's good now," giving him a sixpence, "and then come back and finish your story."

On his return he thus continued – "Well, your honour, the Saint was puzzled what to do, till at last he bethought him of a boat, and sure enough he soon seen a boat fishing just as Terry's boat is now in the very same place. 'God save you,' says he, 'will you lind me a loan of the boat to put these cratures over the river, and I'll give it back to you in a moment.'

"Oh, musha, with all the veins in my heart, your honour,' says the man, bringing in the boat, and Saint Patrick was just putting his foot into it, and calling the bastes after him, when 'Where are you going with that boat?' says a man from the top of the ould castle, but it wasn't ould then, your honour, but a fine bran new one.

'Who's that talking?' says the Saint, quite easy and genteel-like.

'I'm only going to put the bastes acrass, and I'll send her back in a minit.'

" 'Divil a toe you'll put in my boat,' says ould Stephens, or Fitzstephens, as they called him thin, - 'divil a foot you'll put in my boat. I tell you I built this castle, and I built that boat to catch fish for my dinner, and not to make a ferry-boat for the likes of you and your blackguard snakes; come men, turn him out, and go to your work. There's a power of quality coming to dine wud me to-day, and the mistress wants some fish for them', for 'twas a fast day, your honour, by the same token.

"With that Saint Patrick got mighty angry, intirely, 'and that you may never catch a fish in that draught,' says he, 'from this day till the day of judgment,' says he, 'and after it too,' says he, 'and what's more,' says he, 'I'm not behoulding to you,' says he, 'for a boat,' says he; and with that he takes a plate in his hand, puts it on the water, and it turned into a fine ship, and took him and all the snakes and toads, and wild bastes acrass as dry as a bone.' Well, when ould Stephens sees this he got sorry for vexing him, and he sent the men wud the boat to beg pardon, and the Saint forgave him, but he couldn't take the curse off the hole, and to make it surer he put Steven's wife into the bottom of it, for 'twas she put him up to it all, just to vex the Saint, for she knew he was going to banish the frogs and toads, and they say she was a French woman he met in his travels, and they eat every thing, I'm tould, your honour. And maybe ould Stephens hadn't great loss after all, for if he lost the fish he lost the wife too; and that was a comfort, you know – and that's my story, your honour.

34
The Still-House[1]

"Art thou a mourner? Hast thou known
The joy of innocent delights?
Endearing days for ever flown,
And tranquil nights!
O live! and deeply cherish still
The sweet remembrance of the past;
Rely on Heaven's unchanging will
For peace at last."
Montgomery.

"Mick dear, I wish to God you wouldn't go out the night," said the young and handsome Ellen Cooper to her husband, one evening, as they sat by the fire.

"Why so?" he demanded.

"I don't know," she returned; "there is something on my mind like a load that I can't shake off."

"Hooh! nonsense, Ellen; sure I'll be back afore day; an' if you're afeard to stay alone, I'll send Molly Horan over to sleep in the corner."

"I'm not afeard," Mick; I know God is strong, an' I never seen any thing worse than myself; but there's something over me very weighty."

After a few moments pause, Michael replied, "Ellen, dear, I'd willingly stay if I could, but you know I promised to help my cousin Peter; you wouldn't want me to be worse than my word."

"I'd be sorry to do it, Mick; but, any way, this night work is bad. I wish you didn't promise."

"There's no help for spilt milk, Ellen, an' sure its no harm for a man to strive to make the best of his crop, an no price for the corn now."

"Sure he's no worse off nor another, an' he might be content."

"Maybe if you had five or six childer, you wouldn't take it so quite" (quiet).

"It's agin the law, an' you'll not say, Mick, that's right."

"It's a bad law, Ellen, that keeps a man from making the best of his crop."

"That may be - I can't say to the contrary; but, Mick, dear, its the law of the land, an' ought not to be broke."

_ "The ould misthress is comin out in you there," said Michael, laughing. "She didn't know of what shifts poor people is often put to."

"She knew it was wrong to break the law," replied Ellen.

---

[1] Published in *The Dublin Penny Journal*, June 8th 1833. Initialled W. - Ed.

"But sure it's no sin to trick a gauger, Ellen. The misthress was a good woman, but she couldn't know everything."

"She knew what was right and what was wrong, an' we'd not go astray if we minded her bidding," said Ellen, gravely.

"Well, Ellen, acushla, we'll mind it agin; I can't help it this turn; the time is come I must be goin, benaght lahth (blessing be with you). I'll send Molly over;" and taking a tender leave of his wife, the young man hurried out of the house.

Ellen had been brought up about an old lady who resided near the house of her parents, and was, therefore, superior in education and manner to most girls in her station. On the death of her mistress, she was possessed of a few pounds, and having been, for some time, attached to Michael Cooper, they were married. Michael was far inferior to his wife in point of information. He rented a snug cabin, with a few acres of land; but a handsome face and good humour were much greater recommendations in the eyes of an inexperienced girl, and after nearly a year's trial, she did not repent her choice. They were seldom separated, until he was, a short time previous to this period led to assist some of his friends in the process of illicit distillation, and his wife's remonstrances were generally silenced in the manner above related.

"The blessin of God about all here," said Molly Horan, on raising the latch of the door, soon after Michael's departure.

Ellen was sitting where he had left her, one hand supporting her head, and traces of tears were visible on the long dark lashes that shaded her brilliant eyes. She started on hearing the woman's voice, and endeavoured to appear cheerful; but Molly was not so easily imposed on.

"Sure, alanna," she said, "ye needn't let throuble come near ye; the masther (the mother of God save 'im) wont be long out."

"I hope not," was Ellen's reply.

"Asy, dear; ye'll not be so bad out here, if the man goes out awhile," said Molly, with a laugh. Then sinking her voice to a kind of confidential murmur, added, "sure, dear, ye couldn't think a man id be always in the corner fornenst his wife."

"I wouldn't wish it, Molly."

"Faix a hagar, it'd be queer - many's the place a man must go from day-light tal night."

"I don't care a pin, only for the place he's gone to, Molly."

"An sure, avourneen, he's as well there as in his own dacent house (God bless it), an' lashins of fun he'll have wi' the boys. Louersha hene,[1] but a still-house is the pleasant place!"

"But Molly, it is not right to be going against the law."

Molly had, on entering, seated herself in the chimney-corner, her knees nearly touching her chin, charged her dudeen (short pipe), and was puffing away with great

[1] A strong affirmation of assent.

perseverance; she now took it from her mouth, and giving Ellen a look of unqualified amazement, exclaimed: "Chrish chriestha erin, agin the law! Well, but that bates Banagher any way! Sure it's no sin to make a dhrop of potteen. Och hone! God forbid! there's plenty on our poor sowls widout that."

It was in vain that Ellen endeavoured to explain that a breach of the law was wrong. Molly's ideas of breaking the law were different - she affirmed, that "if a body didn't murder, or rob, or steal, they needn't care for all the polis (police) in the world."

Ellen ceased to speak on the subject; but commending her husband to the protection of the Divine Being, in whom she firmly trusted, at the usual hour went to bed, but not to sleep, thinking every sound was Michael's approach, until the light of a spring morning shone through her chamber; then, overcome by watching, she sank into an uneasy slumber.

After having dispatched Molly Horan to his wife, Michael pursued his way to the still-house. He was sincerely attached to Ellen, but thought her opinions of the law too strict; yet, though delighting in the scenes that usually go forward at those places, he would have stayed at home to gratify her, were it not for the promise he had given his cousin, and that his assistance was necessary on that night; but he determined that this was the last time he would go to such a place. While immersed in these reflections, he arrived at the water's edge; the still-house was situated on an island not far from the shore of a large lake, nearly surrounded by mountains. Michael put his fingers in his mouth, and whistling loudly, was presently answered by a corresponding whistle; he replied; and a boat put off from the island, but so cautiously that the dash of the oars could scarcely be heard even when close to the shore. In a low voice he made himself known, and then entering the frail bark, was ferried over in profound silence.

The fresh night breeze was impregnated by the effluvia of fermenting grains that were strewn around the still-house, a miserable cabin with scarcely any covering, and in which, on that night a number of persons were congregated, as the spirits were to be conveyed to the mainland before the morning light.

The murky glare of a large turf fire threw an unearthly shade on the countenances of the men who were, some standing, some sitting, and others recumbent around it, most of them in that state of inebriation denominated half-seas-over, one party smoking another with a pack of cards so much soiled as made it difficult to distinguish spades from diamonds, or clubs from hearts, playing at "five and ten," on their knees; while a third set were attending to the process of distillation.

Michael was made ample amends for the silence of the boatmen, by the universal roar of "Ceade mille phaultha." that burst forth on his entrance.

"An' what kep ye so long?" cried one.

"Och! what knowledge ye want; sure his wife couldn't part 'im, ye fool," replied another.

"It's happy fur them has a purty wife," said a third.

"Let t'yer bother! roared an old man, who was busied about the still. "Mick, boy, come here, and take this; it'll keep the cowld aff yer heart; there's a hard win (wind) on the lough the night;" and he filled a large vessel with the warm liquid, first putting it to his own lips, adding, "Here's confusion to all gaugers and polis!"

"Amin!" was the general response, while Michael drank off a good part of the contents, then reached the vessel to another, who finished it, and, with a hearty smack, declared it was mild as new milk.

During the next two hours, the vessel was frequently replenished, and the scene of blasphemy and ribaldry that accompanied the carouse, was too disgusting for detail.

Michael was usually a sober man; but the uncontroverted proposition that "evil communication corrupts good manners" was exemplified in him; he was soon in a state, if not of total drunkenness, certainly of carelessness as to what he did.

The hour of midnight had some time passed over, when one of the elder and more seasoned members of the party exclaimed, "Come, come, boys, let t'yer drinkin; its time to work; some of the spirits ought to be on land afore this; the polis might be stirrin, comin on day."

"To— wid the polis," replied another; "what div we care for them? They darn't show their nose. We'd smash their daylight out. Let them come now - we're ready."

"Asy, a hagar, asy," said the first, with a sneer; "brag was a good dog; may be if they were hard by ye'd sing another song. Come, boys, its better be sure nor sarry; get some of the vesshels to the boat."

"Never heed, Thady," responded the other; "the gauger has more sense nor to come near uz. I'd brain the first man that put a foot on the island. Time enough to be goin' yet."

However, the more sober of the party thought Thady was right, and began to remove some kegs to the boat. The first load was safely landed on the opposite shore, and two men remained to convey it away. The boat returned for another freight during a general confusion within the still-house, some singing, others talking loudly, and another set swearing at them to quit their blather, an' mind their business. In the midsts of this babel, a man from the outside rushed in, exclaiming in a voice of terror, "The polis! the polis! Be all that's lovely, they're about the house!"

In an instant there was a dead silence; every one seemed paralysed, and the man who was to have performed such feats a short time previously, slunk into a corner behind some sacks. However, the consternation was but momentary; it was determined to resist; the door was made fast with sacks, and whatever they could heap against it. But the assailing party were too strong; the house was forced, and, as the police were entering, one of them was knocked on the head by some person near the door; he fell, and never spoke again. This so enraged his comrades, that a general massacre would have followed, had not the officer used all his influence to prevent it; and finally the greater part of the distillers were made prisoners - when daylight appeared, conveyed to the man-land, and from thence to the jail of the county town.

"Molly! Molly! are you there?" cried Ellen, starting from a disturbed sleep, when the morning was far advanced.

"I'm here, a-lanna, sure I wouldn't leave ye," replied Molly going to the bed-side.

"Is Mick come back? Is it far in the day?"

"He didn't come yet dear; I doubt it's breakfast-time."

"Molly, he said he'd be in before day; I dread something happen'd him."

"What makes ye say that, acushla; maybe they couldn't get the licher (liquor) all to land in time."

"There's that over me I can't shake it off, Molly, I'm sure something happened."

"Lord betune uz an' harum! Don't say the likes of that, dear; sure God is strong."

"I know it, Molly, an' my dependence is on Him; only for that, what I feel now would kill me. Och! I wish Mick would be said by me, an' not go any more to the still-house."

"Ah, then, dear, while a man is on the world he must be neighbourly; and, wid the help of God, sorra hap'orth 'ill happen t'im. Come down, an' take yer breakfast; he'll be back in no time."

"God send!" was Ellen's reply, as she accompanied Molly to the kitchen, and sat down to breakfast, of which she scarcely tasted a morsel.

Before the meal was finished, a neighbouring woman entered, and seating herself in the corner, after the usual salutation, began: "Well, any way its happy fur them wasn't in the island last night."

"What happened?" interrupted Ellen, scarcely able to articulate.

"Is id what happened?" continued the woman; "an' is that all ye know if id? Sure myself thought that every one hard id be this."

"Tell me, tell me at once," exclaimed Ellen, while she trembled exceedingly, and became pale as death.

"What's over her?" said the woman, appealing to Molly.

"She's all through-other."

"For the love of God, tell me what you know, an' don't kill me out," cried Ellen.

"They say," replied the woman, "that the gauger an' the polis cum on them in the still-house last night; there was three men kilt, an' the polis tuk an' put them all in jail the day."

She had scarcely uttered the last word, when Ellen fell to the ground in a state of insensibility; and Molly, clapping her hands, set up the Irish cry.

"Sanwell dhe er in! exclaimed the woman, "what's over ye's all?"

But she gained no information from Molly, who continued to clap her hands, and cry, "Wirra strua! wirra strua" God look down on ye poor sowl lyin there!"

"Faix its very quare," said the other. "Any way, Molly, we ought to rise her up, afeard she die on't."

"True for ye, Shusy; sorra one of me knows what I'm doin. The mother of God help her this day!"

And while endeavouring to restore animation, they still continued to talk.

"A-then Molly, dear, what's over her at all that makes her this way."

"Musha, then, shure ids no wonder, Shusy, an' Mick Cooper to be in the still-house last night, an' six kilt."

"Ids three I toul ye, Molly; an' ye say Mick was makin' a drop of potteen?"

"I didn't say no sich a thing; but a body might go to give a hand to a friend. I dread poor Mick's gone to jail, or he'd be home afore this."

"Ne'er a doubt of it, Molly; every individual, only two or three that run away, was tuk up."

"An' them that's kilt," said Molly; "sure there's no good to take them."

"Wirra, wirra! what news ye tell uz!" replied Shusy.

"No doubt the corner (coroner) 'ill sit on them the day, an' we'll hear all about id."

In some time, poor Ellen revived, and notwithstanding all the women's efforts to dissuade her, set out to learn the fate of her husband; and Molly, whose curiosity was aroused to the highest pitch, accompanied her.

They then learned the true state of the case, which was even more terrible to the afflicted wife than her worst fears had anticipated.

The policeman was killed, and one of his companions swore positively that Michael Cooper gave the blows that deprived him of life. He was, therefore, to be tried for the murder at the ensuing assizes. However, as Cooper solemnly affirmed he had not any missile in his hand, nor was he near the door at the time the blows were given, which some of the men could corroborate, his friends entertained sanguine hopes of his acquittal; and poor Ellen, though suffering great anxiety, at times felt hope that all would end well.

The lady by whom she had been brought up had early instilled the duty of submission to the Divine will; and though, in this instance, the trial was a severe one, yet the good seed produced some fruit, and she was enabled to bear with a degree of fortitude which excited Molly's admiration, who used to say to her cronies, that "sorra one of her ever seen the peel (equal) of Mick Cooper's wife for a fine sodger (soldier), an' has sich dependence out of God; sure she ought to win."

In a short time after the murder the trial came on, and the event showed the futility of human hopes. The prosecution was sustained with great pertinacity; the witness repeatedly swearing he could not possibly be mistaken as to the identity of the prisoner.

Poor Michael's appearance and manner interested a crowded audience; and, therefore, when after a considerable interval, the verdict guilty was returned, a general murmur of compassion ran through the court, which was succeeded by a breathless silence, while the awful sentence of death and dissection was pronounced by the Judge with a faltering tongue and glistening eye. Then a shriek so heart-rending burst forth from under the dock as appalled the stoutest, and added to the general sympathy.

It was poor Ellen; she had, with a strong effort, controlled her feelings until the termination of her earthly hopes; then her anguish became too great for her endurance; with this cry of despair she sank senseless into the arms of the bystanders, and was borne out of court to the house of a friend, where, after a tedious interval, animation returned, which was quickly followed by the birth of a still-born child; fever and delirium succeeded, and for a long time the widowed wife and childless mother remained on the confines of eternity.

Michael suffered the extreme penalty of the law with great firmness; he had heard the tale of his wife's sufferings, from which at that period it was hourly expected she would be released. He expressed a hope of being reunited to her in a better world, and, to the last, solemnly protested his innocence of the crime for which he was about to pay the forfeit - warned his hearers to avoid bad company, saying, though he blessed God he was not guilty of murder; yet, had he taken his wife's advice, and refrained from going to the still-house, he should not then be in that awful situation.

The last rays of the glorious summer's sun was sinking behind the distant mountains, and glowing with mellowed tint on the ivy-covered walls of a ruined building that stood in the centre of a lonely burial ground. No sound was heard, but the call of the rail from the meadows, and the occasional scream of waterfowl that disported on an adjacent sheet of water.

The path that led from the road to this cemetery was, on this evening, trod by a female, muffled in a large cloak, she walked with slow step and down-cast eyes, entering the abode of death by a breach in the dilapidated wall; she knelt by a verdant grave, and her lips poured forth a fervent prayer, the subject of which was only known to the hearer of prayer and her own soul; her bosom heaved, tears coursed each other down a beautiful but pallid face, and throwing herself on the damp grass, she wept long and bitterly.

While thus, as it were, holding communion with departed spirits, a man came up, and regarding her for a moment with a look of intense interest, bend down, touched her arm, and said, in a low voice, "Ellen!" She did not appear to notice this appeal; it was repeated in a more distinct manner, and she replied, "Och! let me alone for a minute; sure I kept up for a long time, an' it'll do me good to be near him now. Och! Mick, dear, dear, why did you leave me alone in the world."

The man brushed a tear from his eye, and said, in a voice choked by emotion, "Ye're not alone, thanks be to God. Look up, Ellen; don't ye know me?"

This seemed to rouse her; she started up exclaiming, "Mick, dear, are you come to take me?" and would have fallen to the earth had not Michael (for he was alive and well) caught her in his arms.

A third person was added to the group; Molly Horan had followed them; by her assistance, Ellen was in some time restored to consciousness, and, in a few words, convinced of the reality of what had the appearance of a supernatural visitation.

When Michael's body, after undergoing the sentence of the law, was taken down, the surgeon of the infirmary, who had known him a long time, caused the remains to be instantly removed, and used all means to resuscitate it, in which he was beyond his most sanguine hopes, successful; but as the man's return to life must be kept secret, he had a coffin, well screwed down, given to his friends with strict orders not to open it, which as the lower orders have a dread of seeing a mangled corse, there was no danger of their doing.

By the unremitting attention of the surgeon, Michael and his wife (though she was ignorant of his existence) began slowly to recover; and when Ellen was strong enough, she removed to her own house, confident that the disfigured remains of her lamented husband were resting among those of his ancestors.

On the evening that Ellen went to the churchyard, Michael returned to his house. Molly Horan, who had continued to reside with Ellen, was, on his appearance, dreadfully terrified; but, after some time, she recovered her reason. Michael followed his wife to his supposed grave and the meeting, already related, took place - Molly saying, "Sure Ellen couldn't but win, she had such great courage an' dependence out of God."

As Michael could not publicly remain in the country, they soon emigrated to the New World, and there, amid a blooming of spring, enjoyed as much happiness as is the lot of human nature.[1]

---

[1] Note: The resuscitation of a person who has been executed by hanging, or, strangulation, may appear too much out of the ordinary course of things: but there are several instances of such on record, and we have no doubt that others have been restored, of which no account, for obvious reasons, have been given.

35
The Garvarry[1]

"He rose - and slowly, sternly, thence withdrew,
Rage in his eye, and threats ———"
BYRON

"I'lllave it to my death, Nancy, me or mine never done im or one belongin' to im a pinsworth of harum;" said the Widow Kelly, one day while gossiping at the house of Nancy Brady.

"Nera bit but its a wondher what makes him be so much agin ye," replied Nancy.

"The Lord forgive im an' every body that leans on the widdy and the orphant, Nancy; but there's one above lookin' at all this," resumed the widow.

"The Mother of God look down on every poor sinner thats in disthress," said Mrs. Brady, with a glance of secret satisfaction round her well-filled and furnished house.

"Och amin, achiernah," replied the widow, "an' the Lord maintain goodness to every one that has it."

"A then, Mary, mysel doesn't think the masthers a real gantleman at all; the ould sort is ever an' always good to the tenants an' the poor," said Nancy.

"Faix an' ye're not wrong," replied Mary. "I know more about im nor ye can, that's only a new comer; sorra one dhrop of gentle blood in his body, good or bad."

"Musha is it in arnest ye are," cried Mrs. Brady; and suspending the evolutions of her spinning-wheel, drew her stool closer to that of the widow, who continued.

"Nera word of lie I'm tellin' ye, shure I'm lookin' at im since he was the bulk of a sod of turf."

"Well, well," replied Nancy, "an as grand as he is."

"Troth an' its jist so," resumed the widow, "His father was a poor man, an' lived out of the end of the house[2] wid my father, God rest his sowl an' as I hard, for I wasn't very big at the time, Paddy Brian hadn't cow or calf."

"Its lek that's this man's father," interrupted Mrs. Brady.

"Yis dear, yis, his father shure enough; an' they say a coire (kind, friendly,) man he was, that struggled hard to rear the family."

"An' what way did they get all the riches?"

[1] Published in the *Dublin Penny Journal*, July 20th 1833. Initialled, W. - Ed.

[2] Living out of the end of a house, means that one cabin is joined to the other.

"Ner a one of me knows; some says the man here, that's Jemmy we used to call'm, got a purse of money in a fair green; more say they ketched a leprehaun[1] and more that it was they got a crock of gould in undher a big stone on the bottom of an ould ditch."

"Any way they have the money," said Mrs. Brady.

"Sorra doubt," replied the widow, "an' cute enough they wer in the beginnin' gettin' up by degrees muryagh, (as it were,) until they tuk land, an' got cows, an' calves, an' sheep, an' horses."

"O wirra what luck some has beyant others," cried Nancy, with a long drawn sigh; "but Mary, dear, how did the man here get it all?"

"Ye see a hegar, he was ever an always cute, so afore they let an to have money, he got the brothers an' sisters all marret an' out of the way; the ould couple died - he left the place, tuk this land an' built the house, an' from plain Jemmy Brian, he's now James O'Brien, Esquire?"

"Its lek, Mary, ye're from the same place."

"Sure, dear, didn't I tell ye his father lived out of the end of the house wid us."

"I mind ye did; an' to be shure ye cum wid im to this land."

"No, avourneen, I was marret an' livin' here long afore he got it, forreer that iver he cum to it at all."

This man's rise in life had been fully as sudden as described by the Widow Kelly; how he came by the means was only known to himself, though various rumours were afloat relative to it. He took leases of large tracts of land, which he again set to others, and became an extensive middleman, as they are termed in Ireland.

Though an illiterate man, Brian was clever; and as wealth poured in, he became haughty and overbearing; he wished to have his humble origin forgotten, but the residence of Kelly's wife on his land was a bar to that, and like the wicked Haman, his wealth and affectation of gentility availed him nothing, so long as Mary Kelly lived near to remind him of what he had been; it was a canker to all his enjoyment. But though in other respects a clever man, in this instance Mr. Brian acted foolishly; instead of conciliating this woman, he took every opportunity of opposing and irritating her, trying all means to get them off his land but in vain. At length Kelly died, and the unrelenting landlord resolved to get rid of the widow. His cruelty need not be detailed; suffice it to say he succeeded in turning the poor woman and her son adrift on the world; and he chuckled in the idea that all traces of his origin would now be obliterated.

But the Mighty Being who had said, "Leave thy fatherless children. I will preserve them alive; and let thy widows trust in me." did not forsake this victim of oppression. A farmer in the neighbourhood, though far from rich, and with a large family, could not look

---

[1] A leprechaun is said to be a lilliputian figure, with a scarlet coat and red nightcap. If any person could be fortunate enough to lay hold on one of those beings, he would be made rich, for they have an intimate knowledge of concealed treasure.

at this act of cruelty, in the depth of winter, unmoved. He gave the widow a cabin with a small garden, and took her son into his employment, and thus defeated O'Brian's plan of sending her out of the country. She endeavoured to assist her son in supporting themselves, by spinning, and buying sheepskins in the season, the wool of which she sold at different markets in the neighbourhood. At this period Pat, the widow's son, was a lad of seventeen, sober and well conducted, esteemed by all who knew him.

Some short time after the conversation above-mentioned between the widow and Mrs. Brady, the latter lost a grown up son; and as they were people considered well to do in the world, crowds came to the wake, knowing it would be a plentiful one, and they were not disappointed, saying to each other, "Any way Phil Brady was givin' his little boy a raal dacent wake, an' no doubt there'd be a fine funeral."

Now Nancy Brady, who sat at the head of the table on which the body of her son was laid out, declared to all who addressed her with the unvarying salutation, "I'm sorry for yer throuble;" that "the heart idin her was breaken' out an' out; and och, och, what did she do to desarve such a crish!" But still Mrs. Brady could cry with the criers, smoke with the smokers, and talk with the talkers.

As the persons, conduct, and affairs of their neighbours, usually form the subject of conversation among the lower orders, and indeed to their shame be it recorded, even of many in the higher classes of life, on the second night of the wake, one subject that occupied a group of idlers around Mrs. Brady, was Mr. Brian and his family.

"A then d'ye tell me so, Darby," said a man, at the same time handing him a pipe; "an' they're of that great lord's family; friends no doubt?" (Friends, as thus used, means relations.)

"Sorra word of lie in id, Ned," replied Darby, "I hard the masther tellin' id to a gantleman."

"What's that ye hard, Darby?" asked Mrs. Brady, who only caught the latter part of what he had said.

"The masther tould a gantleman, an' I by," replied Darby, "that he's related to the great lord of the same name that lives some place in Munsther."

"Nough more a rubbhul than ig ma chauth," (what a tail my cat has,) exclaimed Nancy; "related to a lord, anagh" (an expression of doubt and scorn).

"An'why nat," exclaimed another woman, "some of the lords themselves is no great things."

"Great things here or there," replied Mrs. Brady, "sorra one dhrop of lord's blood in his body."

"How d'ye know, did ye ever see the colour of id?" asked Darby.

"No nor yersel, no more nor me, avourneen," she answered; "an' afther all its truth I'm tellin."

"Maybe ye know, as they know the horses, be the mark of mouth," returned Darby.

"No, dear, nor as ye know the sheep," she retorted; "an' faix its asy to know the good ould stock, the raal blood, from the upstart."

"Sure,Nancy Brady, ye would'nt be afther allegatin' (affirming) sich a thing of the masther," said Darby.

"What?" she demanded.

"That he's an upstart."

"Mind it was yersel said id, Darby Dolan," interrupted Mrs. Brady; then in a lower tone she addressed the woman next her; "an' may be if it was sed its no lie."

"Why so?" asked the woman.

"Bekase," replied Nancy, and she entered into a half whispering detail of the conversation she had with the Widow Kelly.

Darby, who was Mr. Brian's shepherd, and pretended to be greatly attached to him, listened intently, and hearing some half sentences, exclaimed, "This is more of Mary Kelly's lies an' stories; may I never die in sin but she'll be sorry fur id yet."

"What lies?" said Mrs. Brady. "Who knows what Mary Kelly tould me?"

"Many's the one'll know id the night," replied Darby; "but mind I tell ye, that gabby lyin' hag'll be sarry, an' may be more wid her."

"Christ chriestha er in! Darby," said Nancy, "sure ye would'nt go for to tell the masther that I sed any thing agin'm. Och, och, God forbid avourneen; an' I didn't think it no harum to tell what Mary Kelly sed on my own flure."

"Sed here or sed there," replied Darby, after having heard all and much more than was advanced by the widow, "I wondher, Nancy Brady, ye'd sit by an' listen to sich lies of a man that's givin' ye good bread."

A day or two after the wake, the shepherd took the opportunity of his master looking at some sheep, to enter into conversation. After the usual commendations of the stock, and praises of his own carefulness, he began: - "That was a sore crish the Bradys got, sir, God look on them."

The master gave an assenting nod, and Darby continued. "An' maybe they hadn't a great wake an' a fine funeral, sir, God rest the poor boy's sowl."

"Had they," was the concise reply.

"Well, well, sir, any way but the women's gabby; mysel never hard the likes of them fur lies and stories."

"What lies and stories, Darby?" said Mr. O'Brian, seating himself in an attitude that the shepherd well knew was the prelude to a regular gossip; for though usually keeping his people at a great distance, there were times when Mr. O'Brian could lay aside his dignity, and return to his old vulgar habits; and the servants knew how to lead him to this; for it is astonishing how quick sighted they in general are to the foibles of their employers. Darby did not reply till his master had repeated the question, then with a knowing shake of the head, he answered, "Faix it'd be onpossible to mind the half of what a body hears, an' God knows there was a power of talk at the wake."

O'Brian perceiving the shepherd had something to tell, remarked, "But sure Darby, you might remember part of what you heard; no doubt the women were talking of their neighbours."

"Yemay say that any way, sir; and maybe of them id didn't become them to mintion. Musha what mather to me or the like's of me who a body's related to, or about family at all at all."

"Was there any person speaking of my family?" interrupted Mr. O'Brian, for on this point he was very sensitive.

"There's no use in talkin, sir; any way, ye may defy the gabbiest in the parish."

But O'Brian's curiosity was completely aroused, and he insisted on knowing what was said. This was just the point the wily shepherd wished to bring him to; and, with seeming reluctance, he told all, and much more than the Widow Kelly had said to Nancy Brady, and also that it had been a public subject of conversation at the wake.

Scarce able to articulate, so much was he overcome with rage and mortification, Mr. O'Brian declared that he would give fifty pounds, nay, a hundred, to have it in his power to punish Mary Kelly.

"An' sure ye can do id for very little, sir," said Darby. "Can't ye put her in the Bishop's coort, for diffimation an' lies;" and, at the same time, he put his tongue on the other side of his cheek.

To this gibering speech, the master made no reply; but, on turning away, he reiterated his former declaration that he would do any thing to punish the Kellys, and drive them from the country.

Immediately after this, there was a new subject of conversation in the neighbourhood; two of Mr. O'Brian's fat sheep had been stolen; and Darby, according to his own account, said nothing of it for a time, until he searched the bounds, and made every inquiry, but to no purpose. It may be imagined the master was greatly exasperated; he insisted his people should clear themselves. With one voice, they all declared they would take the Garvarry[1] on their innocence. "And the Garvarry you shall certainly take," said O'Brian; "I'll send for it this day."

A young man, who witnessed the swearing, was thus accosted by his mother, on his return: - "Well, Jack, ye wor at Mr. O'Brian's the day."

"Yes," replied he; "an' a sore place it was. The Garvarry cum in it (was brought there), an' great swearin there was."

"Musha, Jack, dear," said another, "what sort of a thing is id at all."

---

[1] St. Barry's Staff, commonly called the Garvarry, it is firmly believed can detect perjury, and that whosoever has the hardihood to swear falsely with it around his neck, is punished by having his face disfigured, so that few are found bold enough to perjure themselves on the Garvarry.

"The very moral (model) of a walking staff, only longer, an' a crook of brass on the tip, wid an ugly smush (face) on id. O wirra! if ye seen it!"

"An' they say," remarked a third, "that if a body swears in the wrong wid that about his neck, his face'll be turned to the back of his head, God bless the mark!"

"Sorra word of lie ye heard," replied Jack.

"A-then, did Darby Dolan put it in his nick?" asked the young man's mother.

"Sure enough he did," said Jack.

"Well, well!" she replied, "but that bates the little dish! The Lord keep us, any way!"

"What makes ye say that?" inquired her son.

"Nothin, dear - och, nothin, avourneen. - God forbid I'd say anythin of e'er a one."

"Isn't them two fine skins I bought for ye," said Pat Kelly, to his mother, one evening, after returning from work.

"Ne'er a better, acushla," she replied; there's great work on them; from who did ye buy them?"

"Sorra, one of me knows - I never seen him afore."

"Well, the morrow, God willin, I'll go to the market, an' its little of the wool I'll have back wid me; an' then, Pat, a hashki[1] ye can buy a new breeches at the fair."

"Ne'er a one of me very bad for them mother; its yersel wants a cloak comin on the winther. Sorra stich I'll buy till ye get it."

"Och! the Mother of God reward ye, avourneen, that always thinks more of the old woman nor yersel. Och! the Lord forgive the man that left the widdy an' the orphant this a way."

"Never heed, mother; he'll not be a pinsworth betther, nor we worse, the last day, for this."

"Och! Pat, alanna ma chru (child of my heart), the Lord fit an' prepare uz for that day, any way."

"God 'save all here!" said Darby, who entered at the same moment.

"God save ye, kindly," replied the widow. "Wont ye cum by to the fire, Darby."

"Sorra bit of me could, Mary; id's a fine evening, thank God. The woman wants a couple of pound of wool; have ye e'er a grain."

"There isn't two betther skins in the counthry nor the little boy bought yesterday;" and she brought forth one to show the length of wool.

"I'll tell the woman," said Darby, and left the house.

He had not been long gone, when Mr. O'Brian and another man returned with him, demanding entrance to search for stolen goods. The poor widow was thunderstruck, and could scarcely say, "Cum in; the nera haporth ever we stole."

"Who says there's any thing stole here?" cried Pat, seizing and brandishing a stick. "I'll tell them to their teeth they're liars."

---

[1] A term of endearment.

"Asy, Pat, alanna - asy, avourneen; don't do any thing rash; let them come in, what do we care, an' nothin they want here?" said the widow, holding her son's arm.

"Come, come, fellow," cried Mr. O'Brian, "we have a warrant to enter. Constable, do your duty."

The constable entered, and seizing on the sheepskins, took them to Mr. O'Brian, who, pointing to the letters, J.O'B., with which they were branded, said they were his property.

"They're mine; I ped for them," replied Pat.

"You'll answer that to the Justice," said the constable; "so come along."

And taking Pat by the arm, with Darby carrying the skins, they set out to the magistrate, who lived within a short distance. Here both O'Brian and his shepherd identified the skins; and, as the young man could not tell who he had bought them from, he was committed to prison, to abide his trial for stealing sheep, the skins of whom were found in his possession.

"And now," thought O'Brian, "I'll at last get rid of this woman and her son; he will, at all events, be transported for life."

It would be vain to attempt a description of what the widow Kelly suffered during the period that elapsed between her son's imprisonment and the assizes. Most people thought his conviction certain, because he could not prove the purchase of the skins, or who he bought them from. Pat Kelly bore an excellent character, and was pitied by the whole neighbourhood. They knew O'Brian's dislike to the widow; and there were some who feared this was a plan laid by wicked people to gratify him by having them sent out of the country.

The wretched mother ceased not night and day to implore the succour of heaven. "Och!" she would say, "we have no other dependence now. My boy, my fine boy, that never did nothin out of the way, to be murthered this a-way!" And Nancy Brady constantly affirmed that, "only they all tuk the garvarry, she'd say some of the min about the land done id; but sure, if they did, their face id be turned round, the Lord save every one!"

So that, though all thought Pat Kelly innocent, they agreed that appearances were greatly aginst him. "An' God look on poor Mary!" they said; "She'll not live one day afther him."

"Good news! good news!" cried a young man, son to the farmer under whom the widow Kelly lived, rushing into the house almost out of breath. "Good news! Poor Pat Kelly's freed; he's innocent." He could utter no more.

"God be thanked!" said his mother; "the widow and orphan, as well as the innocent, are in His blessed keeping. I knew the poor boy had no hand in it. But how was he cleared, Harry?"

"Its little short of a miracle, mother; you'll hardly believe me when I tell you." And he went on to narrate the incidents which were briefly thus: - A man, who lived not far from O'Brian's was, on the evening previous to the assizes sitting at the fire with his wife; he appeared to labour under much uneasiness; she asked what ailed him, and he replied, by desiring her to go into the room for a little, and not come out until he called her. She wondered at this, but obeyed. Now, the room was a small space, close to the fire, the partition wall of which was little more than breast high. The woman had scarcely got inside this frail enclosure, when the man in a tolerably loud voice, began thus: -

"Wall! dear wall! listen to me, an' mind every word I say. I'm in great trouble, wall; there's somethin on my mind that I swore not to tell to man or woman; but, wall, dear, I'll tell id t'ye. Och, och! wall, I'm afeard the Widdy Kelly's little boy 'ill be kilt for stealin them sheep, and he not doin id at all. Darby Dolan is the man that done id; I'll leave id to my death, wall, but he is; he kilt the sheep, an' tuk the meat to a fair, an' he swore me to bring the skins to a market, an' get a strange man to sell them to Pat Kelly, an' no one else; for he heard the masther say, he'd be bether pleased nor twenty sheep to get somethin agin them Kellys, to hunt them, like red shanks, out of the counthry, bekase Mary Kelly cud tell he was no gentleman. An' this is the truth, wall, dear; an' ids but little Darby giv me for helpin 'im; but och! I'll never go to heaven if anythin is done to the poor boy, an' me knowin all about id. So, wall, dear, save 'im if ye can; it'll save my poor sowl, an' I'll leave ye my blessin."[1]

The woman lost no time in taking the necessary steps to save Kelly. Darby was apprehended on the above testimony, and convicted; he made no defence; and, to the joy of the whole court, a very severe sentence was passed upon him.

Mr. O'Brian was so much ashamed of the whole transaction that he left the country for some time, and ceased to persecute the widow, who, with her son, was more than ever respected by the neighbours. And, from this circumstance, the Garvarry fell considerably in the estimation of the upholders of its infallibility.

---

[1] The murderers of a gentleman in the County of — were discovered by the man's telling the circumstances to the wall, his wife being within hearing.

36

Mary Carr, or the Abduction and Rescue[1]

Is there a human form, that bears a heart -
A wretch! a villain! lost to love and truth!
That can, with studied, sly, ensnaring art,
Betray a maiden's unsuspecting youth? — BURNS.

The brilliant sun of a fine morning in August was beaming into a cabin that stood on the side of a retired road. A pole stuck in the thatch, from which depended a rusty horse shoe, indicated the trade of the owner; and in a small hole, intended to represent a window, a fractured jug and footless glass, as plainly as hieroglyphics could do, told that the weary traveller, or determined sot, might be accommodated with mountain dew - in plain language, poteen whiskey.

On this morning the smithy exhibited, in a more than usual degree, the want of regularity. There had been some merry-making in the neighbourhood, at which the heads of the house spent the previous night, and every thing, to use a common phrase, was through other. The master of the house had, after a short sleep in his clothes, arisen, and since that more than once paid a visit to the spirit store of his prudent wife. Some young men, who had been of the night party, dropped in; spirits was called for, as the prelude to a regular drinking bout, when the tramp of a horse was heard, and a loud call, "Is there any one widin," brought the smith to the door.

A man on horseback, with a female on a pillion behind him, required to have a shoe made for his horse, who stripped one, and, in consequence, was lame. But the smith had no coals, therefore how could he make a shoe. The man said he must proceed on his journey, when Vulcan, in a voice rendered almost inarticulate by inebriation, declared, "that poor baste would be entirely knocked up afore they had thravelled a mile iv ground."

"No help for that same," replied the other; "sure I can't be stanin' here all day wid a finger in my mouth - I must be goin' to the next smith."

"Faix, an' ye'll have a long ride," said one of the men from within.

"Is id far off?" asked the equestrian.

"Far off!" growled the smith - "sorra dacent workman, barrin' myself, widin tin mile iv ye."

"Well, I must only put up wid a botch," said the other.

"Sure, iv I had a handful iv coals, the ne'r a minit I'd be makin' a beautiful new shoe," returned the smith.

"That's live horse an' yell get grass," muttered the horseman - "but where could ye get coals?"

[1] Published in *The Dublin Penny Journal*, September 7th 1833. Initialled 'W'. - Ed.

"Hooh, isn't there lashins an' lavins iv coals in the town there beyant," replied Vulcan, staggering towards the horse.

"Musha, and what news ye tell the dacent man, ye drunken brute," exclaimed the mistress of the smithy, rushing out and giving her good man a push towards the door; "go long into the house, doesn't himself know there's plinty iv every goodness in that place, but that wont put a shoe on his cliver baste, God bless id, an' sind him safe over his journey. Ye dirty omodhaun, (fool,) ye couldn't think iv sendin' to them that stud yer frind many's the time, and when ye wor on the shaughran.[1] God look down on me this day, but I'm in a poor way wid ye." Then elevating her voice to a higher key, added, "here, Judy Casey, cum here, acushla - slip over to the still-house, an' Fardy 'ill give ye as much coal-turf as 'll make a shoe for this honest man's baste."

The appearance of the horseman did not warrant her using the epithet gentleman, and she was obliged to pause literally for lack of breath. Judy Casey, a bare-legged, half-clad girl, with staring fiery looks, emerged from the cabin, and set off across the fields in a sling trot, but had not gone many yards when the mistress hallowed after her not to be a minute away, and then begged the equestrians would alight until a shoe could be made.

The man appeared fatigued, and, besides, the cravings of appetite began to annoy him; he, therefore, gladly availed himself of the opportunity to rest - but, previous to alighting, he said, in the Irish language, to those assembled at the door, that the young girl behind him had run away from her parents; he was now bringing her back, and that they should not mind any thing she might say to the contrary.

This was sufficient to attract all eyes to the female, and the young men of the party openly expressed their admiration, exclaiming, "Nough gan nule a colleen ee" - is she not a handsome girl?" Her conductor, who liked not these expressions, replied, in the same language, to this effect - "handsome is that handsome does," and Mrs. Vulcan added her mite, saying, "daughters were ever a trouble to their parents," as she led the girl to a little gloomy space, partitioned off the kitchen, dignified by the title of the room. The man, knowing he should have to wait some time, enquired whether he could have breakfast, adding - "Faix, thravellin' in a raw mornin's a hungry thing."

"Sorra doubt," replied an old woman, who sat smoking in the corner: "maybe ye'd take a blast iv the pipe, it'll draw the win' (wind) aff yer stomick."

"It's little goodness in one house wid me," said the smith - "but, any way, ye'll be welcome to share iv what we have."

"God look down on the poor, it's little they have in this world at all," rejoined the old woman.

"Thrue fur ye," said the horseman - "the poor is hard crushed - God reward them that laves them so."

"Och, amin!" was the response of the woman.

---

[1] At a loss.

"The times is bad enough, to be shure," said a fine intelligent looking young man, who was leaning against the wall, "but there never was a time, iv one was willin' to work, that he wouldn't be able to keep himself above want an' iv they don't work they have no one to blame."

"Work!" repeated the equestrian, contemptuously - "many's the man lives well an' doesn't do a turn iv work."

"Nera one says agin that," replied the young man, who was called Willy Dolan, "but them is gintlemen."

"No, sorra bit - no more nor yerself."

"Then, barrin' they robbed or stole," said Willy Dolan, "what way could they do it, an' then shure it's hung they'd be."

"There's many's the way iv makin' money widout workin' or robbin' either," said the horseman.

"Bethershin (maybe so)," replied Willy, "but ne'r a one iv them can be honest ways, afther all."

"Be gaura, Willy, it's a murther yer mother didn't make a priest or a counsellare iv ye - sure enough ye'd be a great one," remarked the smith.

"Musha, then, Willy," said the old woman, "but I wondher at ye - what do ye know, that never was tin mile from home, comparin' wid this honest man."

"Every one can tell honesty from roguery, Nelly," replied the young man, "an' it would be well for the world iv every one like us was content to earn his bread in honesty, an' not be lookin' for it in any other way. I say that man's a rogue in his heart that would advise a poor boy to the contrary," and looking defiance at the stranger, he left the house.

"Monam ayeah, but Willy Dolan's grand the day - any way, it is a fine thing to have the larnin'," was the remark of the mistress, as she bustled about preparing the breakfast.

James Carr was what is called a man well to do in the world; he held a large farm, and was competent to manage it. He had married early in life, and when in more humble circumstances, a person superior to himself in birth and education, who, nevertheless, made an excellent wife, and brought up their only child, a daughter, much better than girls in her rank usually are brought up. Mary Carr was, indeed, deserving of the admiration she excited in all who beheld her; a very beautiful and modest girl - the delight of her parents and neighbours.

James Carr's landlord was an absentee, and when Mary was about seventeen his son came to the county to transact some business. He saw Mary, and was charmed by her extreme beauty; he went frequently to her father's and, on conversing with her, found, that though very diffident, she was superior to her young companions. He became much attached to her, and sought every opportunity of explaining his sentiments, but Mary never remained an instant alone with him. He then had recourse to a servant woman of Carr's, whom he bribed liberally to plead his cause, but she was not more successful. Owing to the good instructions of her mother, Mary Carr was well aware that the son of her father's landlord could scarcely be honourable in his intentions to her, and, when pressed by the woman to give him a private meeting, she replied -

"I told you often, Peggy, that it's not right for me to be listening to the like of this - he's not fit for me, nor I for him. What would his father and friends say if they heard it?' "

"Hooh, an' what cud they say, an' let them do their best; shure many's the betther nor him marret a counthry girl; an', the heavens may bless yer purty face, ye're a wife for the fill of his masther. Shure, any way, it's no harum to spake civil to him, God help the poor boy, but he has a sore heart."

But this, and many such speeches, were of no avail. Mary would not see him except in her parents' presence. Peggy, afraid her gains would cease if she gave not the young man some hopes, told many lies; and one night, when Mary was asleep, the wretch cut off a lock of her hair,[1] and gave it to the lover as if sent by her. Transported by this apparent proof of her affection, he determined to brave the displeasure of his family and marry her. He mentioned this to a confidential man who lived on the property. This man was named Paddy, and the bitter enemy of James Carr. He expressed the greatest surprise and sorrow for what his young master was meditating, saying it would surely break the ould master's heart. He used many arguments to convince the young man that the Carr's were taking him in, and that he might have the girl on easier terms than matrimony. In fact, Paddy worked so much on him, that he consented to give up his honourable intentions, and agree to a plan, proposed by his adviser namely, that a horse and pillion should be ready on a certain night, at the end of a wood beyond her father's. "An," added Paddy, "I'll engage to make Peggy decoy her out, ready to thravel - ye'll not appear at all - I'll take her to the place ye know, an' thin I'll warrant she's yer own in spite iv the watch."

It is needless to enter into further particulars - the stratagem was successful, and it was the ruffian Paddy, with Mary Carr strapped round his waist, who arrived at the smith's in consequence of his horse having stripped a shoe.

The breakfast was ready, and still the girl with the coal-turf did not make her appearance, though the mistress declared she would be back in a minute - it was time enough - the day was long, and the young girl was tired, a trifle of sleep would do her good. But notwithstanding this, while bustling about, Mrs. Vulcan more than once muttered, "Sorra be in me, Judy Casey, but iv I had a hand on yer lug, I'd put the life in ye." At length the messenger arrived, and, when taxed with delaying, swore, most vehemently, she did not delay one minute; but the mistress sprung across the floor, and would have laid violent hands on her, did not the bystanders interfere and push Judy out of the house.

Mary Carr was invited to partake of the breakfast, but declined; and when, after many delays, owning to the badness of the fire and the drunkenness of the smith, the shoe was fastened on, she was led to the door by the mistress. Paddy, having already got on horseback, desired the smith to put the girl up behind him. While a chair was bringing out to facilitate her ascent, Mary with a blanched cheek, and a voice tremulous from excess of

---

[1] Fact.

agitation exclaimed - "Ah, for the love of God, good Christians, help - will you see a poor girl dragged from her family by a villain? - oh, you couldn't be Irishmen and stand by to see it done. Help me, and may the great God be on your side in time of need!"

"Hould yer prate," roared Paddy; "don't b'lieve a word she says, boys, it's all lies - put her up behind me."

The smith was about to do so, when Willy Dolan, rushing from the crowd, laid his hand on Vulcan's arm, saying - "Mick Kelly, iv you wish for whole bones, don't put a hand on that girl."

"Why so?" demanded the smith.

"Every why," was the answer.

"I tell you, boys, not to heed her," cried Paddy.

"An' I tell ye, boys," exclaimed Willy Dolan, "that's the liar, and the black villain into the bargain; I tell ye she'll never sit on one horse wid ye while I can handle this," and he flourished a stout shillelah with great desterity.

"An', wid the help iv God, that wont be long," said Paddy, pulling a pistol out of his bosom, and ere any person was aware of his intention, firing at Dolan, but, missing the object of his aim, the shot took effect on a young man standing at the extreme edge of the crowd, who, with a loud scream, fell to the ground. For an instant the people appeared as if paralysed, so sudden had been the shot, but they soon rallied.

"Revenge, revenge," shouted Willy Dolan, and in an instant half a dozen cudgels were raised against Paddy, who wisely considered it vain to contend, and, setting off at full gallop, was soon beyond the reach of his enemies.

On hearing the shot Nelly left her place in the corner, and, running up to where the young man was lying, called out that the decent boy was killed, and, clapping her hands, set up the usual cry, in which she was joined by the mistress and Judy Casey.

"Is there any life in him?" asked one of the men.

"Sorra dhrop - he's dead as mutton, an' bleedin' like a pig," replied Nelly.

"Oh, wirra, wirra, what luck my poor cabin had the day," said the hostess; "sorra's name the mudherin' ruffian didn't go some other place an' get a shoe made."

"Ye may thank nobody for that but yerself," retorted her husband.

"Don't bother us, ye brute," she continued, "there's throuble enough at our dour; och, och, who'll tell Nanny Gilaspy that her little boy's a stiff corpse."

" 'An' more was the pity," replied Nelly; "lowersha,[1] it's himself was the clane boy, an' the fine dancer, sorra his equal ever stud on a flure. O, weera deelish, thanks an' praise be to ye, sweet Saver, but it's a little thing knocks the breath out iv a poor sinner, the Lord prepare us for that minit, amin, a chiernah."

---

[1] A strong affirmative.

"Where did the fire hit him, Nelly, dear?" asked one of the people who were collected in a ring about the fallen man.

"The ne'er a ha'porth myself sees an him," she answered, "only a little cut in the side iv his neck, God bless the mark."

"Why but ye bring him into the house?" said another.

"Maybeye want us to be mad," answered Nelly; "no one can tich him till the corner (coroner) cums to hould a jury on him."

"Glory be to God," remarked one, "but death's a poor thing. It's little Barney thought this mornin' the minit was so near."

"Thrue fur ye, Pether; no one knows what's afore him in the mornin'; little fear but ids the young id go - there's Lucause bockagh (lame Luke) that'd be no loss, an' shure he wasn't tuk, glory be to ye, sweet Saver," and Nelly gave three distinct knocks on her bare breast with her clenched hand, while with the other she reached a pipe to the girl, adding - "Judy, alanna, run an' put a bit iv a coal in the pipe, the heart is sore widin me."

All this time the smith and his wife were in consultation at the door, she rocking backwards and forwards; at length they seemed to agree, for she called - "Here, Judy Casey, why but ye go in an' ready the house, sorra good ye'll do stanin' there. Ah, boys, dear, isn't it a wondher but one iv ye steps over for Nancy Gilaspy - Lord comfort her sore heart the day. An' shure another of yees ought to run for the corner, an' not let the poor boy, God rest his sowl, be lyin' an the ground all night." Having issued all these orders in a breath, she turned to Mary Carr, who had sunk on the chair, almost unconscious of what was passing round her, so much had she been terrified. The hostess came close to her, saying, "Ah, thin, that was an unlucky man that cum a near my poor cabin the day, Lord reward him." Mary enquired whether any person was hurt. "Hurted?" exclaimed Mrs. Vulcan - "hurted ye say? - faix, there's a dacent mother's son kilt, an' the like never happened at one dour wid me afore."

"Are you quite certain he is killed?" said Mary.

"Seein''s beleevin'," replied the other, catching Mary's arm, and draggin rather than leading her to where the body lay, surrounded by the people, Nelly smoking and talking vehemently. Mary, on not perceiving Paddy, gained more presence of mind, and said, "Why don't you stop the blood?

"There's no use in id an' he dead," replied Nelly, with a deriding sneer.

But Mary was not deterred; she prevailed on the smith's wife to get cold water and cloths to stop the blood, Nelly all the while growling, "Don't make a fool of yourself, Hetty, sorra dhrop in him more nor a stone."

On cleansing the wound it appeared little more than a scratch. They bathed his face plentifully with cold water, and raised his head to the air; still Nelly said - "Let to yer nonsense, the boy's kilt out and out, he'll never stan' on the green grass agin."

However, in a short time, to Nelly's utter amazement, the young man was restored to animation, and was walking towards the house, when his mother rushed up, like a person deranged, followed by men, women, and children. The young man was not injured; the ball slightly grazed his neck, the shock of which, and extreme terror, deprived him of animation. Many were the exclamations of the crowd on Mary's cleverness, and Nelly was loudest in accusing him of being so weak as to be killed by such a thrifle.

When Willy Dolan had left the house, as before mentioned, he went to where the aperture that gave light to the room opened. In fact, he was smitten by the beauty of Mary, and thought, "iv she run away afore, maybe she'll cum wid me." Mary was leaning with her face at the window, and in tears; she was almost in despair, and did not move on seeing him. He said - "Don't cry, Miss, don't be afeared, yer people wont be angry now yer goin' back agin."

"My people!" exclaimed Mary. "What do you mean?"

"Spake asy," said Dolan - "arn't ye goin' back to yer friends, afther runnin' away from them? - but never heed, ye're not the first that done the like, an' no one 'll cast it up to ye."

"And is this the story the villain invented to destroy me," cried Mary; and in a few words she gave an account of the real state of the case. Such is the force of truth, and perhaps coming with more force from the lips of a beautiful girl, that Dolan gave implicit credit to every word, and exclaimed - "Well, well, the thief iv the world, I knew he wasn't good - he'll pay for this;" then, after a short pause, he added, "Iv ye'll depind on me, Miss, I'll do my best to help ye."

"There'ssomething in your face that tells me you will not deceive a poor girl; I will depind upon you, and may God reward you as you deal with me. Only I trusted in God I wouldn't be able to speak to you now, praise to him, he helped me to go through last night."

"May I never sin, if I could desave any girl, an' ye above all the world," in saying so Willy Dolan's fine face was lighted up with a glow of honest affection; he continued, "When they want to put ye up behind the villen agin, go quitely (quietly) to the dour, ax the boys to help ye, an' lave the rest to me; I must be goin' now." He then went among the young men, and put them up to the rescue, which, as has been seen, was happily effected.

We are limited, and therefore cannot dwell much longer on the affairs of the interesting Mary Carr. It was determined she should proceed back to her parents, accompanied by Willy Dolan, of whom Mrs. Vulcan said - "An' ye needn't be afeard, dear, to go wid Willy Dolan, sorra quieter nor dacenter boy in the counthry, for discreteness an' modesty."

However, before the horse could be got, Mary was overjoyed by the appearance of her father and some of his neighbours. Peggy, on seeing the distraction of Mary's parents when she was missed, repented, and acknowledged her share in the transaction. In consequence, a pursuit was instituted, and, happening to take the same road, they intercepted Paddy in his flight from the smith's, which led to the discovery of Mary.

Paddy was tried at the assizes, and punished for his part in the abduction of Mary Carr; and, in the end, she was married to Willy Dolan.

37

Andrew Murray, or The Effects of Gambling[1]

"A, then, isn't id a great wondher fwhat keeps the boys so long the night," said Molly Sheeran to her husband, as they sat by a brilliant fire on a frosty December evening.

"It's arly yet," was his reply.

"Faix, mysel thinks ids far in the night," she continued: "childer, fwhy but ye wash your feet an' go to bed, an' not be fallin' in the fire wid sleep," and she gave four children, who were lolling in the corners, each a shake to rouse them, but they soon relapsed into sleep again without minding her.

"Is all ready fwhen they do cum, Molly?" asked the husband, who was describing figures in the ashes with a bit of a stick.

"To be shure I'm ready," she replied.

"I doubt the money's low enough wid some iv them, an' they're in no hurry," remarked the man, after a pause.

"The nera bisness they have here 'idout money, Bryan - arrigedh sheesh (money down) for me," replied Molly.

"Stick to that," said Bryan, "an' we'll see more afore mornin'."

"Spake iv the divil an' he'll appear," muttered Molly, as footsteps were heard approaching the door, which she opened.

"God save all here but the cat," said the first of two young men who entered.

"God save ye kindly, boys - but fwhere's Andy Murray?" replied Bryan.

"He's comin'," said the other; "he had to steal out unknownst to the mother an' wife. Happy for them has no wife, an' doesn't care for the mother, he may go out an' cum in as he likes."

"Thrue fur ye," remarked Bryan. "Molly, will I fix the place?"

"Fwhy wouldn't ye," she replied, sharply, adding, "monam own dhoul, childer, iv yees don't go to bed this minit but I'll smash every one iv ye."

This threat sent the drowsy children off, and made more room round the fire, to which Molly invited the young men. Bryan, in the mean time, began to fix the place. On the most level spot, near the fire, he placed a basket, with the bottom upwards, on which was laid a door - this was to answer for a table; three stools and two baskets were to form seats for the party. On the temporary table he put a very small candle, in a most primitive candlestick, viz., a large potato made steady; a bit of chalk, and a small parcel, like a soiled book, completed what Bryan termed fixing the place. He then joined the party around the fire, and put a coal in his pipe.

---

[1] Published in *The Dublin Penny Journal*, October 5th 1833. Initialled 'W'. - Ed.

"Have you any thing for us the night, Molly," asked one of the young men.

"Arra, musha, Tim Casey, did you ever see me empty," she replied, with a sneer.

"Och, glory to ye, Molly," said the other, "it's yersel's the posy."

"I'm thankful t'ye, Jem; troth I wouldn't doubt yer good word; my mother, God rest her sowl, said always a good prowidher (provider) was before an arly riser," replied Molly.

"Iv that's the case," said Tim, "giv us a naggin iv the first shot, afore it was christened, Molly, thigendhou (do you understand)."

"Bad scran t'yer impudence, fwhen did I ever do the like - musha, are ye listenin' t'im, Jim."

"Never heed him, Molly, shure he knows ye'd scorn to do sich a turn."

"Nera word of lie ye say, alanna, it's yer own mother cud tell ye the way I was reared, hot an' warm."

"Fwhat a beau yer granny was," interrupted Tim; bring in the fwhiskey, agus bhe dhe husth (and hold yer tongue)."

Another knock at the door prevented Molly's ready reply, and two men were admitted.

"Welcome, boys, welcome," said Bryan; "cum by the fire - Denis, sit here. Andy Murray, I though ye wouldn't cum the night."

"Iv I was sed by others I wouldn't," returned the person addressed, a fine looking handsome young man.

"No doubt the women was for keepin' ye," said Tim Casey, "but Andy, a mock (my son), never heed them - here's that ye may win, boy," and he tossed off a glass of spirits to the sentiment.

This was a challenge; each of the guests called for spirits, and success to Andy Murray went frequently round - the young man could not avoid returning those pledges, and others equally friendly. While the glass went round, Molly had lit the candle, and Bryan, seating himself at the table, called out, "cum, boys, will ye thry yer luck the night," and taking up the soiled parcel, which was a pack of cards, he began to shuffle them.

"Fhwat's to play for? asked the man called Denis.

"Yer choice thing," replied Bryan - "there's a good fat turkey, or a goose, or the herrins, or a piece iv the sheep;"

It may be necessary to explain that rustic gambling is conducted something on the plan of a lottery. The woman of the house has generally one or more of such articles as those above mentioned, which are purchased by the party to play at a price far above their intrinsic value; each purchase is paid for in equal shares, and the winner of one or more games, at five and twenty, or first fifteen, as is previously agreed on, carries off the prize, which in some cases, is sold again to the original proprietor, and again purchased by the gamblers.

"Well, boys," said Denis, "turkey or goose, herrins or mate, most wotes wins the poll?"

"Maybe we'll play for all - best begin wid the first," replied Tim Casey.

"Dunwid ye," was the general response. The turkey was pronounced middling, Molly named a high price, some objected, and she answered - "Pooh, fwhat signifies id betune five, the winner needn't care, an' the losers, dacent boys, doesn't vali a thrifle."

"Right Molly, right, we don't care a straw," said Denis. "Cum boys, sit down, here's Kelly the rake, the raal gambler, that never stopped at nothin' - faint heart never won fair lady."

All took their seats, settled the game, and were about to begin, when Molly spoke - "Asy, boys, avourneen, fwhere's the money - nera card 'll be pled antil I get id; arrigedh sheesh, Loughrea usage, ever an' always in this house."

"The world for ye, Molly," said Tim Casey, "I warrant ye'll mind yer own."

"Small blame to me for that same," she replied, "iv I don't sorra one iv ye'll do id for me."

"O wirra, fwhat a fool ye are," cried Denis.

"Sorra keeroge (beetle) I'll ate any way, avourneen," returned she, while pocketing the money.

The play then commenced, and there was silence, save the regular knocks on the table as each put down their cards. During the second deal Andrew Murray remarked - "Sorra card I'll play in one house wid ye, Bryan, afther the night, iv you don't get a claner deck (pack) - nera one can see the spots - I was near throwin' away the five fingers badly." Amongst rustic gamblers the five of trumps is so called.

The fate of the turkey was soon decided - Denis won. Next came the goose, and it was carried off by Tim. After this a second edition of whiskey went round, and then a lot of herrings were set up.

"Well, Andy, you an' me has no luck at all the night," said Jem.

"The worse luck now, the betther agin," replied Denis.

Andrew Murray spoke little, but the variations of his countenance showed how much he was interested. When he held good cards it was announced by a flushed cheek and sparkling eye, and when the contrary, he became pale as death.

"Hurrah, boys, the fish is mine," exclaimed Tim Casey - "here's the red rogue, let me see who'll bate it," and he threw the knave of diamonds on the board, with such a thump as sent the potato which held the candle dancing on the floor, and left them in darkness.

"Ye'd betther play no more the night, Andy," said Denis, "ye have no luck, an' maybe the women wouldn't look pleasant at ye the morra."

"Never heed me," replied Murray, "I'm a willin' to lose as any one here, an' as able too - no one can hinder me."

"That's a boy," cried Tim, clapping him on the back, "never knock undher to the women, any way."

"Maybe a woman id crow over ye yet, as great a brag as ye are," answered Molly from the corner.

Another and another stake was purchased and played for, still Murray lost; nor would he accede to the proposal of stopping, he must, he said, have another chance. Now Murray held better cards, and at the commencement of the last game for the stake, Denis and he were equal - in fact, the contest was with them, for the others could have no chance. It was plain to see Andrew held good cards from the glow of his countenance, and the nervous haste with which he played them. When each had but one card to play he said to Denis, "Come, I'll lay any bet I have the game."

"May be so," replied the other coolly, "I'm not fond iv swaggerin', but fwhat'll ye hould?"

Murray pulled out five shillings, saying, "There's all I have, put as much agin it, an' Jim keep it tal the game is done."

"O wirra, we're not rich like ye, Andy; that's too much entirely," said Denis.

"I cow d ye any way," cried Murray exultingly.

"That's fwhat no man done, or woman either," said Denis; - "here Jem, hould this again his five shillings, tal we see who'll win."

And now came the tug of war. — Bryan played a heart, (spades were trumps,) - Tim the king of clubs - Jem the ace of hearts.

"Not bad, faix," said Denis.

Murray's turn came next, and he thundered down the knave of trumps, crying, "That's yer sourt - that'll take the pearl off the piper's eye, I b'lieve." He was gathering up the trick, which would have won the wager and the game, when Denis said, "Asy a hegar, asy; I didn't play yet:" and laying down the five of trumps, quietly took up the trick.

It would be impossible for words to depict the dismay of Murray at the issue of the game. He remained as if entranced, with his eyes fixed, and his hand in the position he had placed it when about to take the trick.

"Heads up, Andy," said Tim Casey, "it's all luck boy - yer turn'll come, out here - never fret."

But Andy did not answer - he appeared to be deep in thought: at length, in a low husky voice, he asked who had played the five?

"Is id who pled the five fingers?" repeated Tim. "Ah boys dear d ye hear that? musha is id dhramin' ye are, Andy. Shure did'nt Denis; an' be the same token won yer five shillings."

"I'm not dhramin," said Murray, with self-possession, "I say it was pled before."

"Nonagh (certainly) it was, many's the time the night," replied Bryan.

"But in this last hand I mane," cried Andrew.

"Arra tunder an ages listen t'm, boys," said Denis; "fwhat makes ye say it was pled in this hand? - that could'nt be."

"It was, and ye're a rogue and a cheat," replied Murray.

"Ye're a liar," exclaimed Denis, turning quite pale.

"No but ye re the grey-headed liar, an' sconce (cheat) to boot," shouted Andrew, starting up in a rage; "ye med me beggar my family, ye villen; be this an be that, iv ye don't give me back my money and the herrins, I'll not lave a whole bone in yer skin afore I quit the house." All this was uttered in the highest tones of passion, and catching up a stick that lay near him, he flourished it over his head.

Jem, who was next him, held his arm, saying, "Are ye mad, Andy? sure it was all fair play."

"It was not, Jem; I must have my own, or - and he added a dreadful imprecation - I'll make him an example on this flure."

"Never heed'm boys," muttered Denis, with blanched cheek; "he's mad or drunk; go home to bed boy, an' ye'll be quieter in the mornin'."

"I'll never quit this tal I get my own," cried Murray.

"You'll have a long stay then," returned Denis with a sneer.

"Hand out my money this minnit, or I'll be beatin' ye fwhile I'm able to stan'," roared Andrew, elevating the stick.

"A then Andy Murray," said Molly, catching his arm, "is'nt id a burnin' shame for ye to be afther risin' sich an alligation in any dacent house; go home avick (my son) an' God bless ye."

"I won't go home tal I have satisfaction out iv that ould rogue;" and before any one was aware of his intention, he had thrown Molly off with such violence as laid her flat on the ground - struck Denis such a blow on the head that he fell backwards insensible, and, in the confusion that ensued, repeated the strokes several times. The table was upset, the candle put out, and even in the dark Murray continued to beat the fallen man. At length, by main force, the stick was wrested from him, and Tim said, "Bryan light the candle; ye kilt the man, Andy: och murdher, murdher, he's dead out an' out - keep the door shut Jem."

After a little the candle was again lit, which revealed a most confused scene. On one side lay Molly, half stunned by the fall, groaning with all her might. In another place Denis was extended, really insensible, and bleeding profusely, Tim holding one of his hands, and exclaiming, "O wirra, wirra, sorra dhrop in him good or bad."

"Fwhat's that you say, Tim Casey," cried Molly, starting up; "id can't be there's a man kilt on my flure — och hone, I'm smashed entirely;" and clapping her hands, set up a loud cry.

"Sorra choke ye," said Bryan, "its not bawlin' we want now. Ye med a nice hand iv my place the night, Andy Murray - looka fwhat ye dun." But there was no answer, and on looking up they found the person addressed had left the house, laying Jem, who guarded the door, also prostrate near it.

Andrew Murray was the only child of his parents, an honest, hard-working couple, who endeavoured to do the best they could for him; but being an only child, he was indulged in every possible way, and particularly by his mother. While his father lived the young man was kept pretty much from bad company; but on the old man's death, which happened when Andrew was about the age of seventeen, though he did not neglect his business, yet he indulged more in rustic dissipation than his mother wished; but she comforted herself with the idea that as he got older he would be more settled. She used to say, - "Young boys is ever so - he'll be settled out here fwhen he's marret."

Andrew was very handsome, possessed an unbounded flow of spirits, was good tempered, (rather an uncommon quality for a pet,) and, as his fond parent constantly affirmed, "as fine a dancer as ever stud on a flure;" - so that he was a welcome guest at every merry-making - the result of which was, that he married before he had completed his nineteenth year, and his mother boasted that her hopes were realized, for some time afterwards he remained more at home, and was attentive to his business. However, before the birth of a son, which took place in less than a year, to the keen eyes of affection Andrew Murray was not what he had been. He began to go out at night, first for short periods - but by degrees his stay was lengthened, so that it sometimes approached the dawn of day when he returned. The consequences of this were obvious: he could not be so regular at work, and his farm suffered. Conscience would frequently interfere, and resolutions of amendment were confidently made. But alas! how frail are the unassisted resolutions of men. They have been beautifully likened to "a morning cloud and the early dew," dissipated by the first rays of the sun.

The downward course is rapid, and so it proved with Andrew Murray; though really attached to his domestic circle, yet he could not resist the lures that were spread to tempt him from home. He got among a set of gamblers who met nightly at Bryan Sheeran's, where, regardless of his mother's advice, his wife's tears, and the endearments of his infant, he continued to dissipate his substance, neglect his business, and let his farm run heavily into arrears. Such was the state of his affairs on the night the catastrophe above mentioned occurred at Sheeran's.

While Andrew Murray was enduring the alternations of hope and despair at the gambling house, his mother and wife were sitting at their spinning wheels, near a dull fire; the season had been broken, and their turf was badly saved. After a long silence, only interrupted by the hum of their wheels, the mother, heaving a deep sigh, said - "The Lord look down on us the night, an' save my poor boy from harum - Jenny dear, there's somethin' over me, - the weight iv the world is on my poor heart."

"Ye're tired spinnin," replied Jenny, "time for ye; throw by the wheel - take a blast iv the pipe - it's far in the night - go to bed."

"I'm not tired, avourneen; I don't care for the pipe; och, och, the great God save ye, Andy, a vick ma chree (son of my heart)."

"Amin, amin," repeated the wife, "wid the help iv God nothen 'ill happen him."

"Maybe so, acushla; the Lord is stronger nor man - but O wirra, I'm in dread - I had a dhrame las night, an' id always cums for bad."

"Dhrames is nothin', mother," said Jenny, "sorra heed I'd give them - go to bed now an' sleep; ye'll be the better iv it."

"Up or down, dear, it's all one; there's throuble greater nor ever afore us - it was a poor day t'ye, alanna, ye joined us at all."

"I never rued it yet, mother; and iv it's allotted for us to have more throuble, welcome be the will of God - I can put up wid it: och, God knows I'd walk the world wid Andy an' ye;"

and the poor young creature, for she was not yet eighteen, took up her apron to dry the tears that were streaming from her eyes.

"The King iv heaven give ye the worth iv yer goodness an' save ye the last day, asthore machree, (pulse of my heart)" was all the old woman could utter; and throwing her arms around her daughter's neck, they wept long and bitterly.

At length footsteps were heard at the door; Jenny hastened to open it, but, to her utter dismay, it was not her husband who entered. Jem came apparently in search of Murray, but, in fact, to warn him to leave the country, saying, "that Denis was kilt out an' out."

We shall not attempt to portray the misery of the wife and mother on hearing those dreadful tidings - the strongest words could scarcely convey an idea of their agony - and succeeding days but added to its poignancy, for Andrew returned not, nor could they hear of him in any quarter. Denis was not killed, but for some time his life was despaired of. During this period Murray's landlord sold every thing on the premises for the rent due - dispossessed the women, and they were thrown on the world pennyless, and almost naked, in the depth of winter, when the ground was covered with snow. As they were much respected by their neighbours, they might have been supported by them, but this they would not accept, and, after a short time, they left the place -

"The world was all before them, where to choose
Their place of rest, and Providence their guide;"

but before their departure they had the consolation of knowing that Denis was recovering.

It was towards evening, on a cold November day, the east wind blowing bitterly, and the sky having all the appearance of snow, that two females were dragging their weary way across a bleak country, in the direction of a few cabins that were seen in the distance. One was old and the other young, and both were faint, and the younger, particularly, was scarcely able to walk; they were clad in the miserable remnants of what had once been decent clothing. Having with difficulty got over a high ditch, the young woman broke a long silence, saying - "Mother, dear, I must sit down - I haven't a bit iv breath, an' there's heat at the back iv this ditch - the cowld is goin' through me."

"We'll rest a little, a lanna," replied the elder, "only don't stay long, ye'll only get worse; the houses is not far off."

"Och, I'm in dread I'll never be able to lave this, the Lord look down on me, an', iv it be his holy will, relieve me."

"Amin, a vourneen; God help ye, only for me an' mine ye might be happy the day."

"I thought nothin iv losing my poor child, he was taken to glory, an' now I'd die happy, mother, iv I could see one sight iv Andy; och, och, is he on the world at all," replied Jenny - for the females were Murray's wife and mother.

"Don't sit here, a haski," said the mother, "the cowld 'ill kill ye out - get up, dear, an' maybe the Lord id hear yer prayer."

"Asy for a minit, mother, tal I get more breath," murmured Jenny, in a faint voice.

After waiting a short time the mother said - "Rise, dear, ye'll only get waker in the cowld." With some effort Jenny arose, and tottered for a few paces forward, the old woman endeavouring to support her; but she would have fallen had not a man, who came behind, caught her.

"The Lord reward ye, honest man," said the old woman, "an' help this crathur to" - but stopping short, she gave a cry of joy, exclaiming - Andy, a cushla me chree - Andy, dear, dear, did ye cum to us agin - O wirra, wirra."

On hearing her mother's exclamation, Jenny suddenly rallied - her strength seemed to return - she gazed on her husband for an instant, threw herself into his arms, looked rapturously up to heaven, and her head fell insensible on his bosom. It was her last exertion, for with it her soul was rendered into the hands of its Maker. But why dwell on this harrowing scene? The mother soon followed her affectionate daughter. Andrew Murray did not long survive; and he died solemnly warning those who surrounded him at the moment, to beware of gambling, by which his fair prospect of happiness in this life had been blighted. "I had land, money, an' respect," he would say - "a good mother, a loving wife, an' a fine child; I beggared an' kilt those I loved best in the world; I am dyin' before twenty one years went over me; I was a gambler. But, thanks be to God, he gave me time to repent, before he tuk me away. Oh, young men, an' ould men, be warned by me, an' see the dreadful fruits of gambling."

38
The Brothers[1]

"The broken soldier kindly bade to stay,
Sat by his fire, and talked the night away;
Wept o'er his wounds, or tales of sorrow done."
Goldsmith.

During the winter of the year 18—, I was residing at the house of a farmer of the better class, in a remote country parish. The master was an intelligent man, who had evidently been reared in a higher sphere than that he now moved in; for at times traces of more cultivated manners would break through the rusticity that association with the lower orders gives; but these evidences of a higher caste were involuntary - they had grown with his growth, and were not exhibited from a vain wish of letting his hearers know he had seen better days; on the contrary, he never repined, but was most thankful to Providence, saying "that the independence flowing from honest industry was sweet indeed." He had a large family; the elder son was not at home during my sojourn; the two next were apprenticed; two girls, of nine and six, with a little curly headed rogue of three years old, were under the care of their mother - a quiet industrious woman.

When weary of reading and the solitude of my chamber, I frequently joined the family circle of my host, who usually assembled in their clean kitchen, around the ample hearth, upon which blazed a huge turf fire. On the most comfortable side was placed a large chair for the master, a smaller one for the mistress, and low stools for the children. The opposite side was sometimes occupied by the servants, but not often, as they were generally employed; but there was frequently some old follower or privileged person staying at the house, who smoked his pipe, or told his tale from that corner, or listened in wondering admiration to the anecdotes of the "strange gentleman, an' lowersha, it was a fine thing to hear him talkin', the Heavens may bless him, an' as asy to speak to him as iv he was the lik iv oursels."

One night when the east wind was blowing keenly, and snow was rapidly clothing all objects in its lustrous mantle, we were gathered around the cheerful fire. In the midst of the joyous laughter and prattle of the little boy, we heard a loud shout from the direction of the public road, which was not far off. While we were debating what it could mean, another cry, as if for help, followed.

"Some accident has happened," said the farmer, turning to the servant man, "go Tom, and see what it is; if there is any person in distress they are welcome to the shelter of my roof."

---

[1] Published in *The Dublin Penny Journal*, January 11th 1834. Initialled 'W' - Ed.

The servant went out, and in a very short time returned, accompanied by a man in the tattered and faded garb of a soldier; a green shade over his eyes, and the manner of his walking told us he was nearly blind. The servant said he had found him sinking down on the roadside. The poor man was placed in a comfortable seat, and the kind hostess gave him some warm drink; after a little he was able to eat, and said he found himself much better, and he blessed the Almighty, and then, for his deliverance from death; adding, that if he had remained out much longer he could not have lived.

"I wonder," I remarked, "you ventured to travel on such a night, and your sight so bad as it appears."

"Indeed, Sir," he replied, "it is, I may say, gone, for I can't see much except in bright sunshine; but I was striving to make the best of my way to some place of shelter, being refused at many of the houses I passed, because, Sir, I had no money."

"May God forgive them that'd turn any creature out such a night as this," exclaimed the mistress.

"By your dress I'd suppose you belonged to the army," said the farmer.

"I did for a great many years," replied the stranger.

"It's not possible," resumed the farmer, "they discharged you without some allowance."

"I have a pension," said the other, "but when I found my sight failing, I left England to go to my native place; I'm a long time travelling from Dublin; I was ill on the way, and at a house where I lodged two nights ago, I was robbed of some clothes, and all the money I had. It is near two months to the next quarter; God only knows what I'm to do until then; but I deserve it all, and more."

"If we were all treated according to our merits," interrupted the farmer, "we'd have another story to tell; but you must talk no more to-night, you want rest; to-morrow, please God, you'll be better able to tell us some of your adventures." Tears of gratitude coursed each other down the poor soldier's care-worn cheeks, as the kind mistress led him to a comfortable bed.

Next day the soldier was much better. I had some conversation with, and found him possessed of intelligence more than his apparent rank in life promised. He was most thankful and grateful to his benevolent entertainers, and above all to the Great Being who implants those humane feelings in the human breast. The farmer was from home all day, but at night, when we were again collected around the social fire-side, the soldier asked his host's permission to give us a brief sketch of his story; it was readily granted, and he thus began: -

"Myparents were in a very respectable line of life, but at my father's death, which happened when I was young, my mother was left with a very limited income to support and educate two sons, of whom I was the eldest. However, being a prudent woman, she got on better than was expected, and when able to fill it I was promised a situation by a friend of the family. My mother early inculcated the principles of religion on her children, so that if they afterwards erred, they could not plead ignorance, having been taught the difference between right and wrong. My brother's disposition and mine were very unlike; he was steady, while I was the contrary; and many were the warnings I received on this account from both mother and brother.

"Many times was I disappointed with regard to the promised situation, and much unhappiness did it cause me. I endeavoured to make myself suppose that my anxiety for employment was to relieve my mother of the burden of my support; but, in fact, it was my longing desire to enter the world, and revel in its highly coloured delights.

"At length I was appointed to the situation, and my destination was a village on the sea coast. Though greatly delighted, I could not avoid feeling deeply at parting those I loved, and the peaceful home of my youth; but my sorrow was greatly mitigated at the prospect of being able to add to their comforts, and perhaps soon see them.

"What the nature of my employment was, is now of no consequence; but I found it would be trifling, as there was another young man in the office. And my anticipations of seeing life were greatly disappointed, as the situation was even more retired than the one I had left; and I had no associate save my colleague in office. I never was fond of reading, therefore many of my leisure hours were spent in rambling along the sea-shore with a gun, sometimes alone, but more frequently accompanied by a son of the person with whom I lodged; a young man whose only acquirements were low dissipation and intrigue. I had often been warned on my love of inferior society - but in vain - the propensity still continued, and in the end I bitterly repented it. However, without resource within, I must have society, and clung to those young men, both of whom were my inferiors in every respect.

"It was early in summer when I arrived at this place, and during the fine weather, time passed very tolerably; but when a severe winter set in, the hours rolled heavily indeed. My colleague, Thompson, often proposed drinking; but reared in habits of strict temperance, I for some time resisted this temptation. Daly, the son of my host, was more successful; he introduced me to the dancing parties of the villagers, and many scenes of low dissipation. But I could not be thus engaged every night, and when obliged to remain at home, Thompson and I had recourse to cards; though the stakes we played for were small, and though I was tolerably successful, yet as time passed over I found my finances running low. I knew it was wrong thus to dissipate my salary, and deprive myself of the power to assist my parent, who, I was aware, stood much in need of it. Yet I had not resolution to fly the temptations continually thrown in my way.

"On parting my mother she said, 'my dear child, beware of running into temptation, or approaching the extreme bounds of innocence; if you do, you may be certain of falling. Seek continual assistance from on high to preserve you.' But I was strong in self-sufficiency: I depended on my own powers, and sought not the only aid that could uphold me. Letters from home frequently arrived that disturbed me much; and from dram drinking, to keep off cold after a wetting, I insensibly began to drink more freely, as I foolishly imagined, to drive away care, that was increasing on me more and more every day, and all the effects of my own wicked conduct. I had an intrigue with a young female in the village, which was discovered by her family, and in an hour of drunkenness I was obliged to marry her.

"So passed the winter, and when spring came I had not a farthing to support myself and wife, nor any to expect for near three months. In this dilemma I applied to Thompson, whom I thought my friend, and with more reluctance than I asked, he lent me a small sum, which I repaid on receiving my salary.

"For some time previous, Thompson and Daly had been engaged in the smuggling trade, which was carried on extensively along the coast, and Daly frequently took trips with the captain of a smuggler that traded at the village. The evening of a quarter day Thompson came to my lodgings, and detailed some news that Daly, who had just returned from a cruise, told him.

" 'And do you know,' he added, 'I think the trade so good, I have sent out a larger venture than usual.'

" 'Take care,' I replied, 'if a hint of this is given at — you may be ruined.'

" 'Nonsense, man,' he said, ' who knows any thing of it, and even if they did, what matter. I'll warrant the great people do jobs in this way themselves.'

" 'May be so, but that is no precedent for us,' was my answer.

" 'Well let the last day be the worst, I won't let a good chance of more than doubling my money slip, and I'd advise you to do the same.'

"I stared at him in astonishment; before I replied, he continued -

" 'Come,come, 'nothing venture nothing win,' you have others to support now, and should endeavour to better yourself; its no sin to do what we can, every one for themselves in this world, and —'

" 'Stop, Thompson,' I exclaimed, putting my hand on his mouth, 'don't finish the saying; but as to my making a venture I have it not in my power; more than the salary I received to day I owe, and must pay."

" 'Didever any one hear such folly,' he cried, 'it would be enough for a child to make such a speech; can't those you owe it to wait, it's well for them to get at it all, and you may never have such an opportunity of making money.'

" 'But if I have paid my creditors already, I cannot get it back,' said I.

" 'Paid it away,' replied he, 'you were in a confounded hurry; get it back, no, you'll never see it again;' adding, after a pause, 'but it is still in your power to do something for yourself.'

" 'In the name of wonder,' I said, 'how can I do any thing without money.'

" 'Do you forget the sum that lies in the office; you might borrow that, it will not be called for until you have it again.'

" 'Are you mad, Thompson, do you really advice me to be guilty of such an act,' I replied in astonishment.

" 'No wonderful act to borrow a sum of money that's not wanting for a short time; there's nothing mad in the idea I'm sure.'

"I could not speak for some time; surprise, and thinking on Thompson's proposal, kept me silent. However, as ours seldom was dry conference, materials for making punch were before us; I mechanically mixed some, and drank it off without well knowing what I did. The money was to a certainty within my reach, having been paid into the office a day or two before, and might not be immediately called for. Thompson continued to enlarge on the benefit of sending out a venture at this time with the greatest fluency, whilst I was silently drinking glass after glass, until I made myself incapable of judging rightly. But I need not enlarge further, you may conceive the result. Before we parted, a bargain was made with a man, whom Thompson had at hand, for certain commodities to be put on board the smuggler, for which I paid him with the money entrusted to my care."

Here the soldier was interrupted by a deep groan from the farmer, and an audible ejaculation from his wife of -

"The Lord be about my poor boys, and keep them in the right way."

After a little the narrator resumed.

"Next morning I was terrified at what I had done; I went to have the bargain annulled, but it was too late, the goods were already on board. For some days I was like a person deranged, I knew not what I did, and I had no comfort from my confidant, who laughed at my silly fears, and said it was a pity one so chicken-hearted had the prospect of making so much money. It would be impossible for me to describe what I suffered during the voyage of the smuggler. I drank myself drunk every night, imagining it drove away care, but the morning brought back my tortures trebly augmented.

"After a long period of miserable uncertainty, Daly returned with the joyful intelligence of the smugglers being on the coast, having made a most successful voyage, but that the cargo could not be landed until the following night, as there was a revenue cutter on the look out. Thompson proposed that I should accompany Daly on board that night, as he feared to leave the place, lest he should be missed; and about the middle of the night we set out in a boat. The moon was shining brightly, and the sea quite calm, so we reached the vessel, which lay about five miles off, before daylight. I was delighted at the success of my venture, and flattered myself, after refunding the money, I should have sufficient to send out a much larger the next trip.

"On the following evening we began to make towards shore, when near the place of anchorage, and considering ourselves quite out of danger, to our great dismay the cutter was seen bearing down on us with all sail. The captain bore away along the coast, but the cutter being a superior sailer, soon came almost up with us. We had on board two pieces of cannon, which were frequently discharged without injury to our pursuer, as we endeavoured to get out to sea, but the cutter, aware of our design, kept on the outside, and when near enough, gave us a full broadside of musketry, which killed one of our men. This kind of running fight continued for some time, when our ammunition being nearly expended, the captain said we must either strike or destroy the vessel, not having sufficient hands to throw the cargo overboard; and as we were not far from shore it was resolved to blow up the ship and endeavour to save ourselves by swimming.

"The resolution was scarcely announced, when in a transport of despair I threw myself into the sea. The destruction of my golden hopes was as nothing to the idea of losing my life. I felt I was not fit to die, and used all exertion to save myself. I was a good swimmer, and the tide beginning to flow, I hoped soon to reach land, which I found was much farther distant than I at first imagined. I felt myself getting weaker - I had a horrible dread of death - which I now deemed inevitable, and bitterly lamented forsaking the paths of virtue. My thoughts of home and loved relatives I cannot explain; they were beyond the power of language to express. The wind rose after I left the smuggler, and I had to combat against a rough sea. In the midst of my despairing reflections, while I felt myself sinking every moment, I was dashed by a huge wave with violence against, as I suppose, a rock, and heard or felt no more.

"When recollection returned, I found myself in bed in a small but neat room, the curtains half drawn, and the light of the window shaded. I felt as if awaking from a deep sleep, and the past events floated in my head like a dream. I endeavoured to sit up, but found I was too weak to do so; I lay for some time gazing around, when an old woman entered; I asked where I was, and what brought me there? she answered -

"Sir, avourneen, year in the house of a good couple, may the Lord reward them; an' d'ye want any thing, dear?"

"Not much wiser by the reply, I again asked how I came there, and at what time last night?'

"Last night!" repeated she, in surprise, 'oh! wirra, Sir, dear, its more nor a fortnight since ye cum; the men goin' to fish foun' ye dead on the shore one mornin' an' brought the masther to see ye; he sed ye'd cum to, an' wid the help iv God, ye did; but ye are in a fever ever since, dear, the Lord be thanked ye cum t'yer mind - I'll tell the misthress.'

"From the mistress, a respectable old lady, who soon visited me, I learned where, and in whose house I was, but she would not allow me to converse, gave me a composing draught, and left me to repose. The next day I was much stronger, and my host came to me; he was indeed a venerable picture of benevolence; taking my hand, he fervently praised God for having restored me to their prayers. He conversed with me in a manner so kindly affectionate, that I concealed nothing from him, and he promised to go where I had been stationed, and see what could be done.

"On his return he told me he had learned that the smuggler escaped during the darkness; that I was supposed to be dead; that Thompson had informed of my taking the money: and was put into my situation for his good conduct.

" 'The villain,' I exclaimed, 'he ruined me to advance himself, but he shall not long enjoy it, I will shoot him.'

" 'Hush, hush,' said my kind host, 'these are the suggestions of the evil one - give not way to them.'

"He continued to explain the sinfulness of my intentions, and that, at all events, I could not venture to appear in the neighbourhood, as if seen I should be prosecuted for robbery; he suggested that I should write to my friends, and begged I would remain at his house until I heard from them. I could not avoid seeing the reasonableness of his remarks, much as I disliked preaching, and agreed to do so. Nothing could exceed their kindness; I was soon restored to my usual health; but days and weeks wore away and I had no letter from home. I knew not what to do; I was weary of my residence, for though those good people realized not in their kindness, yet there was a strictness in their family - such a regular observance of religion, as suited not my taste, vitiated as it was by criminal indulgence.

"After two months, having had no answer to my repeated letters, I became so impatient of the restraints of my abode, that I one night left it clandestinely, and wandered I knew not, cared not whither. But in the darkness I took a wrong turn, and after walking all night, when day dawned, I found myself in the neighbourhood of my former residence. I should have immediately turned my steps another way, but there was some spell over me. I concealed myself among the rocks on the shore all day, intending to quit it at night; indeed I was greatly fatigued and soon fell into a sound sleep.

"It was dark when I emerged from my hiding place, to proceed to a village at some distance, where I was not personally known. I had not gone far on the shore when I saw two persons walking slowly before me, a man and woman, whose figures I thought familiar. I stole softly after them, and found I was not deceived - they were Thompson and my wife; a few words spoken by the latter in a loud tone gave me to understand the nature of their connection. Enraged to madness at the recollection of my wrongs, I grasped a stout stick, my only weapon, and crying, 'villain, the hour of retribution is come,' struck Thompson, while in the act of turning round, such a blow as laid him at my feet; and continued to beat him until actual fatigue obliged me to have done. His companion on hearing the voice, also turned round, and screaming loudly, fell on the strand without motion. I suppose she imagined it was my ghost who had overtaken them. Thompson lay quite still, and thinking I had added murder to my other crimes, I fled quickly, until I left the sea far behind, and found shelter at a late hour in a poor cabin. Early next morning I continued my flight, during which I encountered a party of recruits on their way to embark for foreign service. I hesitated not a moment in enlisting, and the following day left the shores of my native country.

"It would be useless to tell of all the scenes I was an actor in for a series of years; but I still continued my wicked courses, until I was several times brought to death's door. It was while languishing in the ward of an hospital, that a good old man found, and spoke words of comfort, that I trust will never be erased from my bosom. He was a native of the place where I first began to sin, and informed me that Thompson was not killed by the beating I had given him; he suffered under it for a long time, and imagined it was inflicted by a spirit, for it was supposed that I was drowned; my wretched wife did not long survive the fright she had received, and Thompson lost his situation soon after, going no one knew whither.

"Such is my sad story, and if there are any young persons listening, oh! let them beware of straying from the paths of virtue. I am making my way to my native place, but am certain I shall be a solitary being there; my family are, I fear, gone, never having heard from them, though I wrote frequently."

The poor man ceased, and tears flowed from his almost sightless eyes. We were all affected, for there was a melancholy in the tone of his voice that touched the heart. The farmer drew the back of his hand across his eyes, and leaving his seat, went to the other side of the fire. He put his hand on the soldier's shoulder, saying in a low voice, nearly inarticulate from emotion, the single word, "Henry."

"The poor blind man started up, exclaiming -

"Good God! do my ears deceive me, who is it speaks?" and he shook like an aspen-leaf.

"My brother, my dear, my long mourned brother," said the farmer, and they clasped each other in a silent embrace. When at length their emotion a little subsided, the generous soldier disengaging himself from his brother's arms, dropped on his knees, and in the fervour of joy and gratitude uttered aloud his adoration of the Mighty Being who had thus unexpectedly restored him to happiness on earth.

39
The Cock-Fight[1]

The course of our story leads us to the bank of a considerable river, on a lovely evening towards the latter end of April; some of the earlier trees in a wood on the opposite shore, were already clothed in soft green, and among their boughs innumerable tenants of the air were pouring forth their vesper song; not a breeze rippled the calm surface of the stream, now tinged by the roseate hues of the declining sun.

Two girls were seated close to the river in earnest conversation, their cans filled with the pure element, ready to put on their heads.

"Ye wor'n't at the chapel a Sunday, Kitty," said one.

"No;" replied Kitty, "my mother wasn't well."

"I wish ye wor in id, nera one but the sight 'most left my eyes fwhen I seen Nancy Brady."

"Ah fwhy so, Peggy?"

"Orah, Kitty, dear, she was so drest; sorra the leks iver ye seen; a fine new Lighorn-bonnet, wid a power iv yalla ribbins, an a black veil."

"Is it a veil?" interrupted Kitty.

"Aye indeed, a veil, agrah, sorra a many was on her grannys," continued Peggy; "but stay tal ye hear all! A silk coat, my dear, an' a red scarlet shawl near down to her heels; new glous (gloves), an' to be shure, a hankecher in her fist."

"An' a silk coat, too," repeated Kitty, "fwhat color was it?"

"Like a dull green," said Peggy, "I doubt it's a cast off she bought from a dealer - it had'nt the skin iv a new one. Och, iv ye seen her Kitty, sorra one iv her knew iv she was on her head, or her feet, so grand as she was."

"I'm thinkin'" Peggy dear, "ye minded Nancy Brady more nor yer prayers."

"How could I help it, Kitty, wasn't she the shew iv the whole chapel? an' all the boys afther her lik any thin,' an' Frank Davis up to her hip lik a pocket."

"Frank Davis!" exclaimed Kitty.

"Aye indeed," said Peggy, "an' fwhy wouldn't he as well as another, an' faix a handsome boy he is, sorra the lek of him was in the chapel, an' Nancy Brady's very well too, only she put a power iv paint on her face - it was the moral iv the fire."

She might have run on much longer uninterrupted by Kitty, who was immersed in thought. After a silence of some minutes Peggy resumed. "Ah, then, I b'lieve, Kitty, its fwhat ye're thinkin' iv Frank Davis yersel'; I hard it afore, an' yer mother tellin' that she'd never give in to it."

"She didn't say so," replied Kitty.

"Nera word iv lie in it, mysel' was stanin' by."

---

[1] Published in *The Dublin Penny Journal*, January 18th 1834. Initialled, W. - Ed.

"Fwhat can any one say agin him, Peggy?"

"The boy's well enough, Kitty, lowersha, it'd be hard to meet his match, only they say he's too much afther the sport, an' that his masther faults him for it."

"That's some iv Norah's lies, Peggy, bekase he wouldn't marry her daughter."

"Faix, may be so; mysel' doesn't know, only as the people ses."

Just then a loud voice was heard from the hill behind them, calling out -

"Here, Peggy, will ye stay there all night?"

"There's my mother," said the girl, "will ye cum Kitty?"

But Kitty was not in a hurry, and the other putting her can on her head set off. Kitty was disturbed by the gossip of her companion; she had been long attached to Frank Davis, and the flame was mutual. Her mother, who was a widow, did not like the young man: she said he was a gambler, and said truly, that gamblers seldom make good husbands. However, though Kitty heard Frank's love of pleasure very generally commented on, she did not entirely credit it. The boy, she thought, is fond of sport, and why not? sure all boys are so; and she liked a boy to have some spunk (spirit); they always made better husbands than one of your dead-wigs.

It must here be remarked, that the epithet, boy, is common to young men, and indeed men who are not young.

But that Frank Davis should be paying attention to any other, Kitty did not approve. She conceived herself, and very justly, superior to Nancy Brady in personal charms; to be sure she had not a silk coat, nor a Lighorn bonnet with yalla ribbins, an' a black veil, and she would tell him her mind when they met.

Immediately on Peggy's departure, a little boat was pushed from amongst the reeds of the opposite shore, and a man stepping on board, polled it noiselessly across the river, a short way in the rear of where Kitty was sitting; having drawn it ashore, he stole lightly up, and putting his hands on her eyes, cried -

"A penny for yer thoughts."

She quickly disengaged herself, and said gravely -

"I want none iv yer freedom," Frank Davis.

"Don'tmake so free, tal ye're better acquainted," replied the young man, laughing and setting himself close by her, adding, "be the laws, Kitty, ye done it to the life, as cowld lookin' as the snow;" and he took her hand, which she snatched from him.

"Faix, maybe its in arnest ye are," he resumed.

"It's just in arnest I am," she said.

"Hooh, fwhat cum over ye the night?"

"Nothin' at all, thank God, but I might ax fwhat cum over ye this whole week?"

"It's not always I can get out, the masther watches very close - ye know, Kitty, I'd cum iv I could."

"Times was ye would, but times is greatly althered."

"Not wid me, Kitty, I'm always the ould six-and-eight-pence."

"Only fwhen ye meet fine drest girls at the chapel."

"Well, well," interrupted Davis "some gabby person was tellin' ye that I was talkin' to Nancy Brady las' Sunday; och, fwhat news they had."

"An' if ye leked, fwhy not; she's a purty girl, a dacent father an' mother's child an' had grand clothes," said Kitty, endeavouring to speak calmly, though she was greatly agitated, and her eyes filled with tears.

"Iv I leked," repeated Frank, "an' d'ye think, Kitty, bad as I am, I'd ever fancy sich a painted thing?"

"Shure hasn't she a fine Lighorn bonnet, an' a veil?" said Kitty.

"To Bottamy wid her bonnet an' veil to boot," cried Frank, "fwhat do I care for her; ye shouldn't be listenin' to lies."

"It's no lie that ye wor wid her afther mass a Sunday," said Kitty, "an' iv ye think, Frank" - she hesitated and he said -

"Iv I think fwhat, Kitty; I was walkin' a piece wid Nancy Brady a Sunday, but it was to make game iv her, she was so proud. I tould ye often, an' now agin, there isn't a girl in the world wide I care for but yersel," and he added with emotion, "though they say this an' that iv me, I wouldn't tell ye a lie for the boat full iv gould."

There is an old saying, that the falling out of lovers more strongly rivets the chain; and so it happened on the present occasion. Before they parted it was arranged that on the ensuing Monday, being the first after Easter, they were to be married; she was to meet him in the evening, and then proceed to the priest's house.

"An now, Frank dear, said Kitty, "I have one thing to ax ye."

"Ax me any thing in the world, an I'll do it," replied he.

"Its only," and she hesitated a moment, "its only, Frank, that ye won't cock-fight any more."

"Here's my hand an' word for ye, Kitty, that from this day out, I'll shun cock-fights, an' not go agin ye in any thing."

Frank Davis polled his little boat over the river with a light heart that night, for the dearest wish of that heart was about to be realised; he was fondly attached to the pretty Kitty Moore, and longed to call her his own. He was very young, and had made no provision for house-keeping; in fact, had no money save what would be expended on the marriage; but what of that, thought he; I am strong and willing to work, and God never sends mouths into the world, but he sends them bread to eat; it is better to marry than do worse." With these fallacious arguments, too frequently brought forward by our young countrymen and women, Frank Davis put to silence a few qualms of conscience.

The next day was the last of the week, and after Mr. Arden's labourers had been dismissed, and that gentleman was returning to his house, Davis followed him in silence.

"Do you want any thing, Frank?" said Mr. Arden.

"To speak a word, iv ye please, Sir."

"Well, what have you to say?"

"I was wantin' a little money the night, iv its convenient t'yer honor."

"Money, Frank, to be spent in gambling, if so, I shall not give any."

"Shure, Sir, I'm no gambler, I wondher who told ye lies iv me." "I want no one to tell me, Frank, you cannot be ignorant that your work is neglected, or performed in a slovenly manner, and how is your time spent? at cock-fights, ball-alleys, and such like places."

"An' beggin' yer pardon, Sir, shure that's no gamblin."

"Then pray inform me what you term gambling?"

"Playin' wid the cards, pitch-an'-toss, an' the lek, Sir; I never cared for them, sorra card in the deck I know beyant another."

"I trust you may long be so, Frank," said Mr. Arden. He then endeavoured to explain the nature of gaming, and warn the young man against it.

"Well, well, see that now," replied Frank, "I'm thankful to ye, Sir, an never will folly the liks agin."

"Take care, Frank, do not be too confident in your own strength; and now let me tell you, that if you do not give up all such practises we must part. I shall give you the money, and hope it may not be squandered in gaming."

"Wid the help iv God, it won't, Sir."

"Seek that help, Frank, and you may be certain of doing well."

Though passionately fond of the cruel (certainly miscalled royal) pastime of cock fighting, and having, two birds trained for the usual battle on Easter Monday, yet Frank Davis resolved from that time to give it up. His master did not approve of it, and he did not wish to part so good a master; and Kitty Moore, the prettiest girl in the parish, so dearly loved, and so soon to be his wife, wished him to give it up - and he could not deny her any request. He would part his cocks on the following day, and never go to a cock-pit again.

Kitty Moore was early stirring the next morning, not that she had many preparations to make against her marriage. Her wardrobe was not extensive, therefore she had not many choices; but she was restless, and so nervous that every sound startled her. She was about to take an important step without her mother's permission; to unite herself to a person to whom indeed she was warmly attached, but who she feared was greatly addicted to pleasure. But marriage will settle him, she thought, having heard old women frequently say it was the only thing to tame a wild young man.

We have heard dowagers in a more elevated rank of life aver, that reformed rakes make the best husbands; but we think it rather a hazardous experiment for a young female to unite herself to a dissipated man, with the hope of reforming him; in a hundred instances to one it fails. But Kitty Moore was young, and moreover deeply in love, therefore did not pause much to balance consequences.

"It's a fine day," said her mother, "Kitty fwhy but ye go to the chapel; an' shure ye might go to the cock-fights, or the dance afther."

But Kitty did not wish to go out until evening. In the course of the day she sought her friend Peggy, and informed her what was to take place in the evening.

"Didn't I know well," Peggy exclaimed, "ye wor fond iv Frank Davis, an' God knows a dacent clane boy he is, but Kitty, acushla, fwhat does yer mother say?"

"She does'nt know any thing iv it, nor won't for a fwhile," replied Kitty.

"Well the Lord send ye luck, any way: did ye see Frank the day, Kitty?"

"No, I'm to meet him fwhere I tould ye, in the evenin' late, an' Peggy, avourneen, ye won't forget."

"Never fear, Kitty, I'll do it."

What Kitty reminded her friend of, was to meet her after the marriage that they might walk home together.

The full orbed moon was emerging from behind the eastern hills, as Peggy quitted the dance to meet her friend; she had to walk about half a mile, and after getting away from her companions, all was silence, save the occasional bark of a distant dog and the low plaintive notes of the night singing bird. Peggy was tolerably stout-hearted; however, she occasionally looked around with a rather timid air, for the field she was traversing contained one of those forts said to be the favoured resort of the fairies. But Peggy passed through and arrived at the place of meeting without encountering any of the gentry, where a scene awaited her that absorbed every thought.

On the ground lay Kitty Moore, insensible, with Frank Davis kneeling, and holding up her head; his face all smeared with blood and dirt, his head bound with a handkerchief, his clothes torn and muddy. Peggy clapped her hands and stood aghast for a moment.

"Aye, ye may well wondher" said Frank, seeing the gore, but not knowing to whom he spoke, "she's lyin' there, an' I kilt her."

"For God's sake," at length cried Peggy, "fwhat's the matter wid Kitty?"

"Didn't I tell ye I kilt her," replied Davis.

"Ah, Frank, fwhy but ye open her cloak, an' let the win' about her," said Peggy, tearing it open, she then carried water in the hollow of her hand from a pool, with which she plentifully wet Kitty's face; but for a long time in vain, so that the girl, in great alarm, feared her friend was dead. However, she persevered, and at length signs of returning animation began to appear. When Kitty was able to speak she requested to be brought home; Frank Davis wished to accompany them, but this neither would permit. He was reluctantly persuaded to leave them, on Peggy's promising to see him in the morning, and let him know how Kitty had passed the night.

It will be recollected that Frank Davis set out that morning with the determination of parting his cocks, and giving up fighting with them.

"Ye're early on the road the day, Frank," said a friend of his on overtaking him, "goin' to prepare the cocks, no doubt, an' a great fight it'll be; Mr. —, is to have his birds there."

"I'm going to sell my cocks," replied Davis in a hesitating tone.

"Is id sell yer cocks," exclaimed the other, "jokin' ye are."

"Faix, Billy, I'm in arnest."

"The masther won't let ye keep them its lek."

"Shure enough he's not very fond iv sport, but that's not it all out, Billy. I'm goin' to be marret."

"Goin' to be marret!" repeated Billy, stopping short, laying hold of Frank by the shoulder, and staring at him earnestly.

"It's the thruth I tell ye," said Frank.

"Bethershin (maybe so), any way it's quare how quite ye kep it; an' who's the girl?"

"Shure ye might guess."

"Nera one iv me knows; maybe its Peggy Noon."

"No, in troth."

"Ye might see worse in a day's thravel, Frank, but I give it up."

"Fwhat would ye think iv Kitty Moore, Billy?"

"Kitty Moore," repeated Billy, and a dark cloud passed over his brow.

"Isn't she a good girl?" said Frank after a pause.

"Sorra betther," replied the other, assuming a tone of cheerfulness, "an' I wish ye every luck, Frank; but shure that's no reason ye should give up yer fine two cocks, an' sport - there's not the leks iv them in the counthry round."

"They're well trained, Billy, an'll be shure to win, let who's will get them."

"Hooh, man, don't let any one get them, tal ye take one spree out iv them afore ye're tied for life."

"I can't Billy, I gave my hand an' word to Kitty, I wouldn't keep them; any way I'm to be marret the night."

"Neel arugher (no help for it), cum along tal we see fwhat ye'll do wid the cocks."

On arriving at the place, they met many others on the same intent; of course they must treat each other. Naggin led to naggin, and half pint to half pint, for some would not be outdone by others, until the unseasoned heads of the party, among whom was Frank Davis, was tolerably light.

Those who determine to forsake any besetting propensity, should, as a preliminary, avoid being led into temptation; importunity and opportunity are not easily withstood, and so poor Frank Davis found it.

Already elated by the spirits he had drank, the bustle at the cock-pit put to flight all his new formed resolutions, and he was all himself again.

We shall not enlarge on the scene of degradation. Frank entered his cocks against those of Mr.—, they were beaten, and he lost all the money he possessed. He then got completely drunk, and was well drubbed by his friend Billy, who cut him deeply over the eye, and left him nearly insensible in a ditch; for, in fact, Billy was himself fond of Kitty Moore.

It was late in the evening when Frank awoke to consciousness; and perfectly sober, he then recollected his appointment, and how utterly impossible it was for him to fulfil his promise to Kitty; the though was bitter in the extreme, but he determined to go to the place of rendezvous at all events. He bound a handkerchief round his head, and crawled, as well as he was able, to where Kitty had long been waiting with agonised thoughts and fears for his delay, and when he did appear before her in that state, we shall not attempt to describe her feelings: warm and affectionate, they received a shock, time alone could heal; and on hearing him distractedly tell his hopeless tale, animation fled, and in this state she was found by Peggy.

The sequel is soon told. Kitty Moore, before the dawn of the following day, in the presence of Peggy, solemnly promised her mother, never more to see or speak to Frank Davis; and the young man on hearing this death blow to his hopes, enlisted in a regiment bound for foreign service, and left the country, never to return. Dissipation, and the burning sun of a tropical climate, soon finished his career, and he fell, another victim added to the many who are yearly immolated at the shrine of gambling.

40
Archy Conway[1]

On a fine day, late in the lovely month of May, such a day as has been sung by poets, but which the temperature of our Emerald Isle does not often cheer us with, the roads of a certain parish, in a certain county and province in this gem of the ocean, were thronged by groups of people young and old, male and female, hurrying to one common centre - an annual fair held in a field, which was anxiously looked forward to for half the year, and by which the memoranda of the good wives were dated: ask one the age of her child - the answer will be, "so old agin the fair iv Kill;" and among the men it was, "wid the help iv goodness I'll pay ye afther the fair iv Kill;" so that this fair was, as it were, a finger-post to the memories of the neighbourhood. Hither had the crowds been congregating since early dawn; some on one intent, some on another - but all agreeing in the desire of enjoying the pleasures of the fair.

"An' any way, thanks be to goodness, its a fine day," said an elderly female, in the centre of a group of others, who were trotting along barefooted, with petticoats tucked up, and shoes in hand.

"Sorra finer ever cum out iv the sky," replied another, "an' Onny acushla, d'ye mind fwhat a sore day it was this time twel'month: teems iv rain, tundher an' lightnin', an' great big hard snow balls fallin' thick, an' all the sport spiled.

"Nera loss that was, any way, Katty," replied Onny, "only fur it the green id be runnin' wid blood."

"D'ye think they'll strike era stroke the day," asked another woman.

"Iv yeere in the fair afther dinner time, maybe ye'd see that," said Onny.

"Fwhat news ye tell us," retorted the other, "any way they're ruffens iv both sides, an' it's well for them that has no call to the scrub."

"Sorra great things yersel' is," cried Onny, "that he speak in disparagement iv any body; there's them iv both parties, though I don't love or like one side, that's the full iv a masther to any one ever ye had belongin' t'ye, Biddy Moran."

"I didn't know, Onny, ye wor any thing to either party," said the girl.

"Hooh!" that's a wondher dear; wasn't my mother's aunt's husband's cousin marrid to Tom Bruin's aunt's third cousin -fwhy wouldn't I be for the Bruins? - an' any way, that they may win."

"I b'lieve that gridge is long betune them," said one.

"Nigh hand two score years," replied Onny.

"An' fwhat was it put betune them at first?" was another query.

[1] Published in *The Dublin Penny Journal*, July 26th 1834. Initialled, W. - Ed.

"Sorra much, dear," answered Onny; "a hen that was scrapin' oats was kilt be a boy iv the Bruins. A woman iv the Fellins, who owned the hen, fell to beatin' him; his mother cum to save him - the women boxed; iv coorse the men tuk their parts - an' from that day to this there's a gridge betune them."[1]

"No great things to make sich a rout about," said a woman; "it'd be more fitter for them that day to be mindin' their wheels, nor fightin' an drawin' sich a gridge betune the men."

Honor, or Onny, as she was called - a woman of masculine figure and disposition, was on the point of justifying the persons of her own clan, who had been the aggressors in this feud, which was, as she affirmed, of near forty years standing; but a party of young men overtaking them, a scene of bantering and coquetry ensued, which put the women in good humour: when the men passed on there was no further recrimination.

"Well, there's nera cleaner boy in the four walls iv the world nor Archy Conway," remarked Onny, "an' always has the pleasant word for the girls."

"D'ye think, Onny, he'll be marret to Nancy Sweeny?" asked one.

"As lek as not," was the reply.

"He'll be for the Fellins, iv there's strokes the day," said a girl.

"Sorra a blow ever he'll strike for them," answered Onny; "isn't his mother a friend iv Thady Bruin's - oh, yis, indeed, fwhat a fool he is."

They now drew near to the field in which the fair was held, and a general scene of dressing took place: shoes and stockings were put on - petticoats and gowns released from confinement - hair sleeked up and down - shawls, cloaks, and handkerchiefs heaped on each other before they could enter this scene of rustic amusement.

Archy Conway was the son of a widow - a fine-looking young man, who possessed an unbounded flow of spirits which, when among his companions, led him into sundry scrimages as he termed them; in fact, when he was induced to drink more than usual, he was apt to be exceedingly frolicsome. He was foster-brother to a young gentleman in the neighbourhood, who was much attached to him.

Archy's mother, aware of his frailty, endeavoured to keep him as much as possible away from public places, and above all dreaded the annual fair of Kill; knowing all she could urge against his going there would not avail, she went to her foster-child, to request his interference, to keep, if possible, Archy from the fair. For this purpose, on the day previous to the fair, Archy was summoned to the residence of his master; having some idea of the cause, as it was by no means the first time this authority had been resorted to, he went rather unwillingly, and a shade of gloom darkened his handsome features, as he was ushered into the presence of his young master.

"Sit down, Archy," said the gentleman, pointing to a chair - "I wish to speak with you."

---

[1] A fact.

"Yis, Sir," replied Archy, placing himself on the corner of a seat, and in rather a pettish way twirling his hat in one hand.

"Have you got your potatoes finished during this fine weather?" said the young master.

"Not all out, Sir. Shure, Masther Henery, they're down since betune the two Mays - time enough to finish them yet."

"I have frequently endeavoured to convince you, Archy, that your habit of procrastinating is extremely wrong."

"Fwhat's that, Masther Henery?"

"Putting off until to-morrow, what might better be done to-day."

"I'll not be passin' two hours away, Sir; an' sorra sup I'll take, barrin' one glass - won't that do, Sir?"

"I had much rather you did not go at all. What business have you to transact there?"

"Ah then, Masther Henery, ye'er goin' very tight on me entirely; but I promise to —" and, blushing deeply, Archy more vehemently twirled the hat and sent it spinning to the other end of the apartment; after picking it up, he went on: "I promised to meet somebody there, Sir."

Henry smiled while replying, "there would be no use in my saying, Archy, don't go, as you are determined to disobey; but I will say, avoid bad company, and be home early.

Archy promised to do all his master wished; joyfully made his bow, and was hastening off when called back, and enjoined, above all things to beware of fighting. "It is probable," continued Henry, "the Bruins may be defying their adversaries; I desire you will not take part with them."

"Never dread, Sir."

Archy lost no time in arraying himself in "all his best" and hurrying to the fair. The stipulated two hours so passed over, and he thought not of returning; after a further stay he thought it would be soon enough to be goin' till dinner time; sorra bit iv fun he seen yet. — Dinner time went by, and a couple of hours after Onny, with another female, were standing at the outside of a tent. She appeared, amid the babel of confusion that reigned within and without, to be hearkening to some conversation that was carried on in the tent; and to ascertain if she was right as to the speakers, with a piece of stick she perforated a hole in the slight covering sufficient to see through, and putting one eye to it, remained for some time in close espial; then silently touching her companion on the shoulder, motioned her to look through the aperture, and whispered,

"Now, Mary a hagur, if them leaves the tent afore I cum back, mind an' tell me fwhere they go to."

So saying, Onny set off at full speed, muttering as she went. "Maybe, Tim Casey, ye though no one was listenin' to yer villainy; but I'll be up t'ye an' yer faction. Oh, wirra! isn't it a wondher fwhere's Archy Conway; it can't be he went home." She rushed in and out of the tents, like a person deranged, many saying as she drove by them, "that woman's early drunk."

In the mean while the object of her search was enjoying the society of the being he loved best on earth. The pretty Nancy Sweeny had long been admired by Archy, and admiration became love of the most ardent kind; and he had the delight of knowing that his passion was returned. But when did the course of true love run smoothly? The parents of Nancy had a match in contemplation, which they though better; therefore Archy Conway's suit was discouraged by them. Nancy was to have a good fortune, both in money and cattle; consequently she was an object of interest to the youths of the neighbourhood. However, knowing his interest in the damsel's heart, he determined to carry off the prize if he could not obtain her on any other terms; and for the purpose of gaining her consent to this plan, he had drawn her apart from the crowd, and they were in earnest conversation at the rear of a large pedlar's standing, while Onny was in search of him. He had brought forward every argument the eloquence of love prompted, to induce her to run away with him, but in vain.

"Then ye don't care for me," he exclaimed in a tone of passion.

"Archy," replied she, "ye know well I care for ye above the world; an' that I'd thravel Ireland with a bag on my back along with ye."

"It's easy to talk," interrupted Conway, "but fwhy won't ye agree to cum with me, an' sorra bag ye need put on - I've plenty, thanks be to goodness."

"The Lord increase yer store," she answered: "now listen to me, Archy, avourneen - I'll never bring throuble on my father an' mother by goin' away wid any one; but iv they kill me for it, no man, barrin' yersel', will ever put a ring on my finger."

Before he could reply two young men joined them, and Nancy instantly walked away; almost at the same moment Onny arrived, her face flushed, and out of breath.

"Faix I thought the ground opened and swalled ye," she exclaimed in broken accents; "I'm afther killin' myself huntin' for ye through the fair."

She took him aside, and with vehement gestures told him something in a low tone. The effect was electric — his face became inflamed with passion, and, flourishing an oak stick over his head, he leaped up, exclaiming, 'who dare say a word to a Bruin,' and 'huzza for the Bruins,' responded the young men, also cutting the usual caper preparatory to a fight. They then rushed into the fair, sounding the alarm, and in an incredibly short time a number of persons joined them. An instantaneous attack was made on the tent, which soon exhibited but the bare poles without, and within the utmost confusion; Archy all the time calling,

"Come out, Tim Casey - come out ye villain - shew me the Fellin dar shew his head - the Bruins for ever!"

After the first surprise was over, Casey and his party lost no time in escaping, for it would have been madness to contend with the others, who were much more numerous. Archy's party then set out in procession through the fair, leaping, flourishing hats and sticks, and yelling with might and main —

"Down with the Fellins - the Bruins for ever."

On their return in the same order, Archy was, ere he could ward it off, struck with violence by Tim Casey, who had collected a party; Conway soon recovered, and a general battle ensued, to the no small annoyance of the fair, in which the Bruins were victorious, driving their adversaries triumphantly out of the green.

By this time evening was far advanced, and Archy having remained so much longer at the fair than he had promised, set out on his return, but was induced by some companions to step into a shebeen-house on their way, and there they sat drinking a long time. Another party soon afterwards came in, among whom was Tim Casey. Archy rushed at, and would have struck him, did not the landlord and some others prevent him.

"I'll pay ye, ye villain," he exclaimed with fury, while the men were dragging him off, "ye struck me lek a coward."

"Didn't ye first, wid yer party, smash the tent; was I doin' any thing t'ye, only sittin' wid my friends," replied Casey.

"Yes, ye wor match-makin' for a girl that hates ye; I tell ye, Tim Casey, ye'll never put a ring on Billy Sweeny's daughter — never, never," roared Archy.

"That's more nor ye can tell," said Tim.

"I say it, an I'll maintain it till death," cried Conway.

"Whisht, boys, whisht," interrupted the landlord, "its a great shame to hear sich an alligation betune dacent boys."

"Dead or alive I'll be revenged iv ye, Tim Casey," said Archy.

The two rivals were separated, and Tim Casey left the house alone, and proceeded on his way home. Archy followed some time after.

On the day after the fair Archy Conway arose late; he walked into the fields, and throwing himself listlessly on a sunny bank, lay for a considerable time so immersed, not in thought, but in a want of thought, that he heard not a sound, until a smart tap on the shoulder with a switch, and the words -

"What Archy! are you asleep?" aroused him; and starting up with a countenance crimsoned over, he replied, not well knowing what to say,

"Ye freckoned me, Masther Henery."

"I believe so," was the young gentleman's answer; "but how comes it, Archy, you are not at work this fine day."

"I— I—I—I'm not very well, Sir; there's a pain in my head," stammered Archy.

"I thought you were not to have drank more than one glass yesterday, and to return in two hours."

With a little more confidence, Archy replied, "Shure, Masther Henery its not so asy for a body to get out iv a fair as to go into it; so many friends meets one every minit, an' it's onpossible not to drink a little wid them, and that ye know well, Sir."

"I hear there was an engagement between the factions yesterday - I suppose you took a part."

"Sorra haporth there was, Sir, barrin' a bit iv a scrimmage, nothin' worth relatin'."

"But thrifling as it was you were a participator."

"Nera much part I had in it, Sir, only you know I couldn't see my friends—"

His further comments were cut short by the arrival of two policemen; they touched their caps to Mr. Henry, and laying hold on Archy, arrested him on a charge of murder.

"There must be some mistake," said Henry, after a moment's silent surprise.

"None, Sir," replied one of the police respectfully; if you will take the trouble of walking about a mile with us you will meet your father and the jury, when all can be explained to you."

On coming to the place mentioned by the police, they found a great concourse: the coroner, with such a jury as he could muster, and around them men, women, and children; some talking, some standing with uplifted hands, and some bitterly weeping. The crowd made way for Henry, who went up to his father, asking what all this meant.

"It is, indeed, a dreadful business, my dear," replied the Coroner. "A man was this morning found barbarously murdered and suspicion, nay more, strong circumstances tend to criminate Archy Conway."

By the time Henry had arrived, the witnesses were examined, and the jury had given in their verdict of wilful murder against Archy. The amazed young man was led within the circle where the murdered remains lay, the face was so dreadfully beaten in by stones that it was impossible to identify it, except by the clothes, which were positively sworn to. A woman was seated on the ground, with the head of the corpse in her lap, who, when she saw Archy, screaming and clapping her hands, exclaimed,

"Look at yer work, ye murdherin' ruffen - look at my fine boy there that ye kilt, an' he'll never spake to me. Och, Tim Casey, avourneen machree, did yer poor ould mother ever think to see the day ye'd be stretched a disfigured corp; och hone, och hone, fwhat'll I do at all."

The surprise of being immediately brought in contact with a dead body - the screams and words of the afflicted woman, and the charge against himself affected Archy powerfully; he frequently changed colour, and gasped for breath; he once or twice attempted to speak, but his voice was mute, emotion overpowered him.

"Unfortunate young man," said the coroner, "behold the fatal effects of faction, of passion, and drunkenness."

"I wasn't drunk, Sir - I never kilt him nor no other one," sobbed Archy.

The coroner then recapitulated the evidence that had been given, to which Archy replied, "I never kilt him, Sir."

"What became of the deceased afore he left the house, and that you followed?" asked the coroner.

"A then fwhat would I know, Sir - shure I didn't see him good or bad," was the reply.

"Verywell - I don't ask you to say any thing that might criminate yourself," said the coroner, and then directed the prisoner to be removed to the magistrates.

"An' am I to go to jail for fwhat I never dun, nor even cum into my mind. Oh, wirra, wirra, but that's a poor law. Och, Masther Henery, dear, speak to yer father not to kill me this away," and the poor young man wept bitterly, wringing his hands in the agony of despair.

Henry, also much affected, took Archy's hand, and tried to comfort him; explaining that his father could not act otherwise; and he accompanied him to the house of the magistrate, and waited until Archy, more dead than alive, was taken off to prison.

His friends were not prevented seeing him on the appointed days. On one of the days that Henry came to the prison he was accompanied by a female, closely muffled, who Archy conceived to be his mother; and when Henry left them together, saying he would soon return, Archy began —

"Mother, dear, ye oughtn't to be comin' so often this long road; it'll wear ye out entirely."

The female spoke not, but uncovering her head, Archy gave a cry of joy, for it was Nancy Sweeny who stood before him, blushing deeply at her own temerity. Long and fervent was the embrace with which he folded her in his arms; and only in broken accents could he give utterance to his rapture: tears alike of delight and shame chained his tongue.

"I never thought, asthore machree,[1] ye'd see me in this place," he murmured, pressing her more closely to his breast.

"The will iv God be dun," she replied, gently disengaging herself, "the will iv God be dun. Archy, ahashki,[2] I don't b'leeve ye ever dun any harm; ye're the same to me as ever; it can't be the judge 'll heed fwhat they say agin ye."

"Never dread, Nancy; there's no law in the world to hang the innocent; an' God knows, I'm as innocent as the child that's not born."

"I b'leeve ye Archy; I never misdoubted a word ye said yet; but och, och, every one won't be so;" and she took up the corner of her apron to dry the tears that were dimming the lustre of her eyes.

"Nancy," he said, while a deep shade of sadness clouded his brow, "Nancy, iv they hang me," and a convulsive shudder ran through his frame, "iv they hang me, don't grieve, avourneen; forget Archy Conway that loves ye above the world, aye an' thinks iv ye (God forgive me!) more nor iv heaven; forget me asthore, an be—" he could not utter 'happy,' but, bursting into a passion of tears, sobbed long and loudly. Nancy, though suffering as much agitation, endeavoured to comfort him, and gave him the most solemn protestations of never-ceasing affection. But for a length of time she spoke to the winds; at last she threw herself on her knees at his feet, saying,

"Here me, Archy - iv I didn't think more iv ye than all the world, would I come here, unknownst to father or mother - an' now I declare I'll never be the wife iv any man iv I'm not Archy Conway's."

---

[1] Beloved of my heart.

[2] A term of endearment.

Archy raised her up, but the entrance of Henry put a period to the interview.

The awful day of trial at last came round, and Archy's friends hurried to the courthouse with a feverish impatience, though there was not a human probability of his acquittal. Henry stood by the dock, and occasionally the poor prisoner's hand was locked in his. When Archy was called on to plead, he answered with a tolerably steady voice, 'not guilty, my Lord, not guilty - och, God forbid.' But the evidence was most circumstantial; judge, counsel, and jury seemed of the unanimous opinion that a verdict of guilty must be the result.

During the latter part of the trial a slight bustle was heard in court, which the police soon quelled; one of whom put a paper into Henry's hand. When the case on the part of the crown closed, the prisoner, as a matter of course, (for he was generally deemed guilty), was called on for his defence. Henry then whispered something to him; he seemed confounded; the blood rushed suddenly to his face, and as suddenly retreated. Henry again said, 'speak;' and, to the amazement of all, he called loudly, 'Tim Casey;' the man for whose supposed murder he was on trial. To the increased wonder of the hushed spectators, Tim Casey, alive and well, came forward.

When the universal exclamation of surprise and pleasure (for Archy was greatly commiserated) had subsided, Tim Casey proceeded to solve the enigma.

On leaving the public-house the night of the fair, he was warned that the police were in search of him, for some whiteboy offence; he therefore fled without acquainting any of his family; and the man who had been murdered, being dressed exactly as he was on that day, was easily mistaken for him by his family; as, in consequence of the face being disfigured, he was identified merely by his dress.

The case thus made plain, proved the prisoner innocent. The judge told the jury it were needless to charge them. A verdict of not guilty was handed down, and Archy restored to his expecting friends, among whom none experienced more real pleasure and gratitude to the all wise disposer of events than Henry.

The appearance of Tim Casey at this critical moment remains to be briefly accounted for. Onny, in some of her gossipings, got a hint of the matter from a person who had seen Casey in a distant country, but not clear enough to warrant its being made public. She informed Nancy Sweeny, and they both set out in search of him; after many disappointments they were at length successful, and Tim Casey nobly consented to accompany them, careless of consequences, for the purpose of justifying his rival, and they only arrived in the court-house a few moments before the trial ended.

This escape was a useful warning to Archy Conway - he gave up idle meetings and faction quarrels - married Nancy Sweeny, and became industrious and respected by all his neighbours.

41
The Wedding Day[1]

"Then neist outspak, a raucle carlin,
What kent fu' weel to cleek the stirling." - *Burns*

The soft purple haze that succeeds the setting sun of a fine summer day, had diffused itself over the valleys, while the higher grounds yet retained the roseate hue of the glorious luminary; the latest notes of the blackbird were borne on the gale from a coppice, near which stood a cabin of rather better appearance than is usually seen in the more remote parts of Ireland - it could not with propriety be called a cottage, which name implies more of comfort, both internal and external, than the major number of the humble habitations of our father-land exhibit. But cabin or cottage, there it stood, its door open to admit the last rays of light; the floor was earthen - the furniture homely, - a clear turf fire, notwithstanding the season, burned on the hearth - the ashes had been swept up, and it gave it the full force of the idea expressed in the words of the poet -

"A blazing ingle, and a clear hearth-stane."

The furniture was arranged, the floor swept, a table covered with tea apparatus near the fire; an air of tidy comfort reigned through the whole. Two persons were in the house - one, an old woman, sat in the chimney corner, at a spinning wheel, with the usual accompaniment, a pipe in her mouth. The other was also a female, but considerably younger; she was a tall, graceful-looking figure, with tolerably regular features, enlivened by brilliant dark eyes, and a profusion of glossy brown hair, fashionably dressed. Her apparel was plain, but put on with taste; she walked back and forward - now putting some article of furniture to rights - now settling up the fire - again, standing before a small looking-glass that hung against the wall, arranging a curl or placing a pin, with a glance of perfect satisfaction; then stepping to the door, would look intently in one direction for a few moments, return and throw herself into a chair, and again start up. Thus she continued for some time, and not a word was spoken: the old woman mechanically turned her wheel and sucked her pipe, glancing occasionally at her companion's movements. At length the silence was broken by the younger female, saying,

"Well, I wonder will he come to-night?"

The other was deaf, therefore did not hear what was said; the young woman continued —

"He promised - surely it can't be he'll break his word."

[1] Published in the *Dublin Penny Journal*, February 27th 1836. Initialled, W. - Ed.

"What d'ye say, dear - what is it a lanna?" asked the old woman, perceiving the lips of the other move, though she heard not. Receiving no answer, she suspended the motion of her wheel, and said, speaking with the pipe in her mouth,

"Kitty, dear, what's over ye the night, ye're like one was in throuble or throughother?"

"I'm not in trouble then, nor throughother either, as cute as you think yourself," replied Kitty, and her eyes darkened with passion, as she added - "What's that to you what ails me? mind your work; I'm able to take care of myself."

"Sorra doubt iv that," responded the other, and began to ply her wheel.

In a short time the voice of some person singing, was heard approaching; presently an elderly female entered the house, singing

"There was a rigement of Irish Dragoons,
And they were quartered at Derby, O;
The Captain fell in love with a handsome maid,
And her name it was pretty Peggy O."

At the last word, giving her fingers a snap, she said,

"God save all here but the — och, I needn't say cat, for sorra one in it;" then drawing a stool near the old woman, she bawled in her ear.

"I'm proud to see ye well the night, Molly, goodness be thanked — hand us the pipe, avourneen; I'm lost entirely for a blast."

"Ye needn't bawl that away," replied Molly, sharply. "I'm not so hard ov hearin' all out, as people thinks," and she reached the pipe with a frown.

"Och, more power t'yer elbow, a colleen," returned the stranger. "I'm shure its not me ever sed the like iv ye, nor a word, dear - heaven forbid."

"It's little matter whether you did or not," interrupted Kitty; "but, Nelly, I thought you'd send him here tonight."

"Asy, dear, an' I'll tell ye all," replied Nelly, in a lower tone; "any way I'm proud to see ye have the tay wet, for I'm as dhry, as dhry, avourneen, as turf moul in June."

Kitty prepared to satisfy the wants of her guest, who drew her stood nearer the fire - stirred up the turf, and made it blaze more cheerfully. She was a small, thick set woman, of middle-age, with a broad face, and sinister looking dark eyes, and a habit she had of looking from under the lids, gave them even a more suspicious appearance; it is an old true remark, that the person who looks you not fairly in the face, is rather a dubious character. Nelly's black hair was cut straight across her forehead, above which appeared the border of her cap, the rest being all covered by a black silk handkerchief tied under her chin, a shabby though not patched cloak, covered her other garments, and she usually went barefooted. Nelly's occupations were multifarious; she was partly mendicant, fortune-teller, cup-tosser, matchmaker, go-between; cured headaches, with a charmed string, raised the palate of the mouth[1] by means of another charm, and numerous other et ceteras. There were two things Nelly loved supremely, namely, whiskey and tea, and to obtain either of these dearly loved beverages, cared not what sacrifices she made to propriety or truth.

"Well, any way, the heaven's may be their bed that first invinted tay," remarked Nelly, after the third cup; "nera one but it's great drinkin'. an' ye make it so strong, avourneen, that it rises the cockles in one's heart."

Kitty knowing Nelly would not answer questions until her appetite for tea was nearly satiated, now ventured to ask why the person expected so anxiously, did not come.

"That's more nor I can tel," replied Nelly, with the fifth cup in her hand; "but this I know, that I'm nearly frozen waitin' to see 'im, an' was afeard iv the misthress to go near the big house."

"What can be the matter?" said Kitty; "sure he wouldn't be going to give me up after all his promises."

"Hooh, never fear, avourneen, he's too far gone for that - give ye up! - O yes, indeed, to be shure," answered Nelly, with a knowing nod and wink.

"But this is twice he promised, and didn't come," resumed Kitty.

"An' sorra wondher in the same," interrupted Nelly, "many's the one promises, an' can't do it afther; how d'ye know but the misthress sint him some place?"

"Nelly, may be you'd find out in the mornin'; there's another good cup on the pot, don't turn down so soon."

"No, dear, only I want to see what luck's in the cup, an' monam a yeah, but there's all sourts iv good luck," and she pointed out what she called a ring and several other equally apparent things in the confused heap of grounds at the bottom of the cup. "Now, a hegar," she added, "we must do it three times," and her cup with a seventh time filled with the weakened fluid; the omens were equally good; - another cup was swallowed, and on inspecting the grounds, with an exclamation of triumph Nelly declared, they should win; Kitty shook her head, saying, "I hope so."

"Sorra doubt iv id," replied Nelly, and lowering her voice to an almost inaudible whisper, added, "ye know, dear, iv all fails, there's the little powdher that'll make him yer own in spite iv him."

Mrs. Ellard was left a widow with an infant son, the last of a numerous family, who all died young. It will not then be wondered that Charles Ellard was the idol of a mother so circumstanced. Mrs. Ellard was a managing woman, and determined to nurse her son's patrimony to the best advantage during the long minority, while his education, which would have enabled him to appear as a gentleman at the head of this property was woefully neglected. From infancy Charles Ellard never met a contradiction; if he wished for any thing, however preposterous, it was immediately given him, for two reasons, first, his

[1] A swelling of the glands of the throat is thus termed by the ignorant.

mother could not bear to hear him cry, which he was sure to do lustily; and again, she affirmed it was a terrible thing to break a boy's spirit by thwarting him. The poor woman should have recollected, disappointment is the lot of human nature - that few, even of the best regulated minds, endure it with equanimity; and, therefore, that the earlier we are accustomed to meet it, the better for our future comfort. This foolish mother could not part her idol; he was not sent to school, but had a kind of tutor in the house: impatience of contradiction had been fostered in infancy, and as he grew up, it of course gained strength; so Charles only learned when and what he pleased. Mrs. Ellard's remonstrances were met by promises of amendment, for he really loved his parent; but the promises came to nothing; and if the mother was chafed, as sometimes happened, she encountered a burst of passion, or dogged silence. His time, as a boy, was spent in low company and idle pursuits. As he advanced to manhood the same tastes continued. Charles Ellard was the best shot, the most fearless horseman, and able ball-player in the country, and his figure in rustic dances, etc was unrivalled. Too late did the fond parent find her error; she had been indefatigable in the culture of her property, but his mind was a garden of fine plants choked by weeds; there were at times, traces of a better, nobler spirit, but low company, and lower pursuits, nipped them in the bud.

"You must go to school, Charles," said his mother one day when he was past fifteen; "if you go on thus, you will never be able to enter College."

"Go to school, mother!" replied he with a loud laugh.

"Yes, Sir, go to school; is it anything wonderful? - you can never enter college, otherwise.

"It is only wonderful I was not sent to school at the proper time - it is now too late," said Charles, bitterly.

"Ungrateful boy," replied Mrs. Ellard, with tears in her eyes, "I did not expect this from you; have I not done all for the best? - you have had a good tutor at home - if you did not benefit, it is not my fault."

"No dearest mother," said Charles, taking her hand, and speaking with emotion. "You are not to blame, you did all for the best, and the fault is with me; it is now too late to remedy this - college I never meant to enter. I know enough for a country life, and am content; the tutor is unnecessary, you may dismiss him - and now let us have no further arguments on the subject of learning."

"But Charles," she began—

"You know my determination, mother, I shall not depart from it," interrupted he, and left the room.

She knew indeed that he would not, and she felt more bitterly the effects of her ill-judged indulgence: the tutor was dismissed, and from that time Charles troubled his head no more with letters, but entered deeper and deeper into rustic amusements, and sometimes into its dissipation. It was when about the age of nineteen, Charles Ellard became acquainted with the female named Kitty, already before the reader's notice; he was introduced to her by a young rustic, his constant companion in day and night-shooting, the most pernicious of all field-sports in its demoralising effects, the most fatal to soul and body. We shall not now enter on the subject - but a fearful example presents itself, which at some future period we may exhibit as a warning to our youthful readers.

Though Kitty was some years the senior of Charles, she was still handsome, and her manner was better than those of the rank she appeared to move in; she was a stranger lately settled in the neighbourhood - did not appear to want money for moderate expenses, and lived with the old woman whom she called Aunt. Charles was quickly fascinated by the seeming innocence and beauty of this female; he looked to make a conquest on easy terms, but was mistaken. She led him artfully on until his affections were deeply engaged, never permitting him to infringe the strictest bounds of propriety.

Mrs. Ellard frequently saw a woman loitering about the house, but on sending to call her she was gone. This was Nelly, who was Kitty's go-between with Charles. On the afternoon of the day this convenient person was introduced to our readers, Mrs. Ellard was walking in her garden with folded arms, up and down a terrace; she had not taken many turns, when a clear female voice under the hedge sung —

"Whistle and I'll come t'ye my lad,
Let my mother be ever so mad -
Whistle and I'll come t'ye my Joe,
Whether my mother be willing or no."

This was Nelly's usual signal for Charles. Mrs. Ellard looked over and perceived Nelly, dressed as we have introduced her, basking in the sun, that now threw its western beams on the hedge. Determined not to lose the opportunity of speaking this time, the lady stretched more over, so as to be seen, and said,

"What are you doing there my good woman?"

"Sauwall Dhea er in," exclaimed Nelly, starting up, "but ye freckoned the very life out iv me - I thought sorra one was a near me."

"I asked what you were doing there," replied Mrs. Ellard.

"Sorra haporth, good or bad, Madam, only restin' mysel in the heat iv the sun, God help me," replied Nelly, with a low curtsey.

"Where do you live?"

"Nera certain place, Madam - poor Nelly has no cabin, only the good christens gives me lodgin', the Lord bless them, amen achierhah."

"Are you a —" Mrs. Ellard hesitated at the obnoxious word beggar, and added - "how do you get your bread?"

"Is it bread, dear - nera haporth I get barrin' pretes, an' maybe an odd grain iv male - och, och - bread's not for the likes iv me, foreer (alas)."

"Come to the hall-door and you shall have some bread," said Mrs. Ellard.

"The heavens may be yer bed, avourneen - ye're ever an' always good to the poor;" and with tongue thrust out at the other side of her mouth, Nelly proceeded to the hall-door. Mrs. Ellard led her into a room off the hall, shut the door, and seating herself, motioned Nelly to do the same.

"I'm tired sittin', I'm thankful t'yer honor, Madam."

"Sit, woman, when I desire you," said Mrs. Ellard.

Nelly placed herself on the extreme end of a chair, near the door, and taking up the corner of her apron, affected to be very busy with it. After a short pause, the lady resumed -

"I have lately seen you loitering much about this house, and I know not what can bring you, except you come after my son."

"Afther yer son, anagh![1] replied Nelly, laughing; "musha, maybe it's on purpose ye are, Madam - afther yer son! — O wirra, it'd be a nice thing for the likes iv me to be afther a young gentleman - foreer, I'm not young an' purty, now," and with an arch smile Nelly glanced in a mirror opposite, settling the border of her cap.

"You should rather rejoice to be freed from the danger of temptation," said Mrs. Ellard Sharply.

"Every dog has his day, Madam" was Nelly's dry response.

"Then it is not after Mr. Charles you come to this house."

"Musha then, my good lady, what bis'ness would I have wid yer son, Madam? — the Lord forgive ye for evenin' sick a thing to me," said Nelly, affecting to be angry.

"You must have some cause for coming here so often."

"Hooh - many's the bis'ness a poor girl has through the world besides young gentlemen - the less any colleen has to say to them, faix so much the betther for her."

"Quite right, my good woman, I am glad to hear you speak so sensibly," returned the simple lady, duped by the sanctified voice and countenance assumed by Nelly; she resumed - "but I fear there are some in this neighbourhood not of your proper way of thinking."

"Sorra doubt," interrupted Nelly.

"Do you know a young woman who lives in the house by the wood?"

"I hard iv her, Madam," and Nelly continued to look most innocently on the carpet.

"I dread to hear my son has some improper connection with her - do you know anything of it."

Nelly clapped her hands together, threw up her eyes as in amazement, as she answered-

"Och, och, goodness forbid, that'd be the murdher, a lowersha (indeed)."

---

[1] An expression of doubt or scorn.

After a long conversation, Nelly was commissioned to find out the real truth, with a promise of being liberally rewarded, if she was faithful.

"An' masther Charley, Madam; iv I meet him goin' out, what'll I say?"

"There is no danger, he went from home not to return to-day - be you secret and faithful, you shall not serve me for nothing."

"Never fear, Madam, I'll warrant - an' long life t'ye, ye're a good head to the poor, any way."

Nelly went afterwards to Kitty's house, as before related. Kitty's history is soon told; she was the native of a distant country, where her conduct had not been the most correct; she was now living on the wages of her guilt, in the hope of taking in some fool to marry, and as is commonly said, make an honest woman of her, and there was a most encouraging prospect of success with Charles Ellard. In his mind there was a chaos of contending emotions. At one time, he must have Kitty, come what will - he could not live without her; at another, the idea of grieving his mother, who had ever been so kind, gave him pain, and he would not do so; agin, when in Kitty's society, all the better resolutions were abandoned, and passion triumphed; he pleaded earnestly and frequently, but pleaded in vain; for as the old song has it —

"All her discourse was of marriage."

Violent as were the passions of Charles Ellard, indulged as he had ever been, there were periods when the small still voice would make itself heard, and resolutions were formed, to give up idle courses and companions, forget Kitty, and make his mother happy. It is too frequently the lot of the portrayer of nature, to be obliged to record the fragility of good resolutions formed in unassisted human strength.

On the day our tale opens, Charles had a recurrence of those bitter feelings. He had ridden some way from home and returned in a hopeful state of mind, and was preparing to retire early in the evening, when he was informed Mickey Berne wanted to see him. He was the companion of Charles in his sporting excursions, in fact, the confidant of all his rustic pleasures. Ignorant, presuming, dissipated, this young man was the ruin of his master, as confidants too often are, particularly inferiors. Mickey took him some way from the house, and looking cautiously round, said in a whisper—

"Nelly was here the day, Sir - will ye come down to the wood?"

"I have been thinking that I am doing wrong in this business," replied Charles; "it would break my mother's heart."

"Well I knew ye'd cow - ye're not the raal game after all," said Mickey, with a most provoking sneer.

"You are insolent, sirrah," cried Charles, passionately, and clenching his fist, was about to strike, when recollecting he was completely in Berne's power, he desisted, adding — "What do you mean?"

"It's no matter what I mane, iv ye're goin' to turn swadlin' pracher," replied the other, doggedly.

"Would you have me be the death of my mother?"

A long whew, was Mickey's response.

"You know very well, resumed Charles, "she would not survive my marriage with—".

"Bother," interrupted Berne, "the ould woman's tough - sorra fear iv that; a drass (bout) of cryin' or scouldin', is all that'll ail her."

"You must not speak thus of my mother, Mickey," said Charles; then after a pause - "I really know not what to do."

"Sorra one iv ye need be at an amplush (nonplus), iv ye're goin' to give up the poor girl, ye ought to tell her so - come down an' do it at wonst, like a man."

"I believe you are right, Mickey - the sooner I do so the better - my poor mother shall not be made unhappy."

"Bether shin (maybe so)" muttered Mickey, and walked alongside his master to the wood.

We have not space to detail the scene that followed. Kitty wept, raved, fainted, and went through all the evolutions of strong passion, at least appeared to do so. Charles was touched; he hesitated, and remained to comfort her. Mickey judiciously, to console all, proposed a tumbler of punch. Kitty supplied them with it; and two glasses of this insidious beverage caused an almost total revulsion of feeling in Charles; the violence of passion again usurped its sway, and before they parted that night, all matters were arranged for a speedy marriage. She objected to a clandestine union - no *tackem* should ever marry her - it must be done by licence, and in the church. As this could not be done in their own parish, Mickey suggested that Kitty should remove for a week to a large town at some distance, where neither of the parties were known - here they might be married, and return home as if nothing had occurred. This plan was put into practice next day; but before she left home, Kitty had a conference with her ally.

"Nelly, dear," she said, "have an eye to the place till I come back - my aunt is so hard of hearing she's a bad watch."

"Never fear, avourneen; but if ids a fair question where are ye goin' a lanna?"

"To live in the town of — for a week, to be married, and come back."

"Och, the world for ye, Nelly - it's yersel's the girl in the gap; didn't I show ye the ring t'other night, a hagar, an' shure its ye desarves the bouchal gannule (handsome boy) - anyway ye'es 'ill have the bonny childer, the heavens may presarve them."

As the week drew to a close, Charles told his mother he was going for three or four days to pay a visit to a friend. She made no comment, and he set out for the town. When getting the licence, on hearing his name, the vicar-general said, speaking with great deliberation as he filled up the blanks in the paper.

"You are the son of Mr. Ellard of —; take care, young man, I fear you are about to make a foolish match."

While the gentleman was speaking, Charles coloured deeply, and looked despairingly at Berne, his companion, who was standing at his back. He whispered -

"Say ye're the son iv the saddler."

This was not heard by the vicar. Charles instantly replied -

"I am the son of the saddler at —"[1]

"I trust it is as you say," resumed the vicar, looking more earnestly at the young man, "but you are extremely like my friend. I should be sorry his son disgraced himself."

"There's more Paddy Lee's in the world nor one - like's a bad mark," interrupted Mickey.

"Silence, Sir," repeated the minister, "I hope you are not leading the young man astray whoever he may be," and he proceeded to administer the necessary oaths, which both young men subscribed without hesitation, and carried off the license in triumph.

The morning of the wedding-day rose in unclouded splendour, and almost with the glorious luminary of day, Charles Ellard was up. He was that morning to be put in possession of a long sought happiness; yet he was not free from some compunctious thoughts: however, Mickey seeming to dread this, left him not long alone. As early as they could prevail on the clergyman to come, they all met in the church. Kitty was also in a state of feverish anxiety until the knot was tied.

Early as the hour was, curiosity brought some idlers into the church; however, but three persons stood before the altar. The reverend gentleman commenced the service, and proceeded to that part of the exhortation - "Therefore if any man can shew any just cause why they may not be joined together, let him now speak, or else hereafter for ever hold his peace." He paused on pronouncing these words, and ere he resumed, a deep-toned voice from one side of the building exclaimed —

"I forbid the banns."

There was a general movement among the spectators, and the clergyman said —

"Ha! come forward and show cause."

Charles grew red and pale, alternately, and the colour entirely faded from Kitty's countenance, as a tall weather-beaten, ill-clad man, approached; on coming more within the influence of the light, she gazed on him earnestly, and with a fearful scream, fell insensible to the earth.

"What d'ye mane by puttin' us through other this away?" said Mickey, who was the only self-possessed person of the party.

"I claim this woman as my wife[1] - here is the certificate of our marriage," replied the stranger, and reached the paper to the clergyman.

"Who the deuce 'id believe a word ye say? - go long about yer bis'ness," roared Mickey in a violent rage.

---

[1] Fact.

"There's some will, at all events," calmly returned the man, adding, as the policemen came forward - "there's your prisoner - I accuse that man of robbery."

It was now Mickey's turn to be chop-fallen, and he looked more like a corpse than a living person, as he was led trembling out of the church. Before Kitty was recovered from the death-like swoon, Mrs. Ellard joined the party. She did not upbraid her son - but taking his hand,. said in a broken voice —

"Thank Providence, my child - you are rescued."

"Never, I trust, to fall into the same snare," whispered he, and they soon after left the town together.

The sequel must be brief. From the day Mrs. Ellard had conversed with Nelly, that sapient person conceived she should benefit more by serving the lady than Kitty; however, she prudently kept fair with both. It was through her means, Mrs. Ellard became acquainted with Charles plans; and she agreed with Nelly, it was better to come to a point - the marriage could be stopped at the time of celebration. In some of her ramblings through the country, the week before the wedding-day, Nelly encountered a man, to all appearance, a broken soldier; they entered into conversation with much ingenuity and cross-questioning. She made out that he was in search of a wife who believed him dead, and that this wife was Kitty. Such a fortuitous circumstance was beyond her most sanguine expectations, and she resolved to reap the benefit of it. She took him to Mrs. Ellard, and the plan, the *denouement* of which we have described, was settled between them. The night before the soldier met Nelly, he had been robbed, and the following day recognised Mickey Berne as the person who had despoiled him, but at Nelly's instigation forbore taking him up until the morning of the wedding, and brought the police into the church for this purpose.

Thus deprived of the destructive influence of those evil counsellors, Berne and Kitty, Charles Ellard's better principles were more brought into practice; and in the end he became a real source of consolation to his mother, who declared she dated her subsequent happiness from - the wedding day.

W.

OTHER PROSE WORKS

A Petty Sessions' Sketch.[1]

The rain descended in torrents (according to the long-established habit of the weather at the commencement of a romance) as I shouldered my way through the dense throng that surrounded the Court of Petty Sessions in the retired village of —. The peasantry that composed this animated mass, stood "the pelting of the pitiless storm" with all the unconcern of those plumed bipeds "whose nature is to dip the wing in water;" and ever and anon as the high mock-military tone of the sub-constable summoned each particular batch of village litigants to approach the dread tribunal within, the flushed cheek and doffed *caubeen* spoke the alacrity with which they responded to the call.

The sitting magistrates of the day were Conservative Constant, Esquire, who presided, and his able coadjutor, Mr. Penury Plausible. The court-room was spacious and well-lighted - the edifice having been erected for the two-fold purpose of utility and ornament, and, in a great measure, at the expense of the common herd, who were denied the protection of its roof from the rain that poured as if from a bursted water-spout, on their unregarded heads! A few constables occupied the centre of the floor; at a most respectful distance towards its farthest extremity were huddled about a dozen farmers of the better class; while near the bench, and within ear-shot of their worships, sat or stood, according to the wonted degree of allowed familiarity, five or six of those very important personages in Irish society, yelept SHONEENS.

"Call Denis Dooley and Larry Branagin," said the clerk, Mr. Martin Marlaw, who in connexion with the summons server, drove a very profitable trade in the litigious propensities of the peasantry by the issue of summonses, and in which, as evil report suggested, his worship, Mr. Penury Plausible, himself went snacks.

"Pass the names," cried a big manly voice of authority, issuing from the sergeant of police who stood baton in hand, head erect, and cap adjusted on the remotest angle of his cranium, about two paces in advance of his men towards the worshipful bench - "Pass the names."

The call for Denis Dooley and Larry Branagin resounded through the passage, till it reached the thick crowd that occupied the unsheltered area. "Here!" cried a sepulchral tone among the dense congregation - and "Here!" responded a stentorian voice the moment after. Then the dense mass retired to the right and left, leaving an unimpeded avenue to the advancing respondents.

A spectral figure entered the court-room - his countenance was sallow and emaciated; and his footsteps sunk and tottered as the rude policeman urged him forward. His head was bound with a party-coloured handkerchief that appeared stained and stiff from broad blood-marks - blood that did not seem to have been recently shed. Want and sickness and sorrow

[1] Published in *The Nation*, March 11th 1843 as *No. 1.* of "Etchings from Irish Life." Initialled, E.W. - Ed.

had evidently dried up the spring of life within him; and the glazed and sunken eye which at intervals cast a lurid gleam from its hollow socket, told perfectly that recent fever had scathed his burning brain and brow. A man of Herculean form, whose ruffian aspect gleamed darkly within its shaggy overhanging brow, followed close at his heels.

As the wretched being approached to receive the book which Mr. Martin Marlaw tendered, a thrill of horror ran along the chain of human hearts that witnessed this specimen of human misery, in whose core selfish pride and isolation from all the ties of sensibility had not dried up every spring of feeling for kindred flesh. The vulgar herd murmured their sorrow for congenial misery - the distance-keeping farmers groaned at the appalling view - the heaven-born sensation reached the Peelers - the Shoneens found the subtle fluid tingle at their heart-strings as they stared in affectation of wonder that such living death should haunt the walks of men. The Shoneen was the last link of the sympathetic chain. Pity for a brother's woe found no conductor to the bench. The robe of justice haply repels all appeal to sensibility! Mr. Penury Plausible was busied in the tracing of hieroglyphics; and Conservative Constant, Esq., beheld the human edifice sapped by penury and pain, and tottering to its fall, with as much outward unconcern as if his visual nerve took cognisance only of his own "burly groom!"

"The evidence you shall give the court in this cause shall be the thruth, the whole thruth an' nothin' but the thruth, so help yer God. Kiss the book!" said the chairman, Conservative Constant, Esq.[1]

"Neel Berla agum," hollowly answered the miserable man.

"What does the witness say?" interrogated the classic-tongued dispenser of justice.

"That he has no English, plaze your honour," responded the clerk, who always interpreted the vernacular tongue of the untaught peasantry, to the worshipful and learned bench. "Come, come, Mister!" interposed Mr. Penury Plausible, "do not trespass on the public time with your Irish gibberish. If you don't speak English we will dismiss your case altogether."

"O! a virra yealish," exclaimed Dooley, roused to excitement by the hopeless prospect of a dismissal, "an' won't your honour have marcy on me? May God have marcy on yer own sowl at the last hour, an' don't take me short, a yinusil honorig, for I'll hang (betray) myself all out, if ye ax me to spake English. Widn't it answer the inds of justice betther, yer honor, to let me spake the tongue I was christened in, 'specially as Misther Marlaw there, they says, gets a nice pinny for consthring it for the likes of us? O! if a man kilt your honor, as I

[1] The writer of this sketch has often heard a worthy magistrate in a rural district of the south of Ireland swear a witness in this phraseology. His grandfather, who bore a very un-Protestant name, renounced the ancient faith, to preserve a small property, from the effect of these laws which declared that the kingdom of Irish Catholics should not be of this world. The more degenerate grandson, to a holy horror of the creed of his fathers, added ultra-Orange politics to a seemingly utter ignorance of the barbarous tongue of the wild Irish.

was kilt - and left for six weeks on the broad of yer back, God between your honor and harim! with the could sop under ye, and the hate o' the faver in yer brain, an' the druth o' the world in yer heart - would yer honor, I ask, be able to tell yer story in Latin as well as ye could in English, though the owld masther, I hard say, lost a power towards yer larning?"

"That's an impurtinant, siditious ruffian," exclaimed Conservative Constant, Esq., in wrath.

"Constable!" said Justice Plausible, "turn this fellow out - and Marla (turning to the clerk), dismiss the case of Dooley *versus* Branagin *in toto*."

"O! stop, avourneen," cried the alarmed Dooley, "an' as ye won't hear my story in the tongue I know, I'll give it yees in the raimeash of English I have."

After being duly sworn, the plaintiff went on in the following strain: -

"I was coming home, plaze yer honors (to the bench), and, gintlemin as ye are (to the shoneens), I was coming from the last fair of Shanaliss, with a slip of a kaish (small pig) that I had to pay the rint - but the pigs was in no demand, an' no wan axed me the vally of her till I came back. Well, as I was just sayin', Kate Shine, the mother o' my six childre, an' I, wor driving the kaish along, an' talkin' o' wan thing an' another" -

"Ah! Mister, you're wasting the public time with your cock-an'-bull stories. can't you come to the point?" interrupted Mr. Penury Plausible.

"That's the very same thing I'm comin' to, an' I'll get there in a jiffy, I'll be bail," continued Dooley. "But where was I when yer honour put me out? Oh, gudeerigh! sis I , we must fatten this poor kaish, to pay the calls. There's the county cess to pay - bad cess to it! an' the poor rates - they'll lave us poor enough! an' Parson Blackslug's rint-charge - och! that's the blackest charge of all, avourneen; an' a dickey cloak for Kautheen, plase God - who knows her chance, the crather, if a clane boy came across her? an' the brogues for yerself, Kate, asthore; I can get a pair of soles an' welts for those things on my legs; but, above all, the rint must be paid the masther at Lady-day. Kate, avourneen, they'll swally the crather of a kaish up entirely. We must fatten her, sis I, an' get her more bran agin - I was going to say more bran again the next fair - an' I raised my voice, because the woman stopped behind me to drive on the pig.

" 'What whoreson says a word agin the Branagins here or elsewhere?' shouted Larry Branagin just behind me. He was all over a *meer modra-lahee* (a mud-covered dog), bringing in the two sides of the road with his cota-more streeling the gutter behind him. 'Yer sowl to hell,' sis he, 'what rascal spakes a word agin the Branagins?'

"The never a wan here spaking for nor agin' 'em, but yerself, Larry avourneen, sis I; for I was only telling Kate Shine that we should get this crather of a kaish more bran agin the next fair.

" 'Ye war always a sleeveen an' a thraitor, Denis Dooley,' sis Larry Branagin; an' he up with his cleg-alpeen, an' tumbled me. I felt nothin' after the first blow he hot me, till I found myself stretched on the sop in my own cabin, an' Father John preparing me. There I lay for six weeks on the broad of my back, from the hands of Larry Branagin - glory be to God!"

"What have you to say against this charge, Branagin?" demanded the magistrate.

"Musha, never a tittle, a yinusil," was the reply, "but that every word he says is false, as your honor must persave, for he'd hang St. Pether, and prosicute the holy fathers - honour and praise be to 'em.

"Will ye swear to that, friend?" demanded the chairman.

"I'll not swear to his hanging St. Pether, yer honor, till I see him do it," returned Branagin, "but I'll take the book that he wants to hang *me*, that struck him as much as your 'onour did, or the sucking crather I left at home in the lap of the woman that owns me."

"You swear," says Justice Plausible, addressing Dooley, "that this man assaulted and knocked you down on the last fair-day of Shanaliss?"

"I do, plaze yer honor's reverence," said Dooley, emphatically, "and the red blood of my heart that stiffens this owld clout round my head is crying to heaven agin him."

"Donot believe the informing thraitor, yer honor," broke in the defendant, "every man knows that the rogue would impose a pig on a priest. I'm an honest man, yer honor an' may be, yer honor, would put that rogue by till next court-day, when I'll bring Robin Smith, (the bog bailiff's) commendation with me."

At this point of the dispute the clerk took leave to observe that the defendant had not been sworn - a circumstance which seemed to have escaped the notice of the justices. The book was instantly tendered. Branagin took the volume on which to attest the name of the Mighty God. At this moment a twinkle of humour seemed to blend with the sinister expression of his eye. He crossed himself devoutly, bent in deep humility before the tarnished gilt cross that decorated its binding, and then, with great seeming devotion, kissed his - thumb!

"The defendant is not duly sworn - he only kissed his thumb, plaze yer honor," said Marlaw.

"Stand afore me, ye pray-varic-ating thief so help yer God, an' kiss this book," thundered Conservative Constant, Esq.

"I'm sure yer honor wouldn't be afther axing me," replied Branagin, "if yer honor knew the hoult that's of me never to kiss a book; 'twas the last word my father said to me whin he was laving this world - heaven be his bed! 'Larry,' sis he, 'a vic-ma-chree, come here to me (weeps), I'm now going away from yes all, an' I lave it on yer sowl to uphould the character of the sevin ginerations that left ye, an' never put yer lip to a book for judge or jury.' I'll stick by the request of my dying father, yer honor, though I know that Denis Dooley, the thraitor, will hang me; but welcome be the grace o' God! I'm not the first innocent crather, that got the benefit of the law from a perjuring informer!"

The magistrates, after a short consultation, decided that the defendant should pay the plaintiff FIVE SHILLINGS, with costs.

When this decision was announced, Denis Dooley dropped the staff that supported his emaciated frame, and raised his hands to heaven, while his dilated eye expressed the keen intensity of his feelings. "I complain ye to God altogether," he exclaimed, "the murderer who left me low, and the Sassanach who values my blood an' sufferings at a crown! Wouldn't he hang at the 'sizes if he kilt me? an' the dochter said it was only a hair's breadth that saved my life! O, my crathers, my crathers, yer last preaty is sowed to pay the 'potigary, an' get the dhrop o' dhrink to wet my heart! Fari-go-dho! (shame for ever) upon that justice! Mr. Plausible, I seen you sind a garsoon to the threadmill for cutting a twig on Parson Blackslug's land, and —

"Constable," interrupted Mr. Penury Plausible, with rising colour, "take that ruffian to [the] bridewell during the sitting of the court. It will admonish him to show respect to them who administer justice in the Queen's name.

Two policemen then pounced upon the unfortunate Dooley, and hauled him off to the place of durance. He tottered along, the living semblance of a disinterred corpse stalking amid the haunts of men his weeping wife and five children followed close behind.

"Verily, verily," I mentally said, "the POWERS THAT BE hold Irish blood in as slight estimation now as in the olden time —

"——————-, When every Saxon clown
First kill'd his man, and then paid half-a-crown."

Strictures on Murray's English Grammar[1]

When first I undertook the business of teaching in a country town, I found Murray's Grammar in the hands of every boy that sought the sweets of my literary hive. In using this book as the vehicle of grammatical information, I saw that though the rules were well arranged, and the adaptation of the 'Exercises' to these excellent, many of them were mere pyramids of verbiage, beneath which the author's meaning lay darkly interred. In others again, words and the ideas which were intended to be expressed, were at utter variance; and, in short, the work offered anything but a philosophical view of the language. I communicated these thoughts to some village teachers who had honoured me with their notice, but they stood aghast at my presumption. In fact, a tittle uttered against Murray's Grammar, would be in very many quarters, considered as sort of literary blasphemy. I have not the book by me, nor have I at present leisure to mention in detail the many inaccuracies which I have perceived in his book; I present a few from memory, reserving the remarks upon his mode of applying certain forms of the verb, and his rules of syntax, for another paper, in which I intend to show the mode of parsing many sentences of irregular construction, to which Murray's rules do not apply, and which often sadly puzzle the teacher.

1. "To nouns belong number, gender, and case." We are not told what person or case is, though the other properties of the noun have been defined. I shall offer a definition. *Person* is the rank of the noun or pronoun in the estimation of the speaker. Davis's edition says, "cases signify the different terminations which express the relations of one thing to another." This is incorrect, for the terminations of the nominative and objective of nouns have the same form, though these cases express relations entirely different.

2. The distinction of "possessive adjective pronouns" is very incorrect. My, thy, his, theirs, etc., are the possessive case of the personal pronouns, as may be easily proved. "These are *his* books." *His*, a pronoun used instead of the name of the person of whom you speak. "This is *my* hat. *My*, the possessive of *I*, is here put for the person who speaks of himself;

[1] The article was published in the very first issue of *The Schoolmaster's Magazine*, July, 1840, pp. 340-342, and the author is given as 'E. Walsh, Tourin School, Co. Waterford.' The magazine editor prefaces it with the following: "our correspondent will see that we have inserted all of his communication that has any reference to the subject announced. In such cases we do not pledge ourselves to the accuracy of the criticisms, but are satisfied with laying the authority and evidences before our readers. Such notices however, are highly useful, and we recommend the practice of careful and independent examination to others of our readers." - Ed.

and so of the rest. Name them "adjective pronouns," and in frequent instances, such as, *my*, pens, *their* house, *her* slate, they will not agree in gender, number, etc., with their nouns.[1]

3. Murray, after Lowth, says that *self*, in the words myself, thyself, etc., is a noun; on the contrary, they are personal pronouns, as the following form of expression shows: John and myself have finished *our* task; where *our*, the first person, takes the precedence of the third. I shall here observe that the kindred pronouns, myself, himself, ourselves, themselves, are used after a very strange fashion. If the words, himself, themselves, be correct, and agreeable to the ear, why not meself and usselves? Reasoning from analogy, hisself, theirselves, seem the legitimate words; they appear quite as graceful as their twin sisters, and should be again introduced to respectable society.

4. "Own and self, the latter of which has for plural selves, are joined to the possessives." What real information does this announcement convey? We are not told to what class of words "own" belongs. It is the perfect participle of the obsolete verb "owe," to possess; and is yet retained as a participial adjective.

5. "I, is the first person; Thou, the second; He, etc., the third." We should have been told why they are thus ranked. *I*, the representative of the speaker, is *first*, because of the strict and immediate concern one has in all that regards hisself. *Thou*, the second, because the person addressed and who is supposed to be present, is in more immediate connection with the speaker than the person spoken of, who may be absent. *He*, etc., follow the third in order.

6. The neuter pronoun is sometimes used -
1st. To express the subject of any discourse or inquiry;
2nd. The state or condition of any person or thing;
3rd. The person or thing that is considered the cause of any action;
4th. It is used in a singular or plural construction, to represent persons, as it was they that suffered. It was he.

That this tiny imp "it," who, like another Robin Goodfellow, is continually popping its diminutive form into every available cranny of language, should be permitted to elbow

---

[1] [Magazine editor's note]: 'There is an ambiguity in the writer's statement here. If he means that "my," "their," "her," etc., do not agree with *the noun which they modify*, he is right; and no one ever supposed that they should agree with them. But if he means by "the nouns," *the nouns for which they stand*, he is quite wrong. *Her* slate, denotes the slate of one person, and that person a female.'

better folk from their proper position, is a subject of regret. The introduction of "it," in the above-mentioned cases, is quite unnecessary; and the graceful energy of the language, which, like other ill-starred things, has had all its vigour removed for the improvement of its tone, would, in this instance, be restored, if "it," were obliged to attend to its own obscure concerns only.

7. "Who, which, what, etc., when used interrogatively, do not cease to be relative pronouns." Harris maintains the same opinion. Murray says - "The interrogative belongs to a subject, subsequent, indefinite, and unknown, which it is expected the answer should express and ascertain." Is it not absurd to suppose that any pronoun, of whatever class, should belong to a word which is not yet spoken, and the existence of which depends merely on the will of the answer, and which therefore is uncertain and unknown? How can the interrogative, as a relative, agree with its subsequent in gender, number, etc., in sentences like these - "Who have gone to London? which of the ladies is gone? what man is that?" If the answer to the first question be, "John only has gone," "John," the subsequent, does not agree in number, with its relative. If the answer to the second be, "both went," the same occurs. If that to the third should be, "I do not know," the rule appears more strikingly ridiculous.

The words are adjective pronouns, of the interrogative kind, qualifying the noun either expressed or understood.

In the sentence, "What man is that," the noun "man," is nominative after the verb "is" and "what," the adjective pronoun qualifies "man." If "what were a relative in this instance, it would stand without a verb, either expressed or implied, to agree with it. In the sentence, "The house was erected in the year 1800, since *which* time it has passed into many hands," "which" is a demonstrative pronoun.

The Usefulness of Biography[1]

"No study," says Johnson, "can be more delightful or more useful than biography - none can more certainly enchant the heart by irresistible interest, or more widely diffuse instruction to every diversity of condition."

This powerful attraction, which biography must hold over the mind, arises chiefly from the peculiar applicability of each trifling incident to the circumstances and condition of the reader; we feel the probability of being ourselves, at some period or other, placed in a position similar to that of the person whose life is treated of, and, therefore, the narrative excites our special and particular attention, inasmuch as whatever approximates more closely to our own interests is calculated to affect us more sensibly. The pleasures and advantages derived from history and biography are of a different kind - history relates the affairs and events of communities; biography the several actions of individuals. History takes a wide and more extended range, and thus furnishes models by which the public conduct of states may be shaped; biography a narrower and more minute one, and thus affords a standard whereby to regulate the affairs of private men. History tells us of Alexander, as the mighty hero of Macedon, who marched over the extensive plains of Asia, overcame Darius in several engagements, rendered all nations subject to his power, till he had no more countries to subdue, and till the sea alone was able to set boundaries to his conquests; biography more clearly represent him as a man united to us by the common ties of humanity, influenced by the same passions, acting upon the same motives, subject to the same infirmities, and performing all his achievements by the same instruments as ourselves. In the Alexander of history we see the monarch, decked out in his royal vestments, and strutting along proudly upon the vast theatre of the world; in the Alexander of biography we see him behind the curtain, the sparkling of the diadem is gone, the majesty of the sceptre is removed, and he walks along, as one of ourselves, unadorned by the advantitious splendour of attire, or unaided by the accessory exaltation of the dramatic buskin, which tended to magnify him in our view. This characteristic peculiarity of biography arises necessarily from the contractedness of its sphere - in proportion as the variety of topics on which it has to touch are less numerous, so the accuracy with which it can treat of those which it does allude to is the more minute; in history our minds are distracted by the multiplicity of events, and the diversity of characters that are brought before us - we hurry over sieges and battles, the variations of governments and the demolition of states, and thus have not time to stop and examine the separate characters of individual men, which are the chief subjects upon which biography dilates; just as in gazing over a wide extent of country, when the eye can see no limits, the very boundlessness of the prospect prevents us from at once remarking the beauty or deformity of some particular sub-divisions, so, amid the

[1] Published in the *Dublin Penny Journal*, Oct. 10th 1835. Initialled, W. - Ed.

generalities of history, we are unable to analyse complex relations, and though we may draw from them useful lessons, as to the working of governments and the philosophy of states, yet we cannot with facility discover that minute individuality of character by which men are distinguished from one another. History, in fact, is the mine stored with a number of precious gems, but their very variety prevents us from carefully examining the intrinsic value of each. Yet, after all, the intellectual advantages resulting from biography are not to be supposed greater than those resulting from history; if either was to be taken exclusively, no doubt history should be preferred, inasmuch as it givers a more varied and diversified store of general information, and thus affords a greater scope for the exercise of the mental powers, in examining the connection between cause and effect, on a large and extended scale; but biography is chiefly valuable as a supplementary source of pleasure and improvement, where we are not lost amid a multitudinous array of circumstances, but where we can, at leisure, retire from the noise and bustle of public transactions, to view the more minute and perfect development of human character, and the remoter springs of human action when uninfluenced by the voice of crowds, or unagitated by the tumults of passion.

PART FOUR

· POEMS, SONGS · & TRANSLATIONS

(1)

Epistle to Mr. Geoghegan[1]

Forgive me for presuming right
When I this modest strain indite
To thee thou noble thing of light
And high regard
And child of wayward genius bright
And tuneful bard

Ne'er was mine the rhyming trade
No heaven-lit ray the gift betrayed
My horney fist has more essayed
In lonely glen
The labour of the rustic spade
Than poet's pen

But O! one night amid a train
That quaffed the juice of Barleygrain
A song was raised by simple swain
In blissful hour
And thine he said the heavenly strain
of magic power

The soft inspiring song he sung
Was love fraught lay to maidens young
Such as would warble Moore's sweet tongue
To Byron's lyre
I felt the rapturing notes that rung
My bosom fire

And O! I vowed to know thee closer
Thou soul dissolving rhyme-composer
That thou some kind regard may'st show Sir
I dared the crime
For poets hate a plodding proser

---

[1] NLI, MS 8092. The *Epistle* is dated August 24th 1830 and signed 'E Walshe.' Having compared the handwriting in MS 8092 with Walsh's letters in MS 2261, I am satisfied that both are by the same hand. The author gives his address as Barleyhill (near Newmarket, in Co. Cork) and the poem is the earliest datable composition by Edward Walsh.

To write in rhyme
Thy mild indulgence gently fling
Around this artless rhyme I bring
The humble wren may simply sing
Or lonely fly
While the lordly eagles cleaving wing
Explore the sky

Newmarket fair full fast is nearing
O! be thou there sweet endearing
Where whiskey punch in flagons cheering
Will sparkling pass
And friend with bosom friend appearing
O'er the glass

Let worthless wretches dark and drear
Who never to misery gave a tear
Whose God is gold and o'er whose bier
No weeping eye
Be doomed to live unblessed here
And hopeless die.

Give me a social fireside gay
A child of genius near me lay
Let whiskey[1] in sparkling font display
In flask or horn
To keep — victorious sway
John Barley-corn.

Newmarket fair bright Geoghegan
No mood or verse but "may & can"
Pat. — is a plain blunt man
Would gladly walk
From Barleyhill to Moylan's Rock
With thee to talk

[1] The author has not made his final choice of words here: line 3 runs: 'let whiskey/nature/drinks in sparkling font display.' – Ed.

When thou and I have talked our fill
And swigged mayhap a whiskey gill
My cabin stands at Barleyhill
And there's a bed
And nightcap to compose at will
Thy tuneful head

(2)
Address to the Grave[1]

I hail thee cold bed of the weary
Thrice welcome glad couch of repose
Tho' deep thy dark pillow and dreary
Yet there ends the wretched one's woes
Not there shall the salt tear of sorrow
The cheek of affection bedew
Not there shall the sun of the morrow
The pangs of the wretched renew.

Deep slumber eternal I hail thee
Now oft mid the anguish of night
I wished, Ah! could wishes avail me
To wait till the morning's blest light
I'll sleep there the sleep without waking
Till millions from earth & from wave
Arouse at the last trumpet's shaking
And burst from thee sleep of the grave.

(3)
1830[2]

Dear Jack thou man of sooty trade
Of chanter sweet and tuneful quill
Who profferdest thy skilful aid
To help a mourner thro' the shade

---

[1] NLI, MS 8092: Although the *Address* is signed 'E Walshe' the handwriting is unmistakably that of Edward Walsh in MS. 2261.

[2] NLI, MS 8092: The only title given to this poem is '1830.' The handwriting is identical with that in MS 2261.

Of life's sad train of ill
My fire and fun are nearly o'er
And gone for aye my rhyming lore
When first I sung about thy chanter
The muse would rhyme when e'er I'd want her
But now she's fled my hour of need
And faithless left her invalid
To weather like a broken reed
Alas! that e'er this bosom bled
For now believed or promised spoken
Alas! that death low-laid one head
Whose tie to me nought else has broken
Alas! that ever piercing pain
Should burn even to my throbbing brain
That even the tears which comfort brings
Have left this fountain withering
And no soft drop from eyes of mine
Could flow for all my health's decline
Forgive I pray thy care worn friend
Dear Jack! it made me splenetic
When I sat down until thou'st send
The spike for cupplis[?] walking stick
Time was when I could urge my flight
Like fallow deer o'er mountains' height
That sense the wild heaths weakness bend
Beneath my footsteps airy strength
No crag nursed goat could climb like me
The tall rude rocks that mock the sea
Nor ocean bird could lighter lave
His pliant limb in salt sea wave
For long your mourner loved to stray
Where rock bound shore caught ocean spray
And oft the wave delighted rode
Like genius of the deep abode
No worth the day! no worth the hour
That saw the limbs of lightness fail
That saw the youthful poet's power
Neath sorrow's iron sceptre quail
But here's my comfort mid my pain

Jack can mend my walking cane
And when its spike of steel forsake it
God be thankful Jack can make it
Should I wish mid social glee
To steal an hour from pains that rend me
Jack has punch for friends, and me
And God increase it cash to lend me
Or should I want a lightsome tune
Or magic dirge or martial strain
Jack - 'o flying fingers soon
Would raise my drooping heart again
Till every passion by his art
Or pity dearest to my heart
Would rise as swells his tuneful story
I'll rest the muse but I begrime her
Farewell dear Jack. Pray send the spike
And mayest thou with chiming rhyme
Assist thy humble friend and rhymer

(4)
TO ERIN[1]

My country! - too long, like the mist on thy mountains,
The cloud of affliction hath sadden'd thy brow:
Too long hath the blood-rain empurpled thy fountains,
And Pity been deaf to thy cries - until now.

Thou wert doom'd for a season in darkness to languish,
While others around thee were basking in light;
Scarce a sunbeam e'er lighten'd the gloom of thy anguish;
In "the Island of Saints," it seem'd still to be night.

Of thy children, alas! some in sorrow forsook thee,
They could not endure to behold thee distress'd;
In "the land of the stranger" did other's o'erlook thee,
Unworthy the life-stream they drew from thy breast.

---

[1] Reprinted in the DPJ, May 9th 1835, p. 360. A note acknowledges the source as the *Belfast Magazine*. I have failed to locate the original in the surviving issues of the *Belfast Magazine and Literary Journal*, the *Belfast Co-operative Magazine*, and the *New Belfast Magazine*.

And the song of the minstrel was hushed in thy bowers;
For Discord's dire trump, thy lov'd harp was thrown by;
While, strong as the ivy that strangled thy towers,
The gripe of oppression scarce left thee a sigh!

That is past - and for aye let its memory perish;
The day-spring arises, while heaviness ends;
Wake Erin! forbear thy dark bodings to cherish -
The wheel hath revolv'd, and thy fortune ascends!

Yes - thy cause hath been heard - men have wept at thy story -
Alas! that a land of such beauty should mourn!
Have thy children ne'er grac'd the high niches of glory?
Was kindness ne'er known in thy bosom to burn?

Yes, rich as the mines which thy teeming hills nourish,
Are the stores of their genius which nature imparts;
And sweet as the flow'rs in thy valleys that flourish,
The fragrance of feeling that breathes from their hearts!

When stung to despair, in their wildness what wonder
If sometimes their souls from affection might rove?
That frenzy subsiding, their feelings the fonder
Will seek their own halcyon channel of love?

Let the past be forgotten! - Yet shalt thou, fair Erin,
Fling off the base spells which thy spirit enslave;
Thou shalt, like the sea-bird, awhile disappearing,
Emerge with thy plumage more bright from the wave.

Once more 'mong the verdure and dew of thy mountains
The shamrock shall ope its wet eye to the sun,
While fondly the muse shall recline by thy fountain,
And warble her strains to the rills as they run.

And plenty shall smile on thy beautiful valleys
And peace shall return, the long wandering dove;
And religion, no longer a cover for malice,
Shall spread out her wings o'er an Eden of love.

Then turning thy mild harp, whose melody slumbers,
As high on the willow it waves in the breeze,
Let poesy lend thee her liveliest numbers,
To sound thy reveille, thy anthem of praise.

And say unto those that have left thee forsaken -
"Return oh return, to your lone mother's arms!
Other lands in their sons can a fondness awaken;
Shall Erin alone for her race have no charms!

"Oh, blush as ye wander, that it e'er should be taunted,
That strangers have felt, what my own could not feel;
That, when Britons stood forth in my trial undaunted,
My children slunk back, unconcerned in my weal!

"Oh! if yet in your bosom one last spark ye treasure
Of love for the land of your sires - of your birth –
Return! and indulge in the soul-thrilling pleasure,
Of hailing that land 'mong the brightest on earth!"

Then joy to thee, Erin! thy better day breaketh;
The long polar night of thy woe speeds away,
And, as o'er thy chill breast the warm sunlight awaketh,
Each bud of refinement evolves in the ray.

Yet remember - the blossom is barren and fleeting,
As long as the canker of strife, unsubdued,
With its poisonous tooth at the core remains eating -
If e'er thou art *glorious*, thou first must be *good.*

(5)
The Chiefs of Clanawly[1]

A legend of the South.[2]

There's a feast in the hall where Clanawly's chief dwells,
And waking of wild harps, and sounding of shells;
Unclasp'd are the helmets - the wavy plumes now
Bend graceful no more o'er the warrior's brow;
The chiefs are all waiting - did any behold
The princely McAuliff, proud lord of the world?

The night breeze sings cold o'er Clonfert's ancient tomb,
Dallo ripples dark in his wavy woods' gloom;
The guests are impatient - "McAuliff[3] doth hunt

---

[1] The poem was first published in the *Dublin Penny Journal*, January 17th 1835 acknowledging Edward Walsh's authorship. It contains a versification of the legend relating to Ellen, daughter of a McAuliffe chieftain of the wild upland district of north-western Duhallow, traditionally known as *The Dark Mountains of McAuliffe*. See also 'Meelan; a legend of the South' by Edward Walsh, pp. 495ff and a prose version of the *Meelan legend*, in "Meelan's Rock," p. 371ff. - Ed.

[2] Castle McAuliffe, the seat of the chiefs of Clanawly, rose on the bank of the river Daloo, to the left of the road leading from Newmarket to Millstreet, and about a mile from the former. It was a strong building, and towered proudly on a tall cliff that overhung the stream; but the ruin which time and the fire of the invader failed in accomplishing, modern vandalism has completed, and its grass-grown foundations can now hardly be traced. McAuliffe's territory was a mountainous tract, and it yet bears the name of "McAuliffe's Dark Mountains." The last lord of Clanawly was attainted in the rebellion of 1641, with McDonagh of Kanturk, prince of Duhallow, whose uncle McAuliffe was. The popular legends of this race are very curious. McAuliffe, the legend concerning whom we have attempted to portray, rescued the beautiful daughter of a neighbouring chieftain from the "power of fairy," in the manner related in the text; and a wild and spellbound destiny seems to have awaited his posterity by that lady, whom he afterwards married. His son on a certain day, overpowered by the fatigues of the chase, lay down to rest upon the margin of a clear well, which is yet shown as you enter Newmarket from the west; he drank of the water, and, falling asleep, awoke in some hours greatly endued with the spirit of prophecy. These prophecies he uttered in Irish verse. They are yet preserved among the peasantry of Duhallow, and are extremely curious. In one of them, with a mournful prescience, he alludes to the extinction of his own race. This was fulfilled about the year 1828, by the death of a well-known character in the neighbourhood of Newmarket, called John McAuliffe the Active, the last of that noble line; he spent a poor, precarious life - a wanderer in the extensive territory of his ancestors. Meelan, the daughter, we believe, of the last chief of Clanawly, was on her wedding night, conveyed by supernatural agency to a tall cliff on the right bank of the Dallow, over against the ruined church of Clonfert. A huge excavation in the steep hill bears her name, and the peasantry affirm that often, while the shadows of night are falling fast around, her plaintive sounds of lament are heard to wake the echoes that sleep round the rock of her enchantment.

[3] Walsh allows for variety in the spelling of this surname: McAuliff, McAuliffe, etc. – Ed.

The red mountain deer as a chieftain is wont,
Or urging the chase of the wolf from the plain
To his lair in the cliff, does McAuliffe remain?"

Ah, no! for his tall dogs in idleness howl;
Beyond them the gaunt wolf may fearlessly prowl;
The long hunting spear, and the loud hunting horn,
No more in the chase o'er the wide heath are borne;
For the chase of the grey wolf, or red mountain deer,
Doth least in the thoughts of the chieftain appear.

For Ellen, the heiress of all that divide
The bank of the Dallo from the Allo's loud tide,
Is dead. Oh! bethink ye that bosom's dismay,
Which consigns all it loves to the cold reptile's sway:
And never did Love's brilliant fetter entwine
More true heart's, McAuliffe, than Ellen's and thine!

There's wringing of hands - and the mourner's shrill cry,
And the wild *ullalu* of the keener is high;
And the handmaids have strew'd early flowers on the grave
Where Kilcorcoran's alders in solitude wave:
But an old, hoary wizard of visions hath told
A tale which the chieftain forbears to unfold!

And whispers are heard, that fair Ellen survives
Where spells of the fairy bind enchanted lives -
That the bier where the mourners had pour'd their despair,
Held naught but the semblance of young Ellen there!
I wist not what tale did the grey wizard tell -
The breast of the chief holds it closely and well.

But nightly, since Ellen was wrapt in her shroud,
Though the lightning may gleam and the fierce storm be loud,
And though Dallo's dark water his green valley fills,
Increas'd by the streams of his cloud-cover'd hills,
Though blue flash, wild tempest, and wilder wave's flight,
He seeks yon lone crag on the pine-covered height.

There's a feast in the hall - but he climbs the rude steep
When the shadows of darkness are silent and deep;
The breeze that had swept yonder home of the dead,
Was bending the pine on that peak's rugged head,
Where rose through the gloom, on his wonder-struck eye,
A palace where fairies hold festival high!

The essence of all that gives colour to light,
Did with treasures of earth in that structure unite;
And the spirit of music, exalted, refin'd
Like a spell, round the heart of the listener entwin'd,
As he enter'd the portal, and pass'd on to where
Gay pleasure was reigning - for woman was there!

And wine-bowls of brightness the banquet did crown;
In mantle and mail sat old chiefs of renown.
The white bearded harper's wild melody rings,
While the fierce *Eye of Battle*[1] arose on the strings,
And shouts of the brave from the mail-covered throng,
Came blent o'er the board with that wild battle song!

There were bright eyes of beauty, and bosoms of snow,
And maids that were *stolen* long ages ago;
And sea-nymphs that came from their home in the main;
And fairies of ocean, and fays of the plain;
But the chieftain's eye wander'd the bright circle round
In search of young Ellen - and Ellen it found!

The voice of the harp and the hero had fled,
When the mortal appear'd at the feast of the dead;
But *one* who in stature resembled a god,
Cried, "Welcome, O chief, to the crystal abode!"
"Thrice welcome, McAuliffe!" the banquet guests cried.
"Thrice welcome, McAuliffe!" the echoes replied.

[1] *Ros Catha*, or the Eye of Battle, was a warlike air, to the music of which the warriors moved to the fight. It was likewise in high repute at the festive meetings of the chiefs; and, it is said, that its thrilling notes were able to rouse their military ardour to the highest pitch of excitement.

And he who in stature resembled a god,
To the lord of Clanawly right courteously strode,
And led him to where stood a canopied throne,
That with gold and rich jewels all gloriously shone;
Then signed to the harper, who sweetly and well,
Poured the charm of his voice with the *cláirseach's*[1] soft spell.

"All hail, potent lord of Clanawly! - to thee
Thy home long be sacred, thy mountains be free;
May the falchion, thy fathers to victory bore,
Flash vengeance on tyrants till thraldom be o'er.

The heroes are met, at the *cláirseach's* loud call,
To share the glad feast, in the banqueting hall;
But often they gather'd in mantle and mail,
At glory's proud call, for the right of the Gael.

These red bowls of brightness, our banquet-guests drain,
In flavour exceed the famed *boir*[2] of the Dane;
And the chiefs of Kincora ne'er honoured such wine,
As o'er this glad board pours its current divine.

We've maidens like those whose thrice-beautiful eyes,
Lur'd angels to earth, from their home in the skies;
And voices are here, at whose magical will
The tempest of ocean were silent and still.

With the fair and the brave share the banquet of joy,
With music and wine the glad moments employ;
And sirens of sweetness shall warble for thee.
In this hall of our feasting, their songs of the sea.

---

[1] *Cláirseach*. the harp. - Ed.

[2] Tradition affirms that the Danes made a delicious intoxicating liquor, called *boir*, of the mountain heath. Kincora, the residence of Brian Boru, on the bank of the Shannon, was celebrated for its wine-cellars; and when the peasantry would assure you of a hearty welcome to their fireside, they say, in their expressive manner, "Were ours the boir of the Dane, and the wine of Kincora, they should be poured for you."

Then hail, potent lord of Clanawly! to thee
Thy home long be sacred, thy mountains be free;
May the falchion, thy fathers to victory bore,
Flash vengeance on tyrants till thraldom be o'er."

McAuliff then rose, to the brave and the bright:
"In the hall of Clanawly there's feasting to night:[1]
To stay in your palace, that banquet to shun,
My fathers would blush for the shame of their son.
I'll dance but one measure, then quickly retire,
To head the glad feast in the home of my sire.

He bow'd to young Ellen - she blush'd and looked down;
Some beauties grew pale, and some maidens did frown.
Such graceful young dancers 'twere seldom to see,
His stature so noble - so beauteous was she.
"High Heaven defend us," he whispering said,
"There's danger, dear maid, in this measure we tread!"

As quick gleam their steps on the diamond-paved floor,
One hand grasps the lady - they rush to the door -
And one the black dagger[2] whose spell-rending steel
The power of faery would tremble to feel!
Then clasps his fond maid in his ardent embrace
And, gaining the portal, escapes from the place.

There were rushing of lady and chief from the hall
And wailing and woe, would the bravest appal;
But the cock's sudden clarion gave notice of day,
And the hall and the fairy-guests faded away.
So constant in love, and in danger so bold,
Have ye heard of a chief like the lord of the World?

---

[1] To eat or drink at such feasts as this would be the surest way of subjecting himself to fairy spells; and McAuliffe was, doubtless, glad of a fair excuse for evading the influence.

[2] The *Skien Dhu* or black dagger, had irresistible power over the strongest enchantments; its efficacy, even to this day, in destroying fairy spells and killing ghosts, is most devoutly believed; and, to use a phrase of Lord Byron's, 'most incredibly attested.'

(6)
The Spirit of Lough Dergart[1]

A legend of the Shannon[2]

By Lough Dergart's wave, where rude winds roar,
A dark spirit dwelt in time of yore;
And fishermen, fraught with wild affright,
Still shun the curst haunt of the water-sprite.

For often he lur'd the homebound skiff
To the eddy beneath the haunted cliff,
Where the sailors' last shriek and the rocks' reply
Were blended in air with his fiendish joy.

Full often beneath his evil eye
The 'witch'd herd would fall, the harvest die;
And death-dealing shafts the fiend would fling,
As he sported in air on the tempest's wing!

Some horror-fraught deeds of this evil thing,
No legend would say, no bard would sing;
For nothing of ruth could round him dwell,
Who sprung from a witch and a fiend of hell.

His artifice bore to an early tomb
A maid in the pride of beauty's bloom;
I wept o'er her fate long days ago,
And I'll weave in my lay the tale of woe.

This maiden would oft her pathway take
To church by the side of that lonely lake,
And the water-sprite thought, with fell design,
"O! that I could make yon maiden mine!"

---

[1] The poem based on a folk-tale set at Lough *Dergart* (Lough Derg) on the lower Shannon near Killaloe was first published in the *Dublin Penny Journal*, February 14th 1835. - Ed.

[2] Lough Dergart is a large lake formed by the waters of the Shannon, equidistant between Banagher and Limerick. In a novel called the *Monk*, there is a legend much resembling this; but I have given the story exactly as tradition has preserved it among the fishermen that inhabit the banks of Lough Derg.

When the Sabbath bell toll'd, with tone profound,
Though wicked ones hate the sainted sound,
He seeks the bless'd fane; and his angel eye
Of magic would steal a young maiden's sigh.

He shone, a gay knight of noble mien,
The sedge of the lake his armour green;
And the mantle that flow'd o'er his shoulders he
Had form'd from down of the willow tree.

He made a light boat of the wild waves' spray,
To bear to dark doom his fated prey;
And the long lily-leaves the wild lake bore
Were the white-bosom'd sails the bright bark wore.

The high bounding boat soon leaves the land,
The helm well obeys the green knight's hand;
No mortal e'er saw in time gone by
A bright bark so brave - such chieftain high.

And thus have I seen some bright barks brave
All gallantly glide o'er life's wild wave;
How dark were the hearts could say my song,
Of the loud-laughing crew that sail'd along.

He bounds from the well-moor'd bark to shore,
And God's holy house his feet explore,
Where matron and maid admired the mien,
And the blue, laughing eyes of the chieftain green.

He strode up the aisle with stately air,
And sat him beside his maiden fair;
When he press'd her white hand, her eyes betray'd,
And the glow of her cheek, the conquest made.

"My castle is gay in yon lake-girt land,
Where tall forests wave to the breezes bland;
Be queen of that isle, and my own for aye -
To death I'll decline if thou answer 'nay.' "

She falter'd consent - and the nuptial rite
Fast bound the fair maid and the elfin knight;
But the setting sun's gleam o'er blue waves spread,
Soon lighted the bride to her watery bed.

The fresh'ning gale blew the light boat on,
The false castle's towers in the distance shone,
And the falser green knight did thus address
His bride 'mid the waters' loneliness.

"Some brave barks lightly walk the waves when prospering gales pursue,
And things of life that tread the deck may oft such passage rue;
For things of life in bravest barks may tempt the treacherous main,
And quit the shore to which no gale may bear them back again.

"The wise ones say that dangers deep the smoothest waves o'ershade,
And legends tell that genius dark would sigh for mortal maid:
If so, thy blissful bridal bed may be the oozy cave,
A water-sprite the gay green knight to whom the vow you gave.

"You forests, high where breezes sigh, and yonder turrets tall,
Where the mild moon-beam sheds yellow gleam are potent magic all.
At my command uprose that land, and shone those turrets fair;
Lo! from the lake their flight they take, and vanish into air.

"My own beloved bride! for thee I doff this day
disguise,
With all my native loveliness now feast thy
raptur'd eyes;
This form uncouth may give thee joy when you're
bound with potent spell,
Where gnomes of horrid shape appear, and
things of darkness dwell.

"Why shriek? - the tie that made us one, no
earthly power can rend;
Beneath the deep my court I keep, then let us
quick descend.
This day of doom, when yearly come, shall view
the tall bark ride,
And thou be seen, those arms between, thus
sink beneath the tide."

Then blended the boat with its kindred foam,
Then sunk the dark sprite to its watery home,
Then shriek'd the lost maid as her garments white
For an instant were stay'd by the breeze's flight.

Once every year, by sacred doom,
A bark o'er the wave is seen to come;
And the maiden's last shriek is heard to break
The loneliness of the moon-lit lake.

Ye maidens! beware of false ones' sighs,
And shun the warm gaze of eager eyes;
When whispers soft vows some gay green knight,
Be warn'd by the tale of the water-sprite.

(7)
Meelan[1]

A Legend of the South

"———————— "Enchantments drear,
Where more is meant than meets the ear." -*Milton*

'Tis night, and the moon, from her star-clad height,
Flings her marble of silver hue
O'er Clonfert's green graves; and all sparkling bright
Daloo, in her gleam-beams, a sheet of light,
Where murmur its waters blue.

How gloom from afar, o'er the soothing scene,
The tall cliff and wavy wood;
And mournful and grey are the rude rocks between,
Where Castle McAwly[2] stood.

Here frown'd the dark turrets in lordly pride,
Here smil'd the gay chieftain's hall;
The clansmen here marshal'd in order wide,
When war-fires high blazed on the mountain's side,
For battle at glory's call.

Here ne'er shall the string of the *cláirseach* wake;
The songs of the hall are o'er;
No more shall the voice of the victor break,
When home, o'er the mountain, their wild way take,
The kern[3] and crahadore.[4]

---

[1] The poem first appeared in the *Dublin Penny Journal*, April 4th 1835. It is another version of *The Chiefs of Clanawly*, (see pp. 486ff) and *Meelan's Rock* (see pp. 371ff). A ancient Celtic goddess is here presented as the daughter of the McAuliffe chieftain who had his seat at Castle McAuliffe on the banks of the Daloo. Her memory is perpetuated both in the name *Meelin*, a village north west of Newmarket, and *Meelan's Rock* at the Island Wood across the valley from Clonfert graveyard. Tradition attests that her plaintive lament can still be heard by Dallo's banks. - Ed.

[2] The castle of McAuliffe, the chief of Clanawley, stood over the Daloo, on the left hand side of the road to Blackwater-bridge. The foundations are now scarcely visible.

[3] *Kern*: an Irish foot soldier.

[4] *Crahadore*: the taker of spoils.

The clansmen, who battled with Saxon foes,
The chief of the lordly dome;
The bard, at whose call the stout clansmen rose,
In death undistinguished all calm repose -
They are gone to their silent home!

Lo! yonder, where moss-grown the grave-stones lie,
McAuliffe sad-sought the tomb;
He fell not in battle by victor high,
Heart-broken he yielded his latest sigh
For Meelan, his daughter's doom!

Daloo, while thou gildest thy groves between,
Shall the maids of thy sun-lit glade
Twine horror-fraught tales of the nuptial scene
With the olden lays echoed through woodland green,
For Meelan, the gold-haired maid.

And mild as the lambkin, that crops the lea,
And pensive as cowslips pale,
She oft sought the valley alone - for she
Was woo'd by a chieftain of high degree
In yonder dark lonely dale.

O'Herly was gallant, and brave, and gay;
And chronicles ancient tell,
That Malachy bid his fair daughter say,
Who'd kiss her pure cheek on the nuptial day -
Her choice on O'Herly fell.

Fond pair! you have woven in fancy's loom
Sweet garlands of pleasure gay;
Dark destiny withers your garland's bloom,
Yet could beauty, could merit, revoke the doom,
Not yours were this plaintive lay.

The glad nuptial morn arrives; and, lo!
The high notes of joy resound:
The guests are in waiting, a glorious show -
The bards' raptur'd voices all sweetly flow,
To join the wild harp's soft sound.

As blooms the young rose in the sun-beams clear,
With bright pearly dew besprent;
So fair Meelan shone, through the smile and tear,
When the young chieftain soothed each maiden fear,
As they to the altar went.

How glorious the pomp of the lordly train,
That leads the young pair along;
What silver-shod coursers proud paw'd the plain -
Clonfert never saw, in her sacred fame,
So gallant, so fair a throng.

To view the gay pageant the deep crowds press'd,
Warm hearts in hot war's turmoil;
Whose lips, warmly praying, the bright pair bless'd,
As they went where the priests were in surplices dress'd,
To the altar, along the aisle.

The hollow wind whistled the tombs among
The owl, from her ivy tower,
Her harsh nightly notes on the daylight rung,
When young Meelan whispered, with faltering tongue,
Consent to the nuptial power.

The marriage ring wax'd as the moonbeam pale,
And deep was her heart's dark fall,
As the loud tempest gather'd adown the dale,
And the bride and the bridegroom sad sought the vale,
That led to McAuliffe's hall.

The hollow winds whistle - the owlet's cry -
The marriage rings pally glow;
The gloom of the moment - the unconscious sigh -

The lowering dark cloud of the boding sky
Proclaim a sad tale of woe!

The sun hath gone down o'er the mountains steep,
And tinged its glades with gold;
The voice of the banquet is loud and deep -
The last and the latest that hall shall keep -
Clanawly shall e'er behold!

Poor bride! and the handmaids thy chamber spread,
And show'd the gay fragrant flower;
Thou wilt press with thy lover no nuptial bed -
Borne off by enchantment so drear and dread,
From bridegroom and bridal bower!

The revelry rose on the night's dull ear,
The vaulted hall loudly rung,
When Meelan discover'd in wildest fear,
A stranger was seated beside her near,
As "twelve" the strict warder sung.

His flowing locks mock'd the dark raven's plume;
His carriage, commanding high,
Bespoke the proud chieftain; but silent gloom
O'erspread every bosom around the room,
Though none knew the reason why.

His bright eye keen flash'd with unearthly fire,
No mortal might meet its glow;
The guests of the banquet with cold hearts retire,
The bard's fingers ceas'd o'er the trembling wire,
His presence such fears bestow.

Ye guests of the banquet surcease your dread,
Right courteous the stranger tall;
He fills o'er the table the wine bowl red;
He pledges the bride with low-bending head -
The bridegroom and chieftains all.

He leads the young bride in the circling dance,
Most regal his robes were seen;
The banquet-guests view'd him with eyes askance -
The bride, O! she trembled beneath his glance -
Though graceful and gay his mien.

How quick gleam her steps on the marble floor,
And gentle her light foot's sound
In the hall which her white foot oft trod before,
As she led her gay handmaids that marble o'er
To move in the mazy round.

'Tis done - When the murmurs applausive ceased,
The chief led the blooming bride
Where Malachy, 'mid the high chieftains placed,
Presided supreme o'er the nuptial feast,
Then sat by the maiden's side.

"Thy light step, fair bride," the dark stranger said,
"But echoed the music's sound:
With fair, blooming beauties the dance I've led -
Their charms would have vanished, their light step fled,
Wert thou in the mazy round.

"I love a young maid - and her grace is thine,
And thine are her tresses long,
And thine is her dark eye of light divine -
And O! if thou listen to strains of mine,
I'll sing to my fair a song."

She bow'd - and he rais'd some enchanted tone
Ne'er warbled by mortal tongue;
If golden-harp'd seraphs to earth had flown,
The voice of the stranger would seem their own -
And these were the strains he sung:

The song of the Spirit
"Thou knowest where yon mountain uprears its huge head,
Where the hoarse torrent roars down its rude, rocky bed,
There stands my bright palace - high dwelling of air -
And the bride of my bosom shall smile on me there!

"Where the hues of the rainbow, all glorious, unite,
Festooning the hall in gay vapours of light,
Whose diamond-starred pavement now sparkles in sheen,
Far brighter than gems the deep grottos of Lene.[1]

"The soft bridal bed my beloved shall share,
I've pluck'd from the pinions of spirits of air;
And the fairies of ocean, by strong spell beguil'd,
Shall sooth her to slumber with melody wild.

"I know where the waters of loveliness flow,
Whose pure draught can beauty immortal bestow;
And the rose of her cheek, and the snow of her brow,
Shall live through wreck'd ages, as peerless as now!

"My chariot the wild winds - my pathway the sky -
O'er wide earth and ocean unfettered I fly:
And my bright bird of beauty can wing her quick way
On the zephyr's soft pinion, as light fancy may!

"I know where the diamonds of brightness have birth,
In the caves of old ocean and dark womb of earth;
I'll choose for my fairest the rarest of all,
To deck as she pleases the crystal-built hall.

" 'Tis the night of my bridal - I've pass'd it with you:
The morning-star blazes - ye chieftains, adieu!
When yearly this dark night of wonder shall be,
Remember the bridal - and think, think, of me!

---

[1] *Loch Lene*, or the *Lake of Killarney*, remarkable, among its other natural curiosities, for diamonds. Tradition tells that a carbuncle of immense value lies in the bosom of the lake, guarded by enchanted spells.

"High lord of the castle! dark chief of the Wold[1]
The banquet of feasting I leave. But behold!
I'll snatch to my bosom the maid of my vow -
McAuliff's bright daughter, that maiden art thou!

'Tis vain, O rash bridegroom! nor tempt my high power,
I've deck'd for the Meelan the gay nuptial bower!
My train are in waiting - impatient I fly -
My chariot the wild winds - my pathway the sky."

Then rose through the castle the wild guest's fright,
As his strong arm he twin'd her round,
And wing'd through the wide yawning roof his flight:
But ne'er was the bride since that fear-fraught night,
Or the mysterious stranger, found.

To yonder rude cliff, called from Meelan's name,[2]
Through many an olden day -
Where rises the hall of enchanted fame,
Invisible save to the wizard's beam -
The mountain-sprite bore his prey.

At night when the cottagers calm repose,
And silent the grove and green,
Fair Meelan is oft at that dark hour's close,
While swells the sad tale of her fate and woes,
Near her rock of enchantment seen!

---

[1] The father of Meelan, and the last lord of Clanawley, was remarkable for his austere, dark temper. His territory was a mountainous tract, and is yet called "the dark mountains of McAuliffe."

[2] Meelan's Rock is a natural excavation in a huge steep that crowns the right bank of the Daloo, over against the ruined church of Clonfert.

(8)
The Man in the Moon[1]

A Legend[2]

Through optic glass when sages view
The moon's deep vales, her fountains blue,
Her every stream and ocean -
Alas! how vainly proud, they try
To cheat each honest, vulgar eye
With many a wild-goose notion!

Those wits, by light of science led,
With many a tale would turn your head,
Of hills and dales, good lack!
When, lo! each mother's son can spy
A man amid the moon on high,
With bush upon his back.

Since eldest time, from sire to son,
The tale through every age has run -
A tale of truth and wonder.
And from that tale you'll understand,
That man should ne'er with impious hand
His neighbour's substance plunder.

Tradition tells that on a time,
Ere thieving swell'd the list of crime,
Or honesty was fable -
'Twas some long years before the Flood
There lived a farmer, gen'rous good,
Kind-hearted, hospitable.

---

[1] The poem was first published in the *Dublin Penny Journal*, February, 6th 1836. It has an introduction (see note 2 below) initialled E.W. - Ed.

[2] Sir - As I observe in a recent number of your journal, an account of some philosophers having ascertained to a *certainty* that the moon is inhabited, I beg to send you a metrical description of the manner in which the first inhabitant was sent there - at least this is the version of the story given in my part of the country, *Duhallow*.

'Twas to a merry-making warm,
The tenant of a neighbouring farm,
With others, he invited;
And many a bumper o'er his board
Did gaiety and mirth afford,
And many a health was plighted.

Of dishes, there was noblest beef,
(Of dishes, beef thou art the chief,)
And veal, and lamb, and mutton;
And there a fragrant hog's-cheek steam'd,
The which in days of yore was deem'd
Fit dish for any glutton.

The conscious muse, with shame, must own
That knives and forks the board had none,
(How much unlike our vain ones!)
Save one large carving knife, that found
Employment swift the table round,
For ancient days were plain ones.

There sparkled not the vain array,
Of glass and china's bright display,
And little solid food;
Ah, no! the oaken board confess'd,
The meat, its groaning frame compress'd,
Substantial was and good.

I cannot sing what liquor bright,
Of copious stream, enriched the night -
Perhaps 'twas *aqua vitae*;
For say, what beverage dares to vie
What *aqua vitae*, spring of joy,
And boast of topers mighty.

Or whether foreign vintage flow'd,
Or native draughts inspiring glow'd,
Uncertain is the fable;
Yet sure that night, each joyous guest,
Full late, with high-erected crest,
Departed from the table.

The hero of our story, too,
Strode homeward o'er the pearly dew,
Quite happy with his dining;
For modern cit, or ancient clown,
Ne'er strok'd in cabin complacence down
A paunch of better lining.

'Twas on his gen'rous neighbour's grounds,
Adjacent to the well-known bounds
Which told each man's domain,
A hawthorn tree in beauty bloom'd,
And all the scented vale perfum'd
The glory of the plain.

With longing eye the tree he saw,
Regardless of fair Nature's law,
And thus did think, or say -
"This bush a noble fence would make,
Where cattle through my hedges break,
And o'er my pastures stray."

What weapon laid the hawthorn low,
Beneath the felon's midnight blow,
Tradition never knew it;
Old Nick, perhaps, who did suggest
Such bad design to such a guest,
Might bring an axe to hew it.

When Echo told the last stroke's sound,
Which laid the hawthorn on the ground,
The furtive prize he bore;
And all the branches, trailing low,
Full well betray'd his footsteps slow,
The lengthening valley o'er.

Quick panting 'neath th' unholy toil,
His hospitable neighbour's spoil,
Who ill deserv'd the meed;

The villain, first of thieving kind,
To his sad cost did shortly find
How crimes like his succeed.

Great Heaven, with indignation saw
The breach of long-respected law,
And high the thief translated,
Amid the moon's pale silver sheen,
Lest erring sons of men might ween
Such feats were lightly rated.

Through every age, through every year,
And every season, bright or drear,
He freezes or he burns;
And at his back the bush is seen
Clad in all its vernal green,
When blooming spring returns.

Until the dreadful day will come,
When Adam's sons receive their doom,
With bush across his shoulders,
Exalted high the villain stands,
A spectacle to wondering lands,
A warning to beholders.

Then mark the poet's simple theme,
And heed not the stargazer's dream,
My tale doth far exceed it;
For when to steal you are inclined,
Behold the moon, and there you'll find
A lesson, if you heed it.

(9)
The Earl of Desmond and the Banshee[1]

Now cheer thee on, my gallant steed,
There's a weary way before us -
Across the mountain swiftly speed,
For the storm is gathering o'er us.

Away, away, the horseman rides;
His bounding steed's dark form
Seem'd o'er the soft black moss to glide -
A spirit of the storm!

Now, rolling in the troubled sky,
The thunder's loudly crashing;
And through the dark clouds, driving by,
The moon's pale light is flashing.

In sheets of foam the mountain flood
Comes roaring down the glen;
On the steep bank one moment stood
The horse and rider then.

One desperate bound the courser gave,
And plunged into the stream;
And snorting, stemm'd the boiling wave,
By the lightning's quivering gleam.

The flood is past - the bank is gain'd -
Away with headlong speed;
A fleeter horse than Desmond rein'd
Ne'er serv'd at lover's need.

---

[1] Published in the *Book of Irish Ballads*, edited by D.F. MacCarthy, in 1846. The compiler lists it as *anonymous*, but in Walsh's native Araglen Valley and Sliabh Luachra the living tradition recognizes it as his composition. - Ed.

His scatter'd train, in later haste,
Far, far behind him ride;
Alone he's crossed the mountain waste,
To meet his promised bride.

The clouds across the moon's dim form
Are fast and faster sailing,
And sounds are heard on the sweeping storm
Of wild unearthly wailing.

At first low moanings seem'd to die
Away, and faintly languish;
Then swell into a piercing cry
Of deep, heart-bursting anguish.

Beneath an oak, whose branches bare
Were crashing in the storm,
With wringing hands and streaming hair
There sat a female form.

To pass that oak in vain he tried;
His steed refus'd to stir,
Though furious 'gainst his panting side
Was struck the bloody spur.

The moon, by driving clouds o'ercast,
Witheld its faithful gleam;
And louder than the tempest blast
Was heard the banshee's scream.

And, when the moon unveiled once more,
And show'd her palely light,
Then nought was seen save the branches bare
Of the oak-tree's blasted might.

That shrieking form had vanished
From out that lonely place;
And, like a dreamy vision, fled,
Nor left one single trace.

Earl Desmond gazed - his bosom swell'd
With grief and sad foreboding;
Then on his fiery way he held,
His courser madly goading.

For well that wailing voice he knew
And onward hurrying fast,
O'er hills and dales impetuous flew
And reach'd his home at last.

Beneath his wearied courser's hoof
The trembling drawbridge clangs,
And Desmond sees his own good roof,
But darkness o'er it hangs.

He pass'd beneath the gloomy gate,
No guiding tapers burn:
No vassals in the court-yard wait,
To welcome his return.

The hearth is cold in the lonely hall,
No banquet decks the board;
No page stands ready at the call,
To tend his wearied lord.

But all within is dark and drear,
No sights or sounds of gladness -
Nought broke the stillness on the ear,
Save a sudden burst of sadness.

Then slowly swell'd the keener's strain
With loud lament and weeping,
For round a corse a mournful train
The sad deathwatch were keeping.

Aghast he stood, bereft of power,
Hope's fairy visions fled;
His fear's confirmed - his beauteous flower
His fair-hair'd bride - was dead.

(10)
St. Lateerin[1]

When the *slua-shee*[2] appear in lonely dell,
And revels are rife when mortals dream,
And wizards behold - but dare not tell
The spells that are wrought by haunted stream:

When the *shee-geehy*[3] rolls its boding cloud,
And arrows unseen in vengeance fly;
When the voice of the *keener* is wild and loud
O'er the maiden that died by the evil eye:

When the art of the midwife fails to save
The young mother doom'd to *fairy fort*;
When the traveller's lur'd beneath the wave,
Where *Donall na Geela*[4] keeps his court:

What saves in the hour of faery,
When goblins awake and gnomes have sway?
What scatters the ranks of the dread *slua-shee*,
That circle the midnight traveller's way?

Supreme o'er the spirits of earth and sea,
When blessed Lateerin's name is spoken, -
The Druid enchantments fade and flee,
And the spell of the midnight hour is broken.

---

[1] These stanzas introduce the story of *St. Lateerin* (see p. 198) first published in the *Dublin Penny Journal* on May 4th 1833. Despite Walsh's description of it as 'a literal translation of the fragment of a song which rose to a wild and melancholy air amid the tombs and gravestones of Cullin' the song is of his own making. The thrust of the theme is that the invocation of St. Lateerin is a protection from all that might be harmful to the human person. - Ed.

[2] *Slua-shee*: Fairy host.

[3] *Shee geehy*: Fairy wind or tempest, usually those whirling eddied, which raise dust, straw, etc. and are supposed by the country people to be caused by the fairies.

[4] *Donal na Geela*: the Celtic god of the dead and underworld. - Ed.

Thro' regions remote extends her fame,
And many a clime and age can tell,
What pilgrims invoking her holy name,
Drank health at the flow of her *sainted well*!

(11)
Thy Welcome O'Leary[1]

Thy welcome, O'Leary,
Be joyous and high;
As this dwelling of fairy
Can echo reply,
The cláirseach[2] and crothal,[3]
And loud Bara-boo,[4]
Shall sound not a note till
We've music from you.

The bara-boo's wildness
Is meet for the fray,
The crothal soft mildness
For festival gay:
The cláirseach is meeter
For bower and hall.
But thy chanter sounds sweeter -
Far sweeter than all.

When thy fingers are flying
The chanter along,
And the keys are replying
In wildness of song;
Thy bagpipes are speaking

---

[1] The song was published in the *Dublin Penny Journal* of October 18th 1834. The theme of the prose legend relating to *Daniel O'Leary the Duhallow Piper* (see pp. 225ff) is based on an invitation by Sweeney ('The Squire of Kilmeen') to his home in Ballyhoolihan east of Boherbue. O'Leary had a drink too many at the *Wallis Arms* in Millstreet and was sidetracked by the fairies on the banks of the Blackwater at Duarigle. - Ed.

[2] The *cláirseach* is the Irish harp.

[3] The *crothal* was a kind of bell.

[4] The *Bara-boo*: an instrument resembling a trumpet.

Such magical strain,
As minstrels are seeking
To rival in vain.

Shall bards of this dwelling
Admire each sweet tone,
As thy war-notes are swelling,
That erst were their own;
Shall beauties of brightness
And chieftain's of might,
To thy brisk lay of lightness
Dance featly tonight.

The wine of Kincorra,[1]
The bior of the Dane[2]
Shall lighten thy sorrow
Or brighten thy strain;
In the hall of our feasting,
Though many shall dine,
We'll deem thee not least in
The banquet divine.

O'er harper and poet
We'll place thy high seat;
O'Leary, we owe it,
To piper so sweet:
And fairies are braiding,
(Such favourite art thou,)
Fresh laurel, unfading,
To circle thy brow.

Thy welcome, O'Leary,
Be joyous and high;
As this dwelling of fairy

---

[1] *Kincora*, the residence of Brian Boro, on the bank of the Shannon, was famous for its wine cellars.
[2] Tradition affirms that the Danes made a delicious intoxicating liquor of the mountain heath, called 'Bior'. The peasant of the present day, when he would assure you of a hearty welcome, says, "were ours the Bior of the Dane, or the wine of Kincora, it would be poured for you."

Can echo reply;
The cláirseach and crothal
And loud bara-boo,
Shall sound not a note till
We've music from you.

(12)
Mairéad Ní Cheallaigh[1]

Air: *Maighréad Ní Cheallaigh*

"Thy neck was, lost maid!
Than the kanavane[2] whiter;
And the glow of thy cheek
Than the monadan[3] brighter:
But Death's chain hath bound thee
Thine eye glazed and hollow
That shone like a sun-burst,
Young Mairéad Ní Cheallaigh.

At the dance in the village[4]
Thy white foot was fleetest;
Thy voice 'mid the concert
Of maidens was sweetest;
The swell of thy white breast
Made rich lovers follow;

---

[1] One of the most popular of all Walsh's songs, *Mairéad Ní Cheallaigh,* (Mauriade ny Kallagh in Walsh's orthography) was published in the *Dublin Penny Journal*, August 29th 1835. In the story of 'The Duhallow Cowboy' (see pp. 253ff), Walsh puts the words of this touching ballad on the lips of a cow-herd by the Araglen. It is the eternal story of love, passion and betrayal. The characters concerned in the ballad are Daniel O'Keeffe, an 18th-century dispossessed Irish landowner, and Margaret Kelly. In using the name 'Kelly' Walsh may have taken note of local sensibilities in his day: the late Molly Hickey of Gortnacreha, Cullen, told me that the real name of the girl was Margaret O'Callaghan, and that her family who received the blood money kept it in a teapot before using it to acquire land and status. They were known locally as *The Callaghan Taypots*! - Ed.

[2] A plant found in bogs, the top of which bears a substance resembling cotton, and as white as snow. [Irish, *ceannabhán*. - Ed.]

[3] The monadan is a red berry that is found on wild marshy mountains. It grows on an humble creeping plant. [Irish, *monádán*. - Ed.]

[4] In the Kiskeam song tradition, the sequence of the stanzas is altered to begin with the second ('At the dance in the village,' etc) and followed by the first and remaining. - Ed.

And thy raven hair bound them,
Young Mairéad Ní Cheallaigh.

No more shall mine ear drink
Thy melody swelling;
Nor thy beamy eye brighten
The outlaw's dark dwelling;
Or thy soft heaving bosom
My destiny hallow,
When thine arms twine around me,
Young Mairéad Ní Cheallaigh.

"The Moss couch I brought thee
To day from the mountain,
Has drank the last drop
Of thy young heart's red fountain,
For this good *skien*[1] beside me
Struck deep and rung hollow
In thy bosom of treason,
Young Mairéad Ní Cheallaigh.

With strings of rich pearls
Thy white neck was laden,
And thy fingers with spoils
Of the Sasanach maiden:
Such rich silks enrob'd not
The proud dames of Mallow -
Such pure gold they wore not
As Mairéad Ní Cheallaigh.

Alas! that my loved one
Her outlaw would injure -
Alas! that he e'er proved
Her treason's avenger!
That this right hand should make thee
A bed cold and hollow,
When in Death's sleep it laid thee,
Young Mairéad Ní Cheallaigh!

---

[1] A knife.

And while to this lone cave
My deep grief I'm venting,
The Saxon's keen bandog
My footsteps is scenting:
But true men await me
Afar in Duhallow.
Farewell, cave of slaughter
And Mairéad Ní Cheallaigh.

(13)

Harp of Erin Quit thy Slumbers[1]

Air: *Harp of Erin*

Harp of Erin! quit thy slumbers
At the call of Dermid Dhu;
Bid the voice of flowing numbers
Rouse to war the martial crew,
From loud Allo's echoing water,
From sacred Ceadsrue's gentle floods,
From Carrigcashel's ford of slaughter,
From winding Daloo's waving woods;

From Earl of Desmond's mist-wrapt mountain,
Where gushes broad Blackwater's spring;
From blest Lateerin's sainted fountain;
From the silver Araglen:
O'er craggy hill and purple heather
Rush like torrents from the rock,
Led by many a valiant leader,
Bulwark in the battle's shock.

McDonough, prince of wide Duhallow,
Rouse thy chieftains to the fight;
McAuliff's clansmen soon shall follow -
From their marshy mountains' height
The war-cry shrill full wildly waxes,
Where O'Keefe's towering castles soar;

[1] This fine rousing song was published in *The Dublin Penny Journal*, November 23rd 1835. It is to be found in the prose legend, *The Ford of the White Ship* (see pp. 271ff). - Ed.

McSweeny's beamy battle-axes
Thirst to drink the foeman's gore!

Vassals! leave your valleys wasted -
March at freedom's sacred call;
Leave the genial feast untasted,
Diners in the banquet hall -
The eagle craves his banquet gory,
Dash the wine-bowl to the floor,
And feast him in a feast of glory,
Stalwart, kern, and crahadore.

I see the rushing squadrons dealing
Dreadful death and ghastly scar -
I see the firm-set phalanx reeling
'Neath the iron shock of war;
Spears pursuing - Saxons flying -
The sabre's clash - the axe's stroke -
Erin victor - foemen dying
Shrouded in the cannon's smoke!

Terror of the mighty Roman [1]
Conqueror of the warlike Dane [2]
Art[3] the scourge of Saxon foeman -
O'Moore,[4] the shield of battle-plain -

---

[1] Daithi, who succeeded to the monarchy of Ireland in 406, was a prince of the most warlike disposition, and unbounded generosity. In his reign considerable tracts of territory were assigned the ancient Britons that sought shelter in Ireland, as the only country where peace and hospitality were preserved. These grants of land yet retain the names of *Sliabh na Mbreathneach*, or the Welsh Mountains, *Graig na Mbreathneach*, etc. etc. It was the great object of the Irish to give the Romans so much employment abroad, that they would never think of bringing the war into Ireland. It was in the enforcement of this national maxim, that Daithi carried terror and rain to the foot of the Alps, where he was struck dead by lightning in a thunderstorm.

[2] Brian Boro, the Alfred of Ireland, who fell in the memorable battle of Clontarf in 1014, in which 1400 Danes died.

[3] Art Mac Murchad O'Cavanagh, prince of Leinster, who assumed the crown of the province in the reign of Richard the Second, king of England. He cut out sufficient employment for the Saxons during the three succeeding reigns, and died during the minority of Henry the Sixth. It was strongly suspected that he was poisoned by English influence.

[4] Roger O'Moore, a Leinster chieftain contemporary with Edward the Sixth. The unconquered Irish of that period were accustomed to say, "Our trust is in God, our Lady, and Roger O'Moore."

Heroes high in Erin's story -
Source of song to Dermid Dhu -
O! may the memory of your glory
Rouse to war the martial crew!

(14)
Beneath Yon Sad Cypress[1]

Beneath yon sad cypress, where cowslips are dying,
And green grass is glistening with dew,
Low couched in the cold earth, a maiden is lying,
Who once bloom'd as lovely as you;
Till her scorn quench'd the flame of her own constant true love.
He bade the sly traitress a final adieu,
Tho' his flame was but equalled by my flame for you, love,
So tender, so ardent, and true!

When a fond heart more kind caught his faithful devotion,
What wild woes distracted her brain!
Were hers the rich gems in the bosom of ocean,
She'd yield them to bind him again.
He smil'd at her folly - she linger'd forsaken,
And wept, as before wept her lover his woe!
Unpitied - when hopeless her bosom was breaking,
No tear did in sympathy flow.

Beneath yon sad cypress, where cowslips are dying,
And green grass is glistening with dew,
Low couch'd in the cold earth, that maiden is lying,
Who once bloom'd as lovely as you.
Be warn'd by that maid, in her dark bed of sleeping -
Deny not for ever the promise I crave,
Lest the warm bridal touch, be the cold reptile's creeping,
Thy gay nuptial pillow - the grave!

---

[1] Published in the *Dublin Penny Journal*, February 20th 1836, in the story of 'Phelim McCarthy'(see pp. 289ff).- Ed.

(15)
Song of The Demon Nailer[1]

Oft since that fatal time
When Eden's tenants rued me,
Through many an age and clime
I've weary ways pursued me;
On many a heart,
With fraudful art,
I've left a witness token,
That marks it, aye,
My destin'd prey,
If truth on high be spoken.
For this I've to and fro
The earth in many a shape run
But never took, I trow,
Till now, a nailer's apron.

I bid the bellows blow -
I set the hammer ringing -
If one be doomed to woe,
To me is profit springing;
For human souls,
Like these bright coals,
My fiery breath sets glowing -
But oh! the breath
Of woe and death
Through tortur'd spirits blowing!
For this I've to and fro
The earth in many a shape run;
But never took, I trow
Till now, a nailer's apron!

[1] Published in the *Dublin Penny Journal*, March 12th 1836, this song is part of the story of *The Demon Nailer* (see pp. 298ff), a smith with a strong taste for drink, who in a moment of rashness makes a pact with one who turns out to be a demon, and is fiendishly happy as he sings his song. However, the poor smith is rescued from his clutches at the last minute by invoking the 'blessed Saviour.' - Ed.

I smooth the murderer's path
That to his errand bears him;
I rouse the ruffian's wrath
When baleful passion tears him;
O'er many a sleep
I vigil keep,
Suggesting thoughts unholy;
And oft I wear
An aspect fair,
To catch a sinner solely.
For this I've to and fro
The earth in many a shape run;
But never took, I trow,
Till now, a nailer's apron!

(16)
The Fairy Nurse[1]

Air: *Fairy Lullaby.*

Sweet babe! a golden cradle holds thee,
Shuheen sho, lulo lo!
And soft the snow-white fleece enfolds thee!
Shuheen sho, lulo lo!
In airy bower I'll watch thy sleeping,
Shuheen sho, lulo lo!
Where branchy trees to the breeze are sweeping,
Shuheen sho, lulo lo!

When mothers languish broken-hearted,
Shuheen sho, lulo lo!
When young wives are from husbands parted,
Shuheen sho, lulo lo!
Ah! little think the keeners lonely,
Shuheen sho, lulo lo!
They weep some time-worn fairy only,
Shuheen sho, lulo lo!

Within our magic halls of brightness,
Shuheen sho, lulo lo!

---

[1] Published in the *Dublin Penny Journal*, April 23rd 1836, in the story of 'The Doomed Maiden.' (see pp.304ff). - Ed

Trips many a foot of snowy whiteness,
Shuheen sho, lulo lo!
Stolen maidens, queens of Faery,
Shuheen sho, lulo lo!
And kings and chiefs, a Slua-shee[1] airy,
Shuheen sho, lulo lo!

Rest thee, babe! I love thee dearly,
Shuheen sho, lulo lo!
And as thy mortal mother nearly,
Shuheen sho, lulo lo!
Ours is the swiftest steed and proudest,
Shuheen sho, lulo lo!
That moves where the tramp of the host is loudest,
Shuheen sho, lulo lo!

Rest thee, babe! for soon thy slumbers,
Shuheen sho, lulo lo!
Shall flee at the magic keolshee's[2] numbers
Shuheen sho, lulo lo!
In airy bower I'll watch thy sleeping,
Shuheen sho, lulo lo!
Where branchy trees to the breeze are sweeping,
Shuheen sho, lulo lo!

(17)
I've thravelled France an' Spain[3]

I've thravelled France an' Spain, an' likewise in Asia,
Fal de ral, etc., etc.
And spint many a long day at my aise in Arabia,
Fal de ral, etc., etc.
Pur-shoeing of their ways, their sates an' their farims,

---

[1] Fairy hosts.
[2] Fairy music.
[3] This piece of nonsense scarcely deserves a place among Walsh's *verses*. It is found in his story of 'Paddy Corbett's First Smuggling Trip', published in the *Irish Penny Journal*, March 6th 1841 (see pp. 309ff).- Ed.

But sich another place as the lakes o' Killarney
I never saw elsewhere, the air being most charming,
Fal de ral, etc., etc.
There the Muses came to make it their quarters,
Fal de ral, etc., etc.
An' for their ray-creation they came from Castalia,
Fal de ral, etc., etc.
With congregations playing for his lordship,
A viewing of that place, I mean sweet Killarney,
That the music been so sweet, the lake became enchanted,
Fal de ral, etc., etc.

(18)
A Munster Keen[1]

One Monday morning, the flowers were gaily springing,
The skylark's hymn in middle air was singing,
When, grief of griefs! My wedded husband left me,
And since that hour of hope and health bereft me.
Ulla gulla, gulla g'one![2] Etc. etc.

Light of my eyes! My bleeding bosom's pulse;
Calf of the soul which wild despair convulses!
'Twas little thought thy lov'd return would bring me
The heartache and the thousand pangs that wring me.
Ulla gulla, gulla g'one! Etc. etc.

Above the board, when thou art low reclining,
Have parish priests and horsemen high been dining,
And wine and usquebaugh[3], while they were able,
They quaffed with thee – the soul of all the table. –
Ulla gulla, gulla g'one! Etc. etc.

---

[1] The lament was published in the *Dublin Journal of Temperance, Science, and Literature*, June 4th 1842. Curiously, it occurs in one of Walsh's most entertaining stories, namely, 'The Buckaugh's Legend; or, The Wife of the Two Husbands' (see pp. 326ff). The poem is in the heroic mould and has overtones of Eibhlín Dubh Ní Chonaill's *Lament for Art Ó Laoghaire*. - Ed.

[2] Mrs Fihilly [the chief mourner in the story] alone sung the extempore death-song; and the burden of the *ulligone*, or chorus, was taken up by all the females present.

[3] Whiskey. – Ed.

Why did ye die? Could wedded dame adore thee
With purer love than that my bosom bore thee?
Thy children's cheeks were peaches ripe and mellow,
And threads of gold, their tresses long and yellow,
Ulla gulla, gulla g'one! Etc. etc.

Why did ye die? Where Sabbath crowds were brightest,
Thy brogues were blackest, and they shirt was whitest: -
At town and fair, what looks of envy won thee
The fair great coat, these hands I wring had spun thee!
Ulla gulla, gulla g'one! Etc. etc.

In vain for me are pregnant heifer's lowing;
In vain for me are yellow harvests growing;
Or thy nine gifts of love in beauty blooming, -
Tears blind my eyes, and grief my heart's consuming!
Ulla gulla, gulla g'one! Etc. etc.

Pity has plaints whose wailing voice is broken,
Whose finger holds our early wedding token,
The torrents of whose tears have drain'd their fountain,
Whose pil'd-up grief on grief is past recounting,
Ulla gulla, gulla g'one! Etc. etc.

I still might hope, did I not thus behold thee,
That high Knockferin's airy peak might hold thee,
Or Crohan's fairy halls, or Corrin's towers
Or Lene's bright caves, or Cleana's magic bowers.[1]
Ulla gulla, gulla g'one! Etc. etc.

But O! my black despair! When thou wert dying
O'er thee no tear was wept, no heart was sighing, -
No breath of prayer did waft thy soul to glory;
But lonely thou didst lie, and maim'd and gory!
Ulla gulla, gulla g'one! Etc. etc.

[1] Places celebrated in fairy topography.

O! may thy dove-like soul, on whitest pinions,
Pursue her upward flight to God's dominions
Where saints' and martyrs' hands shall gifts provide thee –
And, O! my grief, that I am not beside thee!
Ulla gulla, gulla g'one! Etc. etc.

(19)

A Bird in the Deep Valley Singing[1]

Thou seest where the planets have motion,
In heaven's high vault of night;
The star of my fervent devotion,
One islet of love and light:
O! had I the wing of an angel,
I'd seek yon blue boundless sea,
To dwell in that beautiful islet,
If Mary would fly with me!

Though sorrow too early hath known us,
And gloom wraps our future lot;
Though the children of prudence my blame us,
And proud ones regard us not;
When the magic of hearts that hath bound us
Can scatter these griefs afar -
O! think what a heaven would surround us
In yonder bright lonely star!

Whatever in summer is fairest
Of flower, or shade or green;
Whatever in beauty is rarest,
Should brighten the blissful scene;
We'd slumber in bowers of roses,
Where fountains fall murmuring,
And harps of wild melody waken
When swept by the zephyr's wing.

---

[1] The context of this song is to be found in Walsh's story of 'The Harper' (see pp. 341ff), published in the *Dublin Journal of Temperance, Science and Literature*, July 23rd 1842.- Ed.

There's a voice in that star for us only,
An eye in its liquid ray;
This weeps o'er our destiny lonely -
This whispers us both away!
O! had I the wing of an angel,
I'd seek yon blue boundless sea,
To dwell in that beautiful islet,
If Mary would fly with me!

There's a bird in the deep valley singing,
That charms by his soft vesper song,
And a floweret thrice beautiful springing,
The fairest - the deep vales among:
But the primrose may flourish forsaken,
The thrush vainly sing from his tree;
If Mary were there to awaken
Her wild notes of sweetness for me.

O'er the rock are the bright waters sweeping -
Below waves the green alder grove;
Yon cliff holds the wild echoes sleeping,
That oft wake to accents I love:
The starlight of magical power
Still streams through the old trysting tree;
But Mary, fair star of the bower,
Hath fled the deep valley and me.

We met - and have parted for ever -
We lov'd - and howe'er be her heart,
From mine shall the memory never
Of beautiful Mary depart!
Nor canst thou O'Donovan's daughter,
Permit from remembrance to flee!
The twilight - the rush of wild water -
The bright star - the bower - and me!

(20)
Irish War Song, A.D. 1843[1]

Air: The World is turn'd upside down.

Bright sun! before whose glorious ray
Our Pagan fathers bent the knee;
Whose pillar altars yet can say
When time was young our sires were free;
Who seest how fallen their offspring be,
Our matrons' tears, our patriots' gore;
We swear, before high heaven and thee,
The Saxon holds us slaves no more.

Our sunburst of the Roman foe
Flashed vengeance once in foreign field;
On Clontarf's plain lay scathed low
What power the sea-kings fierce could wield;
Benburb might say whose cloven shield
'Neath bloody hoofs was trampled o'er,
And, by these memories high, we yield
Our limbs to Saxon chains no more,

The *cláirseach*[2] wild, whose trembling string
Had long the "Song of Sorrow" spoke,
Shall bid the wild *Rosc Catha*[3] sing
The curse and crime of Saxon yoke.
And by each heart his bondage broke -
Each exile's sigh on distant shore -
Each martyr 'neath the headsman's stroke -
The Saxon holds us slaves no more.

Send the loud war cry o'er the main -
Your sunburst to the breezes spread:

---

[1] The song was first published in the *Nation* on April 15th 1843. No authorship was acknowledged at the time, but when it became the subject of controversy, it was discovered that Edward Walsh was the author, and the discovery eventually led to his departure from Toureen National School, Co. Waterford. (See *Life* pp. 46ff).- Ed

[2] *Cláirseach*, a harp. - Ed.

[3] *Rosc Catha*: a battle-hymn, a rallying song.

That *slogan* rends the heaven in twain -
The earth reels back beneath your tread.
Ye Saxon despots, hear, and dread!
Your march o'er patriot hearts is o'er -
That shout hath told, that tramp hath said
Our country's sons are slaves no more.

(21)

The Repealers' March[1]

Air: *O'Sullivan's March.*

March to the gathering! - pour from the valley;
Rush from the craggy-cliff's thunder-charged cloud;
Men of the hills from your dark mountains sally,
Where the eagle's cry swells o'er the waterfall loud -
March from the heaths where the red deer are bounding yet,
Where the Gaelic of glory's old tones are resounding yet -
March from the woods where your father's did rally
Which ne'er to the axe of the Sassenach bow'd!

The fiery Mononia , in thunder, has spoken -
The blood of Lagenia burns wild in her vein -
Connacia, the slumber of ages, has broken -
Ultonia's fierce lion refuses the chain!
Heard ye, far nations, the burst of that gathering cry?
All Gaul it awakens - Columbia shouts wild reply -
Sassenach tyrant! what can it betoken?
Foes on the Ocean - fetters in twain!

March to the gathering! glory awaits you;
Go girded in armour of virtue and right -
The stranger and traitor they shudder and hate you,
Tried, firm, and faithful, and stern in your might.
But should not the armour of virtue avail you yet,
And the torch and the steel of the tyrant assail you yet -

[1] The song was published in the *Nation* on July 29th 1843. Walsh's authorship is identified by C.G. Duffy in his personal copy of the *Nation*. - Ed.

While the memory of altar and roof-tree elates you,
Stand firm by your own, in the tyrant's despite.

Stranger and traitor! the sons of the glorious
Proclaim that thy reign of rapine hath fled -
They swear by their fathers in battle victorious,
And the blood of the brave by foul treachery shed -
That Ireland shall be for the Irish a nation yet -
That th' Irish shall find in Old Ireland their station yet -
That vain would thy impotence fetters fling o'er us,
The millions have doom'd thy dark tyranny dead!

(22)
Ninety-Eight![1]

Let all remember ninety-eight, that hour of Ireland's woes -
When rapine red the land o'erspread, the flames of roof-trees rose -
When pity shrieked, and ruffians wreak'd their deadly demon hate,
And gibbets groan'd and widows moaned, in fatal ninety-eight!

In memory save the martyr'd brave, who fell in conflict vain,
By soldiers sword, or shameful chord, or in the convict's chain;
And those whose gore the red lash bore, with tyrants strode elate,
And pitch-caps clung, and tortures wrung, strong hearts in Ninety-Eight!

When memory drear shall cease the tear for those that tyrants crush'd,
May life depart our ingrate heart - our craven tongue be hush'd -
And may his worst of deeds accurs't the despot perpetrate -
If swell not high, the warning cry - Remember Ninety-eight!

And when the yoke, at length, is broke, that binds our island green,
And high acclaim shall swell her name - broad ocean's emerald Queen!
A column fair, of sculpture rare, shall proudly celebrate
The faithful dead, whose blood was shed in fatal Ninety-eight!

---

[1] Published in the *Nation*, August 5th 1843. Walsh's authorship is identified by C.G. Duffy in his personal copy of the *Nation*. - Ed.

(23)
The Voice of Tara[1]

O! that my voice could waken the hearts that slumber cold! -
The chiefs that time hath taken, the warrior kings of old!
O! for Fingal, the pride of all the gallant Fenian crew
To wave his hand - the fight demand - and blow the Baraboo!

O! for the Clan-Morin, the Clana-Deaghadh tall,
Dal Riada's knights of glory, who scaled the Roman wall!
O! for the darts that smote the hearts of Freedom's foreign foe,
When bloodier grew the fierce Crobh-Ruadh[2] o'er bleak Helvetia's snow!

O! for the battle axes that smote the pirate Dane!
O! for the firm Dalcassians that fought on Ossory's plain!
And, O! for those who wrathful rose the Saxon to withstand,
Till traitor arts and recreant hearts betray'd the patriot band!

Alas! our chiefs of glory will list no minstrel's call -
But, o'er their deathless story, can tyrants fling a pall?
Ye'll ne'er disgrace your ancient race, ye sons of fathers brave,
Arise and burst your bounds accurs'd - the tomb contains no slave!

Arise ye, now or never - from heaven the martyr'd brave
Command you to deliver the land they sought to save;

---

[1] Published in the *Nation*, August 19th 1843. Walsh's authorship is identified by C.G. Duffy in his personal copy of the *Nation*. Walsh himself gives a footnote to the effect that the work is a translation from the Irish, but one cannot be certain as to whether this assertion is a literary device or not. – Ed.
Walsh's accompanying note to *The Voice of Tara* reads: 'The original Irish of this song has been preserved in the extensive mountain tract that stretches far into the adjacent counties of Limerick, Cork, and Kerry, between the towns of Newcastlewest, Abbeyfeale, and Castleisland. I have vainly endeavoured to learn the author's name, but the original bears strong marks of its being the production of a Munster bard of the seventeenth century. I took it down, *viva voce*, from a Baccach, who moved a very respectable repertory of wool, butter, and antiquarian lore, among the simple dwellers of the glens. He sung it to that very warlike air, vulgarly named 'The Poacher', in a kind of recitative, with his eyes closed, as if to shut out exterior objects from his inspired vision, and leaning on the top of his staff, as he swayed his body to and fro to the martial sounds. I have rendered the words as literally as possible, hopeless of preserving the abrupt and striking spirit of the Gaelic.'

[2] "The bloody hand," the ensign of the Knights of the Red Branch.

Then swear to die ere despots tie your limbs in bondage chain,
And let the shout ring boldly out o'er listening earth and main!

The fishers of Kilkernan, the men of Greenore Bay -
The dwellers by Lough Dergert, and by the broad Lough Neagh -
Leave boat and oar, and leap ashore, to join the fiery ranks
That come in pride from Galty's side, and from Blackwater's banks,

Where 'stubborn Newre' is streaming - where Lee's green valley smiles -
Where kingly Shannon circles his hundred sainted isles,
They list the call, and woe befall the hapless doomed array,
Who'll rouse their wrath, in war's red path, to strike in freedom's fray.

I see the brave rejoicing - I hear their shouts ascend -
See martyr'd men approving from thrones of brightness bend.
Ye ache my sight, ye visions bright, of all our glory won!
The 'Battle's Eye'[1] hath found reply - my tuneful task is done.

(24)
The Defeat of Strongbow[2]

A.D. 1174[3]

On yonder heath what sounds surprise -
What groans of many dying?
The Crom-a-boo,[4] why doth it rise,
From crag to mountain flying?
Why is the Suire's broad billow red,
And chok'd with recent slaughter?

---

[1] The literal English of *Rosg-Catha*, or the "incentive to Battle" - the war-song of the bard.

[2] Published in the *Nation*, September 2nd 1843. Walsh's authorship is identified by C.G. Duffy in his personal copy of the *Nation*. - Ed.

[3] 1174. The Earl Strongbow marched his forces to plunder Munster, and Roderick O'Connor, king of Connaught, hastened to make resistance. When the English had intelligence of Roderick's approach to give them battle, they invited the foreigners of Dublin to their assistance, who, with all possible speed, marched to Thurles, where they were met by Donal O'Brien at the head of the Dalcassians, by a battalion from West Connaught, and by a numerous and select army of the Clan-Murry, under Roderick. A furious engagement ensued, in which the English were at last defeated. In the battle 1,700 of the English were left dead on the field, and only a few of them survived, who fled with the Earl to his house in Waterford. - *Annals of Dublin,* Translated from the autograph of the *Four Masters* by J. O'Donovan, *D.P. Journal,* vol. I, page 238.

[4] The cry of victory which the Irish women telegraphed through the land from hill to hill.

The Saxon found a robber's bed
Beneath its bloody water!

In Cruachan's Hall,[1] Clan-Murry tall
Shall gather from their highlands -
By Limerick's towers the wild harp's powers
Shall swell o'er Shannon's islands -
For Roderick brave! thy trenchant glave
With Saxon life is gory!
And Donald Mor! thy Dal-Gas[2] bore
Their banner green to glory!

The Saxons came to spoil the land,
And met the land's avengers -
Dark doom and death smote each brigand
Of Murrough of the Strangers![3]
They banquet now the carrion crow -
The grey wolves lap their marrow -
The saint-curs'd men - the unholy foe
That sack'd thy shrine, Kildarra!

Urge on the chase, great Eogan's[4] race!
The Strongbow chief is flying -
His cloven shield is on the field,
His mailed bandit's dying!
The war-axe smote his jointed coat,
His hunted footstep falters;
Marc-Slua, Marc-Slua,[5] your spears pursue
Who robb'd Saint Columb's altars!

---

[1] The palace of the Kings of Connaught, built in the decline of the fourth century by Eochaidh, in honour of the Empress Cruachan.

[2] The posterity of Cormac, called Cas, or the well-beloved, second son of Olioll-Olam, King of Munster, from whom all the great family of Thomond are called Dal-Cas, or Dalcassians.

[3] Dermot McMurrough, King of Leinster, through whom the English first cursed the country, was called by the native *Morough na Gall*, or Morrough of the strangers.

[4] The posterity of Eogan, eldest son of Olioll-Olam, were the great families of Desmond, the McCarthys, O'Callaghans, McAuliffes, etc. etc. McCarthy of Desmond was engaged in this battle.

[5] Irish cavalry.

They spread the board in Waterford
To greet the brave returning -
They feast the wolves - that bandit horde -
Go, change your songs to mourning!
Just Heaven's high lamp reveals them - slain,
Or scatter'd wide and broken,
As erst was strewn the tyrant Dane,
When Erin's wrath was woken!

And thus may close on Erin's foes
The battle-hour forever!
May he who draws in tyrant's cause
Be crown'd with victory never;
But may his death be found beneath
The shafts of freedom's quiver -
Such shafts as they that flew to day
Above the Suir's red river!

(25)
The Songs of the Nation[1]

Air: *Sheela Ni Dhuibhir*

Ye songs that resound in the homes of our island,
That wake the wild echoes by valley and highland,
That kindle the cold with their forefather's story,
That point to the ardent the pathway of glory,
Ye send to the banished,
O'er ocean's far wave,
The hope that has vanished,
The vow of the brave,
And teach each proud despot of loftiest station,
To pale at your spell-word, sweet songs of the nation.

Sweet songs! ye reveal, through the vista of ages,
Our monarchs and heroes, our minstrels and sages,
The splendour of Eamhan,[1] the glories of Teamhar,[2]

---

[1] The song was published in the *Nation* on September 16th 1843. Although it was unsigned, it is authenticated by C.G. Duffy in his personal copy of the paper, and also acknowledged in *The Spirit of the Nation*.- Ed.

When Erin was free from the Saxon defamer -
The green banner flying,
The rush of the Gael,
The Sasanach's dying,
His matron's wild wail -
The glories forgotten, with magic creation,
Burst bright at your spell-word, sweet songs of the nation.

The minstrels who waken these wild notes of freedom,
Have hands for green Erin - if Erin should need 'em;
And hearts for the wronged one, wherever he ranges,
From Zebla to China, from Sionainn[3] to Ganges;
And hate for his foeman,
All hatred above;
And love for dear woman,
The tenderest love;
But chiefest the fair ones whose eyes' animation
Is the spell that inspires the sweet songs of the nation.

(26)

Song of the Penal Days[4]

Air: *Mo Chraoibhín Aoibhin Aulin Ó*

Ye dark-haired youths and elders hoary,
List to the wandering harper's song;
My *cláirseach*[5] weeps my true love's story,
In my true love's native tongue.
She's bound and bleeding 'neath the oppressor,
Few her friends and fierce her foe,
And brave hearts cold who would redress her,
Mo chraoibhín aoibhinn alga ógh.[6]

---

[1] *Eamhain Macha*, Navan Fort, the old capital of ancient Ulster. - Ed.
[2] *Teamhair*, Tara, the seat of the high kings of Ireland. - Ed.
[3] The Shannon River. - Ed.
[4] This touching song was published in the *Nation* on September 16th 1843. It addresses the plight of Ireland during the era of religious persecution, and is set in the year 1720, a time when the country was at one of its lowest points due to the penal code enacted after the breaking of the Treaty of Limerick. - Ed.
[5] *cláirseach*: the harp. - Ed.
[6] *Mo chraoibhín aoibhinn alga ógh*: as 'My fair noble maid.'

My love had riches once, and beauty,
Till want and sorrow paled her cheek;
And stalwart hearts for honour's duty,
They're crouching now like craven sleek.
Oh heaven! that e'er this day of rigour
Saw sons of heroes abject, low,
And blood and tears thy face disfigure,
Mo chraoibhín aoibhinn alga ógh.

I see young virgins step the mountain,
As graceful as the bounding fawn,
With cheeks like heath-flower by the fountain,
And breasts like downy *ceanabhán*;[1]
Shall bondsmen share those beauties ample?
Shall their pure bosoms' current flow
To nurse new slaves for them that trample?
Mo chraoibhín aoibhinn alga ógh.

Around my *clairseach's* speaking measures
Men, like their fathers tall, arise,
Their heart the same deep hatred treasures -
I read it in their kindling eyes;
The same proud brow to frown at danger,
The same long *coulin's*[2] graceful flow,
The same dear tongue to curse the stranger,
Mo chraoibhín aoibhinn alga ógh.

I'd sing ye more, but age is stealing
Along my pulse, and tuneful fires
Far bolder woke my chord, appealing
For craven *Sheamus*[3] to your sires;
Arouse to vengeance, men of bravery,
For broken oaths, for altars low,
For bonds that bind in bitter slavery,
Mo chraoibhín aoibhinn alga ógh.

---

[1] *ceannabhán*: bog cotton. - Ed.
[2] *coulin*: a maid with beautiful hair.
[3] *Sheamus*: King James II of England, who let down the Irish cause.

(27)
What are Repealers?[1]

Air: *Tipperary O!*

Millions who've given their gage, my boy,
Fierce war with oppression to wage, my boy,
Till Erin, once more,
Shall shine as of yore
The land of the hero and sage, my boy!

The land was all Europe's pride, my boy,
Its glory and fame were wide, my boy,
And Roman and Dane,
Who offer'd the chain,
By the sword of its heroes died, my boy!

Her chiefs wax'd faithless and proud, my boy,
And discord's hoarse voice grew loud, my boy;
And, record of shame,
The stranger then came,
And liberty laid in her shroud, my boy.

The land, red rapine long swept, my boy,
And mercy and truth long slept, my boy,
Oh! could you but know
Such tyrants - such woe -
Your young eyes with mine had wept, my boy.

But in the despot's despite, my boy,
The millions arise in their might, my boy,
And swear by the tears
And blood of past years,
To wrest from that despot their right my boy!

They are banded, and firm, and true, my boy,
Resolved to die or to do, my boy,
The young and the old

[1] Published in the *Nation* on November 11th 1843.- Ed.

In the cause are enroll'd,
And I've sworn you one of them, too, my boy!

Ere this vow be unsafe in thy keeping, boy,
May your father bemoan your sleeping, boy,
Where green willows wave
Above your young grave,
And none to condole his weeping, boy!

(28)
The Battle of Callan[1] - A.D. 1261.[2]

Fitz-Thomas went forth to the slaughter and burning,
And the dame by Tra-leigh[3] wish'd the robber's returning,
With the deep-lowing *creach*,[4] with the rich plunder laden -
The altar's blest gold, the rare pearls of the maiden!

Winding down by the Ruachta[5] his lances were gleaming;
Floating, wild as a meteor, his banners were streaming;
He rode with the spoils of all Desmond around him;
But the wrath of the Gael, in its red vengeance, found him!

More swift than the eagle from Skellig's[6] high eyrie,

---

[1] The poem was published in the *Nation* on March 15th 1844. The highly significant Battle of Callan Glen, fought on the slopes of Mangerton near Killarney in 1261, was the first halt to the Norman advance in Munster. - Ed.

[2] During the administration of William Den, Lord Justice of Ireland, the MacCarthys entered Desmond, and by means of an ambuscade, surprised and slew John Fitz-Thomas, ancestor to the FitzGeralds, and his son, Maurice, at Glanarought, in this county (Kerry), which defeat so reduced the FitzGeralds that none of that name durst put a plough into the ground for twelve years, until dissentions arising among the Irish chiefs, the FitzGeralds recovered their former authority. - *Smith's History of the county of Kerry*, page 235.

[3] *Tra-leigh*, the strand of the Leigh. Tralee, the assizes town of the county of Kerry, on an inconsiderable stream, called the Lea, or Leigh.

[4] *Creach* - spoils of cattle.

[5] *Ruachta*, from *Ruacht, a chase or descent*; or perhaps from *Rotta, red water*, a river in Kerry having its rise on Mangerton, and its exit in the bay of Kenmare. It gives its name to the barony of Glanarought.

[6] *Skellig*, more properly Scealg. Islands lying off the coast of Kerry. The Great Scealg is a stupendous rock, nearly inaccessible, except in calm weather, and holds but two places for landing. On a flat, about fifty yards over the level of the sea, are the remains of several chapels that belonged to an abbey of canons regular of St. Austin, founded here, at an early period by St. Finian. For a full description of this island, and the pilgrimages performed there, see *Smith's History of the county Kerry*, page 111, etc.

Than whirlwinds of Corrin in hostings of Faery,
Dark as storm o'er Dun-Mor[1] to the ocean-tir'd toiler,
Burst MacCarthie's fierce wrath on the path of the spoiler!

O'Sullivan Mor, of the mountain and valley,
O'Connor, the chief of the tall-masted galley,
O'Droscoll, the scourge of the *Sassenach* sailor,
Left Cogan's proud daughter[2] a desolate wailer.

For him that hath none from the gaunt wolf to save him,
To staunch the wide wound that the fierce clansman gave him,
To weep the lost chief, with his battle-shield riven,
Cloven down by the war-axe, unhousell'd, unshriven![3]

With the blood of the Rievers that rode to the foray,
From Maing to Moyalla[4] the kirtles are gory;
The saffron-dy'd shirts, by the Cashin and Carrow,
Claim thy care at the fountain, fair maidens, to-morrow!

Chant the deeds of the warriors, in chivalry vying,
The doom of the Rievers, all prostrate or flying,
The false Saxon's fear - as rejoicing thou lavest
The blood-gouts that burst from the breasts of his bravest!

[Note: Walsh's foot note based on Smith's *History* conflates two eras of monastic development, namely the Early Mediaeval Irish Monasticism and the introduction of the Canons Regular of St. Augustine by St. Malachy of Armagh in the 12th-century. - Ed.]

1 *Dun Mór* - the great fortress. A headland in the parish of Dungueen, [i.e. Dunquin], in Kerry, and the most western point in Europe. The peasantry name it *Tigh-mhór* (pronounced *Tee-more*), or More's house, and have given it the same celebrity in Ireland that John o' Groats has received in Scotland.

2 The lady of Maurice, the son of John FitzThomas, who fell with his father at Callan. She was daughter of Lord Cogan, of Carrigaline, in the county of Cork, and mother of Thomas of the Ape, so called from the circumstances of his being carried by a large baboon round the battlements of the castle at Tralee, on the day that the news of the defeat at Callan had arrived. This Thomas was ancestor of the Earls of Kildare.

3 'unhousell'd, unshriven' i.e. without having had the sacraments of *Confession* and *Holy Communion*. – Ed.

4 The Irish name of Mallow, a town in the county of Cork. The Maing, the Cashin, the Carra, are rivers in Kerry.

(29)
Aileen the Huntress[1]

Fair Aileen McCartie, O'Connor's young bride,
Forsakes her white pillow with matronly pride,
And calls forth her maidens (their number was nine)
To the bawn of her mansion, a-milking the kine.

They came at her bidding, in kirtle and gown,
And braided hair, jetty, and golden, and brown,
And form like the palm-tree, and step like the fawn,
And bloom like the wild rose that circled the bawn.

As the Guebre's round tower o'er the fane of Ardfert -
As the white hind of Brandon by young roes begirt -
As the moon in her glory 'mid bright stars outhung -
Stood Aileen McCartie her maidens among.

Beneath the rich kerchief, which matrons may wear,
Stray'd ringleted tresses of beautiful hair;
They wav'd on her fair neck, as darkly as though
'Twere the raven's wing shining o'er Mangerton's snow!

---

[1] This spirited ballad was published in the *Nation* on April 5th 1844. Although the incident recounted only happened about 1731 the whole tenor of the ballad is somewhat mediaeval and in the heroic mould. The poem is not only an insight into the spirit and daring of a great horsewoman but also a rich lesson in history and geography and is particularly poignant for those familiar with the nature of the terrain in question. - Ed.
[Walsh prefaced the poem with the following note] 'The incident related in the following ballad happened about the year 1731. Aileen, or Ellen, was daughter of McCarthy of Clidane, an estate originally bestowed upon this respectable branch of the family of McCarthy More, by James, the seventh Earl of Desmond, and which, passing safe through the confiscations of Elizabeth, Cromwell, and William, remained in their possession until the beginning of the present [19th] century. Aileen, who is celebrated in the traditions of the people for her love of hunting, was the wife of James O'Connor, of Cluain-Tairbh, grandson of David, the founder of the *Siol-i Da*, a well-known sept at this day in Kerry. This David was grandson to Thomas MacTeige O'Connor, of Ahalahanna, head of the second house of O'Connor Kerry, who forfeiting in 1666, escaped destruction by taking shelter among his relations, the Nagles of Monanimy. The present representative of this princely line of O'Connor is nearly connected with the Liberator, O'Connell.'

A circlet of pearls o'er her white bosom lay,
Erst worn by thy proud Queen, O'Connor the Gay,[1]
And now to the beautiful Aileen come down
The rarest that ever shed light on the Laune.[2]

The many-fring'd *falluinn*[3] that floated behind,
Gave its hues to the sunlight, its folds to the wind -
The brooch that refrain'd it some forefather bold
Had torn from a sea-king in battlefield old.

Around her went bounding two wolf dogs of speed,
So tall in their stature, so pure in their breed;
While the maidens awake to the new milk's soft fall,
A song of O'Connor in Carraig's proud hall: [4]

Our galleys on the waves are dancing,
The spear and war-axe brightly glancing;
Rich spoils shall grace McCartie's daughter,
When comes O'Connor from the slaughter -
Love, farewell!
The harp's wild swell
At last proclaims the hour of parting -
Love, farewell!

Last night the warder, lone watch keeping,
Heard the Banshee's voice of weeping;
She wept the brave for battle burning,
Brave for whom there's no returning!
Stay, oh! stay,
O'Connor, gay,
Nor tempt the steel of the false invader
In the fray.

---

[1] O'Connor, surnamed *Sugach*, or the Gay, was a celebrated chief of this race, who flourished in the fifteenth century.

[2] The river Laune flows from the Lakes of Killarney, and celebrated Kerry Pearls are found in its waters.

[3] *Falluinn* - the Irish mantle.

[4] I have placed the song in italics lest it interrupt the visual flow of the ballad. - Ed.

More true to me than cry of fairy,
Thy prayer of faith to the Virgin Mary -
To day shall bleed the Saxon spoiler,
Our nation's curse - our faith's reviler!
Love, farewell!
The harp's wild swell
At length proclaims the hour of parting -
Love, farewell.

As the milk came outpouring, and the song came outsung,
O'er the wall 'mid the maidens a red-deer outsprung -
Then cheer'd the fair lady, then rush'd the mad hound,
And away with the wild stag in airlifted bound.

The gem-fasten'd *falluinn* is dash'd on the bawn -
One spring o'er the tall fence - and Aileen is gone;
But morning's rous'd echoes to the deep dells proclaim
The course of that wild stag, the dogs, and the dame!

By Cluain Tairbh's green border, o'er moorland and height,
The red deer shapes downward the rush of his flight -
In sunlight his antlers all gloriously flash,
And onward the wolf dogs and fair huntress dash.

By Sliabh-Mis now winding (rare hunting I ween!)
He gains the dark valley of Scota the Queen,[1]
Who found in its bosom a cairn-lifted grave,
When Sliabh-Mis first flow'd with the blood of the brave!

By Coill-Cuaigh's[2] green shelter, the hollow rocks ring -
Coill-Cuaigh, of the cuckoo's first song in the spring,
Coill-Cuaigh, of the tall oak and gale-scenting spray -
God's curse on the tyrant that wrought thy decay!

---

[1] The first battle fought between the Milesians and the Tuatha De Danans for the empire of Ireland was at Sliabh Mis, in Kerry in which Scota, an Egyptian princess, and the relict of Milesius, was slain. A valley on the north side of Sliabh Mis, called *Glean Scoithin*, or the vale of Scota, is said to be the place of her interment. The ancient chronicles assert that this battle was fought 1300 years before the Christian era.

[2] *Coill-Cuaigh* - the wood of the cuckoo, so called from being the favourite haunt of the bird of summer, is now a bleak desolate moor. The axe of the stranger laid its honours low.

Now Maing's lovely border is gloriously won,
Now the towers of the island[1] gleam bright in the sun,
And now Ceall-an-Amanach's[2] portals are pass'd,
Where, headless, the Desmond found refuge at last.

By Ard-na-greach[3] mountain, and Avonmore's head -
To the Earl's proud pavilion and panting deer fled -
Where Desmond's tall clansmen spread banners of pride,
And rush'd to the battle, and gloriously died!

The huntress is coming, slow, breathless, and pale,
Her raven locks streaming all wild in the gale;
She stops - and the breezes bring balm to her brow -
But the wolf dog and wild deer, oh! where are they now?

On Réidhlán-Tigh-an-Eárla, by Avonmore's well,
His bounding heart broken, the hunted deer fell;
And o'er him the brave hounds all gallantly died,
In death still victorious - their fangs in his side.

'Tis evening - the breezes beat cold on her breast,
And Aileen must seek her far home in the west;
Yet, weeping, she lingers where the mist-wreaths are chill,
O'er the red deer and tall dogs that lie on the hill!

Whose harp at the banquet told distant and wide
This feat of fair Aileen, O'Connor's young bride? -
O'Daly's - whose guerdon, tradition hath told,
Was a purple-crown'd wine-cup of beautiful gold!

---

[1] "Castle Island" or the "Island of Kerry" - the stronghold of the Fitzgeralds.

[2] It was in this churchyard that the headless remains of the unfortunate Gerald, the 16th Earl of Desmond, were privately interred. The head was carefully pickled, and sent over to the English queen, who had it fixed on London Bridge. This mighty chieftain possessed more than 570,000 acres of land, and had a train of 500 gentlemen of his own name and race. At the source of the Blackwater, where he sought refuge from his inexorable foes, is a mountain called "Reidhlan Tigh-an-Earla," or "The Plain of the Earl's House. He was slain near Castleisland on 11th. November, 1583. [For the story of the Earl mentioned here in Walsh's foot note, see Chapter five of *Where Araglen So Gently Flows* by John J. Ó Ríordáin, CSSR. - Ed.]

[3] *Ard-na-gcreach* - The height of the spoils or armies.

(30)

Versification of the last words of Timothy Scannell, a Munster Peasant. A.D. 1841.[1]

I feel, I feel my prison'd spirit beating
Her fluttering pinion 'gainst this wall of clay,
While sister angels on the wing are waiting
To guide her to the realms of endless day!

She sighs to seek her ancient home - remounting
Where sin and grief and want are ever o'er -
To bask for aye in Truth's eternal fountain,
And drunken be with glory evermore!

O! let mine eye, ere fade its light for ever,
One parting look bequeath this beauteous scene -
Yon golden orb - the rock - the echoing river -
The yellow corn - the grove - the upland green.

Oh! that gaunt want should stalk the sun-lit highland,
That misery's moan should wake the fairy glen,
That sounds around our ocean-cinctur'd island,
The tyrant's tramp on hearts of injured men!

I oft have mark'd our blighted land with wonder -
Heard strong men's curses blent with misery's moans,
And ask'd what arm withheld the vengeful thunder -
Whence sprung the patience of the quiet stones!

And then I begg'd one day from pitying Heaven,
When tyrants, to atone the blood they spilt,
Would to our reeking patriot swords be given -
FATHER forgive me, if the thought were guilt!

For good men say, to bear dark wrong, were better
Than make at freedom's shrine the despot die -

[1] The poem was published in the *Nation* on August 17th 1844. Like so many Irish people before him and since, Timothy Scannell is grappling with the theology of *a just war* and *the right to resist tyranny.*- Ed.

That swords should never sunder slavery's fetter -
I long to learn if thus they think on high!

Think that the valiant men whose steel hath cloven,
And will again, ye brave! the tyrant's crest,
Should have in Heaven no wreath of glory woven -
No song from seraph's harp amid the blest!

Fain would I burst the Saxon bond of slavery -
Fain wait to share in freedom's glorious fray -
Fain see the land exult in stout hearts' bravery -
But Heaven ordains it thus - I must away!

I feel, I feel my prison'd spirit beating
Her fluttering pinion 'gainst this wall of clay,
While sister angels on the wing are waiting
To guide her to the realms of endless day.

(31)
The Death of the Outlaw[1]

The foe's on the mountain,
The Outlaw flees fast,
His rush through the valley's
The fairy-wind's blast!
His raven-dy'd tresses
To the light wind are spread -
The blue bell of beauty
Scarce bends to his tread!

O'er the round hill of Clara
Light vapours are roll'd,

[1] The poem was published in the *Nation* on August 24th 1844. It was initialled E.W. – Ed. [Walsh's Note] 'On the demesne of Henry Wallis, Esq., of Drishane Castle, near Millstreet, in the county of Cork, are some ancient timber trees. It has been remarked of one of these that, from time immemorial, one of its principal boughs has put forth no foliage, while all the other branches of that beautiful tree have had their annual leafy garniture. Tradition saith that on this stricken bough a hunted outlaw hanged himself in his own belt to avoid falling alive into the hands of the remorseless enemy.'

The plains of Duhallow
Are sun-beam'd in gold,
And downward from Tullig
The fierce foemen sweep,
And Avonmore onward
Bathes valley and keep.

By fort and blest fountain
The streamlets take flight -
Old Ceadsru the sacred,
The Araglen bright,
And Brogeen the gentle,
And Daloo the strong,
And Allo that echoes
In Spenser's wild song!

The foe's on the mountain,
His eyeballs are straining;
but Avonmore's woodland
His footstep is gaining;
There's a wild howl behind him,
And suddenly there,
Great God! is he spell-bound,
That son of despair!

The Sassenach sabre
Is gleaming behind;
The bay of the sleuthhound
Sweeps down on the wind;
The ear of his victim
Hath drunk the death-knell;
Why ask if the doom'd one
Be bound with a spell?

Again tells the sleuth-hound
The taint on the gale -
He's startled to motion,
There's death on his trail!
O! Mary the Mother,

How shout the fierce foe!
Adown the deep valley
He bounds like the roe!

His raven-dy'd tresses
To the light breeze are spread,
The bluebell of beauty
Scarce bends to his tread:
He nears the far ash-tree
Of fair spreading bough,
But Mary, the Mother!
What meaneth he now?

He sees the long branches
Wildly wave in the blast,
He hears the keen breezes
Moan hollowly past -
That moan and that motion,
To ear, and to eye,
Seem luring him thither,
The doom'd one - to die!

Again speaks the sleuth-hound
Despair to his breast -
Beneath that dark ash-tree
His hunted feet rest -
One quick-glanced defiance -
He flings the fierce foe -
One long look to Heaven,
His latest, below!

The broad belt around him,
The bough o'er his head,
Are the keys that unclose him,
The gates of the Dead -
How quiver his tall limbs,
How tears the last thrill,
His high-heaving bosom -
But now he is still!

His wild eyes are staring,
There's no friend to close them,
His rigid limbs stiffen,
What hand shall compose them?
His far lonely wake-light,
The autumn moon's ray,
His *Keener* the grey wolf
That howls for his prey!

His soul is unshriven -
Unhallow'd his sod -
Unchanted his prayer -
Who rush'd to his God,
Unholily seeking
The refuge of dole -
O, Saviour that bought him,
Give peace to his soul!

Sped autumn - hoarse winter
Howl'd loud through the grove;
Spring waken'd all nature
To verdure and love -
But never more put forth
Its green leafy pride
The bough where despairing
The suicide died!

(32)
The Revenge[1]

Air: *Uileacán Dubh Ó!*

When boom the guns of the fierce invader,
Uilecán Dubh O![2]
When the tri-colour flouts the breeze of Ben-Edar,[3]
Uilecán Dubh O!

---

[1] The song was published in the *Nation* on September 7th 1844. - Ed.
[2] *Uaill-le-cán dubh O*!: an interjectional phrase, which literally means 'A sad story to relate.'
[3] *Ben-Edar*: Howth Head. - Ed.

To drown in blood th' invading foe,
Shall Erin, as of old, bestow
Her laughing, tall-limb'd warriors? - No!
Uilecán Dubh O!

At Relig-na-Rí[1] the brave men moulder,
Uilecán Dubh O!
Who fac'd a foeman bloodier, bolder,
Uilecán Dubh O!
Who scar'd the haughty host of Rome,[2]
Who seal'd for aye the Sea Kings'[3] doom -
They're cold, they're cold in death's deep gloom,
Uilecán Dubh O!

Sons of sires who fought the Roman,
Uilecán Dubh O!
Who scathed the pride of the Danish foeman,[4]
Uilecán Dubh O!
You lend no ear when bugles sound,
When cannons roar your hills around -
What warrior fights when bleeding bound?
Uilecán Dubh O!

O, traitress false! the foe, the stranger,
Uilecán Dubh O!
Shall be our countless wrongs avenger,
Uilecán Dubh O!
Weep, weep - the martyr'd, mock'd, betray'd,
For Britain draws no battle blade,
Though bale-fires mark the Frenchman's Raid[5] -
Uilecán Dubh O!

[1] *relig na rí*: the graveyard of the kings - near Naas, Co. Kildare. - Ed.
[2] Tradition has it that Nial of the Nine Hostages was fighting on the Continent. - Ed.
[3] Turgesius the Viking. - Ed.
[4] Probably a reference to the Irish victory over the Vikings at the Battle of Clontarf in 1014. - Ed.
[5] 'The Frenchman's Raid' is probably a reference to their landing in Ireland in 1798.

(33)
Eire Mo Chroidhe[1]

Amid the blue waters of ocean is seen
A rock-cinctur'd island of beautiful green,
That shone to far ages, through centuries long
The beacon of glory, the fountain of song,
The cradle of beauty, the shrine of the free,
The empress of nations - Green Eire Mo Chroidhe.
Green Eire Mo Chroidhe.

Like swan of Lough Deargert, its daughter was white,
Its son was like roebuck of Mangerton light -
As soon should that roebuck from wildness be won,
As from virtue that daughter, from valour that son!
O! no island of ocean, though many there be,
Held bright eyes and brave hearts like Eire Mo Chroidhe.
Green Eire Mo Chroidhe.

O weep for the beauteous - oh! sigh for the brave,
Whose passion unhallow'd left Erin a slave,
Low crouching beneath the dark Sassanagh heel,
While warrior and wild wood were smote by his steel:
And red torch and traitor swept mountain and lea,
And God gave to slaughter Green Eire Mo Chroidhe!
Green Eire Mo Chroidhe.

---

[1] The first three stanzas of *Eire Mo Chroidhe* (Ireland of My Heart) were published in the *Nation* on September 28th 1844. The full text was published in the *Wexford Independent*, on October 2nd. of the same year. Thomas Davis, who was editing the *Nation* while C. G. Duffy was taking a short rest in Kerry, refused to publish the last two stanzas and prefaced the remaining three with this incisive comment: "The writer of *Eire Mo Chroidhe* is a man of fine ability, but in these verses, as in many of his, he commits two great faults - he uses uncommon dictionary words when he could more readily have used popular words, and he is unequal. Why did he wind up such sweet generalities as these with yesterday's hurra and a mock miracle?" Always sensitive, Walsh was furious at this public, but in my opinion, justified criticism. Having failed to have the poem published in full Walsh had the song published in the *Wexford Independent*. His anger not only drove him to break with Davis (who had befriended him), but to write anonymous letters to various provincial papers denouncing the *Nation* as being anti-catholic. On his return from Kerry, C. G. Duffy, who knew Walsh better than anybody, while not naming the culprit issued a stern rebuke to him through the columns of the *Nation*, and having done so, continued to befriend Walsh and publish his work. - Ed.

All glory eternal, great Saviour, be thine -
O Mary the mother, we kneel at thy shrine -
'Twas mercy from Heaven that burst the worst yoke
Ever forged by a tyrant - by patriot broke -
When the shout of a Nation rung wild o'er the sea,
Our proud chief hath conquer'd for Eire Mo Chroidhe!
For Eire Mo Chroidhe!

One hope-star arose on the night of our grief,
When Jesus and Mary bestow'd us a Chief,
Cheering hearts that were fainting and cheeks that were pale -
Bringing shame to the wrongers that trampled the Gael -
And joy by Blackwater and Liffy and Lee,
For the day of thy glory, Green Eire Mo Chroidhe!
Green Eire Mo Chroidhe!

(34)

Ma Chraoibhin Aoibhinn Aluin[1]

Air: *Mo Chraoibhín Aoibhin Aulin Ó*

O that my clairseach's chord could borrow,
Ma Chraoibhin Aoibhinn Aluin Og!
Notes of sadness, songs of sorrow,
Ma Chraoibhin etc
Alas! that hearts which wildly bounded,
Should crouch with craven fear astounded,
Ma Chraoibhin etc.

Dungeon walls and chains of iron
Ma Chraoibhin etc.
And murderous men our brave environ,
Ma Chraoibhin etc.
And maid and matron - sister, mother,
Despise the sire, the son, the brother,
Who kindling rage in grief could smother,
Ma Chraoibhin etc.

---

[1] Published in *The Wexford Independent* on October 5th 1844. - Ed.

Slaves accursed, less than women,
Ma Chraoibhin etc.
Who yield them to the Saxon foemen,
Ma Chraoibhin etc.
While bosom soft and blue eye shining:
Are wet and woeful, pale and pining,
That men like beaten whelps are whining,
Ma Chraoibhin etc.

This Coolin grey and tempest-waven
Ma Chraoibhin etc
Was dark as yonder soaring raven,
Ma Chraoibhin etc.
When woke this harp in front of danger -
Red streamed thy steel, each mountain ranger,
And death and fear pursued the stranger,
Ma Chraoibhin etc.

Tall forms like yours, O! trust my story,
Ma Chraoibhin etc.
That wet-shod walked that field of glory
Ma Chraoibhin etc.
Such slogan land assail'd high heaven,
Such hands the grinding steel had driven,
Leaving slavery's fetters riven,
Ma Chraoibhin etc.

I see, I see the glorious rally,
Ma Chraoibhin etc.
They rush from mountain, crag and valley
Ma Chraoibhin etc.
I hear the oath of vengeance taken,
I see the crushing war-axe shaken
And Erin from her bondage waken,
Ma Chraoibhin Aoibhinn Aluin Og!

(35)
O'Donovan's Daughter[1]

Air: *The Juice of the Barley.*

One midsummer's eve, when Bel-fires were lighted,
And the bagpiper's tone call'd the maidens delighted,
I joined a gay group by the Araglen's[2] water[3],
And danced till the dawn with O'Donovan's daughter.

Have you seen the ripe *mónadán*[4] glisten in Kerry,
Have you marked on the Galtees the black whortleberry,
Or *ceannabhán*[5] wave by the wells of Blackwater?
They're the cheek, eye, and neck of O'Donovan's daughter.

Have you seen a gay kidling on Clara's round mountain,[6]
The swan's arching glory on Sheeling's blue fountain,
Heard a weird woman chant what the fairy choir taught her?
They've the step, grace, and tone of O'Donovan's daughter.

Have you marked in its flight the black wing of the raven,
The rosebuds that breathe in the summer breeze waven,
The pearls that lie hid under Lene's magic water?[7]
They're the teeth, lip and hair of O'Donovan's daughter.

Ere the Bel-fire was dimmed or the dancers departed,
I taught her a song of some maid broken-hearted;

---

[1] The song was published in the *Nation* on October 19th 1844. - Ed.

[2] A stream in the western part of the barony of Duhallow in the county Cork.

[3] In Walsh's day and for a century after, Kiskeam people tended to recreate in a commonage by the Araglen water and still known as the *Glouneen*. The living tradition, of which I myself am one of the bearers, is that Edward Walsh met a Mary O'Donovan at the bonfire in the *Glouneen* on St. John's Night. My father told me that John Donovan, the headmaster in Kiskeam National School at the end of the 19th and early 20th century would at times exempt pupils from being examined in their lessons provided they could accurately recite the words of this song. Of all Walsh's songs *O'Donovan's Daughter* is perhaps the one that has most retained its popularity in anthologies. - Ed.

[4] The cranberry, which flourishes only on the wildest mountains.

[5] *Ceanabhán*. The beautiful cotton plant of the bogs whose pendulous spikelets of purest white, dance to the lightest breeze as if they were endowed with life and motion.

[6] A romantic hill [overhanging Millstreet] in the county Cork.

[7] The Lake of Killarney. [a reference to the folk belief that pearls are to be found in Killarney's enchanted Lough Lene. - Ed.]

And that group, and that dance, and that love-song I taught her
Haunt my slumbers at night with O'Donovan's daughter.

God grant, 'tis no fay from Cnoc-Firinn[1] that woos me,
God grant, 'tis not Cliodhna[2] the queen that pursues me,
That my soul lost and lone has no witchery wrought her,
While I dream of dark groves and O'Donovan's daughter!

If spell-bound, I pine with an airy disorder,
Saint Gobnait has sway over Muskerry's[3] wide border;
She'll scare from my couch, when with prayer I've besought her,
That bright airy sprite like O'Donovan's daughter.

(36)

Mo Chraoibhín Cnó[4]

Air: *The Days that are gone.*

My heart is far from Liffey's tide
And Dublin Town;
It strays beyond the southern side

---

[1] A celebrated fairy-hill in the county Limerick, a favourite residence of the fabled Donn, to whom the bards have given the rulership of the fairies of West Munster. - He is said to be one of the sons of Milesius, who, on approaching Ireland, was cast away with his companions, at the mouth of the Shannon. [*Donn Fírinne*, king of the underworld. - *Fírinne* means truth, genuineness, reality. Hence, he rules the place where people face reality. The Irish phrase for saying that a person is dead is a telling one: *tá sé ar shlighidh na firinne*; literally, he is on the way of truth.- Ed.]

[2] *Cliodhna*, is the fairy queen of South Munster. Her royal retreat is at *Carig-Cleena*, a mass of picturesque rocks, five miles southwest of Mallow. She seems to have been, like other royal dames, of a very amorous complexion, and has practised the abduction of young men since time immemorial. [see pp.213ff - Ed.]

[3] A territory extending from Dripsey to Ballyvourney in the county Cork. The lord of this district was O'Flynn, till in the early part of the 14th-century, McCarthy killed the chief, and seized his castle of Macroom. St. Gobnait is the patron saint of that country, and her wells are held in high esteem.

[4] Published in the *Nation*, December 21st 1844, *Mo chraoibín Cnó*, became an instant success in the Dublin of Walsh's day. When Walsh moved to Dublin towards the end of 1843, his wife and family remained in Co. Waterford for some time. It is likely that it was during this interval when he was, on his own admission, very lonely without them that he wrote this beautiful song. (see *Letters*, No.2, Jan 5th 1844). He says that '*Mo chraoibhin cnó* literally means *my cluster of nuts*; but it figuratively signifies *my nut-brown maid*.' The reference is to his wife's strikingly beautiful head of hair: 'for never,' wrote the poet John Keegan, 'did lovelier hair decorate Eve herself in Eden than clusters over the fair brow of *Mo Craoibhín Cno*.' See *Letters*, No. 58. - Ed.

Of Cnoc Maol Donn,[1]
Where Capa Chúinn[2] hath woodlands green,
Where Amhan Mhór's waters flow,[3]
Where dwells unsung, unsought, unseen,
Mo Chraoibhín Cnó,
Lo clustering in her leafy screen,
Mo Chraoibhín Cnó!

The highbred dames of Dublin town
Are rich and fair,
With wavy plume and silken gown,
And stately air;
Can plumes compare thy dark brown hair?
Can silks thy neck of snow?
Or measur'd pace thine artless grace,
Mo Chraoibhín Cnó,
When harebells scarcely show thy trace,
Mo Chraoibhín Cnó?

I've heard the songs by Liffey's wave,
That maidens sung -
They sung their land, the Saxon's slave,
In Saxon tongue -
Oh! bring me here that Gaelic dear
Which cursed the Saxon foe
When thou didst charm my raptured ear,
Mo Chraoibhín Cnó!
And none but God's good angels near
Mo Chraoibhín Cnó!

---

[1] *Cnoc-maol Donn*: The brown bare hill. A lofty mountain between the counties of Tipperary and that of Waterford, commanding a glorious prospect of unrivalled scenery. The eccentric Major Eccles lies interred on its topmost peak, with his horse and gun beside him, at about 2,700 feet above the level of the sea. The day of the funeral is yet remembered among the grey-haired peasantry as a red-letter day in the annals of that district. The major was a scientific scholar, and the author of some works on electricity.

[2] Cappoquin. A romantically situated town on the Blackwater, in the county of Waterford. The Irish name denotes the *head of the tribe of Conn.*

[3] *Amhan-mhor* - The Great River. The Blackwater, which flows into the sea at Youghal. The Irish name is uttered in two sounds, *Oun-Vore*.

I've wandered by the rolling Lee!
And Lene's green bowers -
I've seen the Shannon's widespread sea,
And Limerick's towers -
And Liffey's tide, where halls of pride
Frown o'er the flood below;
My wild heart strays to Amhan Mhór's side,
Mo Chraoibhín Cnó!
With love and thee for aye to bide,
Mo Chraoibhín Cnó.

(37)

Song of the Mermaid[1]

From "The Banshee," a manuscript poem.

Swift streamlet that leavest
Thy bright parent fount -
Ye grey cliffs of granite
That heavenward mount -
Thou dew-burden'd cowslip
And blushing wild rose,
That strew the green mound
Where the sea kings repose!

I hail you - and chiefly
Thou bright fountain-fay
Whose mild rule both streamlet
And valley obey!
From cave of old ocean
I've won my quick flight,
To braid my long hair
In the yellow moon's light.

Our coral-clad bowers
Are bright in the wave;
And gems all resplendent
Shed light in our cave,
Where ocean-nymphs dance to
The wreathed seashell,

[1] The *Song of the Mermaid* was published in the *Nation* on December 28th 1844.- Ed.

While wayward I wander
By streamlet and dell.

Thrice beautiful spirit,
Lone Son of the Rock,[1]
Who lovest the mermaid's
Wild warbling to mock!
If e'er thou hast utter'd
Some wonder-fraught spell
To lure me from ocean,
Sweet sorcerer, tell!

Go slumber, false mocker!
My wild song hath sped,
My long hair is braided,
The mermaid is fled
From streamlet and flower
To ocean's deep wave,
And coral-clad bower,
And gem-lighted cave.

(38)
Bríghidín Bán Mo Stór[2]

Air: *Billy Byrne of Ballymanus.*

I am a wand'ring minstrel man,
And Love my only theme,
I've strayed beside the pleasant Bann,
And eke the Shannon's stream;
I've pip'd and play'd to wife and maid

---

[1] The Irish for Echo is *Mac Allo*, literally *Son of the Rock.*
[2] The song was published in the *Nation* on January 11th 1845. Together with *Mo Chraoibhín Cnó* it captured the hearts of many in the Dublin of the 1840s. The song is for his wife Brighid, whom the poet John Keegan, about 1846, describes as 'a sweet simple-looking, love-inspiring woman of twenty-six years of age, though she looks like a *thackeen* of eighteen.' - Ed.
[Walsh note]: "*Brighdin ban mo stór* is in English *fair young bride*, or *Bridget my treasure*. The proper sound of this phrase is not easily found by the mere English-speaking Irish. The following is the best help I can afford them in the case '*Broo dhoon bawn mu sthoro*.' God forgive them their neglect of a tongue compared with whose sweetness the mincing sibilations of the English are as the chirpings of the cock-sparrow on the house-roof to the soft cooing of the gentle cushat by the southern Blackwater! The proper name Brighit, or Bride, signifies *a fiery dart*, and was the name of the goddess of poetry in the Pagan days of Ireland."

By Barrow, Suir, and Nore,
But never met a maiden yet
Like Bríghidín bán mo stór.

My girl hath ringlets rich and rare,
By Nature's fingers wove -
Loch-Carra's swan is not so fair
As is her breast of love;
And when she moves, in Sunday sheen,
Beyond our cottage door,
I'd scorn the highborn Saxon queen
for Bríghidín bán mo stór.

It is not that thy smile is sweet,
And soft thy voice of song -
It is not that thou fleest to meet
My comings lone and long!
But that doth rest beneath thy breast
A heart of purest core,
Whose pulse is known to me alone,
My Bríghidín bán a stór.

(39)
Battle of Credran[1]
(A.D. 1257)

From the glens of his fathers O'Donnell comes forth
With all Cinel-Conaill,[2] fierce septs of the north -

---

[1] The ballad was published in *The Nation* on May 3rd 1845. - Ed.
[Walsh's prefatory note]: 'A brilliant battle was fought by Geoffrey O'Donnell, Lord of Tirconnell, against the Lord Justice of Ireland, Maurice Fitzgerald, and the English of Connaught, at Credran Cille, Roseede, in the territory of Carburry, north of Sligo, in defence of his principality. A fierce and terrible conflict took place, in which bodies were hacked, heroes disabled, and the strength of both sides exhausted. The men of Tirconnell maintained their ground, and completely overthrew the English forces in the engagement, and defeated them with great slaughter; but Geoffrey himself was severely wounded, having encountered in the fight Maurice Fitzgerald, in single combat, in which they mortally wounded each other. - *Annals of the Four Masters*, translated by Owen Connellan, Esq., published by Geraghty, 8, Anglesea-street, Dublin.'

[2] *Cinel-Conaill* - The descendants of Conall-Gulban, the son of Niall of the Nine Hostages, Monarch of Ireland in the 4th-century. The principality was named Tir-Chonaile, or Tirconnell, which included the county Donegal, and its chiefs were the O'Donnells.

O'Boyle, and O'Daly, O'Duggan, and they
That own, by the wild waves, O'Doherty's sway.

Clan Connor, brave sons of the diadem'd Niall,
Has pour'd the tall clansmen from mountain and vale -
McSweeny's sharp axes, to battle oft bore,
Flash bright in the sunlight by high Dunamore.

Through Innis-Mac-Durin[1] through Derry's dark brakes,
Glentocher of tempests, Slieve Snaght of the lakes,
Bundoran of dark spells, Loch Swilly's rich glen,
The red deer rush wild at the war-shout of men.

O! why through Tir-Chonaill, from Cuil-dubh's dark steep,
To Samer's[2] green border the fierce masses sweep,
Living torrents o'erleaping their own river shore,
In the red sea of battle to mingle their roar?

Stretch thy vision far southward, and seek for reply,
Where blaze of the hamlets glares red on the sky -
Where the shrieks of the hopeless rise high to their God,
Where the foot of the Sassenach spoiler has trod.

Sweeping on like a tempest the Gall-Oglach[3] stern
Contends for the van with the swift-footed kern -
There's blood for that burning, and joy for that wail -
The avenger is hot on the spoiler's red trail.

The Saxon hath gather'd on Credran's far heights
His groves of long lances, the flower of his knights -
His awful cross-bowmen, whose long iron hail
Finds, through Cota and Sciath,[4] the bare heart of the Gael.

The long lance is brittle - the mailéd ranks reel,
Where the Gall-Oglach's axe hews the harness of steel,

---

[1] Districts in Donegal.

[2] *Samer*. - The ancient name of Loch Erne.

[3] *Gall-Oglach* or *Gallowglass*, - the heavy armed foot soldier. *Kern*, or *Ceithernach*. - The light armed soldier.

[4] *Cota*. - The saffron-dyed shirt of the kern, consisting of many yards of yellow linen thickly plaited. *Sciath*. - The wicker shield, as its name imports.

And truer to its aim in the breast of a foeman
Is the pike of a kern than the shaft of a bowman.

One prayer to St. Columb[1] - the battle steel clashes -
The tide of fierce conflict tumultuously dashes;
Surging onward, high-heaving its billow of blood,
While war-shout and death-groan swell high o'er the flood!

As meets the wild billows the deep-centr'd rock,
Met glorious Clan Chonaill the fierce Saxon's shock;
As the wrath of the clouds flash'd the axe of Clan-Chonaile,
'Till the Saxon lay strewn 'neath the might of O'Donnell!

One warrior alone holds the wide bloody field,
With barbed black charger and long lance and shield -
Grim, savage, and gory he meets their advance,
His broad shield up-lifting and crouching his lance.

Then forth to the van of that fierce rushing throng
Rode a chieftain of tall spear and battle-axe strong,
His bracca[2], and geochal[3], and cochal's red fold,[4]
And war-horse's housings, were radiant in gold!

Say who is this chief spurring forth to the fray,
The wave of whose spear holds yon armed array?
And he who stands scorning the thousands that sweep,
An army of wolves over shepherdless sheep?

---

[1] St. *Colum* or *Colum-Cille*, the dove of the Church. - The patron saint of Tyrconnell, descended from Conall Gulban.

[2] *Bracca*. - So called, from being striped with various colours, was the tight-fitting Irula. It covered the ankles, legs, and thighs, rising as high as the loins, and fitted so close to the limbs as to discover every muscle and motion of the parts which it covered - *Walker on Dress of the Irish*.

[3] *Geochal*. - The jacket made of gilded leather, and which was sometimes embroidered with silk.- *ibid*.

[4] *Cochal*. - A sort of cloak with a large hanging collar of different colours. This garment reached to the middle of the thigh, and was fringed with a border like shagged hair, and being brought over the shoulders was fastened on the breast by a clasp, buckle, or broche of silver or gold. In battle, they wrapped the *Cochal* several times round the left arm as a shield. - *ibid*.

The shield of his nation, brave Geoffrey O'Donnell,
(Clar-Fodhla's firm prop is the proud race of Conaill,)[1]
And Maurice Fitzgerald, the scorner of danger,
The scourge of the Gael, and the strength of the stranger.

The launch'd spear hath torn through target and mail -
The couch'd lance hath borne to his crupper the Gael -
The steeds driven backwards all helplessly reel;
But the lance that lies broken hath blood on its steel.

And now, fierce O'Donnell, thy battle-axe wield -
The broad-sword is shiver'd, and cloven the shield,
The keen steel sweeps grinding through proud crest and crown -
Clar-Fodhla hath triumph'd - the Saxon is down!

Thus battled your fathers, the valiant and strong -
Be yours the example, and theirs be the song -
When the hour of dark vengeance to tyrants is due,
I'll shout in your vanguard - O'Donnell a-boo!

(40)

The Death of Fail[2]

(Before Christ 1300)[3]

Hark, O! hark to the voice of woe
That soars above the untrodden highland!

---

[1] This is the translation of the first line of a poem of two hundred and forty-eight verses, written by Firgal og Mac-an-Bhaird on Dominick O'Donnell, in the year 1655. The original line is - "Gaibhle Fodhla fuil Chonaill." - See *O'Reilly's Account of Irish Writers*.

[2] The poem was published in the *Nation* on July 5th 1845. - Ed.

[3] The following ballad, "celebrates the death of Fail, the daughter of Golamh, surnamed *Mile Spainneach* (the Spanish Hero), or Milesius, from whom the Milesian families of Ireland claim descent. This royal dame was wife of Lughaidh, son of Ith, brother of Milesius, in revenge for whose death, by the Tuatha-de-Danann, the sons of Milesius invaded Ireland from Spain, according to the ancient chronicles of the country, more than a thousand years before the Christian era. After the battle of Sleibh Mis, the Milesians moved towards the territory bordering on the river Feale, in Kerry, where one day Lughaidh surprised his lady as she bathed in the river, which has ever since obtained the honour of bearing her name, and so powerful was her sense of shame at the intrusion that she sunk in death on reaching the bank. An instance of matronly modesty unparalleled, perhaps, in any age or clime. Who shall wonder at the virtue of the Christian daughters of our land, with the example of a heathen dame shining bright upon them through the mists of two thousand years ago. - See Keating's *History of Ireland*."

It swells from yon dark vale below -
The darkest vale of the wood-crown'd Island.[1]

Say, O! say, why joy so soon
Forgets the tones that triumph taught her,
When rose from the Mountain of the Moon[2]
The shout of the brave for Danan slaughter.

Caicer the Prophet[3] thus foretold -
"Fated Race! your bosoms' gladness,
'Mid the feast of shells and the harps of gold,
Shall echo'd be by the voice of sadness!"

And when you reach the destin'd Isle,
Your future home through countless ages,
The triumph wild - the foeman's guide -
Shall chequer all your history's pages!

''Twas yester noon fair Fail abode
In the stately tent of royal Lughaidh,[4]
Bright as the eye of heaven[5] she trode
The fragrant hills, the valleys dewy.

She's under the bier, that peerless dame -
Her milk-white breast the death-flowers cover;
The torch is lit for her funeral flame;
He's rearing her *leacht*,[6] her widow'd lover!

---

[1] Wood-crown'd Island. - The first name of Ireland was Inis-na-Bhfiodhbhuidhe, or the Woody Island. - See Dr. Keating's History of Ireland.

[2] Mountain of the Moon. *Sliabh Mis*, in Kerry, where the first battle was fought between the Tuatha-de-Danans and the invading Milesians.

[3] *Caicer, the Prophet.* - Caicer was a Druid who, long before the invasion of the Milesians, foretold that the posterity of Gadelus would obtain possession of a remote western island.

[4] *Lughaidh.* - This proper name is to be sounded as if spelled Lewey. This prince was a celebrated poet. A poem said to have been composed extempore by him, on the death of his wife, is given in *O'Reilly's Irish Dictionary*, at the word *aimbhtheach*, and is supposed to be one of the oldest Irish productions extant.

[5] Eye of Heaven - the sun. This luminary, worshipped by our pagan fathers under the name of *Bel*, or *Beal*, was also called *Sel*, or *Suil*, which literally signifies *eye*, from which the Latin *sol* is evidently taken. From *Sol* or *Suil*, the sun, are traced these Irish words - *solus*, light; *suilbhir*, cheerful; *soleir*, clear; with many others.

[6] *Leacht.*- The pile of circular stones raised in memory of the dead.

Yesternoon she left her summer bower,
Above yon silver-shining water,
To bathe at the bright sun's noon-tide hour,
As was the wont of Spain's fair daughter.

She glided the glassy river on,
No water fairy sporting lighter,
Nor ever did a sailing swan
Stem the stream with bosom whiter.

And now the waters above her skim -
And now her beauteous form's unfolded,
Polish'd as though each pliant limb
Were from far India's ivory moulded!

When Lughaidh, of the clustering ringlets brown,
In distant Spain, who woo'd and won her,
Stole, 'mid the thickening hazels down,
To gaze in maddening rapture on her –

He gaz'd - she was his wedded love,
As bright as Bel[1] through clouds disparted;
Meek as fair Samhain[2] queen above -
His dove-ey'd dame - his tenderhearted!

As she near'd the winding river's bank,
Rapt Lughaidh hail'd his swan returning -
When lo! to earth the matron sank,
Her glowing cheek with blushes burning!

She sank with nought to screen her shame
Save her long, dripping ebon tresses -
Sank cold and pale, the glorious dame,
Amid a husband's wild caresses!

---

[1] *Bel*, or *Beal*. - The god of the sun whose greatest festival we held on the 1st of May. The peasantry still regard the day with due veneration and call it *La-Beal-tinne*, or the *Day of Bel's Fire*.

[2] *Samhain*.- The goddess of the moon. Her festival was held on the 1st of November. The eve of this day is yet distinguished in Scotland and Ireland by many superstitious observances, the most of which may be found in *Burns' Hallow-e'en*. The peasantry call it *Oidche-Shamhna* or *Souna's Night*.

He call'd from death his dying Fail -
Her damp limbs gave their last cold quiver -
And now they chant her funeral wail,
Who died for shame beside the river!

The Druids the smoking pyre[1] enclose,
With holy rites, with censers waving -
In the urn her ashes calm repose,
Who oft repos'd with him that's raving!

The white-stol'd Druids sing, in sooth,
Around the *leacht*, her death of glory;
Her spirit seeks the Land of Youth[2]
Her fame shall live in Gaelic story.

Shall live while maidens' cheeks shall glow -
While matrons cherish her example -
While songs of bards to virtue flow -
While Feale shall seek the ocean ample!

The Summing Up[3]

I never would yield the precious tears
I've wept above this plaintive measure,
For heartless pomps, through lengthening years,
For pearls of price, for countless treasure!

Methought, last night, that Heaven's high choirs
In song contended, each with other -
And the holiest hymn of the golden lyres
Was Fail's blest lay to the Virgin Mother!

---

[1] In the reign of the monarch Eochaidh, or as the name is pronounced, Eochy, *anno mundi* 3,952, the Irish began to bury their dead in graves within the earth. From this remarkable circumstance he was surnamed *Aireamh*, a word which signifies a grave. Before this period the Irish burned the dead, and buried their ashes in urns beneath the *leachts*, or monumental heaps.

[2] The Land of Youth. - A literal translation of *Tír-na-nóige*, the Elysium of the pagan Irish, celebrated as the region of immortal youth.

[3] *Summing-Up*. - At the end of a poem, the Irish poets usually devoted one or two stanzas to the expression of some particular sentiment. This they called the *cangal*, or *binder*, which I translate, the "summing-up." I love to copy these brave old bards, to whom I owe more obligation of thought and power of expression than to the entire corpus of English writers.

(41)
To A Lady[1]

O Lady! thou hast bid me tell
her name who holds my heart from me,
That thou may'st prove, by secret spell,
If she unkind or constant be,
When magic feat and charm are seen,
Around thy hearth, at Hallowe'en.

Through many a stately town I've stray'd
And many a flowery vale of green;
In blazoned hall, in rural shade,
I've beauties bright and beamy seen,
And haply come of matchless grace,
Found in my breast short resting place.

Their memory fled, and left that breast,
Perhaps, a seared and trodden thing,
Which stern misfortune's footstep press'd,
To crush its hopes young blossoming;
And then I swear no nymph for aye
Should haunt my memory's sainted way!

In evil hour, two laughing eyes
My rash oath broke, and bound my spell
Who caused my faithless perjuries
I ne'er have told - I ne'er shall tell,
But on my heart her witching name
Is written with a pen of flame.

O! wouldst thou know her charms, who caught
My fluttering heart in beauty's zone?
Such charms the glorious Grecian wrought
Whom Venus carv'd in living stone -
Charms fill'd with life, and love, and all
That binds a poet beauty's thrall!

---

[1] This poem was written in 1846 and published posthumously in the *Nation* on October 5th 1850. It bears the hallmarks of having being written at Hallowe'en and may have been composed for one of his children - Minnie perhaps. - Ed.

The ivory brow - the pale, pure cheek -
The pouting lip - I leave unsung;
The azure eye, where virtue meek
Sits proudly throned with beauty young -
The ambery hair, whose curls were given
To draw my soul to earth from heaven!

Enchantress fair! as fair and bright
As she I vainly sought and sung -
Demand not, on this magic night,
Thy poet's dame - no wizard tongue
Can break my bondage-link of flame,
Can spell my bird of beauty's name.

(42)
Song to Lesbia[1]

Be mine the rustic peaceful cot,
Remov'd from fortune's strife,
And thee to share my simple lot,
In happy wedded life.
Let Time's rough storms around us swell,
And foamy surges roar,
Secure, within our humble cell,
Content shall guard the door.

Yes, let me draw the blissful scene,
Where woodbine sweetly spread,
And many a fragrant flower between
Shall raise its blooming head
Around our cot; and one dear flow'r
Unrivall'd there shall blow
No rose-bud of our rural bow'r
Decked with so rich a glow.

Thrice pleasing scene of pleasure bright,

[1] The song was published posthumously in the *Nation* on November 30th 1850. It was almost certainly written for his wife. - Ed.

With thee to spend my days;
And hear thee sing (what dear delight!)
Thy happy Edward's lays;
And ne'er shall warmest love depart
From this fond bosom's core,
Till death shall break my constant heart,
And life's last pang be o'er.

(43)
Adown Yon Glen[1]

Adown yon glen, where foaming floods,
In rapid torrents brightly flow -
Where drooping alders slight the woods,
To kiss the crystal tide below.
Where silken zephyrs freshness fling,
O'er moss-clad banks where cowslips blow,
The evening star to me will bring
My own dear Mary, O!

For vulgar souls be Phoebus' light -
For mine the moon's inspiring glow,
When silver clothes the mountains' height,
And liquid fire the streams below;
Then o'er my soul such charms prevail,
For monarch's crowns I'd ne'er forego,
When meets me in the dewy vale;
My own dear Mary, O!

Mild maid! not thine the rose's dye,
But pure thy cheek as mountain snow -
And the azure of thy modest eye
Some seraph stole from Heav'n, I know;
But should that eye's celestial ray,
To other's love a gleam bestow,
I'd tear thee from my heart away,
My own dear Mary, O!

[1] Published posthumously in the *Nation* on December 14th 1850. - Ed.

(44)
There's a Glen of Green Beauty[1]

There's a glen of green beauty, where echoes have spoken,
And waters of brightness o'er rude rocks are flung.
In the glen blooms a bower, (but haply 'tis broken)
Where Mary the strains of her poet oft sung.
Till memory dies in the breast of the weeper,
Those moments of rapture, he'll never forget.
Tho' vanished for aye, like the dream of the sleeper,
I wonder does Mary remember them yet!

O, ne'er shall the bard, in that green blooming bower,
Hear Mary's voice warble his wild song again,
For, young hearts that bounded to passion's soft power,
Misfortune, forever, hath sundered in twain!
As bright eyes might light him o'er life's troubled ocean -
A kinder caress him - but can he forget
The raptures that hallow the heart's first devotion?
I wonder does Mary remember them yet!

Restore him the bloom of a hope early blighted -
Erase from his heart the deep trace of despair -
Recall one wild vow which to Heaven was plighted -
Bid his soul be as pure as when true love was there.
O, never shall peace to his dark soul be spoken,
Shall his couch be unstained with the tear of regret
For pleasures long vanished and tender ties broken -
I wonder does Mary remember them yet!

[1] The song was published posthumously in the *Nation*, January 1st 1855. According to Dan Seán O'Keeffe of Ruhill, Kiskeam, it was written for Mary O'Donovan after his encounter with her in the *Glouneen*, at Kiskeam. See *O'Donovan's Daughter* pp. 549f. - Ed.

(45)
Epistle to a Lady[1]

Dear friend, demand no verse sublime;
For I, who untaught stanzas chime,
Have spent a day of dreary time
At moods and tenses,
Enough to set a man of rhyme
Out o'er his senses.

Ah me! This world's weary school,
Where many a pedant struts by rule,
And many a base and blockhead fool,
In fortun's view,
Bears bitter sway or insult cool
O'er genius true.

Alas, what hearts are tempest driven,
From every hope despairing riven,
Save what the Saviour kind hath given
Ere wretches sink,
Deprived of that last hold, their heaven,
On misery's brink.

And some in gilded galleys glide
Upon the calm, unruffled tide,
Unheeding all the ruin wide,
Of wretches' fall,
They sail secure in gallant pride
At fortune's call.

[1] The poem was published posthumously in the *Nation*, October 1st 1859. Under the heading, 'Unpublished poem of Edward Walsh,' the editorial note reads: 'The daughter of Edward Walsh, his favourite Minnie, transcribes for us the following poem, and another which, shall appear in a future number, from the manuscript of her lamented father, and sends them for publication to the *Nation*.' The poem may have been written for Mrs. Walsh. - Ed.

Ah me, the tide of feeling strong
Quick shoots my burning veins along,
To view each ruthless deed of wrong,
And scene of woe,
When tyrants rule the abject throng
Who crouch below.

But soon this life of sorrow closes,
And when in death my care reposes,
The grave shall be my bed of roses
Blooming gay,
Where one tir'd wretch his head composes
To sleep for aye,

If, when I'm numbered with the dead,
And rank weeds cluster round my head,
These rhymes to kindred ears be led,
And they should crave it,
To trace the bard whose spirit fled
To him who gave it.

Thus should the tale afflictive swell
That round his path misfortune fell,
That fancy wove her garland well,
But fortune blighted,
When o'er his head, and truth to tell,
Dark sorrow lighted.

That oft the teardrop dimm'd his eye,
When ragged misery wandered nigh,
To shun the bursting bosom's sigh
And wretches' moan
Beneath the green graveyard he lie
Unheard, unknown.

That early o'er the Muses' lyre
To wood and wave he swept the wire
And [...] eyes could well inspire
The sacred glow,
Till sadness quench'd the heavenly fire,
And laid him low.

That though by wayward fortune led;
Tho' fading hope that withering fled –
Tho' urged to seek his bitter bread,
Could want be more;
His virgin muse ne'er flattery shed
At rich men's door.

That 'twas his pride, tho' driven again
To drag the deep dark load of pain,
'Mid summer's sun and winter's rain,
A wanderer wild;
To bend he ever did disdain,
To fortune's child.

Lady, I've trespassed on your leisure
In rhyme uncouth, and rudest measure,
But when the Muse, my only treasure,
Prompts the lay,
All gladly at the task of pleasure,
I sing away.

O, set a hair-brained bard like me,
Where headlong waters foaming flee,
Where fairies hold their revelry,
In grove or dell,
Then moves my harp's rude minstrelsy,
By potent spell.

O when my bosom's wont to break,
Or, when my care-crazed head would ache;
The tuneful quill of rhyme I take
To chant the lay,
And every care in Lethe's lake,
Dissolves away.

Whene'er arrives the destined time
That death shall call me to his chime,
Nor deem my folly ought of crime;
O Lady fair,
He'll find me chanting some sweet rhyme
To some sweet air.

And while each act of goodness done,
Be grateful to the Muse's son,
Or poet's meed of praise be won,
By kindness free,
Behold while rhyme's smooth current run
'Twill run for thee.

And lo! Amid the troubles rife,
That mark this chequer'd scene of strife,
May every pleasure mark thy life,
I fervent pray,
Or virtuous maid or faithful wife,
Be thou for aye.

(46)
A Valentine[1]

As the turtle dove seeks the soft wing of his love
When the wild tempest shakes all the terror struck grove,
My fair dove of softness! from life's storm of woe,
I'd shelter my heart in thy bosom of snow,
To dwell in communion with thine.

[1] "A Valentine" was published posthumously in the *Nation*, October 10th 1859. - Ed.

And my life's gleam would live in the light of thine eyes,
And each prayer of my lips were a love-laden sigh,
And angels of mercy would happiness shower
O'er our slumber of peace in our Paradise bower,
My first, my ador'd Valentine.

Oh! be not to me as the Apennine height,
With chill, icy bosom 'neath radiancy bright;
But like the blest sun of a green ocean isle,
To rear the young blossom of hope by thy smile
To flowers and fruitage divine.

Name me, O! name me, beloved of thy breast,
Bright star of my course to love's haven of rest!
O! breathe but that whisper of magic to me,
And I'll fly from this cold world to bliss and to thee,
My first, my ador'd Valentine.

COMPOSITIONS BY EDWARD WALSH?

(47)
Donal Dubh[1]

Air: *She's the dear maid to me.*

My name is Donal Dubh
I'm an outlaw bold and true,
I roam the country through
From Saxon bandits free.
But I loved a maiden fair,
She had dark and glossy hair,
She sold me in despair;
She's the dear maid to me!

Margaret Kelly was her name,
And burning was the flame
That was hidden in her bosom
When first I knew her name.
But her love grew false and cold,
And an outlaw's life she sold,
for the Saxon's worthless gold;
She's the dear maid to me!

My sires were princes grand
Throughout old Ireland;
From many a mighty band,
We held our castles free;
'Till the Saxon's 'gainst us rose:
An outlaw man I rove,
Lamenting my false love.
She's the dear maid to me!

Cursed was the hour
When revenge o'er me had power;
I slew my beauty's flower
When I heard her perjury.

---

[1] This was a very popular song in the Duhallow tradition, and universally understood to be a composition by Edward Walsh. However, I have failed to find a published source acknowledging Walsh's authorship. It has, however, been attributed, erroneously, I believe, to Robert D. Joyce in *Songs of the Gael* ,vol iii, p. 80. - Ed.

This good *scian* by my side,
I struck deep in my bride,
And her life's blood ebbed away;
She's the dear maid to me.

(48)

Lines Written On a View of the Heavens at Night[1]

Infinity of space! - mysterious wonder! -
Too great, too big, for human comprehension! -
Man tries in thought to span thee, but he cannot.
Far, far beyond the reach of thought thou dwellest:
I see thee but in part, and yet around
'Tis one unbounded, measureless expanse -
One limitless, interminable view.
Above me is the vast concavity of heaven,
Spreading around its adamantine arch,
whose azure sweep, enamelled with a thousand stars,
Seems like a sea with isles of living fire.
See how like balls of phosphorus they shine -
How pure and spiritual is their aspect! -
They seem the very eyes of heaven - its ministers of light.
Ye radiant orbs, how vast, how great your distance![2]
And what is Earth amid this mighty scene? -
Earth, that now seems so large and spacious.
'Tis but a round,[3] diminutive, and trembling ball,
That, like the sparkling myriads around,
Wheel on throughout the ample vault of heaven;
For, could we, from some extra-mundane point,
Behold this mighty globe that we inhabit,

---

[1] Published in the *Dublin Penny Journal*, May 14th 1836. It is initialled W. - Ed.

[2] Every little star, though so little in appearance, is really a vast globe like the sun in size and glory. The reason that they appear so diminutive, is owing to their immense and inconceivable distance - so great, that it is supposed a cannon-ball, flying with unabated rapidity, would take seven hundred thousand years before it could reach the nearest of them.

[3] A learned writer remarks, that the loftiest summits of hills, and the greatest ridges of mountains, are no real objection to the globular form of the earth, because they bear no greater proportion to the entire surface of the terraqueous ball than a particle of dust casually dropped on a mathematician's globe bears to its whole circumference; consequently, the rotund figure is no more destroyed in the former case than in the latter.

With all its seas, its mountains, and its lakes,
Its gilded domes and lofty pyramids,
Its noble palaces and splendid halls,
And all the other costly works of man, -
'Twould seem but as yon little drop of gold
That glitters in the firmament above.
But nobler still - surpassing comprehension -
Amazing, inconceivably sublime -
Those many orbs that through the empyrean roll
Are but the central sun of other systems;
And millions, yet unseen, are floating on
Throughout the azure fields of liquid ether.
Thou mighty, grand, and noble contemplation!
Before thee language fails, description droops -
Imagination only can conceive thee,
Unfurl thy wing, then - let me soar aloft -
Bear, bear me onward to yon twinkling star
That trembles on the horizon's utmost verge!
I see - I see another world - a new horizon now -
Another paradrome, which worlds still circuit through -
Another glittering escutcheon, decked
With heaven's armorial bearings.
Surpassing, transcendental greatness!
And where that mighty Power that framed them all -
That vast Omnipotent that ranged them
Each in their respective orbits, that thus they wheel
Through endless ages, still maintain order?
Away, he dwells in fathomless, immensity -
"Afar from mortal eye, or angels' purer ken."
Learn, then, oh man! from this thy littleness -
This lesson ought to teach humility;
For what art thou amid the vast creation?
Thy world is but a fraction of the whole,
And thou thyself an atom placed upon it.

(49)
Matrimony[1]

Hail, wedded bliss! Thou soother of the cares
And ruthless passions of the busy world.
Who rails at thee, and talks of endless strife,
Increas'd expense, or galling slavery,
Rail on unnoticed. Round thy peaceful brow
Love weaves an evergreen; thy sober step
Comfort and *Temperance* support; a train
Of happy cherubs dance along thy path,
And sing of Love's perfection. See the sons
Of rambling impulse gaze with envious eye,
And curse their pleasures, in the common path
Promiscuous plucked, and sigh for such a gem.
Approach not, oh! Ye votaries of wealth!
For wealth is here a secondary good;
They only can be blest whose hearts have known
Mutual affection; hence polluted crew,
For reason and religion both condemn
The sordid motives of your grovelling souls.
How great the solace from the tender smiles
Of wedded love, when sad affliction pours
On our devoted heads a storm of woe.
So felt our parent Adam, when he rov'd
With his lov'd Eve from blissful Paradise.
So felt mankind's sad father, when expell'd
To wander o'er the yet untrodden earth;
His Comfort sooth'd his grief – the briny tear
Kiss'd from his cheek – mixed her sad sighs with his,
And fondly spoke of future happiness.

[1] Published in the *Irish Penny Magazine*, Feb. 28th 1833. Initialled, W.

(50)
To Erin[1]

Not that upon thy plain's the richest treasure
of emerald verdure feeds thy lowing herds -
Not that thy native music's thrilling measure
Hath eloquence deep as inspired words -
Not that thy sons have ever with their swords
Appeared as men, when justice urged them on,
Am I fair island proud to be their son.
But thinking on thee, Erin, when afar,
'Mid strangers' land I wandered, thou to me
Did'st stand alone in radiance like the star
That lit our course, when night set on the sea
That bore me with our vessel far from thee.
In other lands the scene may be as fair -
But where are hearts such as thy children bear?

(51)
The Soldier's Farewell[2]

Farewell to thee, dearest,
No longer I stay,
Valour is calling
To battle away.
The trumpet is sounding,
I hear its wild blast,
One kiss ere I go, love,
Perchance 'tis the last.

---

[1] The sonnet, initialled W, was published in the *Nation*, March 11th 1843, with the following editorial comment, 'W's sonnet is promising for so unpopular a form of versification; but it is only in the hand of a master that it ever has or ever can become very successful. With the exception of Shannon's, we have read few sonnets since Wordsworth's with any pleasure.' There is another poem of the same title which is certainly by Edward Walsh. See pp 483ff. – Ed.

[2] The poem was published in the final issue of the *Dublin Journal of Temperance, Science and Literature* (vol. 2, No 27), 1843 and is initialled by W who seemingly resides at 25, Bachelor's-walk. In 'Answers to Correspondents' of the penultimate issue of the journal there is a note to the effect that an item submitted by "E.W." 'shall meet our attention in our concluding number.' We can only assume that this is the item in question. - Ed.

Farewell to thee, dearest,
The banners now wave,
And I must away
To the field of the brave.
The troops are advancing,
From the uplands they come,
And chargers are bounding
At the roll of the drum.

Farewell to thee, dearest,
The foe now appears,
With glitter of armour
And flashing of spears.
It grieves me to leave thee,
But oh! We must part,
Thou light of my childhood,
Thou lov'd of my heart.

Farewell to theee, dearest,
I'll see thee no more,
Perchance I may fall
On the dread field of gore;
And in tears you will watch, love,
By evening's pale star,
For your soldier's return
Again from the war.

(52)

Our Hopes[1]

Air: *Crúiscín Lán*

No craven blends his moan
With the millions' mighty tone,
As bursting from dark slavery's night
Of tears, and blood, and blame,
But, unscathed in their fame,
They hail the glorious full orb'd sight,

[1] The song was published in the *Nation*, April 20th 1844. It is signed W. - Ed.

Freedom's light,
Rising, Erin! on thy Brave and thy Bright!

One faithful chief of fame,
Transcending all acclaim,
Though the fetters for his strong limbs they weave,
His honour'd name to speak
Blanches every tyrant's cheek,
And thrills the bounding breast of the slave,
Till he crave
Fair Freedom from high heaven or the grave!

And we've men of giant mould,
As true as tested gold,
And fierce as the cloud-cradled flash
That holds his smouldering fire
Suspensive in red ire
''Till the elements all wrathfully clash!
Tyrants rash,
Look better to your fetter and your lash!

The tyrant may enthral -
The chafing chains may gall -
Our leader to the scaffold be led -
Or the traitor's bloody knife
May pour each precious life,
Like the trustful o'er the wine bowl red,
But, ye Dead!
We'll have freedom - by your life-blood shed!

(53)
The Minstrel's Invocation[1]

There's a voice, a voice of sighing,
In the murmuring of the breeze -
There's a dream of grief undying
In the foaming of the seas -
There's a whisp'ring from our mountains,
Cities, valleys, rivers, streams,
And a moaning from our fountains
Like the grief of troubled dreams.

Oh! that voice - it is the sighing
Of the spirits of the dead,
Down by vale and dingle lying,
Where the freeborn fought and bled;
In the forest breezes stealing,
And the murmurs of the sea,
From their lonely graves appealing
To the spirits of the free.

Isle of mist and bardic story,
Isle of many a hero lay,
Where is all thy ancient glory?
Have thine honours passed away?
Oh! that sigh - it is for Freedom -
Freedom to thy father's graves:
Has the voice of Heaven decreed them,
Even in ashes, to be slaves?

Sons of Brian! - sons of Cormac! -
Once the free-born and the free -
Where's your sense of shame and honour?
Where your deeds for minstrelay?
Must the spirit of thy sires
Murmur through thy captive hills?
Have thy hearts not heard the lyres,
That have chaunted of their ills?

---

[1] This poem is initialled 'E_____' in the *Nation* of December 7th 1844. - Ed

Haughty Moore, and brave O'Donnell,
Bold MacDermott and Tyrone,
Heroes of the true Clann Conail,
Hast thou left thy land alone?
Has the Isle of glories martyr'd,
None to succour, none to save?
Are her hopes and freedom barter'd
Since the mighty found a grave?

(54)
Sonnet[1]

I would this dreary pilgrimage were o'er,
Where countless snares my bleeding feet betray.
Sweet dawn arise! my home is far away -
A friendless exile on an alien shore,
I mark the time's advancing breaker's roar;
The tide rolls in to gulf us - yet we stay,
And on a crumbling landmark madly play,
Wasting the priceless hours for evermore.
Rise, sacred dawn! methinks a fresh'ning breeze
From yonder holy mountain skyward springs,
The day is breaking! Courage! now, my heart,
Our lonely skiff shall brave the coldest seas,
For sighs of angels rustle through her wings -
The tear to some, and then in silence we depart.

[1] The sonnet was published in the *Nation*, February 13th 1847. It is signed W. By 1847, Edward Walsh's fortunes were in steep decline, and while we cannot say with certainty that the sonnet is his, the sentiments expressed in it could not have been alien to him at that time. - Ed.

TRANSLATIONS FROM THE IRISH

Walsh's introductory remarks on Irish Popular Poetry[1]

The popular songs and ballads of Ireland are as completely unknown to the great mass of Irish readers, as if they were sung in the wilds of Lapland, instead of the green valleys of their own native land. These strains of the Irish muse are to be found in the tongue of the people only; and while, for past centuries, every means had been used to lead the classes which had partaken, even in the slightest degree, of an English education, into a total disuse of the mother tongue; when the middle and upper ranks, aping the manners of the English settlers located among them, adopted a most un-national dislike to the language of their fathers; when even in the courts of law the sole use of the vernacular was a stumbling-block in the way of him who sought for justice within their precincts, and the youth who may have acquired a smattering of education found it necessary, upon emerging from his native glen into the world, to hide, as closely as possible, all knowledge of the tongue he had learned at his mother's breast; it is no wonder the peasantry should, at length, quit this last vestige of nationality, and assist the efforts of the hedge school-master in its repression. The village teacher had long been endeavouring to check the circulation of the native tongue among the people, by establishing a complete system of espiery in these rustic seminaries, in which the youth of each hamlet were made to testify against those among them who uttered an Irish phrase. This will easily account for the very imperfect knowledge which the rising population of various districts have, at this hour, of the tongue which forms the sole mode of communication between their seniors. The poor peasant, seeing that education could be obtained through the use of English only, and that the employment of the native tongue was a strong bar to the acquirement of the favoured one, prohibited to his children the use of the despised language of his fathers. This transition was, and is still, productive of serious inconvenience to the young and the old of the same household in their mutual intercourse of sentiment. The writer of these remarks has been often painfully amused at witnessing the embarrassment of a family circle, where the parents, scarcely understanding a word of English, strove to converse with their children, who awed by paternal command, and the dread of summary punishment at the hands of the pedagogue, were driven to essay a language of which the parents could scarcely comprehend a single word, and of which the poor children had too scant a stock to furnish forth a tithe of their exuberant thought.

Yet, in this despised, forsaken language are stored up the most varied and comprehensive powers for composition. Who that has heard the priest address his Irish-speaking congregation, and seen the strange power of his impassioned eloquence over the hearts of his hearers - how the strong man, the feeble senior, the gentle girl, were alternately

[1] Published as an introduction to his *Irish Popular Songs* and entitled "Introductory remarks on Irish Popular Poetry." - Ed.

fixed in mute astonishment, kindled into enthusiasm, or melted into tears, as the orator portrayed the mercies of heaven to fallen man - who that has witnessed this, and will not acknowledge its thrilling influence in the affecting simplicity of its pathos, and the energy of its bold sublimity? Who that has heard the peasant-mother lavish upon her infant these endearing expressions, which can hardly be conveyed in a comparatively cold English dress, and not call it the tongue of maternal tenderness? And I trust that he who can read the following songs in the original, will likewise confess that the Irish tongue can also express the most passionate ardour, the most sweetly querulous murmurings of love, and that rendering grief which beats its breast upon the margin of despair.

It has been asserted that there is no language better adapted to lyric poetry than the Irish. That array of consonants which is retained in the words, to show the derivation, and which appears so formidable to the eye of an un-Irish reader, is cut off by aspirates, and softens down into a pleasing stream of liquid sounds, and the disposition of the broad and the slender vowels gives a variety to the ear by their ever-changing melody.

One striking characteristic in the flow of Irish verse must principally claim our notice - namely, the beautiful adaptation of the subject of the words to the song measure - the particular embodiment of thought requiring, it would seem, a kindred current of music to float upon. Or, to vary the figure, the particular tune so exquisitely chosen by the Irish lyricist, seems the natural gait of the subject, whatever they my be, from which it cannot be forced, in a translation, without at once destroying the graceful correspondence which gives its most attractive grace to the original.

Miss Brooke has erred through her versions of the "Reliques" in this respect, and so also, almost generally, have the translators of Mr. Hardiman's "Minstrelsy."

Another grace of the Irish language lies in the number of its synonyms, which enable the poet to repeat the same thought over and over without tiring the ear. Its copiousness permits the raising of a pyramid of words upon a single thought - as, for instance, in the description of a beautiful head of hair, the poet employs a variety of epithets, all of the same cognate race, yet each differing from the other by some slight shade of meaning. The rhymers of later times have carried this peculiarity in a blameable degree. In this species of composition, the translator is quite bewildered, and he seeks, in vain, for equivalent terms in the English tongue to express the graceful redundancies of the original!

In the sentimental and pastoral songs of Ireland, will be found those varied and gorgeous descriptions of female beauty and rural scenery, which have no parallel in the English tongue, and which, as men of learning have asserted, are equalled only in the rich and exuberant poetry of the East. In these Irish songs are to be found none of the indelicate and even gross allusions which so greatly disgrace the lyrical efforts of the best poets of England in the last century. Not but that Irish rhymers have often composed in the censurable manner to which we have alluded; but these reprehensible lays are to be found only in manuscripts, and are never sung by the people.

Some of these popular songs are genuine pastorals, possessing this pleasing feature that while nothing fictitious blends with the strain, and the whole is perfectly true to nature, nothing coarse or vulgar is introduced, to displease the most refined ear, and all the beautiful and glorious objects of nature are pressed into the service of the muse. The bloom of the bean-field is the cheek of the rural nymph; her eye, a freezing star, or the crystal dew-drops on the grass at sunrise; her sudden appearance, a sunburst through a cloud of mist; the majesty of her mien, the grace of the white-breasted swan surveying his arching neck in the mirror of the blue lake; her voice, the cooing of the dove, the magic sounds of fairy music, or the speaking note of the cuckoo when he bids the woods rejoice; her hair either ambery, golden, or flaxen - ringleted, braided, perfumed, bepearled, sweeping the tie of her sandal, or floating on the silken wing of the breeze! The enamoured poet will lead his love over the green-topped hills of the South or West, will show her ships and sails through the vistas of the forest, as they seek their retreat by the shore of the broad lake. They shall dine on the venison of the hills, the trout of the lake, and the honey of the hollow oak. Their couch shall be the purple-blossomed heath, the soft moss of the rock, or the green rushes strewn with creamy agrimony, and the early call of the heath-cock alone shall break their slumber of love!

Allegory was the favourite vehicle of conveying the political sentiment of Ireland in song, at least since the days of Elizabeth. To this figure the poets were inclined by the genius of the tongue, as well as the necessity, which urged to clothe the aspirations for freedom in a figurative dress. Erin, the goddess of the bard's worship, is a beautiful virgin, who has fallen within the grasp of the oppressor - all the terms of his tongue are expended in celebration of the charms of her person, her purity, her constancy, her present suffering, her ancient glory! Her metaphorical names are many: the chief among that class are "Rós geal Dubh," "Graine Mhaol," "Droiman Donn;" or she sometimes appears invested with all the attributes in which the beautiful fairy mythology of the land enwraps the fabled beings of its creation. She leads the poet a devious route to many a rath and fairy place, till at length, amid the shadowy forms of olden bards, and chiefs, and regal dames, and sceptred kings, she bids the wondering mortal proclaim to the Milesan Race that the period was at hand when her faithful friends would burst the bonds of slavery! The "Vision of John MacDonnell" is a beautiful instance of this species of composition, and is also very curious in illustration of the fairy topography of Ireland.

A few specimens to prove our remarks upon the power of Irish verse, may not, perhaps, be unacceptable to the reader. The following noble stanza is from a poem by Eoghan O'Rahilly, a poet of the last century, on a shipwreck which he witnessed on the coast of Kerry. The stanza and its translation are taken from O'Reilly's "Biography of Irish Writers": -

Dob éagnach imirt na tuile re daor-ruathar

Méad na toinne re fuirneach na gaoth guairnéin,
Taobh na loinge 'sa fuirionn air treun-luasgadh,
Aig eigheadh tuitim go grinniol gan dáil fuascailt!

The roaring flood resistless force display'd,
Each whirling blast the swelling surges sway'd,
The vessel burst - alas! the crew she bore
Scream'd in the deep, and sank to rise no more!

Donough MacNamara, a Waterford poet of the last century, in his mock Aeneid, thus describes the roar of the Stygian ferry-man as penetrating the remotest boundaries of creation: -

Do léig se gáir ós ard is béiceach,
Le fuaim a ghotha do chritheadar na spéarthadh,
Do chualadh an chruinne é 'd cuir ifrionn géim ar!

He uttered an outcry and a roar -
At the sound of his voice the heavens were shaken,
All creation heard it, and hell rebellowed!

The following incentive to battle is from the pen of Andrew Magrath, called the *Mangaire Sugach*, another Munster poet: -

Sin agaibh an t-am agus gabhaig le na chéile,
Preabaig le fonn agus planncaig meith-phuic,
Leanaig an fogha ar dhream an éithig,
'S ná h-ionntoigheadh aen le sgáth ó' n-gleó!

The hour hath come - unite your force;
Rush with ardour, and strike the fat he-goats;
Follow up the assault on the perfidious race,
And let none swerve in terror from the conflict!

In "The Boat Song", - one of the songs in the present collection, - the poet thus apostrophises a rock in Blacksod Bay: -

A Dhaoilein, a chroin-charraig gharbh gan sgáth,
Air an ruadh-bharc-so fúm-sa breathnuigh do sháth,

An chuimhin leat, 's an g-cuan-so, go bh-faca tú bád
Gan chontabhairt tonn-bharra gearradh mar táim!

O! Dillon, tempest-beaten rock, all rough and dark!
Look forth, and see beneath me now this bounding bark,
And say, if e'er thou boat beheld within this bay,
Wave mounted, cleaving, confident, like mine today!

The wind agitating the water of the River Funcheon is thus described by one McAuliffe, a blacksmith of Glanmire, near Cork. I would beg of the classical reader to compare this line with that frequently quoted one in the first book of Homer's Iliad: -

Gliong-gothach láidir a g-caithiomh na d-tonn.
Loud-clanging, forceful, wild-tossing the waves.

The following instance from the song of Eadhmonn an Chnoic will shew how the consonant sounds are softened down by aspiration:-

A chuil aluinn dheas na bh-fainneadha g-cas,
Is breagh 'gus is glas do shuile!

Maid of the wreathed ringlets, beautiful, exceedingly fair,
Blue and splendid are your eyes!

And again, in the same song as it is sung in the South of Ireland: -

A chumain sa shearc rachamuidne seal
Fa choillte aig speala drúchta,
Mar a bhfaghadhmuidne breach 'is lon air a nead,
An fiadh 'gus an poc ag buithre;
An ténín is binne air ghéagaibh ag seinim,
An chuaichín air bhárr an úr-ghlais,
Is go bráth ní thiocfa an bás air ar n-goire,
A lár na coille cubhartha!

My hope, my love, we will proceed
Into the woods, scattering the dews,
Where we will behold the salmon, and the ousel in its nest,
The deer and the roebuck calling,

The sweetest bird on the branches warbling,
The cuckoo on the summit of the green hill;
And death shall never approach us
In the bosom of the fragrant wood!

In the allegorical song, *Rós geal Dubh*, the poet's love for his unfortunate country, and his utter despair of its freedom, are thus expressed:

Tá grádh agam am lár dhuit
Le bliaghain anois,
Grádh cráite, grádh cásmhar,
Grádh cíopatha,

Grádh d'fág mé gan sláinte,
Gan rían, gan ruith,
Is go brath, brath, gan aon fhaill agam
Air Rós geal Dubh!

My love sincere is centred here
This year and more -
Love, sadly vexing, love perplexing,
Love painful, sore,

Love, whose rigour hath crush'd my vigour,
Thrice hopeless love,
While fate doth sever me, ever, ever,
From *Rós geal Dubh*!

In the song of "Beautiful Deirdre," the following will illustrate what has been already said of the power of the Irish in the use of synonyms: -

Is camarsach claon, 's is craobhach, chrath-úrlach,
Taithneamhach, teudach, faon-chas, feac-lúaineach
Leabhair-cheart, laobhdha, slaodach, srath-lúbach
A bachall-foilt chaomh-ghlan gheugach fhad-chúrsach.

Her ringlet-hair -
Curve-arching, meandering, spreading, curl-quivering,
Fascinating, string like, plaint-wreathing, restless-swerving,

Free-extending, inclining, abundant, thick-twining,
Mildly-bright branchy, far-sweeping.

The next is a proof of the exquisite feeling of the elegiac muse of our valleys. A lover is weeping over the grave of his betrothed: -

Nuair is dóigh le mo mhuintir go in-bím-se air mo leaba,
Air do thuamba seadh bhí'm sínte ó oidhche go maidin,
Ag cur síos mo chruadhtain, is ag cruadh-ghol go daingion,
Tré mo chailín ciúin stúamaidh, do luadhag liom na leanbh!

When the folk of my household suppose I am sleeping,
On your cold grave till morning the lone watch I'm keeping;
My grief to the night wind for the mild maid to render,
Who was my betrothed since infancy tender!

I shall conclude these quotations with this simile, taken from one of the songs in the present collection: -

Chonairc mé ag teacht chugam í tre lár an t-sléibhe,
Mar réiltion thríd an g-ceó!

I saw her approaching me along the mountain,
Like a star through a mist!

I shall now introduce to the reader's notice some of the poets of the last century, from whose writing many of the songs in this collection are taken. Some of these songs belong to an earlier period. *Rós geal Dubh*, for instance, is supposed to have been composed in the time of Queen Elizabeth; but the names of the writers of some of the best in the collection are now unknown. In these songs, the historian or moral philosopher may trace the peculiar character of our people; and from fragmented phrases and detached expressions, ascertain the "form and pressure" of the times to which they belong, even as the geologist bears away fragments of old world wonders, whence to deduce a theory or establish a truth. He will trace the ardent temper and unbroken spirit of our people in these undefined aspirations for freedom - the allegorical poems; their vehement and fiery love, chastened and subdued beneath the yoke of reason, by deep religious feeling, in their pastoral songs; and in the elegiac strains he will trace the intense feelings that exist in the Irish heart, as the mourner pours his despair over the grave of departed beauty, or sighs, on the margin of a foreign shore, for one green spot in his own loved island which he can never more behold.

These song writers are, doubtless, the lineal descendants of the bards of preceding centuries. Their poems, however, are not works of art; they are, with few exceptions, the efforts of untutored nature - the spontaneous produce of a rich poetic soil. But if these wild lyrics thrill with electric power to the heart, what must be the effect of the finished productions of that happier period when the chiefs of the land protected the craft of the minstrel!

Chief among these poets, as distinguished for his extensive learning and bardic powers, stands John MacDonnell, surnamed Claragh, a native of Charleville, in the County Cork. He was the contemporary and friend of John Toomey, a Limerick poet, celebrated for his convivial temper and sparkling wit. The "Vision," of MacDonnell, with some other pieces, come within the present collection. He was a violent Jacobite, and his poems are chiefly of that character. In his time, the poets held "bardic sessions" at stated intervals, for the exercise of their genius. The people of the districts bordering upon the town of Charleville yet retain curious traditions of these literary contests, in which the candidates for admission were obliged to furnish extempore proofs of poetical ability. O'Halloran in his "Introduction to the History of Ireland," makes honourable mention of this gifted man, and says that he was engaged in writing a history of Ireland in the native tongue. MacDonnell made also a proposal to some gentleman of the County Clare to translate Homer's Illiad into Irish. "From the specimen he gave," says O'Halloran, "it would seem that this prince of poets would appear as respectable in a Gathelian as in a Greek dress."

MacDonnell died in 1754, and was interred near Charleville. His friend and brother poet, John Toomey, wrote his elegy, which may be found in Mr. Hardiman's "Minstrelsy."

Andrew Magrath, surnamed the *Mangaire Súgach*, from whose writings I have largely extracted, was a native of the County Limerick. He practised, for a considerable time, the business of a pedlar, or travelling merchant, an occupation that gave occasion to the designation, *Mangaire Súgach*, which denotes the *Jolly Merchant*. His poems are very numerous, and greatly varied, being chiefly satirical, amatory, and political. This man possessed a genius of the highest order. His humorous pieces abound with the most delicate touches, for, as his occupation of pedlar led him into all grades of society, his discrimination of character was consequently very acute. His love songs are full of pathos, and, so far as I have been able to observe, entirely free from the taint of licentiousness. He, however, lived a vicious, sensual life, and by his irregularities incurred the censure of the Roman Catholic priesthood. It was on occasion of his being refused admittance into the Protestant communion, after his expulsion from the Catholic Church, that he wrote his "Lament," where the portraiture of his strange distress leaves the reader at a loss whether to weep at his misfortune, or laugh at the ludicrous expression of his sorrow.

Owen O'Sullivan, usually named *Eoghan Ruadh*, or *Owen the Red*, from the colour of his hair, was a native of the County Kerry. He lived at a somewhat later period than either MacDonnell or Magrath, and was also, like Magrath, a very eccentric character. O'Sullivan sometimes followed the employment of an itinerant labourer, in which occupation he would make periodical excursions into the Counties of Cork, Limerick, and Tipperary, during the reaping and potato-digging seasons. In the summer months, he would open a hedge school in the centre of a populous district, where the boys of the surrounding hamlets, and the "poor scholars" who usually followed in the wake of Owen's perambulations, were taught to render the Greek of Homer and the usual school range of Latin authors into Irish and English. I should observe that Owen the Red wrote and spoke the English tongue with considerable fluency. Many of his satires, written in that language against the Volunteers of '82, are yet preserved in the neighbourhood of Churchtown and Charleville in the County of Cork.

O'Sullivan's productions are satirical, elegiac, amatory and political. He is the favourite poet of the Munster peasantry, and their appreciation of the potato-digging bard does high credit to their critical discrimination. His strain was bold, vigorous, passionate, and feeling; his only fault being a redundance of language to which he was led by the inclination of the Irish tongue, and his own vehemence of temper. He did in 1784.

The following extract from the life of Owen O'Sullivan, as I have given it in the Jacobite Reliques" will furnish a glimpse of this unfortunate genius: -

"There are doubtless many of my readers who now hear of Owen Roe O'Sullivan for the first time. To them, perhaps, it will be necessary to say, that Owen Roe was to Ireland what Robert Burns, at a somewhat later day, was to Scotland - the glory and shame of his native land. I know no two characters in my range of observation that so closely resemble each other as Burns and Owen Roe. The same poetical temperament - the same desire of notoriety - the same ardent sighings for woman's love - the same embracing friendship for the human family - and the same fatal yearnings after "cheerful tankards foaming," alike distinguished the heaven-taught minstrels. Like Burns, the irregularity of his life obliged the clergymen of his persuasion to denounce him; and, like him, he lashed the priestly order without ruth or remorse - like Burns, he tried the pathetic, the sublime, the humorous, and, like him, succeeded in all. Nor does the parallel end here; they were both born in an humble cottage; both toiled through life at the spade and plough; and both fell, in the bloom of manhood, in the pride of intellect, the victims of uncontrolled passion!"

William Heffernan, more usually called *Uilliam Dall*, or *Blind William*, a native of Shronehill, in the County Tipperary, was contemporary with MacDonnell and Toomey, with whom he often tried his poetic powers in the literary battles of the bardic sessions. He was born blind, and spent the greater part of his life, a poor houseless wanderer, subsisting upon the bounty of others. His pieces are political, elegiac, and amatory. The tenderness of his amatory muse is refined and sweet in the highest degree. His allegorical poem, *Cliona of the Rock*, says Mr. Hardiman, "would in itself be sufficient to rescue his memory from oblivion, and stamp him with the name of poet. The machinery of this ode has been a favourite form of composition with our later bards. They delight in decorating these visionary beings with all charms of celestial beauty, and in this respect, our author appears to have been no mean proficient. His description is heightened with all the glow and warmth of the richest oriental colouring, and the sentiments and language are every way worthy of the subject."

His Caitlin ni Uallachán and other pieces, in this collection, will furnish a fair specimen of his abilities.

Another poet of this century was Donough Roe MacNamara, a native of Waterford, who, finding that the profits of his hedge school, in which he taught Greek and Latin to the peasantry, were inadequate to his support, resolved to try his fortune as a labourer in Newfoundland. He embarked; but on the second day of the voyage, the vessel in which he sailed was chased back upon the Irish coast by a French privateer, and poor MacNamara once more took to the teaching trade. At the suggestion of a Mr. Power, he afterwards wrote a metrical account of his adventure. In this poem he sets out with a description of his poverty - the manner in which the whole parish contributed to fit him out - the fascination of his landlady and her fair daughter, in Waterford - a storm at sea - sea-sickness of the passengers - a vision in which the queen of the fairies takes him to the realm of the departed spirits, where he beholds the shades of Irish warriors, and hears strange political revelations, etc., etc. This mock Aeneid contains passages of extraordinary power, and rare flights of humour. MacNamara also produced many political and amatory songs.

The foregoing are the writers from whose works I have chosen some of the pieces in this collection. Contemporary poets, of whose poems I have not availed myself are Eoghan O'Rahilly, a native of Kerry, a man of learning and great natural abilities. The peasantry of the bordering Counties of Cork, Limerick, and Kerry, yet recite his poems, and cherish the memory of his caustic wit and exquisite humour. O'Halloran makes honourable mention of this poet. Denis and Connor O'Sullivan, brothers, authors of many excellent political and amatory songs, were also natives of Kerry. In the same district, at a somewhat later period, lived Fineen O'Scannell, a man of high poetical merit, the author of many poems. Edmund Wall was also a satirical poet of much celebrity in the County of Cork.

The Reverend William English, a friar of the City of Cork, was a poet, highly facetious and satirical. Timothy O'Sullivan usually named *Teige Gaelach*, a native of the County

Waterford, was also a poet of great celebrity. His works are numerous, consisting of odes, elegies, political songs, and pastorals. His elegy on the death of Denis MacCarthy, of Ballea, in the County Cork, is a beautiful specimen of this species of composition. In early life his conduct was very irregular, and many of his poems licentious; but in after time he became sincerely penitent, and devoted his talents to the composition of sacred poems and hymns, many of which have been collected and published under the title of "Timothy O'Sullivan's Pious Miscellany."

In this passing view of the writers of the last century, I have confined myself to those of the South of Ireland alone. Even many of these I must pass over in silence, and shall close with some account of John Collins, whose genius and learning eminently qualify him to stand among the first of modern writers in Ireland. Collins taught school at Skibbereen, in the County Cork, where he died, in 1816. His poems are held in high estimation; his best production, or perhaps the best in the modern Irish, being his poem on "Timoleague Abbey." Collins has given an Irish translation of Campbell's "Exile of Erin," which admirably provides, if proof were necessary, the power of the Irish language. None will pronounce this translation in any instance inferior to the celebrated original, while, in many passages, the Irish version rises far superior in harmony of numbers and feeling of expression!

In conclusion, I beg leave to say a word or two respecting the songs in this collection. I have admitted nothing among them calculated, in a moral or political point of view, to give offence. I have also been careful to avoid that error which I already censured in others - namely, the fault of not suiting the measure of the translation to the exact song-tune of the original. The Irish scholar will perceive that I have embodied the meaning and spirit of each Irish stanza within the compass of the same number of lines, each for each; and that I have also preserved, in many of the songs, the caesural and demi-caesural rhymes, the use of which produces such harmonious effect in Irish verse. I offer these songs to the public as evidence of the poetic spirit of our people. To the reader who can peruse the original, I have to say, that the English versions are faithful, and, in most instances, perfectly literal transcripts of the Irish; and that our hills and valleys, and milking bawns, and every cottager's fireside, are vocal with hundreds of songs, which want but the aid of a poet, himself one of the people, speaking their tongue, and familiar with its idioms, to recommend them to public notice in an English dress.

It is fit to state that I have copied into this little work some of the songs which Mr. Hardiman has left untranslated in the "Minstrelsy," and also that I have selected from manuscripts some songs which I subsequently found had been already used by Mr. Hardiman. Some of my versions, however, are different from his.

In consequence of the neglected state of the Irish language during the last two centuries, considerable irregularity has arisen among writers in the use of its orthography. This will be apparent to anyone who considers what the fate of a language must be, which, ceasing to be the vehicle of learned instruction, descends to the use of men unskilled in the rules of composition, and ignorant even of the modes of inflecting nouns, or conjugating verbs. The songs in this collection, I am proud to say, are as free as possible from grammatical error, Mr. Owen Connellan, Irish Historiographer to their late Majesties, George IV and William IV, translator of the "Annals of the Four Masters," and author of a "Grammar of the Irish Language, etc., having kindly undertaken to read the Irish throughout, and to correct every apparent error of the text.

E. Walsh.
Dublin, January, 1847.

(55)
The Twisting of the Rope[1]
(*Casadh an tSúgáin*)[2]

Air: *Casadh an tSúgáin.*

What mortal conflict drove me here to roam,
though many a maid I've left behind at home;
Forth from the house where dwelleth my heart's dear hope
I was turned by the hag at the twisting of the rope.

If thou be mine, be mine both day and night;
If thou be mine, be mine in all men's sight;
If thou be mine, be mine o'er all beside -
And oh! that thou wert now my wedded bride.

In Sligo first I did my love behold,
In Galway town I spent with her my gold -
But, by this hand, if thus they me pursue,
I'll teach these dames to dance a measure new.

(56)
The Fair Young Child[3]
(*Páistín Fionn*)

Air: *Páistín Fionn.*

My *Páistín Fionn* is my soul's delight -
Her heart laughs out in her blue eyes bright;
The bloom of the apple her bosom white,
Her neck like the March swans in whiteness.

---

[1] Published in *Irish Popular Songs,* pp 38-41 - Ed.

[2] This is said to be the original song composed to the delightful tune *The Twisting of the Rope.* Tradition thus speaks of its origin: - A Connaught harper, having once put up at the residence of a rich farmer, began to pay such attentions to the young woman of the house as greatly displeased her mother, who instantly conceived a plan for the summary ejection of the minstrel. She provided some hay, and requested the harper to twist the rope which she set about making. As the work progressed, and the rope lengthened, the harper, of course, retired backward, till he went beyond the door of the dwelling, when the crafty matron suddenly shut the door in his face, and then threw his harp out of the window. The version sung in the south of Ireland has some additional stanzas, but I give the song as it is found in Hardiman's *Minstrelsy,* vol. I., where it is left untranslated.

[3] Published in *Irish Popular Songs*, pp. 100-104. - Ed.

Chorus

O! you are my dear, my dear, my dear,
O! you are my dear, and my fair love;
You are my own dear, and my fondest hope here,
And O! that my cottage you'd share, love.

Love of my bosom, my fair *Páistín,*
Whose cheek is red like the rose's sheen;
My thoughts of the maiden are pure, I ween,
Save toasting her health in my lightness!

Chorus

O! you are my dear, etc.

Were I in our village where sports prevail,
Between two barrels of brave brown ale,
My fair little sister to list my tale,
How jovial and happy I'd make me!

Chorus

O! you are my dear, etc.

In fever for nine long nights I've lain
From lying in the hedge-row beneath the rain,
While, gift of my bosom! I hop'd in vain
Some whistle or call might wake ye!

Chorus

O! you are my dear, etc.

From kinsfolk and friends, my fair, I'd flee,
And all the beautiful maids that be,
But never I'll leave sweet *gradh mo chroídhe*[1]
Till death in your service o'ertake me!

Chorus

O! you are my dear, my dear, my dear,
O! you are my dear, and my fair love;
You are my own dear, and my fondest hope here,
And O! that my cottage you'd share, love.

---

[1] *Gradh mo chroídhe*, i.e., 'Love of my heart.' The Irish to be pronounced as if written *Graw mu kree*.

(57)
The Dawning of the Day[1]
(*Faineadh Geal an Lae*)

At early dawn I once had been
Where Lene's[2] blue waters flow,
When summer bid the groves be green,
The lamp of light to glow -
As on by bower, and town, and tower,
And widespread fields I stray,
I met a maid in the greenwood shade,
At the dawning of the day.

Her feet and beauteous head were bare,
No mantle fair she wore,
But down her waist fell golden hair,
That swept the tall grass o'er;
With milking-pail she sought the vale,
And bright her charms' display,
Outshining far the morning star,
At the dawning of the day!

Beside me sat that maid divine,
Where grassy banks outspread -
"Oh, let me call thee ever mine,
Dear maid," I sportive said.
"False man, for shame, why bring me blame?"
She cried, and burst away -
The sun's first light pursued her flight,
At the dawning of the day!

---

[1] Published in *Irish Popular Songs*, pp 40-43. - Ed.
[2] Loch Lene: the most famous of the Lakes of Killarney, Co. Kerry. - Ed.

(58)
The Vision of John MacDonnell[1]
(*Aisling Seán MhicDomhnaill*)[2]

Seán Clarach McDonnell.

One night, my eyes, in seal'd repose,
Beheld wild war's terrific vision -
When, lo! beside my couch arose
The banshee bright, of form Elysian!
Her dark hair's flow stream'd loose below
Her waist to kiss her foot of lightness;
The snows that deck the cygnet's neck
Would fail to peer her bosom's whiteness!

I saw her - mild her angel mien;
Her azure eye was soul subduing;
Her white round breast and lip were seen
The eye of wonder ever wooing,
Her sylph-like waist, her forehead chaste,
Her ivory teeth and taper finger -
'Twas heaven, 'tis true, these charms to view,
'Twas pain within their sphere to linger!

"Fair shape of light! thy lowly slave
Entreats thy race - thy travels' story."
Her white arm gave one beck'ning wave -
She vanish'd like a beam of glory!

---

[1] The song was published in *Reliques*, pp. 18-21, and in *Irish Popular Songs*, pp. 122-129. - Ed.

[2] This allegorical poem, in which the genius of Ireland, impersonated by a queen of Faery leads the charmed mortal through the principal haunts of the fairy host, is valuable, if it were only for its delineation of the mythological topography of the country.
[In an incomplete version of this composition given in the second edition of *Reliques*, pp. 18-21, John O'Daly gives the following note: 'For an account of the Forts and Fairy Mansions, Moats, etc. mentioned in this Poem, see Croker's *Fairy Legends of the South of Ireland*, 3 vols, ed. 1826-28, also his *Researches in the South of Ireland*, O'Flanagan's *Blackwater in Munster*, Mrs. Hall's *Ireland and Its Scenery*, Sir W.R. Wilde's *Boyne and Blackwater*; and for an account of Mananan Mac Lir, see O'Curry's *Tragical Fate of the Children of Lir*, published in the Third Volume of the *Atlantis*, issued by the Catholic University.' - Ed]

My questioning call unheeded all,
My cries above the breezes swelling,
As fill'd with woe I northward go
To Gruach's distant fairy dwelling!

Through fair Senai, through Crochan's hall
I wildly chase the flying maiden;
By fairy fort, by waterfall,
Where weird ones wept with sorrow laden;
My footsteps roam great Aongus' dome,
Above the Boyne, a structure airy;
In hall and moat these wild words float,
"She onwards treads the haunt of Faery!"

Mac Lir, I sought thy proud abode,
Through Creeveroe my question sounded,
Through Temor's halls of state I strode,
And reach'd Cnoc-Fhirinn spell-surrounded,
By Aoivil-roe, 'mid wine-cups' flow,
A thousand maids' clear tones were blending;
And chiefs of the Gael in armed mail,
At tilt and tourney were contending!

The smooth-skin fair, whose witching eye
Had lur'd me from my pillow dreamy,
'Mid shadows hosts was seated high,
Her coal-black tresses wild and streamy -
She said, while shone her proud glance on
The form she knew that long pursued her,
"We much deplore thy wanderings sore,
Now list our wrongs from the fierce intruder."

"Alas!" she said, "my nation's grief,
My prostrate host, my heroes[1] dying,
My wandering exiles, bard, and chief,
In distant regions sadly sighing -
The slaves that plain in Saxon chain,

[1] *An Fear Groidhe*, literally the valiant man, meaning the exiled Charles Stuart. - O'Daly.

My Son exil'd o'er ocean's water;
While beauty's wail o'erloads the gale,
O heaven relieve thee, Erin's daughter!"[1]

"I weep, I weep, my woe-struck bands,
My country, hosts, and chiefs of bravery -
The cold, rude alien spoil'd their lands,
And ground their strength in bitter slavery;
Crush'd weak, obscure, they now endure
Dark sorrow's yoke beneath the stranger;
And the true and high in exile sigh -
Heaven, how I need each brave avenger!"

"Say, O say, thou being bright!
When shall the land from slavery waken?
When shall our hero claim his right,
And tyrant's halls be terror shaken?"
She gives no sign - the form divine
Pass'd like the winds by fairies woken -
The future holds, in Time's dark folds,
The despot's chain of bondage broken!

(59)
From the Cold Sod that's O'er You.[2]
(*A Táim Sínte Air Do Thumba*)

From the cold sod that's o'er you
I never shall sever;
Were my hands twin'd in yours, love,
I'd hold them forever;
My fondest, my fairest,
We may now sleep together;
I've the cold earth's damp odour,
And I'm worn from the weather!

---

[1] *Fiadh-phuic*, i.e. buck goats, meaning the English adventurers, with which the country swarmed after the Cromwellian wars. - O'Daly. [The 4th line in the original of this stanza reads: '*Ag dibirt fiadh-phuic ó na h-alluighe*.' - Ed.]
[2] Published in *Irish Popular Songs*, pp. 144-149. - Ed.

This heart, filled with fondness,
Is wounded and weary;
A dark gulf beneath it
Yawns jet-black and dreary;
When death comes, a victor,
In mercy to greet me,
On the wings of the whirlwind,
In the wild wastes you'll meet me!

When the folk of my household
Suppose I am sleeping,
On your cold grave, till morning,
The lone watch I'm keeping;
My grief to the night wind,
For the mild maid to render,
Who was my betrothed
Since infancy tender!

Remember the lone night
I last spent with you, love,
Beneath the dark sloe-tree,
When the icy wind blew, love;
High praise to the Saviour,
No sin-stain had found you -
That your virginal glory
Shines brightly around you!

The priests and the friars
Are ceaselessly chiding,
That I love a young maiden
In life not abiding;
O! I'd shelter and shield you,
If wild storms were swelling,
And O! my wreck'd hope,
That the cold earth's your dwelling!

Alas, for your father,
And also your mother,
And all your relations,

Your sister and brother,
Who gave you to sorrow,
And the grave 'neath the willow,
While I crav'd, as your portion,
But to share your chaste pillow!

(60)
Eire's Maid is She[1]
(*Béith Eirionn Í*)[2]

William Dall O'Heffernan — Air: *Béith Eirionn Í*

In Druid vale alone I lay,
Oppress'd with care, to weep the day -
My death I ow'd one sylph-like she,
Of witchery rare, *'be n-Eirinn i!*[3]
'Be n-Eirinn i!

The spouse of Naisi, Erin's woe-
The dame that laid proud Ileum low,
Their charms would fade, their fame would flee,
Match'd with my fair, *'be n-Eirinn i!*
'Be n-Eirinn i!

Behold her tresses, unconfin'd,
In wanton ringlets woo the wind,
Or sweep the sparkling dewdrops free,
My heart's dear maid, *'be n-Eirinn i!*
'Be n-Eirinn i!

---

[1] Published in *Reliques*, pp. 78-81; also in *Irish Popular Songs* pp. 114-117. - Ed. [Walsh notes in *Irish Popular songs*, p. 114]: '*Be n-Eirinn i*, literally means *Whoever she be in Ireland.*

[2] This beautiful air was published for the first time from our "Bolg an Dana," in the First Series of our Munster Poets in 1849. The words which accompany it on the present occasion must have been written to perpetuate in song the fame and personal charms of some celebrated fair one who lived in the poet's time. This indeed was generally the custom of the Munster poets, as we have several songs in our "Bolg," written by John Clarach Mac Donnell, Eoghan Rua O'Sullivan, Andrew Magrath, surnamed the "Mangaire Súgach," from his mirth-loving qualities; and by John O'Tuomy the Gay, in praise of a young woman who kept a public house on the banks of the river Maig in the county of Limerick, where the bards did occasionally assemble to drown their sorrows over the glass, and sing their songs. - O'Daly, (1866) p. 79.

[3] Now pronounced *Beih*, and corrupted into "*Be n-Eirinn I.*" - O'Daly (1866) p. 79.

Fierce passion's slave, from hope exil'd,
Weak, wounded, weary, woeful, wild -
Some magic spell she wove for me,
That peerless maid, *'be n-Eirinn i!*
'Be n-Eirinn i!

But O! one noon I climb a hill,[1]
To sigh alone - to weep my fill,
And there Heaven's mercy brought to me
My treasure rare, *'be n-Eirinn i!*
'Be n-Eirinn i!

(61)
King Charles[2]
(*Righ Searlus*)

Seán Clárach Mac Dómhnaill. Ballad. Air: *Over the Hills and Far Away.*

Once I bloom'd a maiden young -
A widow's moans now move my tongue!
My true-love's barque ploughs ocean's spray,
Over the hills and far away!

Chorus:
O! had I worlds I'd yield them now
To place me on his tall barque's prow,
Who was my choice through childhood's day,
Over the hills and far away!

O! may we yet our loved one meet
With joy-bells' chime, and wild drums' beat,
While summoning war-trump sounds dismay
Over the hills and far away!
Chorus: O! had I worlds I'd, etc.

---

[1] *Suighe Finn*, i.e. The resting-place, or watch-tower of Fionn; who being a man of the chase, selected those hills which appeared to him best calculated to afford a fair prospect of the surrounding country. Hence the numerous hills known by that name throughout Ireland, but particularly in Munster. - O'Daly (1866), p. 80.
[2] Published in *Reliques*, pp. 38-41, - Ed.

O! that my hero had his throne,
That Erin's clouds of care were flown,
That proudest prince would own his sway
Over the hills and far away!
Chorus:O! had I worlds I'd, etc.

My bosom's love that Prince afar,
Our king - our joy - our orient star,
More sweet his voice than wild bird's lay
Over the hills and far away!
Chorus:O! had I worlds I'd, etc.

A high green hill I'll quickly climb,
And tune my harp to song sublime,
And chant his praise the livelong day,
Over the hills and far away!

Chorus:
O! had I worlds I'd yield them now,
To place me on his tall barque's prow,
Who was my choice through childhood's day,
Over the hills and far away.

(62)
Expulsion of the Saxon[1]
(*Díth-láithriughadh Gall*)

Eoghan Ruadh Ó Súilleabháin. Ballad. Air: *Staca an Varaga.*[2]

By Blarney's towers I paus'd to ponder,
What deep, dark curse our land lies under,
Chain'd 'neath the foreigner foe.
The homeless horde whose guileful knavery

[1] Published in the *Nation*; also in *Reliques*, pp. 42-47. - Ed.

[2] *Staca an Varaga*, i.e. Market Stake or Cross. Friar Clynn of Kilkenny, under date 1335, in his Annals, published by the Irish Archaeological Society, refers to the Market Cross of Kilkenny, as follows: "Die Jovis in crastino Lucie virginis, erecta magna crux in medio fori Kilkennie; hoc tempore multis ad crucem volantes, crucis signo cum ferro candenti super nudam carnem sunt signati, ut in Terram Sanctum vadant." For further account of these curious antiquarian relics, see *Transactions of the Kilkenny Archaeological Society*, Vol. 2, p. 219. - O'Daly (1866) pp. 42-43.

Coil'd the festering links of slavery
Round hearts where pure pulses flow.
From sires, whose sons are crouching slaves,
Or wanderers wild, or outlaws gory,
Mail-clad sires whose green flag waves
O'er blood-red fields of ancient story,
Where prone groan their offspring of woe.

Lonely and long that hour of weeping,
Hopeless, joyless, tearful - steeping
In salt streams mine eyelids of care!
While thoughts came dark and dismal o'er me,
A form of beauty stood before me,
White bosom'd, heavenly fair!
Her thick, luxuriant ringlets fell,
Or stream'd, the soft-wing'd zephyr gracing,
Or cluster'd o'er her breasts' round swell,
Like sun-wreaths hill of snow enchasing,
Light, bright, and beautiful there.

Lily and rose, with rival power,
To grace her cheek, bestow'd their dower,
Her vermeil, vowless lip to behold,
And pale, pure brown, and ripe eyes' splendour,
Did love-lorn heroes hopeless render,
Slaves chained by tresses of gold.
She's fair as swan by broad, blue lake,
Like snow-hills rise her bosom's heaving;
Her hand can heavenly music wake,
Or draw bright scenes in silken weaving,
Of sea, shore, or battlefield old.[1]

---

[1] Tailc mhic Treoin, the celebrated hero who, pursued Niamh-nuadh-Crothach into Ireland, and gave battle to Fionn mac Cumhail, and the Irish heroes, under whose protection Niamh had placed herself. In this engagement Tailc slew the most renowned of the Fenians, but was afterwards slain by Osgur in single combat, after five days and five nights severe fight, as may be seen by the opposite stanza: -

Feadh chúig n-oidhche, feadh chúig lá,	For five long days and tedious nights
Bhí an dís nár thláith ag gleic,	Both heroes contest dire maintain'd,
Air dít bídh, 's ar bheagán suain,	Their weary limbs not eas'd by rest,
Gur thuit Teilc le buaidh mo mheic.	Or fainting frames by food sustin'd.

Transactions of the Gaelic Society, Dub. 1808. O'Daly (1866), pp. 44-45.

Modest and mild, her words when spoken
Seem ancient strains that bards have woken,
Strains that grace her soft liquid lips;
Faultless and fair, in beauty shining,
Her magic power left maidens pining,
Griev'd deep at their beauty's eclipse.
Low-bending towards the form of light,
In Gaelic old, she lov'd the dearest,
I said, "Fair spirit, whence thy flight,
From friends that love to foes thou fearest,
Aidless far from soldiers or ships?"

"O! be thy lowly slave forgiven,
Who hails thine eye as light from heaven,
And thou now a fay in disguise!
The maid mayhap whose charm ensnaring,
Led Daire's son to warlike Erin,
His North Star the light of thine eyes.
Or ruin'd Emania's hero host,
Or led brave Greece o'er ocean's water,
In tall barks towards the Dardan coast,
To give proud Troy to flames and slaughter,
Dear pledge for Paris's prize."

"Arise," she cried, "let joy possess thee,
Ere harvest's golden glories bless thee,
Thine ear hears the battle cry loud.
Go tell the bards who pine in sadness,
To teach their harp-string songs of gladness,
And raise strains of victory proud!
Each chief shall wave a conqueror's blade,
When war's fierce lash shall scourge the stranger;
From Britain's isle his name shall fade,
When comes old Erin's brave avenger,
To weave the foe a wide, bloody shroud.

"When Spain sends bravest heroes hither,
Oppression's arm shall waste and wither,
By sea, by shore - the despot's reward.
And slavery's chain shall rive asunder,
When Erin's brave 'mid war's wild thunder
In gore bathe the green battle-sward.

No thought of ruth, nor word of peace
By heart be felt, by tongue be spoken,
'Till quenched in blood his light shall cease,
And Saxon power lie crushed and broken" -
Shout loud Amen to the bard!

(63)
Captivity of the Gael[1]
(Géibheann na n-Gaoidheal)

Eoghan Rua Ó Súilleabháin. Air: *Shaun Bui.*[2]

I wander'd the moorland all weary and worn,
Fell sorrow my pathway pursuing;
Revolving what fetters our chain'd limbs have borne,
Sad sighing at Erin's undoing;
Our princes' sad thrall, and our cities' fall,
And wide wasted plains did appal me;
And my tongue cursed that day of the false Saxon's sway,
When Erin was shackled by *Shaun Bui*!

---

[1] The song was published in the *Vindicator*, Belfast, Sat. June 15th 1844 with this prefatory note: 'The following is an English version by Mr. Edward Walsh, (one of the poetical contributors to the *Nation*) of one of a series of Irish Songs, edited by Mr. John Daly, bookseller, Kilkenny.' The song which was also published in *Reliques*, pp. 48-53, with notes as hereunder. - Ed.

[2] 'This air [*Shaun Bui*] is well known in the most remote districts of Munster, particularly in Waterford, Cork and Kerry. It is found with very poor verses, of which the following stanza will suffice to give a just idea: -

Cuirfeadsa an róguire feasda dhá fhóguirt,
A g-Corcadh, a n-Eócaill, 'sa d-Tráighlíghe;
'S ní leómhthadh aon óig-bhean gabhail thoruinn an bóthar,
Le h-eagla an rúguire Seaghan Buidhe!"

Henceforth I'll proclaim the villainous rake,
In Youghal, in Cork, and in Tralee;
As no blithersome young maid can walk the highway,
Through fear of the vagabond *Shaun Bui*!

'The term *Shaun Bui*, *Yellow Jack*, was first applied to the followers of William III. The inflictions endured under the Penal Code, now nearly effaced from the Irish Statute Book, elicited many of these Jacobite songs from the bards of this period; and, showing as they do, the political sentiments of a persecuted people, are calculated to prove the impolicy of such severe class-measures, the ill effects of which are long in the dying out.

'It is an historical fact, that at the Boyne, William's soldiers wore green boughs in their head-gear to distinguish them in battle; and yet our bards quickly named them the *Orange* or *Yellow* race; for, *Shaun Bui*, "Yellow Jack" - is a plain allusion to the complexion of the Anglo-Norman invaders and a synonym for John Bull.' - O'Daly (1866) p. 49.

Where trees woo'd the stream of a valley profound,
And woodbines a bower had bound me,
Fair visions poetic came floating around,
As wild birds pour'd melody round me:
Then burst on my eye a bright star of the sky,
She smiles - and her white teeth enthral me;
'Tis heaven I behold in her features' fine mould,
Though shaded with sorrow by *Shaun Bui*.

Thick, fragrant, and fair fell her bright, shiny locks,
Rare tresses in beauty contending,
Whose long-wreathed ringlets all rivalry mocks,
To her exquisite ankle descending!
And thus wake in song to these bright tresses long
Harps warbling wild as the *ceol-shee*,[1]
More rich than the fleece brought by Jason to Greece
The golden hair sullied by *Shaun Bui*.

The arch of her brow is a soft silky hair,
Her forehead with modesty bright'ning;
To meet the dread light of her blue eye forbear,
There's death in the flash of its lightning!
The red berry's glow, lofty Mangerton's snow,
Ever change on her cheek to enthral thee;
And my heart rent in twain when I thought of her chain
Fast knotted in nuptials to *Shaun Bui*.

Sprightly, yet mild, her fair countenance shone,
Her breast heav'd like billows of ocean;
The heart that throbb'd warm 'neath her emerald zone,
Never bounded to passion's commotion:
As my greedy eye stray'd o'er the beautiful maid,
"Queen of Beauty," I cried, "O recall me
Thy fortune's dark fall that consign'd thee a thrall,
To the cold-hearted Sassenagh, *Shaun Bui!*"

"My grief," said the maiden of heavenly mien,
"Reveals thee my sorrowful story;

[1]Pronounced *Kole-shee*, fairy music. - O'Daly (1866) p. 51.

Dark Niall beheld me, a diadem'd queen,
And Conn added rays to my glory.
But red torch and glaive swept the land of the brave,
And horrors unceasing appal me,
That gave the proud dome for the Sassenagh home,
And the fields of our fathers to *Shaun Bui*.

"And O! the deep gloom of my wild throbbing breast,
That men who should die to avenge her,
See fair Erin smitten, evicted, oppress'd,
In chains of the treacherous stranger!
And O! that the doom of the tyrant were come,
And the salt drops were dried that now fall free,
And a proud nation's force could procure a divorce
From the dull, plodding plunderer, *Shaun Bui*."

I heard the sad tale of the maiden distress'd,
Woe-burden'd and weak at the telling;
My tears' briny stream had its source in my breast,
Where shame and wild anguish were swelling;
And Erin of Love, may the Father above
From the plague of the tyrant recall thee,
And thy young heart rejoice with the spouse of thy choice
When sever'd, forever, from *Shaun Bui*.

(64)
Fair-Hill'd Pleasant Ireland[1]
(*Bán-Chnuic Aoibhin Eirionn*)

Donnchadh Rua MacConmara.

Take a blessing from the heart of a lonely griever,
To fair-hill'd, pleasant Ireland,
To the glorious seed of Ir and Eivir,[2]
In fair-hill'd, pleasant Ireland,
Where the voice of birds fill the wooded vale,
Like the morning harp o'er the fallen Gael -
And oh! that I pine, many long days' sail
From fair-hill'd pleasant Ireland.

---

[1]Published in *Irish Popular Songs*, pp. 154-157. - Ed.

[2] Eibher or Eiver, the son of Ir, who, with his brothers, the sons of Milesius, shared Ireland between them. Ir and his son Eiver had Ulster for their share.

On the gentle heights are soft sweet fountains
In fair-hill'd, pleasant Ireland;
I would choose o'er this land the bleakest mountains
In fair-hill'd, pleasant Ireland -
More sweet than fingers o'er strings of song
The lowing of cattle the vales among,
And the sun smiling down upon old and young,
In fair-hill'd, pleasant Ireland.

There are numerous hosts at the trumpet's warning
In fair-hill'd, pleasant Ireland;
And warriors bold, all danger scorning,
In fair-hill'd, pleasant Ireland -
Oh, memory sad! oh, tale of grief!
They are crush'd by the stranger past all relief;
Nor tower, nor town hath its native chief
In fair-hill'd, pleasant Ireland.

(65)
The Voice of Joy[1]
(*Uaill-guth An Aoibhnis*)

Ulliam Dall O'Heffernan. Ballad.

By Kilmore's woody highland,[2]
Wandering dark and drear,
A voice of joy came o'er me,

---

[1] Published in *Reliques*, pp. 80-83, and in *Irish Popular Songs*. - Ed.
[Note by Walsh/O'Daly]: 'The poet seeing a swarm of bees confused and wild at the loss of the queen bee, accepts the omen as a prognostic of the destruction of the English power in Ireland.'

[2] *Coill Mhor*, i.e., *a large wood*, evidently meaning the wood of Aherlow, which extends from Galbally [Co. Limerick] to Bansha in the County of Tipperary. It is not more than two miles from Shronehill to the South, and fronting the Galtee-mor, and the magnificent chain of mountains from Mitchelstown to Clogheen; presents a scene most beautiful and picturesque. It was in the seclusion of this immense wood the learned Doctor Geoffrey Keating wrote his *Forus Feasa ar Eirinn*; or, *History of Ireland*, more than two centuries back, and of which the Rev. Dr. Todd, S.F., T.C.D. possesses two of the best known MS. copies extant, both being written within Keating's own time, by the ablest scribe of his day, John Mac Torna O'Maolconry, of Sixmilebridge in the county of Clare, A.D. 1646.
It must be in the seclusion of this lonely wood that O'Heffernan sought refuge when composing the present song, in which he foretells that the career of the tyrant Damer would not long survive; and neither did it: for in a few short years after, the tyrant died, leaving the immense wealth which he accumulated by fraud and usury, to scatter and waste away like chaff thrown before the four winds; or to use an Irish phrase, 'Mar leaghaidh cubhair na habhan;' literally, 'as the melting of the froth of the river.' - O'Daly (1866) pp. 80-81.

More holy to mine ear
Than wild harp's breathing dreamy,
Or blackbird's warbling streamy;
No seraph choir could frame me
Such soft music dear!

More sweet than anthems holy
Brought seaward from Rome,
Than spells by wizards spoken
O'er stolen maidens' doom,
Or cuckoo's song inspiring
Where woods green hills environ,
Save love for one fair siren,
It banish'd my gloom.

The golden bees were ranging
The air for a chief -
'Twas freedom's trumpet woken
And dark tyrant's grief;[1]
And George, a homeless ranger,
His tribe, the faithless stranger,
Far banish'd - and their danger,
My glad heart's relief.

If o'er me lay at Shronehill[2]
The hard flag of doom,
And came that sound of sweetness
To cheer the cold gloom -
Death's darksome bondage broken,
My deaf, dull ear had woken,
And, at the spell-word spoken,
I'd burst from the tomb!

---

[1] John Damer, the celebrated usurer. - O'Daly (1866) p. 82.

[2] *Shronehill*, a parish three miles west of Tipperary, and the place of Heffernan's birth; in this district stood Damer's Court, erected more than a century ago. This magnificent mansion was taken down in 1776, and the property now belongs to the Earl of Portarlington. - O'Daly (1866) pp. 82-83.

(66)

The Maid of the Fine Flowing Hair[1]

(Stuairín na m-Bachall Breagh réidh)

The sun hath gone down in the sky,
The stars cease their heavenly way,
The tides of the ocean are dry,
The swan on the lake hath no sway;
The cuckoo but adds to our care,
Who sings from his green, leafy throne,
How the maid of the fine flowing hair
Left Erin in sadness to moan.

Three evils accompany love:
These evils are Sin, Death, and Pain -
And well doth each passing hour prove
Thou'st woven around me their chain.
Oh! maiden that woundedst me sore,
Receive this petition from me,
And heal my fierce pain, I implore,
So God yield His mercy to thee.

Her voice doth the viol surpass,
Or blackbird's sweet notes on the tree,
More radiant than dew-sprinkled grass,
In figure and feature she be:
Her neck like the swan's on the wave,
Her eye hath a light like the sun;
And oh! that my lost heart I gave,
Or saw her who left me undone.

(67)

The Dark Maid of the Valley[2]

(*Bean Dubh an Ghleanna*)

Oh! have you seen my fair one?
The brightest maid of beauty's train,
Who left me thus deploring,

---

[1] Published in *Irish Popular Songs*, pp. 36-39. - Ed.

[2] Published in *Irish Popular Songs*, pp. 42-47. - Ed.

In deep, dark vales, my love-sick pain -
That mild-ey'd, sweet-tongu'd maiden,
Who left a wounded heart to me,
My blessing I bequeath her,
Where'er the gentle maiden be!

Rare artists have engraven
Her slender waist, her beauteous brow,
Her lip with sweetness laden,
That once I thought would truth avow;
Her hand than down far fairer,
More sleek than silk from India's shore;
And oh! in grief I'm pining,
To think I've lost her evermore!

With love my heart was glowing,
When first I spied the lovely fair,
With breast of snowy fairness,
And white teeth, and golden hair -
She shone more bright than Deirdre,[1]
The curse of Meathean chiefs of pride,
Or mild-ey'd beauteous Blanit,[2]
By whom a thousand heroes died!

Fair flower of maids, resign not
My faithful heart for senseless boor,

---

[1] It is said that Deirdre was confined, from the period of her birth, in a fort or tower, by Connor, King of Ulster, because a druid had foretold she would cause great calamity in the kingdom. When she grew up to womanhood, Naois, with his two brothers, bore off the beautiful captive to Scotland, when the king of that country, smitten by the fatal charms of the lady, formed a plan to destroy her lover. They were thus forced to flee from Scotland, and Connor, hearing of their distress, allured them over to Ireland, by promises of pardon, where the three brothers were slain by his order. For this deed of perfidy, Connor, abandoned by his nobles, saw Ulster ravaged from shore to shore, and bathed in the blood of its bravest warriors! See Keating's "Ireland," Haliday's edition, page 371.

[2] Blanit was daughter of the king of the Isle of Man. When the Red Branch Knights plundered that island, this lady, who, it is said, surpassed in beauty all the women of her time, was adjudged to Curaigh MacDaire. Cuchullin claimed her as his prize, but he was overcome by Curaigh in single combat. Sometime after, Cuchullin with a large body of men, attacked and slew Curaigh in his palace. Blanit then departed with Cuchullin into Ulster. Thither did the bard of Curaigh follow her; and one day finding Connor, Cuchullin, and Blanit at the promontory of Cenn Beara, he instantly clasped her with his arms, as she stood on the edge of a steep rock, and flinging himself downward, they were both instantly dashed to pieces! - See Keating's "History of Ireland," Haliday's edition, page 405; and also, "Transactions of the Gaelic Society."

Who rich in worldly treasure,
In all my glorious gifts is poor -
I who, in autumn evening,
Can bid the Gaelic song resound,
Or sing the olden glory
Of Fenian chiefs and kings renown'd.

(68)
The Lady of Alba's Lament for King Charles[1]
(Uaill-Chumhadh na Mna Albanaigh a n-dhiaigh a Céile .i. Rí Séarlus)[2]

Seán Ó Tuama. Ballad. Air: *The White Cockade.*[3]

Oppress'd with grief, I hourly cry,
With bursting heart, and tearful eye-
Since we did thee, fair youth, resign
For distant shores, what woes are mine.

Chorus:
My hero brave, mo ghile mear,
My kindred lover, mo ghile mear,
What wringing woes my bosom knows,
Since cross'd the seas mo ghile mear.[4]

---

[1] Published in *Reliques*, pp. 30-35. - Ed.

[2] The historical characters introduced into this poem are well known to those conversant with Irish history. As the extent of our little book must be very limited, to meet the price at which it is proposed to sell it, we prefer giving the reader original matter instead of illustration; and leave himself to comment, criticise, and illustrate as he pleases. - O'Daly (1866) pp. 31-32.

[3] *The Cnotadh Ban*, literally a *bouquet*, knot, or plume of white ribbon, with which the young women of Munster adorn their hair and head-dress on wedding and other festive occasions. The custom prevailed early in the 17th-century; for we find a poet of that period, *Muiris Mac Dhaibhi Duibh Mic Gearailt*, addressing a young Momonian lady in these beautiful words: -

A chailín donn deas an chnotadh bháin,	O brown-haired maiden of the plume so white -
Do bhuar 's mheall me le h-iomad gradh,	I am sick and dying of thy love,
Tair si liom 's ná déin mo chrádh,	Come now to me and ease my pain,
Mar do thug me greann duit 's dod' chnotabh bán!	I dearly love you and your White Cockade.

The Munster poets wrote many beautiful Jacobite songs to this air; and probably it is on this account that the Scotch claim the air as their own. This air is not generally understood, many persons supposing the White Cockade to mean a military cockade; and with that view doggerel rhymers have polluted the good taste of the public by such low ribaldry as the following: -

A shaighdiuir! a shaighdiuir! a b-fósfádh bean?	O Soldier! O soldier! would you marry a maid
Le h-ím, no le h-ól, no le bualadh an drum.	With butter and milk, or a beat of the drum.

[4] *Mo ghile mear*, literally, my gladdening brightness, my heart's delight, etc., a term of affection, of endearment applied to the Pretender. - O'Daly (1866) p. 34.

No cuckoo's note by fell or flood,
No hunter's cry through hazel wood,
Nor mist-wrapt valley yields me joy,
Since cross'd the seas my royal boy!

Chorus: *My hero brave, etc.*

The sun his golden glory shrouds
In mantle sad of sable clouds;
The threat'ning sky of grief portends,
Since through far realms our lion wends!

Chorus: *My hero brave, etc.*

The minstrel's tuneful song is bann'd,
And bardic grief o'erspreads the land;
Young maidens weep and wail in woe,
Since far from them the prince did go!

Chorus: *My hero brave, etc.*

That haughty, noble, youthful knight,
Of features bland - of spirit light,
Strong-handed, swift, in war's wild throng,
To chase to death the brave and strong!

Chorus: *My hero brave, etc.*

His glancing eyes I may compare
To diamond dews on rose-buds rare,
And love and valour brighten o'er
The features of my bosom's store!

Chorus: *My hero brave, etc.*

His wreathed hair, in graceful flow
Of ringlet rare, falls full below
His manly waist, in yellow fold,
Like silken threads of curling gold!
Chorus: *My hero brave, etc.*

Like Aongus Oge, he bears command,
Or Louis of the trenchant brand,
Or Daire's son, the great Conroy,
Brave Irish chiefs, my royal boy

Chorus: *My hero brave, etc.*

Or Conall, who strong ramparts won,
Or Fergus, regal Rogia's son,
Or Conor, Ulad's glorious king,
Whom harp-strings praise and poets sing.

Chorus: *My hero brave, etc.*

I'll not reveal my true-love's name,
Betimes 'twill swell the voice of fame,
But, O! may heaven, my grief to quell,
Restore the hero safe and well.
Chorus: *My hero brave, etc.*

Wake, wake, the wild harp's wildest sound
Send sparkling flagons flowing round;
Fill high the wine-cups' tide of joy,
This health to thee, my royal boy.

Chorus:
My hero brave, mo ghile mear,
My kindred lover, mo ghile mear,
What wringing woes my bosom knows,
Since cross'd the seas mo ghile mear.

(69)
Reply to the Lady of Alba's Lament[1]
(*Freagradh ar an m-Bean Albanaigh*)

Seán Clárach, ballad. Air: *The White Cockade.*

O royal maid, my bosom's gold!
None can unmoved thy griefs behold;

[1] Published in *Reliques*, pp. 36-39. - Ed.

And O! may heaven's supreme decree
Restore the youth to love and thee!
From realms afar I see him come,
With might to right his injured home,
To hush thy wail, to cheer the Gael,
And sweep the foe o'er ocean's foam.

Unfoil'd in skill, unmatch'd in might,
He'll conquer thrice the foe in fight;
And tyrants proud who swore us slaves,
By Tuaith Luicre's shore, shall find their graves!
Each warrior brave of ancient line,
Where Eoghan, Airt, and Heber shine,
Would dare oppose a host of foes,
To gain his monarch's right divine.

Then gentle reason's tranquil reign
Would bless the earth with peace again;
And winter time and summer day
Would prove propitious like his sway.[1]
With royal crown for monarch meet
Shall Erin's sons great Charles greet;
Each sturdy clown, by Jove, shall drown;
We'll make a sack his winding-sheet!

And Rome shall hold her ancient reign,
Her laws and lore shall aye remain,
And abject George return with shame

---

[1] Tiag Mac Daire Mac Bruadighe. A Thomond Bard, who flourished A.D. 1600, and who took an active part in the "Contention of the Bards," says in his Inaugural Ode, addressed to Donach O'Brien, fourth Earl of Thomond, and published in the Transactions of the Gaelic Society of Dublin, 1808, that God blesses the reign of good princes, by a succession of peaceful and abundant seasons. Thus Connaught appeared under Cathal Mór in the 13th-century: -

I walked entranced
Through a land of Morn.
The sun, with wondrous excess of light,
Shone down, and glanced
Over seas of corn,
And lustrous gardens a left and right etc.
[James Clarence] Mangan. - O'Daly (1866), p. 37.

The starveling boor that first he came!
The priest that hides by cave and fen
Shall rise his honour'd head again;
And to the skies shall hymns arise
From harp, and choir, and minstrel-men!

The Summing Up
May heaven, in mercy to its suppliant's call,
The gourmands quell who hold the Gael in thrall,
Crush, through the western isle, their ruffian sway,
And sweep afar the demon brood for aye!

(70)
The Fair Hills of Eire Ogh[1]
(*Bán Chnuic Éireann Ógh*)[2]

Air: *Uileacán dubh O.*

Beautiful and wide are the green fields of Erin,
Uileacán dubh O!
With life-giving grain in the golden corn therein,
Uileacán dubh O!
And honey in the woods of the mist-wreaths deep,
And in the summer, by the paths, the bright streams leap;
At burning noon, rich, sparkling dew the fair flowers steep,
On the fair hills of Eire Ogh.

How clustering his ringlets, how lofty his bearing,
Uileacán dubh O!
Each warrior leaving the broad bays of Erin,
Uileacán dubh O!
Would heaven grant the hope in my bosom swelling,
I'd seek that land of joy in life's gifts excelling,
Beyond your rich rewards, I'd choose a lowly dwelling
On the fair hills of Eire Ogh.

---

[1] Published in *Irish Popular Songs*, pp. 62-65. - Ed.

[2] *Bán-chnoic Éirean ógh*, literally *the fair Hills of Virgin Ireland.* This song speaks the ardent love of the Irish exile for his native land. It is said to have been written by an Irish student in one of the colleges of France.

Gainful and large are the corn-stacks of Erin,
Uileacán dubh O!
Yellow cream and butter abound ever therein,
Uileacán dubh O!
And sorrel soft, and cresses, where bright streams stray,
And speaking cuckoos fill the grove the livelong day,
And the little thrush so noble, of sweetest-sounding lay,
On the fair hills of Eire Ogh.

(71)

Ros Gheal Dubh[1]

(*An Rós Gheal Dubh*)[2]

A long, way since yesterday
I wildly sped,
O'er mountain steep and valley deep,
With airy tread;
Loch Erne's tide, though its wave be wide,
I'd leap above,
Were my guiding light that sunburst bright -
The *Rós gheal dubh.*

If to the fair you would repair
To sell your flocks,
I pray secure your every door
With bolts and locks;
Nor linger late from the guarded gate
When abroad you rove,
Or the clerk will play through the livelong day
With *Rós gheal dubh.*

---

[1] Published in *Irish Popular Songs*, pp. 56-61. - Ed.

[2] *Rós geal dubh, the white-skinned, black-haired Rose*, is one of those allegorical, political songs, so common in Ireland. The poet sings of his country under the similitude of a distressed maiden, to whom he is ardently attached. In the allusions to the Pope and clergy, we behold the hopes of obtaining assistance from the Catholic powers of Europe. The concluding stanza vividly shews the bloody struggle that would take place ere Rose, his beloved Ireland, would be yielded to the foe. Hardiman's "Minstrelsy" has a different form of this song, but this is the popular version in the south, and is said to be as old as the time of Elizabeth.

My dearest Rose, why should these woes
Dishearten thee?
The Pope of Rome hath sent thee home
A pardon free.
A priestly train, o'er the briny main,
Shall greet my love,
And wine of Spain to thy health we'll drain,
My *Rós gheal dubh.*

My love sincere is centred here
This year and more -
Love sadly vexing, love perplexing,
Love painful, sore,
Love, whose rigour hath crush'd my vigour,
Thrice hopeless love,
While fate doth sever me ever, ever,
From *Rós Gheal Dubh.*

Within thy heart could I claim a part -
One secret share -
We'd shape our flight o'er the wild hills' height
Towards Munster fair.
Branch of beauty's tree, it seems to me
I have thy love;
And the mildest flower of hall or bower
Is *Rós gheal dubh.*

The sea outspread shall be raging red,
All blood the skies,
And crimson war shall shout afar
Where the wild hills rise;
Each mountain glen and mossy fen
In fear shall move,
Some future day, ere thou pass away,
My *Rós gheal dubh.*

(72)
For Ireland I'd not tell Her Name[1]
(Air Éire Ní Ineosain Cia h-Í)[2]

One eve, as I happen'd to stray
By the lands that are bordering on mine,
A maiden came full on my way,
Who left me in anguish to pine -
The slave of the charms, and the mien,
And the silver-ton'd voice of the dame,
To meet her I sped o'er the green -
Yet for Ireland I'd tell not her name!

Would she list to my love-laden voice,
How sooth were my vows to the fair;
Would she make me forever her choice,
Her wealth would increase by my care -
I'd read her our poets' sweet lays,
Press close to my wild heart the dame,
Devote to her beauty the bays;
Yet for Ireland I'd tell not her name!

A maiden young, tender, refin'd,
On the lands that are bordering on mine,
Hath virtues and graces of mind,
And features surpassingly fine;
Blent amber and yellow compose
The ringleted hair of the dame,
Her cheek hath the bloom of the rose;
Yet for Ireland I'd tell not her name!

(Stanzas supplementary to the foregoing):
Sweet poet, incline to my prayer,
For O! could my melodies flow,

---

[1] *Published in Irish Popular Songs,* p. 132-137. - Ed.

[2] The author of this beautiful love song is unknown; but it would seem that he was a native of County Kerry, as this is the most popular song in that part of Munster. Tradition attributes it to a young man who fell violently in love with the affianced bride of his own brother.

I'd sing of your ringleted fair,
If haply her name I could know.
You are censur'd, permit me to say,
Nor grieve I you suffer the blame;
Some blot doth her beauty display,
When for Ireland you'd tell not her name.

Oh, Browne, of the pure spotless fame!
I never would marvel to see
A clown thus consigning to blame
Those charms that so beautiful be;
But you that have roamed by the Lee,
And the scenes of the Suir did proclaim,
Why ask you my secret from me,
When for Ireland I'd tell not her name?

(73)

Leading the Calves[1]

(*Seoladh na n-Gamhnadh*)

One evening mild, in summer weather,
My calves in the wild wood tending,
I saw a maid, in whom together
All beauty's charms were blending.
"Permit our flocks to mix," I said,
" 'Tis what a maiden mild would,
And when the shades of night are fled
We'll lead our calves from the wild wood.

"There grows a tree in the wild wood's breast,
We'll stay till morn beneath it,
Where songs of birds invite to rest,
And leaves and flowers enwreath it.
Mild, modest maid, 'tis not amiss;
'Twas thus we met in childhood;

[1] Published in *Irish Popular Songs*, pp. 46-49 - Ed.

To thee at morn my hand I'll kiss,[1]
And lead the calves through the wild wood.

"With calves I sought the pastures wild;
They've stray'd beyond my keeping;
At home my father calls his child,
And my dear mother's weeping.
The foresters, if here they stray,
Perhaps, in friendship mild, would
Permit our stay till the dawn of day,
When we'll lead our calves from the wild wood."

(74)
The Song of Freedom[2]
(*Duan Na Saoirse*)

An Mangaire Súgach. Ballad. Air: *Duan Na Saoirse.*

All woeful, long I wept despairing,
Dark-blossom'd fainting, wearied, weak,
The foeman's withering bondage wearing,
Remote in the gorge of the mountain bleak;
No friend to cheer my visions dreary,
Save generous Donn,[3] the King of Faery,
Who, 'mid the festal banquet airy,
These strains prophetic thus did speak: -

---

[1] Walsh translates '*Geabhair fós ar barra mo láimh uaim*' as 'To thee at morn my hand I'll kiss' and makes the following comment on it: 'The literal meaning of this line is: "you will receive a kiss from me from out of the top of my hand." It shows that the custom of kissing hands in salutation has prevailed among the Irish peasantry.' - Ed.

[2] Published in *Irish Popular Songs*, pp. 158-163. - Ed.

[3] *Donn Firinneach*, or *Donn the Truthteller*, to whom is attributed, in Irish mythology, the government of the fairies of Munster. His residence is said to be on Cnoc-firinn, a romantic hill in the County of Limerick. The *Mangaire Súgach*, the author of this bold appeal in favour of the exiled house of Stuart, describes Donn as bidding him proclaim to the Brave that the hour had arrived for the last glorious effort on behalf of Charles.
Donn is an historical personage, and is said to have been one of the sons of Milesius, the celebrated king of Spain. When these princes invaded Ireland, more than a thousand years before the Christian Era, Donn, with all his ship's company, was cast away on the west coast of Munster. It is a curious fact that the name of this prince, after the lapse of forgotten ages, is as familiar as a household word among the peasantry of the south!

"Behold how chieftains glorious, regal,
Are bondage-bound, dishonour'd, low;
These churls from Phelim's[1] heirdom legal,
And Eiver's lands, are doomed to go;
For fleets, and Charles brave to lead 'em,
Will reach our shore with promis'd freedom;
Till bursts their might upon the foe.

"And bards shall pour their tuneful treasure,
And minstrels strike their voiceful string,
And Tara wake to music's measure,
And priests be cherished by their king;
And sacred rites and mass-bells sounding,
All Erin's holy domes be found in,
And scattering fear the foe astounding,
While all the Gael exulting sing.

"You've heard the secrets I've unfolden;
To memories true their truths bestow;
And speak, 'twill all the brave embolden,
The treaty broken by the foe:
But now's the hour - your powers uniting,
Arise to crush these he-goats blighting;
And while the race of treachery smiting,
Let none his vengeance wild forego."

---

[1] Feidhlim, son of Tuathal Teachtmar, and father of Conn of the Hundred Battles, was monarch of Ireland at the commencement of the second century of the Christian Era. It was in the person of his father, Tuathal Teachtmar, or the Acceptable, that the Milesian dynasty was restored after the Attacotic rebellion.

(75)
The Boat Song[1]
(*Duan an Bhádóra*)[2]

Bark, scorning every peril of the angry spray,
Safe shelter 'mid the terrors of the storm compass'd way;
When yawning billows redly roll from ocean's cave,
From stern unto quivering mast she ships no wave.

Chorus: -
A flowing tide, a flowing tide,
My secret love, my worldly store,
Flowing - my brave sailing boat.

When draperied in her glorious trim of stainless dye,
The snow-white sails of canvas bleach'd 'neath India's sky,
Saw you her arrowy figure cleave the ocean vast,
God's favourite mounting on the wave before the blast.

Chorus: *A flowing tide, etc.*

"O! Dielion,[3] tempest-beaten rock, all rough and dark,
Look forth, and see beneath me now this bounding bark,
And say, if e'er thou boat beheld within the bay,
Wave-mounted, cleaving, confident, like mine today?"

Chorus: *A flowing tide, etc.*
Then answer'd ancient Dielion thus - "long ages o'er
I've look'd abroad upon the bay that girds the shore,
But look'd in vain, for boat or bark so swift and brave
As thine, and all its gallant crew, to stem the wave!"

---

[1] Published in *Irish Popular songs*, pp. 82-87. - Ed.

[2] *Duan an Bhádóra, the Boatman's Song.* I have copied this spirited sea-song from the second volume of Mr. Hardiman's "Minstrelsy," where it is left untranslated. Mr. Hardiman says that this marine ode is "well known along many parts of the Irish coast, but particularly the west." A translation of this and other Irish songs, by Mr. (now Sir) Samuel Ferguson, will be found in the *Dublin University Magazine* for November 1834.

[3] *Daoilean*, a rock off Blacksod Bay.

Chorus: *A flowing tide, etc.*

* * * * * * * * * * *

Father of Nature! how that boat comes dashing down,
Impetuous where the foamy surges darkly frown -
O! may Thy mercy yield us now the sheltering shore,
Or yonder terror-stricken bark shall whelm us o'er.[1]

Chorus: *A flowing tide, etc.*

(76)
Farewell to the Maig[2]
***(Slán le Máig)*[3]**

An Mangaire Súgach. Air: *Slán le Máigh.*

A long farewell I send to thee,
Fair Maig of corn and fruit and tree,
Of state and gift, and gathering grand,
Of song, romance, and chieftain bland.
Och, och ón! dark fortune's rigour -
Wealth, title, tribe of glorious figure,
Feast, gift - all gone, and gone my vigour,
Since thus I wander lonely!

Farewell for aye to the hearts I prize,
The poets, priests, and sages wise,
And bosom friends, whose boards display,
Fair temperance blent with plenty gay.
Och, och ón, etc.

Farewell to the maids my memories bless,
To all the fair, to their comeliness,
Their sense, their fame, their mildness rare,
Their groups, their wit, their virtue fair.
Och, och ón, etc.

---

[1] There is a want of strict connection between this stanza and the preceding one. The intervening passage necessary to the sense seems to have been lost.
[2] Published in *Irish Popular Songs*, pp. 86-91. - Ed.
[3] Maig: a river of that name in the County Limerick. - Ed.

Farewell to her to whom 'tis due,
The fair skin, gentle, mild-lipp'd, true,
For whom exil'd o'er the hills I go,
My heart's dear love, whate'er my woe.
Och, och ón, etc.

Cold, homeless, worn, forsaken, lone,
Sick, languid, faint, all comfort flown,
On the wild hill's height I'm hopeless cast,
To wail to the heath and the northern blast.
Och, och ón, etc.

If through the crowded town I press,
Their mirth disturbs my loneliness;
And female groups will whisper - see!
Whence comes yon stranger? .Who is he?
Och, och ón, etc.

Thus riven, alas! from bosoms dear,
Amid dark danger, grief and fear,
Three painful months unblest I rove,
Afar from friendship's voice and love.
Och, och ón, etc.

Forc'd by the priest my love to flee,
Fair Maig through life I ne'er shall see;
And must my beauteous bird forego,
And all the sex that wrought me woe.
Och, och ón! my grief, my ruin!
'Twas drinking deep, and beauty wooing,
That caus'd, through life, my whole undoing,
And left me wandering lonely.

(77)

Whiskey - the Soul of Revelry[1]

***(A h-Uiscidhe Chroidhe na n-Anaman*)**

The Bard

Whiskey - soul of revelry!
Low in the mud you seat me -
Possess'd with all your devilry,
I challenge foes to beat me;
Behold my coat to shreds is done,
My neckcloth down the wind has run -
But I'll forgive the deeds you've done,
If you tomorrow meet me.

Whiskey

When after hearing Sunday Mass,
And your good psalm reciting,
Meet me at the wonted place,
'Mid tavern joys delighting,
Where polish'd quarts are shining o'er
The well-cock'd barrels on the floor;
And bring sweet rhymes, a goodly store,
To grace my smiles inviting.

The Bard

My store, my wealth, my cousin bland,
My sister and my brother,
My court, my house, my farm of land,
My stacks - I crave none other;
My labour, horses, and my plough,
My white-fleec'd sheep, my cattle thou,
And far beyond all these I vow
To love you as a mother.

Mild, beautiful, beloved one,
Priz'd o'er all maids and misses,
O! quit me not, or I'm undone,

[1] Published in *Irish Popular Songs*, pp. 96-101 - Ed.

My fathers lov'd your kisses;
My haunting sprite is rum, I trow;
My blood relations, draughts that glow;
My gossip is the punch bowl - O!
I'll haste to share their blisses!

What quarrels dire we both have had
This year of sorrow sable;
But O! my bounding heart is glad
To see you crown the table;
Dear fondling of the nuptial nest,
My father kind, my mother blest,
My upper coat, my inner vest,
I'll hold you while I'm able.

The friends, the very best I saw,
While through the land a rover,
Were brandy, ale, and *usquebaugh* -
Of claret I'm no lover;
This liquor may the clergy bless -
Though great I deem their holiness;
They like the claret ne'ertheless,
When Mass and psalm are over.

(78)
The Peril of Britain[1]
(Anfhochainn Bhreatainn)[2]

Seán Claragh MacDonnell (Ballad). Air: *The Soger Laddie.*

Ye offspring of heroes through centuries olden,
Lend an ear to the tale which the muse hath unfolden,
Though landless your nobles, your chiefs lion-hearted,
From fair *Inis-Fodhla* for ever are parted;

[1] Published in *Reliques*, pp. 26-29. - Ed.

[2] This song bears internal evidence of being written at a time when England was engaged in war with Spain and other countries; and if we are to credit the writer, getting the worst of it. - O'Daly, (1866) pp. 26-27.

There's Philip victorious o'er wide earth and wave;
His allies death-dealing, unsheathed the glaive;
Wild havoc and ruin shall seize the oppressor,
And God's red right arm shall be Erin's redresser.

Whole armies are banded, and heaven their protector,
To scourge the vile soldiers of George the Elector;
By the wrath of the Lord, o'er the wild billow driven,
His fleets seek their harbours, all shattered and riven;
His thousands that march'd to a far, foreign shore,
Have piled the sad fields of defeat in their gore;
Carthagena's dire day gave his brave a red pillow,
And his sails sought Sebastian, in vain, o'er the billow!

Bavaria is mighty in greatness and glory,
The Sultan's in Europe - who'll credit the story?
Vienna's proud ramparts his horsemen beleaguer,
Its empress is tearful - its foeman is eager.
Khevenhuller[1] exiled has from Sicily fled;
Fierce war crush'd his power, his bandits are dead;
Silesia knows Prussia and Poland's infliction,
And Leopold, thy race feel the Lord's malediction!

De Montemar[2] proud to the field is advancing,
With lion-like leaders, with long lances glancing,
With fire and fierce slaughter, with Mars' mighty thunder,
With war's meetest music, with hosts without number -
All Mantua and Milan his mandates obey;
And Tuscany crouches to Philip's high sway,
And Naples hath yielded to Charles the glorious,
Prince sage in the council - in battle victorious.

---

[1] Count Kevenhuller; a distinguished Austrian general who took a conspicuous part in these campaigns. - O'Daly, (1866) p. 28.

[2] Duke de Montemar, who commanded the Spanish army assembled at Rimini, and being joined by the Neapolitan forces, amounted to sixty thousand men, furnished with a large train of artillery, but sickness and desertion made him afterwards run into Naples, where he was followed by the king of Sardinia, as far as Rimini, when he resigned his commission to Count Gages. - O'Daly, (1866) pp. 28-29.

The torch-tossing Louis - a lion in danger,
Sagacious, unshaken, to terror a stranger,
The fierce Gaul has led to the gates of Hanover;
His heel crushes Holland, its glory is over!
And now, while unsheathing his far-flashing brand,
Fell carnage, dark demon, starts forth at his hand;
And George is the game the wild war-hound's pursuing;
There's an end to my theme - to the Saxon red ruin!

(79)
One Clear Summer Morning[1]
(Maidin Gheal t-Samhraidh)

One clear summer morning, near blue Avonree,[2]
A stately brown maiden flash'd full on my way;
More white was her brow than the foam of the sea;
More holy her voice than the fairy choir's lay;
Her slight waist was chalk-white, her foot light and smooth
Glanc'd airlifted over the wild, grassy slope -
"Fair light of the valley," I said to her sooth,
"My heart's health is gone if you yield me no hope!"

At the birth of the maiden a humming bee flew,
With a rich honey-shower to her berry-red lip -
I snatch'd from the fair one the sweet fragrant dew;
'Twas rapture entrancing - but what did I sip?
A sting from her red lip sped swift as a dart
Its way to my bosom - how woeful to say!
'Tis strange that I live with the barb in my heart,
While thousands have died of her love since that day.

---

[1] Published in *Irish Popular Songs*, pp. 128-129. - Ed.

[2] *Abhan-an Righe*, a river in the County Kilkenny. It is called Avonree, or the *King's River*, from the death of the monarch, Niall, who about the middle of the ninth century, was drowned in its waters during a flood, while he was endeavouring to preserve the life of a soldier of his train who had been swept into the current of the river.

(80)

Nelly Bán[1]

(Neillidhe Bhán)

O, sit beside me, Nelly Bán, bright favourite of my heart,
Unless I touch thy snowy neck my life will soon depart;
I'd swim for thee the river Suir, and Shannon's widespread sea;
Thou dost excel the beauteous maids of the town on blue Loch Rea![2]

Were mine the town on blue Loch Rea, Portumna's pleasant streets,
The city of the Battle-ford,[3] and Limerick of the fleets,
Unto thy tribe these precious gifts I gladly would resign,
Could gifts like these incline them, love, to make thee ever mine!

My blessing take to Connaught back, the land of friendship free,
And to my own beloved who is so far from me;
On Thomond's dusky mountain, our meeting place we chose,
Swoll'n Shannon's waves detain'd me - in savage wrath they rose.

I would sooner than my gallant steed - I pass his bridle-rein,
Or heirdom of the wide domain where stately deer are slain;
Than all that reach'd to Limerick of laden fleets this year,
That in the town of blue Loch Rea I could behold my dear!

O! that I were laid in death far on a hill away,
My right hand high extended to feed the bird of prey,
Since Nelly Bán, the theme of bards, I fell in love with thee,
And thy mother says she'll have me not, her son-in-law to be.

---

[1] Published in *Irish Popular Songs*, pp. 112-115. - Ed.

[2] *Baile-loch-readhach*, the town of Loughrea, on the lake of the same name, in the County Galway.

[3] *Baile-áth-cliath*, the Irish name for the city of Dublin. Our historians say that Baile-ath-cliath literally means the Town of the ford of the hurdles; but as cliath might mean either a hurdle or a battle, I have chosen the latter version as better suited to my verse.

(81)
Flower of Brown-Haired Maidens[1]
(Plúr na m-Ban donn Óg)[2]

Air: *Plúr na m-Ban donn Óg.*

Oh! if thou come to Leitrim, sure nought can us sever,
A phlúr na m-ban donn óg!
Wild honey and the mead-cup shall feast us for ever,
A phlúr na m-ban donn óg!
I'll show thee ships and sails, through the vistas grand,
As we seek our green retreat by the broad lake's strand,
And grief would never reach us within that happy land,
A phlúr na m-ban donn óg!

To Leitrim, to Leitrim, in vain thou would'st lead,
Dúirt plúr na m-ban donn óg.
When pale hunger comes, can thy melodies feed me?
Dúirt plúr na m-ban donn óg.
Sooner would I live, and sooner die a maid,
Than wander with thee through the dewy forest glade,
That thou art my beloved, this bosom never said,
Dúirt plúr na m-ban donn óg.

Over the mountain I once met the maiden,
As a star through the mist might glow;
We reach'd while I told her my tale sorrow-laden,
The field of the kine below;
And there, in the hollow by the hedge-row tree,
I plighted her a promise, till life should flee,
To bear all the blame of her true love for me,
Mo phlúr na m-ban donn óg.

---

[1] Published in *Irish Popular Songs*, pp. 90-95. - Ed.

[2] *Plúr na m-ban donn óg, Flower of brown-haired Maidens.* This beautiful song, which breathes the very soul of love and sorrow, seems to have been written at a period when famine afflicted the land. The poet's mistress declines, through dread of hunger, to visit with him the County of Leitrim, maugre all his glorious painting; and he concludes his song with a burst of fierce love, chastened down by grief and Christian resignation.

Alas! my sad heart, that I kiss not thy blushes,
A phlúr na m-ban donn óg,
On a rich, lofty couch, or a heap of green rushes,
Mo phlúr na m-ban donn óg.
Alone, all alone, through the beautiful night,
Laughing in the fulness of our hearts' delight;
Alas! if thou be not mine, how woeful is my plight,
A phlúr na m-ban donn óg!

(82)
Have you been at Carrick?[1]
(*An Raibh tú ag an g-Carraig?*)[2]

Have you been at Carrick, and saw my true-love there?
And saw you her features, all beautiful, bright, and fair?
Saw you the most fragrant, flowering, sweet apple-tree?
Oh! saw you my loved one, and pines she in grief like me?

I have been to Carrick, and saw thy own true-love there;
And saw, too, her features, all beautiful, bright and fair;
And saw the most fragrant, flowering, sweet apple-tree -
I saw thy loved one - she pines not in grief, like thee!

Five guineas would price every tress of her golden hair -
They think what a treasure her pillow at night to share,
These tresses thick-clustering and curling around her brow -
Oh, Ringlet of Fairness! I'll drink to thy beauty now!!

When seeking to slumber, my bosom is rent with sighs -
I toss on my pillow till morning's blest beams arise;
No aid, bright Beloved! can reach me save God above,
For a blood-lake is form'd of the light of my eyes with love!

---

[1] Published in *Irish Popular Songs*, pp. 72-75. - Ed.

[2] This is a song of the South, but there are so many places of the name of Carrick, such as Carrick-on-Shannon, Carrick-on-Suir, etc., that I cannot fix its precise locality. In this truly Irish song, which the pining swain learns that his absent mistress is not love-sick like himself, he praises the beauty of her copious hair, throws off a glass to her health, enumerates his sufferings, and swears to forego the sex for ever; but she suddenly bursts upon his view, his resolves vanish into thin air, and he greets his glorious maid with such a welcome as an Irish lover alone can give!

Until yellow Autumn shall usher the Paschal day,
And Patrick's gay festival come in its train always -
Until through my coffin the blossoming boughs shall grow,
My love on another I'll never in life bestow!

Lo! yonder the maiden illustrious, queen-like, high,
With long-flowing tresses adown to her sandal-tie -
Swan, fair as the lily, descended of high degree,
A myriad of welcomes, dear maid of my heart, to thee!

(83)
Lament of the Mangaire Súgach[1]
(*Uaill Cumhaidh an Mangaire Súgach*)[2]

Beloved! do you pity not my doleful case,
Pursued by priest and minister in dire disgrace?
The churchmen brand the vagabond upon my brow -
Oh! they'll take me not as Protestant or Papist now!

The parson calls me wanderer and homeless knave;
And though I boast the Saxon creed with aspect grave,
He says that claim my Popish face must disallow,
Although I'm neither Protestant nor Papist now!

He swears (and oh! he'll keep his oath) he's firmly bent
To hunt me down by penal Acts of Parliament;
Before the law's coercive might to make me bow,
And choose between the Protestant and Papist now!

The priest me deems a satirist of luckless lay,
Whose merchant-craft hath often led fair maids astray,
And, worse than hunted fugitive all disavow,
He'll take me not a Protestant or Papist now!

---

[1] Published in *Irish Popular Songs*, pp. 64-69. - Ed.

[2] Andrew Magrath, commonly called the *Mangaire Súgach*, or *Jolly Merchant*, having been expelled from the Roman Catholic Church for his licentious life, offered himself as a convert to the doctrines of Protestantism; but the Protestant clergyman having also refused to accept him, the unfortunate *Mangaire* gave vent to his feelings in this lament.

That further, I'm a foreigner devoid of shame,
Of hateful, vile, licentious life and evil name;
A ranting, rhyming wanderer, without a cow,
Who now is deemed a Protestant - a Papist now!

Alas! it was not charity or Christian grace
That urged to drag my deeds before the Scotic race.
What boots it him to write reproach upon my brow,
Whether they deem me Protestant or Papist now?

Lo! David, Israel's poet-king, and Magdaléne,
And Paul, who of the Christian creed the foe had been -
Did heaven, when sorrow filled their heart, reject their vow,
Though they were neither Protestant nor Papist now?

O! since I weep my wretched heart to evil prone,
A wanderer in the paths of sin, all lost and lone,
At other shrines with other flocks I fain must bow.
Who'll take me, whether Protestant or Papist, now?

Beloved! whither can I flee for peace at last,
When thus beyond the Church's pale I'm rudely cast?
The Arian creed or Calvinist, I must avow,
When sever'd from the Protestant and Papist now!

The Summing-up

See Peter th' Apostle, whose lapses from grace were three,
Denying the Saviour, was granted a pardon free;
O God! though the *Mangaire* from him Thy mild laws cast,
Receive him, like Peter, to dwell in THY HOUSE at last!

(84)
Cashel of Munster[1]
(*Caiseal Mumhan*)[2]

I would wed you, dear, without gold or gear, or counted kine,
My wealth you'll be, would fair friends agree, and you be mine.
My grief, my gloom! that you do not come, my heart's dear hoard!
To Cashel fair, though our couch were there but a soft deal board.

O come, my bride, o'er the wild hillside, to the valley low!
A downy bed for my love I'll spread, where waters flow;
And we shall stray where streamlets play, the groves among,
Where echo tells to the listening dells the blackbird's song!

Love, tender, true, I gave to you, and secret sighs,
In hope to see upon you and me, one hour arise,
When the priest's blest voice would confirm my choice and the ring's strict tie,
If wife you be, love, to one but me, love, in grief I'll die!

In church at pray'r first I saw the fair in glorious sheen,
In mantle flowing, with jewels glowing, and frontlet green,
And robe of whiteness, whose fold of lightness might sweep the lea;
Oh, my heart is broken since tongues have spoken that maid for me!

A neck of white has my heart's delight, and breast like snow,
And flowing hair whose ringlets fair to the green grass flow -
Alas! that I did not early die, before the day
That saw me here, from my bosom's dear, far, far away!

---

[1] Published in *Irish Popular Songs*, pp. 168-171. - Ed.

[2] *Caiseal Mumhan, Cashel of Munster*, is the most popular of all the Irish melodies. This will perhaps account for the reason that there is no Irish song of which there are so many corrupt versions as this. I cannot undertake to say that the present is the genuine one, but in its simple pathos it bears strong evidence of authenticity. It was given me by a lady of the County Clare, whose mother, she informed me, was accustomed to sing it, at the advanced age of eighty years.

(85)
Pure Learned Priest![1]
(*A shagairt dhil chaidh*)

Eoghan Rua Ó Súilleabháin.

Pure learned priest! akin to Neill and Art,
Whose power protective cheer'd the poet's heart,
The first in danger's van - (so bards have sung them),
Pray tell thy flock a teacher's come among them.

Well skill'd in ancient Greek and Roman lore,
Fame-laden lays since Erin's days of yore,
And eke the foeman's tongue, upborne by Law,
Whose phrase uncouth distorts the Gaelic jaw.

Upborne by Law which exiles heroes tall,
Which dooms, by traitor's steel, the chieftain's fall,
Dooms Erin's brave no refuge save their God;
And me to wield the village pedant's rod!

Mild man of God, and fair religion's glory,
Deep read in holy tomes and tuneful story,
With thy sweet tongue consign to village fame
What learned lore enwreaths thy poet's name!

[1] Published in *Reliques*, pp. 10-11. It was probably while resident in the region of Annagh, between Charleville and Dromina, in North Cork that Eoghan Rua Ó Súilleabháin composed this church notice announcing the opening of his hedge-school in that locality. - Ed.

(86)
The Cruel Base-Born Tyrant[1]
(*An Bonnaire Fiadh-phuic*)

Seán Clarach MacDonnell (Ballad). Air: *The Fair White Calf.*[2]

What withered the pride of my vigour?
The lowly-sprung tyrant train
That rule all our border with rigour,
And ravage the fruitful plain:
Yet once when the war-trumpet's rattle
Arous'd the wild clansman's wrath,
They, heartless, abandon'd the battle,
And fled the fierce foeman's path!

The loved ones my life would have nourish'd
Are foodless, and bare, and cold;
My flocks by their fountain that flourish'd
Decay on the mountain wold:
Misfortune my temper is trying,
This raiment no shelter yields;
And chief o'er my evils undying,
The tyrant that rules my fields!

Alas! on the red hill where perish'd
The offspring of heroes proud,
The virtues our forefathers cherish'd
Lie pall'd in their blood-stain'd shroud!
And O! for one hero[3] avenger,
With aid o'er the heaving main,
To sweep from *Clar Fodhla*[4] the stranger,
And sever his bondage-chain!

---

[1] Published in *Reliques*, pp. 22-23. - Ed.

[2] This air is very common in Munster, where the original song is well known and sung. We do not know whether Dr. Petrie has published it in the collection he prepared for the Musical Society of Dublin or not. If not, it would be a great drawback upon that learned work, as Moore and Bunting seem to have forgotten it too, and left it unpublished. - O'Daly, (1866) p. 22.

[3] *An Laoch*. The Hero, meaning the Pretender.- O'Daly, (1866) p. 23.

[4] *Clar Fola*, or "Fodhla's Plain," is one of the many names of Ireland. Eire, Banba, and Fodhla, were three queens of the island - hence it is sometimes called Eire's land (whence perhaps "Ireland"), sometimes "Banba's isle," sometimes "Fodhla's plain." etc. This plenitude of synonyms was cherished by the Bards, for poetic reasons. - O'Daly, (1866) p. 23.

(87)

Mac An Cheanaighe[1]

(*Mac An Cheanaighe*)[2]

Aodhgán O'Raithile. Ballad. A.D. 1700.

A vision bless'd my eyes erewhile,
Revealing scenes sublime and airy!
The genius of green Erin's isle,
Stood by my couch, a gorgeous fairy:
Her blue eyes' glow, her ringlets' flow,
And pure, pale brow exceeding any,
Proclaimed, with pride, that at her side
Would sit, her true love, *Mac an Cheanaighe*!

Her voice is sweetest music's sound
To us who for her love are dying:
Proud spouse of Brian, conquest-crown'd,
I mourn the doom that leaves thee sighing!
When Saxon might assails thy right,
I dread, fair queen, belov'd of many,
That o'er thy brow dark sorrow's plough
Shall come, ere cometh *Mac an Cheanaighe*!

Myriads languish for her love,
And burn to clasp her form of beauty;
For her have kings and heroes strove,
Rivals high in love and duty:
But joy's bright trace ne'er lights her face,
She fears her foemen fierce and many;
No hope-fraught ray to cheer her way,
Will come, till cometh *Mac an Cheanaighe*!

---

[1] Published in R*eliques*, pp. 24-27 - Ed.

[2] *Mac an Cheanaighe*, or "the Merchant's Son," means the exiled Stuart. - O'Daly, (1866) p. 25.

"My brethren," said the beauteous maid,
"Were kings supreme and chiefs of glory,
Conn of the blood-red battle blade,
And Art, the theme of ancient story.
And o'er the deep, where tall barks leap,
shall heroes come renown'd and many."
Alas the day! - thy charms' decay
Shall come, ere cometh *Mac an Cheanaighe*!

"There's glory for thy future day,
The banner green shall yet be flying,"
I cried - but 'neath the vision's sway,
In distant Spain I saw her dying!
As burst my cry, she gave reply,
One shriek the wildest far of any -
My bitter grief found no relief,
Till fled thy *keene*r, *Mac an Cheanaighe!*

(88)
The Expected of Ireland[1]
(*Suil-Chabharthadh Eireann*)

Eoghan Ruadh (Ballad). Air: *An Síoda atá ad Bhalluit a Bhuachaill.*[2]

By a green-margin'd stream, at evening, I stay'd,
(Poets are wont to be roaming;)
O'er the dew-sprinkled sward came tripping a maid
Whose charms gave light through the gloaming:

---

[1] Published in *Reliques*, pp. 54-59. - Ed.

[2] This beautiful air originated in the following anecdote. One of those young men, better known among the community as "Poor Scholars," whom a thirst for education, in bygone days, sent from various parts of Ireland to Munster, was accosted in the following manner by a young woman, probably the daughter of his host, in reference to the Wallett, or Satchel, in which he carried his books to school:-

An sioda tá ad Wallet,
An síoda tá ad Wallet,
An síoda tá ad Wallet a bhuachaill,
An síoda tá ad Wallet,
An síoda tá ad Wallet,
Nó abhla do bhlaiseach mna uaisle?

Is it silk that's in your Wallet,
Is it silk that's in your Wallet,
Is it silk that's in your Wallet, my buachaill,
Is it silk that's in your Wallet,
Is it silk that's in your Wallet,
Or apples for ladies to taste of?

To which he replied: -
Ní síoda tá am Wallet,
Ní síoda tá am Wallet,
Ní síoda tá am Wallet a stuaire!
Ní síoda tá am Wallet,
Ní síoda tá am Wallet,
Ná abhla do bhlaiseach mná uaisle!

'Tis not silk I have in my Wallet,
'Tis not silk I have in my Wallet,
'Tis not silk I have in my Wallet, my fair one,
'Tis not silk I have in my Wallet,
'Tis not silk I have in my Wallet,
Nor apples for ladies to taste of? etc. etc.
O'Daly, (1866) p.55.

Air-lifted and light sped the beautiful sprite,
Bearing joy to my breast overladen,
I thought, by my fay, no earth-tainted clay
From Adam had moulded the maiden!

Her long-flowing hair swept her ankle of white,
Golden-ting'd, ringletted, braided,
Odorous tresses, before whose rich light
Proud Jason's fam'd treasure had faded!
O! she was the fairest, the brightest, the rarest.
The gentlest, the simplest, the mildest,
The tunefullest, sweetest, the noblest, the meetest,
For poet in vision the wildest!

Her mild, ample forehead was fair to behold,
Beautiful, polish'd and tender;
Her ripe eye beneath the arch'd brow roll'd,
Darting its arrowy splendour:
The swan's virgin snows, and the hue of the rose,
In her soft, peachy cheek, were contending;
Now white rules alone, now red holds the throne,
And now in rare beauty they're blending!

Her bosom of white, her waist of delight,
Ne'er glow'd to the clasp of a lover:
From her hair-wreathed crown to her glancing foot down,
She triumphs all rivals over!
Her race and her name, he ancestral fame,
Her heroes, for valour's proud duty,
Her history's pages, the laws of her sages,
I question to flowing-hair'd beauty.

"Less fair was the Beauty the Phrygian boy,
Had stolen from Menelaus' bower,
For whom gallant heroes contended with Troy,
Till flames wrapt its ultimate tower,
The fair bosom'd maid in Emania betray'd,
By wiles of a treacherous foeman,
And bright ones that long rais'd the rapture of song,
Should yield to thee, beautiful woman!

"Alas! that the lover his love should not know,
Though sorrow her beauty faded;
Forlorn, I wander, o'erburden'd with woe,
Swayless, unhonoured, unaided;
Poor, shackled, and prone 'neath the tyrant I groan,
While sharp lash and goad ever rend me;
And brave hearts are still (they died on the hill,)
Who'd pour their last life to defend me."

"Lance-bearing warriors numberless, bold,
Death-dealing in hour of danger,
Shall burst, in red battle, the fetters that hold
Our limbs for the Saxon stranger:
When the national sword sweeps that tyrant abhorr'd
From the halls whence our chiefs were driven,
And the chieftains returning, for fierce conflict burning,
Shall raise our proud glory to heaven!"

Go, lead o'er the land a white-bosom'd band,
Proclaiming thy advent regal,
And bring the fair dames to thy true lover, James,[1]
Sweet bard of the line of Nagle.
His heavenly songs speak thy glory and wrongs,
Thy hate of the false Saxon's power,
Or should beauty's bright wing hover mute o'er the string,
He charms the dear bird to his bower!

[1] James Nagle of Cork, a tailor by trade, and a brother of the bard, to whom this song was addressed by Eoghan (Owen) O'Sullivan. - O'Daly, (1866) p. 59.

(89)

Return of King Charles[1]

(*Filleadh Rí Searluis*)

Eoghan Ruadh Ó Súilleabháin. Air: *An Beinsin Luachra* (*The Little Bench of Rushes*).[2]

Alone as I was roaming,
By misty vale of beauty green,
I spied, amid the gloaming
Approaching, a fair young queen;
And as she mov'd in lightness,
Her wreathed ringlets' flaxen flow,
Swept o'er her foot of whiteness,
Like gold wreaths on virgin snow!

She mov'd, a beauteous maiden,
With mild grace and modest mien,
And blue eye laughter laden,
Like dewdrop on rosebud seen;
And cheek of peachy splendour,
And chalk-white teeth of stainless hue,
And form of beauty slender,
That clasp of lover never knew.

---

[1] Published in *Reliques*, pp. 60-65. On the Cork-Kerry border where the song is still in the living tradition it is perhaps better known by the opening words of the first stanza, *I'm Aonar Seal*. - Ed.

[2] The meaning of the word "*Beinsin*" (little Bench) is mistaken by some of our most eminent writers, who suppose it to mean a *Bunch*. In our youthful days it was general custom with the peasantry to go on midsummer eve to the next bog, and cut a *beart luachra* (bundle of rushes), as much as a stout lad could carry home on his back; and this they strewed on benches of stones made for the purpose inside and outside their cottages, where the youth of the neighbourhood spent the evening in their usual pastimes. The custom generally prevailed in the days of our boyhood, but probably has now died away like everything else. The youthful heroine of this song must have been on an excursion of this kind, and no doubt fell in with the amorous Eoghan Rua.

Monsieur Boullaye Le Gouz, who travelled through Ireland in the middle of the seventeenth century, tells us that "Les Irlandois ornent leur chambres de iong, dont ils font leur lits en eté, et de paille en hiver, ils mettent un pied de iong autour de leur chambres, et sur leur fenestres, et plusieurs d'entr'eux ornent leur planchers de rambeaux." - *Les Voyages et Observations du Sieur Boullays Le Gouz*. 4to. *A Paris*, 1657. 476. - O'Daly, (1866) p. 61.

She mocks the vermeil cluster
That forms the quick-beam's coronal;
The snowflake's virgin lustre,
Ere on earth its whiteness fall:
No swan, such neck revealing,
Has o'er his watery mirror hung;
No fairy strain soft stealing,
Like music from her warbling tongue!

"O! beauty-clothed creature!
What star thy dwelling-place hath been?
Or can I scan thy feature,
Unscathed by thy beauty's sheen?
Art thou the fair one[1] burning
With fiercest love, that burst her bower,
And left her lone one mourning,
To share Cuchullain's blissful hour?

"Or Deirdre, beauteous rare one,
The curse of Uladh's land of grief,
Where for the fatal fair one
Were strewn, in battle, king and chief?
Or left the great Mac Dary

---

[1] *An Bheith* (*The Maiden*). This lady was Blathnuid, daughter of the governor of the Isle of Man, who surpassed all the women of her time in exquisite figure and beauty; and though obtained as a prize by Curaigh Mac Daire, on account of the assistance he rendered the heroes of the Red Branch in plundering the island, and the dire contest he had with Cuchullainn afterwards on her account, when he tied him neck and heels, and left him shackled like a captive after cutting off his hair with his sword; yet her attachment was so warm towards Cuchullainn, that she contrived the following stratagem to enable him to obtain her.
She persuaded Curaigh, that he ought to erect a palace for himself that should excel all the royal palaces in the kingdom, and that he might do so by sending the Clanna Deagha to gather all the large upright stones in the kingdom to form this palace. Cuchullain being informed that the Clanna Deagha were scattered over the kingdom, sets out privately, and soon arrived at a wood near the seat of Curaigh, and sends secretly to inform Blathnuid of his arrival, with a large body of troops along with him. She sends him word that she would seal Curaigh's sword, and then as a sign of attack, that she would spill a large vessel of new milk that was in the house into the rivulet which flowed from the castle through the wood where Cuchullain was concealed. Having heard this, in a short time he perceived the stream white with milk, when, sallying out, they forced into the palace and slew Curaigh, who was alone and unarmed, and took Blathnuid away with them to Ulster.
The river was then called Fionghlaise, from being made white with milk. - *Keating*. - O'Daly, (1866) pp. 62-63.

Beside his recent fortress low?
Or laid green Erin weary,
Low-chain'd beneath oppression's blow?"

As strains by haunted fountain,
Thus broke her magic melody: -
"The frail ones thou'rt recounting,
Sweet poet, are no mates for me:
O'er wilds I roam forsaken
To find my royal love again,
While woes my plaints awaken,
And tyrants draw my dearest vein!

"But Charles is returning,
With warriors brave, and flowing sail,
To ease my bosom's burning;
To free, in battle fierce, the Gael!
And when we've quell'd the caitiffs
That made our holy priesthood die,
Green Erin's glorious natives
Shall swell the song of triumph high!

"The priests in dark caves hiding,
Shall altars raise to heaven's King;
The bard, with wolves abiding,
Again shall wake sweet music's string;
When from our fierce oppressors,
We free the land of saint and sage,
Green Erin's bold redressors
Shall hold their fathers' heritage!"

(90)
A Lament for the Gael[1]
(*Caoineadh na nGaoidheal*)

William O'Heffernan the Blind. Ballad. Air: *Shaun Bui* (*Yellow Jack*)

Alas for the records of ages afar,
The chiefs of our olden day's glory,
The shield of the stranger, the valiant in war,
The light of the *Seanachai's* story!
When billows of song
Pour'd their wild tide along,
And minstrels' gay lays might enthral thee;
But our poets to-day
Have a new-fangled lay -
They rhyme to the measure of *Shaun Bui!*[2]

There's Greece and her glory, antiquity's star,
The Caesars of history's pages;
The ancients that gather'd on far-farm'd Senaar,[3]
Our guides through the gloom of past ages:
The Fenians' high sway,
And the proud palmy day,
When Rome fled affrighted from Daithi;[4]

---

[1] Published in *Reliques*, pp. 72-77. - Ed.

[2] The Ballad seems to have been written in ridicule of the Rhymers of that period, with whom the air of *Shaun Bui* was a favourite vehicle of verse. - O'Daly, (1866) p. 72.

[3] *Machaire Shenar*, the Plain of Senar. Fenius Farsa, king of Scythia, being desirous of having a knowledge of the various languages that sprung up before his time, from the confusion of tongues at the Tower of Babel, despatched at his own expense seventy-two learned men to the several countries of the three parts of the world then inhabited; and commanded them to remain abroad for seven years, that each of them might learn the language of the country in which he was located. On their return to Scythia he went to the plain of Shenar, which, according to the Book of Dromsneachta, lies near the city of Athens, where all the youth of the neighbouring nations assembled to be instructed in the languages. - Haliday's *Keating*, p. 225. - O'Daly, (1866) pp. 72-73.

[4] *Daithi*, Darby. Monarch of Ireland, A.D. 398, and last of the Irish Pagan kings. This prince received his death by a thunderbolt at the foot of the Alps, after coming off victorious in one hundred and fifty battles. His army carried his body with them into Ireland, and interred it with great solemnity at Roilig na Riogh, in Cruaghan, after he had governed the island for twenty-three years. - O'Daly, (1866) p. 74.

Lir's[1] offspring of woe,
All forgotten I trow,
If sung not in numbers of *Shaun Bui!*

The discord that brought Beney-Briot[2] to our shore,
The deeds of great Luigh the Long-handed,
When Black-toothed Fergus[3] lay bathed in gore,
That *Eric* the monarch demanded!
When heaps of his slain
Taught Turgesius,[4] the Dane,
How fatal the wrath of the *Ard-Rí*;
Go weave no sweet lay
Of green Erin's proud day,
Or measure your numbers to *Shaun Bui!*

If heroes that perish'd at Clontarf of fame,
To gain their lov'd country's salvation;
Or her who left Breifny[5] to anguish and shame,
For Dermot the curse of his nation:
If Henry the king,
Or Eliza you sing,
Who levell'd our altars, *ma chrá cree!*

---

[1] *Clana Lir*, Children of Lir. The Legend of the Children of Lir has been since time immemorial in high repute, as one of the "Three Tragic Stories of the Irish," or the "Three Sorrows of Story-telling." See the *Atlantis*, Vol. 2, where this affecting tale is published. - O'Daly, (1866) p. 74.

[2] *Beine*. Beney, for whose chivalrous actions, see Keating, Vol. 2, pp. 263-4-5. . - O'Daly, (1866) p. 74.

[3] *Fergus Dubhdheideach*, ie. Fergus the Black-toothed, surnamed from the black colour of his teeth; and for whose fate at the battle of Crionna, where he and his brothers fell at the hands of Lughaidh Lamhfhada, or Looee the Long-handed, see Keating, Vol. 2, pp. 268-69-70. 1809 ed.. - O'Daly, (1866) p. 75.

[4] Turgesius, the Danish tyrant, who usurped the sovereignty of Ireland, A.D. 866, and who inflicted the most excessive cruelties on the Irish people, was, after reducing the country to the lowest set of vassalage, by rapine, plunder, and the sword, slain by Maolsheachluin (Malachy), king of Meath, at a very advanced period of his life. *Keating*, Vol. 2, pp. 99-108. - O'Daly, (1866) p. 75.

[5] *Beith* (the Maid). This lady was *Dearbhfhorguil* (pr. Darvoreguil), wife of Tighearnan O Ruairc (now O'Rourke) king of Breifny, who eloped with Diarmuid Mac Murchadh (now Mac Murrough), king of Leinster, while her husband was on a pilgrimage to St. Patrick's Purgatory, and who, when he returned, determined to be revenged on Mac Murrough, which event is fully recounted by Keating, (Vol. 2, p. 196), and which caused the arrival of the English into Ireland. - O'Daly, (1866) p. 75.

Or Cromwell,[1] whose horde
Gave our priests to the sword,
You'll tune them to numbers of *Shaun Bui!*

Do strains from your harp thro' the heaving heart thrill,
Or are you a pastoral chimer?
When clodpoles approach you by valley or hill,
When wand'ring as wanders your rhymer;
Untaught ev'n to say
Heav'n prosper your way,
Or, may Charles[2] our monarch again be!
They'll aver by their God,
You're the soul of a clod,
If you sing not the measure to *Shaun Bui!*

(91)
The Merry Tailor[3]
(*An Tailiur Aorach*)

William Dall O'Heffernan. Ballad. Air:"*Buachail na mbó 'sa Yimlet.*"

The Tailor[4]
I've rambled full many a mile,
And misery ever pursuing me,

---

[1] *Oliver Cromwell.* We need not refer to the pages of history for the cruelties of this sanguinary fanatic, as our churches, our abbeys and monasteries, sufficiently shew the marks of his sacrilegious hands. The eastern window of the Cathedral of St. Canice, Kilkenny, contained the history of our Saviour from his birth to his Ascension, in emblems of beautifully stained glass, for which Rinuccini, the Pope's Nuncio, when he attended the meeting of the Confederate Catholics, offered £700; but neither the plenitude of the power with which he was invested, nor the distresses of the times, could prevail on the prelate, David Roth, or the Chapter, to comply with his wishes; this beautiful specimen of ancient art remained standing until shattered by the usurper and his vile soldiery. - (Ledwich's *Antiquities*, p. 388). For further particulars about Cromwell see Mr. Prendergast's *History of the Cromwellian Settlement of Ireland*. - O'Daly, (1866) p. 76-77.

[2] Prince Charles, the exile. - O'Daly, (1866) p. 77.

[3] Published in *Reliques*, pp. 84-89. - Ed.

[4] The introduction of the tailor and his amorous woes on this occasion, seems to have been done to furnish a vehicle for the display of the poet's learning. This was vanity quite common at that period with men of the highest literary attainments; and it is no matter of surprise that O'Heffernan would follow their example. In this rapid sketch of female perversity, he displays a considerable knowledge of heathen mythology, and sacred and profane history. To prove that O'Heffernan was a greatly gifted man, we have only to refer the reader to the songs preceding this poem, particularly to "Beih Eirionn I," and the "Voice of Joy," which contain passages of exquisite sweetness and beauty. The hero of this humorous ballad was a David O'Cleary, an eccentric knight of the Thimble, who wasted his earnings among the fair sex till far advanced in life, when finding his expectations fail, introduced himself to O'Heffernan, who composed the song extempore.

Yet still my chief curse was the guile
Of woman, in treachery wooing me!

O'Heffernan's Reply
What matter to tailoring youth,
A shot from their wily battery,
And Solomon wisest, in sooth,
Beguiled by sly female flattery.

Chorus[1]
When writing a stanza divine,
Have wisdom and learning inspiring you;
And shun the false fiend of red wine,
Lest misery ever environ you!

See Sampson, the strong man of old,
Who slaughter'd the Philistine foeman,
How sad is his fate to unfold,
He died by the wiles of a woman!
When writing a stanza divine,

See Hercules, Jupiter's son,
His fall every reader remembers;
Dejanira soon left him undone,
When roasting his carcass to embers!
When writing a stanza divine, etc.

You've listen'd to stories of Troy,
Its heroes and proud pavilions once,
How Helen, the giver of joy,
Gave death to its mighty millions once.
When writing this stanza divine, etc.

You've heard of great Achilles' fame,
As you have abroad been travelling,

---

[1] Our Irish poets had always a fancy for giving a chorus, which is called in Irish "Cur Fa," to their humorous songs; and our bard swayed the palm in this respect. When any of these songs were sung at the hearth of the cottier, of a cold winter evening, as was usually the case, those assembled joined in the chorus, a custom prevalent to this day in Munster. - O'Daly, (1866) pp. 84-85.

And how fair Polyxena came
And guided young Paris's javelin.
When writing a stanza divine, etc.

How Actaeon died a wild deer,
When Dian with antlers adorned him;
Some whisper 'twas meant for your ear,
To prove 'twas in wedlock she horn'd him.
When writing a stanza divine, etc.

You've oft heard a Seanachaí sing,
Of Deirdre the sorrowful story;
How for her great Connor, the king,
Left Uladh's three champions gory.
When writing a stanza divine, etc.

See Conroy, the chief of his clan,
The highway of glory pursuing,
Never met with his match in a man,
Till Blanit consigned him to ruin,
When writing a stanza divine, etc.

See the powerful Talc-mac-Treon
Allur'd by Nea-Nua's tresses,
Beneath Oscar's battle-axe prone,
Died cursing sly Cupid's jesses!
When writing a stanza divine, etc.

There's Fionn Mac Cumhaill[1] the boast
Of Erin's ancient chivalry,
Destroy'd the best man of his host
Through jealousy, green-eyed devilry!
When writing a stanza divine, etc.

---

[1] Fionn Mac Cumhail, the general of the Irish militia, in the reign of Cormac Mac Art, monarch of Ireland, to whose daughter, the princess Grainne, he was married. Grainne, however, forsook her husband Fionn for love of Diarmid O'Duibhne, from whom the present name Dunn or O'Dunn is derived, and eloped with Diarmuid, whom the injured Fionn afterwards slew in battle. For an account of this curious and interesting romance, see the Third Volume of the *Transactions of the Ossianic Society*. - O'Daly, (1866) pp. 88-89.

There are warriors of Meath
Submitting to rapine and slaughter,
Till Turgesius met with his death,
For love of king Malachy's daughter!
When writing a stanza divine, etc.

With Murrough, when *Mór* elopes,
A sorrowful tale for Ireland,
The crown of the country's hopes,
Was driven away from Eireland.
When writing a stanza divine, etc.

Thus fell the valorous Gael,
And fool, look sharp to futurity;
Your 'goose,' if maids hear the tale,
Will be cooked with terrible surety.
When writing a stanza divine,
Have learning and wisdom inspiring you;
And shun the false fiend, red wine,
Lest misery ever environ you!

(92)
Cormac Oge[1]
(Cormac Óg)

The pigeons coo - the spring's approaching now,
The bloom is bursting on the leafy bough;
The cresses green o'er streams are clustering low,
And honey-hives with sweets abundant flow.

Rich are the fruits the hazely woods display -
A slender virgin, virtuous, fair, and gay;
With steeds and sheep, of kine a many score,
Be trout-stor'd Lee[2] whose banks we'll see no more!

---

[1] Published in *Irish Popular Songs*. pp. 48-51. - Ed.

[2] The River Lee, which rises at Gougane Barra, and dividing as it approaches Cork, washes that city on its north and south sides, and, again uniting, forms that beautiful estuary, the harbour of Cork. Spenser speaks of

"The spreading Lee that, like an island fair,
Encloseth Cork with its divided flood."

The little birds pour music's sweetest notes,
The calves for milk distend their bleating throats;
Above the weirs the silver salmon leap,
While Cormac Oge and I all lonely weep.

(93)

Over the Hills and Far Away[1]

(Bharr na g-Cnoc 's an ime g-céin)[2]

Seán Claragh MacDonnell. Air: *Over the Hills and Far Away.*

Once I bloom'd a maiden young,
A widow's woe now moves my tongue;
My true love's barque ploughs ocean's spray,
Over the hills and far away.

Chorus
Oh! had I worlds, I'd yield them now,
To place me on his tall barque's prow,
Who was my choice through childhood's day,
Over the hills and far away!

Oh! may we yet our lov'd one meet,
With joy-bells' chime and wild drums' beat;
While summoning war-trump sounds dismay,
Over the hills and far away!
Oh! had I words, etc.

Oh! that my hero had his throne,
That Erin's cloud of care were flown,
That proudest prince would own his sway,
Over the hills and far away!
Oh! had I worlds, etc.

---

[1] Published in *Irish Popular Song,* pp. 50-53. - Ed.

[2] This song is said to be the first Jacobite effort attempted by MacDonnell. If this be so, the prince whose exile he deplores is James, the son of the deposed monarch, James II, in whose favour the Scotch revolted in the year 1715.

My bosom's love, that prince afar,
Our king, our joy, our orient star;
More sweet his voice than wild bird's lay,
Over the hills and far away!
Oh! had I worlds, etc.

A high, green hill I'll quickly climb,
And tune my harp to song sublime,
And chant his praise the livelong day,
Over the hills and far away!

Chorus
Oh! had I worlds, I'd yield them now,
To place me on his tall barque's prow,
Who was my choice through childhood's day,
Over the hills and far away!

(94)

Beloved of the Flaxen Tresses[1]

(*Muirnín na Gruaige Báine*)[2]

At the *Town of the Isle,*[3] my dear
Abides this long, long year,
Than the summer sun more brightly shining;
Where'er her footsteps go,
Fair honey-flowers will grow,
Even though 'twere winter's dark declining!
If to my net she sped,
'Twould ease my heart and head,
Where cruel love his burning brand impresses;
For all that living be,
I'll choose no mate but thee,
Beloved of the flaxen tresses!

---

[1] Published in *Irish Popular Songs*, pp. 54-57. - Ed.

[2] This beautiful song is preserved in Hardiman's "Minstrelsy," vol. i., but is left there untranslated.

[3] Literally, the Town of the Island - Ballinahinch, in the County of Galway, where was founded, in 1356, a monastery of Carmelite friars. On a small island in the lake of Ballinahinch are the ruins of a castle erected in the time of Elizabeth. A river runs from the lake into Roundstone Bay.

At the bridge of the Avonmore,[1]
I saw my bosom's store,
The maiden of the ringlets yellow -
More sweet her kisses be
Than honey from the tree,
Or festive Spanish wine, of flavour mellow!
Her bosom, globes of white,
Sweet, fragrant, perfect, bright,
Like drifted snow the mountain's breast that presses -
The cuckoo's notes resound,
In winter, where thou'rt found,
Beloved of the flaxen tresses!

Oh! if the boon were mine,
From beauty's ranks divine,
To choose for aye the fairest maiden,
'Twere her to whom sweet lays
Consign the palm of praise,
For whom a thousand hearts with love are laden.
Such maid did once inspire
The Hebrew monarch's lyre;
But, oh! thine eye more dignity expresses -
Relieve my woe, I crave;
Oh! snatch me from the grave,
Beloved of the flaxen tresses!

[1] The Owenmore, a river of the County Mayo, flowing into Blacksod Bay.

(95)
The Cup of O'Hara[1]
(*Cupan Ui h-Eaghra by Carolan*)[2]

Turlogh O'Carolan.
Were I over in Arran,
Or wild Glan-na-Séud,
Where tall barks of swiftness
Bear claret and mead;
'Twas joy to my bosom,
In gladness to sip
O'Hara's bright wine-cup,
Fill'd high to my lip!

Why praise what is sought for
By old man and youth,
While the doctors and sages
(By this hand I am sooth)
Cry, Turlogh, sweet harper,
Come timely to drain
That costly, tall wine-cup,
To the health of brave Kean!

(96)
Amber-hair'd Nora[3]
(*Nóra an Chúil Ómra*)

O! amber-hair'd Nora,
That thy fair head could rest
On the arm that would shelter
Or circle thy breast!
Thou hast stolen all my brain, love,
And then left me alone -
Though I'd cross o'er the main, love,
To call thee mine own!

---

[1] Published in *Irish Popular Songs*, pp. 70-71. - Ed.

[2] *Cupán ui Eaghra*, the Cup of O'Hara. This is one of the celebrated Carolan's songs, and was composed by the harper to celebrate the hospitality of Kean O'Hara, a gentleman of ancient family in the County Sligo.

[3] Published in *Irish Popular Songs*, pp. 76-77. – Ed.

Why, maid of my bosom,
Should falsehood be thine?
Thou hast promis'd to wed me,
Though wealth were not mine;
The dew-sprinkled grass, love,
Scarce feels my light feet,
And, amber-hair'd Nora,
My kisses are sweet!

My fair one is dwelling
By Moy's lovely vale -
Her rich locks of amber
Have left my cheek pale -
May the king of the Sabbath
Yet grant me to see
My herds in the green lanes
Of fair *Baile-ath-Buidhe*!

(97)

The Graceful Maiden[1]

(*An Bhruinneall Mheirbh*)

One morn when mists did hover
The green-wood's foliage over,
'Twas then I did discover
How painful love may be;
A maid, 'mid shades concealing,
Pour'd forth her voice of feeling,
And love came o'er me stealing,
She's a dear maid to me.

When through the valleys roaming,
I see my bright love coming,
Like garden-rose all blooming,
Or flower of the apple-tree;
Bright Venus she's excelling
Fresh from her ocean dwelling,

[1] Published in *Irish Popular Songs*, pp. 78-83. - Ed.

Her soft, round bosom swelling,
Her footfalls light and free.

"Thy love hath left me dying;
The heart where love is lying
Will find what torment trying
Round ruin'd hopes may twine;
And long I've borne the token,
But now it must be spoken,
How thou my heart hast broken,
Who never canst be mine!"

"O! thou of misery telling,
If truth thy tongue's impelling,
I'd ease the pain that's quelling
Thy life, were mine the cure.
But watchful friends surround me,
With promise strict they've bound me,
And if they wandering found me,
What ills might I endure!"

"Tell them, O, light-limb'd maiden,
Thy bloom with grief is fading -
Where groves are foliage-laden,
Thou'lt stray all lonelily:
I'll for thy coming pine, love,
Where the dark wood's boughs entwine, love,
And O! what guilt is thine, love,
If false thou be to me!"

"Alas! how oft thou'st riven
The vow thy lips had given,
While shone the light of heaven,
Or verdure deck'd the plain,
Till sheep, each silly rover,
Would plough the mountain over,
Thou wouldst be my true lover -
But lo! the hope is vain!"

"And now, with white sails flowing,
To Flanders I'll be going;
I'll seek the vineyards growing
In distant Gaul and Spain
Proud maid, no more I'll woo thee;
No more with love pursue thee;
Another mate may sue thee,
And plough for thee the plain!"

(98)
Little Celia Connellan[1]
(*Síle Bheag Ní Choinnealbháin*)

O! pearl-deck'd, beauteous Celia,
My first love of mildness rare!
My life full fast is fading,
My soul is weary, vexed with care;
Come, snowy-bosom'd maiden,
And rove with me the valleys deep,
Or darkest gloom shall seize me,
Till in the pitying grave I sleep!

Come, place the cups before us,
Let choicest wines their brims o'erflow -
We'll drown, in draughts oblivious,
The memory of her breast of snow;
Her neck, that's softer, fairer
Than silk or plumes of snowy white;
For memory wild pursues her
When sever'd from my longing sight!

Were thou and I, dear Smooth-neck!
Of mild cheek and bosom white,
In a summer vale of sweetness
Reposing through the beauteous night;-
No living thing around us
But heath-cocks wild till break of dawn,
And the sunlight of my bosom
Were little Celia Connellan!

[1] Published in *Irish Popular Songs*, pp. 94-97 - Ed.

(99)

The Lullaby[1]

(An Síth Ó)[2]

Eoghan Ruadh Ó Súilleabháin. Ballad.

Hush, baby mine, and weep no more,
Each gem thy regal fathers wore,
When Erin, Emerald Isle, was free,
Thy poet sire bequeaths to thee!

---

[1] Published in *Irish Popular Songs*, pp. 104-11, and in *Reliques*, pp. 66-71. - Ed.

[2] [Walsh's note in *Irish Popular Songs*] The *Seothó*, or Lullaby, was the extempore effusion of Owen Roe O'Sullivan, to soothe the infantile sorrows of an illegitimate child, which one of the victims of his illicit amours had left him. Owen's patience and promises, it is said, were nearly exhausted, when the unfortunate mother, urged by maternal feelings, again returned to claim the child. [Note in *Reliques*] The *Síth Ó (vulgo Shoho*, Lullaby) had its rise in the following manner: - Eoghan Rua, in one of those seasons of fixedness which would sometimes occur, at irregular intervals, in the life of an itinerant, potato-digging poet, squatted down, as our transatlantic brethren would term it, upon the verge of a bog in a rural district in the county of Limerick, when the many-tongued monster, whose wondrous attributes Eoghan often rehearsed from the classic page of Virgil, to many a red-shinned student, had announced the poet's intention of opening the stores of ancient literature in that locality, the Greek-and-Latin-loving *gosoons* hailed with a joy which Irish striplings alone can feel, and when felt can only properly express, the advent of so much wit and learning to their favoured neighbourhood. It was but the work of an hour to raise a turf-built College, some sixty feet long and twelve feet wide, furnished with ranges of seats cut from the neighbouring bog, on which the numerous students might extend their breechless shanks, and luxuriate in all that freedom of motion so utterly unknown among the unhappy worshippers of wisdom at desks and forms. Here the poet continued to tear up ignorance by the roots to the satisfaction of the entire parish, including the priest himself, when on an unfortunate day, entered one of the frail divinities of Eoghan's adoration, in the shape of a fair young woman, who had come to seek him from the last district in which he had been "serenading." She approached the master of the hedge academy, and reproaching him as the author of her shame and sorrow, gave one wild cry, and one endearing kiss to a beautiful babe which she had borne at her bosom, and now laid on her seducer's knee, and departed in audible grief. The reader can conceive the feelings of the unfortunate father, exposed to the jibes of the boys - jibes which no magisterial authority could restrain - and the certain denunciation of Father John on the next Sunday. The scholars had an early dismissal - and anon as the day was wearing late, the young pledge of Eoghan's licentious love, having missed his mamma, set up a squalling which rung shrill and ominous through the deserted hovel. The poet, to still its infantile clamour, administered the extemporary stanzas of the Lullaby, until the weeping mother, urged by material affection, returned again to claim the child, and rid poor Eoghan of a heavy load of affliction.
The historic allusion in this poem will be found in Keating's History of Ireland; Haladay's edition, as far as it goes, is the best to consult; but if O'Mahony's (the reputed American Fenian Head Centre) edition is at hand, published by Haverty of New York in 1858, it is the most accurate, and reliable authority in these matters. - O'Daly, (1866) pp. 66-67.

Hush, baby dear, and weep no more;
Hush, baby mine, my treasur'd store
My heart-wrung sigh, my grief, my groan;
Thy tearful eye, thy hunger's moan!

I'll give the fruit the Phrygian boy
Bestow'd on Venus, queen of joy -
The staff of Pan, the shepherd's God,
And Moses' wonder-working rod.
Hush, baby dear, etc.

The steed of golden housings rare,
Bestrode by glorious Falvey Fair,
The chief who at the Boyne did shroud,
In bloody wave, the sea-kings proud!
Hush, baby dear, etc.

Brian's golden-hilted sword of light,
That flash'd despair on foeman's flight;
And Murcha's fierce, far-shooting bow,
That at Clontarf laid heroes low!
Hush, baby dear, etc.

The courier hound that tidings bore
From Cashel to Bunratty's shore;
An eagle fierce, a bird of song,
And Skellig's hawk, the fierce and strong.
Hush, baby dear, etc.

I'll give, besides, the golden fleece
That Jason bore to glorious Greece;
The harp-sung steed that history boasts,
Cuchullin's - mighty chief of hosts!
Hush, baby dear, etc.

His spear who wrought great Hector's fall,
The mighty javelin of Fingal;
The coat of mail that Connal wore,
The shield that Naois in battle bore.
Hush, baby dear, etc.

Fingal's swift sword of death and fear,
And Diarmid's host-compelling spear;
The helm that guarded Oscar's head,
When fierce Mac Treon beneath him bled.
Hush, baby dear, etc.

Son of old chiefs! to thee is due
The gift Aoife gave her champion true,
That seal'd for aye Ferdia's doom,
And gave young Conlaoch to the tomb.
Hush, baby dear, etc.

Nor shall it be ungiven, unsung,
The mantle dark of Dulaing young,
That viewless left the chief who laid
Whole hosts beneath his battle blade!
Hush, baby dear, etc.

And eke a maid of modest mien,
Of charms beyond the Spartan queen,
Whose awful, soul-subduing charms
Mov'd Priam to dare a world in arms!
Hush, baby dear, etc.

For thee shall sparkle, in my lays,
Rich nectar from young Hebés vase,
Who fill'd the cup in heaven's abode,
For Jove, amid the feast of gods.
Hush, baby dear, etc.

Another boon shall grace thy hand,
Mac Duivne's life-protecting brand,
Great Aongus' gift, when Fenian foe
Pursu'd his path with shaft and bow!
Hush, baby dear, etc.

And dainty rich, and *beoir*[1] I'll bring,
And raiment meet for chief and king;

---

[1] [Walsh's note in *Irish Popular Songs*]: Beoir was delicious liquor, anciently made from mountain heath. Tradition asserts that the Danes alone possessed the secret of preparing it, and also that for this purpose they divided the heathy tracts among them, in preference to the arable land.

But gift and song shall yield to joy -
Thy mother comes to greet her boy!
Hush, baby dear, and weep no more;
Hush, baby mine, my treasur'd store;
My heart-wrung sigh, my grief, my groan,
Thy tearful eye, thy hunger's moan!

(100)
Caitilin Ni Uallachan[1]
(*Caitilin Ni Uallachain*)[2]

William Dall O'Heffernan. Ballad.

How sad our fate, driven desolate o'er moor and wild,
And lord and chief, in gloom and grief, from home exil'd,
Of songs divine, and feasts and wine, and science lorn,
We pine unseen for *Caitilín Ní Uallachán.*

Suppose not now that wrinkled brow, or unkempt hair,
Or long years' rigour did e'er disfigure the queenly Fair -
Her numerous Race would find their place on Erin's lawn,
If the prince had been with his *Caitilín Ní Uallachán.*

Fair were her cheek could we live to wreak the foeman's rout,
And flags would gleam to the breeze's stream o'er victory's shout;
And richest plaid on the happy maid may trail the lawn,
If the prince had been with his *Caitilín Ní Uallachán.*

We raise our eye with suppliant cry to the Lamb of Grace
Who form'd the tide - did the lands divide - gave hills their place -
Who spread around the seas profound, and bay, and lawn -
To change the scene for *Caitilín Ní Uallachán.*

Who Israel led where the Red Sea sped its waves of fear,
His table spread with Heaven's blest bread for forty years,
In favouring hour gave Moses power and freedom's dawn,
Shall come to screen his *Caitilín Ní Uallachán.*

---

[1] Published in *Irish Popular Songs*, pp. 118-121. - Ed.

[2] In this political poem, composed by blind William Heffernan, commonly called *Uilliam Dall*, Ireland is personified under the name of *Caitilín Ní Uallachán*, or Catharine ó Houlihan.

(101)
O Judith, my Dear[1]
(*A Shiobhan a Ruin*)[2]

O, Judith, my dear 'tis thou that hast left me for dead;
O, Judith, my dear, thou'st stolen all the brain in my head;
O, Judith, my dear, thou'st cross'd between Heaven and me,
And 'twere better be blind than ever thy beauty to see!

Thy person is peerless - a jewel full fashion'd with care,
Thou art the mild maiden so modest at market and fair,
With cheek like the rose, and kiss like the store o' the bee,
And musical tones that call'd me from death unto thee!

(102)
The Maid of Ballyhaunis[3]
(*Bruingioll Baile Shamnais*)[4]

Air: *Port Gordon.*

My Mary dear! for thee I die,
O! place thy hand in mine love -
My fathers here were chieftains high,
Then to my plaints incline, love.
O, Plaited-hair! that now we wear
In wedlock's band united,
For, maiden mine, in grief I'll pine,
Until our vows are plighted!

---

[1] Published in *Irish Popular Songs*, pp. 120-123. - Ed

[2] I found these fugitive lines untranslated in Hardiman's "Minstrelsy," and have taken the liberty of transferring them hither, and giving them an English dress, which they very richly deserve. *Siobhan* is Anglicised *Judith* by the Scotch, and *Johanna* by the Irish.

[3] Published in *Irish Popular Songs*, pp. 136-139. - Ed.

[4] *Baile-ath-Shamhnais.* Ballyhaunis, a market town in the barony of Costello, County Mayo. It had a monastery for friars of the order of St. Augustine, endowed by the family of Nagle, who, in after time, took the name of Costello. It subsisted till the reign of James I and at the insurrection of 1641 was restored by some friars of the same order. - Lewis' Topographical Dictionary.
Mr. Hardiman, who leaves this song untranslated in the first volume of the "Minstrelsy," says that it was composed by a friar of the monastery of Ballyhaunis, who fell in love with a beautiful girl of that place. With every respect for the superior information of Mr. Hardiman, I beg to say that this lyric, so creditable to the poetic genius of Connaught, and which stands forth among the happiest efforts of the pastoral muse of Ireland, was, in all likelihood, written by a youthful student of the monastery, as the second stanza bears clear proof that the lover is one not arrived at manhood, and who is subject to his father's control.

Thou Rowan-bloom, since thus I rove,
All worn and faint to greet thee,
Come to these arms, my constant love,
With love as true to meet me!
Alas! my head - its wits are fled,
I've fail'd in filial duty -
My sire did say, "Shun, shun, for aye
That Ballyhaunis beauty!"

But thy *Cúilin Bán*[1] I mark'd one day
Where the blooms of the bean-field cluster,
Thy bosom white like ocean's spray,
Thy cheek like rowan-fruit's lustre,
Thy tones that shame the wild bird's fame
Which sing in the summer weather -
And O! I sigh that thou, love, and I
Steal not from this world together!

If with thy lover thou depart
To the Land of Ships, my fair love,
No weary pain of head or heart
Shall haunt our slumbers there, love -
O! haste away, ere cold death's prey,
My soul from thee withdrawn is;
And my hope's reward, the churchyard sward,
In the town of Ballyhaunis!

(103)
The Lovely Maid[2]
(Ainnir Aluin)

An Mangaire Súgach. Ballad.

Long, long I'm worn and weak,
And pale my wasted cheek;
And groans have rent
Where shafts were sent

---

[1] *Cúilín bán*, fair flowing hair.
[2] Published in *Irish Popular Songs*, pp. 140-143. - Ed.

My inmost soul to seek -
My sense of joy is dead,
The church's wrath I dread;
I'm wild, unwise,
My vigour dies,
My wits are scattered, fled!

The love I do avow
The beauteous Star of Brogha,[1]
Hath heap'd dark blame
Upon my name,
And withering left me now -
Her hair, in wreathed flow,
Falls shining, quivering, low;
Her rich, ripe eye
Bids thousands die
Beneath its arrowy glow!

Lips, precious, musical,
Teeth, chalk-white, close-set, small;
Hand, smooth, and fair;
Form, statelier
Than wave-pois'd swan withal -
Once favouring heaven did will
That, downward o'er the hill,
Beside me came
The light-limb'd dame -
Faint tremblings through me thrill!

Low kneeling to the fay,
I vainly made essay
To melt her heart -
With shriek and start,
She wildly turn'd away:
"Begone!" the virgin said,
"Seducer, thou'st betrayed,
"With deed of guile,
"And tale and wile,
"Full many a Munster maid!"

---

[1] *Brogha*, Bruff, a town in the County Limerick.

(104)

Pulse of my Heart[1]

(*Cuisle mo Chroidhe*)

Air: *Cushla mo Chroidhe*.

Before the sun rose at yester-dawn,
I met a fair maid adown the lawn:
The berry and snow
To her cheek gave its glow,
And her bosom was fair as the sailing swan -
Then, pulse of my heart! what gloom is thine?

Her beautiful voice more hearts hath won
Than Orpheus' lyre of old had done;
Her ripe eyes of blue
Were crystals of dew,
On the grass of the lawn before the sun -
And, pulse of my heart! what gloom is thine?

(105)

Whoe'er she be, I love her[2]

(*Be 'n Eirinn I mo ghradh I*)

An Mangaire Súgach. Ballad.

Through pleasure's bowers I wildly flew,
Deceiving maids, if tales be true,
Till love's lorn anguish made me rue
That one young Fair-neck saw me,
Whose modest mien did awe me,
Who left my life to hover
O'er death's dark shade -
The stainless maid,
Whoe'er she be, I love her!

Her hair like quivering foliage flows,
Her heart no thought of evil knows,
Her face with purest virtue glows,

[1] Published in *Irish Popular Songs*, pp. 142-145- Ed.
[2] ibid., pp. 148-153. - Ed.

Her fame all hate defying -
While for her crowds are dying,
And round death's threshold hover,
Where I, for one,
Am nearly gone -
Whoe'er she be, I love her!

What beauteous teeth, and lip, and neck,
And eye and brow the maiden deck;
What red and white her cheek bespeak!
Like wave-pois'd swan she's fairest,
In virtue high she's rarest;
In her may none discover
One deed to blame -
Mild, modest dame,
Whoe'er she be, I love her!

But since soft ties are round us wove,
Which nought but death can e'er remove,
That balsam-bearing Lip of love
That spell-bound left me dying -
Now far together flying
The ocean-billows over,
Who can divide
From me my bride?
Whoe'er she be, I love her!

But first to Erne's lovely lake,
Where maids are gay, our course we'll take,
Where generous chiefs bright banquets make,
And purple wine is flowing;
Then from our dear friends going,
We'll sail the ocean over,
I and my dame
Of stainless fame -
Whoe'er she be, I love her!

Her secret name I'll not impart,
Although she pierc'd my wandering heart,

With such a death-dispensing dart
As love-sick left me lying,
In fiery torment dying,
Till pity mild did move her -
But wine of Spain
To her we'll drain,
Whoe'er she be, I love her.

(106)
Caitrin, the Daughter of John[1]
(*Caitrin Ní Sheoin*)[2]

Sing the Hunter of Bera[3] who from Ballagh came hither,
Our gates open'd wide to his coming at noon,
And the virgin whose coldness did suitors' hopes wither,
The snow-waisted Caitrin, the daughter of John!

There are tall sons of bravery that pine in her slavery;
Her eye all beguiling - small lips like the rose;
She's a jewel all splendid, of brightest hues blended,
Each gold-wreathed ringlet to her white ankle flows!

Now why should we wonder if thousands surrender,
Like Connor to Deirdre, their hearts to her chain;
Guiding light of the poet, of sun-glancing splendour,
The fairest in Erin of beauty's bright train!

O'er her kindred and nation she holds highest station,
Dispensing rich guerdons to minstrels of song;
Clan-Murray's fair darling - my harp's inspiration,
Bright swan of Lough Glynn, beauteous daughter of John!

---

[1] Published in *Irish Popular Songs*, pp. 156-159. - Ed.

[2] This song is the production of a Connaught bard. It seems to be an effusion in praise of the daughter of a western chief, at whose residence the person whom the minstrel styles the *Hunter of Bera*, had arrived. This spirited outburst of song was certainly a characteristic made of introducing the "Hunter of Bera" to the "Bright Swan of Lough Glynn."

[3] Bera. Bearhaven, a territory in the south-west of the County Cork, the patrimony of the O'Sullivan Bear. *Ballagh*, or *Balla*, a village in the Barony of Claremorris, County Mayo. It has an ancient round tower.

(107)
Owen Roe O'Sullivan's Drinking Song[1]
(*Ól-dán Eoghan Ruaidh Ui Shúilleabháin*)

Eoghan Ruadh Ó Súilleabháin.

This cup's flowing measure
I toast to that treasure,
The brave man whose pleasure
Is quaffing rich wine,
Who deep flagons draining,
From quarrels abstaining,
The morn finds remaining
All joyous divine -
It ne'er shall be mine
To gather vile coin,
To clowns at life's waning,
For aye to resign!

Some churls will come slinking,
To practise cheap drinking,
Where the generous are linking
New joys to the old -
Vile starveling! what matter
If curses should shatter
Your landmarks, and scatter
To strangers your gold!
When laid in the mould,
All naked and cold,
Your dames thus may patter
Your death-song, behold: -

"Let heroes strike under;
At Paris why wonder,
Or Jason, who plunder
From dragons did rive?
The red-branched hero

[1] Published in *Irish Popular Songs*, pp. 162-167. - Ed.

May sink down to zero;
And Caesar and Nero
In vain with him strive.
Let the rich herds arrive
That in Munster survive,
And I'll yield them, my dear, oh!
To clasp thee alive!

"My soul! how grief's arrow
Hath fix'd in my marrow!
O'er that cold coffin narrow
I'll weep evermore -
By the hand of my father!
This moment I'd rather
From the grave thee to gather,
Than gold's yellow store!
All feasts I'll give o'er;
I'm stricken and frore -
Oh, grave at Kilmather,
Be my rooftree and floor!

"My bosom friends inner,
Gather round your poor sinner;
My kerchief and pinner
To pieces shall go.
In the Lee wildly springing,
I'll end this beginning,
His death-song still singing
Who valued me so" -
While round tears thus flow,
And wailing and woe,
To a youth near her clinging;
She beckons alow!

(108)
Come to the Hedgerows[1]
(*O Tar Amach Liomsa*)

O come to the hedgerows
With gay flowers all bright,
When the green fields are smiling
Beneath the sun's light.
Through the green fields we'll wander
The long happy day
While the little birds are singing
Merrily "O come, come away."

O come to the sea-side
To hear the wild waves.
On the dark rocks we'll stand
While the storm wildly raves.
And we'll watch the white sea gulls
Through tempest and spray.
While the mighty ocean rages fierce
And loud, "O come, come away."

(109)
My Pretty Girl Milking the Cow[2]
(*Mo Cailín Deas Crúidhte Na mBó*)

The beam on the streamlet was playing
The dewdrop still hung on the thorn
When a blooming young couple were straying
To taste the mild fragrance of morn.
He sighed as he breathed forth his ditty
And she felt her breast softly to glow
Oh look on your lover with pity
Mo cailín deas crúidhte na mbó.

---

[1] Sr. de Lourdes Gogarty of the Mercy convent Cappoquin told me that this English version is by Edward Walsh.- Ed.

[2] This is the text as given in Sparling's *Irish Minstrelsy*, where the song is entered as *Anon.* - Ed.

While green is your bank's mossy pillow,
Or evening shall weep the soft tear,
Or the streamlet shall steal 'neath the willow,
So long shall thy image be dear.
O fly to these arms for protection,
If pierced by the arrow of woe,
Then smile on my tender affection,
Mo cailín deas crúidhte na mbó.

She sighed as his ditty was ended,
Her heart was too full to reply;
O joy and compassion were blended,
To light the mild beam of her eye.
He kissed her soft hand: "What above thee
Could Heaven in its bounty bestow?"
He kissed her soft cheek: "Ah, I love thee!
Mo cailín deas crúidhte na mbó.

(110)

My Hope, My Love[1]

(*A Chumain sa Sheárc*)

My hope, my love, we will proceed
Into the woods, scattering the dews,
Where we will behold the salmon, and the ousel in its nest,
The deer and the roebuck calling,
The sweetest bird on the branches warbling,
The cuckoo on the summit of the green hill;
And death shall never approach us
In the bosom of the fragrant wood!

[1] Published in the "Introduction" to *Irish Popular Songs*, pp. 20-21. - Ed.

WALSH'S TRANSLATION FROM THE GERMAN?

(111)
The Garden Rose[1]

A garden rose was seen to droop down from its tender stalk,
By a little child, that playfully was sporting on the walk;
The child admired its beauteous hue, and as he gazed he thought,
He'd like to have the lovely thing, 'twas with such fragrance fraught.

He drew him near, 'twas blushing with maturity of bloom,
And all the air was laden with the sweets of its perfume;
He plucked it - with a sudden cry he cast the flower away,
For, closely hid beneath its leaves, a piercing thorn lay.

The rose was scattered on the ground, its loveliness was gone,
The little child was crying now at what the thorn had done.
Weep not, fair child, nor deem it strange, for older ones than thou
Have often felt the secret thorn that thus has hurt thee now.

Look life throughout, its pleasures thus are pleasing to the view,
But, like the rose, a thorn is couched beneath their lovely hue;
Then weep not, weep not, little child, that thus thy hand is torn,
The honeybee still bears a sting, the fairest rose a thorn.

[1] This translation of Goethe's *Heiden Roslein* was published in the *Dublin Penny Journal*, October 10th. 1835 where it was initialled W. If this is the work of Edward Walsh, one has to conclude that he had knowledge of German or was using a pre-existing translation; or is this the work of J.C. Mangan using the initial 'W'? - Ed.

Return of King Charles

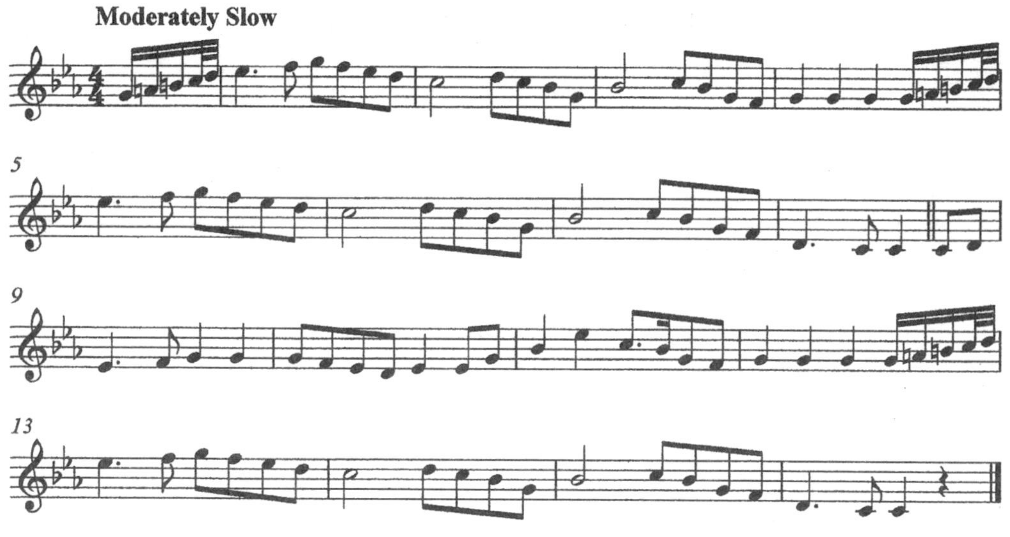

The Expected of Ireland

Captivity of the Gael

Eire's Maid is She

The Lady of Alba's Lament for King Charles

The Twisting of the Rope

Have you been to Carrick?

Black-haired Fair Rose

The Maid of the Fine Flowing Hair

My Pretty Girl milking the Cow

Mo Chraoibhin Aoibhin Aulin

Leading the Calves

The Dark maid of the Valley

Over the Hills and Far Away

Harp of Erin Quit thy Slumbers

The Fair Young Child

One Clear Summer Morning

Cormac Oge

Amber-haired Nora

The Graceful Maiden

Little Celia Connellan

The Dawning of the Day

For Ireland I'd not tell her Name

Farewell to Maig

Caithlin ní Uallachan

The Song of Freedom

The Expulsion of the Saxon

The Fair Hills of Eire Ogh

Donal Dhu

Lament for the Gael

Maid of Ballyhaunis

Pulse of my Heart

Flower of Brown-Haired Maidens

Lullaby

The Cruel Base-Born Tyrant

Appendix II

Opinions of the Press[1] - The *Jacobite Reliques*

We have already noticed the collection of Jacobite relics and other songs in course of publication in penny numbers by Mr. Daly of Kilkenny. It has arrived at the fifth number without any diminution of interest. Each song is accompanied by an interlinear translation, and a metrical version by Mr. Edward Walsh, the writer of some popular poetry in this Journal. We notice it, at present, to extract a favourite relic of great beauty from the last number.

Nothing can be better calculated to promote the reading of the Irish Language among the people than a publication, so popular in price and spirit; and we trust the Catholic Clergy, and the Teetotal Societies will put it in their way." - *Nation.*

We think the public are deeply indebted to Mr. Daly, for the production of this National Work: independently of its value as an addition to our national literature, its influence in a political point of view will be very great, perhaps incalculable. He was a profound Statesman who said, 'Give me the making of a Nation's Songs, and I care not who makes her laws.' - *Limerick Reporter.*

A service will thus be rendered to our National Literature, and many of the sweetest compositions of our ancient bards, will be rescued from that everlasting oblivion to which they were hastening. Another service will be rendered to the country. These Songs for the most part, breathe a spirit of holy patriotism; and their importance, at the present moment, in fanning the flame of nationality, can hardly be over-estimated. - *Kilkenny Journal.*

Mr. Daly of Kilkenny has published the third number of his collection of Irish Songs, giving translations word for word, accompanied by truly beautiful poetical translations by Edward Walsh. Mr. Walsh has been the author of some of the most admire Songs published in the Nation Newspaper, and was previously known to the Irish public, as possessing in a high degree, the talents and acquirements necessary to constitute a successful poet. From the specimens before us, we would anticipate that, in conjunction with Mr. Daly, he will be enabled to make important and truly acceptable additions to the stores of native poetry and music, available to the different classes of the Irish people. The Songs hitherto given are excellent, breathing the genuine spirit of Ireland. - *Wexford Independent.*

We agree with our excellent contemporary, the *Drogheda Argus*, in thinking that they (the Songs) may be rendered subservient to a further purpose, and would afford the most valuable help in leaning the language for the first time. Speaking of one of the Songs, 'The Peril of Britain,' it says 'It is like the rest a Jacobite production, breathing forth the burning

[1] Views on the Walsh-Daly publications in 1844; reprinted in the first edition of *Reliques.*

soul of the enslaved and plundered Irishman, wrapped in his maddening dream of liberation and vengeance. - *Wexford Independent.*

The Songs published by Mr. Daly, we would earnestly recommend to the perusal of men of all classes - those who can sympathise in the sentiments expressed, and those who cannot - those who understand the ancient language of our country, and those who do not; all can derive from them instruction not elsewhere readily acquired. - *Wexford Independent.*

If we were to judge from the excellent arrangement and the beautiful form in which this work before us is brought out, highly creditable to the taste and enterprise of the writer and publisher, we shall say that the matter is worthy of the manner, and the manner of the matter - a rich substance clothed in rich garments; every Irishman should subscribe to the work, it is exceedingly cheap. - *Kerry Examiner.*

Among the 'Signs' which indicate the growing spirit of Nationality in Ireland, not the least worthy of note is the publication of various relics of ancient Irish Poetry. We have before us a series of 'Penny Numbers,' of old Irish Ballads, collected by Mr. John Daly of Kilkenny, and furnished with interlinear translations, for publication, with an English metrical version by Mr. Edward Walsh, who is, we believe, one of the poetical contributors to the Nation Newspaper. They form a valuable help to persons desirous to acquire a knowledge of the Irish Language. - *Drogheda Argus.*

We sincerely wish every success to Mr. Daly's creditable effort to sustain the growing spirit of Nationality, by giving us a collection of Songs in our vernacular tongue, which 'is not dead but speaketh [sleepeth?],' notwithstanding the efforts of foreign tyranny to extinguish it altogether. The Songs are, on the whole, excellent, and afford satisfactory evidence to the facility with which the Irish Language can be brought into poetical or musical composition. The translations are good; and the historical expositions and illustrative notes, at once entertaining and instructive. - *Chronicle & Munster Advertiser.*

We have so often expressed our approbation of the manner in which all parties, concerned in getting out the admirable Irish Songs collected by Mr. Daly, perform their respective duties, that we need now scarcely repeat it. In justice to Mr. Walsh, the poetical translator, however, we feel bound to say that, in the last number we have received, he affords one more convincing proof of a genius equal, if not superior to his original, and this is no mean praise. The Song commenced in the previous number, under the title of 'Captivity of the Gael' - though for brevity's sake, and for different reasons, we may call it Shaun Bui - is continued in the present, and Mr. Walsh's version fully realises the highest anticipations we could form from the happiest and most vigorous of his foregoing efforts. - *Wexford Independent.*

We understand Mr. Daly purposes editing his songs for the future in monthly, instead of weekly parts, as he finds they do not pay the outlay upon their publication in the latter form. We cordially invite public support to his patriotic undertaking. The English versions of the Songs, by Mr. Edward Walsh, are highly creditable to his abilities as a poet. We think them much better than those furnished by Furlong and others of Hardiman's 'Irish Minstrelsy.' - Belfast *Vindicator.*

This is an extremely interesting publication of Irish Songs. They are given in the Vernacular with an interlinear translation, and also translated into beautiful English verse. There are historical illustrative notes by Mr. Daly. The publication as a whole, nationally speaking, is a great credit to the country. Many of the songs are written in a spirit of true poetry. But, instead of a critique, we shall give one or two of the songs at random, which will speak more than any thing we could say. - *Cork Examiner.*

"We have received a number of "Reliques of Irish Jacobite Poetry." We would wish to have those reliques preserved, but with a spirit and sentiment less reprehensible, and not so likely to foster a bad feeling amongst an irritable people, as we Irishmen are. The 'Sketches' could do all that can be required by the most ardent of Erin's sons, and yet advocate a spirit of peace and reconciliation to the rising generation of both countries. One good, however, will be effected by their publication; and [...] good; for we would wish to have it preserved, namely, the desire of learning the Irish language. Is it by their publication that Mr. Smith O'Brien has been induced to study, at this advanced hour of his day-life, the Irish language? We shall be glad to receive the remaining numbers. - *Clare Journal.*

Opinions of the Press - *Irish Popular Songs*

Mr. Walsh has done a service to our national language by his metrical translations, in which we feel quite confident the spirit of the original is preserved as the measure is, so as to emit the 'song-tune' of the Irish ballad. The little volume is brought out in an attractive dress, at a low price, and must prove an accession to our national literary collection. – *Dublin Warder.*

The translation of these songs has brought to his task a thoroughly competent knowledge and appreciation of the Irish language, considerable practice and aptitude for translation, and poetic feeling. Mr. Walsh has done in this instance, what should be done in all cases where the pieces are numerous enough to fill a separate publication, given the translation on the one page, the original on the opposite. The style of the rendering is free, smooth, and pleasing, and not infrequently at once vigorous and harmonious. – *Dublin Weekly Register.*

Appendix III

Emigration to Queensland[1]

Yesterday about four hundred emigrants - men, women, and children - embarked on board the *Erin Go Bragh*, one of the Black Ball Line of Australian packets, for Queensland, Australia. They were principally from Tullamore and its vicinity, in the King's County and were accompanied by the Rev. P. Dunn, a Catholic clergyman who has already resided seven or eight years in the Australian colonies, two or three of which he spent in Queensland. This gentleman is going out expressly with the emigrants, in order to look after them on the way, and to assist them in getting employment as soon after their arrival as possible. The party, in fact was made up by his exertions altogether. On visiting his native place, after his return from Australia, he could not help contrasting the wretched and almost hopeless condition of the poor struggling farmers he saw about him - many of them with eviction constantly impending over their heads, and living in continual dread of utter ruin - with the comfort, prosperity, and independence of those he had left behind in the Australian colonies, and he determined on an effort to lead a number of them at least to a land where their labour and industry would meet with fair protection and reward. Under his advice, accordingly, a number of the inhabitants of Tullamore and its vicinity prepared themselves to quit their native land, and to seek far better fortunes at the other side of the tropics. The colony to which they are going is one which is described as possessing great natural advantages as regards fertility, salubrity and climate, and fitness for trade. It is a new British colony, comprising the whole north-eastern portion of Australia and covers an area equivalent to about three times the area of France, and to ten times the area of England and Wales. The following extract from a small work on the colony, by Mr. Henry Jordan, a member of the Legislative Assembly gives a briefer general description of the face of the country - "The coast line is picturesque, presenting more variety, and features of greater interest and beauty, than most other portions of the Australian sea board. The country is always green, presenting a succession of flats and ridges, well grassed, and finely timbered, or spreading out into extensive plains, waving with nutritious grass, or covered with flowering herbage. Ranges of mountains run parallel with the coast line, at a distance of sixty or seventy miles, with their spurs running out upon the more level lands towards the sea, diversifying the scenery, and giving rise to a multitude of streams and rivers; of these, many are broad and navigable for many miles inland; their banks, formed generally of the best alluvial soil, are finely grassed and wooded." The table lands formed by the mountains in the interior are also extremely rich in soil, and suitable in every respect for pastures. Mr.

---

[1] *North Australian* newspaper, Ipswich, Thursday, May 1st, 1862, p. 4.; copied from the *Cork Examiner*, February 8th. 1862.

Jordan thus describes the climate: - “The climate closely resembles that of Madeira. The temperature is more constant than in many other regions within the isothermal lines. This equalisation is due partly to the sea breeze tempering the heat of the summer, and partly to the copious rains which fall during the hottest months of the year. The peculiar coolness and dryness of the atmosphere, as compared with the latitude, has been explained by the intense and active evaporation which takes place in this part of Australia. The absence of the hot winds that frequently afflict the other Australian colonies further accounts for the comparative coolness of the climate in Queensland. During a large proportion of the year the weather is fine, the sky cloudless, the atmosphere dry, elastic, and exonerating. The summer months (December, January and February) are hot, but not sultry or oppressive. The winter season, when dry (as it almost invariably is), is exceedingly beautiful and agreeable. The mornings and evenings are cool, during the day the air is warm and balmy, the sky brilliantly blue, and the atmosphere singularly transparent.” The soil of the colony is suitable for almost every description of production, and there is no doubt that one day its agricultural products will prove to it a great source of wealth and power, as well as a welcome supply to the inhabitants of less favoured or more densely populated regions. Cotton of the best description and the sugar cane can be cultivated there most successfully. Great advantages are offered to immigrants in the purchase of land, and as wages of mechanics and tradesmen average very high, it is easy for a man of ordinary steady and prudent habits to become in a short time after his arrival - even though without a penny on landing - an independent and prosperous proprietor. It is to this rich and genial region that Father Dunn is leading the party of emigrants whom he induced to fly from the misery and, in many cases, landlord oppression of their own country, to seek positions of comfort, independence, and self-respect elsewhere. Several of the party are taking out a considerable amount of capital to invest in land, but most are going to seek employment. For these latter, however, arrangements have been made by the Right Rev. Dr. Quinn, Catholic Bishop of Brisbane, Queensland, with whom the Rev. Mr. Dunn has been in communication, for enabling all, both male and female, to procure employment as soon as possible after their arrival. Wishing to avoid the troubles, vexations, and accidents of various kinds attendant on going to Liverpool to take shipping, the Rev. Mr. Dunn made arrangements with the Messrs. Baines, the agents for the Black Ball packets, to have on of their ships call at Cork, as the most convenient port, where the emigrants were to meet it; and the *Erin Go Bragh* was accordingly sent here for the purpose. In consequence, however, of the storms which raged in the Channel for several weeks, the arrival of the vessel here was considerably delayed, though the *Retriever*, a powerful steam tug belonging to the new Liverpool Steam-tug Company, was towing her across. She left Liverpool yesterday fortnight, but so severe were the gales which she encountered, that the tug ran short of coals twice, and was obliged to put back to Hollyhead. The unfavourable state of the weather necessarily caused some derangement to the passengers, who arrived in Cork on

Monday week, and were obliged to wait here until yesterday, but by the care and watchfulness of the Rev. Mr. Dunn, and the allowance of 1s 6d a day made by Messrs. Baines to each passenger, they suffered little or no inconvenience beyond the loss of time; and the advice and influence of their reverend director restrained the more impatient and thoughtless from any troublesome display of petulance or vexation at the delay. The attention, however, paid by the gentleman who had come over on the part of the firm to the passengers was very great, and they evinced every anxiety to aid them in every way, so much so that the Rev. Mr. Dunn acknowledged their kindness warmly. Mr. Percival, a gentleman connected with the Steam Tug Company, to whom the tug Retriever belongs, was also most attentive, and showed every readiness to afford what accommodation was in his power. The ship having arrived yesterday morning, the work of embarkation commenced without delay. One of the Citizen's River Steamer Company's boats was employed to take down the passengers and their luggage from Cork, and about five o'clock all were placed safely on board. Nine of the passengers are going as first class and the remainder as intermediate and steerage passengers. The Erin-go-bragh is a very favourable specimen of the improved style of the passenger ship. She is a fine full rigged, copper bottom vessel, of 1,129 tons register, well and strongly built; and her capacity as a sea going vessel was fully tested in the heavy gales she encountered on her passage from Liverpool, when, to quote the language of her captain, "every timber in her was tried" but she arrived here without the slightest damage of any kind. She has a raised quarter deck, under which, on a level with the main deck, run the first and second cabins, both lofty and well ventilated, the former fitted up in the style of luxury to be observed in most or all of the first class packet ships and the latter, though plainly fitted up and with no attempt at ornament or luxury, yet possessing all the requisites that could be had at sea, for the convenience and comfort of passengers. The entire length of the 'tween deck is fitted up for steerage passengers, and the appearance and arrangements of the place, though seen yesterday under very favourable circumstances - being in a state of regular confusion, with the four hundred emigrants and their luggage which had just arrived on board, and with the work of stowing away hardly commenced - afforded a strong and pleasant contrast to the old emigrant ships into which our countrymen formerly crowded in their search for other lands. The height from deck to deck is 8 feet 6 inches at the lowest part, and 8 feet 11 inches, or within one inch of nine feet, at the highest. There are three separate divisions - a partition being raised between each - one for single men, another for married people, and another for unmarried females, and thus those temptations to vice and immorality, the consequences of which on board emigrant ships have been so much deplored, are entirely avoided. The division of the married people is amidships, and it thus separates the other two, the young women's division adjoining it towards the stern, and the young men's towards the bow. The division of the married people is provided with state rooms, thus securing to the different families a good deal of privacy when necessary. Every precaution seems to have been taken for the comfort and convenience of the passengers in the fitting up; the tables are so constructed, that, when not required for use, they can be raised up so as to be entirely out of the way, and to leave room for moving about. The ventilation is also most excellent, the contrivance being such as to secure it thoroughly along the entire of the 'tween decks, and suited for increasing or decreasing it at pleasure. The commander of the vessel, Captain Borlase, evinced a care and anxiety for the care and comfort of all the passengers during the process of embarkation yesterday, which augurs well for them during the voyage; in fact, so arduous did he seem for their comfort and well being, that he intimated his intention of not putting to sea, until all were comfortably arranged and provided with berths, and had their luggage properly stowed. This, it was anticipated, would be accomplished by this afternoon. The Rev. Mr. Dunn will not leave his party until he has seen them all fully provided for in the colony, and should success equal to what he anticipates crown his efforts, he will return for another batch. The Rev. Mr. Dunn expresses himself much gratified with the attention and kindness of the different officials with whom he and his party came in contact in making their arrangements; but he complains of the treatment received at the hands of the Great Southern and Western Railway Company, or rather of their officers. The arrangements with them was that they should supply a special train to start from Tullamore at an early hour in the morning, so as to reach Cork by half-past one. In this respect, however, the engagement was not fulfilled; the train did not arrive until half-past seven in the evening, when it was too late to go in search of suitable lodgings. The parties were, in consequence, obliged to go to boarding houses for the night, which imposed on them much additional expenses. It was also stated that the carriages were in a bad condition and let in the rain.

Appendix IV

Obituary of Adam Edward Walsh[1]

The death occurred yesterday, at his residence, South East Bundaberg, at the ripe age of 83 years 6 months, of Mr. A.E. Walsh, a very old and highly esteemed resident of Bundaberg, and a citizen who, in the primitive days of settlement, had done a full share in working out the development and destiny of the town and district. The deceased gentleman was the eldest son of the union of the late Edward Walsh, the renowned Irish poet and translator, and Bridgid O'Sullivan and was born at Tourin, County Waterford, Ireland on 17th June 1841. At the early age of 11 years he selected a seafaring life, his first voyage being made to America, at a time in world history when conditions were not nearly so comfortable for the sailor as is the case today. At the age of 17 years he joined the United States Reserve Service, in February 1858, continuing his associations therewith until November 1860. On the outbreak of the American Civil War he joined up with the United States navy, being drafted to the Sloop "Macedonia" from which vessel he was discharged from military service in October 1867. Then learning that his mother was seriously ill in Queensland, to which colony she had in the meantime migrated, he set out from San Francisco for this State, arriving here on 20th December of the same year. However the sea seemed to have cast a spell over his spirit for after spending some time in Warwick and Dalby, he was placed in charge of the Moreton Bay Light ship after which he linked up with the Pilot Service, Maryborough, in August, 1874. Being transferred to the Lighthouse Service in January, 1877, the deceased in turn controlled the Sandy Cape and Lady Elliott Island Lighthouse until 12th May, 1878, when he was transferred to the Customs Department, and was stationed at Maryborough. After 10 years service under the late Mr. A.B. Sherridan, sub-collector, he was transferred to Cairns, where after a stay of some ten months, he (owing to the continued ill health of his family) applied for, and was successful in obtaining a transfer to Bundaberg, where he arrived in April, 1888. Continuing in the service in Bundaberg till he reached the retiring age in 1905, since then he had lived in a quiet and well-earned retirement at his home in Boundary Street. He is survived by his widow, three sons and three daughters, namely Messrs, Brian and Edward (Bundaberg) and Minnie (at home), and also by a sister, Mrs. M.F. O'Sullivan of Warwick, to whom all sections of the community will be joined in extending condolence in their period of deep affliction. The funeral will take place at 3 p.m. today leaving deceased's late residence for the General Cemetery, the arrangements being in the hands of Messrs. F.C. Browne and Co.

[1] The *Bundaberg Mail*, Jan. 22nd 1925.

5113859

DEATH

DEATH in the District of Bundaberg in the State of Queensland.

1925 Registered by James Ambrose Murray District Registrar

Marginal notes (if any)	Column		
	1 Number	60	9464
	DESCRIPTION - 2 When died and where	21st January 1925 Boundary Street Bundaberg	
	3 Name and surname; profession, trade, or occupation	Adam Edward WALSH Retired	
	4 Sex and age	Male 83 years 6 months 4 days	
	5 1. Cause of death	Senectus	
	2. Duration of last illness	-	
	3. Medical attendant by whom certified	Egmont Schmidt	
	4. When he last saw deceased ..	18th January 1925	
	6 Name and surname of father .. .. Profession, trade, or occupation ..	Edward Walsh Poet and Translator	
	Name and maiden surname of mother	Bridgid O'Sullivan	
	7 Signature, description, and residence of informant	Certified in writing by Brian S. Walsh, Son, Walker Street, Bundaberg.	
	8 1. Signature of Registrar	Jas. A. Murray	
	2. Date	22nd January 1925	
	3. Place of registration	Bundaberg	
	If Burial or Cremation Registered - 9 When and where buried or cremated	22nd January 1925 Bundaberg General Cemetery	
	By whom certified	F.C. Brown	
	10 Name and religion of minister, and/or names of two witnesses of burial or cremation	M.G. Reuther Lutheran A.G. Stollznow W.C. May	
	11 Where born and how long in Australia States, stating which	Towrin Waterford Ireland 56 years in Queensland	
	If deceased was married - 12 1. Where	Maryborough Queensland	
	2. At what age	33 years	
	3. To whom	Charlotte Josephine Anderson	
	13 Issue living, in order of birth, their names and ages	Living Brian Sarsfield 47 Hilda 45 Minnie 44 Francis 42 Adam Edward 38 Edward 35	years
	Deceased, number and sex	Deceased 1 Male 1 Female	

CAUTION:- Whosoever shall unlawfully alter any Certified Copy of an entry in any Register of Births, Marriages, or Deaths, whether by erasure, obliteration, removal, addition, or otherwise is guilty of a CRIME, and is liable to the punishment by law provided in that behalf. (Vide Sections 486 and 488 of the "Criminal Code.")

I, Desmond Barry Tanner, Registrar-General, do hereby certify that the above is a true copy of an entry in a Register of Deaths kept in the General Registry Office at Brisbane, and I further certify that I am a person duly authorised by law to issue such certificate.

Extracted on 19 November 1999

Exd. by

Tanner

Registrar-General

N.B. Not Valid Unless Bearing the Authorised Seal and Signature of the Registrar-General

Fig. 30. Death Certificate of Adam Edward Charles Walsh, son of Edward & Bridgid.

Appendix V

Obituary of Bridget, wife of Edward Walsh[1]

It is with feelings of much regret that we are called upon to chronicle the demise of a very old and respected lady, in the person of Mrs. Bridget Flynn, mother of Mrs. M.F. O'Sullivan, of Guy-street, and of Mr. E.C. Walsh, of Woodlands, Inglewood. The deceased lady passed away late on Sunday afternoon[2], the cause of death, which was not unexpected, being general break-up of the system. She had been an invalid for many years, and was confined to her room for the past six months, during which time she was cared for with the greatest devotion by her daughter. The late Mrs. Flynn was born in the County of Waterford, near the banks of the Blackwater, and was 77 years of age at the time of her death. She had married twice – first to the late Mr. Edward Walsh, of Cork, Ireland, and then to the late Mr. J.W. Flynn, chemist, of Dalby. Mr. Walsh, her first husband, was one of Ireland's illustrious poets and translator of the "Irish Jacobite Reliques." His works were very much appreciated for the beauty of the verse and the sincerity of the sentiments which permeated them, and at his death in 1859[3] the people of Cork by public subscription had a monument erected to his memory in the local cemetery, thus immortalising his name until the end of time. To show that the poet was not forgotten by his countrymen even after a lapse of years the restoration of the monument, the lettering on which having become obliterated, was made the occasion of a great demonstration in Cork some four years ago. The late Mrs. Flynn leaves three sons and one daughter to mourn her loss, all whom have reached the age of maturity, and are much respected residents of the colony. Deceased earned the respect of all she came in contact for her many sterling qualities. She lived a thoroughly Christian life, and died as we all hope to when our time comes – peacefully and happily. The funeral took place yesterday, and was largely attended, the long *cortege* of carriages and horsemen which followed her remains to their last resting place testifying to the respect that was felt for the deceased lady. The Rev. Father Horan officiated at the grave. We condole with Mrs. O'Sullivan and Mr. Walsh, of Inglewood, in their sad bereavement.

---

[1] *Warwick Examiner and Times*, April 14th 1897, p.3.

[2] In a letter of May 7th 2000, Elizabeth Nunn gave me the following details on the death of her great-great grandmother: "Bridged did not die until 11 April 1897. She is buried at Warwick (Qld) Cemetery and her grave is in excellent repair. (Whenever I go through Warwick I visit her grave). Bridget died on Palm Sunday and, interestingly, the inscription on her grave does not give the date of her death, just that it was on Palm Sunday in 1897. (As an aside, my grandmother, Bridget's grand-daughter, had Bridget as her second given name. When I was a child, I always remember my grandmother making a fuss about Palm Sunday, but never explained why, in my presence anyway. It was only, as an adult, that I realised why when I discovered Bridget's grave)."

[3] The writer confuses the year of Walsh's death (1850) with the date the monument was erected to his memory, an event which happened close on a decade later.

Glossary

a brahir: kinsman, cousin, brother.

a chierhah, achierna: an expletive, Lord!

a chorra, a chorra: friend.

achree, a-chree, achree: term of endearment, darling, love of my heart.

a cuid: a term of endearment.

a cushla: my heart-throb. A term of endearment

a goun: a term of endearment, lit. a *rún*, my secret.

a gragl: a term of endearment, lit. my bright love.

agrah: love.

agus bhe dhe husth: and be quiet!

agus meela failthe, agus mela failte: and a thousand welcomes.

aithir nimhe: the devil, lit. the father of poison.

alanna, alanna ma chree: child, child of my heart.

a-leah, a lea: an exclamation of sorrow or regret.

Amhan-mhor: the Munster Blackwater

amin, a-hiern, amin a chierna, chiernah: the response to a toast, 'Amen Lord!'

a mock: son.

amplush: nonplussed.

anagh: is that so (sometimes with overtones of incredulity or impossibility).

angishore: a person not well fitted for life.

Aodh beg an bridán: Little Hugh of the Salmon.

Araglin, Araglen: a tributary river of the Upper Blackwater in Duhallow, Co. Cork.

aroon: a term of endearment, darling, lit. secret.

arrigedh sheesh: money down!

asthore: a term of endearment, lit. my treasure.

astore machree: a term of endearment, lit. treasure of my heart.

avick: son.

a virra-na-glora: an exclamation of surprise or delight, lit. Oh Mary of Heaven.

avirra yealish: an exclamation, lit. dear Mary!

a vorneen, a vourneen bawn: my darling, my fair darling.

a vrahir: brother, kinsman, cousin.

a will na gerane urth? have you the sharp things on? (i.e. spurs!).

bara-boo: a trumpet-like instrument.

Batha Phadraig: Life of Patrick.

Ben-Edar: Howth Head.

bethersin: may be so! perhaps!

betagh: a low-class person, semi-slave on the land in ancient times.

Bianconi: a coach, named after the Italian entrepreneur of that name.

Bior: a drink made by the Danes (Vikings).
boccagh, boccaughs, buckaugh: a cripple, especially if it is a man of the roads.
bodachs: churls.
borheen: little road.
bouchal gannuile: handsome boy.
Bran: Finn McCool's hound, said to live still in Loch Lene, Killarney.
breshagh: kindling material for a fire.
brien banaha urth aliniv frein: a drop of holy water on you, fair child.
brog, brogues: a shoe, heavy boots.
brohogues: potatoes roasted on embers.
buckeen: a little squire, an upstart.
bulim sciath: a boaster, lit. a shield bearer.
by gar: an exclamation, by God!
cabogues: churls, vulgar persons.
carough: a gambler.
carrig: a rock, a boulder.
carrigawn, carigaun: rough, scabby land.
caubeen: a homespun cap.
ceannabhán, kanavane: bog cotton.
Chiel: child(?).
chora: friend.
Christ Chriestha arin!: the Cross of Christ be upon us!
cione: a dirge, lament.
clachaun: a small settlement of dwellings.
clairseach: the Irish harp.
Clarah: a mountain near Millstreet, Co. Cork.
clashmaclaver: gossip.
Cleena, Cleana, Cliodhna: the fairy queen of South Munster.
clegalpeen, cligh-alpeen: a stout walking stick.
cloheena-greena: a small translucent stone said to be enchanted.
cluhericane: a tiny inhabitant of the fairy world.
Cnoc-maol Donn: Knockmealdown Mountains on Waterford-Tipperary border.
cochal: a cloak.
coire: friendly.
colleen ayrigh: a bright pleasant girl.
collen dubh dheas: lovely dark-haired girl.
coologue, collough, coologue: riding pillion passenger on horse.
Conan Maol, Conan: a member of the Fianna.
cool: the goal line in a match.

Coolin: a fair haired girl.
coollughta, cool-lughta: back corner.
Cormac: a member of the fianna.
corohan: a sailing vessel.
corp an Doul: expletive, my body to the devil, lit. body of the devil.
Corraghs: marshes.
coshering: gathering.
cosh-na-breeda: a traditional tune, lit. by the [river] Bride.
cotamore, cota-more: overcoat.
crahadore: plunderer, taker of spoils.
cran-tubal: a sling.
crathers: creatures, a term of pity, compassion, etc.
creagh, creghs: booty, spoils.
Crohan's fairy halls: the royal residence at Rathcrohan, Co. Roscommon.
Crom: a Celtic god of thunder.
Crom-a-boo: the cry of victory. Long live Crom!
cronans: croonings, hummings, purrings.
crotal, crothal: a bell-sounding instrument.
Cruachan: palace of the kings of Connaught (Crohan's fairy halls) in Roscommon.
crucskeen: a little jug.
cruipper: the strap looped under a horse's tail as part of the harness
Crush Chriest duin: an exclamation, the Cross of Christ to us!
cummer: a ravine, a valley.
cur-an-aigh-an-cuim: 'crooked and straight'
cushla, a-cushla, acushla: a term of endearment, lit. my heart-throb.
dallan: a pillar stone, usually associated with megalithic sites.
Daloo: a Duhallow river which joins the Blackwater near Roskeen Bridge.
Damer: (1630-1720) An English adventurer in Ireland with the reputation of being a wealthy miser.
De Profundis: Ps. 129, repentance, lit. out of the depths.
deanthuis: a make-up, a composition.
deerhogh: the (female) attendant at a holy well or shrine.
Dermid Dhu: Dark Dermot.
Dermid O'Duin, Dearmid: a member of the Fianna.
dhalteen: a term of endearment esp. for a little child, little pet.
dhineushla: sirs, lit. noble persons.
dhinusal, a-yinusal: sir, lit. noble person.
dhokawn: an improvised wind instrument made from holding a piece of strong grass tightly between the thumbs.

dhroundel: jaw.
Donall Caum: The Ó Sullivan Bere.
Donall na Geela: the Celtic god of the dead and the underworld.
donan: wreck.
Doon: A townland south of Kiskeam.
drass: bout.
drimin-dubh: black spotted cow.
drisheen: the stomach of sheep; associated with a special Cork dish.
Drumscartha: a townland near Kiskeam, lit. the hill of the parting.
dudeen: a short-stemmed [clay] tobacco pipe.
dunawn: wreck.
Eamhain Macha: Navan Fort, the old capital of Ulster.
Faire-go-dho: Shame.
fairy fort: ancient circular farmstead, thought to be inhabited by the fairies.
falluin: the Irish mantle.
Fead-a-Pooka: a reputedly haunted area in Kerry, lit. the Marsh of the Pooka.
Fenian: a member of the fianna.
Fian Eirion: Fiana Eirionn: a semi-mythical band of warriors in ancient Ireland.
finan, finane: a long coarse white grass (*fionnán*).
Fingl of McPherson: Finn McCool in McPherson's tales.
flahool: generous.
foreer, foreerb gair!: alas!
freckoned, frickens: frightened, frightens.
Fuan-ma-Cool, Fionn Mac Cumhal: the leader of the fianna.
Fuheroch: an old building, usually roofless, a ruin.
Fuin-traugh: Ventry Harbour in the Dingle Peninsula.
fullbounds: a ferkin of butter specially prepared for tropical markets.
futhill: a garment worn on the neck.
Gall-Oglach: galloglass: heavy-armed foreign mercenary soldier.
galore: plenty.
Galtys: a range of mountains in Co. Tipperary.
garkighs: unfledged birds.
garlagh: a vulnerable child.
garran: gelding.
garvarry: crozier.
gawmogue: a simpleton, a clown.
Glan-a-phrecaun: Glenville, Co. Cork, lit. Glen or Valley of the Raven.
gomulach, gomul: a big ignorant fellow.
gorsoon-bo: cowherd, cowboy.

gosh-rahinee: fern stalk.

Goul Mac Morna, Goul-mac-morin: a prominent member of the fianna.

grawl: a child.

grugh: curds.

hagur, a hagur: a term of endearment.

hashki, ahashki: a term of endearment, dear, love.

Hill of the Parting: Dromscarra, near Kiskeam, Co. Cork.

ignis fatuus: popularly known as 'Jack o' the Lantern,' lit. fool's fire.

inch: land by a river.

instanter: now, immediately.

Introibo: I shall go into; Ps. 29, prayed at the beginning of the Tridentine Mass.

inexpreessibles: trousers.

Juggy: personal name, Judy.

Justice's castle: Duarigle Castle on the Blackwater between Millstreet and Cullen.

kanavane: bog cotton.

Kauth: a girl's name, Catherine, Kathleen (*Cáit*).

keener, keening: mourner, mourning.

keeroge: a beetle.

keenoge, keenogue: a live turf-coal wrapped in tow for carrying in a pocket for kindling a fire elsewhere

keolshee: fairy music.

kern: an Irish foot soldier.

Kerry Dragoons: convoy of Kerry horsemen conveying butter to Cork.

Kildinan: a townland near Rathcormack, Co. Cork.

Kilmeen: an ancient church-site east of Boherbue giving its name to the mediaeval parish of that name.

Kincora, Kincorra: the seat of King Brian Boru in East Clare.

kish, kishogue: a wicker basket; a shapeless mass.

Kiskane: Kiskeam: a village and townland in Western Duhallow, Co. Cork.

kishough: shapeless mass.

Knock-ana-geran-bawn: a place-name in Duhallow, lit. 'the hill of the white gelding.'

Knockfirin: an enchanted hill in Co. Limerick, capital of the Munster fairies.

koelshee: fairy music.

kustha-basha: a little cake kneaded and formed on the hand.

Kyleta-mac-Ronan: a member of the fianna.

lashings-go-leor: plentiful supply.

leacht: a pile of stones raised in memory of the dead.

leprehaun: a leprechaun.

lore: plenty.
loughans: puddles, lit. little lakes.
Lough-guir: Lough Gur, a reputedly enchanted lake near Bruff, Co. Limerick.
Lough Lene: the Lake of Killarney, remarkable in folklore for its diamonds.
Loughrea usage: serious and wholesale financial administrative corruption.
louersha hene: a strong affirmation of assent.
lowersha: indeed, an affirmative.
Lucause bockagh: Luke the cripple, the lame.
lusmore: great herb
ma bochal, maboohil: my boy.
mac allo: an echo.
McNaughton, M'Naughtin, Rev. Fr: appointed Parish Priest of Kilmeen, 1833.
ma cobberigh: my crabbed fellow.
ma colleen bawn: my fair girl.
madra roe: a fox.
mag: faint.
making buttons: nervous, agitated.
ma-launderig: an expression of sorrow or regret.
Mangerton: a mountain in the Killarney area of Co. Kerry.
manim, manima: an exclamation; lit. my soul!
mar dhea, maugiagh: by the way
marcach-na-Shanacloch: the horseman of Shanacloch.
marc-slua: Irish cavalry
marvedy: i.e. maravedi, a small Spanish coin.
mauryagh: as it where, in pretence.
ma-vrone: my sorrow!
meela milloon mulla: an exclamation of wonder, a thousand million praises!
meela murther: an exclamation of astonishment.
Meelan's, Mielan's Rock: A rock in the Island Wood near Newmarket, Co. Cork.
mether: a tall wooden mug.
mhaise: indeed.
monadan: the whortleberry or bill berry.
monam ayeah: an exclamation, my soul indeed!
monam own dhoul: an expletive, my soul from the devil!
moneen: dance a jig.
Morven: a wild district in the West Highlands of Scotland.
mulla gudoa: an exclamation of wonder, lit. praise for ever!
murther maura: an exclamation of horror.
muryagh: by the way, in pretence, as it were.

musha: a casual exclamation, lit. 'if that is so.'
muskauns, miscawn: a small measure, e.g. of butter, whiskey, etc.
napachan: a youngster that has not reached the age of reason.
ne plus ultra: the ultimate, the highest form.
nough gannule a calleen ee: isn't she a comely girl.
O Wirra: an exclamation, lit. O Mary!
Och! hone: exclamation of grief.
Oinseach: a silly girl or woman.
Omedhaun, omodhaun, omadhaun: fool.
Oscar: a prominent member of the fianna.
Osshine: son of Fionn, baptised by Patrick on his return from *Tír na nÓg*.
Pater & Ave: The Lord's Prayer & Hail Mary.
piggin: a small wooden drinking vessel.
pilleen suas: a home-made straw saddle.
Pobble O'Keeffe: between the Araglen & Blackwter in Duhallow, Co. Cork.
poneens: patches.
ramaish, ramish: rubbish, nonsense.
raythilagh: a long single-story traditional dwelling house, a palace.
Rockites: members of a secret, militant, agrarian reform society.
ros-catha: eye of battle, a battle-hymn, war-song, rallying song.
Saggart na bootishy: a popular Irish tune.
Samer: an ancient name for Lough Erne.
Sasanach: an English person, a protestant.
sauvauneen: pet, darling.
sauwall Dhia er in: an exclamation, God save us!
schachraune, shachrawn: at a loss, wandering, down at heel.
sciath: a wicker basket, a shield.
seed of the fire: live embers used to kindling another fire.
shachrawn, shaughran: at a loss, wandering, down at heel.
shanachie, senachie, shanacha: storyteller.
shebeen: an unlicenced spirit-shop.
shee-geehy: a fair wind, especially a whirlwind.
Shemus a cocca, Shemish-a-cocca: cowardly king James II; vulg. Jim the Shit.
shillelah: a stout (blackthorn) stick often used in faction fighting.
shoun-dreed: a druid of ancient times; lit. an old druid.
skail feenight: a story of the fianna, a romantic tale.
skeehogue: a shallow wicker basket.
skien, skein: knife.
skien dhu: black handled knife or dagger: efficacious against fairy spells & for killing ghosts.

sleeveen: sly, slippery person.
slibberigh: a tall slender (young) man.
slua-shee: the fairy host.
smusagh: the innermost part.
smush: face.
sogers: soldiers.
sorra: an exclamation, easy.
sowins: a kind of milk pudding made from grain husks.
sowkins: soul [?]
spalpeen: a day labourer, migrant worker, & by extension, a term of abuse.
spolia optima: best spoils.
sporan nu schilling: a fairy purse.
squire of Kilmeen: Sweeny of Ballyhoolihan. O'Connells are now in occupancy.
stocach: an attendant, a young man.
strahane: stream.
Ta an dhiel urth: the devil is on you/in you.
Teamhair: the Hill of Tara, seat of the high kings of Ireland.
Te Deum: the official song of thanksgiving in the Catholic Church.
thackeen: a young girl.
thigendhou: do you understand?
thraneen: long slender grass, hose.
thrislogue: a step, a spring, a jump, a hop on one leg.
throwing it over: joking, blarney, palaver.
thruckle: a farm-cart, a butt.
Tir-nan-Oge: Irish otherworld, lit. the Land of the Young; Elysium of pagan Irish.
Tubber-na-Treenoda: Trinity Well.
Turk: a mountain with a spectacular waterfall in the Killarney area.
ullagoning, ullagone, ulligone: crying, a cry of lamentation.
usquebaugh: whiskey.
Virra-na-glora!: an exclamation of praise or wonder, lit. O Glorious Mary!
vox faucibus haesit: his voice stuck in his jaws.
Weera deelish: an exclamation, Dear Mary!
Wirra strua!: an exclamation, lit. what a pity Mary!
Wirra wirra: an exclamation, Mary, Mary!
yallow boy, yellow boy: a gold sovereign.
yinusal-a-chree: sir of my heart, my dear sir!.

Bibliography

Primary Sources.

(1) ***Books of Songs & Translations***

Reliques of Irish Jacobite Poetry, Dublin: Samuel J. Machen, 1844.

Irish Popular Songs, Dublin, J. M'Glashan/London: W.S. Orr, 1847.

(2***) Letters***

NLI, MS 2261: Twenty seven letters to John Daly, publisher, Kilkenny.

___MS 8005: Letter to C. G. Duffy.

RIA, MS 12/P19-20.

The Celt, 1857: Eleven letters or fragments of letters in a four-part article by Charles J. Kickham.

The Irishman, March 14th 1866: fragment.

(3) ***Other MS. Material***

NLI, MS 2261: four poems, and a sketch of the life of Eoghan Ruadh Ó Suilleábháin.

___MS 8092: Three poems.

(4) ***Contributions to Newspapers, Journals in order of publication***

"The Midwife": DPJ, 16-2-1833 .

"The Steel Boy": DPJ, 16-3-1833.

"A Legend of Blarney": DPJ, 23-3-1833.

"St. Lateerin": DPJ, 4-5-1833.

"The Charm": DPJ: 20-4-1833.

"Daniel the Outlaw": DPJ, 18-5-1833.

"The Still-House": DPJ, 8-6-1833.

"The Beggarman's Tale": DPJ, 15-6-1833.

"The Goban Saer": DPJ, 6-7-1833.

"Carrig-Cleena": DPJ, 13-7-1833.

"The Garvarry": DPJ, 20- 7-1833.

"The Headless Horseman of Shanacloch": DPJ, 3-8-1833.

"The City of the Lake": DPJ, 17-8-1833.

"Mary Carr, or The Abduction and Rescue": DPJ, 7-9-1833.

"Andrew Murray, or the effects of Gambling": DPJ, 5-10-1833.

"The Brothers": DPJ, 11-1-1834.

"The Cock-fight": DPJ. 18-1-1834.

"Archy Conway": DPJ, 26-7-1834.
"Daniel O'Leary, the Duhallow Piper": DPJ, 18-10-1834.
"The Chiefs of Clanawly": DPJ, 17-1-1835.
"The Spirit of Lough Dergart": DPJ, 14-2-1835.
"Meelan": DPJ, 4-4-1835.
"The Pooka": DPJ, 4-7-1835.
"The Whiteboy": DPJ, 11-7-1835.
"Paddy Doyle's First Trip to Cork": DPJ, 25-7-1835.
"The Duhallow Cowboy": DPJ, 29-8-1835.
"Darby Dooly and his White Horse": DPJ, 19-9-1835.
"The Usefulness of Biography": DPJ, 10-10-1835.
"The Faithful Lovers": DPJ, 24 -10-1835.
"The Ford of the White Ship": DPJ, 23-11-1835.
"Legend of Ossheen the son of Fionn": DPJ, 9-1-1836.
"Jack o' the Lantern": DPJ, 16-1-1836.
"The Man in the Moon": DPJ, 6-2-1836.
"Phelim M'Carthy": DPJ, 20 - 2-1836.
"The Demon Nailer": DPJ, 12-3-1836.
"The Doomed Maiden": DPJ, 30-4-1836.
"Strictures on Murray's English Grammar": *Schoolmasters Magazine*, July1840.
"Paddy Corbett's First Smuggling Trip": IPJ, 6-3-1841.
"The Bald Barrys": IPJ, 17-4-1841.
"The Buckaugh's Legend or The Wife of the Two Husbands": DJTSL, 4-6-1842.
"The Harper": DJTSL, 23-7-1842.
"The Bridal": DJTSL, 23 -7-1842.
"The Rockite Leader": *Nation,* 24-6-1843.
"A Petty Sessions Sketch": *Nation,* 11-3-1843.
"To Erin": *Nation,* 11-3-1843.
"Irish War Song, A.D. 1843": *Nation,* 15-4-1843.
"The Rockite Leader": *Nation,* 24-6-1843.
"The Repealers March": *Nation,* 29-7-1843.
"Ninety Eight": *Nation,* 5-8-1843.
"The Voice of Tara": *Nation,* 19-8-1943.
"The Defeat of Strongbow": *Nation,* 2-9-1843.
"The Songs of the Nation": v 16-9-1843.
"Song of the Penal Days": *Nation,* 16-9-1843.
"What are Repealers?": v 11-11-1843.
"The Battle of Callan": v 15-3-1844.

"Our Hope": *Nation,* 20-4-1844.
"The Lady of Alba's Lament" [tr] *Nation,* 23-3-1844.
"The Expulsion of the Saxon" [tr]: *Nation,* 27-4-1844.
"Battle of Credran": *Nation,* 3-5-1844.
"The Death of Fail": *Nation,* 5-7-1844.
"Versification of the last words of Timothy Scannell": *Nation,* 17-8-1844.
"The Death of the Outlaw": *Nation,* 24-8-1844.
"The Revenge": *Nation,* 7-9-1844.
"O'Donovan's Daughter": *Nation,* 19-10-1844.
"The Minstrel's Invocation": *Nation,* 7-12-44.
"Mo Chraoibhín Cnó": *Nation,* 21-12-1844.
"Song of the Mermaid": *Nation,* 28-12-1844.
"Brighdín Ban Mo Stor": *Nation,* 11-1-1845.
"Aileen the Huntress": *Nation,* 5-4-1845.
"Passages in the life of Daniel O'Keeffe, the Outlaw, surnamed Domhnall na casgadh": *Irish National Magazine:* 13-6-1846 & 20-6-1846.
"Meelan's Rock": *Irish National Magazine:* 20-6-1846.
"I would this dreary pilgrimage were o'er": *Nation,* 13-2-1847.
"The Lady": *Nation,* 5-10-1850.
"Song of Lesbia": *Nation,* 30-11-1850.
"Epistle to a Lady": *Nation,* 1-10-1859.
"A Valentine": *Nation,* 8- 10- 1859.

Secondary Sources

(1) ***Letters***

NLI, MS 2261: eight letters from John Keegan to John Daly.
O'Donoghue, D.J., *Life & Writings of J.C. Mangan* - 2 from John Keegan.
Nation: 17-8-1844 - John (O') Daly to the Editor.
__: 31-8-1850 - A Confederate to the Editor.
__: 31-8-1850 - to the Editor.
CAI, BG 69 B I. 19-12-1850 reply to query.
Celt: 26-12-1857 - letter to C.J. Kickham.
Cork Examiner: 16-6-1858 - Mrs. Walsh to the Editor.
__: 18-6-1858 - C.J.T. to the Editor.
__: 18-6-1858 - McCarthy Downing to the Editor.
Nation: 8-1-1859 - Correspondent to the Editor.
Irish Popular Songs (2nd. ed., 1883): Patrick Traynor to Peter Roe.
Wexford Independent: 16-10-1844 article/letter of unacknowledged authorship.

(2) ***Articles & Notices in Books, Newspapers, Periodicals***

Anon. "Irish Popular Songs" (review), *Irish Quarterly Review*, July 1857, pp.313-37.

— "Reliques of Irish Jacobite Poetry" (Review), in the *Irishman*, Mar. 3rd. 1866.

— "Honouring the Memory of Edward Walsh," *Cork Examiner*, May 15th. 1891.

— "Edward Walsh, Poet and Translator," JCHAS, (II A) 1893, p. 97.

— "Walsh's Poems" JCHAS (II A) 1893, p. 260.

— "Waterford & S.E. Counties Notabilities," *Waterford Archaeological Society Journal* (XII) 1909, pp. 20-24.

— "Hours with Irish Poets. XXV - Edward Walsh" in the *Shamrock*, Feb. 10th. 1877, pp. 298-302.

— "An account of the life of Edward Walsh," *Cork Examiner* 25-7-1936, p.13.

__"The Poet who is closely connected with Millstreet," *Cork Examiner*, 13-2-1974.

— "Brief account of Edward Walsh, poet & patriot," *Corkman*, 9-10-1981, p. 3.

— Part II of same, *Corkman*, 6-8-1982, p. 8.

— The *Kerryman/Corkman*, Friday 15 April 1983.

__ "Profile of poet and school master of Spike Island," *Ireland's Own*, 18-3-1994, p. 11.

— *Southern Star* 12-11-1983, p. 9 or 8.

__ Coleman, James, "The Story of Spike Island," JCHAS, Vol II, No. 13, Jan. 1893: pp.1-8.

Crilly, Daniel, "Charles J. Kickham and Edward Walsh," the *Irish Book Lover*, Vol. III, August 1911, pp 1-2.

Duffy, Charles Gavan, "Edward Walsh" *Nation*, August 24th 1850.

—"Edward Walsh," *Nation*, September 7th 1850.

Edwards, V.,"Edward Walsh: Poet and Schoolmaster," *New Ireland Review*, Vol. IV, Nov. 1895, .158-165.

Gleeson, Timothy, "Edward Walsh, the Irish Poet and Translator. A biographical Sketch, with Poetry," JCHAS, Vol. II, (1893), pp. 145- 208, & Vol. III, (1894), pp. 209-214.

— "Edward Walsh's Poems," an appeal for, JCHAS, Vol II, No. 18, June 1893, p. 117.

Gregg, Frederick J. "Edward Walsh" in *Irish Fireside* NS 1, 1897, p. 316.

Kickham, Charles J. "Edward Walsh" in the *Celt*, Vol. I, (1857) Nos. 19,20,21,22: Dec. 5 - 26 1857.

Lane, J. & B. Clifford, "Profile, account of his work in Cork and sample of poetry," *A North Cork Anthology*, p. 164.

Lee, Sidney, ed. *Dictionary of National Biography*. Vol. LIX. (Smith) London, 1899, p. 213-4.

Lynch, Pat, "The Young Ireland Poet, Edward Walsh," the *Corkman*, 6-8-1982, p.8.

— "The Infamous North Cork Militia" *Charleville & District Historical Journal*, No. 4, (1989) pp 94-95.

Maher, James, (ed), *The Valley Near Slievenamon*, pp. 331-354.

Meagher, J., "Edward Walsh, the poet," the *Southern Star*, 12 - 11 - 1983 p. 8.

McGrath, Kevin, "Writers in the 'Nation,' 1842-5" *Irish Historical Studies* (IV).1949, pp. 189-223.

Murphy, William "C.J. Kickham and Edward Walsh," the *Irish Book Lover*, Vol. III, July, p. 213.

Ó Mathuna, Pilib, "Edward Walsh, the poet from Millstreet," *Agus*, June 1990, pp. 18-19.

Ó Ríordáin, CSSR, John J. "Edward Walsh," *Seanchas Duthalla*, 1986, pp. 8-10.

Roe, Owen, (alias, Eugene Davis) "Hours with Irish Poets: XXV - Edward Walsh," Shamrock, Feb. 10th. 1877, pp. 298-302

—"Hours with the Irish Poets, XXV- Edward Walsh" the *Irishman*, 1877 pp. 298-302.

Tasman, "C.J. Kickham and Edward Walsh," the *Irish Book Lover*, Vol. III, or IV, p. 192.

Thomond, M.H., "Lament for Edward Walsh" in the *Celt*, Mar. 1858, pp. 32-33.

White, James Grove, "An Account of the Yeomanry of Ireland, 1796-1834," JCHAS, II, (1893) pp. 479-509.

Yeats, William B., "Irish National Literature from Callanan to Carleton," the *Bookman*, [viii] July, 1895, (Hodder & Stoughton) London.

(3) ***Public Records and Archives***

NA Education Registers and Salary Books.

ED 1/1S No. 22.

ED 1/13

ED 2/10 Folio 94.

ED 2/212 Folio 43.

ED 4

Quit Rent Office Papers.

CAI, Minute Books of the Board of Guardians.

(4) ***Micro film***

NLI, *Wexford Independent*, October 1844.

Nation, 1843, 1844, 1845, 1855.

Sts. Michael & John's Catholic Parish, Dublin.

Aglish Catholic Parish, Co. Waterford.

Cappoquin, Catholic Parish, Co. Waterford.

St. Mary's Pro-Cathedral Parish, Dublin.

(5) ***Government Publications***

Report on the present state of the disturbed districts, in the S. of Ireland, 1822.

Commissioners of Education in Ireland: 1824, 5, II, 553.

Commissioners to enquiry into Education in Ireland: 1825, II, 530.

Irish Education Inquiry 1826 Education Report, 1826, ii.

Commissioners of National Education in Ireland, Second Report, 1834-35.

The Miseries and Misfortunes of Ireland and The Irish People from the Evidence taken by the Commissioners for Inquiring into the condition of the poorer classes in Ireland, (Reynolds),Dublin, London. 1834.

Parliamentary Gazetteer of Ireland 1844-1845, 3 vols.

(6) ***Personal Interviews***

Mr. Dan Sean O'Keeffe, Ruhill, Kiskeam, Co. Cork.

Mrs. Kit Hickey, née Keeffe, Knockdubh, Cullen, Co. Cork.

Mrs. Mollie Hickey, Gortnacreha, Cullen, Co. Cork.

Mrs. Maureen Phibbs, Blackrock, Blessington, Co. Wicklow.

Mr. James and Nancy O'Riordan, Knockavorheen, Kiskeam, Co. Cork.

An tUas. Tadgh Ó Muineacháin, Gurteen, Banteer, Co. Cork.

Mr. John P. Murphy, Post Office, Kiskeam, Co. Cork.

Dr. Bernard O'Donoghue, Cullen, and Wadam College, Oxford, England.

Sr. De Lourdes Gogarty, Cappoquin, Co. Waterford.

Fr. Timothy Murhpy, Shamrock House, Kiskeam, Co. Cork.

Mrs. Nora Moylan, 132 St. Lawrence Rd., Clontarf, Dublin.

Mrs. Molly J. Neylon NT, Kiskeam, Co. Cork.

Ms. Alice Carter, Girvan, Scotland.

Fr. Martin Slattery, St. John's College, Waterford.

Mrs. Elizabeth Nunn, great-great granddaughter of Edward Walsh, Australia.

(7) ***General Reference Works***

Batterby's *Register for the Catholic World.*

Batterby's *Irish Catholic Directory.*

The *Catholic Directory.*

Guy, *Directory of Munster.*

The *Dublin Almanac & General Register of Ireland.* (Pettigrew) Dublin, 1839 and following i.e. the *Dublin Directory, Thoms Directory.*

Encyclopaedia Britannica. 14th ed. (Wm. Berton) Chicago.

Anon. *National & Historical Ballads of Ireland.* (Gill & Son), Dublin, n.d.

Beckett, J.C. *The Making of Modern Ireland 1603-1923.* 1969 ed. (Faber & Faber) London, 1966.

Breathnach, An tAth. Pádráig, do chruin. *Ceól ár Sínsear.* (Brúin & Nualláin) Baile-Atha-Cliath. 1923.

— *Fuínn na Smól* (Bruin & Nualláin) Baile-Átha-Cliath, 1913.

— eag. *Cnuasachd Bheag Amhrán* (Brúin & Nualláin) Baile-Átha-Cliath.

— ed. *Songs of the Gael.* (Browne & Nolan) Dublin, 1915.

— eag. *Ár gCeól Féinig.* (Brún & Nualláin) B'Átha Cliath, 1920.

Clifford, Brendan. *Duhallow, Notes Towards A History.* (Aubane) Co. Cork.

Colum, Padraic, ed. *Anthology of Irish Verse.* (Boni & Liveright) New York, 1922.

Comerford, Richard V. *Charles J. Kickham, A Biography.* (Wolfhound Press) Dublin, 1979.

Conlon, J.F. *Some Irish Poets and Musicians.* (Litho Press) Middleton, 1974.

Connolly, Peter, ed. *Literature and the Changing Ireland.* (Colin Smythe, Bucks.) 1982.

Connolly, S.J. *Priests and People in Pre-Famine Ireland,* 1780-1845. (Gill & Macmillan) Dublin, 1982.

Cook, John. *The Dublin Book of Irish Verse.* (Hodges Figgis) Dublin, 1909.

Corkery, Daniel. *The Hidden Ireland.* (Gill) Dublin, 1967.

Croker, Thomas Crofton. *Fairy Legends & Traditions of the South of Ireland.* 3 vols. (J. Murray) London.

Culloty, A.T. *On Broken Wing.* (Desmond Publications) 1997.

Cunningham, Rt. Hon.William. *Speeches at the Bar and in the Senate.* (Duffy & Sons) Dublin/London, 1883. (Memoir & notes by John Cashel Hoey).

Daly, Dominic. *The Young Douglas Hyde.* (IUP) Dublin, 1974.

Davis, Thomas. *National and Historical Ballads, Songs, and Poems.* New ed. (Duffy & Sons) Dublin, 1846.

— *Essays and Poems with a Centenary Memoir.* (Gill & Son) Dublin 1945.

Deane, Seamus, Gen. Ed. *The Field Day Anthology of Irish Writing.* 3 vols. (Field Day Publications) Derry, 1991.

Dinneen, Patrick S., ed. *Amhráin Sheagháin Chláraigh Mhic Dhomhnaill.* B.Átha Cliath, 1902.

— *Foclóir Gaedhilge agus Béarla,* Dublin. (Irish Text Society) Dublin,1927.

— *Beatha Eoghain Ruaidh Uí Shúilleabháin,* an dara heagar, (Gaelic League) Dublin, 1902.

Duffy, C.G. et al. *The Spirit of the Nation* or *Ballads and Songs by the writers of the Nation.* (James Duffy) Dublin, 1845.

—*The Ballad Poetry of Ireland*, 4th. ed. (J. Duffy) Dublin, 1846.

—*Young Ireland: A Fragment of Irish History,1840-1850.* (Cassell et al.) London & NY, 1880.

— *Four Years of Irish History, 1845-1849.* (Cassell et al.) London & NY, 1883.

—*The Memoirs of an Irish Patriot 1840-1846.* (Kegan Paul) London 1890.

— *My Life in Two Hemispheres.* 2nd ed., 2 vols. (Fisher Unwin) London, 1898.

Egan, Patrick M. *History, Guide & Directory of county and city of Waterford.* 1895.

Farren, Robert. *The Course of Irish Verse in English.* (Sheed & Ward) London, 1948.

Flanedy, John, ed. *A Special Report of the Proceedings in the case of the Queen against Daniel O'Connell, M.P. John O'Connell, M.P., T. Steele, T.M. Ray, C.G. Duffy, Rev. T. Tierney, Rev. P.J. Tyrrell, John Gray, & R. Barrett.* (J. Duffy) Dublin, 1844.

Flower, Robin. *Love's Bitter Sweet: translations from the Irish Poets of the 16th. & 17th. centuries.* (Cuala Press) Dublin, 1925.

Foster, R.F. *Modern Ireland 1602-1972.* (Penguin Press), Harmondsworth, 1988.

Graves, Alfred P, ed. *The Irish Song Book.* 11th. ed. (Fisher Unwin) London, 1909.

— ed. *Poems of Sir Samuel Ferguson.* (Talbot Press) Dublin, 1916.

— ed. *The Book of Irish Poetry.* (Talbot Press) Dublin, n.d.

Griffith, A., ed. *Meagher of the Sword,* Speeches of Thomas Francis Meagher in Ireland 1846-1848. (Gill & Son) Dublin, n.d.

Hardiman, James, ed. *Irish Minstrelsy.* 2 vols. (Joseph Robinson) London, 1831.

Hayes, Edward. *The Ballads of Ireland.* 2 vols. 7th ed. (James Duffy) Dublin, n.d.

Hogan, Robert, et al. eds. *The Macmillan Dictionary of Irish Literature.* (Greenwood Press) Connecticut, 1979.

Hoagland, Kathleen, ed. *1000 Years of Irish Poetry.* (Devin-Adair Co) NY, 1947.

How, Frederick D. *William Conyngham Plunket, A Memoir.* (Isbister & Co) London, 1900.

Hyde, Douglas. *Abhráin atá Leagtha ar an Reachtúire*. (Gill) B'Áth C. 1903.

— *Love Songs of Connaught.* (I.U.P.) Shannon, 1969.

— *Poems of the Irish.* (Allen Figgis) Dublin, 1963.

— *A Literary History of Ireland.* (T. Fisher Unwin) London, 1899.

Jeffares, A. Norman. *Anglo-Irish Literature.* (Gill & Macmillan) London, 1982.

Joyce, Robert D. *Songs of the Gael.*

Keating, Geoffrey. *The History of Ireland.* (Irish Text Society) Dublin, 1902— .

Kelly, E. *English That For Me & Your Humble Servant.* (Mercier Press) 1990.

Keneally, Thomas. *The Great Shame.* (Chatto & Windus) London, 1998.

Lane, J. & B. Clifford. *A North Cork Anthology*, (Aubane Historical Society) Millstreet, Co. Cork 1993.

Lewis, Samuel. *Topographical Dictionary of Ireland.* 2 vols. (S. Lewis & Co.) London, 1837. Trench, Trubner & Co. 1890.

Lover, Samuel, ed. *Poems of Ireland.* (Ward, Lock & Co), London, 1858.

— *Legends and Stories of Ireland.* Ed. with introductory notes by D.J. O'Donoghue (A. Constable & Co) Westminster, 1899.

— *Songs of Ireland.* (1916) Dublin.

McCarthy, Anne. *James Clarence Mangan Edward Walsh & 19th-century Irish Literature in English.* (Edwin Mellan Press) N.Y., 2000.

McCarthy, Denis F, ed. *The Book of Irish Ballads.* (James Duffy) Dublin, 1846.

— *The Poets & Dramatists of Ireland.* (James Duffy) Dublin, 1846.

— ed. *Book Irish Ballads.* (Duffy), Dublin. n. d.

McCarthy, Justin. *Irish Literature.* (CUA) Washington, 1904.

MacDermott, Martin. *New Spirit of the Nation.* (Fisher Unwin) London, 1894.

M'Gee, Thomas D'Arcy. *The Irish Writers of the 17th. Century.* (Duffy) Dublin, 1846.

McHugh, Roger & Maurice Harmon. *Anglo-Irish Literature from its origins to the present day.* (Wolfhound Press) Dublin 1982.

McKenna, Brian. *A Guide to Information Sources*, vol. 13. (Gala Research Co.) Michigan, 1978.

Mangan, James C., & John O'Daly. *The Poets and Poetry of Munster*, 3rd ed. (J. Duffy & Sons) Dublin, 1883.

Milner, Liam. *Ireland's Heritage: In Black and White.* (Tower Books) Cork, 1989.

— *The River Lee and its Tributaries.* (Tower Books) Cork, 1975.

Mitchel, John . *Jail Journal or, five years in British prisons.* Author's ed. (Cameron, Ferguson & Co.) Glasgow, n.d.

Montague, John, ed. *The Faber Book of Irish Verse.* (Faber & Faber), London, 1974.

Moody, T.W., Martin, F.X., Byrne, F.J., eds. *A New History of Ireland*, VIII. (Clarendon Press) Oxford, 1992.

Ó Brádaigh, Seán, eag. *Songs of 1798*, (Dúchas) B'Átha C., 1982.

O'Connell, John, ed. *Life and Speeches of Daniel O'Connell.* 2 vols. (J. Duffy) Dublin, 1846.

O'Daly, John, ed. *Transactions of the Ossianic Society* for the year 1858. Dublin,1861.

O'Donoghue, D. J., ed. *Poems of James Clarence Mangan.* (Gill), Dublin, 1910.

—*The Poets of Ireland: A Biographical Dictionary*. (The Author) London, 1892.

O'Donovan, John, ed. *Miscellany of The Celtic Society*. Dublin, 1849.

— ed. *Annals of the Kingdom of Ireland*, by The Four Masters, 7 vols. (Hodges, Smith & Co) Dublin, 1856.

Ó Flannghaile, Tomás, ed. *Duanaire na Macaomh*. (Gill & Son) Dublin, 1910.

O'Keeffe, C.M. *Life & Times of Daniel O'Connell*. (J. Mullany) Dubliln, 1864.

O'Kelly, J.J. *Life & Writings of James Clarence Mangan.*

Ó Lochlainn, Colm. *The Complete Irish Street Ballads*. (Pan Books ed.) London, 1978.

—*Anglo-Irish Song Writers*. (Sign of the Three Candles) Dublin, n. d.

O'Reilly, Edward. *An Irish-English Dictionary*. New ed. (Minerva Printing Office) Dublin, 1821.

Ó Ríordáin, CSSR, John J. *Where Araglen So Gently Flows*. (Kerryman) Tralee, 1989.

Ó Tuathaigh, Gearóid. *Ireland Before the Famine 1798-1848. The Gill History of Ireland* (Gill & McMillan) Dublin, 1972.

Power, John. *List of Irish Periodical Publications*.

Power, P.C. *The Story of Anglo Irish Poetry*. (Mercier Press) Cork, 1967.

— *A Literary History of Ireland* (Mercier Press) Cork, 1969.

Rafroidi, Patrick. *Irish Literature in English*. The Romantic Period, 2 vols, (Colin Smythe, Bucks.), 1980.

Read, Donald, and Eric Glasgow *Feargus O'Connor, Irishman & Chartist*. (Edward Arnold) London, 1961.

Shannon-Mangan, Ellen. *James Clarence Mangan: A biography*. (Irish Academic Press) Dublin, 1996.

Sharp, Elizabeth A. *Lyra Celtica*. (Geddes & Colleagues) Edinburgh, 1896.

Sigerson, George. *Bards of the Gael and Gall*. (Talbot Press) Dublin, 1925.

Smith, Charles. *The Ancient and present state of the county of Cork*. 2 vols. (Fenor Press) 1973.

Sparling, H. H. *Irish Minstrelsy: Irish Songs, Lyrics, & Ballads*. (Scott) London, 1887.

Stevenson, Sir John, & Sir Henry Bishop. *Moore's Irish Melodies*, with symphonies and accompaniments. (Gill & a Mhac) Dublin, 1887.

Sullivan, T.D. *Recollections of troubled times in Irish Politics*. (Sealy, Bryers & Walker, and Gill and Son) Dublin, 1905.

Ua Duinnín, Pádráig S. *Amhráin Sheagháin Chlaraigh Mhic Dhomhnaill*. (Chonnradh na Gaedhilge) B.A.C., 1902.

— *Filidhe na Máighe*. (Gill & a Mhac) Baile Átha Cliath, 1906.

— *Beatha Eoghain Ruaidh Uí Shúilleabháin* (Gaelic League) Dublin, 1902.

Various Hands: *Poetry and Legendary Ballads of the South of Ireland.* Cork, 1894.

— National and Historical Ballads of Ireland. (Gill & Son) Dublin, n.d.

Walsh, Edward. *Reliques of Irish Jacobite Poetry*, 2nd ed. (John Daly) Dublin, 1866.

— *Irish Popular Songs*. 2nd ed. J.S.S., (Gill) Dublin, 1883.

Ward, Wilfrid. *The Life of John Henry Cardinal Newman*. 1913 ed. (Longmans, Green & Co) London, 1912.

Welch, Robert. *Irish Poets from Moore to Yeats*. (Colin Smythe, Gerrards Cross) Bucks., 1980.

— *A History of Verse Translation from the Irish*, 1789-1897. New Jersey: (Barnes and Noble Books/ Colin Smythe) Bucks., 1988.

Yeats, William B. *A Book of Irish Verse*, 4th ed., (Methuen & Co) London, 1899.

— *Essays & Introductions*. (Macmillan) London, 1961.

— *Fairy & Folk Tales of the Irish Peasantry*. (W. Scott Ltd) London, n.d.

Index to Letters

Index to Folklore & Other Prose Works

Index to Poems, Songs and Translations

Index of Musical Accompaniments

General Index